COASTAL MAINE

HILARY NANGLE

Stratton
Sugarloaf Mtn
Bingham
Kingfield
Rangeley
Mooselookmeguntic Lake
Skowhegan
Farmington
Belgrade Lakes
Waterville
Bethel
White Mountain National Forest
AUGUSTA
Lewiston
Auburn
Oxford
Long Lake
Fryeburg
Sebago
Cornish
Yarmouth
Brunswick
Freeport
Bath
Wiscasset
Newcastle
Damariscotta
Boothbay Harbor
Monhegan Island
PORTLAND
Casco Bay
Old Orchard Beach
Saco
Biddeford
Alfred
The Kennebunks
Wells
Berwick
Ogunquit
Dover
Eliot
The Yorks
Kittery
NEW HAMPSHIRE
Bangor
Orono
Amherst
Wesley
Eastport
Campobello Island
Lubec
Machias
Grand Manan
Bucksport
Ellsworth
Milbridge
Jonesport
Beals
Great Wass Island
Searsport
Belfast
Blue Hill
Bar Harbor
Winter Harbor
Cadillac Mtn
Acadia National Park
Sedgwick
Lincolnville
Islesboro Island
Mount Desert Island
Camden
Rockport
Penobscot Bay
Deer Isle
Swans Island
Waldoboro
Rockland
Thomaston
Cushing
St. George
Vinalhaven Island
Isle au Haut
ATLANTIC OCEAN
0 25 mi
0 25 km
© AVALON TRAVEL

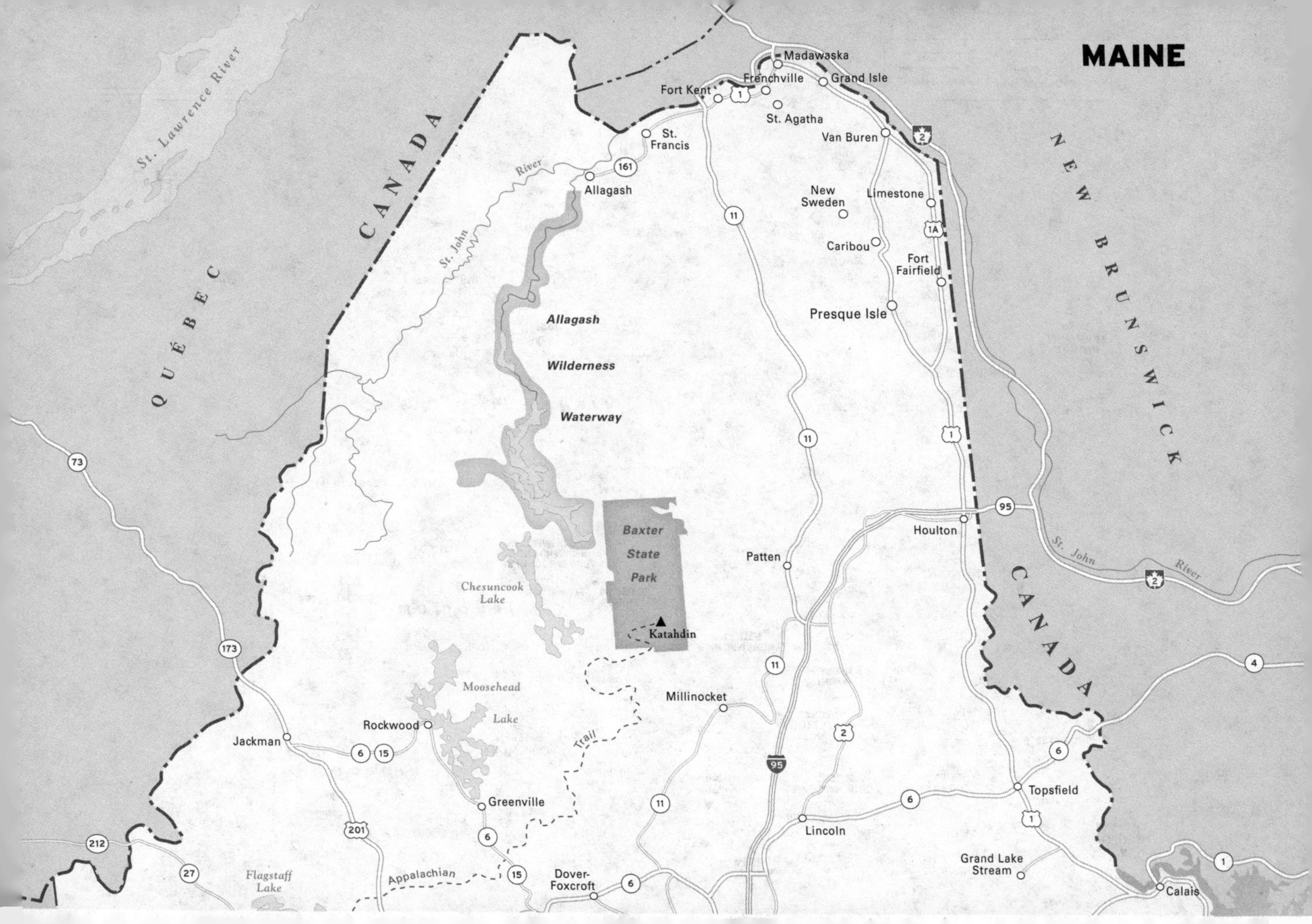
MAINE
QUÉBEC
CANADA
NEW BRUNSWICK
CANADA
St. Lawrence River
St. John River
St. John River
Madawaska
Fort Kent
Frenchville
Grand Isle
St. Agatha
Van Buren
St. Francis
Allagash
New Sweden
Limestone
Caribou
Fort Fairfield
Presque Isle
Allagash Wilderness Waterway
Baxter State Park
Katahdin
Houlton
Patten
Chesuncook Lake
Moosehead Lake
Millinocket
Rockwood
Jackman
Trail
Greenville
Topsfield
Lincoln
Grand Lake Stream
Appalachian
Flagstaff Lake
Dover-Foxcroft
Calais
161
11
1A
1
2
95
73
173
4
6
15
201
212
27
1
2
95
11
6

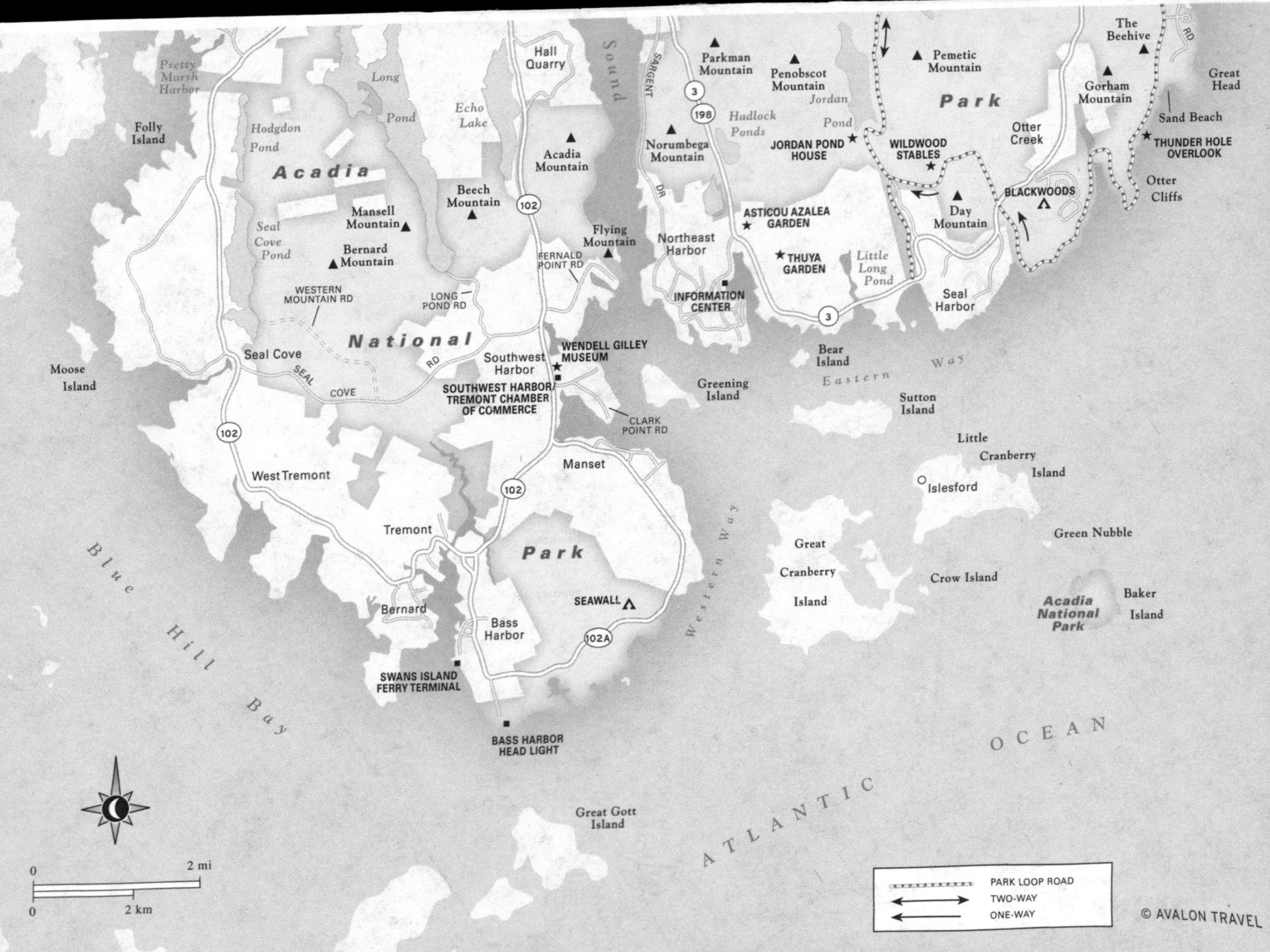

Pretty Marsh Harbor
Long Pond
Echo Lake
Hall Quarry
Sound
SARGENT DR
Parkman Mountain
Penobscot Mountain
Jordan Pond
Pemetic Mountain
The Beehive
Great Head
Folly Island
Hodgdon Pond
Acadia
Acadia Mountain
Norumbega Mountain
Hadlock Ponds
JORDAN POND HOUSE
WILDWOOD STABLES
Park
Otter Creek
Gorham Mountain
Sand Beach
THUNDER HOLE OVERLOOK
Otter Cliffs
RD
Beech Mountain
Mansell Mountain
Seal Cove Pond
Bernard Mountain
Flying Mountain
Northeast Harbor
ASTICOU AZALEA GARDEN
THUYA GARDEN
Little Long Pond
Day Mountain
BLACKWOODS
Seal Harbor
FERNALD POINT RD
WESTERN MOUNTAIN RD
LONG POND RD
INFORMATION CENTER
National
Seal Cove
SEAL COVE RD
Southwest Harbor
WENDELL GILLEY MUSEUM
SOUTHWEST HARBOR/ TREMONT CHAMBER OF COMMERCE
CLARK POINT RD
Moose Island
Greening Island
Bear Island
Eastern Way
Sutton Island
Little Cranberry Island
Islesford
Manset
West Tremont
Tremont
Park
Bernard
Bass Harbor
SEAWALL
Western Way
Great Cranberry Island
Crow Island
Green Nubble
Baker Island
Acadia National Park
SWANS ISLAND FERRY TERMINAL
BASS HARBOR HEAD LIGHT
Blue Hill Bay
Great Gott Island
ATLANTIC OCEAN
102
102A
3
198
0
2 mi
0
2 km
PARK LOOP ROAD
TWO-WAY
ONE-WAY
© AVALON TRAVEL

MOUNT DESERT ISLAND
To Ellsworth
Union River Bay
Marlboro
Hancock Point
Sorrento
Lamoine
Lamoine State Park
Trenton
BAR HARBOR AIRPORT
Eastern Bay
Narrows
BAR HARBOR INFORMATION CENTER
THOMPSON ISLAND INFORMATION CENTER
Frenchman Bay
Salisbury Cove
Hulls Cove
Mount Desert
RD
CROOKED
Alley Island
Town Hill
Lake Wood
HULLS COVE VISITOR CENTER
Bar Island
Porcupine Islands
NORWAY DR
Witch Hole Pond
COLLEGE OF THE ATLANTIC
Indian Point
Blagden Preserve
Western Bay
Green Island
Black Island
Acadia
Bar Harbor
INDIAN POINT
OAK HILL CROSS RD
OAK HILL RD
Somesville
Aunt Betty Pond
PARK LOOP RD
The Thrumcap
Squid Cove
SIEUR DE MONTS SPRING
Eagle Lake
SCHOONER HEAD
Bartlett Island
Bartlett Narrows
Round Pond
Somes Pond
Somes
National
Dorr Mountain
Champlain Mountain
Cadillac Mountain
Pretty Marsh
PRETTY MARSH RD
Sargent Mountain
The Bubbles
Bubble Pond
Schooner Head

Contents

DISCOVER

Coastal Maine

From the glacier-scoured beaches of the Southern Coast, around spruce-studded islands and Acadia's granite shores, to the craggy cliffs Down East, Maine's coastline follows a zigzagging route that would measure about 5,500 miles if you stretched it taut. Eons ago, glaciers came crushing down from the north, squeezing Maine's coastline into a wrinkled landscape with countless bony fingers reaching toward the sea. Each peninsula has its own character, as does each island, each city, and each village. Thanks to its geography, most Maine coast vistas are intimate, full of spruce-clad islands and gray granite and sometimes-forbidding headlands. Now add 64 lighthouses, 90 percent of the nation's lobsters, and the eastern seaboard's highest peak.

When it comes to character, no individuals are more rugged than the umpteenth-generation fishermen who make their living from these bone-chilling waters. Even the summerfolk tend to be different here. Many return year after year, generation after generation, to the same place and the same neighbors and the same pursuits.

Then there's Maine's coastal symphony: waves lapping and crashing, birds crying or singing, fog horns calling and bell buoys ringing, streams gurgling and

Clockwise from top left: buoys; Monhegan Island; lobster; Beachcroft Path; lobster boats in Rockport Harbor; Cape Neddick Light.

leaves rustling. Shore breezes mingle the aromas of pine, balsam, or rugosa rose with the briny scent of the sea. Sometimes you can almost taste the salt in the air.

Lobster, of course, is king, and Maine's seafood is ultra fresh, but don't overlook luscious wild blueberries, sweet Maine maple syrup, delicious farmstead cheeses, and homemade pies sold at roadside stands. Access to this bounty is one reason why talented chefs are drawn to the state.

Even if you don't dine at one of the hot restaurants with nationally known chefs, you can visit cheesemakers, fish smokers, artisan bakers, microbrewers, and organic farmers. But balance that with a classic Maine bean-hole or chowder *suppah*, where you can share a table with locals and, if you're lucky, hear a genuine Maine accent (here's a hint: "Ayuh" isn't so much a word as a sharp two-part intake of breath).

Yes, there's a reason why more than eight million people visit Maine every year, and why longtime summerfolk finally just pick up stakes and *settle* here. Maine boldly promotes itself as "The Way Life Should Be." Spend a little time in this extraordinarily special place and you'll see why.

Clockwise from top left: Campobello sunset; Acadia's carriage roads in autumn; Portland Head Light; Acadia's rocky coast.

Planning Your Trip

Where to Go

Southern Coast

Sand beaches, occasionally punctuated by rocky headlands, are the jewels of Maine's Southern Coast, but this region also oozes history. **Colonial roots** are preserved in historic buildings; **fishing traditions** echo in fish shacks-turned-trendy boutiques; and an **arts legacy** is preserved in museums and galleries. Complementing (or detracting) from these are Route 1's endless **shopping** opportunities: antiques, boutiques, and factory outlets.

Greater Portland

In this compact region are rocky coastline and sand beaches, lighthouses and lobster shacks, coastal islands and **L. L. Bean.** Brine-scented air, cackling gulls, lobster boats, and fishing trawlers give notice that this is a seafaring town, but it's also **Maine's cultural center,** rich in museums and performing-arts centers, and the state's **shopping hub.** Increasingly, Portland's earning national repute as a **destination for culinary travelers.**

Mid-Coast Region

No region of Maine has more **lobster shacks** or as rich a **maritime history** as this peninsula-rich stretch of coastline. Shaped by powerful freshwater rivers, the Mid-Coast is dotted with traditional fishing villages as well as towns that were once thriving ports, mill towns, or shipbuilding centers. The **Maine Maritime Museum** preserves that heritage; **Bath Iron Works** continues it; and the grand homes, brick townscapes, renovated mills, and plentiful shops brimming with maritime treasures and worldly antiques keep it alive.

Whale-watching cruises and kayaking trips depart from Bar Harbor's waterfront.

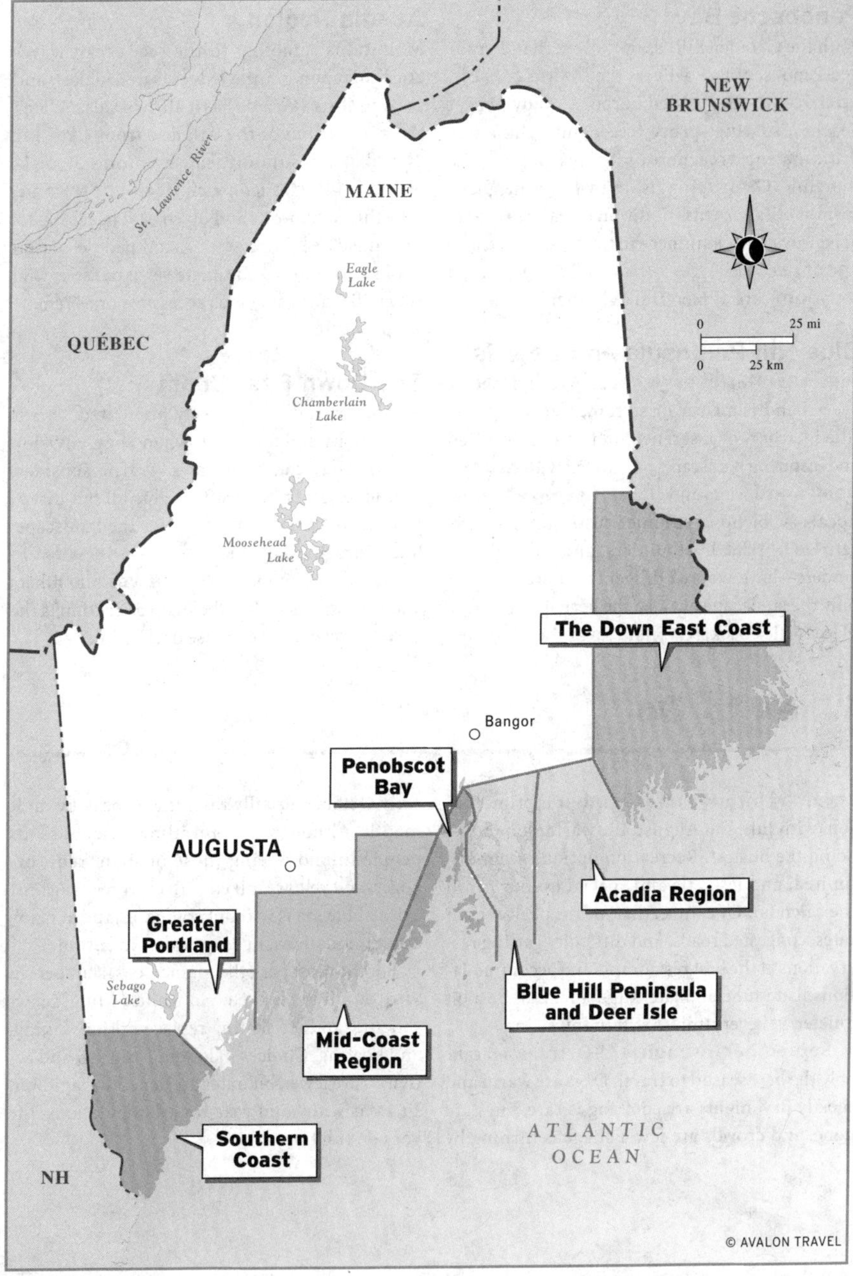

NEW BRUNSWICK
MAINE
St. Lawrence River
QUÉBEC
Eagle Lake
Chamberlain Lake
Moosehead Lake
0
25 mi
0
25 km
The Down East Coast
Bangor
Penobscot Bay
AUGUSTA
Acadia Region
Greater Portland
Sebago Lake
Blue Hill Peninsula and Deer Isle
Mid-Coast Region
Southern Coast
ATLANTIC OCEAN
NH
© AVALON TRAVEL

Penobscot Bay

With the Camden hills as backdrop, island-studded Penobscot Bay delivers the **Maine coast in microcosm.** Boat-filled harbors, sandy pocket beaches, soaring spruce trees, and lighthouses illuminating treacherous ledges pepper the shoreline. Gentrifying fishing villages neighbor cosmopolitan towns; traditional seafarers share driveways with summer rusticators. **Antiques shops, art galleries, artisans' studios,** and **museums** are as plentiful as lobster boats.

Blue Hill Peninsula and Deer Isle

Water, water everywhere. Around nearly every bend is a river or stream, a cove, a boat-filled harbor, or a serene pond. It's an inspired and inspiring landscape, one dotted with **historic homes and forts** and **classic fishing villages.** Locals—a blend of summer rusticators, genteel retirees, artists, boatbuilders, and back-to-the-landers—have worked diligently to preserve not only the landscape but also the heritage. It's a fine place to kick back, relax, and savor the good life.

Acadia Region

Mountains tumbling to the sea, ocean waves crashing upon granite ledges, serene lakes, and soaring cliffs—Acadia has it all, in spades. Watch the sun rise out of the Atlantic from **Cadillac Mountain**'s summit, mosey along **Acadia National Park**'s icon-rich **Park Loop Road,** hike through forests and up coastal peaks, pedal the famed **carriage roads,** and paddle coastal nooks and crannies. Intimate yet expansive, wild yet civilized, Acadia is as accessible or as remote as you desire.

The Down East Coast

Remote, rural, and scarcely populated, this is what many folks picture when they envision Maine. Here the pace slows. Traffic subsides. Fast-food joints and traffic lights all but disappear. **Blueberry barrens** color the landscape; huge tides rule daily life. Two **national wildlife reserves** and numerous **preserves** lure hikers and bird-watchers, but the main attraction is the **rugged and wild** expanse of coastline.

When to Go

Late May through mid-October is prime season, with July and August, the warmest months, being the busiest. Recreation options seem unlimited, and festivals and special events crowd the calendar. Of course, that means peak-season rates, congested roads, and difficulty getting reservations at the best restaurants and accommodations. Late June and late August tend to be a bit quieter, yet everything's still in full swing.

September through mid-October is arguably the best season to travel. Days are warm and mostly dry, nights are cool, fog is rare, bugs are gone, and crowds are few. Foliage is turning by early October, usually reaching its peak by mid-month. Although the prevailing wisdom sends people inland, seeing those brilliant reds, oranges, and yellows mixed with evergreens against a deep blue sea is without compare. And at many accommodations, rates are lower in autumn.

For the most part, the Maine Coast slumbers in **winter,** often blanketed in white. Skiing, snowshoeing, and ice skating replace hiking, biking, and boating. Choices in lodging, dining, and activities are fewer, but rates are generally far lower. In areas with solid year-round populations, life goes on full tilt.

Best of the Maine Coast

Start your tour of the coast with Maine's biggest draws: the three Ls (lighthouses, lobster, and L. L. Bean). Maine's 64 lighthouses stretch from York's Nubble to candy-striped West Quoddy Head, in Lubec. Lobster, of course, can be found practically everywhere along the coast, but the best way to enjoy it is at a no-fuss lobster shack. Bean's ever-expanding campus in Freeport is the massive outdoor retailer's mother ship, but it also has an outlet in Ellsworth.

With more time, continue north up the coast for five days in the Acadia region, followed by some time in the Down East Coast.

Lobster, Lighthouses, and L. L. Bean

If you're arriving by airplane, use Portland International Jetport. This six-day tour heads north up the coast, concentrating on the **Greater Portland, Mid-Coast,** and **Penobscot Bay** regions. Book your first two nights of lodging in Portland, the second two in Damariscotta/Newcastle, and the last two in the Rockland/Camden area.

DAY 1

Try to arrive in **Portland** in time to enjoy an afternoon cruise with **Lucky Catch Lobster Tours;** perhaps you'll catch your dinner. If not, you can still enjoy a lobster on the waterfront.

DAY 2

Loop out to **South Portland** and **Cape Elizabeth** to visit **Spring Point Ledge Light** and **Portland Head Light,** a Maine icon. You won't find a better setting for lunch than **The Lobster Shack,** with views of crashing surf and **Cape Elizabeth Light.** In the afternoon, consider visiting the **Portland Museum of Art** to view masterworks by Maine-related artists or book a sail amid the islands of **Casco Bay.** Still craving lobster? Try an inspired version by one of Maine's nationally recognized chefs (advance reservations recommended). Cap the day

Coastal Maine Botanical Gardens

dinner with a view at Fish House Fish, Monhegan Island

with a midnight shopping run to **L. L. Bean** in Freeport.

DAY 3

Spend the morning at the **Maine Maritime Museum** in Bath, and perhaps enjoy a **lighthouse cruise on the Kennebec River.** For lunch, mosey down to **Five Islands Lobster Company** in Georgetown. Dip down the Boothbay Peninsula to while away what's left of the afternoon at the **Coastal Maine Botanical Gardens.**

DAY 4

Book a day trip to **Monhegan Island** from New Harbor. This car-free, carefree gem, about a dozen miles off the coast, is laced with hiking trails and has earned a place in art history books as the Artists' Island. Lunch? Lobster at **Fish House Fish,** of course. Before or afterward, mosey down to **Pemaquid Point Lighthouse.** Alternatively, poke around the peninsula, visiting **Fort William Henry,** rolling up your sleeves at an authentic lobster shack in **Round Pond,** and browsing **Damariscotta's Main Street shops.**

DAY 5

En route to Rockland, nose over to **Owls Head** to view the lighthouse. In downtown Rockland, tour the **Maine Lighthouse Museum** and **Farnsworth Art Museum.** Grab lunch downtown, and then walk it off by padding out the breakwater to **Rockland Breakwater Light.** Tonight, treat yourself to dinner at **Primo;** make advance reservations for the dining room, or sit in the upstairs counter room or bar, where it's more casual and less pricey.

DAY 6

Hop a ferry to **Vinalhaven Island** and spend the better part of the day exploring: perhaps hiking Lane's Island Preserve, pedaling around the island or paddling protected waters, swimming in the quarries, visiting the historical society museum, and soaking in island life. End the day with a lobster dinner at **McLoon's Lobster Shack** in Spruce Head; it doesn't get any finer.

DAY 7 (MORNING)

Drive or hike to the top of **Mount Battie,** in **Camden Hills State Park,** for panoramic vistas over Penobscot Bay. If time permits, enjoy a morning **lighthouse-themed windjammer cruise** out of Camden harbor, before returning to Portland for you flight home or continuing on to Acadia.

Five Days in Acadia

Book nights 7 and 8 on the Blue Hill Peninsula and nights 9 and 10 on Mount Desert Island.

DAYS 7 (CONTINUED) AND 8

Explore the **Blue Hill Peninsula.** If you're a history buff, head for **Castine;** if you're an arts fan, explore the dozens of studios and galleries peppering the peninsula and adjoining **Deer Isle;** if you're a hiker, plentiful preserves salt the region. You can even take a day boat to a remote section of **Acadia National Park** on Isle au Haut, passing a few lighthouses en route.

DAYS 9, 10, AND 11

Few places in Maine rival **Mount Desert Island** and **Acadia National Park** for scenery and outdoor activities. After stopping at the park's visitor center, drive the **Park Loop,** a perfect introduction to Acadia that covers many of the highlights. Be sure to welcome at least one day by watching the sunrise from the summit of **Cadillac Mountain.** After that, follow your passions: Go hiking, bicycling, or sea kayaking; take a carriage ride; attend a ranger session; board an excursion boat or a whale-watching expedition; visit **Asticou Azalea and Thuya Gardens.** Consider packing a picnic, hopping the passenger ferry to **Winter Harbor,** and spending the better part of one day in the **Schoodic section of Acadia National Park.**

Down East Getaway

Book nights 11 and 12 in Lubec and your final

The Lobster Experience

No Maine visit is complete without a real "lobsta dinnah" at a lobster wharf, a sometimes rough-and-tumble operation within sight and scent of the ocean. Keep an eye on the weather, pick a sunny day, and head out.

If you spot a lobster place with "Restaurant" in its name and no outside dining, keep going. You want to eat outdoors, at a wooden picnic table, with a knockout view of boats, islands, and the sea. Whatever place you choose, the drill is much the same, and the "dinners" are served anytime from noonish until around sunset.

Dress casually so you can manhandle the lobster without messing up your good clothes. If you want beer or wine, call ahead and ask if the place serves it; you may need to bring your own. Carry some insect repellent, in case mosquitoes crash the party.

It's not unusual to see lobster-wharf devotees carting picnic baskets with hors d'oeuvres, salads, and baguettes. I've even seen candles and champagne. Save room for dessert. Many lobster shacks are as renowned for their pies or other homemade delights as the crustacean itself.

Here are a dozen of my favorite lobster shacks salting the Maine coast:

- **Chauncey Creek Lobster Pier, Kittery Point:** For more than 40 years, the Spinney family has operated this popular spot with views toward Pepperrell Cove.
- **The Lobster Shack, Cape Elizabeth:** Ocean views, crashing surf, and even a lighthouse have enticed lobster-lovers to this location since the 1920s.
- **Harraseeket Lunch and Lobster Company, South Freeport:** Take a break from power shopping at L. L. Bean and head to this unfussy spot on the working harbor.
- **Five Islands Lobster Company, Georgetown:** On this working wharf, you can watch sailboats playing hide-and-seek amid the spruce-topped islands in the harbor.
- **Round Pond Lobster Co-op and Muscongus Bay Lobster, Round Pond:** These two share a parking lot and overlook dreamy Round Pond Harbor. The co-op keeps it simple, with lobsters only. Muscongus Bay earns kid-friendly points for its touch tank filled with slimy and spiky sea critters.

McLoon's Lobster Shack

- **Waterman's Beach Lobster, S. Thomaston:** The James Beard Foundation gave Waterman's Beach Lobster, overlooking a working pier and island-studded Mussel Ridge Channel, an award for being an "American Classic."
- **McLoon's Lobster Shack, Spruce Head:** Watch lobstermen unload their catches and savor island-salted views at this off-the-beaten-path spot.
- **Fish House Fish, Monhegan Island:** It doesn't get more in-the-rough than this shack on a beach overlooking Monhegan's harbor.
- **Perry's Lobster Shack and Pier, Surry:** It's worth the drive down Surry Neck to find this tucked-away gem with views to Mount Desert Island.
- **Thurston's Lobster Pound, Bernard:** The two-story, screened-in dining area tops a wharf above Bass Harbor.
- **Lunt's Dockside Deli, Frenchboro:** Hard to beat this spot, overlooking a working harbor on Long Island, eight miles off Mount Desert Island.
- **Quoddy Bay Lobster, Eastport:** Watch the tide change and boats unload their catches on Passamaquoddy Bay.

West Quoddy Head Light

night in Eastport (unless your flight schedule requires otherwise).

DAY 12

Down East Maine beckons. En route to **Lubec,** loop through **Cherryfield** to ogle the architecture and browse the general store or down to Cutler to hike the spectacular trails of the **Cutler Coast Public Preserve.** Be sure to visit Maine's candy-striped lighthouse at **West Quoddy Head State Park,** where you can tour the museum and walk the trail edging the seaside cliffs.

DAY 13

If you've brought your passport or passport card, spend the morning at **Roosevelt Campobello International Park.** Drive to the island's tip to view and perhaps visit **Head Harbour Lightstation.** Otherwise poke around **Lubec** before edging around Cobscook Bay to **Eastport,** home to some of the highest tides on the East Coast. Browse downtown shops and soak up small-town Down East life. When you have a hankering for another lobster meal, **Quoddy Bay Lobster** is the answer.

DAY 14

After catching the sunrise, drive to **Bangor** (allow at least three hours) for your flight home. If you have a late flight out of Portland, connect to I-95 in Bangor (allow an additional 2.5 hours). If you've added a final night in Portland, return via Route 1 and break in **Belfast** for lunch before continuing on to Portland.

Off-Season Escapes

Although it's true that some coastal communities all but roll up the sidewalks after Columbus Day, not all do. Visiting in the off-season, from mid-October through late May, has its merits. Sure, the water's too cold for a swim, except for the annual polar bear dips on New Year's Day, and many outdoor attractions and small museums are shuttered, but there are pluses. Rates are low, crowds are few, and traffic is nonexistent. Winter recreation is a draw, and in bigger cities and college towns, cultural offerings actually increase in winter.

Sun, snow, rain, fog, sea smoke, and ice are all possibilities, which means being prepared for all. In late fall, it's best to avoid the woods unless dressed in hunter orange; in early spring, warm and waterproof boots are a must for slush and mud. In winter, you might walk, snowshoe, or cross-country ski across a beach; glide across a frozen pond; or perhaps even don alpine skis or snowboard or toboggan for a downhill schuss.

The following are good bets for an off-season escape. If you want to avoid the hassles of winter transportation, Portland, Freeport, and Brunswick are all on the Amtrak Downeaster train line, and if you stay downtown in any of them, you won't need a vehicle.

Ogunquit and Kennebunkport

Neither of these two Southern Coast beach towns truly slumbers until after Christmas (and Kennebunkport's **Christmas Prelude** alone is worth a visit), but even then, a handful of restaurants and inns remain open. Winter is best for immersing in the quietude of the season, gazing spellbound at furious ocean waters, or simply hunkering down fireside with a good book and a glass of wine.

Portland

Prefer more action? Maine's cultural hub keeps up the pace in winter with a full slate of theatrical and musical performances. Restaurants remain open, and it's far easier to get a reservation at the

Cross-country skiing is a great winter activity.

Maine Maritime Museum

top tables. On a brilliant day, bundle up and ride an island-bound ferry. On a stormy one, watch surf crash against the craggy shoreline under Portland Head Light. Take advantage of the city's urban trail network and outlying parks.

Freeport

This is the perfect spot to shop till you drop. **L. L. Bean** never closes its doors, and the more than 100 shops and outlets in its shadow keep business hours in winter. Post-Christmas, the sales are abundant, and you won't be fighting for a dressing room. Need a breather from shopping? **Wolfe's Neck Woods State Park** is open and offers winter programs.

Brunswick and Bath

Thanks to **Bowdoin College,** Brunswick's cultural offerings are plentiful in winter. In addition, you can skate on the town mall, forage for treats at the farmers market, and enjoy ocean views. Nearby Bath's downtown is filled with independent shops as well as a Reny's—Maine's favorite discount brand-name store—and the **Maine Maritime Museum** is open.

Rockland and Camden

Museums—including **The Farnsworth Art Museum** and **Owls Head Transportation**—and downtown shops keep Rockland lively year-round, and the January Pies on Parade event draws throngs. Just up the road in Camden, you can ski, snowboard, and toboggan at the **Camden Snow Bowl;** winter hike or cross-country ski at **Camden Hills State Park;** and savor harbor views. Both towns offer active cultural programs and live entertainment.

Mount Desert Island

The island, home to **Acadia National Park,** is mighty quiet in winter, but remains open for snowmobiling, cross-country skiing, snowshoeing, winter hiking, and even, for the hardy, camping. The College of the Atlantic offers lectures and live entertainment, and a handful of restaurants and accommodations are open year-round.

Make-Your-Own Maine

Whether you want to craft furniture, build a boat, sail, or play a musical instrument, there's a learning vacation for you. Here's a sampling.

BUILD A SURFBOARD

York's **Grain Surfboards** is renowned for its handcrafted wooden surfboards, but it also offers surfboard-building classes and a **Surfboard Builder's Fantasy Camp** (207/457-5313, www.grainsurfboards.com). The former are group programs; the latter is a one-on-one weeklong program where you work with a personal board builder to craft your own perfect board.

BUILD A BOAT

Build a boat, a canoe, a classic sea chest, or a remote-control pond yacht. Those are just a sampling from the dozens of boatbuilding and related craft courses offered each summer at the 60-acre waterfront campus of **The WoodenBoat School** (41 WoodenBoat Lane, Brooklin, 207/359-4651, www.thewoodenboatschool.com). There's even a popular family week program. Lodging and meals packages are available.

Word of mouth seems to be the best marketing tool for **The Carpenter's Boatshop** (207/677-2614, www.carpentersboatshop.org) in Pemaquid. Founded in 1979, the boatshop accepts interested applicants of any denomination to join a community dedicated to both spirituality and boatbuilding. Sessions run mid-September-mid-June, and there's no tuition. Room and board are provided. During the summer months, five-day fee-based classes are offered in furniture and boat building.

CRAFT FURNITURE

One-week to nine-month courses are for various woodworking skills, such as furniture making, turning, carving, design and technology, and finishing, are offered at the year-round **Center for Furniture Craftsmanship** (207/594-5611, www.woodschool.org) in Rockport, established in 1993. The center can help arrange lodging and meals.

GO GREEN

Since 1974, the **Shelter Institute** (207/442-7938, www.shelterinstitute.com) in Woolwich has trained neophytes and professionals in energy-efficient home design and construction techniques. Courses take place on the school's 68-acre campus in Woolwich, five miles north of Bath.

The WoodenBoat School

MAKE MUSIC

Learn to play the fiddle by ear at the **Maine Fiddle Camp** (207/443-5411, www.mainefiddle.org) in Montville, held on the grounds of Camp NEOFA in Montville. Campers stay in rustic cabins or tents and enjoy communal meals outdoors, and there's plenty of time to swim or hang out in the afternoon before the evening concerts, dances, and jams. Weekend camps are usually held in June, with weeklong sessions offered in June and August.

You're never too old to learn how to play a musical instrument or to sing. **Summerkeys** (207/733-2316 June 15-Oct. 1, 973/316-6220 Oct. 1-June 15, www.summerkeys.com) in Lubec is a music school without admission requirements. Its premise is inviting: "Come as you are to enjoy the study, the work and the beauty of the Maine Coast." Instruction is offered in numerous musical instruments, including piano, violin, flute, guitar, cello, oboe, and clarinet, as well as in voice. Beginners are welcome.

Hidden Treasure: Antiques and Junktiques

Whether you have a practiced eye or just enjoy the thrill of the hunt, you'll find these the best places to seek genuine collectibles and can't-resist treasures.

WELLS AND VICINITY

Flea market-style shops, antiquarian bookstores, huge barns, and old houses overflowing with "good stuff" line both sides of Route 1 in Wells and nearby towns. Don't miss **R. Jorgensen Antiques,** with 11 rooms of fine European and American antiques, or **Douglas N. Harding Rare Books** for antiquarian volumes and ephemera. Continue up to Kennebunk to **Antiques on Nine** for more finds.

BRUNSWICK AND BATH

Spend a morning shopping in Brunswick. A choice selection fills **Cabot Mill Antiques,** where more than 140 dealers show and sell their wares in the renovated Fort Andross mill complex. Then continue to Bath's **Maine Maritime Museum,** a must for viewing nautical doodads.

WOOLWICH AND WISCASSET

Get an early start for the best pickings at **Montsweag Flea Market.** Afterward, continue north on Route 1, stopping at **Avalon Antiques Market,** a large multidealer shop. Spend the afternoon in downtown Wiscasset prowling through two dozen antiques shops. If time permits, visit two treasure houses in Wiscasset: **Castle Tucker** and the **Nickels-Sortwell House.**

PEMAQUID REGION

Along Route 130, numerous barns have been converted into shops. Return to Route 1 and continue north. Don't miss **Nobleboro Antique Exchange,** a multidealer antiques mall that's much larger than it first appears, or **Maine Antique Toy and Art Museum** in Waldoboro, which also has a shop.

SEARSPORT

Hard to believe any town rivals Wiscasset or Wells for the title Antiques Capital, but Searsport does. Sea captains' homes and big barns now house shops such as **Pumpkin Patch,** which emphasizes Maine antiques, and the **Searsport Antique Mall,** with more than 70 dealers. You'll also find a few roadside flea markets. Learn more about how all these treasures arrived here by visiting the **Penobscot Marine Museum.**

LIBERTY

Stop in Liberty to visit the three floors of antiques at **Liberty Tool Company,** with most of the wares being tools.

Best Hikes

Southern Coast

CUTTS ISLAND TRAIL, RACHEL CARSON NATIONAL WILDLIFE RESERVE, KITTERY

Walk through a coastal preserve on this easy 1.8-mile hike through uplands to a salt marsh. Interpretive panels en route explain the varied habitats.

Greater Portland

MACKWORTH ISLAND, FALMOUTH

Just five minutes from downtown Portland, this 1.5-mile easy amble around the island's vehicle-free perimeter path delivers great views of Casco Bay and Portland Harbor. Don't miss the late governor Percival Baxter's stone-circled pet cemetery.

Mid-Coast

BATES-MORSE MOUNTAIN CONSERVATION AREA, PHIPPSBURG

This relatively easy four-mile round-trip hike crosses a marshland, rises to the summit of 210-foot Morse Mountain, and then descends to Seawall Beach. From the summit, Mount

Southern Coast

Look for ★ to find recommended sights, activities, dining, and lodging.

Highlights

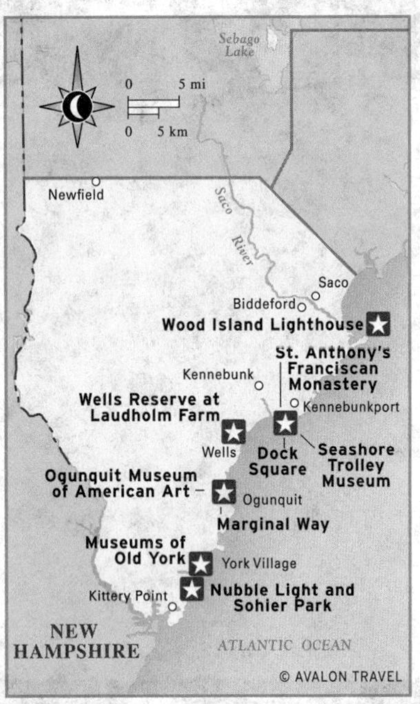

★ **Museums of Old York:** York dates from the 1640s, and on this campus of historic buildings you can peek into early life in the area (page 37).

★ **Nubble Light and Sohier Park:** You'll likely recognize this often-photographed Maine Coast icon, which is the easiest lighthouse to see in the region (page 37).

★ **Ogunquit Museum of American Art:** It's hard to say which is more jaw-dropping, the art or the view (page 46).

★ **Marginal Way:** Escape the hustle and bustle of Ogunquit with a stroll on this paved shorefront path (page 46).

★ **Wells Reserve at Laudholm Farm:** Orient yourself at the visitors center, where you can learn about the history, flora, and fauna of the area, and then take a leisurely walk to the seashore, passing through a variety of habitats (page 47).

★ **Seashore Trolley Museum:** Ding-ding-ding goes the bell, and zing-zing-zing go your heartstrings, especially if you're a trolley fan (page 56).

★ **Dock Square:** Brave the shopping crowds and browse the dozens of fishing shacks-turned-boutiques in the heart of Kennebunkport (page 59).

★ **St. Anthony's Franciscan Monastery:** It's hard to believe this oasis of calm is just a short stroll from busy Dock Square (page 59).

★ **Wood Island Lighthouse:** Tour Maine's second-oldest lighthouse and perhaps even climb the tower (page 71).

Drive over the I-95 bridge from New Hampshire into Maine's Southern Coast region on a bright summer day and you'll swear the air is cleaner, the sky is bluer, the trees are greener, and the roadside signs are more upbeat. "Welcome to Maine: The Way Life Should Be." (Or is it the way life *used* to be?)

Most visitors come to this region for the spectacular attractions of the justly world-famous Maine Coast—the inlets, villages, and especially the beaches—but it's also rich in history. Southernmost York County, part of the original Province of Maine, was incorporated in 1636, only 16 years after the *Mayflower* pilgrims reached Plymouth, Massachusetts. Accordingly, it reeks of history: ancient cemeteries, musty archives, and architecturally stunning homes and public buildings are everywhere here. Probably the best places to dive into that history are the sites of the Museums of Old York in York Harbor.

Geological fortune smiled on this 50-mile ribbon, endowing it with a string of sandy beaches—nirvana for sun worshippers, but less enchanting to swimmers, who need to steel themselves to be able to spend much time in the ocean, especially in early summer before the water temperature has reached a tolerable level.

Complementing those beaches are amusement parks and arcades, fishing shacks-turned-chic boutiques, a surprising number of good restaurants given the region's seasonality, and some of the state's prettiest parks and preserves. Spend some time poking around the small villages that give the region so much character. Many have been gussied up and gentrified quite a bit, yet retain their seafaring or farming bones.

Some Mainers refer to the Southern Coast as northern Massachusetts. Sometimes it can seem that way, not only for the numbers of Massachusetts plates in evidence but also because many former Massachusetts residents have moved here for the quality of life but continue to commute to jobs in the Boston area. The resulting downside is escalating

Previous: Marginal Way; Ogunquit's 3.5 miles of sandy beach. **Above:** Cape Neddick Light, better known as "The Nubble."

Southern Coast

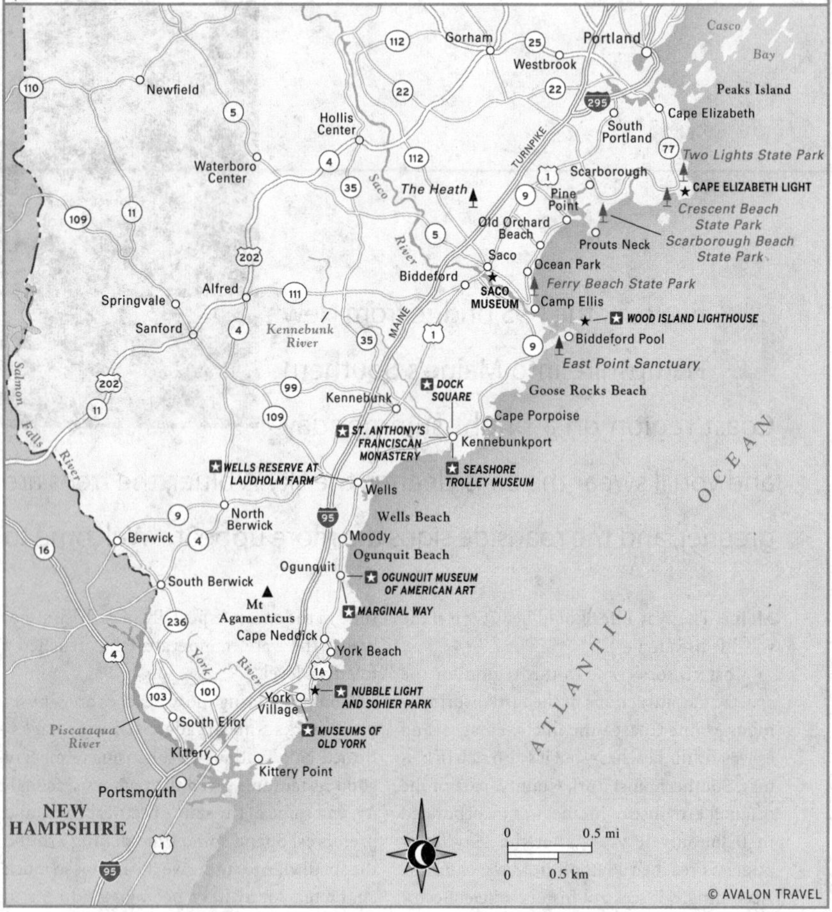

real-estate prices that have forced folks off land that has been in their families for generations and pushed those in traditional seafaring occupations inland. Still, if you nose around and get off the beaten path, you'll find that the real Maine is still here.

PLANNING YOUR TIME

Maine's Southern Coast is a rather compact region, but it's heavily congested, especially in summer. Still, with a minimum of four days, you should be able to take in most of the key sights, including beaches and museums, as long as you don't spend too many hours basking in the sun.

Route 1, the region's primary artery, often has bumper-to-bumper traffic. If you're hopscotching towns, consider using I-95, which has exits for York, Kennebunk, and Saco-Biddeford-Old Orchard Beach. Parking can also be a challenge and expensive, but a trolley system operates in summer and connects most towns, making it easy to avoid the hassles and help the environment.

July and August are the busiest months, with the best beach weather. Spring and fall are lovely, and most attractions are open. In winter, you can walk the beaches without running into another soul, it's easy to get dinner reservations, and lodging prices plummet; the trade-off is that fewer businesses are open.

Kittery

Maine is home to a lot of well-kept secrets, **Kittery** (pop. 9,490) being one of them. Shoppers rarely get beyond the 120-plus outlets along Route 1, but there's equal value in exploring the back roads of Maine's oldest town, settled in 1623 and chartered in 1647. Parks, a small nautical museum, historic architecture, and foodie finds are only a few of the attractions in Kittery and its "suburb," **Kittery Point.** It was also on Kittery's Badger Island that the Continental Navy sloop-of-war *Ranger,* commanded by John Paul Jones, was launched in 1777. The shipbuilding continues at Portsmouth Naval Shipyard on Kittery's Dennet's Island, the first government shipyard in the United States.

SIGHTS

Avoid the outlet sprawl and see the prettiest part of the area by driving along squiggly Route 103 from the Route 1 traffic circle in Kittery through Kittery Point (administratively part of Kittery) and on to Route 1A in York. You can even make a day of it, stopping at the sights mentioned here. Watch for cyclists and pedestrians, as there are no shoulders and lots of blind corners and hills.

Kittery Historical and Naval Museum

Maritime history buffs shouldn't miss the small but well-stocked **Kittery Historical and Naval Museum** (200 Rogers Rd. Ext., near the junction of Rte. 1 and Rte. 236, Kittery, 207/439-3080, www.kitterymuseum.com, 10am-4pm Wed.-Sun. June-Oct., $5 adults, $3 ages 7-15, $10 family). A large exhibit hall and a small back room contain ship models, fishing gear, old photos and paintings, and an astonishing collection of scrimshaw (carved whale ivory).

Lady Pepperrell House

The 1760 Georgian **Lady Pepperrell House** (Pepperrell Rd./Rte. 103, just before the Fort McClary turnoff, Kittery Point) is privately owned and not open to the public, but it's worth admiring from afar. Nearby, across from the First Congregational Church, is the area's most-visited burying ground. Old-cemetery buffs should bring rubbing gear here for some interesting grave markers. The tomb of Levi Thaxter (husband of poet Celia Thaxter) bears an epitaph written for him by Robert Browning.

Fort McClary State Historic Site

Since the early 18th century, fortifications have stood on this 27-acre headland protecting Portsmouth Harbor from seaborne foes. Contemporary remnants at **Fort McClary** (Rte. 103, Kittery Point, 207/384-5160, daily, $3 nonresident adults, $2 Maine adults, $1 ages 5-11 and nonresident seniors, free resident seniors) include several outbuildings, an 1846 blockhouse, granite walls, and earthworks—all with a view of Portsmouth Harbor. Opposite are the sprawling buildings of the Portsmouth Naval Shipyard. Bring a picnic (covered tables and a lily pond are across the street) and turn the kids loose to run and play. It's officially open May 30-October 1, but the site is accessible in the off-season. The fort is 2.5 miles east of Route 1.

Fort Foster

The only problem with **Fort Foster**

(Pocahontas Rd., off Rte. 103, Gerrish Island, Kittery Point, 207/439-3800, 10am-8pm daily late May-early Sept., 10am-8pm Sat.-Sun. Sept.-May, $10 vehicle pass, $5 adults walk-in, $1 children walk-in) is that it's no secret, so parking can be scarce at this 90-acre municipal park at the entrance to Portsmouth Harbor. On a hot day, arrive early. You can swim, hike the nature trails, fish off the pier (state registration required for ages 16 and older), picnic, and investigate the tidepools. Bring a kite; there's almost always a breeze.

ENTERTAINMENT

Kittery Recreation (207/439-3800, www.kitterycommunitycenter.org) presents a **summer concert series** on the common, which varies year to year; most of the concerts are free.

The Dance Hall (7 Walker St., 207/703/2083, www.thedancehallkittery.org), sited in a former Grange hall, hosts concerts, dances, and classes.

SHOPPING

There is no question that you'll find bargains at Kittery's 120-plus factory outlets (www.thekitteryoutlets.com), which are actually a bunch of mini-malls clustered along Route 1. You'll find Calvin Klein, Eddie Bauer, J. Crew, Mikasa, Esprit, Lenox, Timberland, Tommy Hilfiger, Gap, Villeroy & Boch, Barbour, Orvis, Le Creuset, and plenty more (all open daily). Anchoring the scene is the **Kittery Trading Post** (301 Rte. 1, Kittery, 207/439-2700 or 888/587-6246, www.kitterytradingpost.com), a humongous sporting-goods and clothing emporium. Try to avoid the outlets on weekends, when they're especially crowded.

RECREATION

Brave Boat Harbor

Brave Boat Harbor (207/646-9226), one of the Rachel Carson National Wildlife Refuge's 11 Maine coastal segments, is a beautifully unspoiled 7,500-acre wetlands preserve in Kittery Point. There are hiking trails, but the habitat is particularly sensitive here, so be kind to the environment. Take Route 103 to Chauncey Creek Road and continue past the Gerrish Island bridge to Cutts Island Lane. Just beyond it and across a small bridge is a pullout on the left. The 1.8-mile Cutts Island interpretive loop includes a spur ending at a salt marsh. Bring binoculars to spot waterfowl in the marshlands.

Captain and Patty's Piscataqua River Tours

Take a spin around the Piscataqua River Basin with **Captain and Patty's Piscataqua River Tours** (Town Dock, 153 Pepperrell Rd., Kittery Point, 207/439-3655, www.capandpatty.com, $25 adults, $18 under age 10). The 90-minute narrated, historical tour aboard an open launch departs five times daily. En route, Captain Neil Odams points out historic forts, lighthouses, and the naval shipyard.

ACCOMMODATIONS

Put a little *ooh* and *aah* into your touring with a visit to the **Portsmouth Harbor Inn and Spa** (6 Water St., Kittery, 207/439-4040, www.innatportsmouth.com, $165-195). The handsome brick inn, built in 1889, looks out over the Piscataqua River, Portsmouth, and the Portsmouth Naval Shipyard. Five attractive Victorian-style guest rooms, most with water views, are furnished with antiques and have air-conditioning, TVs, Wi-Fi, and phones. There's an outdoor hot tub, and beach chairs are available. Breakfasts are multicourse feasts. Request a back room if you're noise-sensitive, although air-conditioning camouflages traffic noise in summer. Rooms on the third floor have the best views, but these also have handheld showers. Now for the "aah" part: The inn has a full-service spa.

FOOD

Kittery is increasingly a favorite for culinary travelers. The bounty of independent restaurants and specialty food providers expands every season.

Local Flavors

Kittery has an abundance of excellent specialty food stores that are perfect for stocking up for a picnic lunch or dinner. Most are along the section of Route 1 between the Portsmouth bridge and the traffic circle, and five are within steps of one another. At **Beach Pea Baking Co.** (53 Rte. 1, Kittery, 207/439-3555, www.beachpeabaking.com, 7:30am-6pm daily) you can buy fabulous breads and pastries. Sandwiches and salads are made to order 11am-3pm daily. There's pleasant seating indoors and on a patio. Next door is **Golden Harvest** (47 State Rd./Rte. 1, Kittery, 207/439-2113, 9am-7pm daily.), where you can load up on luscious produce. Across the street is **Terra Cotta Pasta Co.** (52 Rte. 1, Kittery, 207/475-3025, www.terracottapastacompany.com, 9am-7pm Mon.-Sat., 10am-5pm Sun.), where in addition to handmade pastas you'll find salads, soups, sandwiches, prepared foods, and lots of other goodies. Count on **Carl's Meat Market** (25 State. Rd., Kittery, 207/439-1557), a butcher shop, for awesome burgers and sandwiches. Let your nose guide you into **Byrne & Carlson** (60 Rte. 1, Kittery, 888/559-9778, www.byrneandcarlson.com), which makes elegant and delicious chocolate for connoisseurs.

Here's a twofold find. **When Pigs Fly** (460 Rte. 1, Kittery, 207/439-4114, www.sendbread.com) earned renown for its old-world artisanal breads made from organic ingredients. Now it's also home to **When Pigs Fly Wood-Fired Pizzeria** (207/438-7036, www.whenpigsflypizzeria.com, 11:30am-9pm Sun.-Thurs., 11:30am-10pm Fri.-Sat., $12-22). Of course there's pizza—Neapolitan style in creative flavor combos—but there are other choices, including house-made charcuterie.

Want a down-home breakfast or lunch? The **Sunrise Grill** (182 State Rd./Rte. 1, Kittery traffic circle, Kittery, 207/439-5748, www.sunrisegrillinc.com, 6:30am-2pm daily, $5-13) delivers with waffles, granola, omelets, Diana's Benedict, salads, sandwiches, and burgers.

Lil's (7 Wallingford Sq., Kittery, 207/703-2800, www.lilscafe.com, 6:30am-4pm Mon.-Fri., 7am-5pm Sat., 7am-4pm Sun.) has earned well-deserved fame for its scratch-made fare, especially its crullers. Breakfast and lunch are available.

Casual Dining

Commitment to using fresh and local foods and a flair for bringing big flavors out of simple ingredients have earned **Anneke Jans** (60 Wallingford Sq., Kittery, 207/439-0001, www.annekejans.net, from 5pm daily, 11am-2pm Sun, $20-35) kudos far beyond Kittery. This is a local hot spot with a lively crowd; reservations are recommended. Gluten-free options are available.

Farm-to-table meets gastropub at **The Black Birch** (2 Government St., Kittery, 207/703-2294, www.theblackbirch.com, 3:30pm-10pm Tues.-Thurs., 3:30pm-11pm Fri.-Sat., $8-19). Upscale comfort foods—such as ricotta gnocchi, poutine and duck confit, and fish and chips—are presented in a menu designed to mix and match and accompanied by a geek-worthy draught beer list.

Ignore the kitschy lighthouse; **Robert's Maine Grill** (326 Rte. 1, Kittery, 207/439-0300, www.robertsmainegrill.com, from 11:30pm daily, $12-32) is a fine place to duck out of the shopping madness and enjoy well-prepared seafood that goes far beyond the usual fried choices, as well as a few landlubber options and a fine selection of Maine craft beers. On Tuesday and Wednesday, community suppers ($14 for three courses) benefit a local nonprofit. Kids' menu available.

Dine inside or out at **Blind Pig Provisions** (2 Badger's Island, Kittery, 207/703-0079, www.blindpigmaine.com, from 11am Wed.-Mon., $12-18), a contemporary gastropub where the evening menu ranges from chicken and waffles to roasted duck breast.

Ethnic Fare

Craving Cal-Mex? Some of the recipes in Luis Valdez's **Loco Coco's Tacos** (36 Walker St., Kittery, 207/438-9322, www.locococos.com, 11am-9pm daily) have been passed down for generations, and the homemade salsas have flavor and kick. If you're feeling really decadent, go for the artery-busting California fries. There are gluten-free and kids' menus too. Most choices are less than $10. Choose from self-serve, dining room, or bar seating.

Chef Rajesh Mandekar blends techniques drawn from Indian, French, and Italian cuisines to create rave-worthy Indian fare at **Tulsi** (20 Walker St., Kittery, 207/451-9511, www.tulsiindianrestaurant.com, from 5pm Tues.-Sun. and noon-2:30pm Sun., $11-23).

Anju Noodle Bar (7 Wallingford Sq., Kittery, 207/703-4298, www.anjunoodlebar.com, noon-9:30pm Sun. and Tues.-Thurs., noon-10 pm Fri.-Sat., $13-18) gets raves for the okonomoyaki and the pork buns. An express lunch menu ($12), including a main course and two sides, is available daily from noon-3:30pm. If you're a hot sauce fan, pick up a bottle or two of the house-made version to spice up your cooking at home.

Chauncey Creek Lobster Pier

Lobster and Clams

If you came to Maine to eat lobster, **Chauncey Creek Lobster Pier** (16 Chauncey Creek Rd., off Rte. 103, Kittery Point, 207/439-1030, www.chaunceycreek.com, 11am-8pm daily mid-May-early Sept., to 7pm Tues.-Sun. early Sept.-Columbus Day) is the real deal. Step up to the window, place your order, take a number, and grab a table (you may need to share) overlooking tidal Chauncey Creek and the woods on the close-in opposite shore. It's a particularly picturesque—and extremely popular—place; parking is a nightmare. BYOB and anything else that's not on the menu.

Lobster-in-the-rough with eye-candy views over Portsmouth are yours at **Morrison's Lobster** (11 Badger's Island West, Kittery, 207/439-2501, 5-8pm Mon.-Wed., noon-9pm Thurs.-Sun.), where you can BYOB.

If clams are high on your must-have list, pay a visit to **Bob's Clam Hut** (315 Rte. 1, Kittery, 207/439-4233, www.bobsclamhut.com, from 11am daily, $10-23), next to the Kittery Trading Post. An institution in these parts since 1956, Bob's is *the* place for fried seafood, especially clams; the tartar sauce is their secret weapon.

GETTING THERE AND AROUND

Kittery is 60 miles or just over an hour via I-95 from Boston, although it can take longer in summer when traffic backs up at tolls. It's about eight miles or 15 minutes to York via I-95. Allow about 20 minutes via Route 1, although traffic can be bumper-to-bumper in the stretch by the outlets.

The Berwicks

Probably the best known of the area's present-day inland communities is the riverside town of South Berwick, thanks to a historical and literary tradition dating to the 17th century, with antique cemeteries to prove it. The 19th- and 20th-century novels of Sarah Orne Jewett and Gladys Hasty Carroll have lured many a contemporary visitor to explore their rural settings, an area aptly described by Carroll as "a small patch of earth continually occupied but never crowded for more than three hundred years."

A ramble through the Berwicks—South Berwick and its siblings—makes a nice diversion from the coast, and because it's off most visitors' radar screens, it's a good alternative for lodging and dining, too.

SIGHTS

Don't blink or you might miss the tiny sign outside the 1774 **Sarah Orne Jewett House Museum and Visitor Center** (5 Portland St./Rte. 4, South Berwick, 207/384-2454, www.historicnewengland.org, 11am-5pm Fri.-Sun. June 1-Oct. 15, $8) smack in the center of town. Park on the street and join one of the tours to learn details of the Jewett family and its star, Sarah (1849-1909), author of *The Country of the Pointed Firs*, a New England classic. The adjacent 1854 Greek Revival-style house is now a visitor center with exhibitions and programs. Books by and about her are available in the gift shop. House tours are at 11am, 1pm, 2pm, 3pm, and 4pm. The house is one of two local Historic New England properties. The house is also open on the first and third Saturdays of the month from Nov. 1-May 31.

The other property is the 18th-century **Hamilton House** (40 Vaughan's Lane, South Berwick, 207/384-2454, www.historicnewengland.org, 11am-5pm Wed.-Sun. June 1-Oct. 15, $10), which crowns a bluff overlooking the Salmon Falls River and is flanked by handsome Colonial Revival gardens. Knowledgeable guides relate the house's fascinating history. It was the setting for Sarah Orne Jewett's *The Tory Lover*, among other things. Tours begin only on the hour, the last at 4pm. In July the **Sunday in the Garden**

the 18th-century Hamilton House in South Berwick

concert series takes place on the lawn ($10 includes a free pass to come back and see the house). Pray for sun; the concert is moved indoors on rainy days. From Route 236 at the southern edge of South Berwick (watch for a signpost), turn left onto Brattle Street and take the second right onto Vaughan's Lane.

Also here is the 150-acre hilltop campus of **Berwick Academy,** Maine's oldest prep school, chartered in 1791 with John Hancock's signature. The coed school's handsome graystone William H. Fogg Memorial Library ("The Fogg") is named for the same family connected with Harvard's Fogg Art Museum. The building's highlight is an incredible collection of dozens of 19th-century stained-glass windows, most designed by Victorian artist Sarah Wyman Whitman, who also designed jackets for Sarah Orne Jewett's books. Thanks to a diligent fundraising effort, the windows have been restored to their former glory.

WORTHWHILE DETOUR

About 25 minutes north of Berwick, via Route 4, is the quiet community of Alfred, home to a Shaker community begun in 1793. In 1931, the Alfred Shakers sold their assets to the Brothers of Christian Instruction and moved in with the Sabbathday Lake Shaker Community. The classic Shaker song *Simple Gifts* is attributed to Alfred Elder Joseph Brackett. Eight original Shaker buildings and a cemetery remain on Shaker Hill, part of the National Register of Historic Places Alfred Shaker Historic District. The Friends of Alfred Shaker Museum maintain the former carriage house as the **Alfred Shaker Museum** (118 Shaker Hill Rd., Alfred, www.alfredshakermuseum.com, 1pm-4pm Wed. and Sat., May-early-Nov., free). Afterward, treat yourself at **Shaker Pond Ice Cream** (148 Waterboro Rd., Alfred, 207/459-5070). Take your cone to **Old Sheep Meadows Nursery** (90 Federal St., Alfred, 207/324-5211, www.oldsheepmeadowsnursery.com), where you can explore five acres of display gardens emphasizing hardy root roses, woodland gardens, daylilies, and pre-Civil War apple trees.

RECREATION

When you're ready to stretch your legs, head to **Vaughan Woods State Park** (28 Oldfields Rd., South Berwick, 207/384-5160, 9am-8pm daily late May-early Sept., park trails accessible year-round, $3 adults, $1 ages 5-11, free over age 65 or under age 5) and wander along the three miles of trails in the 250-acre

Alfred Shaker Museum

riverside preserve. It adjoins Hamilton House and is connected via a path, but there's far more parking at the park itself.

ENTERTAINMENT

Another reason to venture inland is to catch a production at the **Hackmatack Playhouse** (538 School St./Rte. 9, Berwick, 207/698-1807, www.hackmatack.org), midway between North Berwick and Berwick. The popular summer theater, operating since 1972, operates from a renovated barn reminiscent of a past era and has 8pm performances Wednesday-Saturday, a 2pm matinee Thursday, and children's shows. Tickets are $25-30 adults, $20-23 seniors, $10 high school and younger students.

ACCOMMODATIONS

These two inns are sleepers (sorry, couldn't resist). Both are within striking distance of the coast yet provide far more value than similar properties in seaside communities.

Once the headmaster's residence for nearby Berwick Academy, the elegant turn-of-the-20th-century **Academy Street Inn Bed and Breakfast** (15 Academy St., South Berwick, 207/384-5633, year-round, $105-130) has crystal chandeliers, leaded-glass windows, working fireplaces, and high-ceilinged rooms full of antiques. The handsome home, owned by Paul and Lee Fopeano, has five guest rooms with private baths. Full breakfast and afternoon lemonade on the 60-foot screened porch are a real treat.

Innkeepers Ben Gumm and Sally McLaren have turned the outstanding 25-room Queen Anne-style Hurd mansion into the **Angel of the Berwicks** (2 Elm St., North Berwick, 207/676-2133, www.angeloftheberwicks.com, $119-169), an elegant antiques-filled inn. The property, listed on the National Register of Historic Places, has 11-foot ceilings, stained-glass windows, hand-carved friezes, and ornate mantelpieces. There's even a baby grand piano in the music room. Rates include a full breakfast.

FOOD

A local institution since 1960, **Fogarty's** (471 Main St., South Berwick, 207/384-8361, www.fogartysrestaurant.net, 11am-8:30pm daily, $8-20) has expanded through the years from a simple take-out place to a local favorite for inexpensive fresh fare and family-friendly dining. Ask for a river-view table in the back room.

Nature's Way Market (271 Main St.,

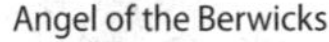
Angel of the Berwicks

South Berwick, 207/384-3210, 8am-9pm Mon.-Fri., 9am-8pm Sat.-Sun.) isn't your ordinary health-food store. In addition to carrying healthful fare, it specializes in locally made specialty foods and a wide array of wine and beer, is a state-licensed liquor store, and also contains a butcher shop where you can purchase made-to-order sandwiches. Stock up here for a picnic in the park.

Relish (404 Main St., South Berwick, 207/384-8249, 5:30pm-9pm Wed.-Sat., $20-34) is an intimate, low-key neighborhood bistro where Linda Robinson and Christine Prunier serve well-crafted dinners with international accents. A gluten-free menu is available. Make reservations: It's worth it.

Thistle Pig (279 Main St., So. Berwick, 207/704-0624, www.thistlepig.com, 11am-10pm Mon. and Thurs.-Sat., 10am-10pm Sun., $16-26). The menu changes frequently to reflect what's fresh and local. Possibilities may include sautéed bluefish, fried pork shoulder, or potato gnocchi.

GETTING THERE

South Berwick is about 11 miles or 20 minutes from Kittery via Route 236. It's about 10 miles or 20 minutes from South Berwick to York via Routes 236 and 91.

The Yorks

Four villages with distinct personalities—upscale **York Harbor,** historic **York Village,** casual **York Beach,** and semirural **Cape Neddick**—make up the **Town of York** (pop. 12,529). First inhabited by Native Americans, who named it Agamenticus, the area was settled as early as 1624, so history is serious business here. High points were its founding by Sir Ferdinando Gorges and the arrival of well-to-do vacationers in the 19th century. In between were Indian massacres, economic woes, and population shuffles. The town's population explodes in summer, which is pretty obvious in July-August when you're searching for a free patch of York Beach sand or a parking place. York Beach, with its seasonal surf and souvenir shops and amusements, has long been the counterpoint to

the Emerson-Wilcox House, one of the historical homes in York Village

York's Old Burying Ground dates from 1735.

genteel York Village, but that's changing with the restoration and rebirth of York Beach's downtown buildings and the arrival of tony restaurants, shops, and condos.

History and genealogy buffs can study the headstones in the Old Burying Ground or comb the archives of the Museums of Old York. For lighthouse fans, there are Cape Neddick Light Station ("Nubble Light") and Boon Island, six miles offshore. Rent horses or mountain bikes on Mount Agamenticus, board a deep-sea fishing boat in York Harbor, or spend an hour hiking the Cliff Path in York Harbor. For the kids there's a zoo, a lobsterboat cruise, a taffy maker, and, of course, the beach.

SIGHTS

★ Museums of Old York

Based in York Village, the **Museums of Old York** (207 York St., York Village, 207/363-4974, www.oldyork.org, museum buildings 10am-5pm Tues.-Sat., 1pm-5pm Sun., early June-mid-Oct., $12 adults or $8 one building, $5 ages 4-16 or $3 one building) are a collection of colonial and postcolonial buildings plus a research library open throughout the summer. Start at the **Jefferds' Tavern Visitor Center** (5 Lindsay Rd., York Village), where you'll need to buy tickets. Don't miss the **Old Burying Ground,** dating from 1735, across the street (rubbings are not allowed). Nearby are the **Old Gaol** and the **School House,** both fun for kids, and the **Emerson-Wilcox House.** About 0.5 mile down Lindsay Road on the York River are the **John Hancock Warehouse** and the **George Marshall Store Gallery** (140 Lindsay Rd.), operated in the summer as a respected contemporary art gallery; across the river is the **Elizabeth Perkins House.** Antiques buffs shouldn't miss the Wilcox and Perkins Houses. Both are open by guided tour; other buildings are self-guided. Visit some or all of the buildings at your own pace. You can walk to some of the sites from the tavern; to reach others you'll need a car, and parking may be limited.

★ Nubble Light and Sohier Park

The best-known photo op in York is the distinctive 1879 lighthouse known formally as **Cape Neddick Light Station,** familiarly "The Nubble." Although there's no access to the lighthouse's island, the **Sohier Park Welcome Center** (Nubble Rd., off Rte. 1A, between Long and Short Sands Beaches, York Beach, 207/363-7608, www.nubblelight.org, 9am-7pm daily mid-May-mid-Oct.) provides the perfect viewpoint (and has restrooms). Parking is limited, but the turnover is fairly good. It's not a bad idea, however, to walk from the Long Sands parking area or come by bike (watch for the road's inadequate shoulders). Weekdays, this is also a popular spot for scuba divers.

Sayward-Wheeler House

Owned by the Boston-based nonprofit organization Historic New England, the 1718 **Sayward-Wheeler House** (9 Barrell Lane

The Yorks

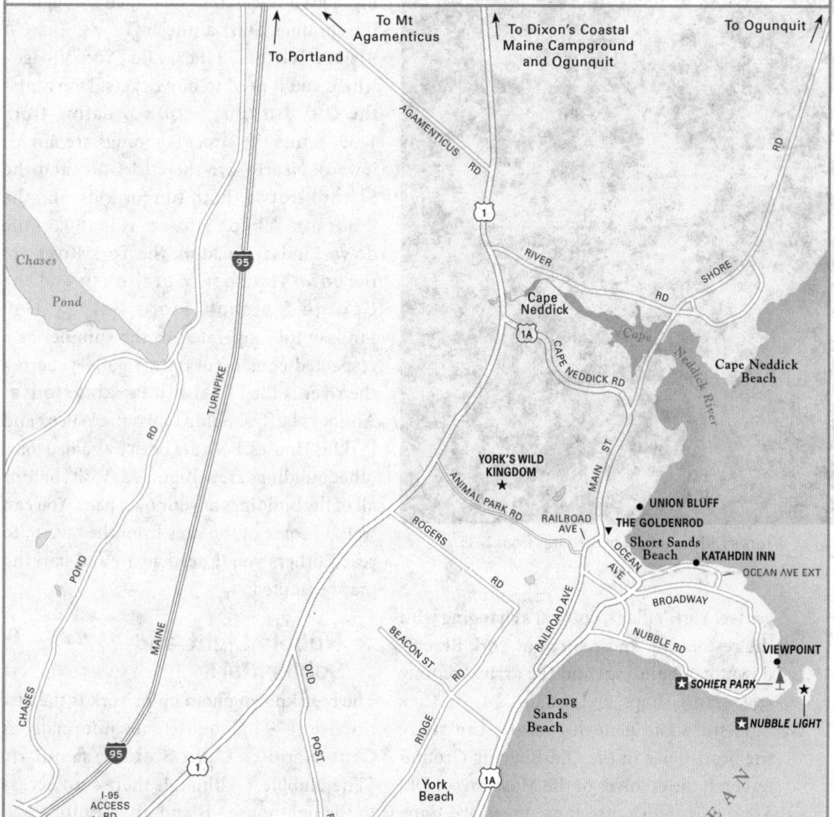

To Mt Agamenticus
To Portland
To Dixon's Coastal Maine Campground and Ogunquit
To Ogunquit
AGAMENTICUS RD
RD
1
95
Chases Pond
RIVER RD
SHORE RD
Cape Neddick
1A
Cape Neddick River
CAPE NEDDICK RD
Cape Neddick Beach
TURNPIKE
RD
MAIN ST
YORK'S WILD KINGDOM
ANIMAL PARK RD
UNION BLUFF
RAILROAD AVE
THE GOLDENROD
ROGERS RD
OCEAN AVE
Short Sands Beach
KATAHDIN INN
OCEAN AVE EXT
BROADWAY
POND
RAILROAD AVE
NUBBLE RD
BEACON ST RD
VIEWPOINT
MAINE
OLD POST RD
SOHIER PARK
CHASES
Long Sands Beach
NUBBLE LIGHT
RIDGE
95
1
York Beach
1A
I-95 ACCESS RD
ATLANTIC OCEAN
STONEWALL KITCHEN
Long Sands Beach
VISITOR CENTER
RD
To New Hampshire
YORK
LONG SANDS
1A
MUSEUMS OF OLD YORK
ST
Lobster Cove
ORGANUG RD
LINDSAY RD
BARRELL LN
WOODBRIDGE RD
Barrells Mill Pond
ST
SENTRY HILL RD
YORK
INN AT TANGLEWOOD HALL
Steedman Woods
York Harbor
York River
WIGGLY BRIDGE
SAYWARD-WHEELER HOUSE
SHIP'S CELLAR PUB
YORK HARBOR INN
CLIFF PATH
SEABURY RD
MORNING GLORY INN
103
Bragdon Island
Harbor Beach
York Harbor
Stage Neck
STAGE NECK INN
Harris Island
0 0.5 mi
0 0.5 km
To New Hampshire
HARRIS ISLAND RD

York's Wild Kingdom has an amusement park geared toward young families.

Ext., York Harbor, 207/384-2454, www.historicnewengland.org, $5) occupies a prime site at the edge of York Harbor. It's open with tours on the hour 11am-4pm the second and fourth Saturday of the month June-mid-October. The house's original period furnishings are all in excellent condition. Take Route 1A to Lilac Lane (Rte. 103) to Barrell Lane and then to Barrell Lane Extension, or access it from the Fisherman's Walk.

York's Wild Kingdom

More than 250 creatures—including tigers, zebras, lions, elephants, and monkeys—find a home at **York's Wild Kingdom** (102 Railroad Ave., off Rte. 1, York Beach, 207/363-4911 or 800/456-4911, www.yorkzoo.com). It's not what you'd call a state-of-the-art zoo, but with its Butterfly Kingdom exhibit and amusement park—with classics such as a Ferris wheel, merry-go-round, kiddie rides, and haunted house—it's a favorite with young families. Other activities include an 18-hole mini golf course, batting cages, a midway with $1 games, an arcade, and go-karts; it's seriously easy to spend a day here. Admission covering the zoo and most rides is $23 adults, $18 ages 4-12, $6 under age 4; an unlimited-rides day pass is $12. Zoo-only admission is $15 adults, $9 ages 4-12, $1 under age 4. There is no fee to simply walk through the amusements area. The zoo is open 10am-6pm daily, late June to late August, closing at 5 pm from late May to late June and late August to late September. Amusement park hours are noon-9:30pm from late June until late August.

ENTERTAINMENT AND EVENTS

Live Music

Inn on the Blues (7 Ocean Ave., York Beach, 207/351-3221, www.innontheblues.com) has live music or a DJ (acoustic, blues, reggae) every night during the summer. The **Ship's Cellar Pub** (480 York St., York Harbor, 800/343-3869) in the York Harbor Inn frequently has live entertainment too. Free concerts are often held at the **Ellis Park Gazebo,** by Short Sands Beach, usually 7pm-9pm early July-early September; check local papers for schedule.

Festivals and Events

Late July-early August, the **York Days** festivities enliven the town with concerts, a road race, sand-castle contests, craft shows, and fireworks.

York Village's **Annual Harvestfest,** in October, includes entertainment, crafts, hayrides, entertainment, and food.

The annual **Lighting of the Nubble** in late November includes cookies, hot chocolate, music, and an appearance by Santa Claus. The best part, though, is seeing the lighthouse glowing for the holidays.

RECREATION

Walks

Next to Harbor Beach, near the Stage Neck Inn, a sign marks the beginning of the **Cliff Path,** a walkway worth taking for its dramatic harbor views in the shadow of elegant summer cottages. On the one-hour round-trip, you'll pass the York Harbor Reading Room, an exclusive club. The path is on private property and traditionally open to the public courtesy of the owners, but controversy surfaces periodically about property rights, vandalism, and the condition of some sections of the walk. Note that it's called the Cliff Path for a reason; it's not a good choice for little ones. Another access point is the Hartley Mason Reservation parkland on Route 1A.

A less strenuous route is known variously as the **Shore Path, Harbor Walk,** or **Fisherman's Walk,** running west along the harbor and river from Stage Neck Road and passing the Sayward-Wheeler House before crossing the Wiggly Bridge, a mini-suspension bridge dating from the 1930s that leads into the **Steedman Woods** preserve. Carry binoculars for good boat-watching and birding in the 16-acre preserve, owned by the Old York Historical Society. A one-mile double-loop trail takes less than an hour of easy strolling.

Mount Agamenticus

Drive to the summit of **Mount Agamenticus** ("The Big A") and you're at York County's highest point. It's only 692 feet, but on a clear day you'll have panoramic views of ocean, lakes, woods, and sometimes the White Mountains. The 10,000-acre preserve (www.agamenticus.org), one of the largest remaining expanses of undeveloped forest in coastal New England, is considered among the most biologically diverse wildernesses in Maine. It includes vernal pools and ponds and is home to rare and endangered species. At the summit are a billboard map of the 40-mile trail network and a memorial to Saint Aspinquid, a 17th-century Algonquian Indian leader. Mountain biking is also hugely popular on Agamenticus. Take a picnic, a kite, and binoculars. In the fall, if the wind is from the northwest, watch for migrating hawks; in winter, bring a sled for the best downhill run in southern Maine. From Route 1 in Cape Neddick, take Mountain Road (also called Agamenticus Road) 4.2 miles west to the access road.

Golf

The **Ledges Golf Club** (1 Ledges Dr., off Rte. 91, York, 207/351-9999, www.ledgesgolf.com) is an 18-hole course with daily public tee times.

Short Sands Beach

Swimming

Sunbathing and swimming are big draws in York, with four beaches of varying sizes and accessibility. Bear in mind that traffic can be gridlocked along the beachfront (Rte. 1A) in midsummer, so it may take longer than you expect to get anywhere. **Lifeguards** are usually on duty 9:30am-4pm mid-June-Labor Day at Short Sands Beach, Long Sands Beach, and Harbor Beach. **Bathhouses** at Long Sands and Short Sands are open 9am-7pm daily in midsummer. The biggest **parking area** (metered) is at Long Sands, but that 1.5-mile beach also draws the most visitors. The scarcest parking is at Harbor Beach near the Stage Neck Inn (two-hour spaces along Route 1A) and at Cape Neddick (Passaconaway) Beach near the Ogunquit town line.

Sea Kayaking

Kayak rentals begin at $55/day single, $75 double, from **Excursions: Coastal Maine Outfitting Company** (1740 Rte. 1, Cape Neddick, 207/363-0181, www.excursionsinmaine.com), or sign up for a half-day tour ($60 ages 14 and older, $50 children). A four-hour basics clinic for ages 16 and older is $85. Excursions is based at Dixon's Campground on Route 1, four miles north of the I-95 York exit.

Harbor Adventures (Harris Island Rd., York Harbor, 207/363-8466, www.harboradventures.com) offers instruction and guided sea-kayaking trips from Kittery through Kennebunkport. Prices begin around $45 for a two-hour harbor tour.

Surfing

Want to catch a wave? For surfing or paddleboard information, lessons, or rentals, call **Liquid Dreams Surf Shop** (171 Long Beach Ave., York, 207/351-2545, www.liquiddreamssurf.com, 8am-8pm daily). It's right across from Long Sands Beach.

Bicycling

Berger's Bike Shop (241 York St., York, 207/363-4070) rents hybrid bikes for $40 full day, $30 half-day; lock and helmet are additional.

Fishing

A local expert on fly-fishing, spin fishing, and conventional tackle is **Eldredge Bros. Guide Service** (1480 Rte. 1, Cape Neddick, 207/373-9269, www.eldredgeflyshop.com). Four-hour guided trips for one or two anglers begin at $300 in freshwater, $350 in saltwater.

ACCOMMODATIONS

Bed-and-Breakfasts

A boutique bed-and-breakfast catering to romantics, the **Morning Glory Inn** (120 Seabury Rd., York Harbor, 207/363-2062, www.morninggloryinnmaine.com, $215-265) has just three guest rooms, all spacious and private and all with doors to private patios or yards, air-conditioning, TVs with DVD players, fridges, Wi-Fi, and plentiful other little amenities. The living room, in the original section of the house, was a 17th-century cottage barged over from the Isles of Shoals; the newer post-and-beam great room doubles as a dining area, where a hot breakfast buffet is served. The property is quiet enough to listen to the birds singing in the gardens; it's truly a magical setting, far removed yet convenient to everything York offers.

Everything's casual and flowers are everywhere at the brightly painted **Katahdin Inn** (11 Ocean Ave., York Beach, 207/363-1824, www.thekatahdininn.com, year-round, $125-165), overlooking the breakers of Short Sands Beach. Longtime owners Rae and Paul LeBlanc appropriately refer to it as a "bed and beach." It was built in 1863 and has always been a guesthouse. Nine smallish guest rooms on three floors, eight of them with water views, have four-poster beds and mostly shared baths. Breakfast is not included, but coffee is always available, the rooms have refrigerators, and several eateries are nearby.

Built in 1889, **The Inn at Tanglewood Hall** (611 York St., York Harbor, 207/351-1075, www.tanglewoodhall.com, $185-245) was once the summer home of bandleaders

Jimmy and Tommy Dorsey. More recently, it was a York Historical Society Decorator Show House. It's an elegant, gracious property within walking distance of the beach, yet a world away. All rooms have TV/DVDs and Wi-Fi; some have gas fireplaces, refrigerators, or private porches. Beautiful woodland gardens are another plus.

Inns

York Harbor Inn (Rte. 1A, York Harbor, 207/363-5119 or 800/343-3869, www.yorkharborinn.com, $209-389) is an accommodating spot with a country-inn flavor and a wide variety of guest-room and package-plan options throughout the year. The oldest section of the inn is a 17th-century cabin from the Isles of Shoals. Accommodations are spread out in the inn, the adjacent Yorkshire House, and four elegantly restored houses, all with resident innkeepers: Harbor Hill and Harbor Cliffs are within steps, and the pet-friendly 1730 Harbor Crest and the Chapman Cottage are about a half-mile away. All have TVs, phones, free Wi-Fi, and air-conditioning; some have four-poster beds, fireplaces, and whirlpools; many have water views. Rates include a generous continental breakfast.

You can't miss the **Stage Neck Inn** (100 Stage Neck Rd., York Harbor, 207/363-3850 or 800/340-9901, www.stageneck.com, year-round, from $325 with breakfast), occupying its own private peninsula overlooking York Harbor. Modern resort-style facilities include an indoor and outdoor pool, tennis courts, golf privileges, a spa, a fitness center, and spectacular views from balconies and terraces. The formal Harbor Porches restaurant (no jeans, entrées $24-38) and the casual Sandpiper Bar and Grille are open to nonguests.

Hotels

For more than 150 years, **The Union Bluff** (8 Beach St., York Beach, 207/363-1333 or 800/833-0721, www.unionbluff.com, from $230) has stood sentry like a fortress overlooking Short Sands Beach. Guest rooms are split between three buildings, all within spitting distance of the beach. Most have ocean views. All have TVs, air-conditioning, and phones; some have fireplaces, whirlpool baths, or oceanview decks. Also on the premises are the Beach Street Grill dining room and a pub serving lighter fare. The best deals are the packages, which include breakfast and dinner. The hotel and pub are open year-round; the restaurant is seasonal. It's probably best to avoid dates when there's a wedding in-house.

Condominium Suites

Fabulously sited on the oceanfront and overlooking the Nubble Light, the high-end **ViewPoint** (229 Nubble Rd., York Beach, 207/363-2661, www.viewpointhotel.com, from $320 night, $1,920 week) has luxuriously appointed 1-3-bedroom suites. All have gas fireplaces; fully equipped kitchens; washer-dryers; TVs; phones; private patios, porches, or decks; and Wi-Fi. On the premises are an outdoor heated pool, a grilling area, gardens, and a playground.

Camping

Dixon's Coastal Maine Campground (1740 Rte. 1, Cape Neddick, 207/363-3626, www.dixonscampground.com, $36-44) has more than 100 well-spaced sites on 26 wooded and open acres. It can accommodate tents and small RVs. Electric and water hookups are available. For something different, reserve a yurt ($120). Facilities include a playground and a good-size outdoor heated pool. It's also the base for Excursions sea kayaking (207/363-0181, www.excursionsinmaine.com).

FOOD

Local Flavors

Stonewall Kitchen (Stonewall Lane, York, 207/351-2712 or 800/207-5267, www.stonewallkitchen.com) concocts imaginative condiments and other food products, many of which have received national awards. Go hungry: An espresso bar and an excellent café (8am-4pm Mon.-Sat.,9am-3pm Sun., $7-15) are on the premises.

Sometimes the line runs right out the door of the low-ceilinged, reddish-brown roadside shack that houses local institution **Flo's Steamed Dogs** (1359 Rte. 1, opposite the Mountain Rd. turnoff, Cape Neddick, no phone, www.floshotdogs.com, 11am-3pm, Thurs.-Tues.). Founder Flo Stacy died in 2000 at age 92, but her legend and her family live on. There is no menu—just steamed Schultz wieners, buns, chips, beverages, and an attitude. The secret? The spicy, sweet-sour hot-dog sauce, allegedly once sought by the H. J. Heinz corporation, but the Stacy family isn't telling or selling. The cognoscenti know to order their dogs only with mayonnaise and the special sauce, not the heretical ketchup or mustard. It's open 11am-3pm, and not a minute later, Thursday-Tuesday year-round.

See those people with their faces pressed to the glass? They're all watching the taffy makers inside **The Goldenrod** (2 Railroad Ave., York Beach, 207/363-2621, www.thegoldenrod.com, 8am-10pm daily), where machines spew out 180 Goldenrod Kisses a minute, for a total of 65 tons a year, and have been at it since 1896. The Goldenrod is an old-fashioned place with a tearoom, a gift shop, an old-fashioned soda fountain with 135 ice cream flavors, and a rustic dining room as well as reasonable prices.

After viewing The Nubble, head across the road to **Dunne's Ice Cream** (214 Nubble Rd., York Beach, 207/363-1277), where unusual flavors complement the standards.

Craving jerk chicken or curried goat? Stop by **Jamaican Jerk Center** (1400 Rte. 1, Cape Neddick, 207/351-3033, www.jamaicanjerkcenter.com, 11am-9pm daily), a seasonal takeout with tables under a tent and on the lawn. There's live reggae music on Saturdays beginning at 4pm. Yes, it's a dive, and service can be slow, but hey, mon, the food's good.

Stop in at the **Gateway Farmers Market** (Greater York Region Chamber of Commerce Visitors Center, Rte. 1, York, 9am-1pm Sat. early-June-early Oct. and Thurs. July-Aug.) and stock up for a picnic. If you still need more, head next door to Stonewall Kitchen.

Tours of **Wiggly Bridge Distillery** (19 Railroad Ave., York Beach, 207/ 363-9322, www.wigglybridgedistillery.com, $13) include tastings of its small batch whiskeys.

Family Favorites

The York Harbor Inn's **Ship's Cellar Pub** (11:30am-11:30pm Mon.-Thurs., 11:30am-midnight Fri.-Sat., 3pm-11:30pm Sun.) attracts even the locals. The menu is the same as in the main dining room (burgers to lobster, $10-39), but the setting is far more casual. The space is designed to resemble the interior of a yacht. The pub doubles as a favorite local watering hole, with live music most nights. Happy hour, with free munchies, 4pm-6pm weekdays, sometimes draws a raucous crowd.

Wild Willy's (765 Rte. 1, York, 207/363-9924, www.wildwillysburgers.com, 11am-8pm Mon.-Sat., $8-10) has turned burgers into an art form. More than a dozen hefty mouthwatering burgers, all made from certified Angus or natural (chemical-free) beef or bison, are available, from the classic Willy burger to the Rio Grande, with roasted green chilies from New Mexico and cheddar cheese. Don't miss the hand-cut fries. Order at the counter before grabbing a seat in the dining area or out on the back deck; the servers will find you when it's ready.

Locals swear by **Rick's All Seasons Café** (240 York St., York, 207/363-5584, 6am-2pm Tues.-Sat., 6am-1pm Sun.), where the prices are low, the food is good, and the gossip is even better. Have patience: Almost everything is cooked to order.

Casual Dining

"Food that loves you back" is the slogan for ★ **Frankie and Johnny's Natural Foods** (1594 Rte. 1 N., Cape Neddick, 207/363-1909, www.frankie-johnnys.com, from 5pm Wed.-Sun. Feb.-Dec., $25-38). Inside the shingled restaurant, wood floors and pine-colored walls provide the background for the vibrant, internationally seasoned fare of chef John Shaw, who trained at the Culinary Institute of America. Vegetarian and vegan choices are always on the menu, along with fish, seafood, and chicken options, and many dishes can be modified for the gluten-sensitive. Portions are huge, breads and pastas are made in-house, and everything is cooked to order, so plan on a leisurely meal. All entrées come with a soup or salad (opt for the house salad—it's gorgeous). Plan on leftovers. Bring your own booze, but leave the credit cards behind, since "plastic is not natural."

The Tavern at Chapman Cottage (370 York St., York Harbor, 207/363-5119, 4pm-9pm daily, $12-15), owned by the York Harbor Inn, serves an extensive menu of tapas-type fare, with options such Baja fish tacos and lamb kefta meatballs as well as heftier choices like veal caprese and lobster brioche ($13-22)

For ocean views paired with a fine dining atmosphere, book a table at the York Harbor Inn's main dining room, **1637** (Rte. 1A, York Harbor, 207/363-5119, www.yorkharborinn.com, 5:30pm-10pm Thurs.-Sun., $10-39).

GiGi's (2 Beach St., York Beach, 207//351-8147, www.gigisyorkbeach.com, from 5pm daily) dishes out decent Italian fare, from pizzas to linguini and clams, with entrees running $22-31. The balcony is ideal for people watching. Inside, the dining areas are sharp and simple. The bar earns raves, and happy hour (3pm-5pm daily) draws a crowd for food and drink specials.

A beautifully restored, rustically elegant farmhouse surrounded by lovely gardens is the setting for the **Velveteen Habit** (37 Ogunquit Rd., Cape Neddick, 207/216-9884, www.thevelveteenhabit.com, 5:30-10pm Wed.-Sun.). The menus change frequently, reflecting what's currently in season in its large backyard gardens and from local purveyors. Most entrees, which might include day-boat halibut or organic chicken, are around $30. Be sure to stroll the gardens before dinner.

Lobster

Locals praise the lobster roll from **The Maine Lobster Outlet** (360 Rte. 1, York, 207/363-9899, www.mainelobsteroutlet.com, 8am-6pm Mon.-Thurs., 8am-7pm Fri.-Sat., 8am-4pm Sun.) as one of the state's best, and say the clam chowder is excellent. It's take-out only. You can also purchase frozen lobster specialty meals here.

Grab an oceanfront seat at **Lobster Cove** (756 York St., York Beach, 207/351-1100, www.lobstercoverestaurant.com, from 8am daily year-round) and watch the waves roll into Long Sands Beach while enjoying lobster or fried seafood.

INFORMATION AND SERVICES

The Maine Tourism Association operates a **Maine State Visitor Information Center** (1 Rte. 95, Kittery, 207/439-1319) in Kittery between Route 1 and I-95, with access from either road. It's chock-full of brochures and has restrooms and a picnic area.

For York-area information, head for the Shingle-style palace of the **Greater York Region Chamber of Commerce** (1 Stonewall Lane, off Rte. 1, York, 207/363 4422, www.gatewaytomaine.org), at I-95's York exit. Inside are restrooms. It's open daily in summer.

GETTING THERE AND AROUND

York is about eight miles or 15 minutes via I-95/Maine Turnpike; allow at least 20 minutes via Route 1, from Kittery. It's about seven miles or 15 minutes via Route 1 to Ogunquit, but allow more time in summer.

The Maine Turnpike, a toll road, is generally the fastest route if you're trying to get between two towns. Route 1 parallels the turnpike on the ocean side. It's mostly two lanes and is lined with shops, restaurants, motels, and other visitor-oriented sites, which means stop-and-go traffic that often slows to a crawl. If you're traveling locally, it's best to walk or use the local trolley systems, which have the bonus of saving you the agony of finding a parking spot.

The seasonal **Shoreline Explorer** (207/324-5762, www.shorelineexplorer.com) trolley system makes it possible to connect from York to Kennebunkport without your car. Each town's system is operated separately and has its own fees. The **York Trolley** (207/748-3030, www.yorktrolley.com) operates between Long and Short Sands Beaches late June-early September. The service ($2 one-way) runs every 30 minutes 10am-10pm. **The Shore Road Shuttle** (207/324-5762, www.shorelineexplorer.com) operates hourly between York's Short Sands Beach and Ogunquit's Perkins Cove late June-Labor Day; ages 5 and younger ride free.

Ogunquit and Wells

Ogunquit (pop. 892) has been a holiday destination since the indigenous residents named it "beautiful place by the sea." What's the appeal? An unparalleled, unspoiled beach, a shorefront path, a dozen art galleries, and a respected art museum with a view second to none. The town has been home to an art colony attracting the glitterati of the painting world since Charles Woodbury came here in the late 1880s. The summertime crowds continue, multiplying the minuscule year-round population. These days it's an especially gay-friendly community too. Besides the beach, the most powerful magnet is Perkins Cove, a working fishing enclave that looks more like a movie set. The best way to approach the cove is via trolley-bus or on foot, along the shoreline Marginal Way from downtown Ogunquit; midsummer parking in the cove is madness.

Wells (pop. 9,589), once part of Ogunquit and since 1980 its immediate neighbor to the north, was settled in 1640. Nowadays it's best known as a long, skinny, family-oriented community with seven miles of splendid beachfront and lots of antiques and used-book shops strewn along Route 1. It also claims two spectacular nature preserves worth a drive from anywhere. At the southern end of Wells, abutting Ogunquit, is **Moody,** an enclave named after 18th-century settler Samuel Moody.

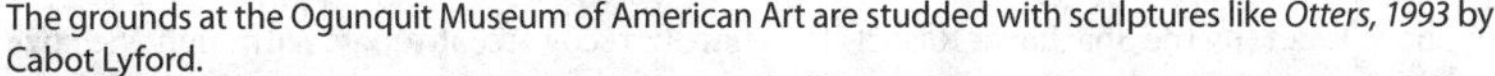

The grounds at the Ogunquit Museum of American Art are studded with sculptures like *Otters, 1993* by Cabot Lyford.

SIGHTS

★ Ogunquit Museum of American Art (OMAA)

Not many museums can boast a view as stunning as the one at the **Ogunquit Museum of American Art** (543 Shore Rd., Ogunquit, 207/646-4909, www.ogunquitmuseum.org, 10am-5pm daily, May 1-Oct. 31, $10 adults, $9 seniors and students, free under age 12), nor can many communities boast such renown as a summer art colony. Overlooking Narrow Cove 1.4 miles south of downtown Ogunquit, the museum prides itself on its distinguished permanent 2,000-piece American art collection. Works by Marsden Hartley, Rockwell Kent, Walt Kuhn, Henry Strater, and Thomas Hart Benton, among others, are displayed in five galleries. Special exhibits are mounted each summer, when there is an extensive series of lectures, concerts, and other programs, including the annual "Almost Labor Day Auction," a social season must. OMAA has a well-stocked gift shop, wheelchair access, and landscaped grounds with sculptures, a pond, and manicured lawns.

No visit to Ogunquit is complete without walking the Marginal Way.

★ Marginal Way

No visit to Ogunquit is complete without a leisurely stroll along the **Marginal Way,** the mile-long paved footpath edging the ocean from Shore Road (by the Sparhawk Resort) to Perkins Cove. It has been a must-walk since Josiah Chase gave the right-of-way to the town in the 1920s. The best times to appreciate this shrub-lined shorefront walkway are early morning or when everyone's at the beach. En route are tidepools, intriguing rock formations, crashing surf, pocket beaches, benches for absorbing the views, and a marker listing the day's high and low tides. When the surf's up, keep a close eye on the kids—the sea has no mercy. A midpoint access is at Israel's Head (behind a sewage plant masquerading as a tiny lighthouse), but getting a parking space is pure luck. The only wheels allowed are strollers and wheelchairs.

Perkins Cove

Turn-of-the-20th-century photos show Ogunquit's **Perkins Cove** lined with gray-shingled shacks used by a hardy colony of local fishermen, fellows who headed offshore to make a tough living in little boats. They'd hardly recognize it today. Although the cove remains a working lobster-fishing harbor, several old shacks have been reincarnated as boutiques and restaurants, and photographers go crazy shooting the quaint inlet spanned by a little pedestrian drawbridge. In the cove are galleries, gift shops, restaurants (fast food to lobster to high-end dining), excursion boats, and public restrooms. I enjoy it best in the early morning, before the crowds arrive. Only a coffee shop at the tip is open then, but you can watch the fishing boats gear up and head out. Parking in the cove is $7 for two hours, but there are some spaces in the back that open up after noon (reserved for local fishermen in the morning).

★ Wells Reserve at Laudholm Farm

Known locally as Laudholm Farm (the name of the restored 19th-century visitors center), **Wells National Estuarine Research Reserve** (342 Laudholm Farm Rd., Wells, 207/646-1555, www.wellsreserve.org) occupies 1,690 acres of woods, beach, and coastal salt marsh on the southern boundary of the Rachel Carson National Wildlife Refuge, just 0.5 mile east of Route 1. Seven miles of trails wind through the property. The best trail is the Salt Marsh Loop, with a boardwalk section leading to an overlook with panoramic views of the marsh and Little River inlet. Another winner is the Barrier Beach Walk, a 1.3-mile round-trip that goes through multiple habitats all the way to beautiful Laudholm Beach. Allow 1.5 hours for either; you can combine the two. Some trails are wheelchair-accessible. The informative exhibits in the **visitors center** (10am-4pm Mon.-Sat., noon-4pm Sun. late May-mid-Oct., 10am-4pm Mon.-Fri. Oct.-Mar., closed mid-Dec.-mid-Jan.) make a valuable prelude for enjoying the reserve. An extensive schedule (Apr.-Nov.) includes lectures, nature walks, and children's programs. Reservations are required for some programs. Trails are accessible 7am-dusk. Late May-mid-October, admission is charged: $5 adults, $1 ages 6-16.

Rachel Carson National Wildlife Refuge

Eleven chunks of coastal Maine real estate between Kittery Point and Cape Elizabeth make up the **Rachel Carson National Wildlife Refuge** (321 Port Rd./Rte. 9, Wells, 207/646-9226, www.fws.gov/refuge/rachel_carson), headquartered at the northern edge of Wells near the Kennebunkport town line. Pick up a *Carson Trail Guide* at the refuge office (parking is limited) and follow the mile-long wheelchair-accessible walkway past tidal creeks, salt pans, and salt marshes. It's a bird-watcher's paradise during migration seasons. Office hours are 8am-4:30pm Monday-Friday year-round; trail access is sunrise-sunset daily year-round. Leashed pets are allowed.

Ogunquit Arts Collaborative Gallery

Closer to downtown Ogunquit is the **Ogunquit Arts Collaborative Gallery** (Shore Rd. and Bourne Lane, Ogunquit, 207/646-8400, www.barngallery.org, 11am-5pm Mon.-Sat., 1pm-5pm Sun. late May-early Oct., free), also known as the Barn Gallery,

Laudholm Farm's trails are open in winter for snowshoeing and cross-country skiing.

featuring the works of member artists, an impressive group. The OAC is the showcase for the Ogunquit Art Association, established by Charles Woodbury, who was inspired to open an art school in Perkins Cove in the late 19th century. Special programs throughout the season include concerts, workshops, gallery talks, and an art auction.

Ogunquit Heritage Museum

Ogunquit's history is preserved in the **Ogunquit Heritage Museum** (86 Obeds Lane, Dorothea Jacobs Grant Common, Ogunquit, 207/646-0296, www.ogunquitheritagemuseum.org, 1pm-5pm Tues.-Sat. June-Sept., free), which opened in 2001 in the restored Captain James Winn House, a 1785 cape house listed on the National Register of Historic Places. Exhibits here and in a new wing focus on Ogunquit's role as an art colony and its maritime heritage, town history, and local architecture.

ENTERTAINMENT

Ogunquit Playhouse

Having showcased top-notch professional theater since the 1930s, the 750-seat **Ogunquit Playhouse** (Rte. 1, Ogunquit, 207/646-5511, www.ogunquitplayhouse.org), a summer classic, knows how to do it right: It presents comedies and musicals, late May-late Oct., with Broadway veterans sprinkled with Hollywood stars. The air-conditioned building is wheelchair-accessible. The box office is open daily in season, beginning in early May; tickets range $44-79. The playhouse also presents a children's series. You can also take a guided **Backstage Tour** ($5 for 45 minutes or $10 for 90 minutes) taking in the dressing rooms, green room, and backstage while picking up insider info on the stars who have played here over the years; call for current schedule. Parking can be a hassle during shows; consider walking the short distance from the Bourne Lane trolley-bus stop.

Live Music

Jonathan's (2 Bourne Lane, Ogunquit, 207/646-4777) is a two-fer find. Downstairs is a casual fine dining restaurant. Upstairs, national headliners often perform in an intimate venue, where every seat has a great view of the stage. A full bar is available until the show starts. Advance tickets are cheaper than at the door, and dinner guests get preference for seats; all show seats are reserved.

Ogunquit Performing Arts (207/646-6170, www.ogunquitperformingarts.org) presents a full slate of programs, including classical concerts, ballet, and theater, at the **Dunaway Center** (23 School Street). The **Wells Summer Concert Series** runs most Saturday evenings early July-early September at the Hope Hobbs Gazebo in Wells Harbor Park. A wide variety of music is represented, from sing-alongs to swing.

FESTIVALS AND EVENTS

Harbor Fest takes place in July in Harbor Park in Wells and includes a concert, crafts fair, parade, and chicken barbecue, along with children's activities.

In August, Ogunquit hosts the annual **Sidewalk Art Show and Sale.**

Capriccio is a performing arts festival in Ogunquit with daytime and evening events held during the first week of September. The second weekend that month, the Wells National Estuarine Research Reserve (Laudholm Farm) hosts the **Laudholm Nature Crafts Festival,** a two-day juried crafts fair with children's activities and guided nature walks.

SHOPPING

Antiques are a Wells specialty. You'll find more than 50 shops with a huge range of prices. The majority are on Route 1. **R. Jorgensen Antiques** (502 Post Rd./Rte. 1, Wells, 207/646-9444) is a phenomenon in itself, filling 11 showrooms in two buildings with European and American 18th- and 19th-century furniture and accessories. **MacDougall-Gionet Antiques and Associates** (2104 Post Rd./Rte. 1,

Wells, 207/646-3531) has been in business since 1959, and its reputation is stellar. The 65-dealer shop, in an 18th-century barn, carries American and European country and formal furniture and accessories.

If you've been scouring antiquarian bookshops for a long-wanted title, chances are you'll find it at **Douglas N. Harding Rare Books** (2152 Post Rd./Rte. 1, Wells, 207/646-8785 or 800/228-1398). Well-cataloged and organized, the sprawling bookshop stocks upward of 100,000 books, prints, and maps at any given time, plus a hefty selection of Maine and New England histories.

Fans of fine craft, especially contemporary art glass, shouldn't miss **Panache** (307 Main St., Ogunquit, 207/646-4878).

RECREATION

Water Sports

BEACHES

One of Maine's most scenic and unspoiled sandy beachfronts, Ogunquit's 3.5-mile stretch of sand fringed with sea grass is a magnet for hordes of sunbathers, spectators, swimmers, surfers, and sand-castle builders. Getting there means crossing the Ogunquit River via one of three access points. For Ogunquit's **Main Beach**—with a bathhouse and big crowds—take Beach Street. To reach **Footbridge Beach,** marginally less crowded, either take Ocean Street and the footbridge or take Bourne Avenue to Ocean Avenue in adjacent Wells and walk back toward Ogunquit. **Moody Beach,** at Wells's southern end, is technically private property, a subject of considerable legal dispute. Lifeguards are on duty all summer at the public beaches, and there are restrooms in all three areas. The beach is free, but parking is $20/day and lots fill up early on warm midsummer days. After 3:30pm some parking is free. It's far more sensible to opt for the frequent trolley-buses.

Wells beaches continue where Ogunquit's leave off. **Crescent Beach** (Webhannet Dr. between Eldredge Rd. and Mile Rd.) is the tiniest, with tidepools, no facilities, and limited parking. **Wells Beach** (Mile Rd. to Atlantic Ave.) is the major (and most crowded) beach, with lifeguards, restrooms, and parking. Around the other side of Wells Harbor is **Drakes Island Beach** (take Drakes Island Rd. at the blinking light), a less crowded spot with restrooms and lifeguards. Walk northeast from Drakes Island Beach and you'll eventually reach **Laudholm Beach,** with great birding along the way. Summer beach-parking fees (pay-and-display) are $16/day or $8/afternoon for nonresidents ($5 for a motorcycle, $25 for an RV); if you're staying longer, a 10-token pass ($80) is a better bargain.

TIDEPOOL EXCURSION

Join marine science educator "Coastal" Carol of **Coast Encounters** (207/831-4436, www.coastencounters.com) on a three-hour, hands-on intertidal excursion, $50/adult, $25/ages 5-18. This is a fabulous way to introduce the kids to the beach. Excursions are geared to all family members, from kids to grandparents. Carol even has a special wheelchair available for handicapped individuals.

BOAT EXCURSIONS

Depending on your interests, you can go deep-sea fishing or just gawking out of Perkins Cove in Ogunquit.

Between April and early November, Captain Tim Tower runs half-day (departing 4pm, $50 pp) and full-day (departing 7am, $85 pp) **deep-sea fishing trips** aboard the 40-foot **Bunny Clark** (207/646-2214, www.bunnyclark.com), moored in Perkins Cove. Reservations are necessary. Tim has a science degree, so he's a wealth of marine biology information. All gear is provided, and the crew will fillet your catch for you; dress warmly and wear sunblock.

Barnacle Billy's Dock at Perkins Cove is homeport for the Hubbard family's **Finestkind Cruises** (207/646-5227, www.finestkindcruises.com, no credit cards). Motorboat options consist of 1.5-hour, 14-mile Nubble Lighthouse cruises; one-hour cocktail cruises; a 75-minute breakfast cruise complete with coffee, juice, and a muffin; and 50-minute lobster-boat trips. Rates run $18-28 adults, $9-14 children. Also available are 1.75-hour sails ($30 pp) aboard **The Cricket,** a locally built wooden sailboat. Reservations are advisable, but usually unnecessary midweek.

EQUIPMENT RENTALS

At **Wheels and Waves** (579 Post Rd./Rte. 1, Wells, 207/646-5774, www.wheelsnwaves.com), bike or surfboard rentals are $30/day, including delivery to some hotels; a stand-up paddleboard is $40, a single kayak is $65, and a double is $65.

Put in right at the harbor and explore the estuary from **Webhannet River Kayak and Canoe Rentals** (345 Harbor Rd., Wells, 207/646-9649, www.webhannetriver.com). Rates begin at $25 solo, $40 tandem for two hours.

Paddle the beach-protected Ogunquit River or the Wells estuaries with a kayak from World Within Sea Kayaking (207/646-0455, 17 Post Rd./Rte. 1, Wells, www.worldwithin.com). A single kayak is $20/hour or $30/two hours, a double is $30/hour, $45/two hours, and a stand-up paddleboard is $25/hour or $35, two hours. It's based at the Ogunquit River Inn and is only open during the high-tide cycle.

Golf

The 18-hole Donald Ross-designed **Cape Neddick Country Club** (650 Shore Rd., Cape Neddick, 207/361-2011, www.capeneddickgolf.com) is a semiprivate 18-hole course with a restaurant and a driving range.

ACCOMMODATIONS

Most properties are open only seasonally.

Ogunquit

MOTELS

You're almost within spitting distance of Perkins Cove at the 37-room **Riverside Motel** (159 Shore Rd., 207/646-2741, www.riversidemotel.com, $199-259), where you can perch on your balcony and watch the action—or, for that matter, join it. Guest rooms have phones, air-conditioning, refrigerators, Wi-Fi, cable TV, and fabulous views. Rates include continental breakfast. The entire 3.5-acre property is smoke-free.

Juniper Hill Inn (336 Main St., 207/646-4501 or 800/646-4544, www.ogunquit.com, year-round, $149-279) is a well-run motel-style lodging on five acres close to downtown Ogunquit, with a footpath to the beach. Amenities include refrigerators, cable TV, coin-operated laundry, a fitness center, indoor and outdoor pools and hot tubs, and golf privileges.

The frills are few, but the **Towne Lyne Motel** (747 Main St./Rte. 1, 207/646-2955, www.townelynemotel.com, $129-189) is a charmer set back from the highway amid manicured lawns. Rooms are air-conditioned and have free Wi-Fi and phone, refrigerators, and microwaves; some have screened porches. Be sure to request a riverside room.

COTTAGES

It's nearly impossible to land a peak-season cottage at **The Dunes** (518 Main St., 207/646-2612, www.dunesonthewaterfront.com, from $185), but it's worth trying. The 12-acre property is under its third generation of ownership, and guests practically will their weeks to their descendants. Nineteen tidy, well-equipped one- or two-bedroom housekeeping cottages with screened porches and wood-burning fireplaces as well as 17 guest rooms are generously spaced on shady, grassy lawns that roll down to the river, with the dunes just beyond. Facilities include a dock with rowboats, a pool, and lawn games. Amenities include Wi-Fi, TVs, phones, and refrigerators. It's all meticulously maintained. In peak season, the one- or two-bedroom cottages require a one- or two-week minimum stay; guest rooms require three nights.

ECLECTIC PROPERTIES

★ **The Beachmere Inn** (62 Beachmere Pl., 207/646-2021 or 800/336-3983, www.beachmereinn.com, year-round, from $190) occupies an enviable oceanfront location on Marginal Way, yet is just steps from downtown. The private, family-owned and -operated property comprises an updated Victorian inn, a new seaside motel, and other buildings, all meticulously maintained and often updated. Pocket beaches are just outside the gate. All rooms have air-conditioning, TVs, phones, and kitchenettes; most have balconies, decks, or terraces; some have fireplaces; almost all have jaw-dropping ocean views. There's also a small spa with a hot tub, steam sauna, and fitness room, and a bistro serving lunch and dinner. Morning coffee and pastries are provided.

It's not easy to describe the **Sparhawk Oceanfront Resort** (41 Shore Rd., 207/646-5562, www.thesparhawk.com, from $230), a sprawling one-of-a-kind place popular with honeymooners, sedate families, and seniors. There's lots of tradition in this thriving six-acre complex—it has had various incarnations since the turn of the 20th century—and the "Happily Filled" sign regularly hangs out front. Out back is the Atlantic Ocean with forever views, and Marginal Way starts right here. It offers a tennis court, gardens, and a heated pool; breakfast is included. The 87 guest rooms in four buildings vary from motel-type (best views) rooms and suites to inn-type suites. There's a seven-night minimum during July-August.

INNS AND BED-AND-BREAKFASTS

When you want to be at the center of the action, book a room at **2 Village Square Inn** (14 Village Square Ln., 207/646-5779, www.2vsquare.com, from $199). The walk-to-everything location puts the beach, Marginal Way, shops, restaurants, and more all within footsteps, if you can tear yourself away from the dreamy views, heated outdoor pool, hut tub, and even on-site massage room. Owners Scott Osgood and Bruce Senecal and manager Peter Hill have earned a reputation as conscientious innkeepers who aim to please. They also operate the **Nellie Littlefield Inn & Spa** (27 Shore Rd., 207/646-1692, www.nliogunquit.com, from $259), a magnificently restored in-town Victorian, and the **Gazebo Inn** (572 Main St., 207/646-3773, www.gazeboinnogt.com, from $239), a carefully renovated 1847 farmhouse and barn within walking distance of Footbridge Beach. All serve a full breakfast buffet. None welcome children. Also under the same ownership is the year-round and child- and dog-friendly **Captain's Quarter's** (207/646-3733, www.captainogt.com, $149-219), a renovated and updated motel. All rooms have a refrigerator and a microwave; some have full kitchens or kitchenettes.

Jacqui Grant's warm welcome, gracious hospitality, and stellar breakfasts combined with a quiet residential location within walking distance of both the village and Footbridge Beach have earned **Almost Home** (27 King's Ln., 207/641-2753, www.almosthomeinnogunquit.com, $155-235) a stellar reputation. She often serves afternoon cheese with wine from her son's California winery. Rooms are spacious and have nice seating areas, and the backyard makes a quiet retreat.

Built in 1899 for a prominent Maine lumbering family, **Rockmere Lodge** (40 Stearns Rd., 207/646-2985, www.rockmere.com, year-round, $198-255) underwent a meticulous six-month restoration in the early 1990s and has seen frequent updates since. Near the Marginal Way on a peaceful street, the handsome home has eight comfortable Victorian guest rooms, all with CD players and cable TV (a massive library of films and CDs is available) and most with ocean views. Rates include a generous breakfast. A wraparound veranda, decks, gardens, a gazebo, and "The Lookout," a third-floor windowed nook with comfy chairs, make it easy to settle in and just watch the passersby on the Marginal Way. Beach towels, chairs, and umbrellas are provided for guests. Pets are not allowed; there are dogs in residence.

The historical **Colonial Inn** (145 Shore Rd., 207/646-5191, www.thecolonialinn.com, from $199) reopened in 2013 after a $4 million restoration that brought the Victorian-era inn in to the 21st century, with amenities including air-conditioning and Wi-Fi. Rooms in the main inn are bright and airy, and some have water views. Family-oriented rooms are located in separate buildings, and some have kitchenettes. It's an easy walk to the beach, but if the ocean's too chilly, the hotel has a heated outdoor pool and hot tub. A continental breakfast buffet is provided. The location puts the best of Ogunquit within footsteps.

Fancy an English countryside-style immersion with spa amenities? Look no further than the **Beauport Inn** (339 Clary Hill Rd., Cape Neddick, 207/361-2400, www.beauportinn.com, from $235), a stone manor on nine acres with a 40-foot lap pool, outdoor hot tub, and indoor Turkish steam room along with four guest rooms and an apartment.

RESORTS

The Cliff House Resort and Spa (Shore Rd., 207/361-1000, www.cliffhousemaine.com), a self-contained complex, sprawls over 70 acres topping the edge of Bald Head Cliff midway between the centers of York and Ogunquit. It's undergoing a complete renovation and is expected to reopen in 2016. The location is spectacular and the facilities and amenities likely will be in keeping with a full-service upscale resort. Call or check the web for current info.

The family-owned **Meadowmere Resort** (74 Main St., 207/646-9661, www.meadowmere.com, from $199) caters to families, with facilities including indoor and outdoor pools, outdoor hot tub, indoor Roman Bath, spacious well-equipped health club and spa, barbeque pits, restaurant, pub, games room, and guest laundry. The 144 guest rooms, spread across five buildings, include suites designed for families, romantics, and honeymooners as well as standard rooms. The location is excellent: Ogunquit Beach, Marginal Way, and downtown shops and restaurants are within 10-15 minutes walking distance (wagons available for towing gear or kids), and it's on the trolley route. This is an ultra-green property, with no chemicals in the pools and an ozone laundry. Also sharing the premises is Jonathan's, a casual fine dining restaurant that often features national caliber shows in an intimate setting. Rates include continental breakfast in season. Open year-round.

Wells

Once part of a giant 19th-century dairy farm, the **Beach Farm Inn** (97 Eldredge Rd., 207/646-8493, www.beachfarminn.com, year-round, $139-159) is a 2.5-acre oasis in a rather congested area 0.2 mile off Route 1. Guests can swim in the pool, relax in the library, or walk 0.7 mile down the road to the beach. Five of the eight guest rooms have private baths (two are detached); third-floor rooms have air-conditioning. Rates include a full breakfast; a cottage rents for $795/week.

Even closer to the beach is **Haven by the Sea** (59 Church St., Wells Beach, 207/646-4194, www.havenbythesea.com, from $250), a heavenly bed-and-breakfast in a former church, now with central air-conditioning. Inside are hardwood floors, cathedral ceilings, and stained-glass windows. The confessional is now a full bar, and the altar has been converted to a dining area that opens to a marsh-view terrace—the bird-watching here is superb. Guest rooms have sitting areas, and the suite has a whirlpool tub and a fireplace. Guests have plenty of room to relax, including a living area with a fireplace. Rates include a full breakfast and afternoon hors d'oeuvres.

FOOD

Ogunquit

LOCAL FLAVORS

The Egg and I (501 Maine St./Rte. 1, 207/646-8777, www.eggandibreakfast.com, 6am-2pm daily, no credit cards) has more than 200 menu choices and earns high marks for its omelets and waffles. You can't miss it; there's always a crowd. Lunch choices are served after 11am.

Equally popular is **Amore Breakfast** (309 Shore Rd., 207/646-6661, www.amorebreakfast.com, 7am-1pm daily). Choose from 14 omelets and eight versions of eggs Benedict (including lobster and a spirited rancheros version topped with salsa and served with guacamole), as well as French toast, waffles, and all the regulars and irregulars.

Eat in or take out from **Village Food Market** (Main St., Ogunquit Center, 207/646-2122, www.villagefoodmarket.com, 6:30am-7pm daily). A breakfast sandwich is less than $3, subs and sandwiches are available in two sizes, and there's a children's menu.

Scrumptious baked goods, tantalizing salads, and vegetarian lunch items are available to go at **Bread and Roses** (246 Main St., 207/646-4227, www.breadandrosesbakery.com, 7am-7pm daily), a small bakery right downtown with a few tables outside.

Harbor Candy Shop (26 Main St., 207/646-8078 or 800/331-5856) is packed with decadent chocolates. Fudge, truffles, and turtles are all made on-site.

ETHNIC FARE

The best and most authentic Italian dining is at **Angelina's Ristorante** (655 Main St./Rte. 1, 207/646-0445, www.angelinasogunquit.com, 4:30pm-10pm daily year-round, $16-35). Chef-owner David Giarusso uses recipes handed down from his great-grandmother, Angelina Peluso. Dine in the dining room, wine room, lounge, or out on the terrace, choosing from pastas, risottos (the house specialty), and other classics.

Another Italian outpost is **Caffe Prego** (44 Shore Rd., 207/646-7734, www.caffepregoogt.com, 11:30am-9pm daily, and 8-11am Sun., $10-25), where owners Donato Tramuto and Jeffrey Porter have created an authentic taste of Tuscany. They've imported Italian equipment and use traditional ingredients to create coffees, pastries, panini, brick-oven pizzas, pastas, salads, and gelati, served inside or on the terrace.

CASUAL DINING

Gypsy Sweethearts (10 Shore Rd., 207/646-7021, www.gypsysweethearts.com, dinner from 5:30pm Tues.-Sun., entrées $19-32) serves inside a restored house, on a deck, and in a garden. It's one of the region's most reliable restaurants, and the creative menu is infused with ethnic accents and includes vegetarian choices. Reservations are advised in midsummer.

Mediterranean fare is finessed with a dollop of creativity and a pinch of Maine flavors at **Five-O** (50 Shore Rd., 207/646-6365, www.five-oshoreroad.com, dinner 5pm-10pm daily, brunch 10am-2pm Sun.), one of the region's top restaurants for casual dining. The menu changes frequently, but the house-made pastas and entrées usually run $20-40. Lighter fare ($10-24) is available until 11pm in the lounge, where martinis are a specialty. Valet parking is available.

Boisterous and lively, **The Front Porch** (9 Shore Rd., 207/646-4005, www.thefrontporch.com, dinner from 5pm Mon.-Fri., from 2pm Sat.-Sun., $2-32) is not for those looking for romantic dining, but it is a good choice for families with divergent tastes. The menu ranges from flatbread pizzas to rack of lamb.

Jonathan's (2 Bourne Lane, Ogunquit, 207/646-4777, www.jonathansogunquit.com, $24-34) is a lovely oasis, a casual fine dining venue with clothed tables and big windows overlooking colorful gardens. Much of the fare is sourced from Chef Jonathan West's own farm (the Mediterranean pasta, with his farm-raised spicy lamb sausage, is excellent). A gluten-free menu available, and lighter fare is served in the bar. Parking isn't a problem. Upstairs is an intimate space where national acts often perform; check the schedule and consider combining dinner with a show.

DINING WITH A VIEW

There's not much between you and Spain when you get a window seat at **MC Perkins Cove** (Oarweed Lane, Perkins Cove, 207/646-6263, www.markandclarkrestaurants.com, 11:30am-3:30pm and from 5pm daily late May-mid-Oct., Wed.-Sun. mid-Oct.-Dec. and Feb.-late May, dinner entrées $25-37). Almost every table on both floors has a view. Service is attentive, and the food is tops and, in keeping with James Beard Award-winning chefs Mark Gaier and Clark Frasier, always fresh. Lighter fare ($12-21) is served in the bar. A jazz brunch ($13-21) is served beginning at 11am Sunday mid-October through mid-December and mid-February through mid-May. Reservations are essential for dinner.

LOBSTER

Creative marketing, a knockout view, and efficient service help explain why more than 1,000 pounds of lobster bite the dust every summer day at **Barnacle Billy's** (Perkins Cove, 207/646-5575 or 800/866-5575, www.barnbilly.com, 11am-9pm daily seasonally). Billy's has a full liquor license; try for the deck, with a front-row seat on Perkins Cove.

Less flashy and less pricey is **The Lobster Shack** (Perkins Cove, 207/646-2941, www.lobster-shack.com, 11am-9pm daily), serving lobsters, meaty lobster rolls, stews, chowders, and some landlubber choices too.

Wells

LOCAL FLAVORS

For scrumptious baked goods and made-to-order sandwiches, head to **Borealis Bread** (Rte. 1, 8:30am-5:30pm Mon.-Sat., 9am-4pm Sun.), in the Aubuchon Hardware plaza.

Pick up all sorts of fresh goodies at the **Wells Farmers Market** (1pm-5pm Wed.) in the Town Hall parking lot (208 Sanford Rd.).

Love doughnuts? You'll love **Congdon's** (1090 Post Rd./Rte. 1, Wells, 207/646-4219, www.congdons.com, 6am-3pm daily), a restaurant and bakery that's been here since 1945.

FAMILY FAVORITES

For fresh lobster, lobster rolls, fish-and-chips, chowders, and homemade desserts, you can't go wrong at the Cardinali family's ★ **Fisherman's Catch** (Harbor Rd./Rte. 1, 207/646-8780, www.fishermanscatchwells.com, 11:30am-9pm daily early May-mid-Oct., $9-26). Big windows in the rustic dining room frame the marsh; some even have binoculars for wildlife spotting. It might seem out of the way, but, trust me, the locals all know this little gem.

A good steak in the land of lobster? You betcha: **The Steakhouse** (1205 Post Rd./Rte. 1, 207/646-4200, www.the-steakhouse.com, 4pm-9:30pm Tues.-Sun., entrées $15-30) is a great big barn of a place where steaks are hand cut from USDA prime and choice corn-fed Western beef that has never been frozen. Chicken, seafood, lobster (great stew), and even a vegetarian stir-fry are also on the menu, and a children's menu is available. Service is efficient, but they don't take reservations, so be prepared for a long wait.

Craving fried clams? **Jake's Seafood** (139 post Rd./Rte. 1, Moody, Wells, 207/646-6771, www.jakesseafoodrestaurant.com, 5am-10pm daily, $9-24) arguably serves the region's best, and its lobster rolls are mighty fine, too. This order-at-the-counter joint has seating indoors and outside. If you want to jaw with the local lobstermen, go for breakfast ($4-9).

FINE DINING

Chef Joshua W. Mather of ★ **Joshua's** (1637 Rte. 1, 207/646-3355, www.joshuas.biz, from 5pm Mon.-Sat, entrées $23-36) grew up on his family's nearby organic farm, and produce from that farm highlights the menu. In a true family operation, his parents not only still work the farm, but also work in the restaurant, a converted 1774 home with many of its original architectural elements. Everything is made on the premises, from the fabulous bread to the hand-churned ice cream. The Atlantic haddock, with caramelized onion crust, chive oil, and wild mushroom risotto, is a signature dish, and it alone is worth coming for. A vegetarian pasta entrée is offered nightly. Save room for the maple walnut pie with maple ice cream. Yes, it's gilding the lily, but you can always walk the beach afterward. Reservations are essential for the dining rooms, but the full menu is also served in the bar.

INFORMATION AND SERVICES

At the southern edge of Ogunquit, right next to the Ogunquit Playhouse, the **Ogunquit Chamber of Commerce's Welcome Center** (Rte. 1, Ogunquit, 207/646-2939, www.ogunquit.org) provides all the usual visitor information and has public restrooms. Ask for the Touring and Trolley Route Map, showing the Marginal Way, beach locations, and public restrooms. The chamber of commerce's annual visitor booklet thoughtfully carries a high-tide calendar for the summer.

Just over the Ogunquit border in Wells (actually in Moody) is the **Wells Information Center** (Rte. 1 at Kimball Rd., 207/646-2451, www.wellschamber.org).

The handsome fieldstone **Ogunquit Memorial Library** (74 Shore Rd., Ogunquit, 207/646-9024) is downtown's only building on the National Register of Historic Places. Or visit the **Wells Public Library** (1434 Post Rd./Rte. 1, Wells, 207/646-8181, www.wells.lib.me.us).

GETTING THERE AND AROUND

Ogunquit is about seven miles or 15 minutes via Route 1, from York. Wells is about six miles or 12 minutes via Route 1 from Ogunquit. From York to Wells, it's about 15.5 miles or 20 minutes on I-95. When traveling in summer, expect heavy traffic and delays on Route 1.

Amtrak Downeaster (800/872-7245, www.amtrakdowneaster.com), which connects Boston's North Station with Portland, Maine, stops in Wells. The Shoreline Explorer trolley connects in season.

The seasonal **Shoreline Explorer** (207/324-5762, www.shorelineexplorer.com) trolley system makes it possible to connect from York to Kennebunkport without your car. Each town's system is operated separately and has its own fees. The **Shoreline Trolley Purple Line-2/Shore Road Shuttle** ($1 one way, $3 day pass, $10 12-ride multipass) operates between Short Sands Beach, in York, and Perkins Cove, Ogunquit; **Shoreline Trolley Route 3/Ogunquit Trolley** ($2 one way, $1.50 ages 10 and under) connects to **Shoreline Trolley Blue Line-4** ($1 one way, $3 day pass, $10 12-ride multipass, 17 and younger ride free), which serves Wells and the Wells Transportation Center (on request only), where the Amtrak Downeaster train stops, and ends in downtown Kennebunk. It connects at the Wells Plaza to **Orange Line-5** ($4 one way/$6 round trip, in-town $2/$3, ages 5-11 half-fare, younger than 5 free), which operates between Wells Beach and Sanford.

The Kennebunks

The world may have first learned of Kennebunkport when George Herbert Walker Bush was president, but Walkers and Bushes have owned their summer estate here for three generations. Visitors continue to come to the Kennebunks (the collective name for **Kennebunk, Kennebunkport, Cape Porpoise,** and **Goose Rocks Beach**) hoping to catch a glimpse of the former first family, but they also come for the terrific ambience, bed-and-breakfasts, boutiques, boats, biking, and beaches.

The Kennebunks' earliest European settlers arrived in the mid-1600s. By the mid-1700s, shipbuilding had become big business in the area. Two ancient local cemeteries—North Street and Evergreen—provide glimpses of the area's heritage. Its Historic District reveals Kennebunk's moneyed past—the homes where wealthy ship owners and shipbuilders once lived, sending their vessels to the Caribbean and around the globe. Today, unusual shrubs and a dozen varieties of rare maples still line Summer Street—the legacy of ship captains in the global trade. Another legacy is the shiplap construction in many houses—a throwback to a time when labor was cheap and lumber plentiful. Closer to the beach in Lower Village stood the workshops of sailmakers, carpenters, and mast makers whose output drove the booming trade to success.

Although **Kennebunkport** (pop. 3,474) draws most of the sightseers and summer traffic, **Kennebunk** (pop. 10,798) feels more like a year-round community. Its old-fashioned downtown has a mix of shops, restaurants, and attractions. Yes, its beaches are also well known, but many visitors drive right through the middle of Kennebunk without stopping to enjoy its assets.

SIGHTS

★ Seashore Trolley Museum

There's nothing quite like an antique electric trolley to dredge up nostalgia for bygone days. With a collection of more than 250 transit vehicles (more than two dozen trolleys on display) from around the world, the **Seashore Trolley Museum** (195 Log Cabin Rd., Kennebunkport, 207/967-2800, www.trolleymuseum.org, $10 adults, $8 seniors, $7.50 ages 6-16) verges on trolley mania. Whistles blowing and bells clanging, restored streetcars do frequent trips (last ride at 4:15pm) on a 3.5-mile loop along a rebuilt portion of the Atlantic Shore Line Railway through the nearby woods. Ride as often as you wish, and then check out the activity in the streetcar workshop, visit three exhibit car-barns, and go wild in the trolley-oriented gift shop. Bring a picnic lunch and enjoy it here. Special events are held throughout the summer, including **Ice Cream and Sunset Trolley Rides** (4:30-7pm Wed.-Thurs., July-Aug. $5, includes ice cream). Here's an interesting wrinkle: Make a reservation, plunk down $60, and you can have a one-hour "Motorman" experience driving your own trolley (with help, of course). The museum is 1.7 miles southeast of Route 1. It's open 10am-5pm daily late May-mid-October and on weekends in May, late October, and during the Christmas Prelude festival.

Ride the rails at the Seashore Trolley Museum.

Walker's Point: The Bush Estate

There's no public access to Walker's Point, but you can join the sidewalk gawkers on Ocean Avenue overlooking George and Barbara Bush's summer compound. The 41st president and his wife lead a low-key, laid-back life when they're here, so if you don't spot them through binoculars, you may well run into them at a shop or restaurant in town. Intown Trolley's regular narrated tours go right past the house, or it's an easy, scenic walk from Kennebunkport's Dock Square. On the way, you'll pass **St. Ann's Church,** whose stones came from the ocean floor, and the paths to **Spouting Rock** and **Blowing Cave,** two natural phenomena that create spectacular water fountains if you manage to be there midway between high and low tides. Right by the compound overlook is **Anchor to Windward,** a 6,000 pound anchor installed by the town in 2009 to honor 41. Another way to view the residence is from the sea aboard the **Schooner Eleanor.**

Wedding Cake House

The **Wedding Cake House** (104 Summer St.,

The Kennebunks

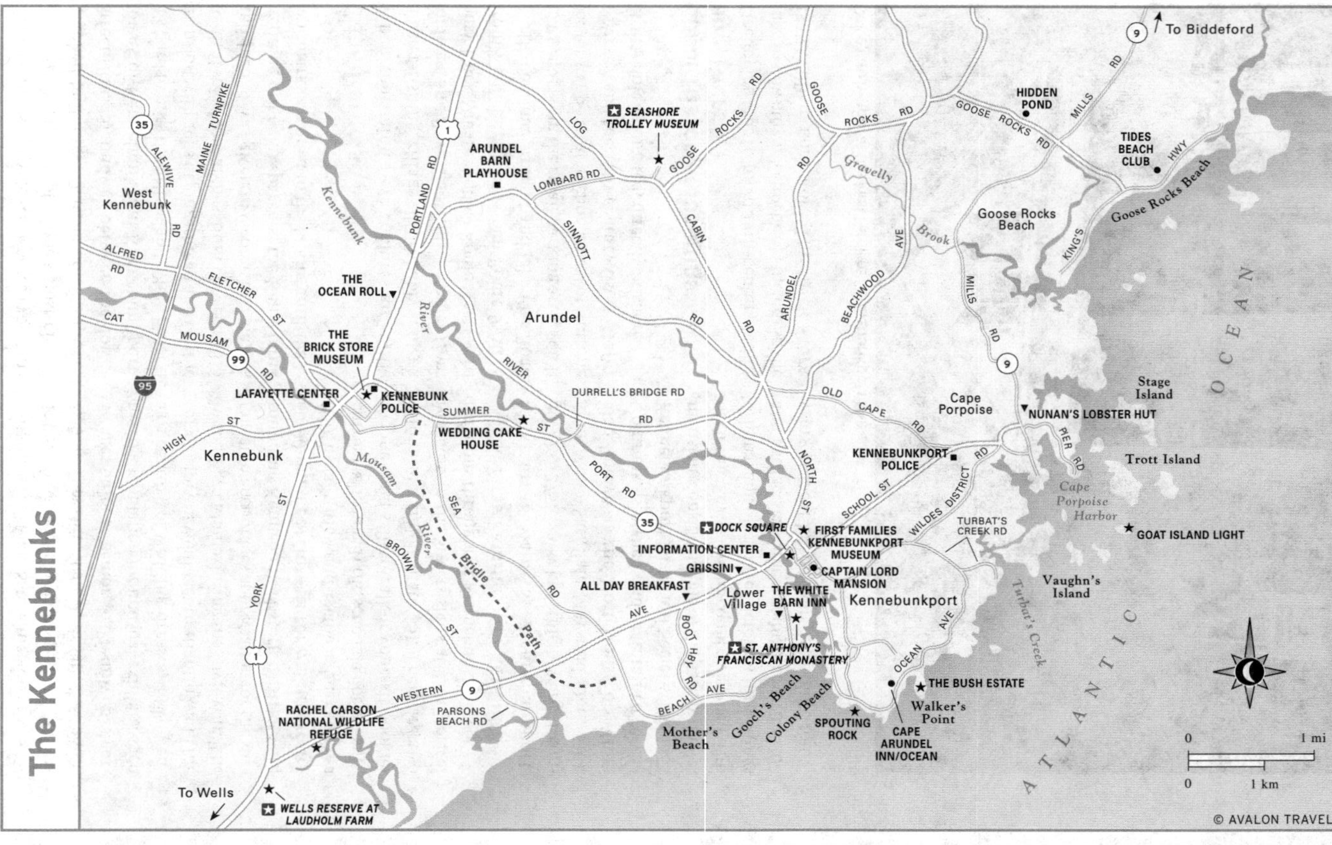

Kennebunk) is a private residence, so you can't go inside, but it's one of Maine's most-photographed buildings. Driving down Summer Street (Rte. 35), midway between the downtowns of Kennebunk and Kennebunkport, it's hard to miss the yellow-and-white Federal mansion with gobs of gingerbread and Gothic Revival spires and arches. Built between 1815 and 1825, it was given to George Bourne as a wedding gift by his parents; the Kennebunk landmark remained in the family until 1983.

Cape Porpoise

When your mind's eye conjures an idyllic lobster-fishing village, it probably looks a lot like **Cape Porpoise,** only 2.5 miles from busy Dock Square. Follow Route 9 eastward from Kennebunkport; when Route 9 turns north, continue straight and take Pier Road to its end. From the small parking area, you'll see lobster boats at anchor, a slew of working wharves, and the 19th-century **Goat Island Light,** now automated, directly offshore.

Local History Museums and Tours

Occupying four restored 19th-century buildings in downtown Kennebunk, including the 1825 William Lord store, **The Brick Store Museum** (117 Main St., Kennebunk, 207/985-4802, www.brickstoremuseum.org, 10am-4:30pm Tues.-Fri., 10am-1pm Sat., $7.50 adult, $3 ages 6016, $6 senior, $20 family) has garnered a reputation for unusual exhibits, such as a century of wedding dresses, a two-century history of volunteer firefighting, and life in southern Maine during the Civil War. The museum encourages appreciation for the surrounding Kennebunk Historic District with 60-90-minute **architectural walking tours** ($5), usually May-mid-October, but call for a current schedule. If the schedule doesn't suit, the museum sells a walk-it-yourself booklet ($16) and a simple map ($5). There are also Museum in the Streets signs at 25 historical locations throughout Kennebunk.

The **First Families Kennebunkport Museum** (8 Maine St., Kennebunkport, 207/967-2751, www.kporthistory.org, 10am-4pm Mon., Sat., late May-mid-Oct., $10), also known as the Nott House or White Columns, is owned and maintained by the Kennebunkport Historical Society. The 1853 mansion, considered one of the best examples of Gothic Revival in the country, is filled with original and often rare Victorian furnishings and artifacts and memorabilia covering 200 years of local history. On 45-minute tours,

Delve into history at the First Families Kennebunkport Museum.

guides relate stories of sea captains, shipbuilders, summerfolk, and presidents. A separate gallery is dedicated to the Bush family. Be sure to visit the restored gardens.

Kennebunk's **Museum in the Streets** (www.themuseuminthestreets.com) comprises 25 sites around town with markers explaining their historical significance.

★ Dock Square

Even if you're not a shopper, make it a point to meander through the heart of Kennebunkport's shopping district, where onetime fishing shacks have been restored and renovated into upscale shops, boutiques, galleries, and dining spots. Some shops, especially those on upper floors, offer fine harbor views. If you're willing to poke around a bit, you'll find some unusual items that make distinctive souvenirs or gifts—pottery, vintage clothing, books, specialty foods, and, yes, T-shirts.

★ St. Anthony's Franciscan Monastery

Long ago, 35,000 Native Americans used this part of town as a summer camp. So did a group of Lithuanian Franciscan monks who in 1947 fled war-ravaged Europe and acquired the 200-acre **St. Anthony's Franciscan Monastery** (Beach St., Kennebunk, 207/967-2011). They ran a high school here 1956-1969, and the monks still occupy the handsome Tudor great house, but the well-tended grounds (sprinkled with shrines and a recently restored sculpture created by Vytautas Jonynas for the Vatican Pavilion at the 1964 World's Fair) are open to the public sunrise-sunset daily. A short path leads from the monastery area to a peaceful gazebo overlooking the Kennebunk River. Pets and bikes are not allowed; public restrooms are available.

ENTERTAINMENT AND EVENTS

Performing Arts

MaineStage Shakespeare (www.mainestageshakespeare.com) performs the bard's works free in Kennebunk's Lafayette Park or, if raining, in Town Hall Auditorium. Check the website for times and locations in Kennebunkport.

Live professional summer theater is on tap at the **Arundel Barn Playhouse** (53 Old Post Rd., Arundel, 207/985-5552, www.arundelbarnplayhouse.com, $35-40), with productions staged in a renovated 1888 barn June-September.

VentiCordi (207/288-6688, www.venticordi.com, $20 adult, $15 senior, $5 ages 18 and younger) presents chamber music concerts at various locations during July and August.

River Tree Arts

The area's cultural spearhead is **River Tree Arts** (35 Western Ave., Kennebunk, 207/967-9120, www.rivertreearts.org), a volunteer-driven organization that sponsors concerts, classes, workshops, exhibits, and educational programs throughout the year.

Festivals and Events

The **Kennebunkport Festival** in early June celebrates art and food with exhibits, social events, food and wine tastings, celebrity chef dinners, and live music. The first two weekends of December mark the festive **Christmas Prelude,** during which spectacular decorations adorn historic homes, candle-toting carolers stroll through the Kennebunks, stores have special sales, and Santa Claus arrives via lobster boat.

The **Village Art Walk** occurs 5-8pm on the second Friday of the month in Kennebunkport's Dock Square, along Ocean Avenue, and in Kennebunk's Lower Village.

Kennebunk Parks and Recreation sponsors **Concerts in the Park,** a weekly series of free concerts 6:30pm-7:30pm Wednesday late June-mid-August in Rotary Park on Water Street. **Third Friday ArtWalks** are held June-September in downtown Kennebunk.

SHOPPING

Lots of small, attractive boutiques surround **Dock Square,** the hub of Kennebunkport, and flow over the bridge into Kennebunk's Lower Village. Gridlock often develops in midsummer. Avoid driving through here at the height of the season. Take your time and walk, bike, or ride the local trolleys. This is just a sampling of the shopping opportunities.

Antiques and Art

English, European, and American furniture and architectural elements and garden accessories are just a sampling of what you'll find at **Antiques on Nine** (81 Western Ave./Rte. 9, Lower Village, Kennebunk, 207/967-0626). Another good place for browsing high-end antiques as well as home accents is **Hurlbutt Designs** (53 Western Ave./Rte. 9, Lower Village, Kennebunk, 207/967-4110). More than 30 artists are represented at **Wright Gallery** (5 Pier Rd., Cape Porpoise, 207/967-5053).

Jean Briggs represents nearly 100 artists at her topflight **Mast Cove Galleries** (Maine St. and Mast Cove Lane, Kennebunkport, 207/967-3453, www.mastcove.com), in a handsome Greek Revival house near the Graves Memorial Library. Prices vary widely, so don't be surprised if you spot something affordable. The gallery often sponsors 2.5-hour evening jazz and blues concerts July-August ($20 donation includes light refreshments). Call for a schedule.

The Gallery on Chase Hill (10 Chase Hill Rd., Kennebunkport, 207/967-0049), in the stunningly restored Captain Chase House, mounts rotating exhibits and represents a wide variety of Maine and New England artists. It's a sibling of the **Maine Art Gallery** (14 Western Ave., Kennebunkport, 207/967-0049, www.maine-art.com), which is right down the street. **Compliments** (Dock Sq., Kennebunkport, 207/967-2269) has a truly unique and fun collection of contemporary fine American crafts, with an emphasis on glass and ceramic ware.

Specialty Shops

Quilt fans should make time to visit **Mainely Quilts** (108 Summer St./Rte. 35, Kennebunk, 207/985-4250), behind the Waldo Emerson Inn. The shop has a nice selection of contemporary and antique quilts.

Most of the clothing shops clustered around Dock Square are rather pricey. Not so **Victorian Affair Boutique** (28 Dock Sq., Kennebunkport, 207/967-9989), which combines designer consignment clothing with new fashions, vintage designer costume jewelry, shoes, and handbags.

Irresistible eye-dazzling costume jewelry, hair ornaments, handbags, scarves, lotions, cards, and other delightful finds fill every possible space at **Dannah** (123 Ocean Ave., Kennebunkport, 207/967-8640), in the Breakwater Spa building, with free customer-only parking in the rear.

Scalawags (3 Dock Square, 207/967-2775) is a bonanza for pet owners, with wonderful presents to bring home to furry pals. If traveling with your pooch, ask about local pet-friendly parks, inns, and restaurants, as well as favorite places for walks.

RECREATION

Parks and Preserves

Thanks to a dedicated coterie of year-round and summer residents, the foresighted **Kennebunkport Conservation Trust** (57 Gravelly Brook Rd., Kennebunkport, 207/967-3465, www.kporttrust.org), founded in 1974, has become a nationwide model for land-trust organizations. The trust has managed to preserve from development several hundred acres of land, including 11 small islands off Cape Porpoise Harbor, and most of this acreage is accessible to the public, especially via a sea kayak. The trust has even assumed ownership of 7.7-acre Goat Island, with its distinctive lighthouse visible from Cape Porpoise, and other coastal vantage points. Check the website for special events and activities.

VAUGHN'S ISLAND PRESERVE

To visit **Vaughn's Island** you'll need to do a little planning, tide-wise, since the 96-acre island is about 600 feet offshore. Consult a tide calendar and aim for low tide close to the new moon or full moon, when the most water drains away. Allow yourself an hour or so before and after low tide, but no longer, or you may need a boat rescue. Wear treaded rubber boots, since the crossing is muddy and slippery with rockweed. Keep an eye on your watch and explore the ocean (east) side of the island, along the beach. It's worth the effort, and there's a great view of Goat Island Light off to the east. From downtown Kennebunkport, take Main Street to Wildes District Road. Continue to Shore Road (also called Turbat's Creek Road), go 0.6 mile, jog left 0.2 mile more, and park in the tiny lot at the end.

EMMONS PRESERVE

Also under Kennebunkport Conservation Trust's stewardship, the **Emmons Preserve** has five trails meandering through 146 acres of woods and fields on the edge of Batson's River (also called Gravelly Brook). The yellow-blazed trail gives best access to the water. Fall colors here are brilliant, birdlife is abundant, and you can do a loop in half an hour. But why rush? This is a wonderful oasis in the heart of Kennebunkport. From Dock Square, take North Street to Beachwood Avenue (right turn) to Gravelly Brook Road (left turn). The trailhead is on the left.

PICNIC ROCK

About 1.5 miles up the Kennebunk River from the ocean, Picnic Rock is the centerpiece of the **Butler Preserve,** a 14-acre enclave managed by the Kennebunk Land Trust (www.kennebunklandtrust.org). Well-named, the rock is a great place for a picnic and a swim, but don't count on being alone. It's an easy .75-mile out and back. Consider bringing a canoe or kayak (or renting one) and paddling with the tide past beautiful homes and the Cape Arundel Golf Club. From Lower Village Kennebunk, take Route 35 west and hang a right onto Old Port Road. When the road gets close to the Kennebunk River, watch for a Nature Conservancy oak-leaf sign on the right. Parking is along Old Port Road; walk down through the preserve to Picnic Rock, right on the river.

Water Sports

BEACHES

Ah, the beaches. The Kennebunks are well endowed with sand, but not with parking spaces. Parking permits are required, and you need a separate pass for each town. Many lodgings

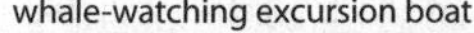
whale-watching excursion boat

provide free permits for their guests—ask when making room reservations. Avoid the parking nightmare altogether by hopping aboard the Intown Trolley, which goes right by the major beaches.

The main beaches in **Kennebunk** (east to west, stretching about two miles) are 3,346-foot-long **Gooch's** (the most popular), Kennebunk (locally called **Middle Beach** or **Rocks Beach**), and **Mother's** (a smallish beach next to Lords Point, where there's also a playground). Lifeguards are on duty at Gooch's and Mother's Beaches July-Labor Day. Ask locally about a couple of other beach options. Mid-June-mid-September you'll need to buy a **parking permit** ($20/day, $75 per/week, $150 for the season) from the **Kennebunk Town Hall** (4 Summer St., 207/985-3675) or at kiosks located at Mother's Beach, Narragansett Point, and Gooch's Beach. **Parsons Beach,** the least known, is a lovely swath with limited parking. Ask for directions and pedal to it instead of driving. Dogs are allowed on Kennebunk's beaches before 9am and after 5pm from June 15 to early September, and all day the rest of the year. Barbara Bush often walks the family canine on Gooch's Beach in the early morning.

Kennebunkport's claim to beach fame is three-mile-long **Goose Rocks Beach,** one of the loveliest in the area. Parking spaces are scarce, and a permit is required late May-early September. **Permits** ($15/day, $50/week, $100 for the season) are available from the **Kennebunkport Police Station** (101 Main St., 207/967-4243, 24 hours daily), **Kennebunkport Town Hall** (6 Elm St.), and **Goose Rocks General Store** (3 Dyke Rd., 207/967-4541). To reach the beach, take Route 9 from Dock Square east and north to Dyke Road (Clock Farm Corner). Turn right and continue to the end (King's Hwy.).

The prize for tiniest beach goes to **Colony Beach** (officially Arundel Beach), near The Colony resort complex. It's close to many Kennebunkport lodgings and an easy walk from Dock Square; no permit is necessary.

BOAT EXCURSIONS

Join Captain Gary aboard the 87-foot **Nick's Chance** (4 Western Ave., Lower Village, Kennebunk, 207/967-5507 or 800/767-2628, www.firstchancewhalewatch.com, $48 adults, $28 ages 3-12, cash only) for the 4.5-hour whale-watching trip to Jeffrey's Ledge, weather permitting. The destination is the summer feeding grounds for finbacks, humpbacks, minkes, the rare blue whale, and the endangered right whale. The boat departs daily late June-early September, weekends only spring and fall, from Performance Marine, in Kennebunk's Lower Village.

Under the same ownership and departing from the same location is the 65-foot open lobster boat **Kylie's Chance,** which departs three times daily in July-August for 1.5-hour scenic lobster cruises ($20 adults, $15 ages 3-12, cash only); the schedule is reduced in spring and fall. A lobstering demonstration is given on most trips, but never on the evening one.

The handsome 55-foot gaff-rigged schooner **Eleanor** (Arundel Wharf, 43 Ocean Ave., Kennebunkport, 207/967-8809, www.gwi.net/schoonersails), built by its captain, Rich "Woody" Woodman, heads out for two-hour sails ($45 pp), usually heading north past Walker's Point, site of the Bush compound, to Cape Porpoise and back, weather and tides willing, one to three times daily during the summer.

OUTFITTERS

Explore the Kennebunk River by canoe or kayak. **Kennebunkport Marina** (67 Ocean Ave., Kennebunkport, 207/967-3411, www.kennebunkportmarina.com) rents single kayaks ($30 for two hours, $50/half-day) and double kayaks and canoes ($50 for two hours, $70/half-day). Check the tide before you depart, and plan your trip to paddle with it rather than against it.

Coastal Maine Kayak & Bike (8 Western Ave., Lower Village, Kennebunk, 207/967-6065, www.coastalmainekayak.com) offers a daylong Cape Porpoise Tour ($85), including guide, instruction, equipment, and snacks; other options are available. Rental kayaks are $40 for three hours or $60 full day; doubles are $65 and $80. Standup paddleboards are $40 for three hours, $65 full day.

If you want to catch a wave, stop by **Aquaholics Surf Shop** (166 Port Rd., Kennebunk, 207/967-8650, www.aquaholic-surf.com). The shop has boards, wetsuits, and related gear both for sale and rental, and it offers lessons and surf camps.

Bicycling

Access to the **Eastern Trail** (www.eastern-trail.org), the 65-mile section of the East Coast Greenway between Kittery and South Portland, is available at the Kennebunk Elementary School, off Alewive Rd., and off the Limerick Road in Arundel.

Coastal Maine Kayak & Bike (8 Western Ave., Lower Village, Kennebunk, 207/967-6065, www.coastalmainekayak.com) rents bikes starting at $10/hour or $35/day.

Golf

Three 18-hole golf courses make the sport a big deal in the area. **Cape Arundel Golf Club** (19 River Rd., Kennebunkport, 207/967-3494), established in 1897, and **Webhannet Golf Club** (8 Central Ave., Kennebunk, 207/967-2061), established in 1902, are semiprivate and open to nonmembers; call for tee times at least 24 hours ahead. In nearby Arundel, **Dutch Elm Golf Course** (5 Brimstone Rd., Arundel, 207/282-9850) is a public course with rentals, pro shop, and putting greens.

ACCOMMODATIONS

Most stay open through the Christmas Prelude festival, with many B&Bs remaining open year-round. This is not an especially budget-friendly area, nor will you find chain motels.

Inns and Hotels

Graciously dominating its 11-acre spread at the mouth of the Kennebunk River, the family-owned **Colony Hotel** (140 Ocean Ave. at King's Hwy., Kennebunkport, 207/967-3331 or 800/552-2363, www.thecolonyhotel.com/maine, from $245) springs right out of a bygone era, and its distinctive cupola is an area landmark. It has had a longtime commitment to the environment, with recycling, waste-reduction, and educational programs. There's a special feeling here, with cozy corners for reading, lawns and gardens for strolling, an oceanview heated swimming pool, room service, 18-hole putting green, tennis privileges at the exclusive River Club, bike rentals, massage therapy, and lawn games. The price of rooms includes breakfast and Wi-Fi. Pets are $30/night. There are no in-room TVs in the main inn.

The **White Barn Grace** (37 Beach Ave., Kennebunk, 207/967-2321, www.white-barninn.com, from $490), with Relais & Châteaux status, is the most exclusive property in the area and also home to one of the Northeast's best restaurants. Many rooms have fireplaces and marble baths with separate steam showers and whirlpool tubs (you can even arrange for a butler-drawn bath). Service is impeccable, and nothing has been overlooked in terms of amenities. There's an outdoor heated European-style infinity pool, where lunch is available, weather permitting, as well as a full-service spa. Guests have use of canoes and bicycles. Hands-on cooking classes are available for $215 per class, $315 with a four-course dinner.

Hay Creek Hotels operates three high-end boutique properties in the area. Guest rooms all have air-conditioning, phones, satellite TV, and video and CD players; bikes and canoes are available for guests. Rates include bountiful continental breakfasts. All but the Beach House are within walking distance of Dock Square. **The Beach House Inn** (211 Beach Ave., Kennebunk, 207/967-3850, www.beachhseinn.com, from $229) faces Middle Beach; splurge on a room with a water view. **The Breakwater Inn, Hotel, and Spa** (127 Ocean Ave., Kennebunkport, 207/967-3118, www.thebreakwaterinn.com, from $209), at the mouth of the Kennebunk River, comprises a beautifully renovated historic inn with wraparound porches and an adjacent, more modern building with guest rooms and a full-service spa. The complex is also home to Stripers Restaurant. Finally, there's **The Yachtsman Lodge and Marina** (Ocean Ave., Kennebunkport, 207/967-2511, www.yachtsmanlodge.com, from $249), an innovative blend of a motel and bed-and-breakfast, with all rooms opening onto patios facing the river and the marina where George H. W. Bush keeps his boat. Pets are allowed here with advance reservation for $25/night.

Families, especially, favor the sprawling riverfront **Nonantum Resort** (95 Ocean Ave., Kennebunkport, 207/967-4050 or 888/205-1555, www.nonantumresort.com, from $260) complex, which dates from 1884. It includes a bit of everything, from gently updated rooms and suites in the main building to modern family suites with kitchenettes in the newer Portside building, where some third-floor rooms have ocean views. Recreational amenities include a small outdoor heated pool, docking facilities, lobsterboat and sailing tours, fishing charters, and kayak rentals. A slew of activities are offered daily, including a children's program. All 115 guest rooms have air-conditioning, Wi-Fi, and TVs; some have refrigerators. Rates include a full breakfast. The water-view dining room is also open for dinner and, in July-August, lunch. Packages, many of which include dinner, are a good choice. Note that weddings take place here almost every weekend.

The **Kennebunkport Resort Collection** (www.kennebunkportresortcollection.com) comprises nine upscale or luxury accommodations in the area, all with the expected amenities. A seasonal dinner shuttle provides transportation between them. Fanciest is **Hidden Pond** (354 Goose Rocks Rd., Kennebunkport, 888/967-9050, from $799), which shares amenities with nearby **Tides Beach Club** (254 Kings Hwy., Kennebunkport, 855/632-3324, www.tidesbeachclubmaine.com, from $439). The family-oriented Hidden Pond resort, tucked in the woods about a mile from Goose Rocks Beach, comprises chic Victorianesque cottages and bungalows, gardens, a spa, a wellness center, outdoor pools, a pool grill, and the fine dining restaurant Earth. The renovated Victorian Tides Beach Club is a hip boutique hotel with a restaurant/lounge on Goose Rocks Beach. A tender oversees beach chairs and umbrellas, provides water, and even delivers lunch. All but two guest rooms at the **Cape Arundel Inn** (208 Ocean Ave., Kennebunkport, 207/967-2125, www.capearundelinn.com, from $309) overlook crashing surf and the Bush estate. The compound comprises the Shingle-style main inn building, the Rockbound motel-style building, and the Carriage House Loft, a large suite on the upper floor of the carriage house; breakfast is included. All guest rooms are air-conditioned and most have fireplaces. Bikes and beach passes, towels, and chairs are provided. Every table in the inn's restaurant (entrées $27-40) has an ocean view. Sixteen additional rooms are on the adjacent the **Olde Fort Estate,** the former stable house of a grand summer resort on 15 acres with an outdoor heated pool. The meticulously renovated 1899 **Kennebunkport Inn** (1 Dock Sq., Kennebunkport, 207/967-2621, from $289) comprises three buildings in the heart of Dock Square. It also has an excellent restaurant, One Dock, as well as piano bar. Rates include a continental breakfast. The **Boathouse Waterfront Hotel** (21 Ocean Ave., Kennebunkport, 207/967-8233, from $299) hangs over the river and is home to David's Restaurant.

Bed-and-Breakfasts

Three of Kennebunkport's loveliest inns are rumored to have been owned by brothers-in-law, all of whom were sea captains. Rivaling the White Barn Inn for service, decor, amenities, and overall luxury is the three-story ★ **Captain Lord Mansion** (Pleasant St., Kennebunkport, 207/967-3141 or 800/522-3141, www.captainlord.com, from $269), which is one of the finest bed-and-breakfasts anywhere. And no wonder: Innkeepers Rick and Bev Litchfield have been at it since 1978, and they're never content to rest on their laurels. Each year the inn improves upon seeming perfection. If you want to be pampered and stay in a meticulously decorated, frequently updated, historical bed-and-breakfast with marble bathrooms (which have heated floors, many with double whirlpool tubs), fireplaces, original artwork, phones, TVs, Wi-Fi, air-conditioning in all guest rooms, and even a few cedar closets, look no further. A multicourse breakfast is served to shared tables. Bicycles as well as beach towels and chairs are available. Afternoon treats are provided.

The elegant Federal-style ★ **Captain Jefferds Inn** (5 Pearl St., Kennebunkport, 207/967-2311 or 800/839-6844, www.captainjefferdsinn.com, $199-399), in the historic district, provides the ambience of a real captain's house. Each of the 16 guest rooms and suites (10 in the main house and 5 more in the carriage house) has plush linens, fresh flowers, down comforters, TVs and DVD players, CD players, Wi-Fi, and air-conditioning; some have fireplaces, whirlpool tubs, and other luxuries. A three-course breakfast and afternoon tea are included. Five rooms, with direct entry, are dog-friendly, at $30/day/dog; pet sitting is available.

The Captain Fairfield Inn (8 Pleasant St., Kennebunkport, www.captainfairfield.com, from $280) is perhaps the most modest architecturally of the three, but it doesn't scrimp on amenities. Guest rooms are divided between traditional and contemporary decor, but all have flat-screen TV/DVDs with Apple TV, iPads, air-conditioning, and Wi-Fi; some have gas fireplaces, double whirlpools, and rainfall showers. The lovely grounds are a fine place to retreat for a snooze in the hammock or a game of croquet. Rates include a four-course breakfast and afternoon cookies.

Slip away from the crowds at the Gott family's antiques-filled ★ **Bufflehead Cove Inn** (B18 Bufflehead Cove Lane, Kennebunkport, 207/967-3879, www.buffleheadcove.com, from $200), a secluded riverfront home in the woods less than a mile from K'port's action. With a location like this and pampering service, you just might not want to stray from the front porch or dock. Rooms have Wi-Fi, flat-screen TVs, and air-conditioning; some have fireplaces and whirlpool tubs. Rates include a full breakfast and afternoon treats and use of beach chairs, umbrellas, and passes.

Far less fussy, the **Old Parsonage Guest House** (15 School St./Rte. 9, Kennebunkport, 207/967-4352, www.oldparsonageguesthouse.com/directions, $99-149) is also far less pricey and, unlike most B&Bs, it welcomes well-behaved children. Three rooms, two sharing a bath, have Wi-Fi. Accommodating innkeepers go out of their way to assist guests and provide a bountiful hot breakfast. The inn is within walking distance of Dock Square.

Neighboring the Wedding Cake House, **The Waldo Emerson Inn** (108 Summer St./Rte. 35, Kennebunk, 207/985-4250, www.waldoemersoninn.com, from $175) has a charming colonial feel, as it should, since the main section was built in 1784. Poet Ralph Waldo Emerson spent many a summer here; it was his great-uncle's home. Three of the six attractive guest rooms have working fireplaces. Rates include a full breakfast. Quilters, take note: In the barn is Mainely Quilts, a well-stocked quilt shop.

Motels

Patricia Mason is the ninth-generation innkeeper at **The Seaside Motor Inn** (80 Beach Ave., Kennebunk, 207/967-4461 or 800/967-4461, www.kennebunkbeach.com, from $249), a property that has been in her family since 1667. What a location! The 22-room motel is the only truly beachfront property in the area. Rooms are spacious, with TVs, Wi-Fi, air-conditioning, and refrigerators. Guests have use of an oceanview hot tub and bicycles. A continental breakfast is included in the rates. Kids ages 12 and younger stay free.

Second-generation innkeepers David and Paula Reid keep the **Fontenay Terrace Motel** (128 Ocean Ave., Kennebunkport, 207/967-3556, www.fontenaymotel.com, from $150) spotless. It borders a tidal inlet and has a private grassy and shaded lawn, perfect for retreating from the hubbub of busy Kennebunkport. Each of the eight guest rooms has air-conditioning, a mini-fridge, a microwave, Wi-Fi, cable TV, and a phone; some have water views. A small beach is 300 yards away, and it's a pleasant one-mile walk to Dock Square.

The clean and simple **Cape Porpoise Motel** (12 Mills Rd./Rte. 9, Cape Porpoise, 207/967-3370, www.capeporpoisemotel.com, from $139) is a short walk from the harbor. All rooms have TV, mini-fridge, and air-conditioning, and some have kitchenettes; rates include a continental breakfast with homemade baked goods, fresh fruit, cereals, and bagels. Also available by the week or month are efficiencies with full kitchens, phones, and one or more bedrooms.

Here's a bargain: The nonprofit **Franciscan Guest House** (28 Beach Ave., Kennebunk, 207/967-4865, www.franciscanguesthouse.com), on the grounds of the monastery, has accommodations spread among two buildings and three other Tudor-style cottages. Decor is vintage 1970s, frills are few, and yes, it's in need of updating, but there are some nice amenities, including TVs, air-conditioning, a saltwater pool, Wi-Fi, and beach passes. The location is within walking distance of the beach and Dock Square. A continental breakfast is included in the rates (hot buffet available, $3), and a buffet dinner is often available (around $17). There is no daily maid service, but fresh towels are provided. Rooms are $109-229, and 1-3-bedroom suites are $190-280.

FOOD

The Kennebunkport Resort Collection operates a dining shuttle between its properties in Kennebunkport and Goose Rocks Beach. It's free for guests at its hotels, but anyone can hop aboard for $5.

Get the lowdown on K'port's food scene on a walking culinary tasting tour with **Maine Foodie Tours** (207/233-7485, www.mainefoodietours.com). Tickets, available online, cost about $55. There's even a dog-friendly tour ($32).

Local Flavors

All Day Breakfast (55 Western Ave./Rte. 9, Lower Village, Kennebunk, 207/967-5132, 7am-1:30pm daily) is a favorite meeting spot, offering such specialties as invent-your-own omelets and crepes, Texas French toast, and the ADB sandwich.

H. B. Provisions (15 Western Ave., Lower Village, Kennebunk, 207/967-5762, www.hbprovisions.com, 6am-9pm daily) has an excellent wine selection, along with plenty of picnic supplies, newspapers, and all the typical general-store inventory. It also serves breakfast and prepares hot and cold sandwiches, salads, and wraps.

Equal parts fancy food and wine store and gourmet café, **Cape Porpoise Kitchen** (Rte. 9, Cape Porpoise, 207/967-1150, 7am-6pm daily) sells sandwiches, salads, prepared foods, desserts, and everything to go with.

Pair a fine wine with light fare at **Old Vines** (141 Port Rd., Lower Village, Kennebunk, 207/967-5766, www.oldvineswinebar.com, from 5pm Mon.-Sat.), an Old World-meets-New World European-style wine/cocktail bar and tapas restaurant housed in a renovated barn. The food is creative and excellent.

Prefer ales? **Federal Jack's** (8 Western Ave., Lower Village, Kennebunk, 207/967-4322, www.federaljacks.com, 11:30am-12:30am) is the brewpub that gave birth to the Shipyard label. Aim for a seat on the riverfront deck. Call in advance for a tour, and if you're serious about brewing, ask about the Maine Brewing Vacation.

Bread and soup, scones and croissants, breakfast or lunch, and even meat pies paired with coffee, tea, beer, or wine—find it all at **Boulangerie, A Proper Bakery** (5 Nasons Ct. #12, Kennebunk, 207/954-3009, www.aproperbakery.com, 7am-5pm Mon.-Sat., 8am-noon Sun.), housed in a beautifully renovated red barn located behind The Pavilion downtown.

The **Kennebunk Farmers Market** sets

up shop 8am-1pm Saturday mid-May-mid-October in the Lafayette Center, just off Route 1 and Storer Street.

Family Favorites

Burgers, pizza, sandwiches, even a turkey dinner with the trimmings—almost everything on the menu is less than $14 at **Duffy's Tavern & Grill** (4 Main St., Kennebunk, 207/985-0050, www.duffyskennebunk.com, from 11am daily). Extremely popular with locals, Duffy's is inside a renovated mill in Lafayette Center. It's an inviting space with exposed beams, gleaming woodwork, brick walls, and big windows framing the Mousam River. If you want to catch the game while you eat, big-screen, high-def TVs make it easy.

Casual Dining

The views complement the food at **Hurricane Restaurant** (29 Dock Sq., Kennebunkport, 207/967-9111, www.hurricanerestaurant.com, from 11:30am daily, entrées $22-50). Thanks to a Dock Square location and a dining room that literally hangs over the river, it reels in the crowds for both lunch and dinner.

Eat well and feel good about it at **Bandaloop** (2 Dock Sq., Kennebunkport, 207/967-4994, www.bandaloop.biz, from 5pm Tues.-Sun., $18-30), a hip, vibrant restaurant where chef-owner W. Scott Lee likes to push boundaries. Lee named the restaurant for the fictional tribe in author Tom Robbins's novels that knew the secret to eternal life. Lee believes the secret is fresh, local, organic, and cruelty-free. Selections vary from meats and fish to vegetarian and vegan prepared with creativity, and include a children's menu.

Floor-to-ceiling windows frame the Kennebunk River breakwater, providing perfect views for those indulging at **Stripers Waterside Restaurant** (Breakwater Inn, 133 Ocean Ave., Kennebunkport, 207/967-5333, www.stripersrestaurant.com, noon-9pm daily), another White Barn Inn sibling, where fish and seafood are the specialties; don't miss the lobster tacos. Most entrées range $22-31. Dress is casual, and valet parking is available.

Chef Peter and his wife, Kate, operate **Pier 77** (77 Pier Rd., Cape Porpoise, 207/967-8500, www.pier77restaurant.com, 11:30am-2:30pm and 5pm-8pm daily, entrées $18-32), which overlooks Cape Porpoise Harbor's lobster boats hustling to and fro. The menu varies from pasta to seafood mixed grill. There's frequent live entertainment, which can make conversation difficult. Reservations are advisable. Practically hidden downstairs is the always-packed **Ramp Bar and Grille** (11:30am-8pm daily), with lighter fare as well as the full menu and a sports-pub decor.

Local is the key word at **50 Local** (50 Main St., Kennebunk, 207/985-0850, www.localkennebunk.com, from 5:30pm daily, $15-43), a bright spot in downtown Kennebunk specializing in local and organic fare. The menu changes daily, but it's easy to cobble together a meal here that fits your appetite and budget.

Portland chef David Turin has expanded his culinary empire with **David's KPT** (207/967-8224, boathouseme.com/davids, from 8:30am daily), a fabulous addition to K'port's restaurant scene. Located at the Boathouse, David's pairs excellent food with the best views in the Dock Square area and a deck that hangs over the river. The menu ranges from pizza and lobster rolls to crispy skin duck breast and osso buco ($15-34).

The views from **Ocean** (208 Ocean Ave., 855/346-5700, www.capearundelinn.com, $31-38, 5-9pm daily) at the Cape Arundel Inn compete for raves with the Chef Pierre Gignac's menu. Savor entrées such as poached lobster or rabbit trio while gazing out at open ocean and Walker Point. A tapas menu is served in the bar.

Get a taste of the White Barn Inn at a fraction of the price at its **bistro** (37 Beach Ave., Kennebunkport, 207/967-2321, www.whitebarninn.com, 6:30pm-9:30pm daily, $18-30), where the menu ranges from pizza and pastas to lobster and steak. Although the dress code is less formal than the main restaurant, you'll still want to spiff up to dine here.

Fine Dining

European country cuisine reigns at **On the Marsh** (46 Western Ave./Rte. 9, Lower Village, Kennebunk, 207/967-2299, www.onthemarsh.com, from 5:30pm daily, entrées $25-43), a restored barn overlooking marshlands leading to Kennebunk Beach. Lighter fare is served in the bar. The space is infused with arts and antiques and European touches courtesy of owner Denise Rubin, an interior designer with a passion for the continent. Dining locations include the two-level dining area, an "owner's table" with a chef's menu, and the kitchen. Service is attentive, but the pace is leisurely. Reservations are essential in midsummer. Special menus include a three-course dinner for $35 on Wednesday evenings and a five-course menu with wine pairings for $54 from 5-6pm on Fridays.

Destination Dining

One of Maine's biggest splurges is **The White Barn Inn** (37 Beach Ave., Kennebunkport, 207/967-2321, www.whitebarninn.com, 6:30pm-9:30pm daily), with haute cuisine and haute prices in a haute-rustic barn. In summer, don't be surprised to run into members of the senior George Bush clan (probably at the back window table). Soft piano music accompanies impeccable service. The four-course (plus extras) fixed-price menu is about $110 per person; add $58 or $85 for wine pairings. For gourmands, consider the nine-course tasting menu (about $165, wine pairings around $100). Reservations are essential—well ahead during July-August—and you'll need a credit card (cancel 24 hours ahead or you'll be charged). The restaurant has relaxed its dress code a bit; jackets are no longer required, but avoid jeans, shorts, and t-shirts—think resort-casual-plus. Although the price is high, the value for the dollar far exceeds that. If you can afford it, dine here.

Also splurge-worthy is **Earth** (at Hidden Pond resort, 354 Goose Rocks Rd., Kennebunkport, 207/967-6550, www.earthathiddenpond.com, from 5:30pm daily, $18-40), where consulting chef Ken Orringer hangs his toque in Maine. The farm-to-fork cuisine includes handmade pastas, house-made charcuteries, wood-oven pizzas, and entrées such as local seafood paella, duck, and short ribs. The dining room is rustic, and the garden views sublime.

Lobster and Clams

Nunan's Lobster Hut (9 Mills Rd., Cape Porpoise, 207/967-4362, www.nunanslobsterhut.com, from 5pm daily) is an institution. Sure, other places might have better views, but this casual dockside eatery with indoor and outdoor seating has been serving lobsters since 1953.

Adjacent to the bridge connecting Kennebunkport's Dock Square to Kennebunk's Lower Village is another time-tested classic, **The Clam Shack** (Rte. 9, Kennebunkport, 207/967-2560, www.theclamshack.net, lunch and dinner from 11am daily May-Oct.). The tiny take-out stand serves perhaps the state's best lobster rolls, jam-packed with meat and available with either butter or mayo, and dee-lish fried clams.

Lobster and crab rolls and chowders are the specialties at **Port Lobster** (122 Ocean Ave., Kennebunkport, 207/967-2081, www.portlobster.com, 9am-5pm daily), a fresh-fish store with takeout just northeast of Dock Square.

Pair your lobster with a view of Goat Island Light at **Cape Pier Chowder House** (79 Pier Rd., Cape Porpoise, 207/967-0123, www.capeporpoiselobster.com, from 11am daily).

The Ocean Roll (207/985-8824, www.mainelobsterrolls.com, 11am-8pm daily), an extremely popular, seasonal food truck selling fresh lobster rolls and fried seafood, is usually parked at the corner of Ross Avenue and Route 1 in Kennebunk.

INFORMATION AND SERVICES

The **Kennebunk-Kennebunkport-Arundel Chamber of Commerce** (16 Water St., Kennebunk, 207/967-0857, www.visitthekennebunks.com) produces an excellent area guide to accommodations, restaurants, area maps, bike maps, tide calendars, recreation, and beach parking permits. It maintains a seasonal kiosk at 1 Chase Hill in Lower Village.

Check out **Louis T. Graves Memorial Public Library** (18 Maine St., Kennebunkport, 207/967-2778, www.graveslibrary.org) or **Kennebunk Free Library** (112 Main St., 207/985-2173, www.kennebunklibrary.org).

Public restrooms are at Gooch's and Mother's Beaches and at St. Anthony's Franciscan Monastery, and in the Dock Square parking area.

GETTING THERE AND AROUND

Kennebunk is about five miles or 10 minutes via Route 1 from Wells. Kennebunkport is about 6.5 miles or 12 minutes via Routes 1 and 9 from Wells. Connecting Kennebunk and Kennebunkport are four miles of Route 9. From Kennebunk to Biddeford, it's about nine miles or 17 minutes via Route 1. Allow longer for summer congestion in each town.

Amtrak Downeaster (800/872-7245, www.amtrakdowneaster.com) connects Boston's North Station with Portland, Maine, with stops in Wells, Saco, and Old Orchard Beach (seasonal). It connects with the seasonal **Shoreline Explorer** (207/324-5762, www.shorelineexplorer.com) trolley system, which operates between York and Kennebunkport. Each town's system is operated separately and has its own fees. The **Shoreline Trolley Aqua Line-7/Kennebunk Shuttle** ($1 one way, $3 day pass, $10 12-ride multipass, free for children under 18) connects Line Blue Line-4 (serving the Wells Transportation Facility and the Downeaster) with downtown Kennebunk, Lower Village, and Kennebunk's beaches.

Shoreline Trolley Line 6/Intown Trolley (207/967-3686, www.intowntrolley.com, $16, $6 ages 3-17) operates as a narrated sightseeing tour throughout Kennebunk and Kennebunkport. It originates in Dock Square and makes regular stops at beaches and other attractions. The entire route takes about 45 minutes, with the driver providing a hefty dose of local history and gossip. Seats are park bench-style. You can get on or off at any stop.

The best fried clams in the Kennebunks come from The Clam Shack.

Old Orchard Beach Area

Seven continuous miles of white sand beach have been drawing vacation-oriented folks for generations to the area stretching from Camp Ellis in Saco to Pine Point in Scarborough. Cottage colonies and condo complexes dominate at the extremities, but the center of activity has always been and remains Old Orchard Beach.

In its heyday, **Old Orchard Beach's pier** reached far out into the sea, huge resort hotels lined the sands, and wealthy Victorian folk (including Rose Fitzgerald and Joe Kennedy, who met on these sands in the days when men strolled around in dress suits and women toted parasols) came each summer to see and be seen.

Storms and fires have taken their toll through the years, and the grand resorts have been replaced by endless motels, many of which display "Nous parlons français" signs to welcome the masses of French Canadians who arrive each summer. They're joined by young families who come for the sand and surf, and T-shirted and body-pierced young pleasure seekers who come for the nightlife.

Although some residents are pushing for gentrification and a few projects are moving things in that direction, **Old Orchard Beach** (pop. 8,624) remains somewhat honky-tonk, and most of its visitors would have it no other way. French fries, cotton candy, and beach-accessories shops line the downtown, and as you get closer to the pier, you pass arcades and amusement parks. There's not a kid on earth who wouldn't have fun in Old Orchard—even if some parents might find it all a bit much.

Much more sedate are the villages on the fringes. The **Ocean Park** section of Old Orchard, at the southwestern end of town, was established in 1881 as a religious summer-cottage community. It still offers interdenominational services and vacation Bible school, but it also has an active cultural association that sponsors concerts, Chautauqua-type lectures, films, and other events throughout the summer. All are open to the public.

South of that is **Camp Ellis.** Begun as a small fishing village named after early settler Thomas Ellis, it is crowded with longtime

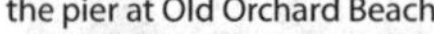
the pier at Old Orchard Beach

summer homes that are in constant battle with the sea. A nearly mile-long granite jetty—designed to keep silt from clogging the Saco River—has taken the blame for massive beach erosion since it was constructed. But the jetty is a favorite spot for wetting a line and for panoramic views off toward Wood Island Light (built in 1808) and Biddeford Pool. Camp Ellis Beach is open to the public, with lifeguards on duty in midsummer. Parking—scarce on hot days—is $2/hour.

As you head north from Old Orchard, you'll pass **Pine Point,** another longtime community of vacation homes. Services are few, and parking is $10/day.

Most folks get to Old Orchard by passing through **Saco** (pop. 18,482) and **Biddeford** (pop. 21,277), which have long been upstairs-downstairs sister cities, with wealthy mill owners living in Saco and their workers and workplaces in Biddeford. But even those personalities have always been split—congested commercial Route 1 is part of Saco, and the exclusive enclave of Biddeford Pool is, of course, in below-stairs Biddeford.

Saco still has an attractive downtown, with boutiques and stunning homes on Main Street and beyond. Once blue-collar Biddeford is now one of southern Maine's hotspots. It's home to the magnificent Biddeford City Theater and the University of New England, and as a Main Street community it's getting a much-needed sprucing up. Another Biddeford hallmark is its Franco-American tradition, thanks to the French-speaking workers who sustained the textile and shoemaking industries in the 19th century. The mills on the Saco River Island between the two cities are being rehabbed to house restaurants, shops, offices, and condos, while honoring their past with a museum.

SIGHTS

Saco Museum

Founded in 1866, the **Saco Museum** (371 Main St., Saco, 207/283-3861, www.dyerlibrarysacomuseum.org, noon-4pm Tues.-Thurs. and Sun., noon-8pm Fri., 10am-4pm Sat. June-Dec., $5 adults, $3 seniors, $2 ages 7-18) rotates selections from its outstanding collection, including 18th- and 19th-century paintings, furniture, and other household treasures. Lectures, workshops, and concerts are also part of the annual schedule. Admission is free after 4pm Friday.

★ Wood Island Lighthouse

The all-volunteer **Friends of Wood Island**

Mills along the Saco River are being rehabbed to house restaurants, shops, studios, and accommodations.

Light (207/200-4552, www.woodislandlighthouse.org) is restoring Maine's second-oldest lighthouse, which was commissioned by President Thomas Jefferson, built in 1808 (reconstructed in 1858) on 35-acre Wood Island and abandoned in 1986. In July-August the Friends offer 1.5-hour guided tours ($15 adults, $8 children, recommended donation) of the two-story keeper's house and 42-foot-tall stone tower, relating tales of former keepers and their families to bring the site to life. You can even climb the 60 stairs to the tower's lantern room for splendid views. The tour departs from Vine's Landing in Biddeford Pool. Once on the island, it's about a half-mile walk to the site. Reservations are accepted within one week of the tour date; see the website or call for a current schedule.

Harmon Museum

Dip into Old Orchard Beach's history at the Old Orchard Beach Historical Society's **Harmon Museum** (4 Portland Ave., Old Orchard Beach, 207/934-9319, www.harmonmuseum.org, 10am-4pm Tues.-Fri., 10am-2pm Sat., free). Religious groups, the famed Pier, destructive fires, Ocean Park, transportation, and celebrities are all covered with displays, artifacts, and memorabilia. Interesting anytime, but a great rainy-day activity.

Biddeford Mills Museum

Very much a work in progress, the **Biddeford Mills Museum** (2 Main St., Biddeford, 207/229-6387, www.biddefordmillsmuseum.org) offers tours of the former textile mills, including their underground canals. The two-hour tours are guided by former mill workers who share their stories along with the history of the mills; call or check the website for current schedule and fees.

ENTERTAINMENT

At 6pm every Thursday, late June-Labor Day, **free concerts** are staged in Old Orchard's Memorial Park, followed by **fireworks** set off by the pier at 9:45pm.

Family concerts and other performances are staged at the outdoor **Seaside Pavilion** (8 Sixth St., Old Orchard Beach, 207/934-2024, www.seasidepavilion.org).

The BallPark (E. Emerson Cummings Blvd., Old Orchard, 207/205-6160, www.oldorchardbeachballpark.com) hosts concerts, shows, and other events.

The **Temple** (Temple Avenue, Ocean Park), a 19th-century octagon that seats more than 800, is the venue for Saturday- or Sunday-night concerts (7:30pm, $15 adults) and many other programs throughout the summer.

Designed by noted architect John Calvin Stevens in 1896, the 500-seat **City Theater** (205 Main St., Biddeford, 207/282-0849, www.citytheater.org), on the National Register of Historic Places, has been superbly restored, and the acoustics are excellent even when Eva Gray, the resident ghost, mixes it up backstage.

A rainy-day godsend, the **IMAX Theater** (779 Portland Rd./Rte. 1, Saco, 207/282 6234, www.cinemagicmovies.com) has digital sound, stadium seating, a restaurant, and online ticketing.

EVENTS

La Kermesse (www.lakermessefestival.com), meaning "the fair" or "the festival," is Biddeford's summer highlight, when nearly 50,000 visitors pour into town in late June to celebrate the town's Franco-American heritage. Local volunteers go all out to plan block parties, a parade, games, a carnival, live entertainment, and traditional dancing. Then there's *la cuisine franco-américaine;* you can fill up on *boudin, creton, poutine, tourtière, tarte au saumon,* and crepes (although your arteries may rebel).

The **Biddeford+Saco Art Walk** (www.biddefordsacoartwalk.com/) takes place the last Friday of each month.

In July the parishioners of St. Demetrios Greek Orthodox Church (186 Bradley St., Saco, 207/284-5651) mount the annual **Greek Heritage Festival,** a three-day extravaganza of homemade Greek food, traditional Greek music and dancing, and a crafts fair. Be sure to tour the impressive, $1.5-million, domed church building.

The beaches come to life in July with the annual **Parade and Sandcastle Contest** in Ocean Park.

One weekend in mid-August, Old Orchard Beach's **Beach Olympics** is a family festival of games, exhibitions, and music benefiting Maine's Special Olympics program.

RECREATION

Parks and Preserves

Saco Bay Trails (www.sacobaytrails.org), a local land trust, has produced a helpful trail guide ($10) that includes the Saco Heath, the East Point Sanctuary, and more than a dozen other local trails. The Cascade Falls trail, for example, is a half-mile stroll ending at a waterfall. Copies are available at a number of Biddeford and Saco locations, including the Dyer Library, or from Saco Bay Trails. Trail information is also on the organization's website.

EAST POINT SANCTUARY

Owned by Maine Audubon (207/781-2330, www.maineaudubon.org), the 30-acre **East Point Sanctuary** is a splendid preserve at the eastern end of Biddeford Pool. Crashing surf, beach roses, bayberry bushes, and offshore Wood Island Light are all features of the two-part perimeter trail, which skirts the exclusive Abenakee Club's golf course. Allow at least an hour; even in fog, the setting is dramatic. During spring and fall migrations it's one of southern Maine's prime birding locales, so you'll have plenty of company at those times, and the usual street-side parking may be scarce. It's poorly signposted (perhaps deliberately), so you'll want to follow the directions: From Route 9 (Main Street) in downtown Biddeford, take Route 9/208 (Pool Road) southeast about five miles to the Route 208 turnoff to Biddeford Pool. Go 0.6 mile on Route 208 (Bridge Road) and then turn left onto Mile Stretch Road. Continue to Lester B. Orcutt Boulevard, turn left, and go to the end. Be careful: There's poison ivy on the point.

THE HEATH

Owned by The Nature Conservancy, 1,200-plus-acre **Saco Heath Preserve** is the nation's southernmost "raised coalesced bog," where peat accumulated through eons into two above-water dome shapes that eventually merged into a single natural feature. (A bit of esoterica: This is the home of the rare Hessel's hairstreak butterfly.) Pick up a map at the parking area and follow the mile-long, self-guided trail through the woods and then into the heath via a boardwalk. The best time to visit is early-mid-October, when the heath and woodland colors are positively brilliant and insects are on the wane. You're likely to see deer and perhaps even spot a moose. The preserve entrance is on Route 112 (Buxton Road), two miles west of I-95. Pets are not allowed in the preserve.

FERRY BEACH STATE PARK

When the weather's hot, arrive early at **Ferry Beach State Park** (95 Bay View Rd., off Rte. 9, Saco, 207/283-0067, $6 nonresident adults, $4 Maine resident adults, $2 nonresident seniors, $1 ages 5-11), a pristine beach backed by dune grass on Saco Bay. In the 117-acre park are changing rooms, restrooms, a lifeguard, picnic tables, and a 1.7-mile trail network winding through woodlands, marshlands, and dunes. Later in the day, keep the insect repellent handy. It's open daily late May-late September but accessible all year; trail markers are removed in winter.

Tours

Join **Nonesuch Oyster Tours** (www.nonesuchoysters.com) aboard the *Oys-Tour* for a cruise of Nonesuch Oyster Farm, sited in a tidal estuary nature preserve frequented by eagles, sturgeon, and seals. Tours include tasting six freshly harvested oysters. Tours (noon and 2pm, Thurs.-Sun., $50 pp) depart from Pine Point.

Amusement Parks

If you've got kids or just love amusement parks, you'll find Maine's best in the Old Orchard area, where sand and sun just seem to complement arcades and rides perfectly. (All of these parks are seasonal, so call or check websites for current schedule.)

The biggie is **Funtown/Splashtown USA** (774 Portland Rd./Rte. 1, Saco, 207/284-5139 or 800/878-2900, www.funtownsplashtownusa.com). Ride Maine's only wooden roller coaster; fly down New England's longest and tallest log flume ride; free-fall 200 feet on Dragon's Descent; get wet and go wild riding speed slides, tunnel slides, raft slides, and river slides or splashing in the pool. Add a huge kiddie-ride section as well as games, food, and other activities for a full day of family fun. Ticketing options vary by the activities included and height, ranging $25-36 for "Big" (48 inches and taller), $20-27 for "Little" (38-48 inches tall) and "Senior" (over age 60), and free for kids under 38 inches tall.

Three miles north of Funtown/Splashtown USA, **Aquaboggan Water Park** (980 Portland Rd./Rte. 1, Saco, 207/282-3112, www.aquabogganwaterpark.com, 10am-6pm daily late June-Labor Day) is wet and wild, with such stomach turners as the Yankee Ripper, the Suislide, and the Stealth, with an almost-vertical drop of 45 feet—enough to accelerate to 30 mph on the descent. Wear a bathing suit that won't abandon you in the rough-and-tumble. Also, if you wear glasses, safety straps and plastic lenses are required. Besides all the water stuff, there are mini-golf, an arcade, go-karts, and bumper boats. A day pass for all pools, slides, and mini-golf is $20 (48 inches and taller), $16 (under 48 inches tall), and $5 (under 38 inches tall). Monday is $12 general admission. A $30 superpass also includes two go-kart rides and unlimited bumper-boat rides.

The biggest beachfront amusement park, **Palace Playland** (1 Old Orchard St., Old Orchard, 207/934-2001, www.palaceplayland.com) has more than 25 rides and attractions packed into four acres, including a giant waterslide, a fun house, bumper cars, a Ferris wheel, roller coasters, and a

Golf

Tee off at the **Biddeford-Saco Country Club** (101 Old Orchard Rd., Saco, 207/282-5883) or the challenging 18-hole par-71 **Dunegrass Golf Club** (200 Wild Dunes Way, Old Orchard Beach, 207/934-4513 or 800/521-1029).

Water Sports

Gone with the Wind (524 Pool St., Biddeford Pool, 207/283-8446, www.gwtwonline.com) offers two tours, afternoon and sunset, with prices varying with the number of people on the tour (for two people it's about $85 pp). Wetsuits are supplied. The most popular trip is to Beach Island. Also available are rentals ($40 half-day, $65 full day).

Bare Knee Point Kayak Rentals (45 Camp Ellis Ave., Saco, 207/283-4455, www.bareknee pointkayaks.com) makes kayaking easy with an option for a 45-minute ride up the Saco River, allowing you to paddle back with the current. Rentals are $25/two hours solo, $40 tandem; add the upriver cruise for $10 pp.

Baseball

Baseball fans might consider a mosey inland to watch the **Sanford Mariners** (Roberts St., Sanford, 207/324-0010, www.sanfordmainers.com), which play in the New England Collegiate Baseball League. The team's home stadium, built in 1915 and rebuilt in 1997 after a fire, is famed as the site where, on Oct. 1, 1919, Babe Ruth hit is last homer as a member of the Red Sox. Tickets are $5 adults, $3 students/seniors.

ACCOMMODATIONS

The area has hundreds of beds—mostly in motel-style lodgings. The chamber of commerce is the best resource for motels, cottages, and the area's more than 3,000 campsites.

Palace Playland, Old Orchard Beach

24,000-square-foot arcade with more than 200 games. An unlimited pass is $32/day; a kiddie pass good for all two-ticket rides is $24; two-day, season, and single tickets are available.

The **Old Orchard Beach's pier,** jutting 475 feet into the ocean from downtown, is a mini-mall of shops, arcades, and fast-food outlets. Far longer when it was built in 1898, it has been lopped off gradually by fires and storms. The current incarnation has been here since the late 1970s.

The Old Orchard Beach Inn (6 Portland Ave., Old Orchard Beach, 207/934-5834 or 877/700-6624, www.oldorchardbeachinn.com, year-round, $135-200) was rescued from ruin, restored, and reopened in 2000. Built in 1730, and most recently known as the Staples Inn, the National Historic Register building has 18 antiques-filled guest rooms with air-conditioning, phones, and TVs. Continental breakfast and afternoon tea are included in the rates; a two-bedroom suite is $425-450.

Practically next door is **The Atlantic Birches Inn** (20 Portland Ave./Rte. 98, Old Orchard Beach, 207/934-5295 or 888/934-5295, www.atlanticbirches.com, $121-230), with 10 air-conditioned guest rooms split between a 1902 Victorian designed by John Calvin Stevens and a 1920s bungalow. Breakfast is hearty continental, and there's a swimming pool. The beach is an easy walk. It's open all year, but call ahead off-season.

Two family-owned, beachfront motels, both with pools, have been recently renovated: **The Beachwood Motel** (29 W. Grand Ave., Old Orchard Beach, 207/934-2291, www.beachwood-motel.com, $210-265) and **The Edgewater Motor Inn** (57 W. Grand Ave., Old Orchard Beach, 800/203-2034, www.theedgewatermotorinn.com, $179-289). Both are in Old Orchard's hub, so don't expect quiet nights.

FOOD

Old Orchard Beach

Dining is not Old Orchard's strong point, but it is a bonanza for cheap eats. Stroll Main Street and out to the pier for hot dogs, fries, pizza, and ice cream.

All-day breakfast and a menu that tops out at $10 makes part-convenience-store/order-at-the-counter **Tami Lyn's Place** (126 W. Grand Ave., 207/934-4292, www.tamilynsplace.com,

6am-9pm daily) popular for inexpensive family meals.

For casual dining, **Joseph's by the Sea** (55 W. Grand Ave., 207/934-5044, www.josephsbythesea.com, 7am-11am and 5pm-9pm daily, entrées $23-33) is a quiet shorefront restaurant amid all the hoopla. Request a table on the screened patio. The menu is heavy on seafood, but there are choices for steak lovers. Reservations are advisable in midsummer.

Escape the OOB madness at **Yellowfin's Restaurant** (5 Temple Ave., Ocean Park, 207/934-1100, www.yellowfinsrestaurantme.com, from 5pm daily, $18-25), which offers casual fine dining, with entrees such as Yellowfin ahi tuna, almond-crusted haddock, and filet marsala; BYOB.

Saco

Craving fast-ish food? The Camire family operates Maine's best homegrown option, **Rapid Ray's** (189 Main St., 207/283-4222, www.rapidrays.biz, 11am-12:30am Mon.-Thurs., 11am-1:30am Fri.-Sat.), a downtown institution for more than 50 years. Burgers, steamed dogs, lobster rolls, and clam cakes are served at the standing-room-only joint.

Super soups and sandwiches come from **Vic & Whits** (206 Main St., 207/284-6710, 8am-8pm Mon.-Sat., 8am-1pm Sun.), which also has a nice selection of retail wine, beer, and Maine cheeses.

The New Moon Restaurant (17 Pepperell Sq., 207/282-2241, 7:30am-2pm daily and 5pm-9pm Thurs.-Sat.) serves rave-worthy breakfasts and lunches in a cheerful yellow house. On Friday and Saturday nights, it offers dinners with entrées ($16-24) such as chicken saltimbocca and filet mignon medallions.

For gluten-free Venezuelan eats, stop into **Luis's Arepera & Grill** (213 North St., 207/286-8646, www.luisareperaandgrill.com, 11am-8pm Mon.-Fri.) for take-out fare ($5-20).

Located on Saco Island in renovated factory building #3, **The Run of the Mill Public House & Brewery** (100 Main St., 207/571-9648, www.therunofthemill.net, 11:30am-9pm Sun.-Thurs., to 10pm Fri.-Sat., $8-18) is a 14-barrel brewpub with seasonal outdoor deck seating overlooking the river. Expect pub-fare classics with a few surprises.

At **Huot's Seafood Restaurant** (Camp Ellis Beach, Saco, 207/282-1642, www.huotsseafoodrestaurant.com, 11:30am-8:30pm Tues.-Sun., $9-31), under third-generation management, the menu is huge, portions are large, and prices are reasonable. It's a good value for fresh seafood; children's menu available and there's a take-out window.

Biddeford and Biddeford Pool

For a town grounded in Franco-American culture, Biddeford is getting increasingly hip with expanding and interesting choices.

Love biscuits? You'll love **Biscuits & Company** (25 Alfred St., 207/710-2333, 7:30am-2pm Wed.-Sat., 9am-1pm Sun.), an especially popular spot for breakfast and lunch.

If Biddeford has a living room, it's **Elements** (265 Main St., 207/710-2011, www.elementsbookscoffeebeer.com, 7am-6pm Mon., 7am-8pm Tues.-Thurs., 7am-11pm Fri., 9am-11pm Sat., 9am-6pm Sun.), a combination bookstore, coffee and craft-beer bar, and café serving light fare ($6-13) and offering weekend entertainment.

Maine's oldest diner is the **Palace Diner** (18 Franklin St., 207/284-0015, www.palacedinerme.com, 8am-2pm daily), a 1926 Pollard that was towed to Maine from Lowell, Massachusetts, by horses in the same year that Lindberg flew over the Atlantic. Today, it's tucked off Main Street next to City Hall.

Buffleheads (122 Hills Beach Rd., 207/284-6000, www.buffleheadsrestaurant.com, 11:30am-2pm and 5pm-9pm daily, closed Mon. off-season, $10-28) is an off-the-tourist-trail family dining find with spectacular ocean views and a strong local following. The kids can munch on pizza, burgers, spaghetti, and other favorites while adults savor well-prepared seafood with a home-style spin or landlubber classics. Lobster pie is a perennial favorite. Hills Beach Road branches off Route 9 at the University of New England campus.

Take your lobster or fried seafood dinner to an oceanfront picnic table on the grassy lawn behind **F. O. Goldthwaite's** (3 Lester B. Orcott Blvd., Biddeford Pool, 207/284-8872, 7am-7:30pm daily, $4-market rates), an old-fashioned general store. Salads, fried seafood, sandwiches, and kid-friendly fare round out the menu.

INFORMATION AND SERVICES

Sources of visitor information are **Biddeford-Saco Chamber of Commerce and Industry** (207/282-1567, www.biddefordsacochamber.org), **Old Orchard Beach Chamber of Commerce** (207/934-2500 or 800/365-9386, www.oldorchardbeachmaine.com), and **Ocean Park Association** (207/934-9068, www.oceanpark.org).

The **Dyer Library** (371 Main St., Saco, 207/282-3031, www.sacomuseum.org), next door to the Saco Museum, attracts scads of genealogists to its vast Maine history collection. Also check out **Libby Memorial Library** (Staples St., Old Orchard Beach, 207/934-4351, www.ooblibrary.org).

GETTING THERE AND AROUND

Biddeford is about five miles or 10 minutes via Route 1 from Kennebunk. From Biddeford to Portland, it's about 18 miles or 25 minutes via I-95 and I-295; allow at least a half-hour via Route 1. Downtown Biddeford is about a mile via Route 9 from downtown Saco. From Saco to Old Orchard Beach is about four miles or at least 10 minutes via Route 9, the Old Orchard Beach Road, and Route 5, but it can take twice that in summer traffic.

Amtrak Downeaster (800/872-7245, www.amtrakdowneaster.com) connects Boston's North Station with Brunswick, Maine, with stops in Wells, Saco, Old Orchard Beach (seasonal), Portland, Freeport, and Brunswick. If you're thinking about a day trip, take the train and avoid the traffic and parking hassles.

The **Biddeford-Saco-Old Orchard Beach Transit Committee** (207/282-5408, www.shuttlebus-zoom.com) operates three systems that make getting around simple. The **Old Orchard Beach Trolley** (10am-midnight daily late June-Labor Day) operates three routes on a regular schedule that connect restaurants and campgrounds. You can flag it down anywhere en route. Fare is $1-2/ride; children under age 2 ride free. **ShuttleBus Local Service** provides frequent weekday and less-frequent weekend service (except on national holidays) between Biddeford, Saco, and Old Orchard Beach. One-way fare is $1.25 ages five and older; exact change is required. **ShuttleBus InterCity Service** connects Biddeford, Saco, and Old Orchard with Portland, South Portland, and Scarborough. Fares vary by zones, topping out at $5 for anyone over age 5.

Greater Portland

When national magazines highlight the 10 best places to live, eat, work, or play, Greater Portland often makes the list. The very things that make the area so popular with residents make it equally attractive to visitors. Small in size but big in heart, Greater Portland entices visitors with the staples—lighthouses, lobster, and L. L. Bean—but wows them with everything else it offers. It is the state's cultural hub, with performing arts centers, numerous festivals, and varied museums; it's also a culinary destination, with nationally recognized chefs as well as an amazing assortment and variety of everyday restaurants; and finally, despite its urban environment, it has a mind-boggling number of recreational opportunities. No wonder the National Heritage Trust named it a Distinctive Destination.

Portland's population hovers around 66,000, but when the suburbs are included, it climbs to nearly 250,000, making it Maine's largest city by far. Take a swing through the bedroom communities of Scarborough (pop. 18,919), Cape Elizabeth (pop. 9,015), and South Portland (pop. 25,002), and you'll better understand the area's popularity: easily accessible parks, beaches, rocky ledges, and lighthouses are all minutes from downtown, along with a slew of ferry-connected islands dotting Casco Bay. Head north through suburban Falmouth (pop. 11,185) and Yarmouth (pop. 8,349) and you'll arrive in Freeport (pop. 7,879), home of mega-retailer L. L. Bean. En route, you'll still see the vestiges of the region's heritage: sailboats and lobster boats, traps and buoys piled on lawns or along driveways, and, tucked here and there, farmstands brimming with fresh produce.

Greater Portland also marks a transitional point on Maine's coastline. The long, sandy beaches of the Southern Coast begin to give way to islands and a coastline edged with a jumble of rocks and ledges spliced with rivers and coves.

It's tempting to dismiss Portland in favor of seeking the "real Maine" elsewhere along the coast, but the truth is, the real Maine is here. And although Portland alone provides plenty to keep a visitor busy, it's also an excellent base

Previous: Portland is a working seaport; Portland's waterfront. **Above:** directions in Freeport are often given using the Big Indian as a reference point.

Look for ★ to find recommended sights, activities, dining, and lodging.

Highlights

★ **The Old Port and the Waterfront:** Plan to spend at least a couple of hours browsing the shops, dining, and enjoying the energy of this restored historic district (page 83).

★ **Portland Museum of Art:** This museum houses works by masters such as Winslow Homer, John Marin, Andrew Wyeth, Edward Hopper, and Marsden Hartley as well as Monet, Picasso, and Renoir (page 86).

★ **Victoria Mansion:** This house is considered one of the most richly decorated dwellings of its period remaining in the country (page 86).

★ **Portland Observatory:** Climb the 103 steps to the orb deck of the only remaining maritime signal tower on the eastern seaboard. You'll be rewarded with views from the White Mountains to Casco Bay's islands (page 87).

★ **Portland Head Light:** This lighthouse, commissioned by President George Washington, sits on the rocky ledges of Cape Elizabeth (page 90).

★ **Lobstering Cruise:** Go out on a working lobster boat in Portland Harbor, see the sights, and perhaps return with a lobster for dinner (page 98).

★ **Casco Bay Tour:** Take a three-hour tour on the mail boat, which stops briefly at five islands en route (page 111).

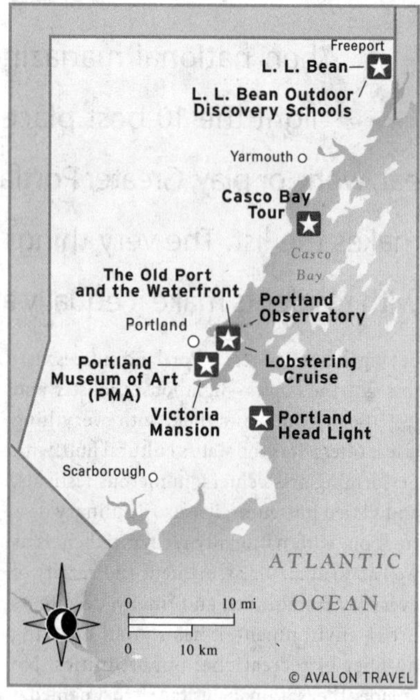

★ **L. L. Bean:** The empire's flagship store is in Freeport. No trip to this shopping mecca is complete without a visit (page 116).

★ **L. L. Bean Outdoor Discovery Schools:** Don't miss the opportunity for an inexpensive introduction to a new sport (page 119).

for day trips to places such as the Kennebunks, Freeport, Brunswick, and Bath, where more of that real Maine flavor awaits.

PLANNING YOUR TIME

July and August are the most popular times to visit, but Greater Portland is a year-round destination. Spring truly arrives by mid-May, when most summer outfitters begin operations at least on weekends. September is perhaps the loveliest month of the year weather-wise, and by mid-October those fabled New England maples are turning crimson.

To do the region justice, you'll want to spend at least three or four days, more if your plans call for using Greater Portland as a base for day trips to more distant points. You can easily kill two days in downtown Portland alone, what with all the shops, museums, historical sites, waterfront, and neighborhoods to explore. If you're staying in town and are an avid walker, you won't need a car to get to the must-see sights on the peninsula.

You *will* need a car to reach beyond the city (although the Amtrak Downeaster train connects to Wells, Old Orchard, Freeport, and Brunswick). Allow a full day for a leisurely tour through South Portland and Cape Elizabeth and on to Prouts Neck in Scarborough.

Rabid shoppers should either stay in Freeport or allow at least a day for L. L. Bean and the 100 or so outlets in its shadow. If you're traveling with a supershopper, don't despair. Freeport has parks and preserves that are light-years removed from the frenzy of its downtown, and the fishing village of South Freeport offers seaworthy pleasures.

HISTORY

Portland's downtown, a crooked-finger peninsula projecting into Casco Bay and today defined vaguely by I-295 at its "knuckle," was named Machigonne (Great Neck) by the Wabanaki, the Native Americans who held sway when English settlers first arrived in 1632. Characteristically, the Brits renamed the region Falmouth (it included present-day Falmouth, Portland, South Portland, Westbrook, and Cape Elizabeth) and the peninsula Falmouth Neck, but it was 130 years before they secured real control of the area. Anglo-French squabbles spurred by the governments' conflicts in Europe drew in the Wabanaki from Massachusetts to Nova Scotia. Falmouth was only one of the battlegrounds, and it was a fairly minor one. Relative calm resumed in the 1760s only to be broken by the stirrings of rebellion centered on Boston. When Falmouth's citizens expressed support for the incipient revolution, the punishment was a 1775 naval onslaught that wiped out 75 percent of its houses, which created a decade-long setback. In 1786, Falmouth Neck became Portland, a thriving trading community where shipping flourished until the 1807 imposition of the Embargo Act. Severing trade and effectively shutting down Portland Harbor for a year and a half, the legislation did more harm to the fledgling colonies of the United States than the French and British it was designed to punish.

In 1820, when Maine became a state, Portland was named its capital. The city became a crucial transportation hub with the arrival of the railroad. The year after the Civil War ended, the city suffered a devastating blow: Exuberant Fourth of July festivities in 1866 sparked a conflagration that virtually leveled the city. The Great Fire spared only the Portland Observatory and a chunk of the West End. Evidence of the city's Victorian rebirth remains today in many downtown neighborhoods.

After World War II, Portland slipped into decline for several years. The city's waterfront revival began in the 1970s and continues today, despite commercial competition from South Portland's Maine Mall. Congress Street has blossomed as an arts and retail district, public green space is increasing, and an influx of immigrants is changing the city's cultural makeup. With the new century, Portland is on a roll.

Greater Portland

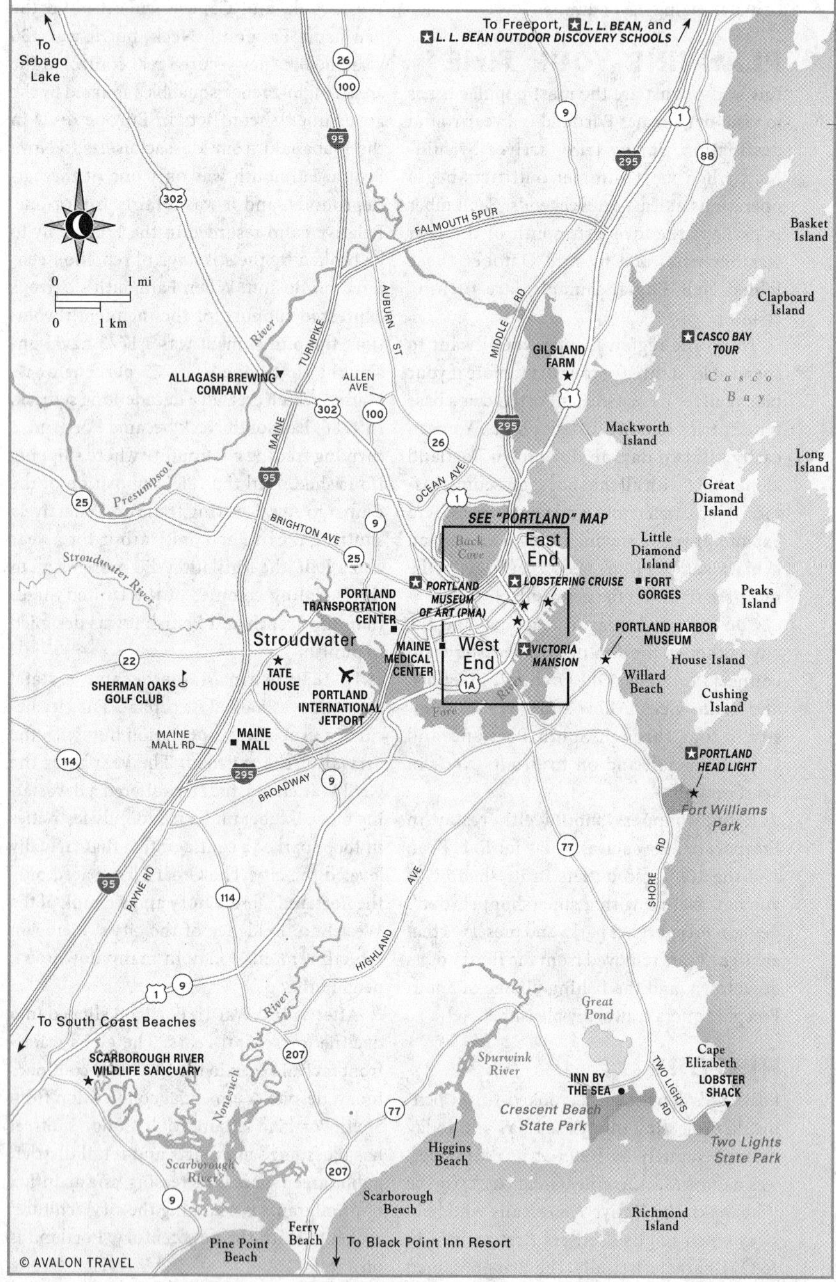

Portland

Often compared to San Francisco (an oft-cited but never-verified statistic boasts that it vies with San Francisco for the title of most restaurants per capita), Portland is small, friendly, and easily explored on foot, although at times it may seem that no matter which direction you head, it's uphill. The heart of Portland is the peninsula jutting into Casco Bay. Bordering that are the Eastern and Western Promenades, Back Cove, and the working waterfront. Salty sea breezes cool summer days and make winter ones seem even chillier. Unlike that other city by the bay out West, snow frequently blankets Portland December-March.

Portland is Maine's most ethnically diverse city, with active refugee resettlement programs and dozens of languages spoken in the schools. Although salty sailors can still be found along the waterfront, Portland is increasingly a professional community with young, upwardly mobile residents, transplants, and early retirees spiffing up Victorian houses and infusing new energy and money into the city's neighborhoods.

The region's cultural hub, Portland has world-class museums and performing arts centers, active historical and preservation groups, an art school and a university, a symphony orchestra, numerous galleries and coffeehouses, and enough activities to keep culture vultures busy well into the night, especially in the thriving, handsomely restored Old Port and the up-and-coming Arts District.

Portland is also a playground for lovers of the sports and outdoors, with trails for running, biking, skating, and cross-country skiing, water sports aplenty, and a beloved minor-league baseball team, the Sea Dogs. When city folks want to escape, they often hop a ferry for one of the islands of Casco Bay or head to one of the parks, preserves, or beaches in the suburbs.

Still, Portland remains a major seaport. Lobster boats, commercial fishing vessels, long-distance passenger boats, cruise ships, and local ferries dominate the working waterfront, and the briny scent of the sea—or bait—seasons the air.

PORTLAND NEIGHBORHOODS

The best way to appreciate the character of Portland's neighborhoods is on foot. So much of Portland can (and should) be covered on foot that it would take a whole book to list all the possibilities, but several dedicated volunteer groups have produced guides to facilitate the process.

Greater Portland Landmarks (207/774-5561, www.portlandlandmarks.org) is the doyenne, founded in 1964 to preserve Portland's historic architecture and promote responsible construction. The organization has published more than a dozen books and booklets, including *Discover Historic Portland on Foot,* a packet of four well-researched walking-tour guides to architecturally historic sections of Portland's peninsula: Old Port, Western Promenade, State Street, and Congress Street. It's available online or for $6 at local bookstores, some gift shops, and the **Visitor Information Center** (14 Ocean Gateway Pier, 207/772-5800). Ask about guided walking tours highlighting neighborhoods or sights. Self-guided tours can be downloaded from the Landmarks website.

★ The Old Port and the Waterfront

Tony shops, cobblestone sidewalks, replica streetlights, and a casual upmarket crowd (most of the time) set the scene for a district once filled with derelict buildings. Scores of boutiques, enticing restaurants, and entertaining buskers make this a fun area to visit year-round. Nightlife centers on the Old Port,

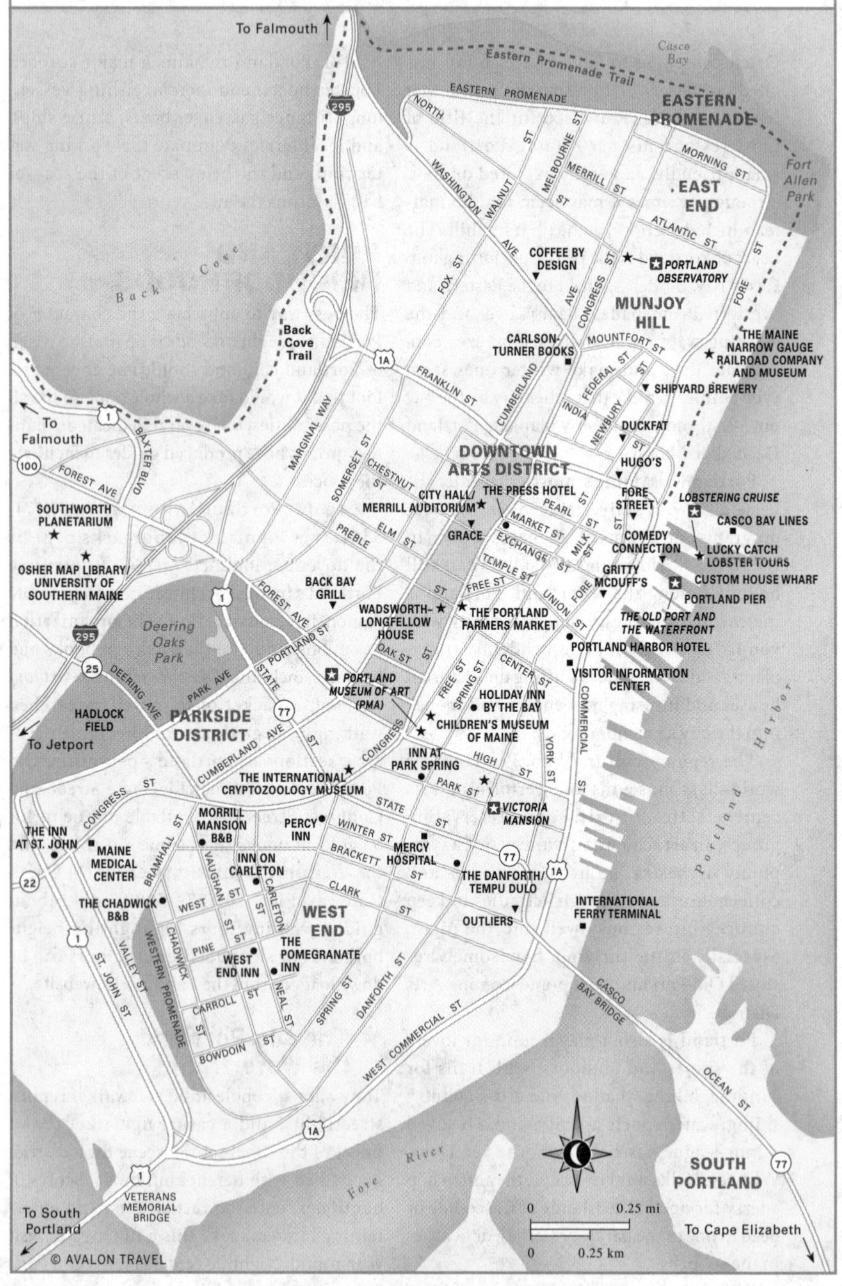
Portland
To Falmouth
Casco Bay
Eastern Promenade Trail
EASTERN PROMENADE
EASTERN PROMENADE
NORTH ST
MELBOURNE ST
MORNING ST
MERRILL ST
EAST END
Fort Allen Park
WASHINGTON AVE
WALNUT ST
ATLANTIC ST
Back Cove
COFFEE BY DESIGN
PORTLAND OBSERVATORY
FOX ST
CONGRESS ST
MUNJOY HILL
FORE ST
Back Cove Trail
CARLSON-TURNER BOOKS
MOUNTFORT ST
THE MAINE NARROW GAUGE RAILROAD COMPANY AND MUSEUM
FRANKLIN ST
CUMBERLAND AVE
FEDERAL ST
SHIPYARD BREWERY
INDIA ST
NEWBURY ST
DUCKFAT
To Falmouth
BAXTER BLVD
MARGINAL WAY
SOMERSET ST
DOWNTOWN ARTS DISTRICT
HUGO'S
FOREST AVE
CHESTNUT ST
CITY HALL/ MERRILL AUDITORIUM
THE PRESS HOTEL
FORE STREET
LOBSTERING CRUISE
SOUTHWORTH PLANETARIUM
PEARL ST
CASCO BAY LINES
PREBLE ST
ELM ST
GRACE
MARKET ST
EXCHANGE ST
COMEDY CONNECTION
LUCKY CATCH LOBSTER TOURS
OSHER MAP LIBRARY/ UNIVERSITY OF SOUTHERN MAINE
MILK ST
TEMPLE ST
GRITTY MCDUFF'S
CUSTOM HOUSE WHARF
BACK BAY GRILL
FREE ST
UNION ST
PORTLAND PIER
Deering Oaks Park
FOREST AVE
WADSWORTH-LONGFELLOW HOUSE
THE PORTLAND FARMERS MARKET
THE OLD PORT AND THE WATERFRONT
PORTLAND ST
OAK ST
PORTLAND HARBOR HOTEL
DEERING AVE
PARK AVE
STATE ST
CENTER ST
VISITOR INFORMATION CENTER
PORTLAND MUSEUM OF ART (PMA)
FREE ST
SPRING ST
HOLIDAY INN BY THE BAY
Portland Harbor
HADLOCK FIELD
PARKSIDE DISTRICT
CHILDREN'S MUSEUM OF MAINE
To Jetport
CUMBERLAND AVE
CONGRESS ST
INN AT PARK SPRING
YORK ST
COMMERCIAL ST
HIGH ST
THE INTERNATIONAL CRYPTOZOOLOGY MUSEUM
PARK ST
CONGRESS ST
STATE ST
VICTORIA MANSION
MORRILL MANSION B&B
PERCY INN
THE INN AT ST. JOHN
MAINE MEDICAL CENTER
BRAMHALL ST
WINTER ST
BRACKETT ST
MERCY HOSPITAL
INN ON CARLETON
VAUGHAN ST
CARLETON ST
THE DANFORTH/ TEMPU DULO
CLARK ST
THE CHADWICK B&B
WEST ST
WEST END
OUTLIERS
INTERNATIONAL FERRY TERMINAL
PINE ST
WEST END INN
THE POMEGRANATE INN
ST. JOHN ST
VALLEY ST
WESTERN PROMENADE
CHADWICK ST
CARROLL ST
NEAL ST
SPRING ST
DANFORTH ST
CASCO BAY BRIDGE
BOWDOIN ST
WEST COMMERCIAL ST
OCEAN ST
Fore River
SOUTH PORTLAND
VETERANS MEMORIAL BRIDGE
To South Portland
0 0.25 mi
0 0.25 km
To Cape Elizabeth
© AVALON TRAVEL

Shops and restaurants line the streets of the rejuvenated Old Port.

and a few dozen bars keep everyone hopping until after midnight. Police keep a close eye on the district, but it can get a bit dicey after 11pm on weekends.

Congress Street and the Downtown Arts District

Bit by bit, once-declining Congress Street is being revitalized, showcasing the best of the city's culture. Galleries, artists' studios, coffeehouses, cafés, and bistros as well as libraries, museums, and performing arts centers are all part of the ongoing renaissance.

West End

Probably the most diverse of the city's downtown neighborhoods, and one that largely escaped the Great Fire of 1866, the West End includes the historically and architecturally splendid Western Promenade, Maine Medical Center (the state's largest hospital), the city's best bed-and-breakfasts, a gay-friendly community with a laissez-faire attitude, and a host of cafés and restaurants as well as a few niches harboring the homeless and forlorn. A self-guided architectural tour of this National Historic Register-listed Victorian Western Promenade neighborhood, with Italianate, Queen Anne, Gothic, and Colonial Revival homes, can be downloaded from **Greater Portland Landmarks** (207/774-5561, www.portlandlandmarks.org).

Munjoy Hill and the East End

A once slightly down-at-the-heels neighborhood enclave with a pull-'em-up-by-the-bootstraps attitude, Portland's East End is rapidly gentrifying. Munjoy Hill is probably best known for the distinctive wooden tower crowning its summit. Named for George Munjoy, a wealthy 17th-century resident, this district has a host of architectural and historic landmarks, including the Eastern Cemetery, which is on the National Register of Historic Places, and the Eastern Promenade and Fort Allen Park, with spectacular harbor views.

Bayside and Parkside

A Babel of languages reverberates in these districts just below and west of Portland City Hall. Bayside experienced the arrival of refugees—Cambodian, Laotian, Vietnamese, Central European, and Afghan families—from war-torn lands during the 1980s and 1990s. Nowadays you'll hear references to Somali Town, an area named for all the resettled refugees from that shattered country. Others have come from Sudan and Ethiopia. Portland's active Refugee Resettlement Program has assisted all of them, and many newcomers have become entrepreneurs, opening restaurants and small markets catering to their compatriots, but increasingly gaining customers among other residents, too.

Stroudwater

Off the downtown peninsula at the western edge of Portland, close to the Portland Jetport, is the historic area known as Stroudwater, once an essential link in Maine water transport. The 20-mile-long **Cumberland and Oxford Canal,** hand-dug in 1828, ran through here as part of the timber-shipping route linking Portland Harbor, the Fore and Presumpscot Rivers, and Sebago Lake. Twenty-eight wooden locks allowed vessels to rise the 265 feet between sea level and the lake. By 1870 trains took over the route, condemning the canal to oblivion. The site is now the 85-acre Fore River Sanctuary, a lovely preserve with trails and a waterfall. The centerpiece of the Stroudwater area today is the historic 18th-century Tate House.

SIGHTS

★ Portland Museum of Art

Three centuries of art and architecture can be discovered at Maine's oldest (since 1882) and finest art museum, the **Portland Museum of Art** (7 Congress Sq., 207/775-6148, recorded info 207/773-2787 or 800/639-4067, www.portlandmuseum.org, 10am-5pm Sat.-Sun. and Mon.-Thurs., 10am-9pm Fri. and third Thursday, closed Mon. mid-Oct.-late May, $12 adults, $10 seniors and students, $6 ages 6-17, free 5pm-9pm every Fri.). The museum's top-flight collection of American and impressionist masters and fine and decorative arts is displayed in three architecturally stunning connected buildings: the award-winning Charles Shipman Payson building, designed by I. M. Pei and opened in 1983; the newly restored Federal-era McLellan House; and the Beaux Arts L. D. M. Sweat Memorial Galleries, designed by noted Maine architect John Calvin Stevens. The museum also has a well-stocked gift shop and an excellent café that's open for lunch daily (11am-4pm) and dinner Friday until 8pm. Check the website for current family activities, lectures, and other events, including **Movies at the Museum** ($8), showcasing foreign, classical, and art films. Plan well in advance if you want to pair a museum visit with a tour of the **Winslow Homer Studio** on nearby Prouts Neck—the 2.5-hour tours ($55) depart from the museum and are limited to 10 participants. Call for the current schedule. The studio is a don't-miss for fans of the American master.

Victoria Mansion

★ Victoria Mansion

The jaws of first-time visitors literally drop when they enter the Italianate **Victoria Mansion** (109 Danforth St., 207/772-4841, www.victoriamansion.org, 10am-4pm Mon.-Sat., 1pm-5pm Sun. May 1-Oct. 31, special hours in Dec., $15 adults, $13.50 seniors, $5 ages 6-17, $35 family, no senior discount in holiday season), also called the Morse-Libby Mansion. It's widely considered the most magnificently ornamented dwelling of its period remaining in the country. The National Historic Landmark is rife with Victoriana: carved marble fireplaces, elaborate porcelain and paneling, a freestanding mahogany staircase, gilded glass chandeliers, a restored 6-by-25-foot stained-glass ceiling window, and unbelievable trompe l'oeil touches. It's even more spectacular at Christmas, with yards of roping, festooned trees, and carolers; this is the best time to bring kids, as the house itself may not particularly intrigue them. The mansion was built in the late 1850s by Ruggles Sylvester Morse, a Maine-born entrepreneur

the Portland Observatory

whose New Orleans-based fortune enabled him to hire 93 craftspeople to complete the house. The interior, designed by Gustave Herter, retains virtually all of the original furnishings. Guided 45-minute tours begin every half-hour on the quarter-hour in season; tours are self-guided during the holidays.

★ Portland Observatory

Providing a head-swiveling view of Portland (and the White Mountains on a clear day), the octagonal red-painted **Portland Observatory** (138 Congress St., 207/774-5561, www.portlandlandmarks.org, 10am-5pm daily late May-mid-Oct., last tour at 4:30pm, $10 adults, $8 seniors, $5 ages 6-16) is the only remaining marine signal tower on the eastern seaboard. Built in 1807 at a cost of $5,000 by Captain Lemuel Moody to keep track of the port's shipping activity, the tower has 122 tons of rock ballast in its base. Admission in those days (when only men were allowed to climb the 103 interior steps) was 12.5 cents. Today, admission includes the small museum at the tower's base and a guided tour to the top.

The Longfellow Connection

A few blocks down Congress Street from the Portland Museum of Art, you can step back in time to the era of Portland-born poet Henry Wadsworth Longfellow, who lived in the now carefully restored **Wadsworth-Longfellow House** (485 Congress St., 207/774-1822, www.mainehistory.org, 10am-5pm Mon.-Sat., noon-5pm Sun. May 1-Oct. 31, last tour 4pm, special holiday hours Nov.-Dec., $15 adults, $12 seniors and students, $3 ages 6-17, includes the museum). Longfellow was here as a child in the early 1800s, long before the brick mansion was dwarfed by surrounding high-rises. Wadsworth and Longfellow family furnishings fill the three-story house, owned by the Maine Historical Society. On 45-minute tours, savvy guides provide insight into Portland's 19th-century life. Don't miss the urban oasis—a wonderfully peaceful garden—behind the house (same hours, free). At the adjacent **Maine Historical Society Museum**, you can take in the Maine Historical Society's exhibits chronicling five centuries of life in Maine and find an extensive collection of Maine history books in the gift shop. Admission for the museum alone is $8 adults, $7 seniors, $2 children. The center also offers **historical walking tours** for $15 pp; call for schedule.

Maine Narrow Gauge Railroad Company and Museum

A three-mile ride along Portland's waterfront is the highlight of a visit to the **Maine Narrow Gauge Railroad Company and Museum** (58 Fore St., 207/828-0814, www.mngrr.org, 9:30am-4pm Sat.-Thurs., noon-4pm Sun. early May-late Oct., $3 adults, $2 seniors and ages 3-12, free with train ticket) owns more than three dozen train cars and has others on long-term loan, most from Maine's five historic narrow-gauge railroads, the last of which

Lighthouses Tour

Whether in a car or on a bike, it's easy to loop through South Portland and Cape Elizabeth on a lighthouse tour.

Begin just over the Casco Bay Bridge from downtown Portland on Route 77, take Broadway, and continue to Spring Point Marina, turning left at the stop sign and then right onto Madison Street to nine-acre Bug Light Park. A paved walkway leads to Portland Breakwater Lighthouse, also known as Bug Light, built in 1875. Also here is a memorial commemorating the Liberty ships built on this site during World War II. There's a plan to build an outdoor performing arts center adjacent to the park.

Retrace your route to Broadway and cross it, turning left on Fort Street until it ends at **Southern Maine Community College (SMCC),** overlooking the bay. The best time to come here is evenings and weekends, when there's ample parking. Unless it's foggy (when the signal is deafening) or thundering (when you'll expose yourself to lightning), walk out along the 9,000-foot granite breakwater to the **Spring Point Ledge Light** (207/699-2676, www.springpointlight.org), with fabulous views in every direction. Volunteers usually open it 11am-3pm Saturday and usually Sunday, mid-June-early September ($5; children must be at least 51 inches tall to enter the light). Also here are picnic benches, the remains of Fort Preble, and the **Spring Point Shoreline Walkway,** a scenic three-mile path with views to House, Peaks, and Cushings Islands. At the end of the path you'll reach crescent-shaped **Willard Beach,** a neighborhood spot with restrooms, a snack bar, and those same marvelous views.

From the SMCC campus, return on Broadway to the major intersection with Cottage Road and bear left. Cottage Road becomes Shore Road at the Cape Elizabeth town line. Loop into Fort Williams Park and make a pilgrimage to **Portland Head Light,** with **Ram Island Ledge Light** in the distance, before continuing on Shore Road to its intersection with Route 77. Bear left, follow it to Two Lights Road, and follow the signs to 40-acre **Two Lights State Park.** Almost a pocket park, it has picnicking and restroom facilities, but its biggest asset is the panoramic ocean view from atop a onetime gun battery. Summer admission is $4.50 nonresident adults, $3 Maine resident adults, $1.50 nonresident seniors, $1 ages 5-11.

Before or after visiting the park, continue on Two Lights Road to the parking lot at the end, where you'll see the signal towers for which Two Lights is named. There's no access to either, and only one still works. If you haven't brought a picnic for the state park, there are few places finer to enjoy the view and a lobster than at **The Lobster Shack.**

closed in 1943. You can board a number of the cars and see others undergoing restoration. Train rides along the 2-foot rails operate on the hour, 10am-3pm, $10 adults, $9 seniors, $6 ages 3-12. The track edges Casco Bay along the Eastern Promenade; it's a short but enjoyable excursion that's a real kid-pleaser. The museum also operates special excursions including ice cream trains, rails and ales, and Polar Express trains.

Portland Science Center

The **Portland Science Center** (68 Commercial St., Maine Wharf, 207/812-3850, www.portlandsciencecenter.com,) opened in 2015 as an edu-tainment center. It hosts major traveling exhibitions, such as *Body Worlds*, that engage, entertain, and inform viewers. Admission rates and hours vary by show.

Children's Museum of Maine

Here's the answer to parents' prayers: a whole museum in downtown Portland catering to kids. At the **Children's Museum of Maine** (142 Free St., 207/828-1234, www.kitetails.com, 10am-5pm Mon.-Sat., noon-5pm Sun., $10, free for children under 18 months, $2 admission 5pm-8pm first Fri. of each month, $4 for Camera Obscura only) lots of hands-on exhibits encourage interaction and guarantee involvement for a couple of hours.

The International Cryptozoology Museum

An eight-foot-tall likeness of a Bigfoot greets visitors at former university professor and author Loren Coleman's **International Cryptozoology Museum** (11 Avon St., 207/518-9496, www.cryptozoologymuseum.com, 11am-4pm Mon. and Wed.-Sat., call to confirm hours, $7 adults, $5 ages 12 and younger). Coleman is a renowned expert in cryptozoology, the story of hidden animals such as bigfoot, the Loch Ness monster, and the abominable snowman. He has amassed a collection of artifacts such as skulls and footprint castings that lend credence to the existence of these rumored beasts, as well as kitsch that includes movie props and souvenir memorabilia. This is always a big hit with kids.

Southworth Planetarium

Under a 30-foot dome with comfy theater seats and a state-of-the-art laser system, the **Southworth Planetarium** (Science Building, University of Southern Maine, 70 Falmouth St., 207/780-4249, www.usm.maine.edu/planet) presents astronomy shows, with ticket prices around $6. Take Exit 6B off I-295 and go west on Forest Avenue to Falmouth Street (a left turn). The Science Building is on the left past the parking lot.

Osher Map Library

Love maps? You'll love the University of South Maine's **Osher Map Library** (314 Forest Ave., 207/780-4850, www.oshermaps.org, 10am-4pm Tues.-Wed., 10am-8pm Thurs. 10am-2pm Sat., free) with more than 300,000 maps, including works on cosmography, astronomy, navigation, geography, and history, as well as globes, atlases, books, and scientific instruments dating from the late 15th century. Exhibitions feature rare and historic works drawn from the collection. Bring a sweater; the air-conditioning is set for preservation standards. There's free parking in the USM garage on Surrenden Street, off Bedford Street.

Tate House

Just down the street from the Portland International Jetport, in the Stroudwater district, is the 1755 **Tate House** (1270 Westbrook St., 207/774-6177, www.tatehouse.org, 10am-4pm Wed.-Sat., 1pm-4pm Sun., last tour 3pm, mid-June-mid-Oct., $12 adults, $10 seniors, $5 ages 6-12), a National Historic Landmark owned by the Colonial Dames of America. Built by Captain George Tate, who was

Portland Head Light was commissioned by George Washington and first lit in 1791.

prominent in shipbuilding, the house overlooks the Stroudwater River and has superb period furnishings and a lovely 18th-century herb garden with more than 70 species. Tours last 40 minutes. Cellar-to-attic architecture tours ($15) are offered and garden tours (free) are available by advance reservation.

★ Portland Head Light

Just four miles from downtown Portland in Cape Elizabeth, Fort Williams feels a world away. This oceanfront town park, a former military base, is home to **Portland Head Light** (1000 Shore Rd., Cape Elizabeth, 207/799-2661, www.portlandheadlight.com, dawn-dusk daily). Commissioned by President George Washington and first lit in 1791, it has been immortalized in poetry, photography, and philately. The surf here is awesome—perhaps too awesome, as the *Annie C. Maguire* was shipwrecked below the lighthouse on Christmas Eve 1886. There's no access to the 58-foot automated light tower, but the restored keeper's house has become **The Museum at Portland Head Light** (10am-4pm daily late May-Oct. 31, 10am-4pm Sat.-Sun. late spring and late fall, call to confirm dates, $2 adults, $1 ages 6-18). It's filled with local history and lighthouse memorabilia. From downtown Portland, take Route 77 and then Broadway, Cottage Road, and Shore Road; the route is marked.

ENTERTAINMENT AND EVENTS

The best places to find out what's playing at area theaters, cinemas, concert halls, and nightclubs are the *Portland Phoenix* (www.portlandphoenix.com) and the *Go* supplement in the Thursday edition of the *Portland Press Herald* (www.mainetoday.com). Both have online listings; hard copies are available at bookstores and supermarkets. The *Phoenix* is free.

Nightlife

LIVE MUSIC

The Portland Conservatory of Music presents free weekly **Noonday Concerts** at First Parish Church (425 Congress St., 207/773-5747, www.portlandconservatory.org) at 12:15pm most Thursdays October-early April. The music varies widely—perhaps jazz, classical, or choral.

Portland Parks and Recreation sponsors **Summer in the Parks** (207/756-8275, July-Aug., free), an evening concert series and a midday kids' performance series in downtown parks.

Young, or young at heart? Take the ferry to Peaks Island for **Reggae Sundays** (late May to early Sept.) on the deck at Jones Landing (at the ferry landing, Peaks Island, 207/766-4400).

BREWPUBS AND BARS

Portland is a beer town, with an ever-increasing number of microbreweries and brewpubs. It's also vigilant about enforcing alcohol laws, so bring valid identification. Bars close at 1am.

Not only is **Gritty McDuff's** (396 Fore St., Old Port, 207/772-2739, www.grittys.com) one of Maine's most popular breweries, but its brewpub was the state's first, and opened in 1988. The menu includes pub classics such as fish-and-chips and shepherd's pie as well as burgers, salads, and sandwiches. Gritty's books live entertainment fairly regularly. Tours are available by appointment. Gritty's also has a branch in Freeport.

A longtime favorite pub, **$3 Dewey's** (241 Commercial St., Old Port, 207/772-3310, www.threedollardeweys.com) is so authentic that visiting Brits, Kiwis, and Aussies often head here to assuage their homesickness. Inexpensive fare, 36 brews on tap, free popcorn, and frequent live music make it a very popular spot.

Far newer on the scene is **Little Tap House** (106 High St., 207/518-9283), a bright spot with 14 taps and a farm-to-table gastropub menu.

Especially popular in the late afternoon and early evening is **J's Oyster** (5 Portland Pier, 207/772-4828), a longtime fixture (some might call it a dive) on the waterfront known for its raw bar and for pouring a good drink.

Of all Portland's neighborhood hangouts, **Ruski's** (212 Danforth St., 207/774-7604) is the most authentic—a small, usually crowded onetime speakeasy that rates just as highly for breakfast as for nighttime schmoozing. Expect basic homemade fare for under $10, plus darts and a big-screen TV. Dress down or you'll feel out of place.

Other dress-down neighborhood bars are **Rosie's** (330 Fore St., 207/772-5656, www.rosies-oldport.com) and **Blackstones** (6 Pine St., 207/775-2885, www.blackstones.com), Portland's oldest neighborhood gay bar.

Beer geeks, here's your happy place. Family-friendly **Novare Res Bier Cafe** (4 Canal Plaza, 207/761-2437, www.novareresbiercafe.com) carries nearly 500 bottled beers from around the world and has more than 25 rotating taps. Pair them with selections from the meat-and-cheese bar, sandwiches, or small plates.

West of I-295, **The Great Lost Bear** (540 Forest Ave., 207/772-0300, www.greatlostbear.com) has 78 brews on tap, representing more than 45 Maine microbreweries plus others from the Northeast. The bear motif and the punny menus are a bit much, but the scratch-made pub-style fare is very good. It's a kid pleaser.

COCKTAILS

For more upscale tippling, where bartenders are elevated to mixologists noted for creative concoctions, head for **Hunt & Alpine** (75 Market Street, 207/747-4754, www.huntandalpineclub.com), **The Bearded Lady's Jewel Box** (644 Congress St., 207/747-5384), or the **Top of the East** (157 High St., 207/775-5411), a glass-walled lounge with divine sunset views topping the Westin Hotel.

BARS WITH ENTERTAINMENT

Scope out the scene when you arrive; the *Portland Phoenix* has the best listings. Most clubs have cover charges. The coolest venue with the hottest acts is **Port City Music Hall** (504 Congress St., 207/899-4990, www.portcitymusichall.com), a three-floor entertainment emporium. **Asylum** (121 Center St., 207/772-8274, www.portlandasylum.com) caters to a young crowd with dance jams, CD release parties, DJ nights, and live bands. **Geno's** (625 Congress St., 207/221-2382) has been at it for years—an old reliable for rock music with an emphasis on local bands. **Blue** (650A Congress St., 207/774-4111, www.portcityblue.com) presents local artists and musicians in an intimate, cozy space and serves beer, wine, tea, and light fare; traditional Irish music is always featured on Wednesday evening, and jazz on Saturday.

Performing Arts

MERRILL AUDITORIUM

The magnificently restored **Merrill Auditorium** (20 Myrtle St., box office 207/874-8200, www.porttix.com) is a 1,900-seat theater inside Portland City Hall on Congress Street with two balconies and one of the country's only municipally owned pipe organs, the magnificent, recently restored **Kotzschmar Organ** (207/553-4363, www.foko.org); guided organ tours are offered during the concert season.

Special events and concerts are common at Merrill, and the auditorium is also home to a number of the city's arts organizations. The **Portland Symphony Orchestra** (207/842-0800, www.portlandsymphony.org) and presenting organization **Portland Ovations** (207/773-3150, www.portlandovations.org) have extensive, well-patronized fall and winter schedules; the PSO presents three summer Independence Pops concerts as well. The **Portland Opera Repertory Theatre** (207/879-7678, www.portopera.org) performs a major opera each summer. In addition, there are films, lectures, and other related events throughout July.

Tickets for these organizations are available through **PortTix** (207/942-0800, www.porttix.com).

ONE LONGFELLOW SQUARE

Diverse programming is the hallmark of **One Longfellow Square** (207/761-1757, www.

onelongfellowsquare.com), an intimate venue for performances and lectures at the corner of Congress and State Streets.

STATE THEATRE

The **State Theatre** (609 Congress St., 207/956-6000, www.statetheatreportland.com), built in 1929 with art deco, Spanish, and Italian decor elements, hosts national touring artists as well as up-and-comers.

PORTLAND STAGE COMPANY

Innovative staging and controversial contemporary dramas are typical of the **Portland Stage Company** (Portland Performing Arts Center, 25A Forest Ave., 207/774-0465, www.portlandstage.org), established in 1974 and going strong ever since. Equity pros present half a dozen plays each winter season in a 290-seat performance space.

See what's playing at the State Theatre.

Events

Summer brings plentiful events, including the **Old Port Festival,** one of the city's largest festivals, usually the first weekend of June. It has entertainment, food and crafts booths, and impromptu fun in Portland's Old Port. The **Greek Heritage Festival,** usually the last weekend of June, features Greek food, dancing, and crafts at Holy Trinity Church (133 Pleasant St.).

Some of the world's top runners join upward of 500 racers in the **Beach to Beacon Race,** held in late July-early August. The 10K course goes from Crescent Beach State Park to Portland Head Light in Cape Elizabeth.

In mid-August the **Italian Street Festival** showcases music, Italian food, and games at St. Peter's Catholic Church (72 Federal St.). Artists from all over the country set up in 350 booths along Congress Street for the annual **Sidewalk Arts Festival** in late August.

The big October wingding is the **Harvest on the Harbor,** a celebration of all things food- and wine-related with tastings, dinners, exhibits, and special events.

The **Maine Brewers' Festival,** the first weekend in November at the Portland Exposition Building, is a big event that expands every year thanks to the explosion of Maine microbreweries; there are samples galore. From Thanksgiving weekend to Christmas Eve, **Victorian Holiday** in downtown Portland harks back with caroling, special sales, concerts, tree lighting, horse-drawn wagons, and Victoria Mansion tours and festivities.

SHOPPING

The Portland peninsula is thick with non-cookie-cutter shops and galleries. The Old Port/Waterfront and Arts District have the highest concentration, but more and more are opening on the East End.

Bookstores

Longfellow Books (1 Monument Way, 207/772-4045) sells new and used books and hosts readings. **Carlson-Turner Books** (241 Congress St., 207/773-4200 or 800/540-7323), on Munjoy Hill, has an extensive used-book inventory.

Art Galleries

Portland has dozens upon dozens of studios and galleries. A great way to discover them is on the **First Friday Artwalk** (www.firstfridayartwalk.com) on the first Friday evening of each month, when in-town galleries host exhibition openings, open houses, meet-the-artist gatherings, and other artsy activities.

Galleries specializing in contemporary art include **June Fitzpatrick Gallery** (112 High St., 522 Congress St., 207/699-5083, www.junefitzpatrickgallery.com), **Aucocisco** (89 Exchange St., 207/553-2222, www.aucocisco.com), specializing in contemporary fine art, and **Greenhut Galleries** (146 Middle St., 207/772-2693, www.greenhutgalleries.com), specializing in contemporary Maine art and sculpture. More than 15 Maine potters—with a wide variety of styles and items—market their wares at the **Maine Potters Market** (376 Fore St., 207/774-1633, www.mainepottersmarket.com).

Specialty Shops

Check out the latest home accessories from Maine-based designer **Angela Adams** (131 Middle St., 207/774-3523).

Woof: The company store for **Planet Dog** (211 Marginal Way, 207/347-8606, www.planetdog.com) is a howling good time for dogs and their owners. You'll find all sorts of wonderful products, and Planet Dog, whose motto is to "think globally and act doggedly," has established a foundation to promote and serve causes such as dog therapy, service, search and rescue, bomb sniffing, and police dogs.

Ferdinand (243 Congress St., 207/761-2151) is chock-full of eclectic finds, including screen prints, jewelry, vintage clothing, and cards created on the owner's letterpress.

The stained-glass artwork is irresistible at **Laura Fuller Design Studio** (129 Congress St., 207/650-6989).

SOST Linen (5 South St., 774/234-7678) is a must for locally designed and made linen clothing and home wares.

RECREATION

Parks, Preserves, and Beaches

Greater Portland is blessed with green space, thanks largely to the efforts of 19th-century mayor James Phinney Baxter, who had the foresight to hire the famed Olmsted Brothers to develop an ambitious plan to ring the city with public parks and promenades. Not all the elements fell into place, but the result is what makes Portland such a livable city.

TRAIL NETWORK

Portland Trails (305 Commercial St., 207/775-2411, www.trails.org), a dynamic membership conservation organization incorporated in 1991, is dedicated to creating and maintaining a 50-mile network of hiking and biking trails in Greater Portland. It already has 31 mapped trails to its credit, including the 2.1-mile Eastern Promenade Trail, a landscaped bay-front dual pathway circling the base of Munjoy Hill and linking East End Beach to the Old Port, and a continuing trail connecting the Eastern Prom with the 3.5-mile Back Cove Trail, on the other side of I-295. Trail maps are available on the website. Snowshoe rentals ($10/day) are available weekdays from the office. The group also holds organized walks ($5 nonmembers)—a great way to meet some locals. Better still, join Portland Trails ($35/year) and support its ambitious efforts.

DOWNTOWN PENINSULA

Probably the most visible of the city's parks, 51-acre **Deering Oaks** (Park Ave. between Forest Ave. and Deering Ave.) is best known for the quaint little duck condo in the middle of the pond. Other facilities and highlights here are tennis courts, a playground, horseshoes, rental paddleboats, a snack bar, the award-winning Rose Circle, a worth-attending farmers market (7am-noon Sat.), and, in winter, ice skating. After dark, steer clear of the park.

At one end of the Eastern Promenade, where it meets Fore Street, **Fort Allen Park**

Winslow Homer

the Winslow Homer Studio in Prouts Neck

Discovering Maine in his early 40s, Winslow Homer (1836-1910) was smitten—enough to spend the last 27 years of his life on Prouts Neck, a granite-tipped thumb of land edged with beaches reaching into the Atlantic in Scarborough, just south of Portland. Homer painted some of his greatest works—masterpieces such as *Weatherbeaten, The Fog Warning,* and *The Gulf Stream*—at this oceanfront studio, taking inspiration from the crashing surf, craggy shores, stormy seas, and dense fog. Standing in the studio puts you right at the scene, and the docent-led tours will explain the artist's importance in American art.

Originally the carriage house for Homer's *The Ark,* the adjacent house owned by Homer's brother Charles, the studio was moved 100 feet and converted to living quarters in 1883 by Portland architect John Calvin Stevens, one of the founders of the Shingle style. The piazza, pergola, and later the painting room were added.

The simplicity of the studio, with its bead-board wall and ceiling, tongue-and-groove floor, and brick fireplace, is pure Maine cottage. Some original furnishings and artifacts add context to understanding Homer. These include the *Snakes! Snakes! Mice!* sign he painted to scare off ladies who might be inclined to visit; the window in which he etched his name; the writings on the wall, such as *Oh what a friend chance can be when it chooses;* and a book of family photographs. Copies of his artwork, displays, and a slide show of images are exhibited in the painting room, or "the factory," as he called it. Especially intriguing are the Civil War sketches he made for *Harper's Weekly* while embedded with the Army of the Potomac.

The views from the second-floor piazza are the same as when Homer lived here. Gazing at the open Atlantic, listening to waves crash, gulls cry, and the wind rustling the trees, and maybe wrapped in the damp hush of fog, is perhaps the best place to begin to truly understand Homer's inspiration. After absorbing the view and walking to the oceanfront, you'll see the Homer works at the museum with a far deeper understanding of what made this genius tick.

Homer's ties with the Portland Museum of Art date back to his 1893 exhibition, which included *Signal of Distress.* On the centennial of Homer's death, the museum opened its Charles Shipman Payson wing, honoring the man who funded it and donated 17 paintings by the artist. The museum acquired Homer's studio, a National Historic Landmark, in 2006, opening it to the public after a six-year project to restore it to its 1910 appearance. The 2.5-hour tours are limited to 10 participants and cost $55 for the public, $30 for museum members. They depart the museum on a schedule that varies by season and permissions. It's wise to make reservations months in advance.

overlooks offshore Fort Gorges (coin-operated telescopes bring it closer). A central gazebo is flanked by an assortment of military souvenirs dating as far back as the War of 1812. All along the Eastern Prom are walking paths, benches, play areas, and even an ill-maintained fitness trail—all with that terrific view. Down by the water is **East End Beach,** with parking, token sand, and the area's best launching ramp for sea kayaks or powerboats. Friends of the Eastern Promenade (www.easternpromenade.org), founded in 2006, helps restore and preserve the landscape and sponsors a free summer concert series on Thursday evenings.

WEST OF THE DOWNTOWN PENINSULA

Looping around tidal **Back Cove** is a 3.5-mile trail for walking, jogging, or just watching the sailboards and the skyline. Along the way, you can cross Baxter Boulevard and spend time picnicking, playing tennis, or flying a kite in 48-acre **Payson Park,** where parking is available.

Talk about an urban oasis: The 85-acre **Fore River Sanctuary** (sunrise-sunset daily), managed by Portland Trails, has two miles of blue-blazed trails that wind through a salt marsh, link with the historic Cumberland and Oxford Canal towpath, and pass near **Jewell Falls,** Portland's only waterfall. From downtown Portland, take Congress Street West (Rte. 22) past I-295 to the Maine Orthopedic Center parking lot at the corner of Frost; park in the far corner.

Listed on the National Register of Historic Places, 239-acre **Evergreen Cemetery** (207/797-4597, 672 Stevens Ave., www.friendsofevergreen.org) is Portland's largest urban space. Begun in the mid-1850s and modeled after Mount Auburn Cemetery in Cambridge, Massachusetts, it's an excellent example of a rural cemetery, a garden-like place favored by 19th-century romantics. You'll find tree-lined paths, hiking trails, ponds, vistas, and plenty of history. Docents offer **historic walking tours** (5pm Thurs., 2pm Sun., $7), or download a map and explore on your old. In May, bird-watchers are here to see warblers, thrushes, and other migratory birds that gather in the ponds and meadows. During peak periods it's possible to see as many as 20 warbler species in a morning, including the Cape May, bay breasted, mourning, and Tennessee. Naturalists from Maine Audubon often are on-site helping to identify birds.

CAPE ELIZABETH

Fort Williams (www.fortwilliamspark.com, free), a 90-acre, town-owned oceanfront park on the site of a former military base, offers much more to explore beyond Portland Head Light. Walk the trails, explore ruins of the Goddard Mansion, prowl through fortifications, play tennis, or dip your toes into the surf at the rocky beach. Warning: There's a strong undertow here. The grassy headlands are great places to watch the boat traffic going in and out of Portland Harbor. Bring a picnic lunch or purchase food from one of the food trucks—and don't forget a kite.

Crescent Beach State Park (Rte. 77, www.parksandlands.com, $6.50 nonresident adults, $4.50 Maine resident adults, $1.50 senior nonresidents, $1 ages 5-11), a 243-acre park with a mile-long beach, changing rooms, a lifeguard, restrooms, picnic tables, and a snack bar, is a favorite with families.

Directly offshore is **Richmond Island** (www.ramislandfarm.com), a 226-acre private preserve that's accessible by boat and open to visitors who respect the island's ecology; do not walk on the breakwater or use the island's dock; no dogs permitted. A two-mile path skirts the perimeter, taking in four beaches, dunes, a lake, woodlands, and grasslands. Wildlife includes sheep, deer, bald eagle, blue herons, and more. Primitive camping is available on four sites with a permit; call 207/799-0011. An island map is available on the website.

SCARBOROUGH

Scarborough Beach Park (Black Point Rd./Rte. 207, 207/883-2416, www.scarboroughbeachstatepark.com, $6.50 nonresident adults, $4.50 Maine resident adults, $2 children), a long stretch of sand, is the best beach for big waves. Between the parking area and the lovely beach you'll pass Massacre Pond, named for a 1703 skirmish between resident Native Americans and wannabe residents (score: Indians 19, wannabes 0). The park is open all year for swimming, surfing (permit required), beachcombing, and ice skating, but on weekends in summer the parking lot fills early. Lifeguards are on duty on sunny days from mid-June to early September. Purchase snacks or rent chairs, umbrellas, and boogie boards ($5 each) at The Shack.

At 3,100 acres, **Scarborough Marsh**

(Pine Point Rd./Rte. 9, 207/883-5100, www.maineaudubon.org, 9:30am-5:30pm daily mid-June-early Sept., 9:30am-5:30pm Sat.-Sun. late May and Sept.), Maine's largest salt marsh, is prime territory for bird-watching and canoeing. Rent a canoe (from $16 for 1 hour) at the small nature center operated by Maine Audubon and explore on your own. Or join one of the 90-minute guided tours (call for the schedule, $13). Other special programs, some geared primarily for children, include wildflower walks, art classes, and dawn bird-watching trips; all require reservations and reasonable fees. Also here is a walking-tour trail of less than one mile. Pick up a map at the center.

Overlooking the marsh is 52-acre **Scarborough River Wildlife Sanctuary** (Pine Point Rd./Rte. 9), with 1.5 miles of walking trails that loop to the Scarborough River and past two ponds.

FALMOUTH

A 65-acre wildlife sanctuary and environmental center on the banks of the Presumpscot River, **Gilsland Farm** (20 Gilsland Farm Rd., 207/781-2330, www.maineaudubon.org, dawn-dusk daily) is state headquarters for Maine Audubon. More than two miles of easy, well-marked trails wind through the grounds, taking in salt marshes, rolling meadows, woodlands, and views of the estuary. Observation blinds allow inconspicuous spying during bird-migration season. In the **education center** (9am-5pm Mon.-Sat., noon-4pm Sun.) are hands-on exhibits, a nature store, and classrooms and offices. Fees are charged for special events, but otherwise it's all free. The center is 0.25 mile off Route 1.

Once the summer compound of the prominent Baxter family, Falmouth's 100-acre **Mackworth Island** (sunrise-sunset daily year-round), reached via a causeway, is now the site of the Governor Baxter School for the Deaf. Limited parking is just beyond the security booth on the island. On the 1.5-mile vehicle-free perimeter path, which has great Portland Harbor views, you'll meet bikers, hikers, and dog walkers. Just off the trail on the north side of the island is the late governor Percival Baxter's stone-circled pet cemetery, maintained by the state at the behest of Baxter, who donated this island as well as Baxter State Park to the people of Maine. From downtown Portland, take Route 1 across the Presumpscot River to Falmouth Foreside. Andrews Avenue (third street on the right) leads to the island.

Walking Tours

PORTLAND FREEDOM TRAIL

Pick up a copy of this free map and brochure (also available online) detailing a **self-guided walking tour** of 16 marked sights related to Portland's role in Maine's Underground Railroad (www.portlandfreedomtrail.org). Among the highlights are the Abyssinian Meeting House, the third-oldest African American meetinghouse still standing in the United States (a National Historic Landmark placed on the National Trust's 11 Most Endangered Properties list in 2013); the First Parish Unitarian Universalist Church, where abolitionist William Lloyd Garrison spoke in 1832; and Mariners' Church, location of an antislavery bookstore and print shop that printed the first Afrocentric history of the world.

PORTLAND WOMEN'S HISTORY TRAIL

Another **self-guided walking tour,** this one details four loops—Congress Street, Munjoy Hill, State Street, and the West End—with about 20 stops on each. Among the sites: a long-gone chewing-gum factory where teenage girls worked 10-hour shifts. The trail guide is available online for $8.50 in selected bookstores and at the **Maine History Museum gift shop** (489 Congress St., 207/879-0427).

GREATER PORTLAND LANDMARKS

Greater Portland Landmarks (207/774-5561, www.portlandlandmarks.org) offers seasonal walking tours of various Portland neighborhoods or themes. These change frequently, so call. It also offers downloads for self-guided tours of the Churches on the Peninsula, Congress Street, The Old Port, and Western Promenade.

Food and Beverage Tours

Maine's culinary renown has sprouted a number of tour options.

Just as the name promises, **Maine Foodie Tours** (10 Moulton St., 207/233-7485, www.mainefoodietours.com) delivers a taste of Maine. The **Culinary Walking Tour** ($45) visits vendors selling everything from cheese to lobster to chocolate in the Old Port; **Culinary Delights Trolley Tour** ($49) includes both onboard and in-shop tastings; **Sips, Smugglers, and Speakeasies** ($49) crawls through the city's pubs. Other options include **Eat Dessert First!, Bike and Brews,** and a progressive island dinner cruise.

Look for the keg topping the flagpole at **Shipyard Brewery** (86 Newbury St., 207/761-0807, www.shipyard.com). Full brewery tours are offered on Tuesday evenings; make reservations well in advance. Free, 30-minute tours at **Allagash Brewing Company** (50 Industrial Way, 207/878-5385, www.allagash.com) are by online reservation. **Geary's Brewing Company** (38 Evergreen Dr., 207/878-2337, www.gearybrewing.com) offers tours by appointment. You can also get a personal tour at **Rising Tide Brewing Co.** (103 Fox St., 207/370-2337).

For a more thorough immersion into the local brew scene, book a tour on **The Maine Brew Bus** (207/200-9111, www.mainebrewbus.com, $40-75) or **Maine Beer Tours** (207/553-0898, www.mainebeertours.com, $54). Minimum age is 21; ID required.

What? You'd rather have wine? Step out on a guided, two-hour, educational wine walk (from $40) or cruise (from $65) with sommelier Erica Archer of **Wine Wise** (207/619-4630, www.winewiseevents.com).

Stop by **Maine Mead Works** (51 Washington Ave., 207/773-6323, www.mainemeadworks.com) for a tour and tasting of the company's fermented honey drinks; call for a current schedule.

Land-and-Sea Tours

Various commercial operators offer area land-and-sea tours, but frankly, none is first-rate. Guides on each often present incorrect information. Still, such tours are a good way to get the city's general layout.

The best of the lot is the 1.75-hour narrated Portland City and Lighthouse Tour in a trolley-bus by **Portland Discovery Land and Sea Tours** (Long Wharf, 207/774-0808, www.portlanddiscovery.com, $22 adults, $16 children). You can combine this tour with a 90-minute Lighthouse Lovers cruise on Casco Bay. The combined price is $40 adults, $48 children.

Bicycling

The **Bicycle Coalition of Maine** (207/623-4511, www.bikemaine.org) has an excellent website with info on trails, events, organized rides, bike shops, and more. Another good resource is **Casco Bay Bicycle Club** (www.cascobaybicycleclub.org), a recreational cycling club with rides several times weekly. Check the website for details.

For rentals (hybrids $25/day) and repairs, visit **Cycle Mania** (65 Cove St., 207/774-2933, www.cyclemania1.com).

View five lighthouses and enjoy a fancy lunch on a half-day tour with **Summer Feet Cycling Adventure** (866/857-9544, www.summerfeet.net, $95). Summer Feet offers plenty of other options, from full day to week-long trips, including self-guided bicycling tours for which it makes all arrangements and moves luggage.

The best locales for island bicycling—fun for families and beginners but not especially challenging for diehards—are Peaks and Great Chebeague Islands, but do remember to follow the rules of the road.

Golf

Public courses are plentiful in Greater Portland, but you'll need an "in" to play the private ones. Free advice on helping you choose a course is offered by **Golf Maine** (www.golfme.com).

Consider just Greater Portland's 18-hole courses. **Sable Oaks Golf Club** (505 Country Club Dr., South Portland, 207/775-6257, www.sableoaks.com) is considered one of the toughest and best of Maine's public courses. Since 1998, **Nonesuch River Golf Club** (304 Gorham Rd./Rte. 114, Scarborough, 207/883-0007 or 888/256-2717, www.nonesuchgolf.com) has been drawing raves for the challenges of its par-70 championship course and praise from environmentalists for preserving wildlife habitat; there's also a full-size practice range and green. The City of Portland's **Riverside Municipal Golf Course** (1158 Riverside St., 207/797-3524) has an 18-hole par-72 course (Riverside North) and a nine-hole par-35 course (Riverside South). Opt for the 18-hole course.

Ferries and excursion boats crowd wharves along the waterfront.

Sea Kayaking

With all the islands scattered through Casco Bay, Greater Portland is a sea-kayaking hotbed. The best place to start is out on Peaks Island, 15 minutes offshore via the Casco Bay Lines ferry. **Maine Island Kayak Company** (MIKCO, 70 Luther St., Peaks Island, 207/766-2373, www.maineislandkayak.com) organizes half-day, all-day, and multiday local kayaking trips as well as national and international adventures. An introductory half-day tour in Casco Bay is $70 pp; a full day is $110 pp and includes lunch. Reservations are essential. MIKCO also does private lessons and group courses and clinics (some require previous experience).

★ Lobstering Cruise

Learn all kinds of lobster lore and maybe even catch your own dinner with **Lucky Catch Lobster Tours** (170 Commercial St., 207/233-2026 or 888/624-6321, www.luckycatch.com, $25 adults, $22 seniors, $20 ages 13-18, $15 ages 2-12). Captain Tom Martin offers three different 80-90-minute cruises on his 37-foot lobster boat. On each cruise (except late Saturday and all day Sunday, when state law prohibits it), usually 10 traps are hauled and the process and gear are explained. You can even help if you want. Any lobsters caught are available for purchase after the cruise for wholesale boat price (and you can have them cooked nearby for a reasonable rate). Wouldn't that make a nice story to tell the folks back home?

Boat Excursions

Down on the Old Port wharves are several excursion-boat businesses. Each has carved out a niche, so choose according to your interest and schedule. Dress warmly and wear rubber-soled shoes. Remember that all cruises are weather-dependent.

Portland Discover—Land & Sea Tours (Long Wharf, 207/774-0808, www.portlanddiscovery.com) offers a Lighthouse Lovers Cruise and a Sunset Lighthouse Cruise ($22 adults, $16 children).

Cruise up to 20 miles offshore seeking whales with **Odyssey Whale Watch** (Long

Wharf, 170 Commercial St., 207/775-0727, www.odysseywhalewatch.com, $48 adults, $38 under age 12). Four- to five-hour whale watches aboard the *Odyssey* depart daily June-early September as well as on spring and fall weekends. (Go easy on breakfast that day, and take preventive measures if you're motion-sensitive.) Odyssey also offers Deep Sea Fishing trips for cod ($69) and mackerel ($35); bait and tackle are provided.

Sail quietly across the waters of Casco Bay aboard a windjammer with **Portland Schooner Company** (Maine State Pier, 56 Commercial St., 207/766-2500, www.portlandschooner.com, late May-Oct., $39 adults, $15 age 12 and under). Four to six two-hour sails are offered daily on two schooners, the 72-foot *Bagheera* and the 88-foot *Wendameen*, both historical vessels designed by John G. Alden and built in East Boothbay. Overnight windjammer trips also are available for $250 pp, including dinner and breakfast.

Spectator Sports

A pseudo-fierce mascot named Slugger stirs up the crowds at baseball games played by the **Portland Sea Dogs** (Hadlock Field, 271 Park Ave., 207/879-9500 or 800/936-3647, www.portlandseadogs.com, $9-11), a AA Boston Red Sox farm team. The season schedule (early Apr.-Aug.) is available after January 1.

The home court for the **Red Claws** (207/210-6655, www.maineredclaws.com, $8-30), an NBA development team for the Boston Celtics, is the **Portland Expo** (239 Park Ave.). Home ice for the Portland Pirates (207/Pirates, www.portlandpirates.com, $17-25), a Florida Panthers affiliate, is the Cross Insurance Arena.

ACCOMMODATIONS

Downtown Portland

INNS AND BED-AND-BREAKFASTS

All of these are in older buildings without elevators; stairs may be steep. With the exception of the Inn at St. John, all are in the West End.

Chic and stylish, **The Danforth** (163 Danforth St., 800-991-4266, www.danforthinn.com, from $325), honors its siting in a handsome 18th-century brick mansion but updates it with contemporary verve accented with Southeast Asian art and antiques. Service is impeccable at this elegant, nine-room luxury inn, which also offers an excellent restaurant and lounge. A menu breakfast is included.

Railroad tycoon John Deering built **The Inn at St. John** (939 Congress St., 207/773-6481 or 800/636-9127, www.innatstjohn.com, $99-260) in 1897. The comfortable (if somewhat tired) and moderately priced 39-room hostelry is a good choice for value-savvy travelers who aren't seeking fancy accommodations. Some rooms share baths. The inn welcomes children and pets and even has bicycle storage. Cable TV, Wi-Fi, air-conditioning, free local calls, free parking, and a meager continental breakfast are provided. Reimbursement for taxi from the airport or transportation center is available at a fixed price. Most guest rooms have private baths (some are detached); some have fridges and microwaves. No elevator. The downside is the lackluster neighborhood—in the evening you'll want to drive or take a taxi when going out. It's about a 45-minute walk up and over the hill to the Old Port, or around $10 via taxi.

Staying at **The Pomegranate Inn** (49 Neal St. at Carroll St., 207/772-1006 or 800/356-0408, www.pomegranateinn.com, from $299) is an adventure in itself, with faux paintings, classical statuary, contemporary art, antiques, and whimsical touches everywhere—you'll either love it or find it a bit much. The elegant 1884 Italianate mansion has seven guest rooms and a suite, all with air-conditioning, TV, and Wi-Fi, and some with fireplaces.

Take a carefully renovated 1830s town house, add contemporary amenities and a service-oriented innkeeper, and the result is the **Morrill Mansion Bed and Breakfast** (249 Vaughan St., 207/774-6900 or 888/566-7745, www.morrillmansion.com, $169-249), on the West End. Six guest rooms and one suite are spread out on the second and third floors. No frilly Victorian accents here—the decor is understated yet tasteful, taking advantage of hardwood floors and high ceilings. You'll find free Wi-Fi and local calls and a TV with a DVD player in each room. It's near the Maine Medical Center.

In the same neighborhood is **The Chadwick Bed & Breakfast** (140 Chadwick St., 800/774-2137, www.thechadwick.com, $250). All four rooms have electric fireplaces, air-conditioning, flat-screen TVs with DVD players, iPod docking stations, and Wi-Fi, and a DVD library is available. Guests have use of a lovely backyard garden. Here's a nice service: If you need to depart before the full breakfast is served, a bagged breakfast is provided.

Guests are treated like royalty with plush linens and memorable breakfasts at **The Inn on Carleton** (46 Carlton St., 207/775-1910 or 800/639-1779, www.innoncarleton.com, $195-225), a masterfully updated and decorated 1869 Victorian with a convenient location in the city's West End. Although all guest rooms have private baths, two are detached.

Former travel writer Dale Northrup put his experience to work in opening the **Percy Inn** (15 Pine St., 207/871-7638 or 888/417-3729, www.percyinn.com, $129-209) in a handsome brick townhouse conveniently located just off Longfellow Square. The air-conditioned guest rooms are furnished with phones, CD players, TV/VCRs, wet bars, and refrigerators. There's even a 24-hour pantry. It's best suited for independent-minded travelers who don't desire much contact with the host or other guests, as public rooms are few and the innkeeper, although always accessible, is rarely on-site. Breakfast is a continental buffet. If you're noise-sensitive, avoid accommodations that open directly into the pantry, kitchen, or breakfast room.

A new owner has breathed new life into **The Inn at Park Spring** (135 Spring St., 207/774-1059 or 800/427-8511, www.innatparkspring.com, $195-295), housed in an 1835 brick townhouse, just steps from most Arts District attractions. Four handsome guest rooms have air-conditioning and phones, and some have Internet access. A bi-level suite has a kitchenette, living room, and private patio and entrance. There's a guest fridge on each floor. Rates include a full breakfast.

The Georgian-style **West End Inn** (146 Pine St., 800/338-1377, www.westendbb.com, $189-239), built in 1877, received a facelift in 2013, updating the six rooms with contemporary amenities such as Wi-Fi and flat-screen TVs. One room has a detached bath, another a private deck. The decor blends traditional furnishings with fun and contemporary accents. A full breakfast and afternoon refreshments are served.

FULL-SERVICE HOTELS

Extra! Extra! In 2015, ★ **The Press Hotel** (19 Exchange St., 207/808-8800, www.thepresshotel.com, from around $370) opened in a downtown building that previously housed the state's largest newspaper. The 110-room boutique hotel, a Marriott Autograph Collection property, honors the building's journalistic heritage with a contemporary décor accented with art installations, vintage newsroom-inspired furnishings, wallpapers printed with quirky newspaper headlines, and carpets patterned with jumbled type. The location is the city's best, at the head of the Old Port where it intersects with the downtown, and just across from City Hall. Other plusses include an excellent restaurant, a lobby lounge, and fitness room.

The **Portland Harbor Hotel** (468 Fore St., 207/775-9090 or 888/798-9090, www.portlandharborhotel.com, from $339), an upscale boutique hotel in the Old Port, is built around a garden courtyard. Rooms are plush, with chic linens, duvets, down pillows on the beds, Wi-Fi, and digital cable TV; marble and granite bathrooms have separate soaking tubs and showers. Complimentary bike rentals are available, and the hotel offers a free local car service. Valet parking is $18. There's a cozy lounge, and the restaurant has 24-hour room service. Also on the premises are a fitness

The Inn by the Sea is an especially dog-friendly beachside resort.

room and spa services. The best splurge is the suites. Ice Bar, an ice sculpture event where you can order your favorite libation from bars made of ice, is held the last weekend of January in the hotel's courtyard and draws a crowd.

You might have trouble finding the **Portland Regency** (20 Milk St., 207/774-4200 or 800/727-3436, www.theregency.com, from $285): This hotel, registered with the National Trust for Historic Preservation as a historic property, is secreted in a renovated armory in the heart of the Old Port. The nicest rooms are the renovated ones, especially those on the fourth floor with decks. Perks include Wi-Fi and free shuttles to all major Portland transportation facilities. Be forewarned: Room configurations vary widely—some provide little natural window light or are strangely shaped. All have LCD TVs, minibars, and air-conditioning. A restaurant, spa, and fitness center are on-site. Valet parking is $12 per night.

Yes, it's a chain, and yes, it's downright ugly, but the **Holiday Inn by the Bay** (88 Spring St., 207/775-2311 or 800/345-5050, www.innbythebay.com, from $210) provides a lot of bang for the buck. It's conveniently situated between the waterfront and the Arts District. Rooms on upper floors have views either over Back Cove or Portland Harbor; Wi-Fi is free, as is a local shuttle service. It also has an indoor pool, a sauna, a fitness room, on-site guest laundry facilities, a restaurant, and a lounge.

The Burbs

South of Portland are two upscale beachfront inns. Especially splurge-worthy and well suited for families is the ultra- green, oceanfront ★ **Inn by the Sea** (40 Bowery Beach Rd./Rte. 77, Cape Elizabeth, 207/799-3134 or 800/888-4287, www.innbythesea.com, from around $559), just seven miles south of downtown Portland. Guests stay in handsome rooms, suites, and two-bedroom cottages, most with kitchens or expanded wet bars, comfy living rooms, and big views. This is perhaps southern Maine's most contemporary luxury property, with a cozy lounge, a full-service spa, and a small cardio room. Big windows frame ocean views at **Sea Glass** (207/299-3134, entrées $24-34), offering all meals daily. Other facilities include an outdoor pool, a *boules* court, wildlife habitats, and a private boardwalk winding through a salt marsh to the southern end of Crescent Beach State Park. By reservation, dogs are honored guests; they're welcomed with bowls and bed, receive turndown treats, and have their own room-service and spa menus. Even better, the hotel has a successful foster dog program, so you might end up heading home with a furry friend.

The **Black Point Inn Resort** (510 Black Point Rd., Prouts Neck, Scarborough, 207/883-2500 or 800/258-0003, www.blackpointinn.com, from $530 including breakfast and dinner) is a classic, unpretentious seaside hotel with a genteel vibe. The historic Shingle-style hotel opened in 1878 at the tip of Prouts Neck, overlooking Casco

Bay from one side and down to Old Orchard from the other. Now owned by a local partnership, the inn has returned to its roots, catering to wealthy rusticators. Guests have access to a private, oceanfront 18-hole golf course and tennis courts, the Cliff Walk around the point (passing American master Winslow Homer's studio, recently opened to the public by reserved guided tour departing from the Portland Museum of Art), and a lovely trail-laced woodland sanctuary that has ties to Homer's family. **The Point Restaurant** (6pm-8:30pm daily, $28-38), a fine dining venue, is open to nonguests by reservation; the less-fussy **Chart Room** (8am-10am and 11:30am-9pm daily, $10-18) serves lighter fare. Both are underwhelming, but Portland's nearby. Don't miss cocktails on the porch at sunset, with views over beach and water to distant Mount Washington. A hefty 18 percent service charge is added to daily rates.

Only a narrow byway separates **The Breakers Inn** (2 Bay View Ave., Higgins Beach, Scarborough, 207/883-4820, www.thebreakersinn.com, $215 daily, from $1,200 weekly) from the sands of Higgins Beach. This is an old-timey bed-and-breakfast in a turreted, porch-wrapped three-story Victorian. It was built in 1900, converted to an inn in 1932, and has been operated by the Laughton family since 1956. Every room in the main inn has an ocean view, including two in the basement. Interior stairways are steep and narrow. Fancy or frilly, this isn't; you're paying for location, not amenities or decor. Breakfast is included; picnic lunches are available. Transportation is available from Portland's transportation hubs. No credit cards.

FOOD

Named "America's Foodiest Small Town" by *Bon Appétit* magazine in 2009, downtown Portland alone has more than 100 restaurants, so it's impossible to list even all the great ones—and there are many. The city's proximity to fresh foods from both farms and the sea makes it popular with chefs, and its growing immigrant population means a good choice of ethnic dining too. If you're especially into the food scene, check www.portlandfoodmap.com, which tracks openings and closures and links to reviews.

You can also check the "Community News" listings in each Wednesday's *Portland Press Herald*. Under "Potluck," you'll find listings of **public meals,** usually benefiting nonprofit organizations. Prices are always quite

The Black Point Inn Resort is located on Prouts Neck, near the studio of painter Winslow Homer.

low (under $10 for adults, $2-4 for children), mealtimes quite early (5pm or 6pm), and the flavor local.

When you need a java fix, **Coffee by Design** (620 Congress St., 67 India St., 43 Washington Ave., 207/879-2233) is the popular local choice, not only for its fine brews but also for its support of local artists and community causes.

The Portland Farmers Market sets up on Wednesday on Monument Square and on Saturday in Deering Oaks Park.

Here is a choice selection of restaurants, by neighborhood, with open days and hours provided for peak season. Some don't list a closing time—that's because they shut the doors when the crowd thins. Make reservations, especially in July-August.

The Old Port and the Waterfront

If there is a cruise ship in port, avoid restaurants clustered in the heart of the waterfront during lunch.

LOCAL FLAVORS

All of these venues are west of the Franklin Street Arterial between Congress and Commercial Streets.

Best known for the earliest and most filling breakfast around, **Becky's Diner** (390 Commercial St., 207/773-7070, www.beckysdiner.com, 4am-9pm daily) has more than a dozen omelet choices, just for a start. It also serves lunch and dinner, all at downright cheap prices.

Enjoy pizza with a view at **Flatbread Company** (72 Commercial St., 207/772-8777, www.flatbreadcompany.com, 11:30am-10pm daily), part of a small New England chain. The all-natural pizza is baked in a primitive wood-fired clay oven and served in a dining room with a wall of windows overlooking the ferry terminal and Portland Harbor. Vegan options are available.

For gourmet goodies, don't miss **Browne Trading Market** (Merrill's Wharf, 262 Commercial St., 207/775-7560). Owner Rod Mitchell became the Caviar King of Portland by wholesaling Caspian caviar, and now he's letting the rest of us in on it. Fresh fish and shellfish fill the cases next to the caviar and cheeses. The mezzanine is literally wall-to-wall wine, specializing in French.

When you're craving carbs, want pastries for breakfast, or need to boost your energy with a sweet, follow your nose to **Standard Baking Company** (75 Commercial St., 207/773-2112), deservedly famous for its handcrafted breads and pastries.

Humble sandwiches, hot dogs, and fries get treated like adults at **Blue Rooster Food Co.** (5 Dana St., 207/747-4157, www.bluerooster-foodcompany.com, 9am-6pm Sun.-Thurs., 9am-2am Fri.-Sat.), a good spot for cheap eats anytime, but especially appreciated for its after-the-bars-close hours.

Seeking to recreate the pastry shop experience that exists throughout Paris, Food & Wine-lauded chef Steve Corry and his wife, Michelle, drew upon her French heritage in opening **Portland Patisserie** (46 Market St., 207/553-2355, www.portlandpatisserie.com, 7am-8pm daily). Stop in for elegant pastries, freshly baked breads, house-made chocolates, and crepes, as well as soups, salads, quiches, and charcuterie-and-cheese plates. There is a small seating area. For full service, visit adjacent Petite Jacqueline.

CASUAL DINING

Executive Chef Josh Berry presides over the open kitchen at **Union Restaurant** (119 Exchange St., 207/808-8700, www.thepresshotel.com/union, 7am-10pm daily, $20-36) sited in The Press Hotel. Berry created the handsome, farm-to-table restaurant in consultation with James Beard award winners Clark Frasier and Mark Gaier. The menu gives local fare a contemporary spin.

One of the city's hottest restaurants, **Central Provisions** (414 Fore St., 207/805-1085, www.central-provisions.com, 11am-2pm and 5-10pm daily) earned national kudos as one of 2014's best new restaurants for its creative and fresh approach to small-plate dining. Upstairs is an open kitchen with counter seating as well as tables; downstairs is a bar serving Prohibition-era cocktails. The mix-and-match menu offers raw, cold, hot, and hearty preparations ($4-18). No reservations.

Chef-entrepreneur Harding Lee Smith's **The Grill Room** (84 Exchange St., 207/774-2333, www.thegrillroomandbar.com, 11:30am-2:30pm Mon.-Sat. and from 5pm daily, $18-39) turns out excellent wood-grilled meats and seafood.

SEAFOOD

Ask around and everyone will tell you the best seafood in town is at **Street and Company** (33 Wharf St., 207/775-0887, www.streetandcompany.net, opens 5:30pm daily, $22-36). Fresh, beautifully prepared fish is what you get, often with a Mediterranean flair. Tables are tight, and it's often noisy in the informal brick-walled rooms.

For lobster in the rough, head to **Portland Lobster Company** (180 Commercial St., 207/775-2112, www.portlandlobstercompany.com, 11am-10pm daily). There's a small inside seating area, but it's much more pleasant to sit out on the wharf and watch the excursion boats come and go. Expect to pay in the low $20 range for a one-pound lobster with fries and slaw. Other choices ($8-23) and a kids' menu are available.

Fore Street restaurant's Sam Hayward inked Portland on the foodie map by winning Maine's first James Beard award in 2004. His newest endeavor is **Scales** (68 Commercial St./Maine Wharf, 207/805-0444, www.scalesrestaurant.com), a harborfront seafood emporium. The emphasis is on traditional New England favorites, such as steamed lobster, fresh Gulf of Maine fish, a raw bar, and fried oyster and clams, as well as killer chowders and lobster rolls, all prepared with skilled precision and beautifully presented. From 5:30 pm daily; lunch in season.

ETHNIC FARE

Sushi approaches an art form at **Miyake** (468 Fore St., 207/871-9170, www.miyakerestaurants.com, 11:30am-2pm and 5:30pm-9pm Mon.-Sat.). Trained in both French and classical Japanese techniques, chef Masa Miyake has developed a following far beyond Maine for his innovative sushi crafted from primarily local ingredients, including vegetables, fowl, and pork raised on his farm. A four-course tasting menu is $55, the omakase chef's-tasting menu is $70, and à la carte options are $13-18.

Petite Jacqueline (46 Market St., 207/553-7044, www.bistropj.com, 11:30am-9:30pm Mon.-Thurs., 11:30am-10:30pm Fri.-Sat., 9am-2pm and 5-9:30pm Sun., $19-26) has earned national accolades for its authentic French bistro cuisine. It's located in the same building as sibling Portland Patisserie.

Top-notch for northern Italian cuisine is **Vignola Cinque Terre Ristorante** (36 Wharf St., 207/347-6154, www.vignolamaine.com, from 5pm daily, noon-2:30pm Sat., 10am-2:30pm Sun., $12-30). Chef Lee Skawinski is committed to sustainable farming, and much of the seasonal and organic produce used comes from the restaurant owners' Laughing Stock Farm and other Maine farmers.

The Corner Room Kitchen and Bar (110 Exchange St., 207/879-4747, www.thefrontroomrestaurant.com, from 11:30am Mon.-Sat., 9am-3pm Sat., 4pm-9pm Sun., $16-29), one of popular local chef Harding Lee Smith's restaurants, takes its cue from rustic Italian fare, with hearty and delicious pizzas, pastas, and panini.

Pasta doesn't get much more authentic than that served at **Paciarino** (468 Fore St., 207/774-3500, www.paciarino.com, 11:30am-2:30pm Mon.-Sat. and 6pm-9pm daily, $15-22). Owners Fabiana De Savino and Enrico Barbiero moved here from Milan in 2008, and they make their pastas and sauces fresh daily using recipes from De Savino's *nonna*.

Chef Damian Sansonetti arrived in Portland with a distinguished pedigree, and he's living up to expectations with his rustic, authentic, southern Italian fare at ★ **Piccolo**

(111 Middle St., 207/747-5307, www.piccolomaine.com, 5pm-10pm Tues.-Sun., 10:30am-2pm Sun., $19-25). Expect a fabulous, leisurely meal professionally served. The restaurant only seats 20, so reservations are a must.

Irish fare with a Maine accent fills the menu at **Ri-Ra** (72 Commercial St., 207/761-4446, www.rira.com/portland, from 11:30am Mon.-Fri., from 10 am Sat.-Sun.). Entrées in the glass-walled second-floor dining room, overlooking the Casco Bay Lines ferry terminal, are $10-22. The ground-floor pub, elegantly woody with an enormous bar, is inevitably stuffed to the gills on weekends—a great spot for such traditional fare as corned beef and cabbage as long as you can stand the din. They don't take reservations, so be prepared to wait, especially on weekends.

Fresh farm-to-table pan-Mediterranean cuisine the specialty at **Tiqa** (327 Comercial St., 207/808-8840, from 11am Mon.-Sat., from 10am Sun., $20-35), a light and bright contemporary restaurant serving kefta and kabobs in addition to dishes from Italy, Morocco, Egypt, North Africa, Tunisia, Turkey, Portugal, and Spain.

DESTINATION DINING

Plan well in advance to land a reservation at ★ **Fore Street** (288 Fore St., 207/775-2717, www.forestreet.biz, 5:30pm-10pm Sun.-Thurs., 5:30pm-10:30pm Fri.-Sat., entrées from $20). Chef Sam Hayward, renowned for his passionate and creative use of Maine-sourced ingredients, won the James Beard Award for Best Chef in the Northeast in 2004 and has been featured in many foodie publications. Hayward excels at elevating simple foods to rave-worthy dishes. The renovated former warehouse has copper-topped tables, an open kitchen, and industrial chic decor—but quiet it's not. Make reservations well in advance, or show up early to try to land one of the handful of unreserved tables.

Arts District and Downtown

These restaurants are clustered around Danforth Street and along and around Congress Street.

LOCAL FLAVORS

Can't make up your mind? Peruse the reasonably priced fare available at **Public Market House** (28 Monument Sq., 207/228-2056, www.publicmarkethouse.com, 8am-7pm Mon.-Sat., 10am-5pm Sun.), with vendors selling meats, cheeses, breads, sandwiches, pizzas, burritos, coffees, and soups.

Well off most visitors' radar screens is **Artemisia Café** (61 Pleasant St., 207/761-0135, 11am-2pm Tues.-Fri., 9am-2pm Sat.-Sun., 5pm-8:30pm Wed.-Sat., $14-27), a cheery neighborhood café with a creative menu drawing on international influences.

Nosh Kitchen Bar (551 Congress St., 207/553-2227, www.noshkitchenbar.com, 11:30am-1am Mon.-Sat., 4pm-1am Sun.) updates the concept of New York-style deli fare with a fresh-and-local twist. The setting is sleek, with a granite bar on one side, copper-topped tables on the other, and comfy lounge-like seating at the entry. Nosh serves inspired sandwiches and burgers and, well, noshing fare ($10-21). Fries are offered in flavors including bacon-dusted and salt-and-vinegar and accompanied by a tempting array of dipping options.

ETHNIC AND VEGETARIAN FARE

Slip into sleek **Emilitsa** (547 Congress St., 207/221-0245, www.emilitsa.com, from 5pm Tues.-Sat., $18-35) for finely crafted authentic Greek food paired with Greek wines.

At ★ **Tempu Dulo** (163 Danforth St., 207/879-8755, www.tempodulu.restaurant), a sleek fine dining restaurant located in the Danforth Inn, Chef Lawrence Klang blends techniques and flavors honed from his classical European training with those learned during a culinary immersion in Southeast Asia, and adds a Maine accent; think banana leaf-steamed lobster with Bali spice, a bok choi spring roll, and coconut turmeric rice. Choose from a three-course menu ($67), a chef's-tasting Indonesian rijsttafel ($87), and a lobster-tasting menu ($98).

Nationally lauded chef Cara Stadler's **Bao Bao Dumpling House** (133 Spring St., 207/772-8400, www.baobaodumplinghouse.com, 11:30am-11pm Wed.-Sat., 11:30am-9pm Sun.) is a must for traditional and inspired dumplings and other small plate dishes. Six dumplings range $6-10; other dishes top out around $14.

Masa Miyake's **Pai Men Miyake** (188 State St., 207/541-9204, www.miyakerestaurants.com, 11:30am-11pm daily, $7-16) is a traditional Japanese noodle bar serving miso and ramen soup along with amazing pork gyoza and pork buns.

Duck into chef-owner Asmeret Teklu's **Asmara** (51 Oak St., 207/253-5122, 11:30am-10:30 Tues.- Sat., 3-9 pm Sun., $13-17) to be transported to eastern Africa. Traditional Eritrean and Ethiopian dishes, a mix of mild to spicy curried stews, and vegetarian plates are served on *injera*, spongy flat bread made from teff flour that doubles as an eating utensil (silverware is available, if you ask). Entrées are generous and come with a salad and choice of vegetable. Service is leisurely; this is a one-woman show.

Ever-popular **Local 188** (685 Congress St., 207/761-7909, www.local188.com, from 5:30pm daily and 9am-2pm Sat.-Sun.) serves fabulous Mediterranean-inspired food with a tapas-heavy menu. It doubles as an art gallery, with rotating exhibits. Most tapas selections are less than $10; heartier choices and entrées begin at $21. There is free parking behind the building.

Authentic Thai—not the Americanized version, but the kind of food you might purchase from a street vendor in Bangkok—is served in a very non-Thai, cool-yet-sophisticated space at **Boda** (671 Congress St., 207/347-7557, www.bodamaine.com, 5pm-12:45am daily). Make a meal out of small plates or opt for an entrée ($14-19); vegetarian and gluten-free dishes are available.

Vegan and vegetarian cuisine comes with an Asian accent at **Green Elephant** (608 Congress St., 207/347-3111, www.greenelephantmaine.com, 11:30am-2:30pm Mon.-Sat. and from 5pm daily, $11-15). There's not one shred of meat on the creative menu, but you won't miss it.

Little Lad's (482 Congress St., 207/871-1636, www.littlelads.com, 11am-6pm Sun.-Fri.) is a no-frills vegan café, where the $6.99 lunch buffet, served 11am-3pm Mon.-Fri., might include chick-in cacciatore or bean stroganoff. Also available are sandwiches and sweets. Don't miss the herbal popcorn.

CASUAL DINING

Fun, whimsical, and artsy describes most restaurants in the Arts District, but not **Five Fifty-Five** (555 Congress St., 207/761-0555, www.fivefifty-five.com, from 5pm daily and 9:30am-2pm Sun., $28-35), where chef Steve Corry was named by *Food & Wine* magazine as one of the top 10 Best New Chefs in the country. Fresh, local, and seasonal are blended in creative ways on his ever-changing menu, which is divided into small plates, green plates, savory plates, cheese plates, and sweet plates. A five-course tasting menu is around $70. If you can't afford to splurge in the main restaurant, Corry serves lighter fare in the lounge.

A longtimer in the Portland dining scene, **David's** (22 Monument Sq., 207/773-4340, www.davidsrestaurant.com, 11:30am-3pm Mon.-Fri. and from 5pm daily, $12-30) serves pizzas, pastas, and updated familiar fare. Never one to rest on his laurels, chef-owner David Turin opened **David's Opus 10** an 18-seat fixed-price restaurant within this one in 2012, and has an equally popular restaurant in South Portland.

Dining at **Grace** (15 Chestnut St., 207/828-4422, www.restaurantgrace.com, from 5pm Tues.-Sat., $19-40) is a heavenly experience. The restaurant is located in a masterfully renovated mid-19th-century Gothic Revival church that's listed on the National Register of Historic Places. Equally well thought out is the menu, which draws from local foods.

Be sure to have a reservation if you're going

before the theater to **BiBo's Madd Apple Café** (23 Forest Ave., 207/774-9698, www.bibosportland.com, 11am-2pm Wed.-Fri. and from 5:30 Wed.-Sat., 10am-2pm Sun., $17-20)—it's right next to the Portland Performing Arts Center. On the other hand, it's popular anytime thanks to chef Bill Boutwell ("BiBo"). There's no way of predicting what will be on the bistro-fusion menu.

For tapas, head to **Sur Lie** (11 Free St., 207/956-7350, www.sur-lie.com, from 4pm Tues-Sat. and 10am-2pm Sun., $6-20), where the menu ranges from fried oysters to hanger steak.

West End

Have breakfast or lunch or pick up prepared foods at **Aurora Provisions** (64 Pine St., 207/871-9060, www.auroraprovisions.com, 8am-6:30pm Mon.-Sat.), a combination market and café with irresistible goodies, most made on the premises.

Superb thin-crust pizzas made from all-natural ingredients in usual and unusual flavor combos emerge from the wood-fired oven at **Bonobo** (46 Pine St., 207/347-8267, www.bonobopizza.com, 11:30am-2:30pm Wed.-Fri., noon-4pm Sat., and from 4pm daily, $10-17).

Chef Abby Harmon's **Caiola's Restaurant** (58 Pine St., 207/772-1110, www.caiolas.com, from 5:30pm Mon.-Sat. and 9am-2pm Sun., entrées from $14) delivers comfort food with pizzazz in a cozy neighborhood bistro. This little gem is off most visitors' radar screens, but locals fill it nightly.

The decor is chic and sophisticated without being stuffy and the fare matches it at **Outliers Eatery** (231 York St., 207/747-4166, www.outlierseatery.com, 5pm-11pm Tues.-Sat., 10am-3pm Sun., $15-27). The menu is simple, with servers explaining that day's preparation. It's all fresh and local, though it's not a place for a quiet meal.

Bayside

Portlanders have long favored **Bayside American Café** (98 Portland St., 207/774-0005, www.baysideamericancafe.com, 7am-1:45pm daily) for its breakfasts and brunches ($7-15), where the menu is humongous. They don't take reservations on weekends, so expect to wait in line.

Breakfast is served all day at the **Miss Portland Diner** (140 Marginal Way, 207/210-6673, www.missportlanddiner.com, 7am-3pm Sun.-Mon., 7am-9pm Tues.-Sat.), a 1949 Worcester Diner (car no. 818) that was rescued, restored, and reopened in 2007. Snag a counter stool or a booth in the original dining car, not the addition, then treat yourself to breakfast for dinner. Sure, there are more traditional choices—soups, sandwiches, wraps, burgers, dogs, comfort foods, seafood plates and platters, or nightly dinner specials (most choices range $7-12)—but breakfast and diners go together like bacon and eggs. An added bonus: Parking is plentiful and free.

For a lovely meal in a fine dining setting, reserve a table at the **Back Bay Grill** (65 Portland St., near the main post office, 207/772-8833, www.backbaygrill.com, 5-10pm Tues.-Sat.). A colorful mural accents the serene dining room; arts and crafts wall sconces cast a soft glow on the white linen-draped tables. The menu, which highlights fresh, seasonal ingredients, isn't innovative but is well prepared, and the wine list is long and well chosen. Service is professional. Entrées are $19-36.

East End

These dining spots are all east of the Franklin Street Arterial. Poke around this end of the city, and you'll find quite a few ethnic hole-in-the-wall places on and around Washington Avenue. It's an ever-changing array, but if you're adventurous or budget-confined, give one a try.

LOCAL FLAVORS

Chocoholics take note: When a craving strikes, head to **Dean's Sweets** (475 Fore St., 207/899-3664) for adult-flavored dark-chocolate truffles made without nuts.

If you're a tea fan, don't miss **Homegrown Herb & Tea** (195 Congress St., 207/774-3484, www.homegrownherbandtea.com), an Ayurvedic shop that blends black, green, and herbal teas and serves light fare, including a delightful lavender shortbread.

The most incredible fries come from ★ **Duckfat** (43 Middle St., 207/774-8080, www.duckfat.com, 11am-10pm daily, $8-14), a casual joint owned by James Beard Award-winning chef Rob Evans. Fries—fried in duck fat, of course—are served in a paper cone and accompanied by your choice of six sauces; the truffle ketchup is heavenly. Want to really harden those arteries? Order the *poutine*—Belgian fries topped with Maine cheese curd and homemade duck gravy. In addition, Duckfat serves panini, soups, salads, and really good milk shakes; wine and beer are available.

Mainers love their Italian sandwiches, and **Amato's** (71 India St., 207/773-1682, www.amatos.com, 6:30am-11pm daily, entrées $10-16) is credited with creating a drool-worthy sub, usually made with ham, cheese, tomatoes, green peppers, black olives, and onions wrapped in a doughy roll and drizzled with olive oil. Also available are calzones, salads, and other Italian-inspired foods. Amato's has outlets throughout southern Maine; this one has outdoor patio seating.

Micucci's Grocery Store (45 India St., 207/775-1854) has been serving Portland's Italian community since 1949. It's a great stop for picnic fixings, prepared takeout pizzas and sandwiches, and a nice selection of inexpensive wines.

Ever had a mashed potato pizza? You can get one as well as other intriguing choices at **Otto Pizza** (225 Congress St., 207/358-7551, www.ottoportland.com, from 11:30am daily). Otto's has a second Portland location at 576 Congress St., in the downtown Arts District.

Huge portions at rock-bottom prices make **Silly's** (40 Washington Ave., 207/772-0360, www.sillys.com, 11am-9pm Wed.-Fri., 9am-9pm Sat.-Sun., $10-16) an ever-popular choice among the young and budget-minded. The huge menu has lots of international flair along with veggie, vegan, gluten-free, and dairy-free options. A separate menu lists milk shakes in dozens of wacky flavors. The decor: vintage kitsch, 1950s Formica and chrome, and Elvis. The same menu is served at adjacent **Silly's with a Twist,** which also serves alcohol.

Traditional Salvadorian foods (think Mexican with attitude) have turned hole-in-the-wall **Tu Casa** (70 Washington Ave., 207/828-4971, www.tucasaportland.com, 11am-9pm Sun.-Fri.) into a must-visit for in-the-know foodies. It's also a budget find, with almost everything on the menu going for less than $10.

Just try *not* to walk out with something from **Two Fat Cats Bakery** (47 India St., 207/347-5144)—oh, the cookies! The breads! The pies!

CASUAL DINING

A trio of restaurants from Beard-nominated chef/owners Andrew Taylor and Mike Wiley line the seaward side of Middle Street. First was **Hugo's** (88 Middle St. at Franklin St., 207/774-8538, www.hugos.net, from 5:30pm Mon.-Sat.), where the weekly changing tasting menu (from $45) showcases fresh and local fare from the sea, forest, and field and foraged and farmed. Next came **Eventide Oyster Co.** (86 Middle St., 207/774-8538, www.eventideoysterco.com, 11am-midnight daily), a fave of food guru Andrew Zimmern that has also won national accolades. The menu includes nearly two dozen oysters and other shellfish paired with sauces, as well as other seafood; mix and match from $3, with entrées around $25. In 2015, they added **The Honey Paw** (78 Middle St., 207-774-8538, www.thehoneypaw.com, $15-42), a "non-denominational noodle bar" serving dishes such as Vietnamese chili lobster and Szechuan bouillabaisse.

Just down the street, try the **East Ender** (47 Middle St., 207/879-7669, www.eastender-portland.com. 11:30am-10pm Mon.-Sat., and 11am-3pm and 5-9pm Sun., $15-28), which delivers complex flavors, such as miso-marinated black cod, cold smoked burger, and a divine lobster tostada, and **Ribollita** (41

Middle St., 207/774-2972, www.ribollitamaine.com, from 5pm Mon.-Sat., $13-20), a small, casual trattoria that's justly popular for its rustic Italian fare; just be in the mood for a leisurely meal.

Blue Spoon (89 Congress St., 207/773-1116, www.bluespoonme.com, 11:30am-3pm Mon.-Fri., 9am-2pm Sat., and from 5pm Mon.-Sat, $14-28) was one of the first upscale eateries on Portland's gentrifying East End. Chef-owner David Iovino, who studied at the French Culinary Institute, has created a warm and welcoming neighborhood gem.

Chef Guy Hernandez and sommelier Stella Hernandez are the creative geniuses behind **Lolita Vinoteca + Asador** (90 Congress St., 207/775-5652, www.lolita-portland.com, from 11am Wed.-Mon., $10-24) a sophisticated restaurant that emphasizes small bites with big flavors. Think charcuterie and cheese and toasts from a wood-fired grill, but don't neglect the bigger offerings.

The Burbs

Pair a visit to Portland Headlight and Fort Williams with a lobster roll from **Bite Into Maine** (Fort Williams, Cape Elizabeth, 207/420-0294, www.biteintomaine.com, 11am-sellout daily), a mobile food truck also serving vegetarian sandwiches, ice cream, and desserts.

Great sunset views over Portland's skyline, a casual atmosphere, and excellent fare have earned **Saltwater Grille** (231 Front St., South Portland, 207/799-5400, www.saltwatergrille.com, from 11:30am daily, dinner entrées $13-30) an excellent reputation. Dine inside or on the waterfront deck.

If you're venturing out to Cape Elizabeth, detour into **The Good Table** (527 Ocean House Rd./Rte. 77, Cape Elizabeth, 207/799-4663, www.thegoodtablerestaurant.net, 11am-9pm Tues.-Wed., 8am-9pm Thurs.-Sat., 8am-2pm Sun., entrées $9-20). Lisa Kostopoulos's popular local restaurant serves home-style favorites as well as Greek specialties.

Dine al fresco at **The Well at Jordan's Farm** (21 Wells Rd., Cape Elizabeth, 207/831-9350, 5pm-9pm Tues.-Sat., $20-26), where Jason Williams, a Culinary Institute of America grad, creates dinners from the working farm's bounty and other ingredients sourced locally. Everything is made from scratch. Seating is on picnic tables on the lawn and in a gazebo or at the four-stool kitchen bar. In an interesting twist, all prices on the four- or five-item menu are suggested. Cash only. BYOB.

Sea Glass (40 Bowery Beach Rd./Rte. 77, Cape Elizabeth, 207/299-3134, entrées $16-39), at the Inn by the Sea, pairs well prepared food with divine views. Dine indoors or on the deck, enjoying entrees such as sea scallops filet mignon, or an updated lobster bake. Sea Glass is open for breakfast, lunch, and dinner daily.

Every Mainer has a favorite lobster eatery (besides home), but **The Lobster Shack** (222 Two Lights Rd., Cape Elizabeth, 207/799-1677, www.lobstershacktwolights.com, 11am-8pm daily late Mar.-mid-Oct.) tops an awful lot of lists. Seniority helps—it's been here since the 1920s. There is scenery as well: a panoramic vista in the shadow of Cape Elizabeth Light. The menu has seafood galore, along with burgers and hot dogs for those who'd rather not have lobster. Opt for a sunny day; the lighthouse's foghorn can kill your conversation when the fog rolls in.

INFORMATION AND SERVICES

The **Visitor Information Center of the Convention and Visitors Bureau of Greater Portland** (14 Ocean Gateway Pier, 207/772-5800, www.visitportland.com) has info and public restrooms. The **Portland Downtown District** (207/772-6828, www.portlandmaine.com) and **LiveWork Portland** (www.liveworkportland.org) have helpful sites.

Check out the **Portland Public Library** (5 Monument Sq., 207/871-1700, www.portlandlibrary.com).

In the Old Port area, you'll find **public restrooms** at the Visitor Information Center

(14 Ocean Gateway Pier), Spring Street parking garage (45 Spring St.), Fore Street Parking Garage (419 Fore St.), and Casco Bay Lines ferry terminal (Commercial St. and Franklin St.). On Congress Street, find restrooms at Portland City Hall (389 Congress St.) and the Portland Public Library (5 Monument Sq.). In Midtown, head for the Cumberland County Civic Center (1 Civic Center Sq.). In the West End, use Maine Medical Center (22 Bramhall St.).

GETTING THERE AND AROUND

Portland is about 100 miles or two hours via I-95 from Boston, although during peak travel periods it can take longer because of congestion and toll lines. It's about 26 miles or 45 minutes via Route 1 from Kennebunk. It's about 17 miles or 20 minutes via Route 295 to Freeport.

The clean and comfortable **Portland Transportation Center** (100 Thompson Point Rd., 207/828-3939) is the base for **Concord Coachlines** (800/639-3317, www.concordcoachlines.com) and the **Amtrak Downeaster** (800/872-7245, www.amtrakdowneaster.com). Parking is $4/day, and the terminal has free coffee, free newspapers (while they last), and vending machines.

The **Metro** (207/774-0351, www.gpmetrobus.net $1.50/ride, $5/day pass, exact change required) bus service makes it easy to get around the city. Route 1 loops the downtown peninsula, stopping at the Portland Transportation Center, **Greyhound Bus** (www.greyhound.com), and **Casco Bay Lines ferry service** (www.cascobaylines.com); Route 8 services the West End, Old Port, Waterfront, and Bayside. Route 5 services **Portland International Jetport** (207/774-7301, www.portlandjetport.org).

Taxis charge $1.90 for the first 0.1 mile plus $0.30 for each additional 0.1 mile; minimum fare is $5; airport fares add $1.50 surcharge.

It's getting easier to get around Portland thanks to bike lanes on some roads. For bicycle rentals (from $25/day) and repairs, visit **Cycle Mania** (65 Cove St., 207/774-2933, www.cyclemania1.com). Also see **Portland Trails** (207/775-2411, www.trails.org) for mapped routes.

Parking

Street parking (meters or pay stations) is $1/hour. Parking garages and lots ($2-4/hour, $8-27/day) are strategically situated all over downtown Portland, particularly in the Old Port and near the civic center. Some lots accept Park and Shop stickers, each valid for one free hour, from participating merchants. The Casco Bay Lines website (www.cascobaylines.com) has a useful map listing parking lots and garages and their fees.

For winter parking-ban information, call 207/879-0300.

Casco Bay Islands

Casco Bay is dotted with so many islands that an early explorer thought there must be at least one for every day of the year and so dubbed them the Calendar Islands. Truthfully, there aren't quite that many, even if you count all the ledges that appear at low tide. No matter; the islands are as much a part of Portland life as the Old Port.

★ CASCO BAY TOUR

Casco Bay Lines (Commercial St. and Franklin St., Old Port, 207/774-7871, www.cascobaylines.com), the nation's oldest continuously operating ferry system (since the 1920s), is the lifeline between Portland and six inhabited Casco Bay islands. What better way to sample the islands than to take the three-hour ride along with mail, groceries, and island residents? The Casco Bay Lines Mailboat Run stops—briefly—at **Long Island, Chebeague, Cliff,** and **Little Diamond** and **Great Diamond Islands.** Departures are 10am and 2:15pm daily mid-June-early Sept., 10am and 2:45pm in other months. Fares are $15.50 adults, $13.50 seniors, and $7.75 ages 5-9.

The longest cruise on the Casco Bay Lines schedule is the nearly six-hour narrated summertime trip (late June-early Sept., $26 adults, $22.50 seniors, $12 ages 5-9) with a two-hour stopover on **Bailey Island,** departing from Portland at 10am daily. Dogs ($3.75) on leashes and bicycles ($7) need separate tickets.

For a shorter island hop, choose any of the island ferry runs and simply stay aboard for the round-trip.

PEAKS ISLAND

Peaks Island is a mere 20-minute ferry ride from downtown Portland, so it's no surprise that it has the largest year-round population. Historically a popular vacation spot—two lodges here were built for Civil War veterans—it was known as Maine's Coney Island at the turn of the 20th century.

Although you can walk the island's perimeter in 3-4 hours, the best way to see it is via bike (extra ferry cost $6.50 adults, $3.25 children), pedaling around clockwise. It can take less than an hour to do the five-mile island circuit, but plan to relax on the beach, savor the

Portland's skyline from Peaks Island

views, and visit the museums. Rental bikes are available on the island from Brad Burkholder at **Brad and Wyatt's Bike Shop** (115 Island Ave., Peaks Island, 207/766-5631, 10am-6pm daily, $10/2 hours-$20/day).

Other ways to see the island are on a 75-minute golf-cart tour with **Island Tours** (207/766-5514, www.peaksislandtours.com, $18 adults, $10 children); on a **taxi tour** with Island Transportation System (207/518-000, $10 pp; or on a rental golf cart with **Mike's Carts** (207/239-1777, $20/hour). Advance reservations are advised for all.

Civil War buffs have two museums worth visiting. The **Fifth Maine Regiment Center** (45 Seashore Ave., Peaks Island, 207/766-3330, www.fifthmainemuseum.org, noon-4pm Mon.-Fri., 11am-4pm Sat.-Sun. July 1-early Sept., 11am-4pm Sat.-Sun. late May-July 1 and early Sept.-mid-Oct., $5 donation) is a Queen Anne-style cottage built by Civil War veterans in 1888 that now houses exhibits on the war and island history. Just a few steps away is the **Eighth Maine Regimental Memorial** (13 Eighth Maine Ave., Peaks Island, 207/329-3530, www.8thmainepeaksisland.com, 11am-4pm daily, $5 requested donation). Tours detail the building's fascinating history and its collection of artifacts pertaining to the Eighth Maine as well as material on the island, World War II, and more.

Another museum perhaps worthy of a visit just for its quirkiness is the **Umbrella Cover Museum** (207/939-0301, www.umbrellacovermuseum.org, call for hours, donation), where owner Nancy 3. Hoffman (yes, 3) displays her Guinness World Record collection.

Bring a flashlight and waterproof footwear if you want to prowl around the World War II-era **Battery Steele.** It's located on the ocean side of the island and well camouflaged with greenery, now, but easy to find with a map. Free maps are available near the ferry dock; detailed color maps are also available for $6 in island stores, but I found the $1 color map available at Brad and Wyatt's Bike Shop handy for a day trip.

Accommodations

The **Inn on Peaks Island** (33 Island Ave., 207/766-5100, www.innonpeaks.com, from $199) overlooks the ferry dock and has jaw-dropping sunset views over the Portland skyline; no island roughing it here. The spacious cottage-style suites have fireplaces, sitting areas, and whirlpool baths.

On the other end of the Peaks Island luxury scale is the extremely informal and communal **Eighth Maine Living Museum and Lodge** (13 Eighth Maine Ave., 207/329-3530 or 239/789-7859, www.8thmainepeaksisland.com, from $150), a rustic shorefront living-history hostel-style lodge overlooking White Head Passage. Fifteen bedrooms sharing three baths and a huge shared kitchen allow you to rusticate in much the same manner as the Civil War vets who built this place in 1891 with a gift from a veteran who had won the Louisiana Lottery.

Food

Both **The Cockeyed Gull** (78 Island Ave., 207/766-2880, www.cockeyedgull.com, noon-8:30pm daily, entrées $10-27) and the **Shipyard Brewhaus** (33 Island Ave., 207/766-5100, www.innonpeaks.com, 11am-9pm daily, $9-24) have inside dining as well as outdoor tables with water views.

GREAT CHEBEAGUE

Everyone calls Great Chebeague just "Chebeague" (shuh-BIG). Yes, there's a Little Chebeague, but it's a state-owned park and no one lives there. Chebeague is the largest of the bay's islands—4.5 miles long by 1.5 miles wide—and the relatively level terrain makes it easy to get around. Don't plan to bring a car; it's too complicated to arrange. You can bike the leisurely 10-mile circuit of the island in a couple of hours, but unless you're in a hurry, allow time to relax and enjoy your visit.

Stop by the **Museum of Chebeague History** (137 South Rd., 207/846-5237, www.chebeaguehistory.com 10am-4pm Mon.-Sat., 1-4pm Sun.) for an intro to the island's history.

If the tide is right, cross the sand spit from The Hook and explore **Little Chebeague.** Start out about two hours before low tide (preferably around new moon or full moon, when the most water drains away) and plan to be back on Chebeague no later than two hours after low tide.

Back on Great Chebeague, when you're ready for a swim, head for **Hamilton Beach,** a beautiful small stretch of sand lined with dune grass and not far from the Chebeague Island Inn. Also on this part of the island is **East End Point,** with a spectacular panoramic view of Halfway Rock and the bay.

For a golfing adventure, play the nine-hole **Great Chebeague Golf Club** (207/846-0478, www.chebeagueislandgolf.com), which includes a tee box shared with a lobsterman.

Accommodations

Get that old-timey island experience at the **Chebeague Island Inn** (61 South Rd., Chebeague Island, 207/846-5155, www.chebeagueislandinn.com, from $250), an unfussy historical inn that's been gently updated. Rooms are small and some share baths. The restaurant serves all meals (breakfast is included), but it's hit or miss.

Food

Visitors to Chebeague Island have a few food choices. **Calder's Clam Shack** (108 North Rd., Chebeague Island, 207/846-5046, www.caldersclamshack.com, 11:30am-8pm Tues.-Sun.), a grab-and-go takeout, serves burgers, pizza, chowders, salads, sandwiches, and of course, fried seafood. **The Niblic** (207/846-4146, www.chebeagueislandboatyard.com), at the Chebeague Island Boat Yard, has sandwiches, soups, chowders, and baked goods as well as a nice selection of Maine-made gifts. The **Slow Bell Café** (207/846-3078), the island's bar, offers pub fare and dinner specials, along with live entertainment on weekends.

GREAT DIAMOND

A century ago, nearly 1,000 personnel were stationed here at Fort McKinley, the largest of five military complexes in Portland Harbor. Now most of the car-free island is a self-contained private community listed on the National Register of Historic Places. The barracks and officers' quarters are now private homes; the quartermaster's storehouse is the Diamond's Edge Restaurant; the quartermaster's office houses an art gallery and museum; and the blacksmith shop is the General Store. Overnight guests have access to the amenities,

A ferry approaches Great Diamond.

which include walking trails, pebble beaches, and bicycle rentals ($10/day) from the store. Day-trippers can enjoy the restaurant, store, volunteer-operated **Fort McKinley Museum** (http://fortmckinleymuseum.weebly.com), a historical trail, or arrange for a tour of the private community (email tours@diamond-cove.com).

Accommodations

Step inside the **Inn at Diamond Cove** (22 McKinley Ct., 207/805/9836, www.innatdiamondcove.com, from $300), and it's hard to believe the tony, contemporary accommodations were once occupied by soldiers. All rooms have wet bars, and most have balconies, though none has a water view. The inn has its own restaurant serving all meals (open to non-guests by reservation) as well as a heated pool.

Food

Diamond's Edge Restaurant (Diamond Cove, 207/766-5850, www.diamondsedgerestaurantandmarina.com, 11:30am-2:30pm and 5-9pm Tues.-Sun., $16-40), located within steps of the Diamond Cove ferry dock, has tables inside, on the porch, and on the lawn. Service can be hit or miss, but the food is excellent. If you need to catch a specific return ferry, make sure to let your server know in advance.

For a quick bite to eat, pick up sandwiches, pizza, and other goodies at the **General Store,** located less than 50 yards behind the restaurant.

EAGLE ISLAND

Seventeen-acre **Eagle Island** (207/624-6080, www.pearyeagleisland.org, 10am-5pm mid-June-early Sept., $3 Maine resident, $4.30 non-resident, $1 ages 5-11), a National Historic Site, juts out of Casco Bay, rising to a rocky promontory 40 feet above the crashing surf. On the bluff's crest, Robert Edwin Peary, the first man to lead a party to the North Pole without the use of mechanical or electrical devices, built his dream home. It's now a state historic site that's accessible via an excursion boat from Freeport. The half-day trip usually includes a narrated cruise to the island and time to tour the house, filled with Peary family artifacts, and wander the nature trails. Trails are usually closed until approximately mid-July to protect nesting eider ducks.

Peary envisioned the island's rocky bluff as a ship's prow and built his house to resemble a pilot house. Wherever possible, he used indigenous materials from the island

Robert Edwin Peary's Eagle Island home is open to visitors who arrive via Atlantic Seal Cruises.

in the construction, including timber drift, fallen trees, beach rocks, and cement mixed with screened beach sand and small pebbles. From the library, Peary corresponded with world leaders, adventurers, and explorers such as Teddy Roosevelt, the Wright brothers, Roald Amundsen, and Ernest Shackleton, and planned his expeditions. Peary reached the North Pole on April 6, 1909, and his wife, Josephine, was on Eagle Island when she received word via telegraph of her husband's accomplishment. After Peary's death in 1920, the family continued to spend summers on Eagle until Josephine's death in 1955. The family then donated the island to the state of Maine. A free self-guided audio tour is available at the Welcome Center, where you can view a 10-minute video about Peary and the island.

GETTING THERE

Ferries provide regularly scheduled transportation to most islands. Water taxis provide alternative transportation.

Casco Bay Lines (207/774-7871, www.cascobaylines.com) has service to **Peaks Island, Little Diamond, Great Diamond, Diamond Cove, Long Island, Chebeague Island,** and **Cliff Islands.** Round-trip tickets for each are in the range of $8-12 adult, $4-6 child/senior, $6.50 adult bike, $3.25 child bike.

Chebeague Transportation Company (207/846-3700, www.chebeaguetrans.com) ferries between causeway-connected Cousins Island, Yarmouth, and Chebeague Island. Round-trip fares are $16 adult, $3.50 ages 6-11. Parking in CTC's lots is $15-20, which includes shuttle to the ferry dock.

Atlantic Seal Cruises (207/865-6112, www.atlanticsealcruises.com), owned and operated by Captain Tom Ring, departs Town Wharf, in South Freeport, for twice-daily 2.5-hour cruises ($35 adults, $25 ages 5-12, $20 ages 1-5) to **Eagle Island.** The trip includes a lobstering demonstration (except Sunday, when lobstering is banned).

Freeport

Freeport has a special claim to historic fame—it's the place where Maine parted company from Massachusetts in 1820. The documents were signed on March 15, making Maine its own state.

At the height of the local mackerel-packing industry, countless tons of the bony fish were shipped out of South Freeport, often in ships built on the shores of the Harraseeket River. Splendid relics of the shipbuilders' era still line the streets of South Freeport, and no architecture buff should miss a walk, cycle, or drive through the village. Even downtown Freeport still reflects the shipbuilders' craft, with contemporary shops tucked in and around handsome historic houses. Some have been converted to bed-and-breakfasts, others are boutiques, and one even disguises the local McDonald's franchise.

Today, Freeport is best known as the mecca for the shop-till-you-drop set. The hub, of course, is sporting giant L. L. Bean, which has been here since 1912, when founder Leon Leonwood Bean began making his trademark hunting boots (and also unselfishly handed out hot tips on where the fish were biting). More than 120 retail operations now fan out from that epicenter, including many shops carrying Maine-made products. You can find almost anything in Freeport, except maybe a convenient parking spot in midsummer.

The town offers plenty for nonshoppers too. You can always find quiet refuge in the town's preserves and parks, along with plenty of local color at the Town Wharf in the still honest-to-goodness fishing village of South Freeport.

An orientation note: Don't be surprised to receive directions (particularly for South

Freeport) relative to "the Big Indian"—a 40-foot-tall landmark at the junction of Route 1 and South Freeport Road. If you stop at the Maine Visitor Information Center in Yarmouth and continue on Route 1 toward Freeport, you can't miss it.

SHOPPING

In Freeport, shopping is the biggest game in town. Anyone who visits is likely to darken the door of at least one shop.

★ L. L. Bean

If you visit only one store in Freeport, it's likely to be "Bean's." The whole world beats a path to **L. L. Bean** (95 Main St./Rte. 1, 207/865-4761 or 800/341-4341, www.llbean.com)—or so it seems in July-August and December. Established as a hunting and fishing supply shop, this giant sports outfitter now sells everything from kids' clothing to cookware on its ever-expanding downtown campus, with separate Hunting & Fishing; Home; and Bike, Boat & Ski stores. Look for the outlet store—a great source for deals on equipment and clothing—in the Village Square Shops across Main Street.

Until the 1970s, Bean's remained a rustic store with a creaky staircase and a closet-size women's department. Then a few other merchants began arriving, Bean's expanded, and a feeding frenzy followed. The Bean reputation rests on a savvy staff, high quality, an admirable environmental consciousness, and a no-questions-asked return policy. Bring the kids—for the indoor trout pond and the aquarium-viewing bulb, the clean restrooms, and the "real deal" outlet store. The main store's open-round-the-clock policy has become its signature; if you show up at 2am, you'll have much of the store to yourself, and you may even spy vacationing celebrities or the rock stars who often visit after Portland shows.

Outlets and Specialty Stores

After Bean's, it's up to your whims and your wallet. The stores stretch for several miles up and down Main Street and along many side streets. Pick up a copy of the *Official Map and Visitor Guide* at any of the shops or restaurants, at one of the visitor kiosks, or at the **Hose Tower Information Center** (23 Depot St., two blocks east of L. L. Bean). All the big names are here, as are plenty of little ones—don't overlook the small shops tucked on the side streets.

SIGHTS

Desert of Maine

Okay, so maybe it's a bit hokey, but talk about sands of time: More than 10,000 years ago, glaciers covered the region surrounding the **Desert of Maine** (95 Desert Rd., 207/865-6962, www.desertofmaine.com, early May-mid-Oct., $12.50 adults, $7.75 ages 13-16, $6.75 ages 4-12). When they receded, they scoured the landscape, pulverizing rocks and leaving behind a sandy residue that was covered by a thin layer of topsoil. Jump forward to 1797, when William Tuttle bought 300 acres and moved his family here along with his house and barn and cleared the land. Now jump forward again to the present and tour where a once-promising farmland has become a desert wasteland. The 30-minute guided safari-style tram tours combine history, geology, and environmental science and an opportunity for children to hunt for "gems" in the sand. Decide for yourself: Is the desert a natural phenomenon? A human-made disaster? Or does the truth lie somewhere in between?

Harrington House and Pettengill Farm

A block south of L. L. Bean is the **Harrington House** (45 Main St./Rte. 1, 207/865-3170, www.freeporthistoricalsociety.org, 9am-5pm Mon.-Sat. late May to mid-Oct., 10am-4pm Tues.-Fri. mid Oct.-late May, free), home base of the Freeport Historical Society. Pick up walking maps detailing Freeport's architecture for a small fee. Displays pertaining to Freeport's history and occasional exhibits by local artists are presented in two rooms in the restored 1830 Enoch Harrington House, a property on the National Register of Historic Places.

Also listed on the register is the society's **Pettengill Farm,** a 140-acre 19th-century saltwater farm comprising a circa-1810 saltbox-style house, woods, orchards, a salt marsh, and lovely perennial gardens. The farmhouse is open only during the annual Pettengill Farm Days in the fall, or by appointment, but the grounds are open at all times. From Main Street, take Bow Street 1.5 miles and turn right onto Pettengill Road. Park at the gate, and then walk along the dirt road for about 15 minutes to the farmhouse.

Eartha

She's a worldly woman, that Eartha. The **DeLorme Mapping Co.** (Rte. 1, Yarmouth, 207/846-7000, www.delorme.com/about/eartha.aspx) is home to the world's largest rotating and revolving globe, a three-story-tall spherical scale model of Earth. Eartha, as she's known, measures 41 feet in diameter with a 130-foot waist and weighs nearly three tons. She spins in DeLorme's glass-walled lobby, making her visible to passersby, but she's best appreciated up close and, well, as personal as you can get with a monstrous globe. Each continent is detailed with mountains and landforms, vegetation and civilization. She can be viewed 9:30am-5pm Monday-Friday. Take Route 1 south from downtown Freeport to the I-295 Exit 17 interchange; DeLorme is on the left.

Blueberry Pond Observatory

Prepare to be wowed by the night sky at the **Blueberry Pond Observatory** (355 Libby Rd., Pownal, 207/688-4410, www.blueberryobservatory.com), where you'll get exclusive viewings of constellations, planets, nebulas, asteroids, and galaxies. Guided two-hour tours, which include extensive viewing and digital astronomy pictures, cost $140 for the first adult and $20 for each additional adult; children 12 and younger are free. One-hour tours, which don't include photography, are half the cost.

Chocolate Tour

Take a 30-minute tour through **A. Wilbur's Candy Factory** (174 Lower Main St., 207/865-4071, $3.50) and enjoy plentiful samples while seeing how the chocolates and novelties are made.

The Big Indian

This 60-foot-tall landmark statute, created by Rodman Shutt in 1968, has welcomed visitors to Freeport since 1969. Originally commissioned by the Casco Bay Trading Post, it was restored in 2005.

ENTERTAINMENT

Shopping seems to be more than enough entertainment for most of Freeport's visitors, but don't miss the **L. L. Bean Summer Concert Series** (800/341-4341, ext. 37222). At 7:30pm most Saturdays early July-Labor Day weekend, Bean's hosts free big-name family-oriented events in Discovery Park, in the Bean's complex (95 Main St./Rte. 1). Arrive early—these concerts are *very* popular—and bring a blanket or a folding chair.

RECREATION

Parks, Preserves, and Other Attractions

MAST LANDING AUDUBON SANCTUARY

Just one mile from downtown Freeport, **Mast Landing Audubon Sanctuary** (Upper Mast Landing Rd., 207/781-2330, www.maineaudubon.org, free) is a reprieve from the crowds. Situated at the head of the tide on the Harraseeket River estuary, the 140-acre preserve has 3.5 miles of signed trails weaving through an apple orchard, across fields, and through pines and hemlocks. The name? Ages ago it was the source of masts for the Royal Navy. To find it, take Bow Street (across from L. L. Bean) one mile to Upper Mast Landing Road and turn left. The sanctuary is 0.25 mile along on the left.

WOLFE'S NECK WOODS STATE PARK

Five miles of easy to moderate trails meander through 233-acre **Wolfe's Neck Woods State Park** (Wolfe's Neck Rd., 207/865-4465, www.parksandlands.com, $4.50 nonresident adults, $3 Maine resident adults, $1 ages 5-11), just a few minutes' cycle or drive from downtown Freeport. You'll need a trail map, available near the parking area. The easiest route (and partly wheelchair-accessible) is the Shoreline Walk, about 0.75 mile, starting near the salt marsh and skirting Casco Bay. Sprinkled along the trails are helpful interpretive panels explaining various points of natural history—bog life, osprey nesting, glaciation, erosion, and tree decay. Guided tours are offered at 2pm daily mid-July-late August, weather permitting. Leashed pets are allowed. Adjacent **Googins Island,** an osprey sanctuary, is off-limits, but you can spy the nesting birds from the mainland (binoculars help). From down town Freeport, follow Bow Street (across from L. L. Bean) for 2.25 miles; turn right onto Wolfe's Neck Road (also called Wolf Neck Rd.) and go another 2.25 miles.

WOLFE'S NECK FARM

Kids love **Wolfe's Neck Farm** (10 Burnett Rd., 207/865-5433, www.wolfesneckfarm.org), a 626-acre saltwater farm dedicated to sustainable agriculture and environmental education. Visit with farm animals and enjoy the farm's trails and varied habitats—fields, forests, seashore, and gardens—at no charge. **Barnyard and organic garden tours** are held on Saturdays and Sundays during the summer months ($5). On the once-monthly **tractor-pulled Haywagon History Tours** (10am-noon Sat., $6 ages 13 and older) of the farmlands and Wolfe's Neck point, guides enthusiastically share Freeport's history and the region's ecology and weave in plenty of entertaining stories; advance reservations are requested, and a minimum of six guests is required. Bicycle ($18-22) and kayak ($30) rentals are available. Pumpkin hayrides are offered in the fall.

Mast Landing Audubon Sanctuary

WINSLOW MEMORIAL PARK

Bring a kite. Bring a beach blanket. Bring a picnic. Bring a boat. Bring binoculars. Heck, bring a tent. Freeport's 90-acre oceanfront town-owned playground, **Winslow Memorial Park** (207/865-4198, www.freeportmaine.com, $4) has a spectacular setting on a peninsula extending into island-studded Casco Bay. Facilities include a boat launch ($3-5), a campground ($25-35, no hookups), a fishing pier, a volleyball court, scenic trails, a playground, restrooms, picnic facilities, and a sandy beach (the best swimming is at high tide, and there is no lifeguard). On Thursday evenings in July-August, local bands play. The park is 5.5 miles from downtown. Head south on Route 1 to the Big Indian (you'll know it when you see it), go left on South Freeport Road for one mile to Staples Point Road, and follow it to the end.

BRADBURY MOUNTAIN STATE PARK

Six miles from the hubbub of Freeport, you're in tranquil, wooded 590-acre **Bradbury Mountain State Park** (Rte. 9, Pownal, 207/688-4712, www.parksandlands.com, $4.50 nonresident adults, $3 Maine resident adults, $1 ages 5-11), with facilities for picnicking, hiking, mountain biking, and rustic camping, but no swimming. Pick up a trail map at the gate and take the easy 0.4-mile round-trip Mountain Trail to the 485-foot summit, with superb views east to the ocean and southeast to Portland. It's gorgeous in fall. Or take the Tote Road Trail, on the western side of the park, where the ghost of Samuel Bradbury himself allegedly occasionally brings a chill to hikers in a hemlock grove. A playground keeps the littlest tykes happy. The camping fee is $19/site for nonresidents, $11 for residents. The park season is May 15-October 15, but there's winter access for cross-country skiing. Hawk Watch takes place mid-March-mid-May. From Route 1, cross over I-95 at Exit 20 and continue west on Pownal Road to Route 9 and head south.

★ L. L. Bean Outdoor Discovery Schools

Since the early 1980s, the sports outfitter's **Outdoor Discovery Schools** (888/552-3261, www.llbean.com) have trained thousands of outdoors enthusiasts to improve their skills in fly-fishing, archery, hiking, canoeing, sea kayaking, winter camping, cross-country skiing, orienteering, and even outdoor photography. Here's a deal that requires no planning: **Discovery Series Courses** ($25, includes equipment) provide 1.5-2.5-hour lessons in sports such as kayak touring, fly casting, archery, clay shooting, snowshoeing, and cross-country skiing. All of the longer fee programs, however, plus canoeing and camping trips, require preregistration well in advance. Some of the lectures, seminars, and demonstrations held in Freeport are free, and a regular catalog lists the schedule. Bean's waterfront **Flying Point Paddling Center** hosts many of the kayaking, saltwater fly-fishing, and guiding programs and is home to the annual **PaddleSports Festival** in June, with free demonstrations, seminars, vendors, lessons, and more.

L. L. Bean Kids' Camp

No need to drag your little ones through the outlets or find a sitter when you want to enjoy an adult-oriented experience. Enroll your child, ages 7-12, for a day or a week in Bean's summer **Kids' Camp** (888/552-3261, www.llbean.com). They'll have a blast exploring Maine's great outdoors with skilled instructors and counselors. Activities include canoeing, kayaking, stand-up paddleboarding, archery, fishing, crafts, nature walks, and more. All equipment is provided; you'll need to provide lunch and snacks. You can even arrange for early or late pickup for an additional fee. Rates vary with schedule.

Boat Excursions

Atlantic Seal Cruises (Town Wharf, South Freeport, 207/865-6112, www.atlanticsealcruises.com), owned and operated by Captain Tom Ring, makes two three-hour cruises ($35 adults, $25 ages 5-12, $20 ages 1-4) daily to 17-acre **Eagle Island** (www.pearyeagleisland.org), a State Historic Site once owned by Adm. Robert Peary, the North Pole explorer. The trip includes a lobstering demonstration (except Sunday, when lobstering is banned). Once a week, Ring offers a daylong excursion to **Seguin Island** ($55 ages 10 and older, $40 children), off the Phippsburg Peninsula, where you can climb the light tower and see Maine's only first-order Fresnel lens, the largest on the coast.

Kayak, Canoe, and Bike Rentals

Ring's Marine Service (Smelt Brook Rd., South Freeport, 207/865-6143, www.ringsmarineservice.com) rents single kayaks for $35, tandems for $50, and canoes for $30 (all prices per day), with longer-term rentals and delivery available. Bikes are $18 for a half-day.

ACCOMMODATIONS

Downtown

One of Freeport's pioneering bed-and-breakfasts is on the main drag, but away from much of the traffic, in a restored house where Arctic explorer Adm. Donald MacMillan once lived. The 19th-century **White Cedar Inn** (178 Main St., 207/865-9099 or 800/853-1269, www.whitecedarinn.com, $179-378) has seven attractive guest rooms and a two-bedroom suite with antiques, air-conditioning, and Wi-Fi; some have gas fireplaces. The full breakfast will power you through a day of shopping.

Two blocks north of L. L. Bean, the ★ **Harraseeket Inn** (162 Main St., 207/865-9377 or 800/342-6423, www.harraseeketinn.com, $235-315) is a splendid 84-room country inn with an indoor pool, cable TV, air-conditioning, phones, and Wi-Fi; many rooms have fireplaces and hot tubs. One room is decorated with Thomas Moser furnishings; otherwise, decor is colonial reproduction in the two historical buildings and a modern addition; some rooms have a fireplace, woodstove, or whirlpool tub. The inn is especially accessible, so it's a prime choice for anyone with mobility issues. Rates include a hot-and-cold buffet breakfast and afternoon tea with finger sandwiches and sweets—a refreshing break. Pets are permitted in some guest rooms for $25, which includes a dog bed, a small can of food, a treat, and dishes. Ask about packages, which offer great value. Children 12 and younger stay free. The inn is home to two excellent dining venues, and it's long been a leader in the farm-to-table movement. Free transportation is provided to and from the Amtrak station.

Three blocks south of L. L. Bean on a quiet side street shared with a couple of other bed-and-breakfasts is **The James Place Inn** (11 Holbrook St., 207/865-4486 or 800/964-9086, www.jamesplaceinn.com, $174-199). Innkeepers Robin and Tori Baron welcome guests to seven comfortable guest rooms, all with air-conditioning, Wi-Fi, flat-screen TVs, and DVD players; a few have double whirlpool

Shop Local in Freeport

Unlike many outlet centers across the country, Freeport has an excellent mix of local Maine stores in addition to the big name national company stores. L.L. Bean is the biggie, but you'll find close to three dozen stores with Maine roots. Here's a sampling:

- **Brahms Mount** (115 Main St., 207/869-4026): blankets, linens, and throws woven on antique shuttle looms
- **Brown Goldsmiths & Co.** (115 Mechanic St., 207/865-4126): handcrafted jewelry
- **Cuddledown** (574 Rte. 1, 207/865-1713): bedding, sleepwear, and linens
- **Edgecomb Potters** (8 School St., 207/865-1705): porcelain pottery
- **Georgetown Pottery** (148 Main St., 207/865-0060): hand-painted porcelain pottery
- **Island Treasure Toys** (20 Bow St., 207/865-7007): heirloom-quality children's toys
- **Jill McGowan** (56 Main St., 207/865-0909): the great white shirt
- **Maine Woolens** (124 Main St., 207/865-0755): wool and cotton blankets
- **R.D. Allen Freeport Jewelers** (13 Middle St., 207/865-1818): Maine tourmaline jewelry
- **Sea Bags** (6 Bow St., 207/939-3679): nautically inspired totes made from recycled sails
- **A. Wilbur's Candy Shoppe** (11-13 Bow St., 207/865-4071): chocolates
- **When Pigs Fly** (21 Main St., 207/865-6006): old world-style artisan breads
- **Wicked Whoppies** (32 Main St)., 207/865-3100: Maine's official snack

tubs, and one has a private deck and fireplace. If the weather is fine, enjoy breakfast on the inn's deck. After shopping, collapse on the hammock for two with a home-baked treat.

Beyond Downtown

Three miles north of downtown is the **Maine Idyll** (1411 Rte. 1, 207/865-4201, www.maineidyll.com, $76-136), a tidy cottage colony operated by the Marstaller family for three generations. It is a retro throwback and a find for budget-bound travelers. Twenty studio to three-bedroom pine-paneled cottages are tucked under the trees. The Ritz this is not, but all have refrigerators, microwaves, Wi-Fi, and TVs; some have kitchenettes; most have fireplaces. A light breakfast is included. Well-behaved pets are welcome for $4.

The family-run ★ **Casco Bay Inn** (107 Rte. 1, 207/865-4925 or 800/570-4970, www.cascobayinn.com, $111-141) is a bit fancier than most motels. It has a pine-paneled lounge with a fieldstone fireplace and a guest Internet station as well as Wi-Fi throughout. The spacious guest rooms have double sinks in the bath area, and some have a refrigerator and a microwave. A continental breakfast with a newspaper is included.

Camping

For anyone seeking peace, quiet, and low-tech camping in a spectacular setting, ★ **Recompence Shore Campsites** (134 Burnett Rd., 207/865-9307, www.freeportcamping.com, $26-48) is it. Part of Wolfe's Neck Farm Foundation, the eco-sensitive campground has 130 wooded tent sites and a few hookups, many on the farm's three-mile-long Casco Bay shorefront. Kayak, canoe, and bicycle rentals are available; swimming depends on the tides. Facilities include a playground and snack bar with Wi-Fi. Take Bow Street (across from L. L. Bean) to Wolfe's Neck Road, turn right, go 1.6 miles, then turn left on Burnett Road. Three pet-friendly oceanfront camping cabins are $130-170, plus $10/pet. Lobster bakes are held most Saturday evenings.

FOOD

Freeport has an ever-increasing number of places to eat, but there are nowhere near enough to satisfy hungry crowds at peak dining hours on busy days. Go early or late for lunch, and make reservations for dinner.

Local Flavors

South of downtown, **Royal River Natural Foods** (443 Rte. 1, 207/865-0046) has a small selection of prepared foods, including soups, salads, and sandwiches, and there is a seating area.

Craving a proper British tea? **Jacqueline's Tea Room** (201 Main St., 207/865-2123, www.jacquelinestearoom.com) serves a four-course Afternoon Tea, by reservation only, for about $25 pp in an elegant setting. Seatings for the two-hour indulgence are between 11am and 1pm Tuesday-Saturday. No reservations are necessary for the Cream Tea, which includes two scones, condiments, and a pot of tea. It is served 10:30am-2:30pm Tuesday-Saturday.

At the Big Indian **Old World Gourmet Deli and Wine Shop** (117 Rte. 1, 207/865-4477, www.oldworldgourmet.com, 9am-3pm Mon.-Sat.), the offerings are just as advertised, with sandwiches, soups, salads, and prepared foods. There are a few tables inside, but it's mostly a to-go place.

Can't decide what to eat? **Freeport Public Market** (20 Bow St., 207-865-9478, www.freeportmarket.com) is the answer. Under one roof are order-at-the-counter shops serving pizza and subs, smoothies and juices, crepes, and soups.

When you want to grab a quick lunch, **Li's Chinese Express Food Cart** (corner of Middle and Bow Streets, 347/323-5341, 11am-6pm daily) is just the spot for spring rolls and wok dishes.

Pair climbing Bradbury Mountain with breakfast or lunch at **Edna and Lucy's** (407 Hallowell Rd., Pownal, 207/688-3029, 8am-3pm Wed.-Fri., 8am-4pm Sat.-Sun.). The house-made doughnuts are a must.

Casual Dining

The Harraseeket Inn (162 Main St., 207/865-9377 or 800/342-6423) has two restaurants. The woodsy-themed ★ **Broad Arrow Tavern** (11:30am-10:30pm daily $12-36), just two blocks north of L. L. Bean but seemingly a world away, is a perfect place to escape shopping crowds and madness. The food is terrific, with everything made from organic and naturally raised foods. Can't decide? Opt for the extensive all-you-can-eat lunch buffet (11:30am-2pm Mon.-Sat., $18) that highlights a bit of everything. In early 2013, the inn teamed with the Maine Organic Farmers and Gardeners Association and the Maine Farmland Trust and completely renovated and enlarged its main restaurant, renaming it **Maine Harvest** (5:30pm-9pm daily, dinner entrées $20-38). The restaurant showcases not only farm-to-table fare but also the people who make it happen and the story behind preserving and cultivating organic farmland in the state. The menu emphasizes creative pairings and artistic presentations. Brunch (11:45am-2pm Sun., $26) is a seemingly endless buffet, with whole poached salmon and Belgian waffles among the highlights.

Good wine and fine martinis are what reels them into **Conundrum Wine Bistro** (117 Rte. 1, 207/865-0303, from 4:30pm Tues.-Sat., $12-38), near Freeport's Big Indian, but the food is worth noting too. Dozens of wines by the glass will keep most oenophiles happy. The food, varying from pork ramen and cheese platters to burgers and roasted salmon, helps keep patrons sober.

Ethnic Fare

Dine indoors or out on the tree-shaded patio at **Azure Italian Café** (123 Main St., 207/865-1237, www.azurecafe.com, from 11:30am daily). Go light, mixing selections from antipasto, *insalate,* and *zuppa* choices, or savor the heartier entrées ($18-38). The service is pleasant, and the indoor dining areas are accented by well-chosen contemporary Maine artwork. Live jazz is a highlight some evenings.

Down the side street across from Azure is **Mediterranean Grill** (10 School St., 207/865-1688, www.mediterraneangrill.biz, from 11am daily., entrées $18-34). Because it's off Main Street, the Cigri family's excellent Turkish-Mediterranean restaurant rarely gets the crowds. House specialties such as moussaka, lamb chops, and *tiropetes* augment a full range of kebab and vegetarian choices. Or simply make a meal of the appetizers—the platters are meals in themselves. Sandwiches and wraps are available at lunch.

Good food and attentive service has made **Thai Garden** (491 Rte. 1, 207/865-6005, 11am-9pm daily, $8-15), located south of downtown, an ever-popular choice.

Lobster

In South Freeport, order lobster in the rough at **Harraseeket Lunch and Lobster Company** (36 Main St., Town Wharf, South Freeport, lunch counter 207/865-4888, lobster pound 207/865-3535, www.harraseeket lunchandlobster.com, 11am-8:45pm daily summer, 11am-7:45pm daily spring and fall, no credit cards). Be prepared for crowds and a wait in midsummer. Fried clams are particularly good here, and they're prepared either breaded or battered. BYOB.

Far more peaceful is **Day's Seafood Takeout** (1269 Rte. 1, Yarmouth, 207/836-3436, www.dayscrabmeatandlobster.com, from 11am daily), with picnic tables out back overlooking a tidal estuary.

INFORMATION AND SERVICES

Freeport Merchants Association (Hose Tower, 23 Depot St., 207/865-1212 or 800/865-1994, www.freeportusa.com) produces an invaluable foldout map-guide showing locations of all the shops, plus sites of lodgings, restaurants, visitor kiosks, restrooms, and car and bike parking.

Just south of Freeport is the **Maine Visitor Information Center** (Rte. 1 at I-95 Exit 17, Yarmouth, 207/846-0833), part of the statewide tourism-information network. Also here are restrooms, phones, picnic tables, vending machines, and a dog-walking area.

GETTING THERE AND AROUND

Freeport is about 18 miles or 20 minutes via Route 295 from Portland. It's about 10 miles or 15 minutes via Route 295 to Brunswick. You'll need a car to explore beyond the downtown area.

Some **Amtrak Downeaster** (800/872-7245, www.amtrakdowneaster.com) trains stop in Freeport. The station is downtown, eliminating the need for a car unless you want to explore beyond the shops and in-town activities.

Mid-Coast Region

In contrast to the Southern Coast's gorgeous sandy beaches, the Mid-Coast region is characterized by a deeply indented shoreline with snug harbors and long, gnarled fingers of land. Even though these fingers are inconvenient for driving and bicycling, this is where you'll find picture-book Maine in a panorama format. Lighthouses, fishing villages, country inns, and lobster wharves pepper the peninsulas. The Mid-Coast, as defined in this chapter, stretches from Brunswick to Waldoboro.

The Bath-Brunswick area is one of the least touristy areas of the coast. Not that visitors don't come, but this area has a strong and varied economic base aside from tourism, which means that no matter when you visit, you'll find shops, restaurants, and lodgings open and activities scheduled. Bowdoin College and Bath Iron Works also contribute to a population more ethnically diverse than in most of Maine, and there's an active retiree population. Still, as you drive down the peninsulas that reach seaward from Bath and Brunswick, the vibrancy gives way to traditional fishing villages pressed by the hard realities of maintaining such lifestyles in the modern world.

Wiscasset still clings to the nickname of prettiest village in Maine, but for many travelers heading through on Route 1, Wiscasset is nothing but a headache. Traffic often backs up for miles, inching forward through the bottleneck village. Although many are just glad to get through it, those who take time to explore Wiscasset are rewarded with multitudes of antiques shops and lovely architecture.

The tempo changes northeast of Wiscasset. Traffic eases, and there's less roadside development. Detour down the Boothbay and Pemaquid Peninsulas, and you'll be rewarded with the Maine of postcards. These two peninsulas appear unchallenged as home to more lobster-in-the-rough spots than elsewhere on the coast, and Maine's creative economy is blossoming here, as evidenced by the abundant artists' and artisans' studios.

PLANNING YOUR TIME

Route 1 is the primary artery connecting all the points in the Mid-Coast region, and

Previous: fishing shack in the Harpswells; Pemaquid Point Light. **Above:** the Damariscotta Pumpkinfest.

Look for ★ to find recommended sights, activities, dining, and lodging.

Highlights

★ **Bowdoin College:** This beautiful shady campus is home to the Bowdoin College Museum of Art, the Peary-MacMillan Arctic Museum, and the Maine State Music Theater (page 128).

★ **Maine Maritime Museum:** It's easy to while away a half-day enjoying this museum's exhibits and riverfront setting (page 139).

★ **Coastal Maine Botanical Gardens:** This seaside garden comprises 250 acres of well-planned exhibits, trails, and art (page 157).

★ **Burnt Island Tour:** Step back in history and visit with a lighthouse keeper's family circa 1950 (page 159).

★ **Pemaquid Point Lighthouse:** It's hard to say which is Maine's prettiest lighthouse—but Pemaquid's is right up there. It's also depicted on the Maine state quarter (page 171).

★ **Colonial Pemaquid and Fort William Henry:** A beautiful setting overlooking John's Bay, a partially reconstructed fort, and remnants from one of the first British settlements in America make this site well worth a visit (page 172).

★ **Lobster in the Rough:** Lobster wharves abound in Maine, but the Pemaquid Peninsula has a concentration of scenic spots for lobster lovers (page 183).

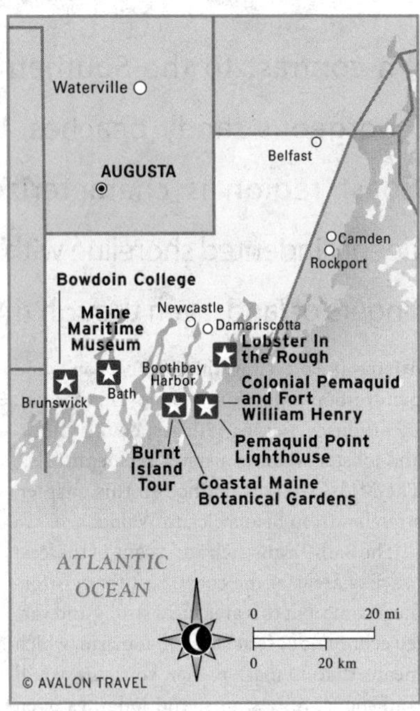

Mid-Coast Region

Wiscasset, a major bottleneck, is smack-dab in the middle. For this reason, it's best to split your lodging and explorations into two parts: south of Wiscasset and north of Wiscasset. Even then, driving down the long fingers of land requires patience. The towns south of Wiscasset are less touristy than those on the Boothbay or Pemaquid Peninsulas, with Orr's and Bailey's Islands and the Phippsburg Peninsula being the best places to sprout roots for old-time summer flavor.

To cover the region, you'll need 4-5 days. Antiques mavens should concentrate their efforts in Bath, Wiscasset, and Damariscotta. Allow at least two days to appreciate the fine museums in Brunswick and Bath, and another day to tour Wiscasset's historical house museums and nearby fort. If you're an avid or even aspiring kayaker, you'll want time to puzzle through the nooks and crannies of the coastline in a boat, and if you value parks and preserves, this region offers plenty worth your time.

Brunswick Area

Brunswick, straddling Route 1, was incorporated in 1738 and is steeped in history. It's home to prestigious Bowdoin College, classic homes and churches, several respected museums, and year-round cultural attractions.

Brunswick (pop. 20,278) and **Topsham** (pop. 8,784) face each other across roiling waterfalls on the Androscoggin River. The falls, which Native Americans knew by the tongue-twisting name of Ahmelahcogneturcook ("place abundant with fish, birds, and other animals"), were a source of hydropower for 18th-century sawmills and 19th-20th-century textile mills. Franco-Americans arrived in droves to beef up the textile industry in the late 19th century, but eventually lost their jobs in the Great Depression. Those once-derelict mills now house shops, restaurants, and offices.

Brunswick is also the gateway to the **Harpswells** (pop. 4,740), a peninsula-archipelago complex linked by causeways, several bridges, and a unique granite cribstone bridge. Scenic back roads on Harpswell Neck inspire detours to the fishing hamlets of **Cundy's Harbor, Orr's Island,** and **Bailey Island,** and once you're here, it's easy to want to linger.

SIGHTS

★ Bowdoin College

Bowdoin College (Brunswick, 207/725-3000, www.bowdoin.edu) got its start nearly 150 years before the now-defunct Naval Air Station landed on the nearby Brunswick Plains. Founded in 1794 as a men's college with a handful of students, Bowdoin, coed since 1969, now has 1,750 students. The college has turned out such noted graduates as authors Nathaniel Hawthorne and Henry Wadsworth Longfellow, sex pioneer Alfred Kinsey, U.S. president Franklin Pierce, Arctic explorers Robert Peary and Donald MacMillan, U.S. senators George Mitchell and William Cohen, and a dozen Maine governors. Massachusetts Hall, the oldest building on the 110-acre campus, dates from 1802. The stately Bowdoin pines, on the northeast boundary, are even older. The striking **David Saul Smith Union,** occupying 40,000 square feet in a former athletic building on the east

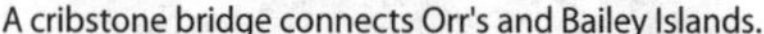
A cribstone bridge connects Orr's and Bailey Islands.

side of the campus, has a café, a pub, a lounge, and a bookstore open to the public. Call for information on admissions and **campus tours** (207/725-3100) and on **concerts, lectures,** and **performances** open to the public (207/725-3375).

Photos and artifacts bring Arctic expeditions to life at the small but fascinating **Peary-MacMillan Arctic Museum** (Hubbard Hall, 207/725-3416, www.bowdoin.edu/arctic-museum, 10am-5pm Tues.-Sat., 2pm-5pm Sun., free). Among the specimens are animal mounts, fur clothing, snow goggles, and Inuit carvings—most collected by Arctic pioneers Robert E. Peary and Donald B. MacMillan, both Bowdoin grads. Permanent exhibits highlight the natural and cultural diversity of the Arctic. The small gift shop specializes in Inuit books and artifacts.

An astonishing array of Greek and Roman artifacts is only one of the high points at the **Bowdoin College Museum of Art** (Walker Art Building, 207/725-3275, www.bowdoin.edu/art-museum, 10am-5pm Tues.-Sat., 10am-8:30pm Thurs., 2pm-5pm Sun., free). Designed in the 1890s by Charles McKim of the famed McKim, Mead, and White firm, it's a stunning neoclassical edifice with an interior rotunda and stone lions flanking the entry. In 2007 the museum was expanded and modernized, adding a striking bronze-and-glass entry pavilion to preserve the facade while also achieving accessibility. The college's prized Assyrian reliefs, previously in the magnificent rotunda, were moved to a glass-walled addition facing Brunswick's Park Row. The renovated museum is far more user-friendly, and a fitting setting for the impressive permanent collection of 19th- and 20th-century American art and other works.

Pejepscot Historical Society Museums

Side by side in an unusual cupola-topped duplex facing Brunswick's Mall (village green) are two museums operated by the **Pejepscot Historical Society** (207/729-6606, www.pejepscothistorical.org): the **Pejepscot Museum & Research Center** (159 Park Row, Brunswick, 10am-4pm Tues.-Sat., free) and the **Skolfield-Whittier House** (161 Park Row, Brunswick, tours on the hour 10am-3pm Wed.-Sat. late May-mid-Oct., $8.50 adults, $4 ages 6-16). Focusing on local history, the museum has a collection of more than 50,000 artifacts and mounts an always-interesting special exhibit each year. The 17-room Skolfield-Whittier House, on the right side of

Bowdoin College Museum of Art

the building, looks as though the owners just stepped out for the afternoon. Unoccupied 1925-1982, the onetime sea captain's house has elegant Victorian furnishings and lots of exotic artifacts collected on global seafaring stints.

The Pejepscot Historical Society also operates the **Joshua L. Chamberlain Museum** (226 Maine St., Brunswick, 207/729-6606, tours on the hour 10am-3pm Tues.-Sat., 1pm-3pm Sun., $8.50 adults, $4 ages 6-16). Across from First Parish Church, it commemorates the Union Army hero of the Civil War's Battle of Gettysburg, who's now gaining long-overdue respect. The partly restored house where Chamberlain lived in the late 19th century (and where Henry Wadsworth Longfellow had lived 30 years earlier) is a peculiar architectural hodgepodge with six rooms of exhibits of Chamberlain memorabilia, much of it Civil War-related. A gift shop stocks lots of Civil War publications, especially ones covering the Twentieth Maine Volunteers. A combination ticket for both historical houses is $15 adults, $6.50 children.

Also under the museum's umbrella is the **Brunswick Women's History Trail.** With more than 20 points of interest, the trail covers such national notables as authors Harriet Beecher Stowe and Kate Douglas Wiggin along with lesser-known lights, including naturalist Kate Furbish, pioneering Maine pediatrician Dr. Alice Whittier, and the Franco-American women who slaved away in the textile mills at the turn of the 20th century. A booklet ($1) is available from the museum; the tour is also mapped online.

Uncle Tom's Church

Across the street from the Chamberlain museum is the historic 1846 **First Parish Church** (9 Cleveland St. at Bath Rd., Brunswick, 207/729-7331), a Gothic Revival (or carpenter Gothic) board-and-batten structure crowning the rise at the head of Maine Street. Scores of celebrity preachers have ascended this pulpit, and Harriet Beecher Stowe was inspired to write *Uncle Tom's Cabin* while listening to her husband deliver an antislavery sermon here. Arrive here before noon any Tuesday early July-early August, when guest organists present 40-minute lunchtime concerts (12:10pm-12:50pm) on the 1883 Hutchings-Plaisted tracker organ, followed by a building tour. A $5 donation is requested. At other times, the church is open by appointment.

The Peary-MacMillan Arctic Museum is located on the Bowdoin College campus.

Joshua L. Chamberlain, Civil War Hero

When the American Civil War began in 1861, Joshua Chamberlain was a 33-year-old logic instructor at Bowdoin College in Brunswick; when it ended, in 1865, Chamberlain earned the Medal of Honor for his "daring heroism and great tenacity in holding his position on the Little Round Top." He was designated by Ulysses S. Grant to formally accept the official surrender of Confederate General John Gordon (both men represented the infantry). He later became governor of Maine (1867-1871) and president of Bowdoin College, but Chamberlain's greatest renown, ironically, came more than a century later—when 1990s PBS filmmakers focused on the Civil War and highlighted his strategic military role.

Joshua Lawrence Chamberlain was born in 1828 in Brewer, Maine, the son and grandson of soldiers. After graduating from Bowdoin in 1852, he studied for the ministry at Bangor Theological Seminary and then returned to his alma mater as an instructor.

With the nation in turmoil in the early 1860s, Chamberlain signed on to help, receiving a commission as a lieutenant colonel in the Twentieth Maine Volunteers in 1862. After surviving 24 encounters and six battle wounds and having been promoted to general (brigadier, then major), Chamberlain was elected Republican governor of Maine in 1866—by the largest margin in the state's history—only to suffer through four one-year terms of partisan politics. In 1871, Chamberlain became president of Bowdoin College, where he remained until 1883. He then dove into speechmaking and writing, his best-known work being *The Passing of the Armies*, a memoir of the Civil War's final campaigns. From 1900 to 1914, Chamberlain was surveyor of the Port of Portland, a presidential appointment that ended only when complications from a wartime abdominal wound finally did him in. He died at the grand old age of 86.

Brunswick's Joshua L. Chamberlain Museum, in his onetime home at 226 Maine Street, commemorates this illustrious Mainer, and thousands of Civil War buffs annually stream through the door in search of Chamberlain "stuff." To make it easier, the Pejepscot Historical Society has produced a helpful map titled "Joshua Chamberlain's Brunswick," highlighting town and college ties to the man—his dorm rooms, his presidential office, his portraits, even his church pew (number 64 at First Parish Church). Chamberlain's gravesite, marked by a reddish granite stone, is in Brunswick's Pine Grove Cemetery, just east of the Bowdoin campus.

Biennially, the museum celebrates **Chamberlain Days** with a symposium that concentrates on his roles in the war and in Maine. Typically, events include lectures by authors and scholars; field trips to places of interest connected with Chamberlain's life; tours of his home, concentrating on the most recent restoration work; musical or dramatic performances; and group discussions.

Brunswick Literary Art Walk

Cast your eyes downward while walking along Maine Street. Four bronze plaques recognize Brunswick's most famous writers: Henry Wadsworth Longfellow, Nathaniel Hawthorne, Harriet Beecher Stowe, and Robert P. T. Coffin. Each plaque bears a quote from the author commemorated.

Brunswick Fish Ladder

If you're in town mid-May-late June, plan to visit **Central Maine Power's Brunswick Hydro** generating station, straddling the falls on the Androscoggin River and the Brunswick-Topsham town line (Lower Maine St., next to Fort Andross). A glass-walled viewing room lets you play voyeur during the annual ritual of anadromous fish heading upstream to spawn. Amazingly undaunted by the obstacles, such species as alewives (herring), salmon, and smallmouth bass make their way from saltwater to freshwater via a 40-foot-high, 570-foot-long artificial fish ladder. The viewing room, which maxes out at about 20 people, is open 1pm-5pm Wednesday-Friday June-September.

ENTERTAINMENT

The **Maine State Music Theatre** (Pickard Theater, Bowdoin College, box office 1 Bath

Rd., Brunswick, 207/725-8769, www.msmt.org) has been a summer tradition since 1959. The renovated state-of-the-art air-conditioned theater brings real pros to its stage for four musicals (mid-June-late Aug., $36-50). Nonsubscription tickets go on sale in early May. Performances are at 8pm Tuesday-Saturday; matinees are staged at 2pm on an alternating schedule—each week has matinees on different days. No children under age four are admitted, but special family shows ($7-12) are performed during the season.

The **Bowdoin International Music Festival** (box office 12 Cleveland St., Brunswick, 207/725-3895, www.bowdoinfestival.org) is a showcase for an international array of classical talent of all kinds late June-early August. The six-week festival, part of an international music school, presents a variety of concert opportunities—enough that there's music almost every night of the week. Venues vary and tickets range from free to $40. Call or check the website for the current schedule.

Second Friday Art Walks (207/725-4366) take place in downtown Brunswick 5pm-8pm on the second Friday of the month May-September. Gallery openings, wine tastings, light refreshments, and other activities are usually part of the mix.

Music on the Mall presents family band concerts at 6pm-8pm Wednesday (Thursday if it rains) in July-August on the Brunswick Mall, the lovely park in the center of town.

FESTIVALS AND EVENTS

The first full week of August, the **Topsham Fair** is a weeklong agricultural festival with exhibits, demonstrations, live music, oxen pulls, contests, harness racing, and fireworks at the Topsham Fairgrounds.

The third Saturday of August, the **Maine Highland Games,** sponsored by the St. Andrew's Society of Maine, mark the annual wearing of the plaids—but you needn't be Scottish to join in the games, watch the Highland dancing, or browse the arts and crafts booths. (Only a Scot, however, can appreciate that unique concoction called haggis.)

SHOPPING

Downtown Brunswick invites leisurely browsing, with most of the shops concentrated on Maine Street. Take special care when crossing the four-lane-wide street, and do so only at marked crosswalks.

Art, Crafts, and Antiques Galleries

The **Bayview Gallery** (58 Maine St., Brunswick, 800/244-3007) specializes in contemporary New England artists.

More than 140 dealers show and sell their wares at **Cabot Mill Antiques** (14 Maine St., 207/725-2855), in the renovated Fort Andross mill complex next to the Androscoggin River.

Part gallery, part resource center, **Maine Fiberarts** (13 Maine St., Topsham, 207/721-0678, www.mainefiberarts.org) is a must-stop for anyone interested in fiber-related artwork: knitting, quilting, spinning, and basketry. If you're really interested in finding artists and resources statewide, check out the online resources.

Nearly two dozen local artists exhibit their works in varied media at **Sebascodegan Artists Gallery** (4 Orrs Island Rd., Rte. 24, Great Island, Harpswell, 207/833-5717).

Bookstore

With an eclectic new-book inventory that includes lots of esoterica, **Gulf of Maine Books** (134 Maine St., Brunswick, 207/729-5083) has held the competition at bay since the early 1980s. The fiction selection is particularly good, as are the religion, health, and poetry sections. Poet, publisher, and Renaissance man Gary Lawless oversees everything.

RECREATION

Parks and Preserves

In the village of Bailey Island, a well-maintained path edges the cliffs and passes the **Giant Stairs,** a waterfront stone stairway of mammoth proportions. To get there, take

Route 24 from Cooks Corner toward Bailey Island and Land's End, keeping an eye out for Washington Avenue, on the left about 1.5 miles after the cribstone bridge. (Or drive to Land's End, park the car with the rest of the crowds, survey the panorama, and walk 0.8 mile back along Route 24 to Washington Avenue from there.) Turn onto Washington Avenue, go 0.1 mile, and park at the Episcopal church (corner of Ocean St.). Walk along Ocean Street to the shorefront path. Watch for a tiny sign just before Spindrift Lane. Don't let small kids get close to the slippery rocks on the surf-tossed shoreline. The same advice holds for Land's End, where the rocks can be treacherous.

Thank the **Brunswick-Topsham Land Trust** (108 Maine St., Brunswick, 207/729-7694, www.btlt.org), founded in 1985, for access to the 11-acre shorefront **Alfred Skolfield Preserve,** historically a portage site for Native Americans and later home to a shipyard. One of the two blue-blazed nature-trail loops skirts a salt marsh, where you're apt to see egrets, herons, and ospreys in summer. Take Route 123 (Harpswell Rd.) south from Brunswick about three miles; when you reach the Middle Bay Road intersection (on the right), continue on Route 123 for 1.1 miles. Watch for a small sign and a small parking area on the right.

Tucked behind the Harpswell town office, off the Mountain Road linking Route 123 with Route 24, the **Cliff Trail** is a 1.5-mile loop that follows the shoreline along Strawberry Creek, passes through forests with fairy houses, and rises to 150-foot cliffs with dreamy views over Long Reach.

Nearly four miles of trails wind through fields and forests and edge cliffs on the 118-acre **Bowdoin College Coastal Studies Center,** a spectacular chunk of oceanfront tipping an Orr's Island peninsula. It's likely you'll have the seven trails practically to yourself. To find it, take Route 24 south and then turn right on Bayview Road (just under two miles beyond the bridge). Keep right at the fork. When the road turns to gravel, continue to a parking area with an info kiosk where you can pick up a trail map.

Swimming

Thomas Point Beach (29 Meadow Rd., Brunswick, 207/725-6009 or 877/872-4321, www.thomaspointbeach.com, 9am-sunset daily mid-May-Sept., $4 adults, $2 ages 3-12) is actually 85 acres of privately owned parkland with facilities for swimming (lifeguard on duty, bathhouses), fishing, field sports, picnicking (500 tables), and camping (75 tent and RV sites for $26; no water or sewer hookups, but electricity and a dump station are available). No pets, skateboards, or motorcycles are allowed. The sandy beach is tidal, so the swimming "window" is about two hours before high tide until two hours afterward; otherwise, you're wallowing in mudflats. The same timing applies to kayakers and canoeists. Toddlers head for the big playground; teenagers gravitate to the arcade and the ice cream parlor. From Cooks Corner, take Route 24 south 1.5 miles, turn left, and follow signs for less than two miles to the park.

A popular, family-oriented spot for freshwater swimming is **White's Beach** (Durham Rd., Brunswick, 207/729-0415, www.whitesbeachandcampground.com, $3.50 adults, $2.50 seniors and under age 13). The sandy-bottomed pond maxes out at nine feet. In mid-July the campground hosts a popular family bluegrass festival. Park facilities include a snack bar, a playground, hot showers, and campsites ($22-33). From Route 1 just south of the I-95 exit into Brunswick, take Durham Road 2.2 miles northwest.

Boat Excursions

Departing at noon from the Cook's Lobster House wharf (Cook's Landing) in Bailey Island (off Rte. 24), a large sturdy **Casco Bay Lines ferry** (207/774-7871, www.cascobaylines.com, $16 adults, $7.50 ages 5-9) does a 1.75-hour nature-watch circuit of nearby islands, including Eagle Island, the onetime home of Admiral Robert Peary (there are no stopovers on these circuits). Reservations aren't needed.

Sea Escape Charters (Bailey Island, 207/833-5531, www.seaescapecottages.com) operates two- to six-hour sails aboard the Schooner *Alert* ($40-100/adult, $32-80/child), a 70-foot Maine-built windjammer. Trips operate out of Sea Escape Cottages, one- or two-bedroom well-equipped cottages with full kitchens and oceanside decks, along with three suites that rent for $165-199/night or $955-1,175/week.

Sea Kayaking

H2Outfitters (Orr's Island, 207/833-5257 or 800/205-2925, www.h2outfitters.com) has been a thriving operation since 1978. Based in a wooden building on the Orr's Island side of the famed cribstone bridge, this experienced company organizes guided trips, including island camping; all gear is included. A three-hour tour is $75 pp for two. If you're up for a full day of paddling, opt for the Eagle Island tour ($125 pp for two).

Seaspray Kayaking (207/443-3646 or 888/349-7772, www.seaspraykayaking.com) has bases on the New Meadows River in Brunswick and Sebasco Harbor Resort in Phippsburg as well as rental centers in Georgetown and at Hermit Island Campground, Small Point. The New Meadows base is particularly good for those nervous about trying the sport. Rentals are $15-25 for the first hour, $5-10 for each additional hour, and $25-50/day. Equipment options include solo and tandem kayaks, recreational kayaks, surf kayaks, paddleboards, and canoes. Tours, led by registered Maine Guides, vary from sunset paddles to three-day expeditions and include moonlight paddles, island-to-island tours, and inn-to-inn tours. Rates begin at $50 adults. A striper-fishing kayak tour, including tackle and instruction, is $85.

If you're an experienced sea kayaker, consider exploring Harpswell Sound from the boat launch on the west side of the cribstone bridge; kayaks can also be put in at Mackerel Cove, near Cook's Lobster House. A launch with plentiful parking is at Sawyer Park on the New Meadows River, on Route 1 just before you cross the river heading north.

ACCOMMODATIONS

Motels and Inns

The Brunswick Hotel and Tavern (4 Noble St., Brunswick, 207/837-6565, www.thebrunswickhotelandtavern.com, $180-280), opened in 2011, is adjacent to the station where Concord Coachlines bus stops and Amtrak's Downeaster dock; it's also across from the town green and within steps of Bowdoin College. Historical photographs hung throughout and nods to Bowdoin's polar bear mascot offset the contemporary decor. Amenities include a locally popular restaurant with an outdoor patio and a fitness room. A dog-friendly room is available.

Continue another mile down Route 24, cross the cribstone bridge, and you'll come to Chip Black's **Bailey Island Motel** (Rte. 24, Bailey Island, 207/833-2886, www.baileyislandmotel.com, $140), a congenial, clean, no-frills waterfront spot with 11 guest rooms and wowser views. Kids under 10 stay for free; age 10 and older are $15 extra. Continental breakfast is included, and guest rooms have Wi-Fi, cable TV, and a small fridge. A dock is available for boat launching.

Looking rather like the film set of an old-fashioned tearjerker, the family-run **Driftwood Inn** (81 Washington Ave., Bailey Island, 207/833-5461, www.thedriftwoodinnmaine.com, no credit cards) has 25 rustic pine-paneled guest rooms in four buildings (some with a private toilet and sink; all with shared showers), six housekeeping cottages, a saltwater pool, a stunning view, a dining room, and a determinedly take-us-as-we-are ambience. There are no frills, period, but it has oceanfront porches, games, and rare old-fashioned simplicity. You'll sleep at night listening to the waves crash on the rocky shore. It's all on three oceanfront acres near the Giant Stairs. The dining room, open to non-guests by reservation, serves solid Maine fare with an emphasis on seafood late June-early

September for $18-30; breakfast is $7.25. Meals aren't offered during spring and fall. Rooms are $80-130, and cottages rent by the week ($685-1,000). Dogs are allowed in the cottages.

Bed-and-Breakfasts

Right downtown, facing the tree-shaded Mall, is ★ **The Brunswick Inn** (165 Park Row, Brunswick, 207/729-4914 or 800/299-4914, www.brunswickbnb.com, year-round, from $180), a stately 30-room Federal mansion built in 1848. Fine art from a local gallery hangs throughout the inn, complementing the handsome decor. Fifteen comfortable guest rooms are split between the main house and the renovated Carriage House (with two fully accessible guest rooms); all have Wi-Fi and phones, and some have TVs. There's also a small cottage with a kitchen. Inside the main inn is a laid-back lounge with occasional entertainment.

Within walking distance of downtown Brunswick, but across the bridge spanning the Androscoggin River, is the **Black Lantern B&B** (57 Elm St., Topsham, 888/306-4165, www.blacklanternbandb.com, $110-125), Tom and Judy Connelie's lovely 1860s riverfront home. All guest rooms are decorated with an emphasis on comfort, and two have water views. Judy's quilts will warm you on a cool night.

On the outskirts of town, in a rural location smack-dab on Middle Bay, is **Middle Bay Farm Bed and Breakfast** (287 Pennellville Rd., Brunswick, 207/373-1375, www.middlebayfarm.com, year-round, $170-190), lovingly and beautifully restored by Phyllis Truesdell, who bought the property after it sat all but abandoned for a decade. Once the site of the Pennell Brothers Shipyard, the farmhouse and sail loft now house guests seeking an away-from-it-all yet convenient location. Four water-view guest rooms in the 1834 farmhouse are decorated with antiques and have TVs and video players. Also in the main house is a living room with fireplace and grand piano. Two suites in the sail loft each have a living room with a kitchenette and two tiny bedrooms, and they share an open porch. All guests receive a full breakfast in the water-view dining room. Bring a sea kayak to launch from the dock if you'd like.

At the 1761 **Harpswell Inn** (108 Lookout Point Rd., South Harpswell, 207/833-5509 or 800/843-5509, www.harpswellinn.com, year-round), innkeepers Anne and Dick Moseley operate a comfortable, welcoming,

The Brunswick Inn

antiques-filled oasis on 2.5 secluded water-view acres. It's tough to break away from the glass-walled great room, but Middle Bay sunsets from the porch can do it. In fall, the foliage on two little islets in the cove turns brilliant red. The bed-and-breakfast has seven guest rooms ($155-190), three suites ($240-260), and four cottages ($1,050-1,580/week). Prices are slightly higher for one-night stays.

Thirteen miles south of Cooks Corner, **The Log Cabin** (Rte. 24, Bailey Island, 207/833-5546, www.logcabin-maine.com, $179-339) has nine nicely decorated guest rooms with phones, TVs and video players, private decks facing the bay, and, weather permitting, splendid sunset views to the White Mountains. Four guest rooms have kitchen facilities; some have gas fireplaces or whirlpool tubs. There's also an outdoor heated pool. Full breakfast is included; dinner ($18-34) is available.

FOOD

Local Flavors

★ **Wild O.A.T.S. Bakery and Café** (149 Maine St., Tontine Mall, Brunswick, 207/725-6287, www.wildoatsbakery.com, 7am-5pm daily) turns out terrific made-from-scratch breads and pastries, especially the breakfast kind, in its cafeteria-style place. (Just so you know, the name stands for Original and Tasty Stuff.) It has inside and outside tables, moderate prices, good-for-you salads, and great sandwiches.

For food on the run—no-frills hot dogs straight from the cart—head for Brunswick's Mall, the village green where **Danny's on the Mall** (no phone) has been cooking dirt-cheap tube steaks since the early 1980s.

Fat Boy Drive-In (Bath Rd./Old Rte. 1, Brunswick, 207/729-9431, 11am-8pm daily, no credit cards) is a genuine throwback—a landmark since 1955, boasting carhops, window trays, and a menu guaranteed to clog your arteries. Onion rings, frappés, and BLTs are specialties. Aim for the second Saturday in August, when the annual Sock Hop takes place.

Choose from about 30 flavors of gelato and *sorbetto* at **The Gelato Fiasco** (74 Maine St., Brunswick, 207/607-4002, 11am-11pm daily). You can find these to-die-for gelati statewide, but this is ground zero.

A favorite for chowder is **Salt Cod Cafe** (1894 Harpswell Islands Rd., Orr's Island, 207/833-6210, 8am-5pm daily), with a primo location overlooking the cribstone bridge. Sandwiches, wraps, rolls, and baked goods are also available.

The chocolates, truffles, and bark made by Melinda Harris Richter are divine at **Island Candy Company** (Harpswell Islands Rd., Orr's Island, 207/833-6639, 11am-8pm daily in season), and there are baked goods, ice cream, and a lovely garden, too.

The **Brunswick Farmers Market** sets up rain or shine on the Mall (village green) 8am-2pm Tuesday and Friday May-November; Friday is the bigger day. **The Brunswick-Topsham Land Trust Farmers' Market** takes place from 8:30am-12:30pm Saturday at Crystal Spring Farm, Pleasant Hill Road. You'll find produce, cheeses, crafts, condiments, live lobsters, and serendipitous surprises, depending on the season.

Family Favorites

Just over the bridge from Brunswick, in the renovated Bowdoin Mill complex overlooking the Androscoggin River, the **Sea Dog Brewery** (1 Main St., Topsham, 207/725-0162, www.seadogbrewing.com, 11:30am-1am daily, $10-26) has seating inside and on a deck overhanging the river. The menu ranges from burgers and sandwiches to full-plate entrées. It offers frequent acoustic entertainment, and there are games for kids, a video arcade, and pool tables.

Ethnic and Eclectic Fare

Greek fisherman's stew, saltimbocca alla Romana, handmade organic pastas, and *arancini* are just a few of the Greek and Italian choices that might appear on the seasonally changing menu at ★ **Trattoria Athena** (25 Mill St., Brunswick, 207/721-0700, www.trattoriaathena.com, 5pm-9pm Tues.-Sat.,

$18-26). The dining area is small, with a cozy rustic vibe that complements the cuisine. This gem, about a block off Maine Street, is worth finding. Sister restaurant **Enoteca Athena** (97 Main St., 207/721-0100, www.enotecaathena.com, from 3:30pm Mon.-Sat., $13-20) is a casual wine bar with a menu focused on rustic Greek and Italian fare.

You'll find decent sushi and Japanese specialties at **Little Tokyo** (72 Maine St., Brunswick, 207/798-6888, www.littletokyomaine.com, 11:30am-9:30pm daily, entrées $12-25).

★ **Tao Yuan** (22 Pleasant St., Brunswick, 207/725-9002, www.tao-yuan.me, 5-9pm Tues.-Thurs., 5pm-10pm Fri.-Sat.) wows guests with fresh and innovative Asian cuisine masterfully prepared by chef-owner Cara Stadler, who trained with master chefs in France and China and has been nominated for a Beard award. Tapas-sized portions run $7-18. Also available are 15-course tasting ($68) and pre-theater ($48 before 6pm) menus.

Generous portions, moderate prices, efficient service, and narrow aisles are the story at **The Great Impasta** (42 Maine St., Brunswick, 207/729-5858, www.thegreatimpasta.com, 11am-9pm Mon.-Thurs., 11am-10pm Fri.-Sat., $15-26), a cheerful, informal eatery where the garlic meets you at the door. There are gluten-free choices and a "bambino menu" for the kids.

Eclectic doesn't begin to describe **Frontier Cafe** (Mill 3, Fort Andross, 14 Maine St. at Rte. 1 overpass, Brunswick, 207/725-5222, www.explorefrontier.com, 11am-9pm Sun. and Tues.-Thurs., 11am-10pm Fri.-Sat., kitchen closes one hour earlier, entrées $12-26), a combination café, gallery, and cinema inspired by founder Michael Gilroy's world travels. The menu includes wonderful market plates emphasizing the cuisine of a country or region—Spain, France, the Middle East, Italy, or global—as well as other worldly flavors, burgers, and vegetarian and vegan options. Desserts are homemade, and there's also a kids' menu. Wine and beer are served. Films are screened, and there are frequent events and entertainment.

World-class beer is the focus at **Ebenezer's Brew Pub and Lively Brewing Co.** (112 Pleasant St., Brunswick, 207/373-1840, www.lionspridepub.com, 11:30-1 am Mon.-Sat., 9-1am Sun.), where the Maine-accented pub favorites menu ($8-30) is geared around the brews. In addition to the in-house brews on draft, some rather obscure pours (emphasis on Belgian) are drawn from 35 handblown glass taps.

Hip, funky, and full of personality describe **El Camino** (15 Cushing St., Brunswick, 207/725-8228, www.elcaminomaine.com, 5pm-9pm Tues.-Sat.), which uses fresh, local, and often organic ingredients to create innovative Cal-Mex fare such as crabmeat-and-avocado quesadillas. Prices top out around $18, although specials are more.

Pho fans will find it as well as other Vietnamese fare at **Lemongrass** (212 Maine St., Brunswick, 207/725-9008, www.lemongrassme.com, 11am-2:30pm and 4-9pm Tues.-Sun., $9-16).

Lobster and Seafood

You want fresh? You want simple? **Erica's Seafood** (Basin Point Rd., Harpswell, 207/833-7354, www.ericasseafood.com, 11am-7pm daily), a seasonal takeout on a working wharf overlooking Casco Bay, delivers on both counts. The menu includes lobster and crabmeat rolls, fried seafood, chowders, and burgers. The only seating is on picnic tables.

Arguments rage endlessly about who makes the best chowder in Maine, but ★ **The Dolphin Marina and Chowder House** (Dolphin Marina, 515 Basin Point Rd., South Harpswell, 207/833-6000, www.dolphinmarinaandrestaurant.com, 11:30am-8pm daily May 1-Oct. 31, $10-36) tops lots of lists for its fish chowder, accompanied by a blueberry muffin. Equally famed is its lobster stew; plus, you can't beat the scenic 13-mile drive south from Brunswick or the spectacular sea and island views through the rounded row of windows of its new, waterfront building.

Other good bets for lobster, along with chowders and fried seafood, are **Gurnet Trading Co.** (602 Gurnet Rd./Rte. 24, Brunswick, 207/729-7300, www.gurnettrading.com), serving lunch and dinner daily overlooking Buttermilk Cove and **Morse's Cribstone Grill** (1945 Harpswell Islands Rd., Bailey Island, 207/833-7775, www.morsescribstonegrill.com, 11:30am-9pm Mon.-Sat., noon-8pm Sun.), perched on the shorefront adjacent to the bridge.

INFORMATION AND SERVICES

Area information is provided by the **Southern Midcoast Chamber of Commerce** (877/725-8797, www.midcoastmaine.com) and the **Harpswell Business Association** (www.harpswellmaine.org).

Check the website of **Curtis Memorial Library** (23 Pleasant St., Brunswick, 207/725-5242, www.curtislibrary.com) for excellent local resources and guides.

GETTING THERE AND AROUND

Brunswick is about 10 miles or 15 minutes via Route 295 from Freeport. It's about nine miles or 15 minutes via Route 1 to Bath.

The **Amtrak Downeaster** (800/872-7245, www.amtrakdowneaster.com) makes two daily trips between Boston and Brunswick, with Maine stops in Saco, Wells, Old Orchard (seasonal), Portland, and Freeport en route.

Bath Area

One of the smallest in area among Maine's cit ies, **Bath** (pop. 8,514), packs a wallop in only nine square miles. Like Brunswick, it straddles Route 1 and edges a river, but Bath's centuries of historical and architectural tradition and well-preserved Victorian downtown have earned it a prized designation: The National Trust for Historic Preservation named it a Distinctive Destination.

Giant cranes dominate the riverfront cityscape at the huge Bath Iron Works complex, source of state-of-the-art warships—your tax dollars at work. Less evident (but not far away) is the link to the past: Just south of Bath, in Popham on the Phippsburg Peninsula, is the poorly marked site where a trouble-plagued English settlement, a sister colony to Jamestown, predated the Plymouth Colony by 13 years. (Of course, Champlain arrived before that, and Norsemen left calling cards even earlier.) In 1607-1608 settlers in the Popham Colony managed to build a 30-ton pinnace, *Virginia of Sagadahoc,* designed for transatlantic trade, but they lost heart during a bitter winter and abandoned the site.

Bath is the jumping-off point for two peninsulas to the south—**Phippsburg** (pop. 2,216, of Popham Colony fame) and **Georgetown** (pop. 1,042). Both are dramatically scenic, with glacier-carved farms and fishing villages. Drive (bicycling is best left to experienced pedalers) a dozen miles down any of these fingers and you're in different worlds.

Across the Sagadahoc Bridge from Bath is **Woolwich** (pop. 3,072), from where you can continue northeastward along the coast or detour northward on Route 128 to the hamlet of Day's Ferry. Named after 18th-century resident Joseph Day, who shuttled back and forth in a gondola-type boat across the Kennebec River, the picturesque village has a cluster of 18th- and 19th-century homes and churches—all part of the Day's Ferry Historic District. The village's Old Stage Road saw many a stagecoach in its day; passengers would ferry from Bath and pick up the stage here to travel onward.

SIGHTS

Bath Iron Works

Known locally as BIW or The Yard, **Bath Iron Works** has been building ships on this

50-acre riverfront site since 1890. Currently its roughly 5,700 employees build destroyers for the U.S. Navy. BIW is open to the public for launchings, when it's a mob scene with hordes of politicos, townsfolk, and military pooh-bahs in their scrambled eggs and brass. The best way to get a peek at the workaday world behind the gates is on a Bath Iron Works Trolley Tour with the Maine Maritime Museum.

★ Maine Maritime Museum

Spread over 25 acres on the Kennebec River is the state's premier marine museum, the **Maine Maritime Museum** (243 Washington St., Bath, 207/443-1316, www.mainemaritimemuseum.org, 9:30am-5pm daily, $15 adults, $13.50 seniors $10 ages 6-16). On the grounds are five original 19th-century buildings from the Percy and Small Shipyard (1897-1920), a late-Victorian home and hands-on exhibits, but the first thingk you see is the architecturally dramatic **Maritime History Building,** locale for permanent and temporary displays of marine art and artifacts and a shop stocked with nautical books and gifts. Bring a picnic (or purchase lunch at the seasonal Even Keel Snack Bar) and let the toddlers loose in the children's pirate's play area. Then either wander the campus on your own or join one of the guided tours. Don't miss the boat shop, where volunteers build and restore small vessels. Shipyard demonstrations are held on a rotating schedule, and brown-bag lectures are often given. In summer, weather permitting, the museum sponsors a variety of special river cruises; call for information. May-mid-October the museum offers fascinating one-hour **Bath Iron Works Trolley Tours** ($30 adults, $15 under age 17, includes two-day museum admission) conducted by former BIW employees. You'll need to reserve a week or longer in advance; it's well worth the effort. Pair it with a one-hour cruise to view the yard from the river. The museum is open year-round; the Percy and Small Shipyard is year-round but in winter only as conditions permit, with reduced-price admissions.

Bath Walking Tours

Sagadahoc Preservation (www.sagadahocpreservation.org), founded in 1971 to rescue the city's architectural heritage, details self-guided walking and driving architectural tours on its website. Sagadahoc Preservation also offers an annual house tour, usually in June; check the website for details.

ENTERTAINMENT AND EVENTS

Bath's most diversified entertainment setting is the **Center for the Arts at the Chocolate Church** (804 Washington St., Bath, 207/442-8455, www.chocolatechurch.com), a chocolate-brown board-and-batten structure built in 1846 as the Central Congregational Church. Year-round activities at the arts center include music and dance concerts, dramas, exhibits, and children's programs.

At 7pm every Tuesday and Friday mid-June-August, the **Gazebo Concert Series** brings live entertainment to Bath's Library Park.

The **Third Friday Art Walk** takes place 4-7pm on the third Friday of the month June-September.

Throughout the summer, the **Maine Maritime Museum** (207/443-1316) schedules special events, often hinging on visits by tall ships and other vessels. Some of the visiting boats are open to the public for an extra fee.

November-April, 50 dealers show their wares at the monthly **Bath Antiques Shows** (www.bathantiquesshows.com, $4) at the Bath Middle School.

The **Drummore Bay Concert Hall** (526 Main Rd./Rte. 209, Phippsburg, 207/446-7199, http://drummorebayconcerthall.com), a renovated Grange hall, is the site of a summer concert series.

SHOPPING

Front and Center Streets are lined with fun, independent shops.

Bath is home to **The Mustard Seed Bookstore** (74 Front St., Bath, 207/389-4084)

Bath Area

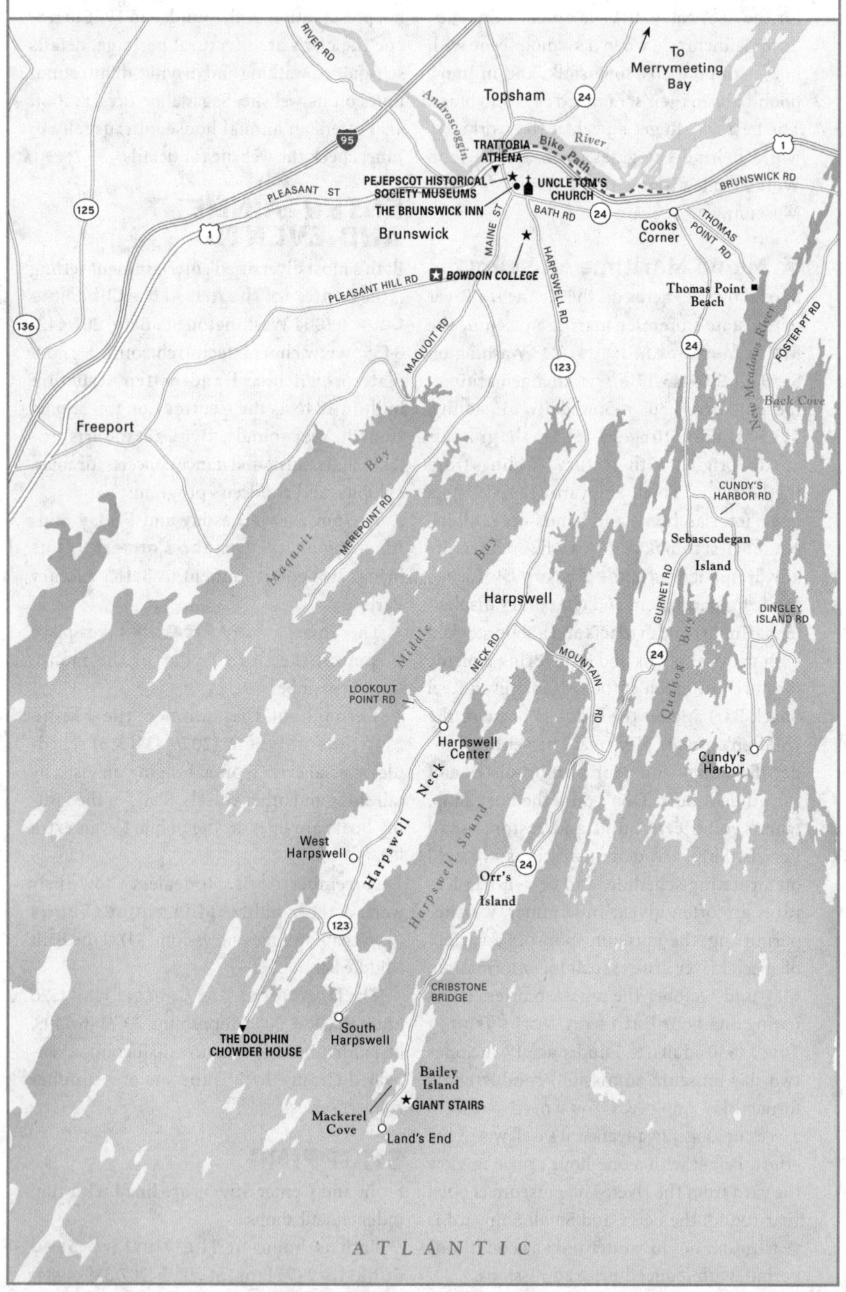
To Merrymeeting Bay
RIVER RD
Topsham
24
Androscoggin River
95
Bike Path
1
TRATTORIA ATHENA
PEJEPSCOT HISTORICAL SOCIETY MUSEUMS
UNCLE TOM'S CHURCH
THE BRUNSWICK INN
PLEASANT ST
125
1
Brunswick
MAINE ST
BATH RD
24
BRUNSWICK RD
Cooks Corner
THOMAS POINT RD
HARPSWELL RD
BOWDOIN COLLEGE
PLEASANT HILL RD
136
MAQUOIT RD
Thomas Point Beach
24
New Meadows River
FOSTER PT RD
123
Back Cove
Freeport
Bay
CUNDY'S HARBOR RD
MEREPOINT RD
Maquoit
Bay
Sebascodegan Island
GURNET RD
Harpswell
DINGLEY ISLAND RD
Middle
NECK RD
MOUNTAIN RD
24
Quahog Bay
LOOKOUT POINT RD
Harpswell Center
Cundy's Harbor
Harpswell Neck
Harpswell Sound
West Harpswell
24
Orr's Island
123
CRIBSTONE BRIDGE
South Harpswell
THE DOLPHIN CHOWDER HOUSE
Bailey Island
GIANT STAIRS
Mackerel Cove
Land's End
ATLANTIC

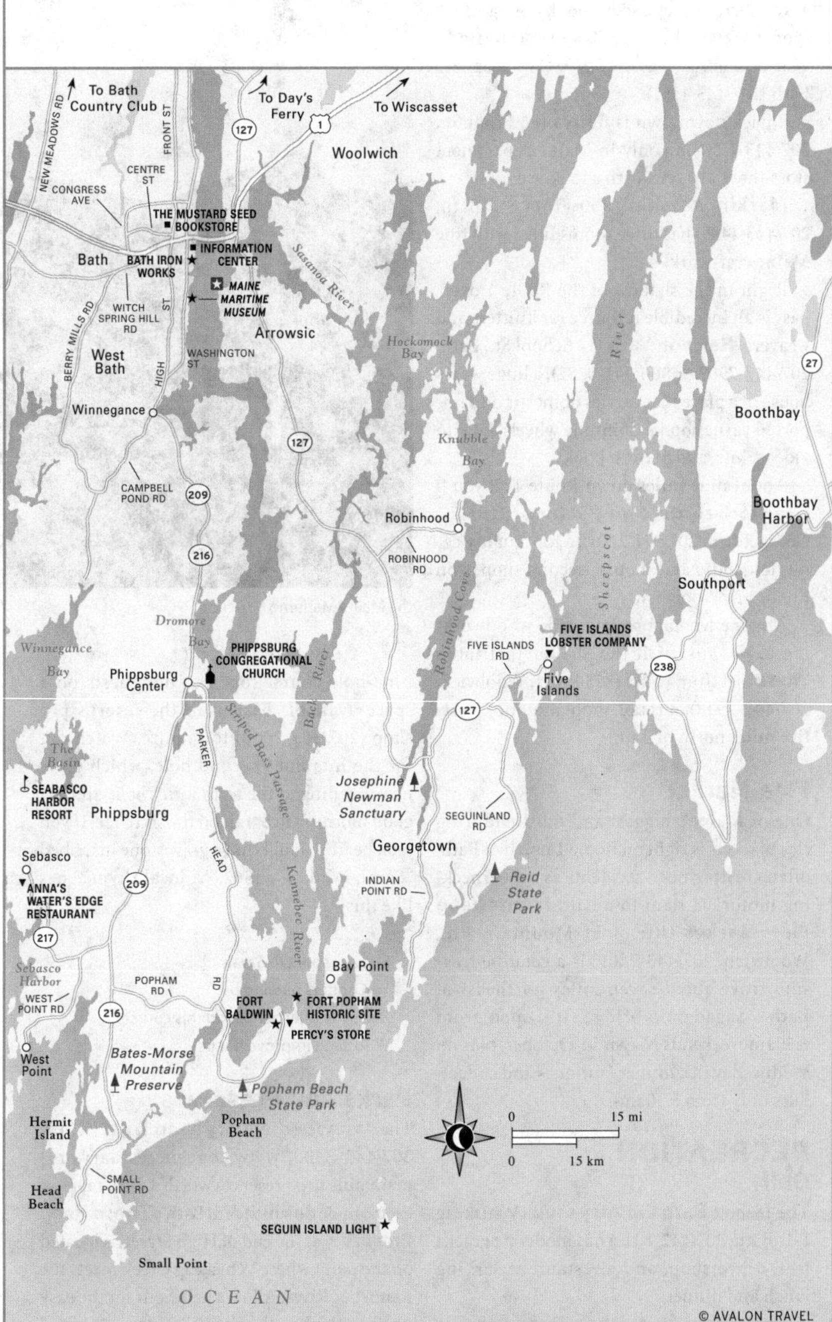
To Bath Country Club
To Day's Ferry
To Wiscasset
Woolwich
NEW MEADOWS RD
FRONT ST
CENTRE ST
CONGRESS AVE
THE MUSTARD SEED BOOKSTORE
INFORMATION CENTER
Bath
BATH IRON WORKS
MAINE MARITIME MUSEUM
Sasanoa River
WITCH SPRING HILL RD
BERRY MILLS RD
HIGH ST
Arrowsic
West Bath
WASHINGTON ST
Hockomock Bay
Winnegance
Knubble Bay
Boothbay
CAMPBELL POND RD
Boothbay Harbor
Robinhood
ROBINHOOD RD
Southport
Dromore Bay
Winnegance Bay
PHIPPSBURG CONGREGATIONAL CHURCH
Phippsburg Center
Back River
Robinhood Cove
Sheepscot River
FIVE ISLANDS RD
FIVE ISLANDS LOBSTER COMPANY
Five Islands
Striped Bass Passage
PARKER HEAD RD
The Basin
SEABASCO HARBOR RESORT
Phippsburg
Josephine Newman Sanctuary
SEGUINLAND RD
Georgetown
Sebasco
ANNA'S WATER'S EDGE RESTAURANT
Kennebec River
INDIAN POINT RD
Reid State Park
Sebasco Harbor
WEST POINT RD
POPHAM RD
Bay Point
FORT BALDWIN
FORT POPHAM HISTORIC SITE
PERCY'S STORE
West Point
Bates-Morse Mountain Preserve
Popham Beach State Park
Hermit Island
Popham Beach
0
15 mi
0
15 km
SMALL POINT RD
Head Beach
SEGUIN ISLAND LIGHT
Small Point
OCEAN
127
1
209
216
217
238
27
© AVALON TRAVEL

a wonderful independent bookstore and tea shop. For cheap beach reads and eclectic finds, visit **The Library Bookstore** (194 Front St., Bath, 207/443-1161).

Smack downtown is **Renys** (86 Front St., 207/443-6251), an only-in-Maine department store that's always worth a look-see.

Markings Gallery (50 Front St., Bath, 207/443-1499) has three rooms filled with fine Maine craftwork.

Right in the shadow of the Route 1 overpass is an incredible resource for knitters and weavers, **Halcyon Yarn** (12 School St., Bath, 207/442-7909 or 800/341-0282), a huge warehouse of a place that carries domestic and imported yarns, looms, spinning wheels, how-to videos, kits, and pattern books.

About nine miles down Route 127, you'll come to **Georgetown Pottery** (Rte. 127, Georgetown, 207/371-2801), a top-quality ceramics studio and shop. A second shop is on Route 1 in Woolwich.

Anyone who appreciates fine woodworking tools *must* visit the Shelter Institute's **Woodbutcher Tools** (873 Rte. 1, Woolwich, 207/442-7938), a retail shop and bookstore, five miles north of Bath.

Flea Market

One of Maine's biggest and most enduring flea markets is right on Route 1 north of Bath, often creating near-accidents as rubbernecking motorists slam to a halt. **Montsweag Flea Market** (Rte. 1 at Mountain Rd., Woolwich, 207/443-2809) is a genuine treasure trove about seven miles northeast of Bath's Sagadahoc bridge. It's open from 6:30am weekends May-mid-October, plus on Wednesday in summer (antiques and collectibles only from 5:30am).

RECREATION

Golf

The 18-hole **Bath Country Club** (Whiskeag Rd., Bath, 207/442-8411) has moderate greens fees, a pro shop, and a restaurant serving lunch and dinner.

The **Sebasco Harbor Resort** has a nine-hole course, open to nonguests on a space-available basis; call the resort's pro shop (207/389-9060) to inquire. Watch out for the infamous second hole, which gives new meaning to the term *water hole,* and say good morning to Sarah on the sixth tee: If you look nearby, you'll find a gravestone inscribed "Sarah Wallace—1862." A local rhyme goes like this:

> Show respect to Sarah
> You golfers passing by;
> She's the only person on this course
> Who can't improve her lie.

the Maine Maritime Museum

Parks and Preserves

The **Kennebec Estuary Land Trust** (KELT, 207/442-8400, www.kennebecestuary.org) maintains two preserves worth a visit; maps of each can be downloaded. Bath's **Thorn Head Preserve,** at the end of High Street, is located on the point where Whiskeag Creek meets the Kennebec River. Allow a half-hour for the easy walk to the headland and its stone "picnic" table with views toward Merrymeeting Bay. Allow longer if you want to explore any of the side trails. The **Whiskeag Trail,** a five-mile nonmotorized multiuse urban path, connects the preserve to the Bath YMCA. For terrific views of this section of coast, hike the loop trail to the bedrock summit of Georgetown's **Higgins Mountain.** The Route 127 trailhead is on the right, 7.6 miles south of Route 1.

BATES-MORSE MOUNTAIN CONSERVATION AREA

Consider visiting Phippsburg's lovely 600-acre **Bates-Morse Mountain Conservation Area** only if you are willing to be conscientious about the strict rules for this private preserve. A relatively easy four-mile round-trip hike takes you through marshland (you'll need insect repellent) and to the top of 210-foot Morse Mountain, which has panoramic views, and then down to privately owned Seawall Beach. On a clear day you can see New Hampshire's Mount Washington from the summit. No pets or vehicles are allowed, and there are no facilities; stay on the preserve road and the beach path at all times, as the side roads are private. Least terns and piping plovers—both endangered species—nest in the dunes, so avoid this area, especially mid-May-mid-August. Morse Mountain is a great locale for spotting hawks during their annual September migration southward. Pick up a map (and the rules) from the box in the parking area on Morse Mountain Road (marked private), off Route 216 just under a mile south of the intersection with Route 209.

PHIPPSBURG HIKING TRAILS

The **Phippsburg Land Trust** (207/443-5993, www.phippsburglandtrust.org) has prepared a handy free brochure with a map detailing more than a dozen preserves, most with trails. Four—Center Pond, Ridgewell, Spirit Pond, and Sprague Pond—have trail guides available at trailhead boxes. The land trust also hosts guided walks mid-June-mid-September.

JOSEPHINE NEWMAN SANCTUARY

A must-see for any nature lover, the 119-acre **Josephine Newman Sanctuary** (Rte. 127, Georgetown), has 2.5 miles of blazed loop trails winding through 110 wooded acres and along Robinhood Cove's tidal shoreline. Josephine Oliver Newman (1878-1968), a respected naturalist, bequeathed her family's splendid property to Maine Audubon (207/781-2330, www.maineaudubon.org),

Bath is especially proud of its ship-building heritage.

which maintains it today. The 0.6-mile self-guided trail is moderately difficult, but the rewards are 20 informative markers highlighting special features: glacial erratics, reversing falls, mosses, and marshes. The easiest route is the 0.75-mile Horseshoe Trail, which you can extend for another mile or so by linking into the Rocky End Trail. No pets or bikes are allowed. To find this hidden gem, take Route 127 from Route 1 in Woolwich (the road to Reid State Park) for 9.1 miles. Turn right at the sanctuary sign and continue up the narrow, rutted dirt road (ideally no one will be coming the other way) to the small parking lot. A map of the trail system is posted at the marsh's edge and available in the box.

ROBERT P. TRISTRAM COFFIN WILDFLOWER SANCTUARY

The New England Wildflower Society (www.newfs.org) owns the 177-acre trail-laced **Robert P. Tristram Coffin Wildflower Sanctuary** bordering Merrymeeting Bay in Woolwich. It is home to more than 100 species of wildflowers. To find it, take Route 127 north for 2.2 miles, then Route 128 for 4.5 miles, and look for a small parking area on the left.

Swimming

POPHAM BEACH

On hot July and August weekends, the parking lot at **Popham Beach State Park** (Rte. 209, Phippsburg, 207/389-1335, www.parksandlands.com, $6 nonresident adults, $4 Maine resident adults, $2 nonresident seniors, free Maine resident seniors, $1 ages 5-11), 14 miles south of Bath, fills up by 10am, so plan to arrive early at this huge crescent of sand backed by sea grass, beach roses, and dunes. Facilities include changing rooms, outside showers, restrooms, and seasonal lifeguards. It's officially open April 15-October 30, but the beach is accessible all year.

HEAD BEACH

Just off Route 216, about two miles south of the Route 209 turnoff to Popham Beach, is **Head Beach,** a sandy crescent that's open daily until 10pm. A day-use parking fee ($8) is payable at the small gatehouse; there's a restroom on the path to the beach and a store within walking distance. No pets.

REID STATE PARK

If I had to pick my favorite coastal state park, it would be **Reid** (Seguinland Rd., Georgetown, 207/371-2303, www.

Library Park, downtown Bath

parksandlands.com, $6.50 nonresident adults, $4.50 Maine resident adults, $2 nonresident seniors, free Maine resident seniors, $1 ages 5-11). Surf crashes on One Mile and Half Mile beaches, eagles and osprey soar overhead, kids splash in the lagoon or hunt for seaborne treasures in pools left by the receding tide, and birds nest in the sand dunes and marshlands. Trails lace the 765 acres, but for the biggest reward for the smallest effort, ascend Griffith Head and take in the sweeping seascape views. Facilities include changing rooms with showers, picnic tables, restrooms, and snack bars. The park—14 miles south of Route 1 in Woolwich and two miles off Route 127—is open daily year-round. In winter, bring cross-country skis and glide along the shoreline. Plan to arrive early on summer weekends, when parking is woefully inadequate.

Just 0.5 mile beyond the road to Reid State Park is **Charles Pond,** where the setting is unsurpassed for freshwater swimming in the long, skinny pond. You'll wish this were a secret too, but it isn't. There are no facilities.

Boat Excursions

The 50-foot ***Yankee*** operates out of Small Point's Hermit Island Campground Monday-Saturday throughout the summer. You can go on nature cruises, enjoy the sunset, or visit Eagle Island; the schedule is different each day, and rates vary widely by trip. Call for information and reservations (207/389-1788).

The **MV *Ruth,*** a 38-foot excursion boat, runs cruises out of Sebasco Harbor Resort late June-Labor Day. You don't need to be a Sebasco guest to take the trips, but reservations are essential. The schedule changes weekly, but possible options are a Cundy's Harbor lunch cruise, a sunset cruise, and a pirates excursion, with trips ranging 1-2 hours. Call the resort (207/389-1161) for the current week's schedule and rates.

If you prefer a custom tour, call **River Run Tours** (207/504-2628, www.riverruntours.com). Whether you want to view lighthouses or wildlife or cruise upriver to Swans Island, Captain Ed Rice has a cruise for you. Boat rate is $120/hour while cruising, $50/hour for standby. His comfortable pontoon boat accommodates six; plan on at least two hours.

The easiest access to Seguin Island (www.seguinisland.org) is via the **Seguin Island Ferry** (207/841-7977, www.fishntripsmaine.com, $30), which departs from the harbor near Fort Popham; call for current schedule. Most trips allow about three hours to tour the lighthouse, hike the trails, visit the museum, and picnic.

Canoeing and Kayaking

Close to civilization yet amazingly undeveloped, 392-acre **Nequasset Lake** is a great place to canoe. You'll see a few anglers, a handful of houses, and near-wilderness along the shoreline. Personal watercraft and motors over 10 hp are banned. Take Route 1 from Bath across the bridge to Woolwich. Continue to the flashing caution light at Nequasset Road; turn right and go 0.1 mile. Turn left, and left again, into the parking area for the Nequasset Stream Waterfront Park, a popular swimming hole. Launch your canoe and head upstream, under Route 1, to the lake.

Seaspray Kayaking (888/349-7774, www.seaspraykayaking.com) operates from bases at the New Meadows Kayaking Center in West Bath, Hermit Island in Phippsburg, and Sebasco Harbor Resort in Sebasco Estates, with rentals available at Hermit Island Campground on Small Point. Hourly canoe, paddleboard, or kayak rentals begin at $15-25 plus $10 for each additional hour, up to $20-50 daily, with longer-term rates and delivery available. A variety of guided tours are also offered, with half-day sea kayaking options for $50 adults, $25 children, and specialty paddles, such as sunset or moonlight, for $450 pp.

Fishing Charters

Cast a line for stripers, bluefish, pike trout, and smallmouth bass with **Kennebec Tidewater Charters** (207/737-4695, www.kennebectidewater.com). Captain Robin

Looping Around the Phippsburg Peninsula

Thanks to a map and brochures produced by the Phippsburg Business Association and Phippsburg Land Trust (www.phippsburglandtrust.org) and an online guide from the Phippsburg Historical Society (www.phippsburghistorical.com), it's easy to spend the better part of a day or longer exploring the peninsula that extends south from Bath.

About two miles south of Bath is a causeway known as **Winnegance,** a Wabanaki name usually translated as "short carry" or "little portage." Native Americans crossed here from the Kennebec River to the New Meadows River.

It's another 1.3 miles to the **Dromore Burying Ground** (on the right), with headstones dating from 1743. The next mile opens up with terrific easterly views of Dromore Bay. Right in the line of sight is state-owned, 117-acre Lee Island, which is off-limits May-mid-July to protect nesting eagles and waterfowl.

Next you're in **Phippsburg Center,** alive with shipbuilding from colonial days until the early 20th century. Hang a left onto Parker Head Road. After the Phippsburg Historical Museum (2pm-4pm Mon.-Fri. summer), in an 1859 schoolhouse, and the Alfred Totman Library, turn left onto Church Lane to see the "Constitution Tree," a huge English linden planted in 1774, in front of the 1802 **Phippsburg Congregational Church.**

Parker Head Road continues southward (watch out for speed bumps) and meets Route 209, which leads to **Popham Beach State Park.** Continue to the end of Route 209 for the **Fort Popham Historic Site,** where parking is woefully inadequate in summer. Youngsters love this place—they can fish from the rocks, explore the 1865 stone fortress, picnic on the seven-acre grounds, and create sand castles on the tiny beach next to the fort. Resist the urge to swim, though; the current is dangerous, and there's no lifeguard. Across the river is Bay Point, a lobstering village at the tip of the Georgetown Peninsula. **Percy's Store** (207/389-2010), by the way, with a handful of tables, is a good bet for pizza, picnic fare, fried dough, and fishing tackle.

Across the cove from the fort is Fort Baldwin Road, a one-lane-wide winding road leading to the shorefront site of the 1607 Popham Colony. Climb the path up Sabino Hill to what's left of World War I-era **Fort Baldwin.** Bring a flashlight if you want to explore the three sections of ruins.

Backtrack about four miles on Route 209, turn left onto Route 216, and head toward **Small**

Thayer, a Master Maine Guide, offers freshwater and saltwater cruises beginning at $300 for four hours. Tackle is provided, and instruction is available. Catch-and-release is encouraged.

ACCOMMODATIONS

Bath

Find elegance and comfort at the **Inn at Bath** (969 Washington St., Bath, 207/443-4294 or 800/423-0964, www.innatbath.com, $170-245). Guest rooms in the 1810 Greek Revival-style inn are decorated with antiques, and each has air-conditioning, a TV and video player, Wi-Fi, and a phone. Two have wood-burning fireplaces, and two have two-person whirlpool tubs. Dogs are a possibility. One room is wheelchair-accessible.

Phippsburg Peninsula

The trouble with staying at the ★ **Sebasco Harbor Resort** (Sebasco Rd., Sebasco Estates, 207/389-1161 or 800/225-3819, www.sebasco.com), a self-contained resort on 575 waterfront acres, is that between the beautiful setting and the bountiful offerings, you might not set foot off the premises during your entire vacation. Situated at the mouth of the saltwater New Meadows River, 12 miles south of Bath, Sebasco has attracted families who return year after year since 1930, when it opened. Sebasco changed hands in 1997, and owner Bob Smith has brought the resort up to 21st-century standards while keeping its old-style rusticity. You'll have to look far and wide to find a better family resort. Scattered around the well-tended property

passageways at the Fort Popham Historic Site

Point. Go about 0.9 mile to Morse Mountain Road, on the left, which leads to the parking area and trailhead for the **Bates-Morse Mountain Preserve.** Farther south are Head Beach and Hermit Island.

Returning northward on Route 216, you'll hook up with Route 209 and then see a left turn (Rte. 217) to Sebasco Harbor Resort. Take the time to go beyond the resort area. When the paved road goes left (to the Water's Edge Restaurant), turn right at a tiny cemetery and continue northward on the Old Meadowbrook Road, which meanders for about four miles along the west side of the peninsula. About midway along is **The Basin,** regarded by sailors as one of the Maine Coast's best "hurricane holes" (refuges in high winds). As you skirt The Basin and come to a fork, bear right to return to Route 209; turn left and return northward to Bath.

are the main lodge and a variety of cottages (1-10 bedrooms; the two-bedroom units with a shared living room are a great choice for families), a main lodge, a four-story cupola-topped lighthouse building edging the harbor, and two suites buildings, Harbor Village and the waterfront Fairwinds Spa, with more contemporary amenities. All have private baths, phones, and cable TV; many have water views; some have refrigerators or kitchenettes or full kitchens. Rates begin around $199; kids under age 12 are free; pets are $25/night. Rates that include breakfast and dinner are an additional $48 pp (no charge for children under age 11 when dining with an adult and from the kids' menu). Weekly summer events include a Sunday-evening reception and grand buffet, lobster bakes, bingo, live entertainment, and the twice-weekly Camp Merrit children's program ($20/day, includes lunch). Recreational facilities include two all-weather tennis courts, a nine-hole championship golf course and a three-hole regulation course for beginners and families, the state's largest outdoor saltwater pool, boat tours aboard the *Ruth*, sailing trips, sea-kayak excursions, mountain-bike tours, candlepin bowling, horseshoes, a playground, a well-equipped fitness center, bike rentals ($10/five hours or $18/day) and as much or as little organized activity as you want.

Magnificent gardens surround **Edgewater Farm Bed and Breakfast** (71 Small Point Rd./Rte. 216, Sebasco Estates, 207/389-1322 or 877/389-1322, www.ewfbb.com, $140-225), Carol and Bill Emerson's comfy, unfussy

19th-century farmhouse, just south of the turnoff to Popham Beach and close to the access for Morse Mountain. Families usually choose the carriage house, where kids can play in the huge recreation room. A brunch-size breakfast served in the solarium benefits from organic produce grown on the four-acre grounds. Then there's the four-foot-deep indoor lap pool, a hot tub outside on the deck, and the Benedictine labyrinth Bill created in a wooded grove. English, Spanish, a bit of French, and German are all spoken. Pets are welcome for $25.

Rock Gardens Inn (Rte. 218, Sebasco Estates, Phippsburg, 207/389-1339, www.rockgardensinn.com, from $170 pp d) hosts numerous artists' workshops, and no wonder: It sits on its own peninsula, and the pretty grounds are landscaped with wild and cultivated flowers. Guests stay in one of three inn rooms or 10 cottages and have use of an outdoor heated pool and sea kayaks. Rates include breakfast and dinner—and the weekly lobster cookout. Sebasco Harbor Resort is just steps away, and guests have access to its facilities as well. Ask about all-inclusive art workshops.

Step back in history at ★ **The 1774 Inn** (44 Parker Head Rd., Phippsburg Center, 207/389-1774, www.1774inn.com, $180-260), a magnificently restored four-square Georgian colonial property, listed on the National Register of Historic Places, with an 1870 ell and barn. Many colonial details have been preserved, including shutters with peepholes and strong bars to defend against attack, paneled wainscoting, ceiling moldings, fluted columns, and wide-plank pine floors. Most of the eight guest rooms (all but two with private baths) have views of the Kennebec River. All are spacious and furnished with antiques. Outside, the inn's four acres roll down to the river. Rates include a full breakfast and evening snacks.

You can walk to beaches or forts from **Stonehouse Manor** (907 Popham Rd., Phippsburg, 877/389-1141, www.stonehouse-manor.com, $220-320), a National Historic Register-listed bed-and-breakfast with distant ocean views, lovely gardens and an enviable location on Silver Lake. The graceful 1896 mansion-style cottage's architectural features include leaded stained-glass windows and oak pocket doors. Rooms are spacious, and the feeling is like being on a private estate. Breakfasts are a treat.

Georgetown Peninsula

Imagine the perfect Maine seaside inn, and likely it resembles **Grey Havens Inn** (96 Seguinland Rd., Georgetown, 855/473-9428 or 207/371-2616, www.greyhavens.com, $215-395). Innkeepers Eve and Dick Roesler and Chuck Papachristos have thoroughly renovated and updated this 1904 Shingle-style classic with two turrets, front porch, and dreamy views over lobster boats, spruce-fringed islands, and rockbound coast. Public rooms flow, with a massive stone hearth dominating the living room. Guest rooms are comfy and simply decorated in coastal cottage style. Rates include a continental breakfast. The inn's restaurant, Blue, serves dinner, $20-30, Tuesday-Sunday (although it closes for functions).

It's hard to tear yourself away from the scenery and sanctuary at **The Mooring Bed and Breakfast** (132 Seguinland Rd., Georgetown, 207/371-2790 or 866/828-7348, www.themooringb-b.com, $165-210), the original home of Walter Reid, who donated Reid State Park to the state. His great-granddaughter Penny Barabe and her husband, Paul, have beautifully restored the house, situated on lovely oceanfront grounds with island-studded views. Each guest room has a water view and air-conditioning. There's plenty of room to spread out, including the appropriately named Spanish room. A full breakfast, afternoon wine and cheese, and freshly baked sweets are included.

Even more secluded is **Coveside Bed & Breakfast** (6 Gotts Cove Lane, Georgetown, 207/371-2807 or 800/232-5490, www.coveside-bandb.com, $165-235), an enviable spot on five oceanfront acres near Five Islands. Tom and

Carolyn Church have four guest rooms in the main house and three in the adjacent cottage, all with water views. Some rooms have fireplaces; one has a whirlpool tub. Carolyn's pastry-chef skills are evident at breakfast. Wi-Fi is available, and a separate building has a TV and exercise room. Guests have use of bicycles and a canoe, gardens, and the dock on Gotts Cove.

Camping

Plan to book in January if you want a waterfront campsite in midsummer at the Phippsburg Peninsula's **Hermit Island Campground** (6 Hermit Island Rd., Phippsburg, 207/443-2101, www.hermitisland.com, no credit cards). With 270 campsites (no vehicles larger than pickup campers; no hookups) spread over a 255-acre causeway-linked island, this is oceanfront camping at its best. The well-managed operation has a store, a snack bar, a seasonal post office, boat rentals, boat excursions, trails, and seven private beaches. The hub of activity (and registration) is the Kelp Shed, next to the campsite entrance. Open and wooded sites run $$40-65 mid-June-Labor Day, $37 early and late in the season. Three small cabins rent for $445-1,175 per week in season. Reservations for a week's stay or longer and for Memorial Day and Labor Day weekends can be made by mail beginning in early January and by phone in early February (call for the exact date). Reservations for stays of less than one week are accepted after March 1. It's open mid-May-Columbus Day, but full operation is really June-Labor Day. The campground is at the tip of the Phippsburg Peninsula. Pets are not allowed.

FOOD

Local Flavors

In Waterfront Park on Commercial Street, the **Bath Farmers Market** operates 8:30am-noon every Saturday May-October.

For breakfast, lunch, or sweets, drop into the **Starlight Café** (15 Lambard St., 207/443-3005, 7am-2pm Mon.-Fri., 8am-2pm Sat.), a too-cute and too-tiny basement space across a side street from the Customs House. It's bright and cheerful, and the food is hearty and creative; cash only.

Some argue that the state's best thin-crust pizza (and praiseworthy garlic knots) comes from the ovens at **The Cabin** (552 Washington St., Bath, 207/443-6224, www.cabinpizza.com, 10am-10pm Sun.-Thurs., 10am-11pm Fri.-Sat., no credit cards), a somewhat rough-and-tumble working-class joint that's been a local fave since 1973. It's across from Bath Iron Works. Avoid it during BIW shift changes (3pm-5pm Mon.-Fri.).

The **Winnegance General Store and Café** (36 High St., Bath, 207/443-3300, 6am-6pm Mon.-Sat., 6am-4pm Sun.), snugged on a corner with views over the Kennebec River and Winnegance Lake, is a fine place for breakfast, lunch, or fresh-baked treats.

A wonderful multifaceted find is Susan Verrier's **North Creek Farm** (24 Sebasco Rd., Phippsburg, 207/389-1341, www.northcreekfarm.org, 9am-6:30pm daily, lunch 11:30am-3:30pm Mon.-Sat., brunch 9am-2pm Sun.), an 1850s saltwater farm with fabulous organic gardens, including ornamental display gardens and lots of rugosa roses (a specialty—Susan has written two books on them). Visitors can meander down by a waterfall, creek, and salt marsh. Inside the barn is a small store stocked with garden and gourmet goodies and a small café, where delicious soups and sandwiches are made to order. There are a handful of tables indoors, as well as chairs and tables scattered in the gardens.

On the Georgetown Peninsula, **Five Islands Farm** (1375 Rte. 127, Five Islands, 297/371-9383, www.fiveislandsfarm.com) is a fine stop for picnic fixings, with an excellent assortment of Maine cheeses along with breads, meats, chips, salsa, and even wine.

The **Georgetown Country Store** (Five Islands Rd., 207/371-2106, 7am-7pm daily) earns kudos for its lobster rolls as well as other fare, which can range from clam fritters to house-made chili specials.

Barbecue

Finger-licking Memphis-style barbecue, along with other Southern specialties, is served in big quantities at **Beale Street Barbeque and Grill** (215 Water St., Bath, 207/442-9514, www.mainebbq.com, 11am-9pm Sun.-Thurs., 11:30am-9pm daily, $11-30). Everything's made on the premises. Find it next to the municipal parking lot.

Casual Dining

Kate and Andy Winglass operate **Mae's Café and Bakery** (160 Centre St. at High St., Bath, 207/442-8577, www.maescafeandbakery.com, 8am-2pm daily), a longtime local favorite bakery and café with seating indoors and on a front deck. It's *the* place to go for brunch (reservations are essential on weekends). Most choices are in the $9-13 range. Rotating art shows enliven the open and airy dining rooms.

The cool and contemporary Danish decor matches the food at **Solo Bistro** (128 Front St., Bath, 207/443-3373, www.solobistro.com, from 5pm Mon.-Sat., $18-30), a sophisticated storefront restaurant downtown where the choices might range from a bistro burger to butter-poached lobster. A nightly three-course fixed-price menu is usually around $25. There's live jazz most Friday nights.

Dining with a View

All the places listed here are seasonal.

Even if you're not staying at **Sebasco Harbor Resort** (Rte. 217, Sebasco Estates, 207/389-1161 or 800/225-3819, www.sebasco.com), you can dine in either of its two waterfront restaurants, both with gasp-evoking sunset views and both with children's menus. Binoculars hang by windows in the **Pilot House** (5:30pm-8:30pm Mon.-Sat., dinner entrées $18-32), the more formal of the two, so diners can get a better view of the boats or birds happening by. Below it is the casual **Ledges** (11:30am-10pm daily, $8-24), with indoor and outdoor seating and a menu including sandwiches, pizzas, lobster, and comfort favorites.

A few notches above a seafood shack, **Anna's Water's Edge Restaurant** (75 Black's Landing Rd., Sebasco Estates, 207/389-1803, www.thewatersedgerestaurant.com, 11am-9pm daily $5-35) has serene views over island-salted Casco Bay. The menu ranges from hot dogs to lobster, with plentiful fried fish, sandwiches, and even pastas and steak. Keep it simple for the best experience.

Gaze at seals playing in the Kennebec River, at Fort Popham, and out to open ocean from **Spinney's Restaurant** (987

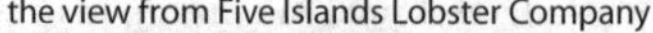
the view from Five Islands Lobster Company

Rte. 209, Popham Beach, 207/389-2052, www.spinneysrestaurant.com, 8am-9pm daily, entrées $13-30, sandwiches and hot dogs less). Food varies in quality from year to year, but you can't beat the view, and you can keep it budget-friendly by coming for breakfast.

Big windows frame sigh-worthy views at **Blue** (96 Seguinland Rd., Georgetown, 855/473-9428 or 207/371-2616, www.greyhavens.com, 5:30pm-9pm Tues.-Sun.), the restaurant at the Grey Havens Inn. White-draped tables are comfortably spaced in the wood-floored and beadboard-walled and -ceilinged dining room. Chef Esau Crosby's menu emphasizes locally sourced fare and may include choices such as lazy lobster or tournedos of beef, most running $20-30.

Lobster in the Rough

Just over a mile beyond the turnoff to Reid State Park, you'll reach the end of Route 127 at Five Islands. Here you'll find ★ **Five Islands Lobster Company** (1447 Five Islands Rd., Five Islands, Georgetown, 207/371-2990, www.fiveislandslobster.com, 11:30am-7pm daily, weekends only spring and fall.), known for its slogan: "Eat on the dock with the fishermen, but best avoid the table by the bait-shack door." Here you can pig out on lobster rolls, better-than-usual onion rings, crab cakes, and, if you must, burgers and hot dogs. Dress down, BYOB, and enjoy the end-of-the-road ambience of this idyllic spot.

INFORMATION AND SERVICES

Visitor Information

A visitors center is located in Bath's renovated train station (restrooms available), adjacent to the Bath Iron Works main yard. It's open year-round with brochure racks and staffed by volunteers May-October. Request copies of the *City of Bath Downtown Map and Guide* and the *Guide to Southern Midcoast Maine*.

Online information is available from **Main Street Bath** (www.visitbath.com), the city's website (www.cityofbath.com), and the **Southern Midcoast Chamber of Commerce** (877/725-8797, www.midcoastmaine.com).

Check out **Patten Free Library** (33 Summer St., Bath, 207/443-5141, www.patten.lib.me.us).

Find **public restrooms** at Bath City Hall (55 Front St.), Patten Free Library (33 Summer St.), Sagadahoc County Courthouse (752 High St.), the visitors center, and in summer only at Waterfront Park (Commercial St.).

GETTING THERE AND AROUND

Bath is about 10 miles or 15 minutes via Route 1 from Brunswick. It's about 12 miles or 20 minutes via Route 1 to Wiscasset, but allow up to double that in summer for congestion in Wiscasset.

The **Bath Trolley** (www.cityofbath.com) circulates through the area, with each one-way trip costing $1.

Wiscasset Area

Billing itself as "The Prettiest Village in Maine," **Wiscasset** (pop. 3,732) works hard to live up to its slogan, with quaint street signs, well-maintained homes, and an air of attentive elegance.

Wiscasset ("meeting place of three rivers"), incorporated as part of Pownalborough in 1760, has had its current name since 1802. In the late 18th century it became the shire town of Lincoln County and the largest seaport north of Boston. Countless tall-masted ships sailed the 12 miles up the Sheepscot River to tie up here, and shipyards flourished, turning out vessels for domestic and foreign trade. The 1807 Embargo Act and the War of 1812 delivered a one-two punch that shut down trade and temporarily squelched the town's aspirations, but Wiscasset yards soon were back at it, producing vessels for the pre-Civil War clipper-ship era—only to face a more lasting decline with the arrival of the railroads and the onset of the Industrial Revolution.

The Davey Bridge, built in 1983, is the most recent span over the Sheepscot. The earliest, finished in 1847, was a toll bridge that charged a horse and wagon $0.15 to cross, pedestrians $0.03 each, and pigs $0.01 apiece. Before that, ferries carried passengers, animals, and vehicles between Wiscasset and Edgecomb's Davis Island (then named Folly Island).

Wiscasset is notorious for midsummer gridlock. Especially on weekends, traffic backs up on Route 1 for miles in both directions—to the frustration of drivers, passengers, and Wiscasset merchants. The state Department of Transportation has tested traffic medians, stoplights, and other devices, but nothing has solved the problem. A bypass has been under discussion for years, but not-in-my-backyard opposition to every route has halted progress. (When you stop in town, try to park pointed in the direction you're going; it's impossible to make turns across oncoming traffic.)

SIGHTS

In 1973 a large chunk of downtown Wiscasset was added to the National Register of Historic Places, and a walking tour is the best way to appreciate the Federal, Classical Revival, and even prerevolutionary homes and commercial buildings in the Historic District. Listed here are a few of the prime examples. See www.wiscasset.org for 28 properties listed on the National Historic Register and a walking map. If you do nothing else, swing by the homes on High Street.

Historic Houses

Historic New England (207/882-7169, www.historicnewengland.org) owns two Wiscasset properties within easy walking distance of each other. Both are open for tours (every half hour 11am 4pm Wed. Sun. June-mid-Oct., $5 each).

Once known as the Lee-Tucker House, **Castle Tucker** (Lee St. and High St.) was built in 1807 by Judge Silas Lee and bought by sea captain Richard Tucker in 1858. The imposing mansion has Victorian wallpaper and furnishings, Palladian windows, an amazing elliptical staircase, and a dramatic view over the Sheepscot River. In 1997, Jane Tucker, Richard's granddaughter, magnanimously deeded the house to Historic New England.

The three-story **Nickels-Sortwell House** (121 Main St.) looms over Route 1, yet it's so close to the road that many motorists miss it. Sea captain William Nickels commissioned the mansion in 1807 but died soon after its completion. For 70 or so years it was the Belle Haven Hotel before Alvin and Frances Sortwell's meticulous Colonial Revival restoration in the early 20th century.

Lincoln County Jail and Museum

Wiscasset's Old Jail (133 Federal St., Wiscasset, 207/882-6817, noon-4pm

Sat.-Sun. June-mid-Oct., $5 adults, free under 16), completed in 1811, was the first prison in the District of Maine (then part of Massachusetts). Amazingly, it remained a jail—mostly for short-timers—until 1953. Two years after that the Lincoln County Historical Association took over, so each summer you can check out the 40-inch-thick granite walls, floors, and ceilings; the 12 tiny cells; and historic graffiti penned by the prisoners. Attached to the prison is the 1837 jailer's house, now the Lincoln County Museum, containing antique tools, the original kitchen, and various temporary exhibits. A Victorian gazebo overlooking the Sheepscot River is a great spot for a picnic. From Main Street (Rte. 1) in downtown Wiscasset, take Federal Street (Rte. 218) 1.2 miles.

Fort Edgecomb

Built in 1808 to protect the Sheepscot River port of Wiscasset, the **Fort Edgecomb State Historic Site** (Eddy Rd., Edgecomb, 207/882-7777, 9am-5pm daily late May-early Sept., $3 nonresident adults, $2 Maine resident adults, $1 ages 5-11) occupies a splendid three-acre riverfront spread ideal for picnicking and fishing (no swimming). Many summer weekends, the encampments on the grounds of the octagonal blockhouse make history come alive with Revolutionary reenactments, period dress, craft demonstrations, and garrison drills. It's off Route 1; take Eddy Road just north of Wiscasset Bridge and go 0.5 mile to Fort Road.

Wiscasset, Waterville, and Farmington Railway

Also historic, but a bit more lively and fun for kids, is the **Wiscasset, Waterville, and Farmington Railway** (97 Cross Rd., Sheepscot, 207/882-4193, www.wwfry.org, 9am-4pm Sat. year-round and Sun. late May-Oct.), a museum commemorating a two-foot-gauge common carrier railroad that operated in the early part of the 20th century, from Wiscasset in the south to Albion and Winslow in the north. On the grounds are a museum in the old station (free admission) and train rides along the mainline track running north from Cross Road, on the original roadbed ($7 adults, $4 children 4-12). Trains depart Sheepscot regularly between 10am-3:30pm on weekends; the schedule is a bit complicated, so check the website for spring and fall operation. From Route 1 in Wiscasset, take Route 218 north 4.7 miles to a four-way intersection and turn left on Cross Road to the museum.

the Nickels-Sortwell House in Wiscasset

Head Tide Village

Head Tide Village, an eminently picturesque hamlet at the farthest reach of Sheepscot River tides, is worth a detour, especially in autumn. From Wiscasset, follow Rte. 218 north for about eight miles and then turn right on Rte. 194 to find this idyllic pocket, listed on the National Register of Historic Places. From the late 18th century to the early 20th, Head Tide (now part of the town of Alna) was a thriving mill town, a source of hydropower for the textile and lumber industries. All that's long gone, but hints of that era come from the handful of well-maintained 18th- and 19th-century homes in the village center.

Up the hill, the stunning 1838 **Head Tide Church,** another fine example of local prosperity, is usually open 2pm-4pm Saturday July-August. Volunteer tour guides point out the original pulpit, a trompe l'oeil window, a kerosene chandelier, and walls lined with historic Alna photographs.

Head Tide's most famous citizen was the poet **Edwin Arlington Robinson,** born here in 1869. His family home, at the bend in Route 194, is not open to the public. Perhaps his Maine roots inspired these lines from his poem "New England":

> Here where the wind is always north-northeast
> And children learn to walk on frozen toes.

Just upriver from the bend in the road is a favorite swimming hole, a millpond where you can join the locals on a hot summer day. Not much else goes on here, and there are no restaurants or lodgings, so Head Tide can't be termed a destination, but it's a village frozen in time—and an unbeatable opportunity for history buffs and shutterbugs.

FESTIVALS AND EVENTS

Wiscasset's daylong **Annual Strawberry Festival and Country Fair** (St. Philip's Episcopal Church, Hodge St., 207/882-7184) celebrates with tons of strawberries along with crafts and an auction on the last Saturday in June. The church is also the site of **Monday-night fish-chowder suppers** mid-July-mid-August. Reservations are advised (207/882-7184) for these popular 5:30pm suppers.

An **Art Walk** takes place 5pm-8pm the last Thursday of the month June-September.

A summer highlight at Watershed Center for the Ceramic Arts (207/882-6075, www.watershedceramics.org) is its annual **Salad Days,** a fundraising event held on a Saturday in July. For a $35 donation, you choose a handmade pottery plate, fill it from a piled-high buffet of fruit and veggie salads, and are part of an old-fashioned picnic social—and you even get to keep the plate. Afterward, there's plenty of time to explore the center's 32 acres.

SHOPPING

Natural beauty products and bamboo clothing fill Kelley Belanger's fun shop, **In the Clover** (85A Main St., Wiscasset, 207/882-9435).

Antiques and Art

It's certainly fitting that a town filled end-to-end with antique homes should have more than two dozen solo and group antiques shops.

Right downtown, **Blythe House Antiques** (161 Main St., Wiscasset, 207/882-1280) has multiple dealers exhibiting in room settings. French and English antiques are the specialty at **Daybreak Manor** (106 Rte. 1, Wiscasset, 207/882-9786), which also has formal gardens, a winery, and an apiary. Both fine art and antiques are sold at **French and Vandyke** (8 Federal St., Wiscasset, 207/882-8302).

European and American 19th- and 20th-century painters are the broad focus at **Wiscasset Bay Gallery** (67 Main St./Rte. 1, Wiscasset, 207/882-7682 or 888/622-9445, www.wiscassetbaygallery.com), which schedules high-quality rotating shows throughout the season.

In the handsome open spaces of an early-19th-century brick schoolhouse, the

Maine Art Gallery (15 Warren St., Wiscasset, 207/882-7511, www.maineartgallery.org) was founded in 1954 as a nonprofit organization to showcase contemporary Maine artists.

Two miles south of town is the **Avalon Antiques Market** (563 Rte. 1, Wiscasset, 207/882-4239, www.avalonantiquesmarket.com), a huge red barn of a place filled with more than 100 dealers showing on three floors.

ACCOMMODATIONS

Bed-and-Breakfasts

Named after a famous Maine clipper ship, Paul and Melanie Harris's **Snow Squall Inn** (5 Bradford Rd. at Rte. 1, Wiscasset, 207/882-6892 or 800/775-7245, www.snowsquallinn.com, $107-182) is a renovated mid-19th-century house on the edge of downtown. Inside are four lovely guest rooms and three family suites, all with phones, air-conditioning, and Wi-Fi, and two with fireplaces. Melanie is a licensed massage therapist and a vinyasa yoga instructor; Paul is a professionally trained chef. It's open all year, but only by reservation November-April.

Wiscasset's antiques shops are within easy walking distance of the **Newkirk Inn** (33 Washington St., Wiscasset, 207/522-3127, www.newkirkinn.com, $105-145), an 1870 Greek Revival with four air-conditioned guest rooms. Breakfast is continental. Dogs allowed with crate.

Then there's **The Squire Tarbox Inn** (1181 Main Rd./Rte. 144, Westport Island, 207/882-7693 or 800/818-0626, www.squiretarboxinn.com, mid-Apr.-Dec., $139-199), an elegantly casual bed-and-breakfast and inn that doubles as a working organic farm. Accomplished Swiss chef-owner Mario De Pietro and his wife, Roni, have continued the inn's reputation for dining excellence. Eleven rooms, some with fireplaces, are divided between the late-18th-century main house and the early-19th-century carriage house; those in the main house are more formal. Rates include breakfast, and the dining room is open to nonguests by reservation for dinner. Also on the property are walking paths, a rowboat, mountain bikes, a working pottery, and a working farm, with organic vegetable gardens, chickens, and goats. A few guest rooms are pet-friendly ($15/stay). From downtown Wiscasset, head southwest four miles on Route 1 to Route 144. Turn left and go about 8.5 scenic miles to the inn.

Step back in time at **Wabi Sabi Cottage** (111 Sheepscot Rd., Alna, 207/687-2200, www.wabisabicottage.com, $145-195), Joan Thompson's combination bed-and-breakfast, café, and antiques shop in a riverside cottage designed by the former resident architect of Colonial Williamsburg. The decor is pure 19th century, and one of the two guest rooms has back-to-back Victorian clawfoot tubs in the oversized bathroom. Breakfast is continental weekdays and full on weekends.

Motels

Fairly close to Route 1 but buffered a bit by century-old hemlocks, the well-maintained **Wiscasset Motor Lodge** (Rte. 1, Wiscasset, 207/882-7137 or 800/732-8168, www.wiscassetmotorlodge.com, $79-108) has been updated over the years with pine and red oak harvested and milled on the eight-acre property. Guest rooms have phones, TVs, Wi-Fi, and air-conditioning; a light breakfast is included in summer. Ask for a room in the back building if you're noise-sensitive.

FOOD

Across Federal Street from the Nickels-Sortwell House in downtown Wiscasset is the lovely **Sunken Garden,** an almost-unnoticed pocket park created around the cellar hole of a long-gone inn. It's a fine place for a picnic.

Local Flavors

Let's start with the obvious: **Red's Eats** (Main St. and Water St., Wiscasset, 207/882-6128, 11am-11pm Mon.-Sat., noon-6pm Sun., early May-mid-Oct.). This simple take-out stand has garnered national attention through the decades for its lobster rolls stuffed with the meat from a whole lobster. It's easy to spot because of the line. Expect to wait, perhaps for an hour or more. Is it worth it? I don't think so, but others rave about the cold lobster rolls, the fried fish, the hot dogs, and the wraps. If you're planning on one of Red's lobster rolls, ask someone who has just bought one the price before you get in line and make sure you have enough cash (no credit cards). Of course, you can skip the wait with a quick walk across Main Street to the Town Wharf, where **Sprague Lobster** (22 Main St., Wiscasset, 207/882-2306) has set up a competing stand that many locals prefer. Lines are rare, and the lobster rolls also contain the meat from an entire crustacean.

Adjacent to Red's is **QT's Ice Cream Parlor** (47 Railroad Ave., 207/701-7293), serving Lear's Old Fashioned Ice Cream, a local favorite.

Back up the street is **Treat's** (80 Main St., Wiscasset, 207/882-6192, 10am-6pm Mon.-Sat., noon-5pm Sun.), a superb source of gourmet picnic fixings: sandwiches, soups, wine, cheese, condiments, and artisanal breads.

Family Favorites

Two miles southwest of downtown Wiscasset, **The Sea Basket Restaurant** (303 Rte. 1, Wiscasset, 207/882-6581, www.seabasket.com, 11am-8pm Wed.-Sun. Mar.-Dec., $4-22) has been serving hearty bowls of lobster stew and good-size baskets of eminently fresh seafood since 1981. The fried fish is almost healthful, thanks to convection-style frying using trans fat-free oil. Not a place to seek out, but decent on-the-road food.

In a high-visibility location across Route 1 from Red's Eats, **Sarah's Cafe** (Main St./Rte. 1 and Water St., Wiscasset, 207/882-7504, www.sarahscafe.com, 11am-8pm daily, $7-16) is the home of huge "whaleboat" and "dory" sandwiches, homemade soups, pizza, vegetarian specials, and an ice cream fountain. Lobster meat shows up in salads, burritos, quesadillas, wraps, croissants, and more. The deck has front-row seats on the Sheepscot River. Food is reliably mundane and the service can be sluggish and indifferent, but crayons keep kids busy.

Casual Dining

Pizzas, paninis, and entrees such as mixed seafood stew and chicken Alfredo are served at **Little Village Bistro** (65 Gardiner Rd./Rte. 27, Wiscasset, 207-687-8232, http://littlevillagebistro.com, 4-9pm Tues-Sat., $14-26), a cozy Italian-accented restaurant that turns out excellent fare. Choices range from

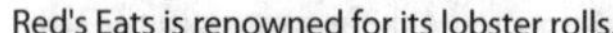
Red's Eats is renowned for its lobster rolls.

sandwiches and pizzas to entrees such as crab-stuff haddock and crispy seared duck breast. There's a kids menu, with $5 choices. Make reservations; it's tiny.

Well off the beaten path on an island connected to the mainland by a bridge is **The Squire Tarbox Inn** (1181 Main Rd./Rte. 144, Westport Island, 207/882-7693 or 800/818-0626, www.squiretarboxinn.com, dinner Wed.-Mon. mid-June-mid-Oct., Thurs.-Sat. April and May and November and December, entrées $28-33), a working organic farm where Swiss chef Mario De Pietro serves memorable meals. The Continental entrées, such as rack of lamb, Swiss-style veal, and Maine crab cakes, are served in an elegantly rustic dining room. Monday night is pizza night. Off-season, Thursday nights are Swiss night, with appropriate cuisine served. Ask about cooking classes. Reservations required.

INFORMATION AND SERVICES

The **Wiscasset Area Chamber of Commerce** (207/882-9600, www.wiscasset-chamber.com) has info on members.

Check out **Wiscasset Public Library** (21 High St., Wiscasset, 207/882-7161, www.wiscasset.lib.me.us).

Find **public restrooms** on the Town Wharf, Water Street, and the Lincoln County Court House.

GETTING THERE AND AROUND

Wiscasset is about 12 miles or 20 minutes via Route 1 from Bath, but allow up to twice that in summer. It's about 13 miles or 20 minutes via Routes 1 and 27 to Boothbay Harbor. It's about 8 miles or 15 minutes via Route 1 to Damariscotta.

Boothbay Peninsula

East of Wiscasset, en route to Damariscotta, only a flurry of signs along Route 1 in Edgecomb hints at what's down the peninsula bisected by Route 27 and framed by the Sheepscot and Damariscotta Rivers. Drive southward down the Boothbay Peninsula Memorial Day-Labor Day and you'll find yourself in one of Maine's longest-running summer playgrounds.

The three peninsula towns of **Boothbay** (pop. 3,120), **Boothbay Harbor** (pop. 2,165), and, connected by a bridge, **Southport Island** (pop. 606) are a maze of islands and peninsulas. When Route 27 arrives at the water, having passed through Boothbay, you're at Boothbay Harbor ("the Harbor"), scene of most of the action. The harbor itself is a boat fan's dream, loaded with working craft and pleasure yachts. Ashore are shops and galleries, restaurants and inns, and one-way streets, traffic congestion, and pedestrians everywhere. But don't despair; it's easy to escape the peak-season crowds in one of the numerous parks and preserves, fine places for a hike or a picnic. Hop on an excursion boat to an offshore island, for a whale watch, or for an evening sail around the bay.

Try to save time for quieter spots: East Boothbay, Ocean Point, Southport Island, the Coastal Maine Botanical Gardens, or even just over the 1,000-foot-long footbridge stretching across one corner of the harbor. Cross the bridge and walk down Atlantic Avenue to the Fishermen's Memorial, a bronze fishing dory commemorating the loss of hardy souls who've earned a rugged living here by their wits and the sea. Across the street is Our Lady Queen of Peace Catholic Church, with shipwright-quality woodwork.

SIGHTS

★ Coastal Maine Botanical Gardens

The shorefront **Coastal Maine Botanical Gardens** (Barters Island Rd., Boothbay, 207/633-4333, www.mainegardens.org,

Boothbay Peninsula

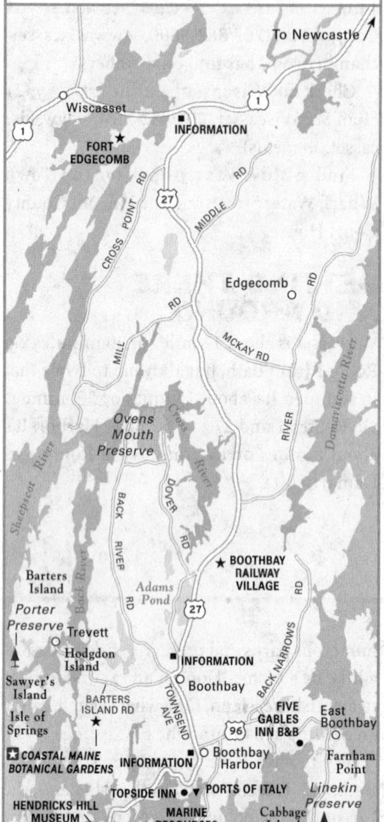

9am-6pm daily July Aug., to 5pm daily mid-Apr.-June and Sept.-Oct., $16 adults, $14 seniors, $8 ages 3-17) are masterful, yet still in their youth. The nonprofit project, designed to preserve more than 125 acres of woodlands with a trail network and landscaped pocket "theme" gardens, has grown to encompass 250 acres, with formal gardens, paths, herb and kitchen gardens, woods walks, a fairy village, a five-senses garden, and nearly a mile of waterfront. Artwork is placed throughout. A magical children's garden encourages imagination, play, and discovery in a setting drawing from Maine-related children's literature such as *Blueberries for Sal* and *Miss Rumphius*. Operating from the garden's landing are **Sheepscot River Cruises** (207/633-6598), which offers guided one-hour tours ($25 adult, $15 kids) aboard the Beagle, an electric vessel, and **Tidal Transit**, which offers three-hour sea-kayaking tours (call the garden for details, $45). The visitors center has an excellent café (10am-4pm), a library, and a gift shop. Pick up a map and explore on your own, or join a free docent-led tour (11am and 1pm Thurs. and Sat.). Allow at least two hours, although you could easily spend a full day here. Other garden activities include lectures, the Maine Fairy House Festival, and a Kitchen Garden Dinner series. Entrance to the preserve is on Barters Island Road, about 1.3 miles west of Boothbay Center.

Boothbay Railway Village

When George McEvoy's mother ordered him to find a new home for his growing collection of historical memorabilia, including automobiles and defunct narrow gauge and downsized Maine Central Railroad artifacts, McEvoy purchased 15 acres in Boothbay, Maine, constructed a three-quarter-mile narrow gauge track, and in May 1965, opened the **Boothbay Railway Village** (Rte. 27, Boothbay, 207/633-4727, www.railwayvillage.org, 9:30am-5pm daily early June-mid-Oct., $10 adults, $5 ages 3-18). Fifty-plus years later, meticulously restored, coal-fired steam trains loop through an ever-expanding village comprising 24 buildings, including a functioning steam-boiler workshop, on the now-30-acre campus that feels like a life-size train set. Historical buildings saved and relocated here include Maine Central and Belfast & Moosehead stations, the Boothbay Town Hall, and the Spruce Point Chapel. Exhibits, which range from the significant (60-plus antique vehicles) to the mundane (600 salt-and-pepper sets), help visitors make the connection between industry, everyday life, and the railway. Train rides also operate on weekends from late May until daily opening in June and for a Halloween ride on the last weekend in October.

★ Burnt Island Tour

Visit with a lighthouse keeper's family, climb the tower into the lantern room, and explore an island during a living- and natural-history program presented by the Maine Department of Marine Resources on **Burnt Island** (207/633-9559, www.maine.gov/dmr/education.htm, $25 adults, $15 ages 3-11). The tour is offered in July-August; call for current schedule. Travel via excursion boat from 21st-century Boothbay Harbor to Burnt Island, circa 1950, where actors portray the family of lighthouse keeper Joseph Muise, who lived here 1936-1951. During the three-hour program, you'll spend time with the light keeper, his wife, and each of his children, learning about their lifestyles and views on island life. Historical documents, photographs, and lenses, from 1821 to the present, are displayed in the 45-foot covered walkway between the house and tower. You may climb the spiral stairway up to the lantern room and see how the lighthouse actually functions. On an easy hike, a naturalist explains the island's flora, fauna, and geology and recounts legends. During free time, you may hike other trails, listen to a program on present-day lobstering and Maine fisheries, go beachcombing, fish for mackerel off the dock, or just relax and enjoy it all.

Marine Resources Aquarium

A 20-foot touch tank, with slimy but pettable specimens, is a major kid magnet at the **Marine Resources Aquarium** (McKown Point Rd., West Boothbay Harbor, 207/633-9559, www.maine.gov/dmr/education.htm, 10am-5pm daily late May-early Sept., 10am-5pm Wed.-Sun. Sept., $7 adults, $5 seniors, $3 ages 3-12), operated by the Maine Department of Marine Resources. Exhibits in the hexagonal aquarium include rare lobsters (oversize,

the Coastal Maine Botanical Gardens

albino, and blue) and other Gulf of Maine creatures; new residents arrive periodically. Educational programs include laboratory tours, sport-fishing lessons, and talks. Self-guiding leaflets are available. Consider bringing a picnic—it's a great setting. At the height of summer, parking is limited, and it's a longish walk from downtown around the west side of the harbor, so plan to take the free local trolley-bus.

Southport Island

The nautical shortcut of Townsend Gut separates Boothbay Harbor from **Southport Island**. The island is ideal for a drive-about (or a pedal-about, for experienced cyclists), following Route 27 south to the island's tip and returning north on Route 238. En route are plentiful glimpses of island-salted ocean waters, especially if you explore some of the side roads. Here are a few other noteworthy sights.

A historic 1810 Cape-style building, carefully restored, is the 11-room home of the **Hendricks Hill Museum** (Rte. 27, West Southport, 207/633-1102, www. southportmainehistory.com, 11am-3pm Tues., Thurs., and Sat. July-Aug., donation), a community attic filled with all kinds of workaday tools and utensils and fascinating maritime memorabilia. The museum is about two miles south of the Southport Island bridge, on the right, in the center of West Southport.

From the Southport Village General Store, where you can pick up sandwiches for a picnic, decent lobster rolls, and baked goodies, among other treats, it's just a hop down Beach Road to **Hendricks Head,** with a nice sandy beach and lighthouse views.

At the island's tip is the **Southport Memorial Library** (207/633-2741, 9am-4pm and 7pm-9pm Tues. and Thurs., 9am-4pm Sat.). Displayed inside is a huge collection of mounted tropical butterflies along with 10 signed and numbered Roger Tory Peterson prints.

ENTERTAINMENT

The renovated 1894 **Opera House** (86 Townsend Ave., Boothbay Harbor, 207/633-5159, www.boothbayoperahouse.com) hosts concerts, lectures, dramas, and special events.

Ask locally about the **Boothbay Playhouse,** which closed and was listed for sale in 2015.

The **Lincoln Arts Festival** (207/633-3913, www.lincolnartsfestival.net) presents concerts—classical, pops, choral, and jazz—and

Ride through the Boothbay Railway Village.

other arts-related events at various locations on the Boothbay Peninsula late June-late September.

Early July-August is a great time for music in Boothbay Harbor. Free **band concerts** at 7:30pm on Thursday are performed on the Memorial Library lawn (4 Oak St.). Bring a blanket or folding chair.

Mid-June-mid-October there's live entertainment weekends at **McSeagulls** (14 Wharf St., Boothbay Harbor, 207/633-5900, www.mcseagullsonline.com), which also serves decent food 11:30am-9pm daily.

Mine Oyster (16 Wharf St., 207/633-6616, www.mineoyster.net) has live entertainment, with an emphasis on dance bands.

EVENTS

The **Fishermen's Festival** is a colorful early-season celebration, held the third weekend of April, and includes the Miss Shrimp Princess pageant, a lobster-crate race, plentiful seafood and chowder, contests such as trap hauling, scallop and clam shucking, fish filleting, and net mending, and the blessing of the fleet to ensure a successful summer season. There's also a real steal—a lobster-eating contest you can enter for about $5.

June is the month for **Windjammer Days,** two days of festivities centering on traditional windjammer schooners. Highlights are the Windjammer Parade, harbor-front concerts, plenty of food, and a fireworks extravaganza.

In early August the **Boat Builders Festival** features shipyard and boat tours, food, and kids' activities.

RECREATION

Parks and Preserves

BOOTHBAY REGION LAND TRUST

The **Boothbay Region Land Trust** (137 Townsend Ave., Boothbay Harbor, 207/633-4818, www.bbrlt.org) has preserved more than 1,700 acres, including six islands, with more than 30 miles of trails available. Individual preserve maps as well as a general brochure-map with driving directions are available at the information centers, the trust office, and at trailhead kiosks. The trust also offers a free series of summertime guided walks and paddles in the various preserves, along with talks. A free guide, available at local businesses and info centers, provides details and access points. Here's just a sampling of the possibilities.

Most popular is the **Porter Preserve,** a 19-acre property bordering the Sheepscot River. Follow the moderately easy 0.86-mile

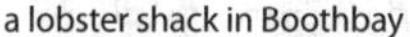

a lobster shack in Boothbay

loop trail and be rewarded with spectacular views, especially at sunset. You might even spy some seals lolling in the ledges at low tide. To get there, take Route 27 south to the monument in Boothbay Center. Bear right on Cory Lane and go 0.3 mile, bearing right again on Barters Island Road for 12.2 miles (perhaps stopping at the Trevett Country Store for lobster rolls or subs to go). Turn left on Kimballtown Road, for 0.5 mile, then left at the fork onto Porter Point Road. Park in the small lot just beyond the cemetery.

The 146-acre **Ovens Mouth Preserve** has almost five miles of trails on two peninsulas linked by a 93-foot bridge. The 1.6-mile trail on the east peninsula is much easier than the 3.7 miles of trails on the west peninsula. To get there, from the monument in Boothbay Center, travel 1.7 miles north and then go left on Adams Pond Road. Bear right at the fork and then continue 2.2 miles. To get to the east peninsula, bear right at the junction onto the Dover Road Extension. Proceed to the end of the tarred road to the parking lot on the left. To get to the west peninsula, bear left at the junction and continue 0.15 mile to the parking area on the right.

In East Boothbay, on the way to Ocean Point, is the 94.6-acre **Linekin Preserve,** stretching from Route 96 to the Damariscotta River. The 2.3-mile white-blazed River Loop (best done clockwise) takes in an old sawmill site, a beaver dam, and great riverfront views. You'll meet a couple of moderately steep sections on the eastern side, near the river, but otherwise it's relatively easy. To get there, take Route 96 for 3.8 miles and look for the parking area and trailhead on the left.

KNICKERCANE ISLAND

This gem is ideal for a picnic, perhaps with a lobster roll from the Trevett Country Store. The island is connected via a bridge, making it a pleasant place to stroll or, if you're brave, swim. Also here is an honest-to-God lobster pound (no, not the kind that serves the tasty crustaceans, but rather the impoundment area for them). The island is off the Barters Island Road causeway. To find it, from Boothbay Center follow signs for the Coastal Maine Botanical Center, then continue until you come to open water on both sides of the road; the parking area is on the left.

BARRETT PARK

On the east side of the harbor, Barrett Park is an oceanfront park on Linekin Bay, with shade trees, picnic tables, swimming, and restrooms. To find it, take Atlantic Avenue and turn left on Lobster Cove Road (at the Catholic church).

Boat Excursions

Two major fleet operators provide practically every type of sea adventure imaginable. Boothbay Harbor's veteran excursion fleet is **Cap'n Fish's Cruises** (Pier 1, Wharf St., Boothbay Harbor, 207/633-3244 or 800/636-3244, www.boothbayboattrips.com, $19-35 adults, $10-20 children). Cap'n Fish's 150-passenger boats do nine varied, mostly 2-3-hour cruises. There's bound to be a tour length and itinerary (seal-watching, lobster-trap hauling, lighthouses, Damariscove Harbor, puffin cruises, and more) that piques your interest. Pick up a schedule at one of the information centers and call for reservations. Cap'n Fish's is the best choice for **whale-watching,** offering three-four-hour trips departing daily mid-June-mid-October. Tours cost $54 adults, $32 ages 6-14, with a rain check if the whales don't show up. Reservations are advisable, especially early and late in the season and on summer weekends. No matter what the weather on shore, dress warmly and carry more clothing than you think you'll need. Motion-sensitive children and adults should plan ahead with appropriate medication. Cap'n Fish's also runs 2.5-hour puffin-sighting tours to Easter Egg Rock, circling the island once or twice for the best views. Cruises are offered once weekly in June, then three times weekly in July-late August ($35 adults, $15 children).

The harbor's other big fleet is **Balmy Days Cruises** (Pier 8, Commercial St., Boothbay Harbor, 207/633-2284 or 800/298-2284,

Damariscove Island

Summering Wabanakis knew it as Aquahega, but Damerill's Cove was the first European name attributed to the secure, fjord-like harbor at the southern tip of 210-acre Damariscove Island in 1614, when Captain John Smith of the Jamestown Colony explored the neighborhood. By 1622, Damerill's Cove fishermen were sharing their considerable codfish catch with starving Plimoth Plantation colonists desperate for food. Fishing and farming sustained resident Damariscovers during their up-and-down history, and archaeologists have found rich deposits for tracing the story of this early island settlement about seven miles south of Boothbay Harbor.

Rumors persist that the ghost of Captain Richard Pattishall, decapitated and tossed overboard by Indians in 1689, still roams the island, accompanied by the specter of his dog. The fog that often overhangs the bleak, almost-treeless low-slung island makes it easy to fall for the many ghost stories about Pattishall and other one-time residents. In summer, the island is awash with wildflowers, bayberries, raspberries, blackberries, and rugosa roses.

Since 2005, most of 1.7-mile-long Damariscove has been owned by **The Boothbay Region Land Trust** (1 Oak St., 2nd Fl., Boothbay Harbor, 207/633-44818, www.bbrlt.org). Day-use visitors are welcome on the island anytime, but the northern section (called Wood End) protects the state's largest nesting colony of eiders—nearly 700 nests. Damariscove Island became a National Historic Landmark in 1978. Dogs are not allowed.

Access to the island is most convenient if you have your own boat. Enter the narrow cove at the southern end of the island. You can disembark at the dock on the west side of the harbor, but don't tie up here or at the adjacent stone pier. Two guest moorings and two courtesy dinghies are available. The Boothbay Region Land Trust sometimes offers special trips. Summertime caretakers live in the small cabin above the dock, where a trail map is available. Stay on the trail (watch out for poison ivy) or on the shore and away from any abandoned structures; the former Coast Guard station is privately owned.

www.balmydayscruises.com), operating three vessels on a variety of excursions. The *Novelty* does daily one-hour harbor tours ($18 adults, $9 ages 3-11). Reservations usually are not necessary. The 31-foot Friendship sloop *Bay Lady* offers 90-minute sailing trips ($26 adults, $18 children) daily in summer. Reservations are wise for the *Bay Lady* as well as for the fleet's most popular cruise, a daylong trip to Monhegan Island ($38 adults, $19 ages 3-11) on the *Balmy Days II*, departing at 9:30am and returning at 4:15pm daily early June-late September, plus extended weekends in late May and early October. The three-hour round-trip allows about 3.5 hours ashore on idyllic Monhegan Island.

A far smaller and more personal experience is offered by **Appledore Cruises** (20 Commercial St., Boothbay Harbor, 207/633-6598, www.schoonereastwind.com, $32 adults, $25 kids). A trip aboard *Schooner Eastwind*, a 65-foot traditional wooden schooner built in 2004, is more than a day sail—it's an adventure. Herb and Doris Smith not only built this schooner, but also sailed around the world in their previous boats through the years, providing fodder for many tales. They take passengers on 2.5-hour cruises to the outer islands and Seal Rocks up to four times daily. The boat departs from Fisherman's Wharf.

Kayaking and Bicycling

From Memorial Day weekend through September, **Tidal Transit** (18 Granary Way, Chowder House Building, Boothbay Harbor, 207/633-7140, www.kayakboothbay.com), near the footbridge, will get you afloat with 2-3-hour guided lighthouse, wildlife, or sunset sea kayaking tours for around $45-50; full and multiday tours are available, too. It also offers tours from the Coastal Maine Botanical Garden.

For do-it-yourselfers, Tidal Transit rents

single kayaks ($25 one hour-$55/day), tandem kayaks ($35 one hour-$75/day), stand-up paddleboards ($15/half-hour -$45/half-day) and bicycles ($10 half-day, $15 full day).

SHOPPING

Artisans' galleries pepper the peninsula. Galleries, boutiques, and novelty shops crowd Boothbay Harbor, providing plenty of browsing for all budgets and tastes. Here are a few worth seeking out.

A visit to the **Villard Gallery** (57 Campbell St., Boothbay Harbor, 207/633-3507, www.villardstudios.com) is a must for fans of fine-art crafts. Kim and Philippe Villard split their lives between Boothbay Harbor and southern France, where they live in the midst of a national park. Philippe is a talented sculptor, and Kim an equally talented painter. They collaborate on woodcuts and handmade books, and the results are in collections and museums. Call in advance if you want a demonstration of the process. They have works in all price ranges, from poster prints to the actual woodblocks themselves.

Antiques store or museum, you decide: The **Palabra Shop** (53 Commercial St., Boothbay Harbor, 207/633-4225) has 10 rooms chock-full of antiques and collectibles. It's also home to the world's largest collection of Moses bottles, viewable by appointment.

One of the state's best fine-art galleries, **Gleason Fine Art** (31 Townsend Ave., Boothbay Harbor, 207/633-6849, www.gleasonfineart.com) specializes in Maine art from the 19th-21st centuries. The gallery is light, bright, and a pleasure to browse. Even if you have no interest in buying, stop in to see works by some of Maine's top talents.

Also displaying a fine selection of predominantly Maine-related art is **Studio 63 Fine Art Gallery** (53 Townsend Ave., Boothbay harbor, 207/633-2755, www. studio53fineart.com).

Ae Home (93 Townsend Ave., Boothbay Harbor, 207/315-5221, www.aeceramics.com), is a studio/gallery where talented Alison Evans creates hand molded and glazed ceramic dishware and tabletop accessories in natural shapes inspired by the Maine coast.

At **Eventide Epicurean Specialties** (5 Boothbay House Hill, Boothbay Harbor, 207/350-4244), you can taste your way through dozens of olive oils and balsamic vinegars and pick up other specialty foods, such as breads, cheeses, and chocolates.

The Balmy Days excursion boat transports passengers from Boothbay Harbor to Monhegan Island.

The views from the Newagen Seaside Inn on Southport Island are dreamy.

ACCOMMODATIONS

If you want to concentrate your time in downtown Boothbay Harbor, shopping or taking boat excursions, stay in town and avoid the parking hassles. Although the town practically rolls up the sidewalks in the winter, a few businesses do stay open year-round. Lodgings that do so are noted; others are seasonal, usually mid-May-mid-October.

Classic Inns

To get away from it all, book in at the **Newagen Seaside Inn** (Rte. 27, Southport, 207/633-5242 or 800/654-5242 outside Maine, www.newagenseasideinn.com, mid-May-Sept., from $200), an unstuffy, updated, full-service inn with casual fine dining and views that go on forever. Renovated guest rooms are split among the Main Inn; the Little Inn, where rooms have private decks, TVs, and kitchenettes; and seven cottages. There's a long rocky shore, a nature trail, and a spa, plus tennis courts, a pool and hot tub, cruiser bikes, guest rowboats, a game room, candlepin bowling, and porches just for relaxing. Rates include a generous buffet breakfast. The dining room is open to nonguests by reservation for dinner 5:30pm-9pm daily; entrées run $19-36, but lighter fare is available. The inn is six miles south of downtown Boothbay Harbor.

Over in East Boothbay, the **Ocean Point Inn** (Shore Rd., East Boothbay, 207/633-4200 or 800/552-5554, www.oceanpointinn.com, $99-349) wows with spectacular sunset views and an easygoing ambience that keeps guests returning generation after generation. Lodgings on the sprawling complex comprise an inn, a lodge, a motel, apartments, and cottages. Most guest rooms have ocean views; all have mini-fridges, phones, cable TV, Wi-Fi, and air-conditioning; some have kitchenettes. The rates, which include a hot buffet breakfast, reflect that this is an older property, and some accommodations are tired; updating is in progress. Also on the premises are a restaurant and tavern with fabulous ocean views, a pier, an outdoor heated pool, a hot tub, and Adirondack-style chairs set just so on the water's edge. The best deals are the packages.

For those who require luxury touches, the **Spruce Point Inn and Spa** (Atlantic Ave., Boothbay Harbor, 207/633-4152 or 800/553-0289, www.sprucepointinn.com) is the answer. Accommodations are traditional inn rooms and cottages and condos, all with private decks, mini-fridges, and TVs; some have fireplaces, kitchenettes, and whirlpool tubs. Decor and prices vary widely. The inn holds big weddings on many weekends, so try for midweek. Peak rates begin around $400. Amenities at the 57-acre resort include a full-service spa and fitness center, freshwater and saltwater pools, tennis courts, rocky shorefront, and a shuttle bus to downtown (about 1.5 miles, although it seems farther). Children's programs are available. Dining choices range from poolside to pub-style to fine dining, with prices to match each setting. It's pet friendly.

Linekin Bay Resort (92 Wall Point Rd., Boothbay Harbor, 207/633-2494 or

866/847-2103, www.linekinbayresort.com), a classic old-timey summer sporting camp on 20 wooded oceanfront acres, is moving on up. New owners began updating and rebuilding the dated and worn lodges and cabins in 2016, with plans to upgrade the waterfront and enhance the children's program. Summer season rates ($155-190 per adult, $50-115 per child, plus 10 percent amenity fee) include lodging, all meals, recreational programs, kids' camps, sailing instruction, as well as use of the tennis courts, heated saltwater pool, sailboats, canoes, and kayaks. Pet-friendly accommodations are available, $40/stay.

Bed-and-Breakfasts

Topping an in-town hill with sigh-producing views over the inner and outer harbors, and yet just a two-minute walk to shops and restaurants, is ★ **Topside Inn** (60 McKown St., Boothbay Harbor, 207/633-5404 or 888/633-5404, www.topsideinn.com, from $185), a solid 19th-century sea captain's home with two annexes. Innkeepers Buzz Makarewicz and Mark Osborn keep updating the nicely renovated property, opting for a handsome décor with a touch of seaside whimsy. Guest rooms in the three-story main inn are mostly spacious, with nice views. Good books are plentiful, and the rockers on the wraparound porch and Adirondack chairs on the lawn are perfect places to read or relax. The annexes have motel-type guest rooms done in bed-and-breakfast style; all have decks and most have at least glimpses of the ocean. All guest rooms have flat-screen TVs and Wi-Fi. Rates in all buildings include breakfast, a self-serve cold buffet with a hot entrée that's served to the table. Hot beverages are available all day; beer, wine, and cocktails are available as are cheese and charcuterie plates; and on most afternoons home-baked cookies magically appear in the guest pantry.

Next door is **The Harbor House** (80 McKown St., Boothbay Harbor, 800/856-1164, www.harborhouse-me.com, $145-195), a mansard-roofed house with six rooms (one pet-friendly, one with detached bath) and a great wraparound porch. Breakfast is a buffet, with a hot entrée. Some rooms have great water views.

In town and on the water, the **Blue Heron Seaside Inn** (65 Townsend Ave., Boothbay Harbor, 207/633-7020 or 866/216-2300, www.blueheronseasideinn.com, year-round, $240-285) opened in 2003 after a complete restoration. The uncluttered, bright interior belies the Victorian vintage. Large guest rooms are accented with antiques and collectibles from Boothbay natives Phil and Laura Chapman's years overseas. Each room has a waterfront deck, air-conditioning, a fridge, a microwave, an LCD HDTV, Wi-Fi, and a phone; some also have a fireplace and a whirlpool tub. A dock with kayaks and a paddleboat is available. A full breakfast is elegantly served on Wedgwood china.

Cozy Harbor Bed & Breakfast (Pratt's Island Rd., 207/633-3546, www.cozy-harbor.com, $150) is sited in a harborside white frame house. Guests have a choice of two rooms sharing 1.5 baths, but innkeeper Sandra Seifert will only rent both rooms to people traveling together; no sharing with strangers, here. The guestrooms, breakfast room, and living room with TV all have water views, and there's a dock across the street.

Escape the hustle and bustle of Boothbay Harbor at the ★ **Five Gables Inn B&B** (107 Murray Hill Rd., East Boothbay, 207/633-4551 or 800/451-5048, www.fivegablesinn.com, $165-265), which began life as a no-frills summer hotel in the late 19th century. It's gone steadily upmarket since then. Unique touches include wonderful murals throughout and window seats in the gable rooms. All but one of the 16 light and airy guest rooms have Linekin Bay views, and some have fireplaces. The living room is congenial, the gardens are gorgeous, and the porch goes on forever. Rates include a multicourse breakfast and afternoon tea. The inn, on a side road off Route 96 in the traditional boatbuilding hamlet of East Boothbay, is 3.5 miles from downtown Boothbay Harbor. Arriving by boat? One mooring is available for guests.

Pining to stay in a lighthouse? Splurge at **The Inn at Cuckolds Lighthouse** (Cuckolds Island, off Southport, 855/212-5252, www.innatcuckoldslighthouse.com, from $450), an ultra-lux two-suite escape in an 1892 lighthouse complex on a private island. Transportation is provided; it's about 15 minutes from the Southport landing to the island. Suites are stocked with nibbles, breakfast and afternoon tea are included; lunch and dinner are available for $65 for a three-course meal to $75 for a Maine lobster bake. Note: no children under age 18.

Motels and Hotels

Since 1955, the Lewis family has owned and operated the **Mid-Town Motel** (96 McKown St., Boothbay Harbor, 207/633-2751, www.midtownmaine.com, $95), a spotless, no-frills vintage motel that's within steps of everything. It's a classic: clean, convenient, and cheap, and the owners couldn't be nicer folks.

Every room at the lakefront **Beach Cove Hotel & Resort** (38 Lakeview Rd., Boothbay Harbor, 207/633-0353 or 866/851-0450, www.beachcovehotel.com, $99-220) has a water view, a balcony or deck, air-conditioning, Wi-Fi, a mini-fridge, and a microwave. The renovated property, about one mile from downtown, is extremely popular with families who appreciate its beach, dock, heated saltwater pool, canoes, and rowboats. A light continental breakfast is included.

Camping

With 150 well-maintained wooded and open sites on 45 acres, **Shore Hills Campground** (553 Rte. 27, Boothbay, 207/633-4782, www.shorehills.com, $29-52) is a popular big-rig destination where reservations are essential in midsummer. Tenters should request a wooded site away from the biggest RVs. Leashed pets are allowed, and there's a shuttle service to Boothbay Harbor.

Much smaller, and smack on the ocean, is **Gray Homestead Oceanfront Camping** (21 Homestead Rd., Southport, 207/633-4612, www.graysoceancamping.com, $37-50), a family-run campground with 40 RV and tenting sites as well as cottages and condos. A stone beach, a pier, laundry facilities, kayak rentals, and lobsters—live or cooked—are available. There's even a small sandy beach.

FOOD

Boothbay Harbor is not a culinary destination. Go for the views and enjoy the region, but don't expect to be wowed by the food.

Local Flavors

Three general stores deliver local flavors with some fancy touches. It's worth the drive over to Trevett to indulge in a lobster roll from the **Trevett Country Store** (207/633-1140), just before the bridge connecting Hodgdon and Barters Islands. Stop into the **Southport General Store** (443 Hendricks Hill Rd., 207/633-6666), serving Southport Island since 1882, for breakfast, pizzas, sandwiches, burgers, baked goods, and a decent wine selection. On the east side, the **East Boothbay General Store** (255 Ocean Point Rd./Rte. 96, East Boothbay, 207/633-4503) has been serving locals since 1893. These days, it sells wine and specialty foods in addition to pizzas (including an awesome breakfast version), sandwiches, and baked goods.

"Free beer tomorrow" proclaims the sign in front of **Bet's Famous Fish Fry** (Village Common, Rte. 27, Boothbay), a take-out stand that's renowned for its generous portions of fresh haddock fish-and-chips perfectly prepared (hint: unless you're starving, often a half-order will feed two). There's a nice seating area with picnic tables and a garden.

Blue Moon (54 Commercial St., Boothbay Harbor, 207/633-2220, from 7:30 a.m. daily) is a tiny spot worth seeking out for breakfast and lunch fare. Try to snag one of the porch tables hanging over the harbor.

The seasonal **Boothbay Area Farmers Market** sets up on the Town Commons, Boothbay, 9am-noon Thursday.

Casual Dining

Real Northern Italian fare prepared by a

real Italian chef is the lure for ★ **Ports of Italy** (47 Commercial St., Boothbay Harbor, 207/633-1011, www.portsofitaly.com, 4:30pm-9:30pm daily, $17-30). Owner Sante Calandri hails from Perugia, but more recently spent 23 years in New York City. This isn't a red-sauce place; expect well-prepared and innovative fare, with delicious homemade pastas and especially good seafood.

The Watershed Tavern (301 Adams Pond Rd., Boothbay, 207/633-3411 11am-9pm Mon.-Sat., www.watershedtavern.com, $10-15), at the Boothbay Craft Brewery, serves panini, burgers, wood-oven pizzas, and heartier fare. A brewery tour is available for $5 pp.

For spectacular sunset views, take a spin out to the **Ocean Point Inn** (Shore Rd., East Boothbay, 207/633-4200 or 800/552-5554, www.oceanpointinn.com, 7:30am-10am and 6pm-9pm daily, $110-30). The lobster stew is rave-worthy, and a children's menu is available. Non-guests are also welcome at the full hot breakfast buffet, $14.

The tapas menu complements the views from the third-floor deck at **Boat House Bistro** (12 The By-Way, Boothbay Harbor, 207/633-0400, www.theboathousebistro.com, 11:30am-10pm daily). There are plenty of other options, but the tapas, pizzas, soups, and salads ($8-15) are the way to go.

The **Thistle Inn** (55 Oak St., Boothbay Harbor, 207/633-3541, www.thethistleinn.com, from 5pm Tues.-Sun., $25-35) is a two-fold find, with a finer dining restaurant serving entrees such as cornmeal-crusted haddock and filet mignon as well as a casual pub offering burgers, pizzas, and crab cakes.

Lobster in the Rough

Boothbay Harbor and East Boothbay seem to have more eat-on-the-dock lobster shacks per square inch than almost anywhere else on the coast, but, frankly, they're all overcrowded and overpriced, and don't deliver an authentic experience.

The best of the in-town lot is **The Lobster Dock** (49 Atlantic Ave., Boothbay Harbor, 207/635-7120, www.thelobsterdock.com, 11:30am-8:30pm daily), where lobsters are delivered twice daily; now that's fresh. Although there are a few choices for landlubbers—even PBJ for kids—lobster and fish are the prime attraction. It's right on the harbor, so the views are superb. Expect to wait in line.

Far more authentic and well worth the splurge is **Cabbage Island Clambakes** (Pier 6, Fisherman's Wharf, Boothbay Harbor, 207/633-7200, www.cabbageislandclambakes.com). Touristy, sure, but it's a delicious adventure. Board the excursion boat *Bennie Alice* at Pier 6 in Boothbay Harbor, cruise for about an hour past islands, boats, and lighthouses, and disembark at 5.5-acre Cabbage Island. Watch the clambake in progress, explore the island, or play volleyball. When the feast is ready, pick up your platter, find a picnic table, and dig in. A cash bar is available in the lodge, as are restrooms. When the weather's ifty, the lodge and covered patio have seats for 100 people. For about $65 (no credit cards), you'll get two lobsters (or half a chicken), chowder, clams, corn, an egg, onions, potatoes, blueberry cake, a beverage, and the boat ride. Clambake season is mid-June-mid-September. The 3.5-hour trips depart at 12:30pm Monday-Friday, 12:30pm and 5pm Saturday, and 11am and 1:30pm Sunday.

The only item on the menu at **Shannon's Unshelled** (11 Granary Way, Boothbay Harbor, www.shannonsunshelled.biz, 11am-sold out daily), a take-out, is a lobster roll, made with the meat of a whole lobster and served on a buttered bun with a side of sea-salted butter.

Oliver's (36 Cozy Harbor Rd., Southport, 207/633-8888, www.oliversrestaurant.com, 11:30am-8pm daily, $15-30) has a stunning location overlooking the harbor and serves a full, if pricey, menu with an emphasis on seafood.

INFORMATION AND SERVICES

Providing info about their members are the **Boothbay Harbor Region Chamber of Commerce** (207/633-2353, www.

boothbayharbor.com) and the **Boothbay Chamber of Commerce** (207/633-4743, www.boothbay.org).

Check out **Boothbay Harbor Memorial Library** (4 Oak St., Boothbay Harbor, 207/633-3112, www.bmpl.lib.me.us). Thursday evenings in July-August there are band concerts on the lawn.

Find **public restrooms** at the municipal parking lot on Commercial Street (next to Pier 1), the municipal lot at the end of Granary Way, Saint Andrews Hospital, the town offices, the library, and the Marine Resources Aquarium.

GETTING THERE AND AROUND

Boothbay Harbor is about 13 miles or 20 minutes via Routes 1 and 27 from Wiscasset. It's about 15 miles or 35 minutes to Damariscotta via Routes 27 and 1.

The Rocktide Inn operates free trolleybuses on continuous scheduled routes during the summer.

Pemaquid Region

At the head of the Pemaquid Peninsula, the riverfront towns of **Damariscotta** (pop. 2,218) and her conjoined twin, **Newcastle** (pop. 1,752), anchor the southwestern end of the Pemaquid Peninsula, while **Waldoboro** (pop. 5,075) anchors the northeastern end. Along the peninsula are **New Harbor** (probably Maine's most photographed fishing village), **Pemaquid Point** (site of one of Maine's most photographed lighthouses), and historic ports reputedly used by Captain John Smith, Captain Kidd, and assorted less-notorious types. Here too are a restored fortress, Native American historic sites, antiques and crafts shops galore, boat excursions to offshore Monhegan, and one of the best pocket-size sandy beaches in Mid-Coast Maine.

On Christmas Day 1614, famed explorer Captain John Smith anchored on Rutherford Island, at the tip of the peninsula, and promptly named the spot Christmas Cove. Today it is one of three villages that make up the town of South Bristol, the southwestern finger of the Pemaquid Peninsula. **Bristol** (pop. 2,755) and **South Bristol** (pop. 892), covering eight villages on the bottom half of the peninsula, were named after the British port city.

As early as 1625, settler John Brown received title to some of this territory from the Wabanaki sachem (chief) Samoset, an agreeable fellow who learned snippets of English from English cod fishermen. *Damariscotta* (dam-uh-riss-COT-ta), in fact, is a Wabanaki word for "plenty of alewives [herring]." The settlement here was named Walpole but was incorporated in 1847 under its current name.

Newcastle, incorporated in 1763, earned fame and fortune from shipbuilding and brick-making—which explains the extraordinary number of brick homes and office buildings throughout the town. In the 19th century, Newcastle's shipyards sent clippers, Down Easters, and full-rigged ships down the ways and around the world.

Route 1 cuts a commercial swath through Waldoboro without revealing the attractive downtown—or the lovely Friendship Peninsula, south of the highway. Duck into Waldoboro and then follow Route 220 south 10 miles to Friendship for an off-the-beaten-track drive.

Waldoboro's heritage is something of an anomaly in Maine. It's predominantly German, thanks to 18th-century Teutons who swallowed the blandishments of General Samuel Waldo, holder of a million-acre "patent" stretching as far as the Penobscot River. In the cemetery at the Old German Church, on Route 32, the inscription on a 19th-century marker sums up the town's early history:

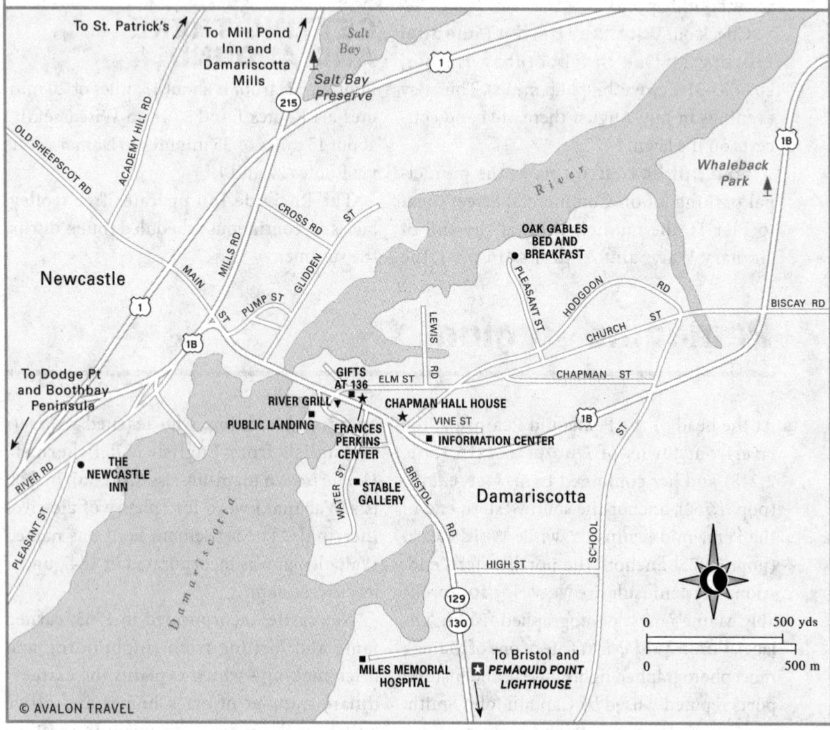

This town was settled in 1748, by Germans who emigrated to this place with the promise and expectation of finding a populous city, instead of which they found nothing but a wilderness; for the first few years they suffered to a great extent by Indian wars and starvation. By perseverance and self-denial, they succeeded in clearing lands and erecting mills. At this time [1855] a large proportion of the inhabitants are descendants of the first settlers.

It sure makes you wonder why Waldo's name stuck to the town.

After the mill era, the settlers went into shipbuilding in a big way, establishing six shipyards and producing more than 300 wooden vessels, including the first five-masted schooner, the 265-foot *Governor Ames,* launched in 1888. Although the *Ames*'s ill-supported masts collapsed on her maiden voyage, repairs allowed her to serve as a coal hauler for more than 20 years, and many more five-masters followed in her wake. It's hard to believe today, but Waldoboro once was the sixth-busiest port in the United States. At the Town Landing, alongside the Medomak River, a marker describes the town's shipyards and shipbuilding heritage.

SIGHTS

Chapman-Hall House

Damariscotta's oldest surviving building is the Cape-style **Chapman-Hall House** (270 Main St., Damariscotta, noon-4pm Sat.-Sun. early June-mid-Oct., $5), built in 1754 by Nathaniel Chapman, whose family tree includes the legendary John Chapman, better known as Johnny Appleseed. Highlights are a 1754 kitchen and displays of local shipbuilding memorabilia. The house, on the National Register of Historic Places, was meticulously restored in the styles of three different eras. Don't miss the antique roses in the back garden. It's now cared for by the Lincoln County Historical Society (www.lincolncountyhistory.org), which organizes docent-led tours.

★ Pemaquid Point Lighthouse

One of the icons of the Maine Coast, Pemaquid Point's lighthouse has been captured for posterity by gazillions of photographers and is depicted on a Maine state quarter. The lighthouse, adjacent keeper's house, and picnic grounds are a town park. Also on the premises is an art gallery. Admission to the grounds, payable at the gatehouse, is $2 (age 12 and older). The lighthouse grounds are accessible all year, even after the museum closes for the season, when admission is free. The point is 15 miles south of Route 1 via winding two-lane Route 130.

Commissioned in 1827, **Pemaquid Point Light** (www.lighthousefoundation.org) stands sentinel over some of Maine's nastiest shoreline—rocks and surf that can reduce any wooden boat to kindling. Now automated, the light tower is licensed to the American Lighthouse Foundation and is managed by the Friends of Pemaquid Point Lighthouse. Volunteers *aim* to open the tower 10:30am-5pm daily late May-mid-October, weather permitting. There is no charge for the tower, but donations are appreciated. Still can't get enough? Newcastle Square Vacation Rentals (207/563-6500, www.mainecoastcottages.com) manages a one-bedroom apartment available for weekly rental ($1,200) in the keeper's house. Proceeds benefit preservation.

The adjacent **Fisherman's Museum** (207/677-2494, 9am-5pm daily mid-May-mid-Oct., donation), in the former light keeper's house, points up the pleasures and perils of the lobstering industry and also has some lighthouse memorabilia.

While here, visit the **Pemaquid Art Gallery** (207/677-2752), displaying juried works by the Pemaquid Group of Artists since 1928.

Bring a picnic and lounge on the rocks below the light tower, but don't plan to snooze. You'll be busy protecting your food from the dive-bombing gulls and your kids from the treacherous surf.

Three national flags fly over Fort William Henry.

★ Colonial Pemaquid and Fort William Henry

At the **Colonial Pemaquid State Historic Site** (end of Huddle Rd., 207/677-2423, friendsofcolonialpemaquid.org, 9am-5pm daily late May-early Sept., $3 nonresident adults, $2 Maine resident adults, non-resident seniors kids free), signed from Route 130 in New Harbor, visitors can gain a basic understanding of what life was like in an English frontier settlement. The 19-acre complex, listed on the National Register of Historic Places, comprises a museum and visitors center, Fort William Henry, the Fort House, the remnants of a village, an 18th-century cemetery, a picnic area, a pier and boat ramp, and restrooms, all spread out on a grassy point sloping to John's Bay and bordered by McCaffrey's Brook, the Pemaquid River, and Pemaquid Harbor. Bring a picnic, bring a kite, bring a kayak, let the kids run—but do take time to visit the historic sites (a kids' activity book is available for $1). Demonstrations, tours, lectures, and reenactments are part of the site's summer schedule.

Three national flags fly over the ramparts of **Fort William Henry,** a reconstruction of a fort dating from 1692, the second of three that stood here between 1677 and the late 18th century. The forts were built to defend the English settlement of Pemaquid, settled between 1625 and 1628, from the French. From the rebuilt western tower, you'll have fantastic views of John's Bay and John's Island, named for none other than Captain John Smith; inside are artifacts retrieved from archaeological excavations of the 17th-century trading outpost.

The square white Fort House, which dates to the late 1700s, houses a research library and archaeology lab as well as a gift shop.

Exhibits at the museum and visitors center focus on regional history, from early Native American life through the colonial period. Selections from the more than 100,000 artifacts uncovered during archaeological digs here are displayed, along with a diorama of Pemaquid Village.

Take time to wander the village, 14 cellar holes of 17th- and 18th-century dwellings, a forge, a trading post, a jail, and other early buildings, all marked with interpretive signs. Also visit the burying ground. Note that rubbings are not permitted, as they could damage the fragile old stones.

Historical Houses of Worship

One of the oldest houses of worship in Maine that still holds services, **The Old Walpole Meeting House** (Rte. 129, Bristol Rd.,

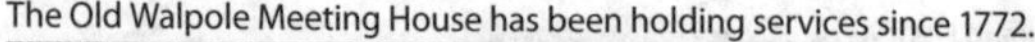
The Old Walpole Meeting House has been holding services since 1772.

Walpole, www.oldwalpolemeetinghouse.org), built in 1772, remains remarkably unchanged, with original hand-shaved shingles and handmade nails and hinges. The balcony—where African American servants were once relegated—is paneled with boards more than two feet wide. The meetinghouse is 3.5 miles south of Damariscotta and 0.25 mile south of where Routes 129 and 130 fork. The Walpole Barn, across the main road, has keys, if you want to peek inside.

The beautifully restored **Harrington Meeting House** (Old Harrington Rd., off Rte. 130, 2pm-4:30pm Mon., Wed., and Fri. July-Aug., donation), begun in 1772 and completed in 1775, now serves as Bristol's local-history museum—town-owned and run by the Pemaquid Historical Association. Behind it is an old cemetery that's fascinating to explore.

A remnant of Waldoboro's German connection is the **Old German Church** (Rte. 32, Waldoboro, 207/832-7742, www.oldgermanmeetinghouse.com, 1pm-4pm daily July-Aug.) and its cemetery. The Reformed Lutheran church, built in 1772 on the opposite side of the Medomak River, was moved across the ice in the winter of 1794. Inside are box pews and a huge hanging pulpit. One of the three oldest churches in Maine, it lost its flock in the mid-19th century when new generations no longer spoke German. An annual, afternoon German service is held on the first Sunday of August.

Built in 1808, **St. Patrick's Catholic Church** (Academy Hill Rd., Damariscotta Mills, Newcastle, 207/563-3240, 9am-sunset daily), a solid brick structure with 1.5-foot-thick walls, a rare crypt-form altar, and a Paul Revere bell, is New England's oldest Catholic church in continual use. Academy Hill Road starts at Newcastle Square in downtown Newcastle; the church is 2.25 miles from the square and one mile beyond Lincoln Academy.

St. Andrew's Episcopal Church (Glidden St., Newcastle, 207/563-3533), built in 1883, is nothing short of exquisite, with carved-oak beams, a stenciled ceiling, and, for the cognoscenti, a spectacular Hutchings organ.

Frances Perkins Center

For insight into the life of the first female presidential cabinet member in U.S. history, visit the **Frances Perkins Center** (170A Main St., 207/563-3374, www.francesperkinscenter.org, 10am-2pm Tues.-Sat.). In addition to the small museum honoring the U.S. Secretary of Labor, 1933-45, the center often organizes guided tours ($20) of the nearby Perkins Homestead, a 57-acre working farm and brickyard under consideration as a National Historic Landmark.

Old Rock Schoolhouse

Docents garbed in period costumes welcome visitors to the one-room **Old Rock Schoolhouse** (158 Rock Schoolhouse Rd., 1-3 pm Wed. and Sun.), a stone structure dating from 1837 that's one of Maine's oldest schoolhouses.

The Thompson Ice House

On a Sunday morning in February (weather and ice permitting), several hundred helpers and onlookers gather at Thompson Pond, next to the **Thompson Ice House** (1264 Rte. 129, South Bristol, www.thompsonicehouse.com), for the annual ice harvest. Festivity prevails as a crew of robust fellows marks out a grid and saws out 12-inch-thick ice cakes, which are pushed up a ramp to the ice-storage house. More than 60 tons of ice is harvested each year. Sawdust-insulated 10-inch-thick walls keep the ice from melting in this building first used in 1826 and now listed on the National Register of Historic Places. In 1990 the house became part of a working museum (1pm-4pm Wed. and Fri.-Sat. July-Aug., donation), with ice tools and a window view of the stored ice cakes. The grounds, including a photographic display board depicting a 1964 harvest, are accessible for free all year. The site is 12 miles south of Damariscotta on Route 129.

Return of the Alewives

If you're in the Damariscotta area in May and early June, don't miss a chance to go to Damariscotta Mills to see the annual **Alewife Run.** During this time, more than 250,000 alewives (*Alosa pseudoharengus,* a kind of herring) make their way from Great Salt Bay to their spawning grounds in freshwater Damariscotta Lake, 42 feet higher. Waiting eagerly at the top are ospreys, gulls, cormorants, and sometimes eagles, ready to feast on the weary fish. Connecting the bay and the lake is a man-made stone-and-masonry "fish ladder" (www.damariscottamills.org), a zigzagging channel where you can watch the foot-long fish wriggle their way onward and upward. The ladder was built in 1807; restoration is ongoing. A walkway runs alongside the route, and informative display panels explain the event. It's a fascinating historical ecology lesson. To reach the fishway, take Route 215 for 1.6 miles west of Route 1. When you reach a small bridge, cross it and take a sharp left down a slight incline to a small parking area. Walk behind the fish house to follow the path to the fish ladder. Try to go on a sunny day—the fish are more active, and their silvery sides glisten as they go.

Waldoborough Historical Society Museum

The **Waldoborough Historical Society Museum** (1164 Main St., Waldoboro, www.waldoborohistory.us, noon-3pm Wed.-Mon. late June-early Sept., free) is a three-building roadside complex just 0.1 mile south of Route 1 at the eastern end of town. On the grounds are the 1857 one-room **Boggs Schoolhouse,** the 1819 **Town Pound** (to detain stray livestock), and two buildings filled with antique tools, toys, and utensils along with period costumes, antique fire engines, and artifacts from the shipbuilding era.

Maine Antique Toy and Art Museum

Indulge your inner child at the **Maine Antique Toy and Art Museum** (Rte. 1, Waldoboro, 207/832-7398, 10am-4pm Wed.-Mon. late May-mid-Oct., noon-4pm Sat.-Sun. mid-Oct.-Christmas, $5). The museum houses an extensive collection of antique toys and original comic art. See how Mickey Mouse first appeared or browse a collection of Lone Ranger memorabilia. This museum is geared to nostalgic adults, not kids—you'll find all the old favorites, including Popeye, Felix the Cat, Betty Boop, Snow White, Pogo, and Yoda.

ENTERTAINMENT

Two struggling arts centers provide year-round programs. **River Arts** (170 Business Rte. 1, Damariscotta, 207/563-1507, www.riverartsme.org) doubles as a gallery. Neoclassic on the outside, art deco within, the **Waldo Theatre** (916 Main St., Waldoboro, 207/832-6060, www.thewaldo.org) was built as a cinema in 1936. Restored in the mid-1980s, it presents concerts, plays, films, lectures, and other year-round community events.

Lincoln County Community Theater (Theater St., Damariscotta, 207/563-3424, www.lcct.org) owns and operates the historic Lincoln Theater, dating from 1867. It also presents musicals and dramas, concerts, films, and more.

Salt Bay Chamberfest (207/522-3749, www.saltbaychamberfest.org) presents concerts in August.

FESTIVALS AND EVENTS

In mid-August, **Olde Bristol Days** features a crafts show, a parade, road and boat races, live entertainment, and fireworks. Damariscotta's people pleasers are the **Pemaquid Oyster Festival** in September and **Pumpkinfest,** a family pleaser with food, entertainment, and competitions, in October.

SHOPPING

Downtown Damariscotta has a nice selection of independent shops, galleries, and boutiques. Parking in summer is a headache; the municipal lot behind the storefronts has a three-hour limit, and it's often full. You can usually find spots on some of the side streets.

Antiques and Antiquarian Books

Antiques shops are numerous along Bristol Road (Rte. 130), where many barns have been turned into shops selling everything from fine antiques to less-pedigreed "old stuff." Serious antiques aficionados will find plenty to browse and buy along this stretch of road.

The multidealer **Nobleboro Antique Exchange** (104 Atlantic Hwy./Rte. 1, Nobleboro, 207/563-6800, www.antiquex.net) is housed in a light-blue building that goes on and on, with more than 100 display areas on three levels. The selection is diverse, from period antiques to 20th-century collectibles.

The **Art of Antiquing** (4 Back Shore Rd., Round Pond, 207/529-5300, www.theartofantiquing.com) specializes in antiques and art sourced in Europe and the United Kingdom.

Art Galleries

Worth a visit for the building alone, the **Stable Gallery** (26 Water St., Damariscotta, 207/563-1991, www.stablegallerymaine.com), just off Main Street, was built in the 19th-century clipper-ship era and still has original black-walnut stalls—providing a great foil for the work of dozens of Maine craftspeople. Lining the walls are paintings and prints from the gallery's large "stable" of artists.

You'll find a carefully curated selection of Maine-made fine and folk arts and crafts as well as artisan chocolates at **Gifts at 136** (136 Main St., Damariscotta, 207/563-1011), an especially fine shop with works in all price ranges.

In his **River Gallery** (79 Main St., Damariscotta, 207/563-6330), dealer Geoff Robinson specializes in 19th- and early-20th-century European and American fine art—a connoisseur's inventory.

Betcha can't leave without buying something from **Pemaquid Craft Co-op** (Rte. 130, New Harbor, 207/677-2077), with 15 rooms filled with high-quality works by 50 Maine artisans.

A delightful little off-the-beaten-path find is **Tidemark Gallery** (902 Main St., Waldoboro, 207/832-5109), showing fine arts and crafts from local artists.

The **Philippe Guillerm Gallery** (882 Main St., Waldoboro, 207/701-9085) showcases the works of Guillerm, who travels the world via boat in winter collecting driftwood, which he fashions into amazing works of art.

Specialty and Eclectic Shops

The Pemaquid Peninsula is fertile ground for crafts and gifts, and many of the shop locations provide opportunities for exploring off the beaten path. Artists' studios and galleries are plentiful.

The inventory at **Sherman's Maine Coast Book Shop and Café** (158 Main St., Damariscotta, 207/563-3207) always seems to anticipate customers' wishes, so you're unlikely to walk out empty-handed. You'll find a superb children's section, helpful staff, and always something tempting in the café.

Weatherbird (Main St. and 72 Courtyard St., Damariscotta, 207/563-8993) is a double find. The Main Street shop specializes in women's clothing, and off the alley behind it is the original store, stocked with housewares, wines, toys, cards, and gourmet specialties.

All sorts of fabulous finds, including specialty foods, wine, books, and Swan Island Blankets, fill the **Walpole Barn** (Rte. 129, Walpole, 207/563-7050, www.thewalpolebarn.com), Warren and Deb Storch's retirement fun. Browse home and garden products, whimsies, gourmet foods, and even wines.

Another delightful shop in a barn, **The Good Supply** (2016 Bristol Rd., Pemaquid, 207/607-3121) specializes in goods crafted by Maine artists and artisans.

The Granite Hall Store (9 Backshore Rd.,

off Rte. 32, Round Pond, 207/529-5864) is an old-fashioned country store with merchandise ranging from toys to Irish imports. The "penny" candy, fudge, ice cream, and the old-fashioned peanut-roasting machine captivate the kids.

Bells reminiscent of lighthouses, buoys, and even wilderness sounds are crafted by **North Country Wind Bells** (544 Rte. 32, Round Pond, 877/930-5435, www.northcountrybells.com). Factory seconds are a bargain.

Renys

Whatever you do, don't leave downtown Damariscotta without visiting **Renys** (207/563-5757 or 207/563-3011), with stores on each side of Main Street; one sells clothing, the other everything else (although that mix might change). If you can recognize the edges of cutout labels, you'll find clothes from major retailers at discounted prices. Stock up on housewares, munchies, puzzles, toiletries, shoes, and whatever else floats your boat; the prices can't be beat. And don't miss the old fashioned soda fountain.

RECREATION

Parks and Preserves

Residents of the Pemaquid Peninsula region are incredibly fortunate to have several foresighted local conservation organizations, each with its own niche and mission. The result is dozens of trail-webbed preserves. For good descriptions of trails throughout Lincoln County, purchase Paula Roberts's *On the Trail in Lincoln County* ($15.75), which describes and provides directions to more than 60 area walking trails. It's available at Salt Bay Farm, which benefits from its sale. Another excellent resource is *PWA Hike and Paddle Pocket Guide,* available for a $2 donation from the Pemaquid Watershed Association (207/563-2196, www.pemaquidwatershed.org).

SALT BAY FARM

Headquarters of the **Damariscotta River Association** (DRA, 110 Belvedere Rd., Damariscotta, 207/563-1393, www.damariscottariver.org, 9am-5pm Mon.-Fri.), founded in 1973, the Salt Bay Farm Heritage Center is a late-18th-century farmhouse on a farm site. Pick up maps, brochures, and other information on the more than 2,900 acres and 22 miles of shoreline protected and managed by the DRA. More than two miles of trails cover Salt Bay Farm's fields, salt marsh, and shore frontage and are open to the public sunrise-sunset daily year-round. DRA also has a healthy calendar of events, including bird-watching tours, natural-history trips, and concerts. To reach the farm from downtown Newcastle, take Mills Road (Rte. 215) to Route 1. Turn right (north) and go 1.4 miles to the blinking light (Belvedere Rd.). Turn left and go 0.4 mile.

SALT BAY PRESERVE HERITAGE TRAIL

Across Great Salt Bay from the DRA Salt Bay Farm is the trailhead for the **Salt Bay Preserve Heritage Trail,** a relatively easy three-mile loop around Newcastle's Glidden Point that touches on a variety of habitat and also includes remnants of oyster-shell middens (heaps) going back about 2,500 years. This part of the trail is protected by the federal government; do not disturb or remove anything. To reach the preserve from Newcastle Square, take Mills Road (Rte. 215) about two miles to the offices of the *Lincoln County News* (just after the post office). The newspaper allows parking in the northern end of its lot, but stay to the right, as far away from the buildings as possible, and be sure not to block any vehicles or access ways. Walk across Route 215 to the trailhead and pick up a brochure-map.

WHALEBACK PARK

How often do you get to see ancient shell heaps? **Whaleback Park** is an eight-acre public preserve designed to highlight what remains of the Glidden Midden, ancient oyster-shell heaps across the river from the park viewpoint. (The midden is also visible, but not as easily, from the Salt Bay Preserve Heritage Trail.) Informational signs explain the history of the midden, allegedly the largest such human artifact north of Florida. The "mini mountain" of castoffs was even vaster until the 1880s, when a factory harvested much of it to make lime. The trailhead and parking is on Business Route 1 opposite and between the Great Salt Bay School and the Central Lincoln County YMCA.

DODGE POINT PRESERVE

In 1989 the state of Maine acquired the now 521-acre **Dodge Point Preserve**—one of the stars in its crown—as part of a $35 million bond issue. To sample what the Dodge Point Preserve has to offer, pick up a map at the entrance and follow the Old Farm Road loop trail, and then connect to the Shore Trail (Discovery Trail), heading clockwise, with several dozen highlighted sites. Consider stopping for a riverside picnic and swim at Sand Beach before continuing back to the parking lot. Hunting is permitted in the preserve, so November isn't the best time for hiking. The Dodge Point parking area is on River Road, 2.6 miles southwest of Route 1 and 3.5 miles southwest of downtown Newcastle.

TRACY SHORE PRESERVE

Walk through a woodland wonderland that extends to ledgy shorefront along Jones Cove in South Bristol. Old cellars, moss-covered trails, lichen-covered rocks, a vernal pool, old pasture grounds, and spectacular views highlight this little-known gem, owned by the DRA. It has cliffs and lots of slippery rocks, so be watchful of children. You can connect to another preserve, Library Park, on a link crossing busy Route 129. The trailhead and parking are at the intersection of Route 129 and the S Road, 8.7 miles south of the split from Route 130.

LA VERNA PRESERVE

Roughly 3.5 miles south of the Round Pond post office on Route 130, you'll find this splendid 120-acre **shorefront preserve,** with 2.7 miles of hiking trails passing through woodlands, overgrown farmland, and forested wetlands to 3,600 feet of spectacular ocean frontage. Download a map from the Pemaquid Watershed Association (www.pemaquidwatershed.org).

RACHEL CARSON SALT POND

If you've never spent time studying the variety of sea life in a tidal pool, the **Rachel Carson Salt Pond** is a great place to start. Named after the famed author of *Silent Spring* and *The Edge of the Sea,* who summered in this part of Maine, the salt pond was one of her favorite haunts. The whole point of visiting a tidepool is to see what the tide leaves behind, so check the tide calendar (in local newspapers, or ask at your lodging) and head out a few hours after high tide. Wear rubber boots and beware of slippery rocks and rockweed. Among the many creatures you'll see in this 0.25-acre pond are mussels, green crabs, periwinkles, and starfish. Owned by The Nature Conservancy, the salt pond is on Route 32 in the village of Chamberlain, about a mile north of New Harbor. Parking is limited. Across the road is a trail into a 78-acre inland section of the preserve, most of it wooded. Brochures are available in the registration box.

Golf

The nine-hole **Wawenock Country Club** (Rte. 129, Walpole, 207/563-3938), established in the 1920s, is a challenging and popular public course.

Swimming

The best bet (but also the most crowded) on the peninsula for saltwater swimming is town-owned **Pemaquid Beach Park** (www.bristolparks.org), a lovely tree-lined sandy crescent. There is no lifeguard, but there are cold-water showers and bathrooms and a nature center with exhibits, and the snack bar serves decent food. Admission is $4 for anyone over age 12. The gates close at 7pm (restrooms close at 5pm). The beach is just off Snowball Hill Road, west of Route 130.

A much smaller beach is the pocket-size sandy area in **Christmas Cove** on Rutherford

Island. Take Route 129 around the cove and turn to the right, and then right again down the hill.

One of the area's most popular freshwater swimming holes is **Biscay Pond,** a long, skinny body of water in the peninsula's center. From Business Route 1 at the northern edge of Damariscotta, take Biscay Road (turn at McDonald's) three miles to the pond (on the right, heading east). On hot days, this area sees plenty of cars; pull off the road as far as possible.

Farther down the peninsula, on Route 130 in **Bristol Mills,** is another roadside swimming hole, between the dam and the bridge.

Boat Excursions

At 9am each day mid-May-early October, the 60-foot powerboat *Hardy III* departs for **Monhegan,** a Brigadoon-like island a dozen miles offshore where passengers can spend the day hiking the woods, picnicking on the rocks, bird-watching, and inhaling the salt air. At 3:15pm everyone reboards, arriving in New Harbor just over an hour later. The cost is $36 adults, $20 ages 3-11, $5 dogs, and reservations are required. Trips operate rain or shine, but strong seas can affect the schedule. Early June-late September there's also a second Monhegan trip—used primarily for overnighters—departing New Harbor at 2pm daily. Early and late in the season, Monhegan trips operate only Wednesday, Saturday, Sunday, and holidays. The *Hardy III* also operates daily 1.5-hour **puffin-watching tours** (5:30pm mid-May-late Aug., $28 adults, $12 ages 2-11), and one-hour **seal-watching tours** (noon daily mid-June-early Sept. and Sept. weekends, $15 adults, $12 children). **Hardy Boat Cruises** (Rte. 32, New Harbor, 207/677-2026 or 800/278-3346, www.hardyboat.com) is 19 miles south of Route 1, based at Shaw's Fish and Lobster Wharf. Parking is $4/day at a nearby baseball field.

Damariscotta River Cruises (Schooner Landing, 888/635-4309, www.damariscottarivercruises.com, $30 adult, $15 kids) offers two-hour cruises on the Damariscotta River, with options including oyster farms and seal-watching, happy hour, and reggae. It also offers specialty cruises, such as oyster and wine tasting, for $50. There's a full bar as well as snacks available for purchase.

Canoeing and Kayaking

Midcoast Kayak (47 Main St., Damariscotta, 207/563-5732, www.midcoastkayak.com) has rentals and offers guided tours and lessons on

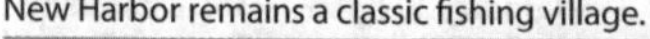

New Harbor remains a classic fishing village.

Muscongus Bay and the Damariscotta River. Three-hour to full-day tours range $50-110 and include all sorts of options. If you would rather do it yourself, recreational kayaks and sea kayaks are available at rates beginning at $28 for two hours. Instruction and delivery are also available.

Operating from a base near Colonial Pemaquid is **Maine Kayak** (113 Huddle Rd., New Harbor, 866/624-6351, www.mainekayak.com). Guided options include sunset paddles, wildlife paddles, puffin paddles, paddle-and-sail, half-day and full-day trips, and a variety of overnights. Rates begin at $40 for the shorter trips. Kayak and stand-up paddleboard rentals begin at $25.

If you have your own boat or just want to paddle the three-mile length of **Biscay Pond,** you can park at the beach area and put in. Another good launching site is a state ramp off Route 1 in **Nobleboro,** at the head of eight-mile-long **Lake Pemaquid.**

Two preserves are accessible if you have your own boat. Owned by the Damariscotta River Association, 30-acre **Menigawum Preserve (Stratton Island)** is also known locally as Hodgdon's Island. It's at the entrance to Seal Cove on the west side of the South Bristol peninsula. The closest public boat launch is at The Gut, about four miles downriver—a trip better done *with* (in the same direction as) the tide. The best place to land is Boat House Beach, in the northeast corner—also a great spot for shelling. Pick up a map from the small box at the north end of the island and follow the perimeter trail clockwise. At the northern end, you'll see osprey nests; at the southern tip are Native American shell middens—discards from hundreds of years of marathon summer lunches. (Do not disturb or remove anything.) You can picnic in the pasture, but camping and fires are not allowed. Stay clear of the abandoned home site on the island's west side. The preserve is accessible sunrise-sunset.

Named for a 19th-century local woman dubbed "The Witch of Wall Street" for her financial wizardry, **Witch Island Preserve** is owned by Maine Audubon. The wooded 19-acre island has two beaches, a perimeter trail, and the ruins of the "witch's" house. A quarter of a mile offshore, it's accessible by canoe or kayak from the South Bristol town landing, just to the right after the bridge over The Gut. Put in, paddle under the bridge, and go north to the island.

ACCOMMODATIONS

Inns

Innkeeper Julie Bolthuis has breathed new life into ★ **The Newcastle Inn** (60 River Rd., Newcastle, 207/563-5685 or 800/832-8669, www.newcastleinn.com, from $200), an 1860s sea captain's home with 14 guest rooms and suites (all with air-conditioning and Wi-Fi, some with TV, fireplace, or whirlpool tub) spread out between the main inn and carriage house. The lovely grounds descend to the edge of the Damariscotta River. Julie serves a full breakfast, on the patio when the weather cooperates, stocks a pantry that includes a bottomless cookie jar, and offers a pub just for guests. One room is dog-friendly ($35/day).

Within easy walking distance of Pemaquid Light and 16 miles south of Route 1, **The Bradley Inn** (3063 Bristol Rd./Rte. 130, New Harbor, 207/677-2105 or 800/942-5560, www.bradleyinn.com, from $180) is a restored late-19th-century three-story inn with restaurant, carriage house, and a cottage amid lovely gardens. Some accommodations have a water view, fireplace, or both; one has a full kitchen. Room rates include full breakfast and afternoon tea.

Almost on top of Pemaquid Light is the rambling and delightfully old-fashioned **Hotel Pemaquid** (3098 Bristol Rd./Rte. 130, New Harbor, 207/677-2312, www.hotelpemaquid.com, mid-May-mid-Oct., $100-180). Seventeen miles south of Route 1 but just 450 feet from the lighthouse (you can't see it from the inn, but you sure can hear the foghorn), the hotel has been welcoming guests since 1900; it's fun to peruse the old guest registers. Hang out in the large, comfortable parlor or on the wraparound veranda. The owners have gently renovated the property, updating and improving everything without losing the Victorian charm or quirks of an old seaside hotel. Don't expect fancy or fussy, but it now has flat-screen TVs, in-room refrigerators, Wi-Fi, and a guest laundry. The inn building has guest rooms with private and shared baths as well as suites. Other buildings have motel-style units with private baths. Apartments, cottages, and suites begin at $210. For the Victorian flavor of the place, request an inn room or a suite. There is no restaurant, but The Bradley Inn and The Sea Gull Shop are nearby.

Bed-and-Breakfasts

Martha Scudder provides a warm welcome for her guests at **Oak Gables Bed and Breakfast** (Pleasant St., Damariscotta, 207/563-1476 or 800/335-7748, www.oakgablesbb.com, year-round, $120). At the end of a pretty lane, this 13-acre hilltop estate overlooks the Damariscotta River. Despite a rather imposing setting, everything's homey, informal, and hospitable. Four spacious second-floor rooms, which can be joined in pairs, share a bath; a guest wing ($175/night, $975/week) has a full kitchen, a private bath, and a separate entrance. The heated swimming pool is a huge plus, as is the boathouse deck on the river. Guests can harvest blackberries from scads of bushes. Also on the grounds are a three-bedroom cottage ($1,400/week), a river-view one-bedroom apartment ($185/night, $1,100/week), and a studio apartment ($175/night, $975/week), which is usually booked up well ahead.

Wake up with a dip after a restful sleep at the ★ **Mill Pond Inn** (50 Main St./Rte. 215, Damariscotta Mills, Nobleboro, 207/563-8014, www.millpondinn.com, $150, no credit cards). The 1780 colonial was restored and converted into an inn in 1986 by delightful owners Bobby and Sherry Whear. The five guestrooms have water views; two have detached bathrooms. After a full breakfast, snooze in a hammock, watch for eagles and great blue herons, pedal a bicycle into nearby Damariscotta, or canoe the pond, which connects to 14-mile-long Damariscotta Lake. Bobby, a Registered Maine Guide, offers fishing trips and scenic tours of the lake in his restored antique Lyman lapstrake (clinker-built) boat. Use of bicycles and a canoe is free for guests. The inn is just a five-minute drive from downtown Damariscotta, but a world away.

The mansard-roofed **Inn at Round Pond** (1442 Rte. 32, Round Pond, 207/809-7386, www.theinnatroundpond.com, year-round, $175-185) commands a sea captain's view of the harbor as it presides over the pretty village of Round Pond. It's an easy walk to a waterfront restaurant, two dueling lobster pounds, an old-timey country store, and a few galleries and shops. Each of four good-sized, air-conditioned rooms has harbor views and sitting areas. There are no TVs and no locks, but there's no reason for either. A full breakfast is included.

About three miles south of town is **Blue Skye Farm** (1708 Friendship Rd., Waldoboro, 207/832-0300, www.blueskyefarm.com, $120-165), Jan and Peter Davidson's bed-and-breakfast in a gorgeous 18th-century farmhouse set amid 100 acres with trails, gardens, and lawns (but close to the road, so noise can be a problem for the sensitive). Original wall stencils by Moses Eaton decorate the entry. Breakfast is provided, and guests have full use of the country kitchen to prepare other meals. Other common rooms include the dining room, screened-in sunroom, and a sitting room that's stocked with games and a fireplace. Five guest rooms, three with private baths, are meticulously decorated.

Cozy, comfy, and cluttered with good reads and beloved treasures, **La Vatout** (218 Kaler's Corner, Waldoboro, 207/832-5150, www.levatout.com, $105-145) is a find for those who want a taste of down-home Maine. Innkeeper Dominika Spetsmann and resident artist Linda Mahoney provide a warm welcome to their 1830s farmhouse with four guest rooms (two sharing a bath) surrounded by organic gardens and home to a resident cat and dog. The only indoor public area is the dining room, where hearty breakfasts are crafted from local eggs, meats, fish, and grains, along with garden produce. For a real treat, consider the art workshops or nature packages, including one that allows you to forage for wild mushrooms with Maine mushroom guru David Spahr, and then return to the inn to prepare a meal.

Motels and Cottage Colonies

You'll have to plan well in advance to snag one of the humble **Ye Olde Forte Cabins** (18 Old Fort Rd., Pemaquid Beach, 207/677-2261, www.yeoldefortecabins.com, from $115/day, $575/week). These rustic, no-frills cabins have edged a grassy lawn dropping to John's Bay since 1922. Each has at least a toilet and a sink, but a shower house and a well-equipped cookhouse are part of the colony. Although guests are expected to clean up after themselves when using the kitchen, management keeps the place immaculate. The small private beach is a great place to launch a kayak. The cabins are less than 25 yards from Colonial Pemaquid and Fort William Henry.

Dan Thompson is the third-generation innkeeper at **The Thompson House and Cottages** (95 South Side Rd., New Harbor, 207/677-2317, www.thompsoncottages.net, $450-1,850/week), a low-key, step-back-in-time complex of mostly waterfront rooms, apartments, and cottages split between two mini peninsulas. Most have fireplaces; none has a TV. Rowboats are available, and there's a library with games, books, and puzzles.

Now, here's a bargain. Up a long winding driveway behind Moody's Diner is **Moody's Motel** (Rte. 1, Waldoboro, 207/832-5362, www.moodysdiner.com, $67-87), in business since 1927; it's likely that little has changed in the meantime. Expect nothing more than a clean and well-run property, and you'll be content. The retro motel and tourist cabins all have screened porches, TVs, and Wi-Fi; a few have kitchenettes. Pets are $10.

Camping

A favorite with kayakers is **Sherwood Forest Camping** (Pemaquid Trail, New Harbor, 800/274-1593, www.sherwoodforestcampsite.com, $31-41). Facilities include a small camp store, rec room, and a laundry. The campground is just 800 feet from Pemaquid Beach. Two-bedroom rental cabins are $750/week.

FOOD

Local Flavors

DAMARISCOTTA

The absolute best breakfasts and mighty fine lunches come from **Crissy's Breakfast and Coffee Bar** (212 Main St., 207/563-6400, www.cbandcb.com, 8am-2pm daily, $5-12). Savor killer croissants, excellent eggs, and gluten-free rice bowls, along with internationally inspired lunch items in one of three pleasant dining rooms.

For baked goods, sandwiches, soups, and gourmet goodies to go, head to **Weatherbird** (1168 Elm St., 207/563-8993, 8am-5:30pm Mon.-Sat.). Eat at one of the handful of tables out front or take it to the waterfront.

Check out the Moxie memorabilia while enjoying breakfast, lunch, sweets, and coffee at **S. Fernald's Country Store** (50 Main St., Damariscotta, 207/563-8484, 8am-6pm Mon.-Sat., 9am-5pm Sun.). The candy by the pound is a real kid-pleaser.

King Eider's Pub (2 Elm St., Damariscotta, 207/ 563-6008, www.kingeiderspub.com,11:30am-9pm daily) is the place for oysters, crab cakes, single-malt scotches, and good times.

The burgers, lobster rolls, and sweet-potato fries earn raves at **Larson's Lunch Box** (430 Main St., 207/563-5755, 11am-4pm Thurs.-Tues., to 7pm July-Aug.), a no-frills take-out stand with a few picnic tables.

Another take-out, **The Village Grill** (Biscay Rd., 207/563-2278), has earned a solid rep for its barbecue, but it also offers burgers and fried seafood.

In a barn-style building at the northern edge of Damariscotta, **Round Top Ice Cream** (Business Rte. 1, 207/563-5307) has been dishing out homemade ice cream since 1924.

Rising Tide Natural Foods Market (323 Main St., 207/563-5556, www.risingtide.coop, 8am-8pm daily), a thriving co-op organization since 1978, has all the natural and organic usuals, plus a self-service deli section with soups, sandwiches, salads, and entrées; indoor seating is available.

The **Damariscotta Area Farmers Market** sets up 9am-noon on Friday mid-May-October at Salt Bay Heritage Center (Belvedere Rd., just off Route 1) and 3pm-6pm Monday at Rising Tide Market (323 Main St.).

DOWN THE PENINSULA

You won't find a cozier, less expensive, or more welcoming home-based bakeshop than **Dot's Bakery** (1233 Rte. 32, Round Pond, 207/529-2514, 8am-5pm Thurs.-Mon.). Muffins, pies, doughnuts, soups, breads, and even buttermilk pancakes, sandwiches, and pizza are on the menu. Dine in on the central table or take it to go. Call ahead to order pie.

Abundant Bakery (11 Leeman Hill Rd., New Harbor, 207/677-2235), located across from the public landing, bakes breads, cookies, scones, muffins, pies, and bars, including to-die-for lemon squares.

Big portions of house-made comfort foods have given tiny **Deb's Bristol Diner** (1267 Bristol Rd./Rte. 130, Bristol, 207/563-8005, 6 am-2pm Mon.-Tues. and Thurs.-Sat., 7am-noon Sun.), a sibling of Deb's in Waldoboro, a huge local following.

Just around the corner from Colonial Pemaquid, **The Cupboard Cafe** (137 Huddle Rd., New Harbor, 207/677-3911, www.thecupboardcafe.com, 8am-3pm Tues.-Sat., 8am-noon Sun.) is a homey cabin serving fresh-baked goods, breakfasts, and a nice choice of fresh salads, burgers, sandwiches, and specials. Almost everything is made on the premises; the cinnamon and sticky buns are so popular, they've spurred a mail-order business.

WALDOBORO

At the corner of Routes 1 and 220, opposite Moody's Diner, is the warehouse-y building that turns out **Borealis Breads** (1860 Atlantic Hwy./Rte. 1, 207/832-0655, 8:30am-5:30pm Mon.-Sat., 9am-4pm Sun.). Using sourdough starters (and no oils, sweeteners, eggs, or dairy products), owner Jim Amaral and his crew produce baguettes, olive bread, lemon fig bread, rosemary focaccia, and about a dozen other inventive flavors; each day has its specialties. A refrigerated case holds a small selection of picnic fixings (sandwich spreads, juices). Great soups, salads, and excellent sandwiches are available to go.

Each fall around mid-September, a tiny, cryptic display ad appears in local newspapers: "Kraut's Ready." Savvy readers recognize this as the announcement of the latest batch of Morse's sauerkraut—an annual ritual since 1918. The homemade kraut is available in stores and by mail order, but it's more fun (and cheaper) to visit the shop, the **Kraut House** (3856 Washington Rd./Rte. 220, 207/832-5569 or 800/486-1605, www.morsessauerkraut.com, 9am-6pm Thurs.-Tues.), which also has a small restaurant (10:30am-4pm Mon.-Tues. and Thurs.-Fri., 8am-4pm Sat.-Sun.) serving traditional German fare, including sandwiches such as a classic Reuben, liverwurst, or sausage; homemade pierogies; sausages; and pork schnitzel, all $6-14. Big serve-yourself jars of Morse's pickles are on the tables. While waiting, feast on tastings in the shop. The red-painted farm store also carries Aunt Lydia's Beet Relish, baked beans, mustard, maple syrup, and other Maine foods as well as a mind-boggling selection of hard-to-find and unusual northern European specialties, cheeses, meats, and preserved fish. It's eight miles north of Route 1.

Truck drivers, tourists, locals, and notables have been flocking to **Moody's Diner** (Rte. 1 and Rte. 220, 207/832-7785, www.moodysdiner.com, 5am-9:30pm Mon.-Sat., 6am-9pm Sun., $5-15) since the early 1930s, when the Moody family established this classic eatery on a Waldoboro hilltop. The antique neon sign has long been a Route 1 beacon, especially on a foggy night, and the crowds continue, with new generations of Moodys and considerable expansion of the premises. It has gone beyond dinerdom; expect hearty, no-frills fare and such calorific desserts as peanut butter or walnut pie. After eating, you can buy the cookbook.

Moody's has longevity, but **Deb's Diner** (1495 Rte. 1, 207-832-6144, 6am-2:30pm Mon-Sat., 7-11am Sun.) has won over legions of fans with its house-made fare, which ranges from baked goods to chowders, with all seafood sourced from local fishermen.

The Narrows Tavern (15 Friendship St., 207/832-2210, 11:30am-1am daily, $8-18) is a convivial watering hole with a family-friendly attitude and activities ranging from cribbage to live music.

Casual Dining

DAMARISCOTTA

A reliable standby in downtown Damariscotta, next to the Damariscotta Bank and Trust, the **Salt Bay Café** (88 Main St., 207/563-3302, www.saltbaycafe.com, 7:30am-9pm daily) has a loyal following thanks to its imaginative, reasonably priced cuisine and cheerful, plant-filled setting. Vegetarians have their own menu, with more than two-dozen choices. Most dinner entrées are $15-22, but hefty sandwiches are also available.

Chef Rick and Jean Kerrigan own ★ **Damariscotta River Grill** (155 Main St., 207/563-2992, www.damariscottarivergrill.com, 11am-9:30pm daily, entrées $8-24), a reliable favorite where the open kitchen offers carefully prepared foods with an emphasis on fresh seafood. Add $8 to the price of any entrée to include a salad or soup and a dessert. The artichoke fondue is worth fighting over. Choose a table in the back with a river view, if available.

Bridging the gap between pub and restaurant is the **Newcastle Publick House** (52 Main St., Newcastle, 207/563-3434, www.newcastlepublickhouse.com, 11am-11pm Sun.-Thurs., 11am-midnight Fri.-Sat., $8-24). Emphasis is on organic, natural, and local foods, including Pemaquid oysters, and pub favorites such as shepherd's pie or lamb shanks braised in Geary's London porter. The craft beer menu is another draw.

DOWN THE PENINSULA

The Anchor (34 Anchor Inn Rd., Round Pond, 207/529-2600, www.theanchorrestaurant.com, 11am--9pm daily mid-May-mid-Oct., entrées $20-30), tucked away on the picturesque harbor in Round Pond, always attracts a crowd with a menu that emphasizes seafood, but has other options too. Reservations are advisable on summer weekends. After Labor Day, the schedule can be a bit erratic; call to confirm hours.

Coveside Restaurant (105 Coveside Rd., Christmas Cove, South Bristol, 207/644-8282, www.covesiderestaurant.com, 11am-9pm daily, $10-28), based at a marina on Rutherford Island, just off the end of the South Bristol peninsula, is open for lunch and dinner as well as light meals. Grab a seat on the deck and watch a steady stream of boaters and summer vacationers during the cruising season. The food quality and service efficiency varies since it's a leased operation, but when it's on, it's hard to beat.

Location, location: Right next to Pemaquid Light is **The Sea Gull Shop** (3119 Bristol Rd., Pemaquid Point, 207/677-2374, www.seagullshop.com, 7:30am-3pm Tues.-Thurs., to 8pm Fri-Mon., entrées $17-33), a seasonal gift shop, restaurant, and ice cream spot with big views and decent food—pancakes and muffins, for instance, overflowing with blueberries. BYOB; call ahead for hours in spring and fall.

Pair exploring Fort William Henry with lunch or dinner at **The Contented Sole** (at Fort William Henry, 207/677-3000, www.thecontentedsole.com, 11:30am-9pm daily, $10-20), a quirky waterfront seafood shack with a menu ranging from seafood to pizza. Dine indoors or outside on the dock, which is dog-friendly.

★ Lobster in the Rough

The Pemaquid Peninsula must have more eat-on-the-dock places per capita than any place in Maine. Some are basic no-frills operations; others are big-time commercial concerns. Each has a loyal following.

The biggest and best-known lobster wharf is **Shaw's Fish and Lobster Wharf** (Rte. 32, New Harbor, 207/677-2200 or 800/772-2209, 11am-8pm daily). You can also order steak, margaritas, and oysters at the wharf raw bar. Fried seafood dinners run $8-20.

Facing each other across the dock in the hamlet of Round Pond are two of my all-time favorite lobster shacks, **Round Pond Lobster Co-Op** (207/529-5725) and **Muscongus Bay Lobster** (207/529-5528). Muscongus has enlarged in recent years, so it has a bigger menu and covered seating, but tiny Round Pond Lobster keeps it simple and oh-so-fresh. Both usually open around 10am daily for lunch and dinner and close around sunset. At either, bring the go-withs, from wine and cheese to bread and chocolates.

Other seasonal lobster wharves salting the peninsula are **Pemaquid Seafood** (32 Co-Op Rd., Pemaquid Harbor, 207/677-2642), the no-frills, lobster-only **South Bristol Fishermen's Co-op** (35 Fire Rd. 16., South Bristol, 207/644-8224), and **Broad Cove Marine Services** (374 Medomak Rd., Bremen, 207/529-5186), a low-key sleeper.

INFORMATION AND SERVICES

The **Damariscotta Region Chamber of Commerce** (207/563-8340, www.damariscottaregion.com) publishes a free annual information booklet about the area.

Skidompha Library (Main St., Damariscotta, 207/563-5513, www.skidompha.org) also operates a used-book shop and a gallery and offers a film series and talks. Also check out **Waldoboro Public Library** (958 Main St., Waldoboro, 207/832-4484, www.waldoborolibrary.org).

GETTING THERE AND AROUND

Damariscotta is about eight miles or 15 minutes via Route 1 from Wiscasset. It's about 10 miles or 15 minutes via Route 1 to Waldoboro, and about 15 miles or 30 minutes via Route 130 to Pemaquid Point. From Pemaquid Point it's about 23 miles or 40 minutes via Route 32 to Waldoboro. From Waldoboro, it's about 12 miles or 20 minutes via Route 1 to Thomaston or about 20 miles via Routes 1 and 90 to Camden.

Penobscot Bay

Look for ★ to find recommended sights, activities, dining, and lodging.

Highlights

★ **Monhegan Historical and Cultural Museum:** View an impressive collection of masters at this museum adjacent to the Monhegan Lighthouse (page 199).

★ **The Farnsworth Art Museum and the Wyeth Center:** Three generations of Wyeths are represented in this museum, which also boasts an excellent collection of works by Maine and American masters (page 204).

★ **Owls Head Transportation Museum:** View a fabulous collection of vintage airplanes, automobiles, and even bicycles, many of which are flown, driven, or ridden during weekend special events (page 205).

★ **Rockland Breakwater:** Take a walk on this nearly mile-long breakwater to the lighthouse at the end (open on weekends). It's an especially fine place to watch the windjammers sail in or out of Rockland Harbor (page 206).

★ **Owls Head Light State Park:** The views of Penobscot Bay are spectacular, and it's a great place for a picnic lunch (page 208).

★ **Camden Hills State Park:** If you have time, hike the moderate trail to the summit for a gull's-eye view over Camden Harbor and Penobscot Bay. If not, take the easy route and drive (page 228).

★ **Penobscot Marine Museum:** Learn what life was *really* like during the Great Age of Sail in a town renowned for the number and quality of its sea captains (page 247).

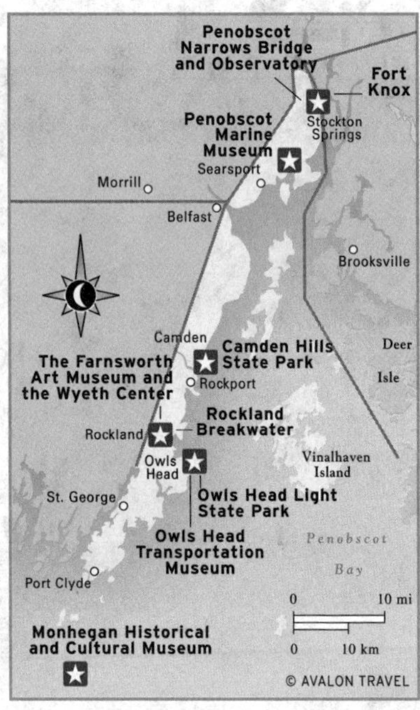

★ **Fort Knox:** A good restoration, frequent events, and secret passages to explore make this late-19th-century fort one of Maine's best (page 251).

★ **Penobscot Narrows Bridge and Observatory:** On a clear day, the views from the 420-foot-high tower, one of only three in the world, extend from Mount Katahdin to Cadillac Mountain (page 252).

The rugged and jagged shoreline edging island-studded Penobscot Bay is the image that has lured many a visitor to Maine. The coastline here ebbs and flows, rising to rocky headlands, dropping to protected harbors, and linking quiet fishing villages with comparatively cosmopolitan towns. Although the state considers this to be part of the Mid-Coast, this region has a different feel and view, one framed by coastal mountains in Camden and Lincolnville and accented by an abundance of islands.

From Thomaston through Prospect, no two towns are alike except that all are changing, as traditional industries give way to arts- and tourism-related businesses. Thomaston's Museum in the Streets, Rockland's art galleries, Camden's picturesque mountainside harbor, Lincolnville's pocket beach, Belfast's inviting downtown, Searsport's sea captains' homes, and Prospect's Fort Knox all invite exploration, as do offshore, ferry-linked islands.

From salty Port Clyde, take the mail boat to Monhegan, an offshore idyll known as the Artists' Island. From Rockland and Lincolnville Beach, car and passenger ferries depart to Vinalhaven, North Haven, Matinicus, and Islesboro. All are occupied year-round by hardy souls, and joined in summer by less-hardy ones. Except for Matinicus, they're great day-trip destinations.

If what appeals to you about a ferry trip is traveling on the water, get a taste of the Great Age of Sail by booking a multiday cruise aboard one of the classic windjammer schooners berthed in Rockland, Rockport, and Camden. Or simply book a day sail or sea-kayak excursion.

Although it's easy to focus on the water, this region is rich in museums and art galleries, antiques and specialty shops, some of the state's nicest inns, and many of its better restaurants.

Most folks arrive in July-August, but autumn, when turning leaves color the hills and are reflected in the sea, the days remain warm, and nights are cool, is an ideal season to visit, especially for leaf peepers who want to get off the beaten track. And in winter, when snow

Previous: the Windjammer Parade sails by Rockland Breakwater Light; a traditional fishing harbor. **Above:** the Penobscot Narrows Observatory.

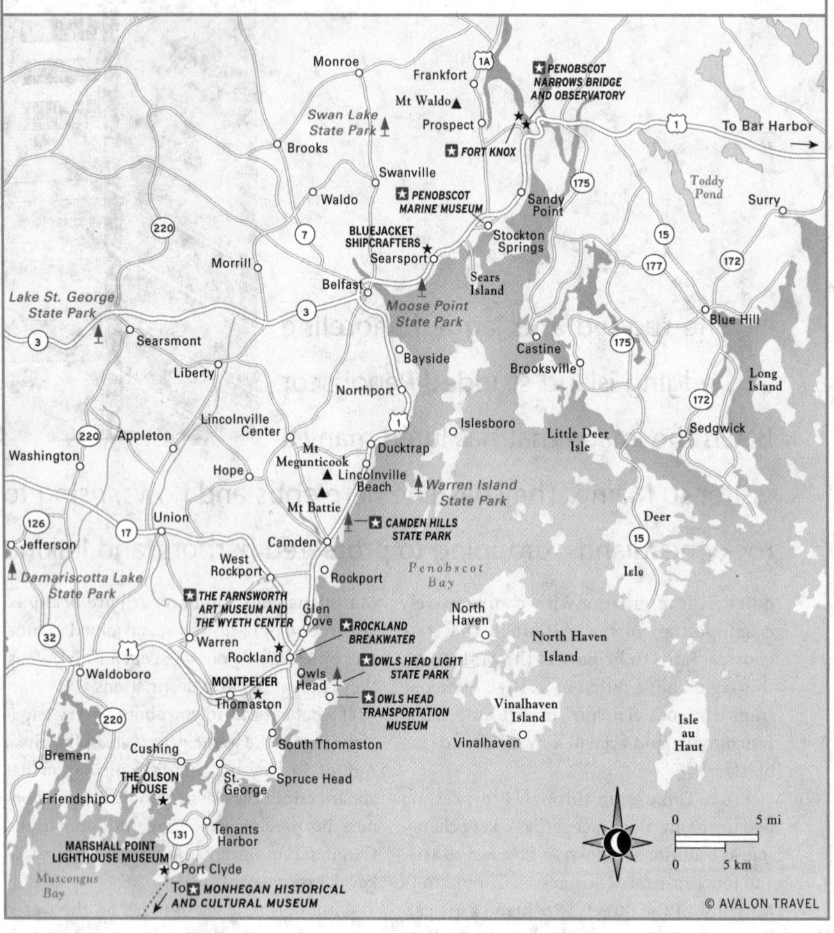

blankets the Camden Hills, you can ski while gazing out over Camden Harbor.

PLANNING YOUR TIME

To hit just the highlights, you'll need at least three days. If you want to relax a bit and enjoy the area, plan on 4-5 days. Make it a full week if you plan on overnighting on any of the offshore islands. In general, lodging is less expensive in Rockland, Belfast, and Searsport than it is in Camden. In any case, head for Monhegan or Vinalhaven on a fine day and save the museums for inclement ones.

Two-lane Route 1 is the region's central artery, with veins running down the peninsula limbs. Yes, traffic backs up, especially in Camden (and in Thomaston on the Fourth of July, when it's closed for a parade), but it rarely stops moving. If your destination is Rockland, take I-95 to Augusta and then Route 17 East; if it's Belfast or north, take I-95 to Augusta and then Route 3 East. Route 90 is a nifty bypass around Thomaston and Rockland, connecting Route 1 from Warren to Rockport. For a less direct route, the **Georges River Scenic Byway** is a 50-mile rural inland route, mostly along Route 131, between Port Clyde and Liberty. It parallels the coast, but it meanders through farmlands and tiny villages and by lakes and rivers, with antiques shops and farm stands along the way. It's simply gorgeous in autumn.

Thomaston Area

Thomaston (pop. 1,558) is a little gem of a town and is becoming more so each year, thanks to the razing of the old Maine State Prison. It's also the gateway to two lovely fingers of land bordering the St. George River and jutting into the Gulf of Maine—the Cushing and St. George Peninsulas.

In 1605, British adventurer Captain George Waymouth sailed up the river now named after him (the St. George River was originally called the Georges River). A way station for Plymouth traders as early as 1630, Thomaston was incorporated in 1777 and officially named after General John Thomas, a Revolutionary War hero.

Industry began with the production of lime, which was used for plaster. A growing demand for plaster, and the frequency with which the wooden boats were destroyed by fire while carrying loads of extremely flammable lime, spurred the growth of shipbuilding and its related infrastructure. Thomaston's slogan became "the town that went to sea."

Seeing the sleepy harbor-front today, it's hard to visualize the booming era when dozens of tall-masted wooden ships slid down the ways. But the town's architecture is a testament and tribute to the prosperous past. All those splendid homes on Main and Knox Streets were funded by wealthy ship owners and shipmasters who understood how to occupy the idle hands of off-duty carpenters.

SIGHTS

Knox Museum

As you head north out of Thomaston on Route 1, you'll come face-to-face with an imposing colonial hilltop mansion at the junction with Route 131 South. Dedicated to the memory of General Henry Knox, President George Washington's secretary of war, **Montpelier** (Rte. 1 and Rte. 131, Thomaston, 207/354-8062, www.generalknoxmuseum.org, 10am-4pm Wed.-Fri. and 10am-1pm on non-even Sat., late May-early Sept., $10 adults, $8 seniors, $4 ages 5-13, $20 family; last tour 1 hour before closing), home to the **Knox Museum,** is a 1930s replica of Knox's original Thomaston home. The mansion today contains Knox family furnishings and other period antiques, all described with great enthusiasm during the hour-long tours. A gift shop run by the Friends of Montpelier carries books and other relevant items. Concerts, lectures, and special events occur here periodically throughout the summer; General Knox's birthday is celebrated with considerable fanfare in July. Do call for the current schedule, as the museum is also often open on weekends for special events.

Museum in the Streets

Montpelier is the starting point for a three-mile walking, cycling, or, if you must, driving tour of nearly 70 sites in Thomaston's **National Historic Landmark District.** Pick up a copy of the tour brochure at one of the local businesses. Included are lots of stories behind the facades of the handsome 19th-century homes that line Main and Knox Streets; the architecture here is nothing short of spectacular. Much of this history is also recounted in the Museum in the Streets, a walking tour taking in 25 informative plaques illustrated with old photos throughout town.

EVENTS

Thomaston's **Fourth of July,** an old-fashioned hometown celebration reminiscent of a Norman Rockwell painting, draws huge crowds. A spiffy parade—with bands, veterans, kids, and pets—starts off the morning at 11am, followed by races, crafts and food booths, and lots more. If you need to get *through* Thomaston on the Fourth of July, do it well before the parade or well after noon; the marchers go right down Main Street (Rte. 1), and gridlock forces a detour.

The region's Finnish heritage is celebrated at **Finn Fling Day** at the Finnish Heritage House in mid-September.

SHOPPING

Thomaston has a block-long shopping street (on Rte. 1), with ample free parking out back behind the stores.

The **Maine State Prison Showroom Outlet** (Main St./Rte. 1 at Wadsworth St., Thomaston, 207/354-9237) markets the handiwork of inmate craftsmen. Some of the souvenirs verge on kitsch; the bargains are wooden bar stools, toys (including dollhouses), and chopping boards. You'll need to carry your purchases with you; prison-made goods cannot be shipped.

At the southern end of Thomaston, in a renovated chicken barn, is **Thomaston Place Auction Gallery** (51 Atlantic Hwy./Rte. 1, Thomaston, 207/354-8141, www.thomastonauction.com), the home of Kaja Veilleux, a longtime dealer, appraiser, and auctioneer. Auctions occur frequently, with previews beforehand.

Just south of Thomaston is **Lie-Nielsen Toolworks** (Rte. 1, Warren, 800/327-2520, www.lie-nielsen.com), crafting heirloom-quality hand tools for connoisseurs. Ask about workshops.

CAMPING

Located on the Thomaston-Cushing town line, 35-acre **Saltwater Farm Campground** (Wadsworth St./Cushing Rd., Cushing, 207/354-6735, www.saltwaterfarmcampground.com) has 37 open and wooded tent and RV sites ($35-54) overlooking the St. George River. Cabins go for $75. Facilities include a bathhouse, heated pool, hot tub, laundry, store, and play area. The river is tidal, so swimming is best near high tide; otherwise, you're dealing with mudflats.

FOOD

Often overlooked by visitors (but certainly not by locals) is casual **Thomaston Café and Bakery** (154 Main St./Rte. 1, Thomaston, 207/354-8589, www.thomastoncafe.com, 11am-2pm and 5:30pm-8pm Wed.-Sat., and 10am Sun., and Wed.-Sat., entrées $19-22). Chef/owner Ryan Jones' menu changes daily to offer the best from his organic farm. Possibilities may include grass-fed beef stroganoff or line-caught swordfish.

Fresh seafood, including a raw bar and to-die-for fried oysters, have earned **The Slipway** (24 Public Landing, Thomaston, 207/354-4155, www.theslipwaymaine.com, 11:30am-9:30pm daily, $10-24) a solid following. Aim for a fine day, when you can dine on the dock (best at higher tides), although the views are equally fine from the porch and dining rooms.

INFORMATION AND SERVICES

The **Penobscot Bay Region Chamber of Commerce** (800/223-5459, www.mainedreamvacation.com) is the area's best resource.

The **Thomaston Public Library** (42 Main St., Thomaston, 207/354-2453) occupies part of the Greek Revival Thomaston Academy.

GETTING THERE AND AROUND

Thomaston is 12 miles or 18 minutes via Route 1 from Waldoboro. It's about 15 miles or 25 minutes via Route 131 to Port Clyde, and about 5 miles or 10 minutes via Route 1 to Rockland.

Cushing Peninsula

Cushing's recorded history goes back at least as far as 1605, when someone named "Abr [maybe Abraham] King"—presumably a member of explorer George Waymouth's crew—inscribed his name here on a ledge (now private property). Since 1789, settlers' saltwater farms have sustained many generations, and the active Cushing Historical Society keeps the memories and memorabilia from fading away. But the outside world knows little of this. **Cushing** (pop. 1,534) is better known as "Wyeth country," the terrain depicted by the famous artistic dynasty of N. C., Andrew, and Jamie Wyeth and assorted other talented relatives.

If you're an Andrew Wyeth fan, visiting Cushing will give you the feeling of walking through his paintings. The flavor of his Maine work is here—rolling fields, wildflower meadows, rocky tidal coves, broad vistas, character-filled farmhouses, and some well-hidden summer enclaves.

SIGHTS

Broad Cove Church

Andrew Wyeth aficionados will recognize the **Broad Cove Church** as one of his subjects—alongside Cushing Road en route to the Olson House. It's open most days, so step inside and admire the classic New England architecture. The church is also well known as the site of one of the region's best beanhole bean suppers, held on a Saturday in mid-July and attracting several hundred appreciative diners. From Route 1 in Thomaston, at the Maine State Prison Showroom Outlet, turn onto Wadsworth Street and go six miles, then bear left at the fork; the church is 0.4 mile farther, on the right.

The Olson House

Many an art lover makes the pilgrimage to the **Olson House** (11am-5pm Tues.-Sun., July 1-early Oct., noon-5pm late May-July, $10, $17 with Farnsworth admission), a famous icon near the end of Hathorne Point Road. The early-19th-century farmhouse appears in Andrew Wyeth's 1948 painting *Christina's World* (which hangs in New York's Museum of Modern Art), his best-known image of the disabled Christina

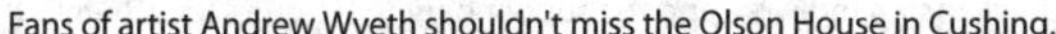

Fans of artist Andrew Wyeth shouldn't miss the Olson House in Cushing.

Beanhole Beans

"To be happy in New England," wrote one Joseph P. MacCarthy at the turn of the 20th century, "you must select the Puritans for your ancestors...[and] eat beans on Saturday night." There is no better way to confirm the latter requirement than to attend a beanhole bean supper—a real-live legacy of colonial times, with dinner baked in a hole in the ground.

Generally scheduled, appropriately, for a Saturday night (check local newspapers), a beanhole bean supper demands plenty of preparation from its hosts—and a secret ingredient or two. (Don't even think about trying to pry the recipe out of the cooks.) The supper always includes hot dogs, coleslaw, relishes, home-baked breads, and homemade desserts, but the beans are the star attraction. Typically, the suppers are also alcohol-free. They are not only feasts, but also bargains, never setting you back more than about $10.

The beans at the Broad Cove Church's **annual mid-July beanhole bean supper,** served family-style at long picnic tables, are legendary—attracting nearly 200 eager diners. Minus the secrets, here's what happens.

Early Friday morning: Church volunteers load 10 pounds of dry pea and soldier (yellow eye) beans into each of four large kettles and add water to cover. The beans are left to soak and soften for 6-7 hours. Two or three volunteers uncover the churchyard's four rock-lined beanholes (each about three feet deep), fill the holes with hardwood kindling, ignite the wood, and keep the fires burning until late afternoon, when the wood has reduced to red-hot coals.

Early Friday afternoon: The veteran chefs parboil the beans and stir in the seasonings. Typical additions are brown sugar, molasses, mustard, salt, pepper, and salt pork (much of the secret is in the exact proportions). When the beans are precooked to the cooks' satisfaction, the kettle lids are secured with wire and the pots are lugged outdoors.

Friday midafternoon: With the beans ready to go underground, some of the hot coals are quickly shoveled out of the pits. The kettles are lowered into the pits and the coals replaced around the sides of the kettles and atop their lids. The pits are covered with heavy sheet metal and topped with a thick layer of sand and a tarpaulin. The round-the-clock baking begins, and no one peeks before it's finished.

Saturday midafternoon: Even the veterans start getting nervous just before the pits are uncovered. Was the seasoning right? Did too much water cook away? Did the beans dry out? Not to worry, though—failures just don't happen here.

Saturday night: When a pot is excavated for the first of three seatings (about 5pm), the line is already long. The chefs check their handiwork and the supper begins. No one seems to mind waiting for the second and third seatings—while others eat, a sing-along gets under way in the church, keeping everyone entertained.

Olson, who died in 1968. In 1991, two philanthropists donated the Olson House to the Farnsworth Art Museum in Rockland, which has retained the house's sparse, lonely, and almost mystical ambience. The clapboards outside remain unpainted, the interior walls bear only a few Wyeth prints (hung close to the settings they depict), and it is easy to sense Wyeth's inspiration for chronicling this place. To find it, from the Broad Cove Church, continue just over one mile, then turn left onto Hathorne Point Road. Go another 1.9 miles to the house. Tours are offered on the hour.

St. George Peninsula

The St. George Peninsula is actually better known by some of the villages scattered along its length—**Tenants Harbor, Port Clyde, Wiley's Corner, Spruce Head**—plus the smaller neighborhoods of Martinsville, Smalleytown, Glenmere, Long Cove, Hart's Neck, and Clark Island. Each has a distinct personality, determined partly by the different ethnic groups—primarily Brits, Swedes, and Finns—who arrived to work the granite quarries in the 19th century. Wander through the Seaview Cemetery in Tenants Harbor and you'll see the story: row after row of gravestones with names from across the sea.

A more famous former visitor was 19th-century novelist Sarah Orne Jewett, who holed up in an old schoolhouse in Martinsville, paid a weekly rental of $0.50, and wrote *The Country of the Pointed Firs,* a tale about "Dunnet's Landing" (Tenants Harbor).

Today the picturesque peninsula has saltwater farms, tidy hamlets, a striking lighthouse, spruce-edged tidal coves, an active yachting harbor, and at the tip, the tiny fishing village of Port Clyde, which serves as a springboard to offshore Monhegan Island.

Port Clyde is likely the best-known community here. (Fortunately, it's no longer called by its unappealing 18th-century name: Herring Gut.) George Waymouth explored Port Clyde's nearby islands in 1605, but you'd never suspect its long tradition. It's a sleepy place, with a general store, low-key inns, a few galleries, and pricey parking.

SIGHTS

Marshall Point Lighthouse Museum

Not many settings can compare with the spectacular locale of the **Marshall Point Lighthouse Museum** (Marshall Point Rd., Port Clyde, 207/372-6450, www.marshallpoint.org, 1pm-5pm Sun.-Fri., 10am-5pm Sat. late May-mid-Oct., free), a distinctive 1857 lighthouse and park overlooking Port Clyde, the harbor islands, and the passing lobsterboat fleet. Bring a picnic and let the kids run on the lawn (but keep them well back from the shoreline). The museum, in the 1895 keeper's house, displays lighthouse and local memorabilia. The grounds are accessible year-round. Take Route 131 to Port Clyde and watch for signs to the museum.

SHOPPING

Art

The St. George Peninsula has been attracting artists for decades, and galleries are abundant. Some have been here for years, and others started up yesterday; most are worth a stop, so keep an eye out for their signs. In early August, a number of renowned artists usually coordinate an open-studio weekend.

Overlooking the reversing falls in downtown South Thomaston, **The Old Post Office Gallery** (Rte. 73, South Thomaston, 207/594-9396, www.artofthesea.com) has 11 rooms filled with marine art and antiques: ship models, prints, paintings, sculpture, scrimshaw, and jewelry.

Used Books

Drive up to the small parking area at **Lobster Lane Book Shop** (Island Rd., Spruce Head, 207/594-7520) and you'll see license plates from everywhere. The tiny shop, in a crammed but well-organized shed that has been here since the 1960s, has 50,000 or so treasures for used-book fans. For a few dollars, you can stock up on a summer's worth of reading. The shop, open noon-5pm Sat.-Sun., is just under a mile east of Route 73, with eye-catching vistas in several directions (except, of course, when Spruce Head's infamous fog sets in).

General Store

Despite periodic ownership changes, **Port**

Clyde General Store (Rte. 131, Port Clyde, 207/372-6543) remains a characterful destination, a two-century-old country store with ever-increasing upscale touches. Stock up on groceries, pick up a newspaper, order breakfast or a pizza, or buy a sweatshirt (you may need it on the Monhegan boat). The current owner has gussied it up even more and added a shop and a gallery featuring Wyeth works upstairs.

RECREATION

Swimming and Beachcombing

Drift Inn Beach, on Drift Inn Beach Road (also called Candy's Cove Road), isn't a big deal as beaches go, but it's the best public one on the peninsula, so it gets busy on hot days. The name comes from the Drift Inn, an early-20th-century summer hotel. Drift Inn Beach Road parallels Route 131, and the parking lot is accessible from both roads. Heading south on the peninsula, about 3.5 miles after the junction with Route 73, turn left at Drift Inn Beach Road, then continue 0.2 mile.

Sea Kayaking

The St. George Peninsula is especially popular for sea kayaking, with plenty of islands to add interest and shelter. **Port Clyde Kayaks** (Rte. 131, Port Clyde, 207/372-8128, www.portclydekayaks.com) offers half-day, sunset, and full-moon ($60) guided kayaking tours around the tip of the peninsula, taking in Marshall Point lighthouse and the islands.

If you have kayaking experience, you can launch on the ramp just before the causeway that links the mainland with Spruce Head Island, in Spruce Head (Island Rd., off Rte. 73). Parking is limited. A great paddle goes clockwise around Spruce Head Island and nearby Whitehead (there's a lighthouse on its southeastern shore) and Norton Islands. Duck in for lunch at Waterman's Beach Lobster. Around new moon and full moon, plan your schedule to avoid low tide near the Spruce Head causeway, or you may become mired in mudflats.

Boat Excursions

The best boating experience on this peninsula is a passenger-ferry trip from Port Clyde to offshore **Monhegan Island**—for a day, overnight, or longer. The trip isn't cheap, and parking adds to the cost, but it's a "must" excursion, so try to factor it into the budget. Port Clyde is the nearest mainland harbor to Monhegan; this service operates all year. **Monhegan-Thomaston Boat Line** (Port Clyde, 207/372-8848, www.monheganboat.com) uses two boats, the ***Laura B.*** (70 minutes each way) and the newer ***Elizabeth Ann*** (55 minutes). Round-trip tickets are $35 adults, $20 ages 2-12. Leave your bicycle in Port Clyde; you won't need it on the island. Reservations are essential in summer, especially for the 10:30am boat. With advance payment, tickets are held until one-half-hour before departure; there's a $5 fee for cancellations, with no refunds within 24 hours. Parking in Port Clyde is $7/day. If a summer day trip is all you can manage, aim for the first or second boat and return on the last one; don't go just for the boat ride.

During the summer, the Monhegan-Thomaston Boat Line also offers 2.5-hour sightseeing cruises, on a varied schedule, including a Puffin and Nature Cruise and a Lighthouse Cruise. Each costs $30 adults, $10 children.

The ***Linderin Losh*** lobster boat tours ($42) depart from the Port Clyde General Store for a 2.5-hour Wyeths by Water excursion highlighting locations featured in works by N. C. and Andrew Wyeth as well as a lobstering demonstration. For reservations and details, call 207/372-6600.

ACCOMMODATIONS

No accommodations on the peninsula are contemporary or modern; for upscale lodgings, stay in Rockland or Camden.

Inns

The East Wind Inn (Mechanic St., Tenants Harbor, 207/372-6366, www.eastwindinn.com, $165-250) overlooks a dreamy island-dotted harbor. Built in 1860 and originally used as a sail loft, it has a huge veranda, a cozy parlor, harbor-view rooms, and a quiet dining room. Guest rooms, suites, and apartments are divided between the main inn and the spiffed-up 19th-century former sea captain's home; all have Wi-Fi, and TVs are available upon request. Rates include a full breakfast.

The decidedly old-fashioned **Craignair Inn** (5 Third St./Clark Island Rd., off Rte. 71, Spruce Head, 800/320-9997, www.craignair.com, $120-215), built in 1928 to house granite workers, is an unfussy, unpretentious spot with a quiet oceanfront location overlooking the causeway connecting Spruce Head to Clark Island and beyond to open seas. Guest rooms are split between the main inn and the meeting house annex; some share baths. Note: There is no elevator, nor is there a bellman. Rates include breakfast. Pets are allowed in some rooms for $20/night. The inn has an excellent water-view dining room (entrées $19-28).

Bed-and-Breakfasts

Two sister properties, the dog-friendly, circa 1820s **Ocean House** (870 Rte. 131, Port Clyde, 207/372-6691) and the **Seaside Inn & Barn Café** (5 Cold Storage Rd., Port Clyde, 207/372-0700), an 1850s sea captain's home, are both part of Linda Bean's Perfect Maine empire (www.lindabeansperfectmaine.com). Guestrooms in both are unpretentious; some share baths and some have harbor views. Expect steep stairs and no a/c. Rates range $129-249 and include breakfast. The Seaside's barn houses a café and a gallery. From either, you're within steps of the Monhegan boat.

The ocean laps at the front—or is it back—yard of **Erika's B&B By the Sea** (4 Water St., Spruce Head, 207/691-7124, www.erikasbnb.com), a seaside cottage with two private rooms with separate entrances and serene views, one with a queen bed on the second floor ($159) and one with twin beds on the first floor ($129). A full breakfast is included, and a one-hour private powerboat cruise is available for $75.

Camping

The third generation now operates **Lobster Buoy Campsites** (280 Waterman's Beach Rd., South Thomaston, 207/594-7546, $28-38), a no-frills oceanfront campground with 40 sites, 28 with water and electric, all with fire ring and picnic table. Bathhouses are adequate but basic, with coin-op showers. You can launch a canoe or kayak from the small, rocky beach. Most sites are open, and Lookout Beach is reserved for tenting. For privacy, opt for sites 24-27, which edge the campground and have shrubbery between them.

FOOD

Local Flavors

Don't be surprised to see the handful of tables occupied at the **Keag Store** (Rte. 73, Village Center, South Thomaston, 207/596-6810, 5am-9pm Mon.-Sat., 6am-8pm Sun.), one of the most popular lunch stops in the area. (Keag, by the way, is pronounced "gig"—short for "Wessaweskeag.") Roast-turkey sandwiches with stuffing are a big draw, as is the pizza, which verges on the greasy but compensates with its flavor—no designer toppings, just good pizza. Order it all to go and head across the street to the public wharf, where you can hang out and observe all the comings and goings.

Eat in or just pick up excellent pastries, sandwiches, and even fried foods to go at the **Schoolhouse Bakery** (Rte. 73, Tenants Harbor, 207/372-9608, 7am-2pm Tues.-Sat.).

Yardbird Canteen (686 Port Clyde Rd., Port Clyde, 207/372-2068, 11am-7pm Mon. and Wed-Sat., noon-5pm Sun.), a roadside takeout with outdoor seating, serves good, reasonably priced fare, including lobster rolls, fried seafood, and barbeque, along with some creative specials.

Casual Dining

For a relaxing dinner with a gorgeous view, mosey on over to the **Craignair Inn**

Restaurant (Clark Island Rd., off Rte. 71, Spruce Head, 800/320-9997, www.craignair.com, from 5:30pm Tues.-Sun. in season, entrées $19-30). Big windows in the dining room frame Clark Island and the ocean beyond, and the food complements the view.

White tablecloth dining, harbor views, and good food are the draws at the **Wan-e-set Restaurant** (7:30-9:30am Mon.-Fri., 7:30-10:30am Sat.-Sun., and 6-9 pm Mon.-Tues.-and Thurs.-Sat.) located in The Eastwind Inn. Breakfast runs $6-14; dinner, which might include sea scallops or filet mignon, runs $21-24. For a more casual meal, opt for the **Quarry Tavern** (5-9pm Thurs.-Sun.), where choices such as lobster mac-n-cheese or a fried shrimp and scallop plate run $8-16.

Lobster in the Rough

These open-air lobster wharves are the best places in the area to get down and dirty and manhandle a steamed or boiled lobster.

The dreamy spruce-cropped island views alone are worth the trip to ★ **McLoon's Lobster Shack** (327 Island Rd., Spruce Head, 207/593-1382, www.mcloonslobster.com, 11am-7pm daily), but this off-the-beaten-path shack dishes out mighty fine lobster, lobster rolls, lobster stew, crab cakes, and house-made desserts such as strawberry shortcake and blueberry pie. It's well worth finding. BYOB.

A broad view of islands in the Mussel Ridge Channel is the bonanza at **Waterman's Beach Lobster** (343 Waterman's Beach Rd., South Thomaston, 207/596-7819, www.watermansbeachlobster.com, 11am-7pm Wed.-Sun., no credit cards). This tiny operation has a big reputation: It won a James Beard Award.

Bring your own wine to McLoon's Lobster Shack.

It turns out lobster, clam, and mussel dinners, fat lobster and crabmeat rolls, and superb pies as well as hot dogs and grilled cheese. Step up to the window and place your order. Service can be slow, but why rush with a view like this? Choose a good day; there's no real shelter from bad weather. BYOB. The wharf is on a side road off Route 73 between Spruce Head Village and South Thomaston; watch for signs on Route 73.

GETTING THERE AND AROUND

Port Clyde is about 15 miles or 25 minutes via Route 131 from Thomaston.

Monhegan Island

Eleven or so miles from the mainland lies a unique island community with gritty lobstermen, close-knit families, a longstanding summertime artists' colony, no cars, astonishingly beautiful scenery, and some of the best birdwatching on the eastern seaboard. Until the 1980s, the island had only radiophones and generator power; with the arrival of electricity and real phones, the pace has quickened a bit—but not much. Welcome to **Monhegan Island.**

But first a cautionary note: Monhegan has remained idyllic largely because generations of residents, part-timers, and visitors have been sensitive to its fragility. When you buy your ferry ticket, you'll receive a copy of the regulations, all very reasonable, and the captain of your ferry will repeat them. *Heed them, or don't go.*

Many of the regulations have been developed by The Monhegan Associates, an island land trust founded in the 1960s by Theodore Edison, son of inventor Thomas Edison. Firmly committed to preservation of the island in as natural a state as possible, the group maintains and marks the trails, sponsors natural history talks, and insists that no construction be allowed beyond the village limits.

The origin of the name *Monhegan* remains up in the air; it's either a Maliseet or Micmac name meaning "out-to-sea island" or an adaptation of the name of a French explorer's daughter. In any case, Monhegan caught the attention of Europeans after English explorer John Smith stopped by in 1614, but the island had already been noticed by earlier adventurers, including John Cabot, Giovanni da Verrazzano, and George Waymouth. Legend even has it that Monhegan fishermen sent dried fish to Plimoth Plantation during the Pilgrims' first winter on Cape Cod. Captain Smith returned home and carried on about Monhegan, catching the attention of intrepid souls who established a fishing and trading outpost here in 1625. Monhegan has been settled continuously since 1674, with fishing as the economic base.

In the 1880s, lured by the spectacular setting and artist Robert Henri's enthusiastic reports, gangs of artists began arriving,

The top of Lighthouse Hill has panoramic views of Monhegan Island.

Ten Rules for Monhegan Visitors

- Smoking is banned everywhere except in the village.
- Rock climbing is not allowed on the wild headlands on the back side of the island.
- Preserve the island's wild state—do not remove flowers or lichens.
- Bicycles and strollers are not allowed on island trails.
- Camping and campfires are forbidden island-wide.
- Swim only at Swim Beach, just south of the ferry landing—if your innards can stand the shock. Wait for the incoming tide, when the water is warmest (and this warmth is relative). It's wise not to swim alone.
- Dogs must be leashed; carry bags to remove their waste.
- Be respectful of private property; stay on the trails. (As the island visitors guide puts it, "Monhegan is a village, not a theme park.")
- If you're staying overnight, bring a flashlight; the village paths are very dark.
- Carry the island trail map when you go exploring; you'll need it.
- Carry a trash bag, use it, and take it off the island when you leave.

lugging their easels here and there to capture the surf, the light, the tidy cottages, the magnificent headlands, fishing boats, even the islanders' craggy features. American, German, French, and British artists have long come here, and they still do; well-known painters associated with Monhegan include Rockwell Kent, George Bellows, Edward Hopper, James Fitzgerald, Andrew Winter, Alice Kent Stoddard, Reuben Tam, William Kienbusch, and Jamie Wyeth.

Officially called Monhegan Plantation, the island has about 60 year-rounders. Several hundred others summer here. A handful of students attend the tiny school through eighth grade; high-schoolers have to pack up and move "inshore" to the mainland during the school year.

At the schoolhouse, the biggest social event of the year is the Christmas party, when everyone brings casseroles, salads, and desserts to complement a big beef roast. Kids perform their Christmas play, Santa shows up with presents, and dozens of adults look on approvingly. The islanders turn out en masse for almost every special event at the school, and the adults treat the island kids almost like common property, feeling free to praise or chastise them any time it seems appropriate—a phenomenon unique to isolated island communities.

For years, Monhegan's legislated lobster-fishing season perversely began on December 1 (locally known as Trap Day), but in 2007 it was moved forward to October 1, making it possible for visitors to view the action. An air of nervous anticipation surrounds the dozen or so lobstermen after midnight the day before as they prepare to steam out to set their traps on the ocean floor. Of course, with less competition from mainland fishermen that time of year, and a supply of lobsters fattening up since the previous season, there's a ready market for their catch. But success still depends on a smooth "setting." Meetings are held daily during the month beforehand to make sure everyone will be ready to "set" together. The season lasts into June.

Almost within spitting distance of Monhegan's dock (but you'll still need a boat) is whale-shaped **Manana Island**, once the home of a former New Yorker named Ray

Phillips. Known as the Hermit of Manana, Phillips lived a solitary sheepherding existence on this barren island for more than half a century until his death in 1975. His story had spread so far afield that even the *New York Times* ran a front-page obituary when he died. (Photos and clippings are displayed in the Monhegan Museum.) In summer, youngsters with skiffs often hang around the harbor, particularly Fish Beach and Swim Beach, and you can usually talk one of them into taking you over for a fee. (Don't try to talk them down too much or they may not return to pick you up.) Some curious inscriptions on Manana (marked with a yellow *X* near the boat landing) have led archaeologists to claim that Vikings even made it here, but cooler heads attribute the markings to Mother Nature.

One last note: Monhegan isn't for the mobility-impaired. There's no public transportation, and roads are rough and hilly.

When to Go

If a day trip is all your schedule will allow, visit Monhegan between Memorial Day weekend and mid-October, when ferries from Port Clyde, New Harbor, and Boothbay Harbor operate daily, allowing 5-8 hours on the island—time enough to do an extensive trail loop, visit the museum and handful of shops, and picnic on the rocks. Other months, there's only one ferry per day from Port Clyde, and only three per week November-April, so you'll need to spend the night—not a hardship, but it definitely requires planning.

Almost any time of year, but especially in spring, fog can blanket the island, curtailing photography and swimming (although usually not the ferries). A spectacular sunny day can't be beat, but don't be deterred by fog, which lends an air of mystery you won't forget. Rain, of course, is another matter; some island trails can be perilous even in a misty drizzle.

Practicalities

Monhegan has no bank, but there are a couple of ATMs. Credit cards are not accepted everywhere. Personal checks, traveler's checks, or cash will do.

The only public restroom is on Horn Hill, at the southern end of the village (behind the Monhegan House). A donation of $0.50 is requested; don't complain, just drop what you can into the slot to help defray maintenance costs. It's a mere pittance to help keep the island clean.

Electricity is *very* expensive on the island (about $0.70/kilowatt hour, compared with a national average of $0.09). Ask before plugging in a charger for your phone at any restaurant, shop, or other private business, and don't be surprised if you're turned down.

SIGHTS

Monhegan is a getaway destination, a relaxing place for self-starters, so don't anticipate organized entertainment beyond the occasional lecture or narrated nature tour. Bring sturdy shoes (maybe even an extra pair in case trails are wet), a windbreaker, binoculars, a camera, and perhaps a sketchpad or a journal. If you're staying overnight, bring a flashlight for negotiating the unlighted island walkways, even in the village. For rainy days, bring a book. (If you forget, there's an amazingly good library.) In winter, bring ice skates for use on the Ice Pond.

★ Monhegan Historical and Cultural Museum

The **Monhegan Lighthouse**—activated in July 1824, automated in 1959, and now on the National Register of Historic Places—stands at the island's highest point, Lighthouse Hill, an exposed summit that's also home to the **Monhegan Historical and Cultural Museum** (207/596-7003, www.monhegan-museum.org, 11:30am-3:30pm daily July-Aug., hours vary June and Sept., $5) in the former keeper's house and adjacent buildings. Overseen by the Monhegan Historical and Cultural Museum Association, the museum has been updated in recent years and is well worth visiting. Exhibits displayed throughout the Keeper's House blend artwork by

American icons such as Rockwell Kent and James Fitzgerald with historical photos and artifacts downstairs and an emphasis on flora, fauna, and the environment upstairs. The lighthouse tower is open once or twice weekly; call or check the website for current schedule. Outbuildings have tools and gear connected with fishing and ice cutting, traditional island industries. The assistant light keeper's house, restored top to bottom as a handsome art gallery, provides a climate-controlled environment for an annual exhibition drawing from works in the museum's impressive collection as well as outside sources. A volunteer is usually on hand to answer questions. Interesting note: Only works by deceased artists are shown, since there are so many talented artists on the island. The museum also owns two buildings designed and built by Rockwell Kent and later owned by James Fitzgerald (www.jamesfitzgerald.org). The house is maintained as a historic house museum, and Fitzgerald's works are displayed in the studio. It's open twice weekly; call for current schedule.

Artists' Studios

Nearly 20 artists' studios are open to the public during the summer (usually July-August), but not all at once. At least five are open most days—most in the afternoon (Monday has the fewest choices). Sometimes it's tight timewise for day-trippers who also want to hike the trails, but most of the studios are relatively close to the ferry landing. An annually updated map-schedule details locations, days, and times. It's posted on bulletin boards in the village and is available at lodgings and shops.

Winter Works is a crafts co-op and **Lupine Gallery** (207/594-8131) showcases works by Monhegan artists. When you get off the ferry, walk up the hill; one's on the left, and the other is dead ahead. You can't miss them—and shouldn't.

Monhegan Brewing Company

Lobsterman Matt Weber, son of a brewer, and his wife, Mary, a teacher, operate **Monhegan Brewing Company** (Lobster Cove Rd., 207/975-3958, www.monheganbrewing.com). Opened in 2013, they began with Lobster Cove APA and Shipwreck IPA as well as two nonalcoholic sodas. The Webers are working with the Monhegan Island Farm Project, which composts the waste barley. Stop by the tasting room, open 11am-6pm daily, July-Aug., with fewer hours in the fall, to see what's brewing and enjoy a pint in the trap-enclosed outdoor seating area.

The Monhegan Historical and Cultural Museum

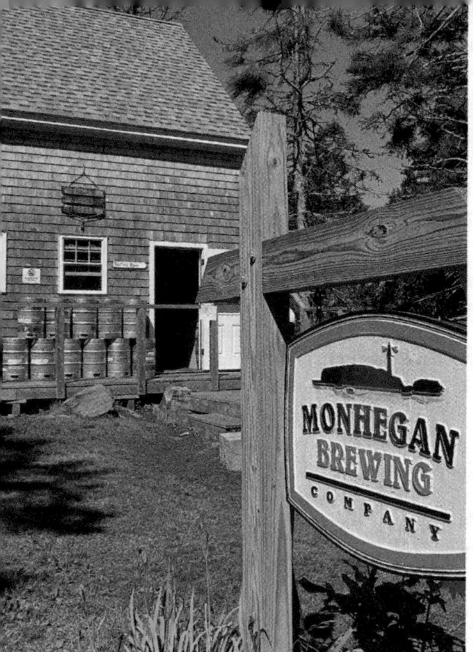

After hiking, quench your thirst at Monhegan Brewing Company.

RECREATION

Hiking and Walking

Just over half a mile wide and 1.7 miles long, barely a square mile in area, Monhegan has 18 numbered hiking trails, most of them easy to moderate, covering about 12 miles. All are described in the *Monhegan Associates Trail Map* (www.monheganassociates.org), available at mainland ferry offices and island shops and lodgings or on the website. (The map is not to scale, so the hikes can take longer than may be apparent.)

The footing is uneven everywhere, so Monhegan can present major obstacles to those with disabilities, even on the well-worn but unpaved village roads. Maintain an especially healthy respect for the ocean here, and don't venture too close; through the years, rogue waves on the island's back side have claimed victims young and old.

A relatively easy **day-tripper loop,** with a couple of moderate sections along the back side of the island, takes in several of Monhegan's finest features starting at the southern end of the village, opposite the church. To appreciate it, allow at least two hours. From the Main Road, go up Horn Hill, following signs for the **Burnthead Trail** (no. 4). Cross the island to the **Cliff Trail** (no. 1). Turn north on the Cliff Trail, following the dramatic headlands on the island's back side. There are lots of great picnic rocks in this area. Continue to Squeaker Cove, where the surf is the wildest, but be cautious. Then watch for signs to the **Cathedral Woods Trail** (no. 11), carpeted with pine needles and leading back to the village.

When you get back to Main Road, detour up the **Whitehead Trail** (no. 7) to the museum. If you're spending the night and feel energetic, consider circumnavigating the island via the **Cliff Trail** (nos. 1 and 1-A). Allow at least 5-6 hours for this route; don't rush it.

An excellent companion for hiking is the **Monhegan Island Nature Guide,** available widely on the island for $20.

Bird-Watching

One of the East Coast's best bird-watching sites during spring and fall migrations, Monhegan is a migrant trap for exhausted creatures winging their way north or south. Avid bird-watchers come here to add rare and unusual species to their life lists, and some devotees return year after year. No bird-watcher should arrive, however, without a copy of the superb *Birder's Guide to Maine*.

Predicting exact bird-migration dates can be dicey, since wind and weather aberrations can skew the schedule. Generally, the best times are mid-late May and most of September into early October. If you plan to spend a night (or more) on the island during migration seasons, don't try to wing it—reserve a room well in advance.

Around-the-Island Tour

On most days, the **Balmy Days excursion boat** makes a half-hour circuit around the island 2pm-2:30pm for a nominal fee. Ask at the ferry dock.

ACCOMMODATIONS

The island has a variety of lodgings from rustic to comfortable, but none are luxurious. Pickup trucks of dubious vintage meet all the ferries and transport luggage to the lodgings. For cottage renters, Monhegan Trucking charges a small fee for each piece of luggage.

The best lodging is the **Island Inn** (207/596-0371, www.islandinnmonhegan.com, $170-420), an imposing three-story hotel dating from 1816 that commands a prime chunk of real estate overlooking the harbor. Most guest rooms have been updated, but retain the simplicity of another era, with painted floors, antique oak furnishings, and comfy beds covered with white down duvets. Just try to resist the siren song of the Adirondack chairs on the expansive veranda and lawns overlooking the ferry landing. Rates for the 32 harbor- and meadow-view guest rooms and suites (some with shared baths) include full breakfast. Add $5 pp daily gratuity and $10/room for a one-night stay.

In the heart of the village, **Monhegan House** (207/594-7983 or 800/599-7983, www.monheganhouse.com, late May-Columbus Day, $160-224), built in 1870, is a large four-story building with 28 guest rooms. All but two suites ($224) have shared baths; most are on the second floor, with a few powder rooms on the third floor. Don't miss the loose-leaf notebook in the lobby. Labeled *A Monhegan Novel*, it's the ultimate in shaggy-dog sagas, created by a long string of guests since 1992. A $3 pp service fee covers breakfast and housekeeping; there may be a $5 pp surcharge for one-night stays. Children are welcome; ages 4-12 are $19, ages 13 and older are $29.

A more modernized hostelry, **Shining Sails** (207/596-0041, www.shiningsails.com, $150-225) lacks the quaintness of the other inns, but the two guest rooms and five efficiencies are comfortable, convenient to the dock, and have private baths. Breakfast (included only in season) is meager continental. "Well-supervised" children are welcome. An additional four apartments ($165-235) are in a separate building. Shining Sails also manages more than two dozen weekly-rental cottages and apartments, with rates beginning around $800/week in season.

The funkiest lodging, and not for everyone, is **The Trailing Yew** (207/596-0440, www.trailingyew.com, $150, no credit cards). Spread among six rustic buildings are 35 guest rooms, most with shared baths (averaging five rooms per bath and not always in the same building) and lighted with kerosene (about 12 have electricity). Rates include breakfast, taxes, and gratuities; kids are $45-65, depending on age. Dinner is available in the old-fashioned, low-key 50-seat dining room, served family-style, and also open to nonguests by reservation for dinner at 5:45pm and for breakfast at 7:45am. Bring a sleeping bag in spring or fall; rooms are unheated.

FOOD

Everything is quite casual on the island, and food is hearty and ample, albeit pricey. None of the restaurants have liquor licenses, so buy beer or wine at one of the stores or the Barnacle Café, or bring it from the mainland. In most cases hours change frequently, so call first.

Prepared foods, varying from pastries to sandwiches and salads, are available from **Barnacle Café** (207/596-0371), under the same ownership as the nearby Island Inn; **The Novelty** (207/594-4926), behind and operated by The Monhegan House; **Black Duck Emporium** (207/596-7672); and **L. Brackett & Son** (207/594-2222), a grocery with prepared foods. The restaurant at the **Island Inn**, open to nonguests for breakfast and dinner from 6pm daily, has an excellent dinner menu with entrées ($19-34) emphasizing seafood; BYOB. It's also open for lunch, 11:30am-1:30pm daily.

Islanders and visitors flock to the **Monhegan House Café**, overlooking the village, for breakfast and dinner (entrées $22-27).

You can't get much rougher for lobster in the rough than **Fish House Fish** (Fish Beach, 11:30am-7pm daily). Lobster and crabmeat rolls, locally smoked fish, and homemade stews and chowders are on the menu, as well as fresh lobster. I've found the lobster rolls to be on the meager side; opt instead for the whole crustacean. Take it to the picnic tables on the beach and enjoy.

INFORMATION AND SERVICES

Several free brochures and flyers, revised annually, will answer most questions about planning a day trip or overnight visit to Monhegan. Ferries supply visitors with the *Visitor's Guide to Monhegan Island* and sell the Monhegan Associates Trail Map ($1). Both are also available at island shops, galleries, and lodgings. In addition, info is available at www.monheganwelcome.com and www.monhegan.info.

Monhegan's pleasant little Jackie and Edward Library was named after two children who drowned in the surf in the 1920s. The fiction collection is especially extensive, and it's open to everyone.

Also check the Rope Shed, the community bulletin board next to the meadow, right in the village. Monhegan's version of a bush telegraph, it's where everyone posts flyers and notices about nature walks, lectures, excursions, and other special events. You'll also see the current Monhegan Artists Studio Locations map.

GETTING THERE AND AROUND

Ferries travel year-round to Monhegan from Port Clyde at the end of the St. George Peninsula. Seasonal service to the island is provided from New Harbor by **Hardy Boat Cruises** and from Boothbay Harbor by **Balmy Days Cruises.**

Part of the daily routine for many islanders and summer folk is a stroll to the harbor when the ferry arrives, so don't be surprised to see a good-size welcoming party when you arrive. You're the live entertainment.

Monhegan's only vehicles are a handful of pickup trucks owned by local lobstermen and li'l ol' trucks used by **Monhegan Trucking.** If you're staying a night or longer and your luggage is too heavy to carry, they'll be waiting when you arrive at the island wharf.

Rockland

A "Share the Pride" campaign—kicked off in the 1980s to boost sagging civic self-esteem and the local economy—was the first step in the transformation of **Rockland** (pop. 7,297). Once a run-down county seat best known for the aroma of its fish-packing plants, the city has undergone a sea change, and in 2010 was named a Distinctive Destination by the National Trust for Historic Preservation. The expansion of the Farnsworth Museum of American Art and the addition of its Wyeth Center was a catalyst. Benches and plants line Main Street (Rte. 1), while independent stores offer appealing wares and coffeehouses and more than a dozen art galleries, along with the new Maine Center for Contemporary Art, attract a diverse clientele. Rockland Harbor is now home to more windjammer cruise schooners than neighboring Camden (which had long claimed the title "Windjammer Capital"). If you haven't been to Rockland in the last decade, prepare to be astonished.

Foresighted entrepreneurs had seen the potential of the bayside location in the late 1700s and established a tiny settlement here called "Shore Village" (or "the Shore"). Today's commercial-fishing fleet is one of the few reminders of Rockland's past, when multimasted schooners lined the wharves—some to load volatile cargoes of lime destined to become building material for cities all along the eastern seaboard, others to head northeast toward the storm-racked Grand Banks and the lucrative cod fishery there. Such hazardous pursuits meant an early demise for many a local seafarer, but Rockland's 5,000 or so residents were enjoying their prosperity in the late 1840s. The settlement was home to more than two dozen shipyards and dozens of lime kilns, was enjoying a construction boom, and boasted a newspaper and regular steamship service. By 1854, Rockland had become a city.

Today, Rockland remains a commercial hub—with Knox County's only shopping plazas (no malls, but the big-box stores have arrived), a fishing fleet that heads far offshore, and ferries that connect nearby islands. Rockland also claims the title of "Lobster Capital of the World" thanks to Knox County's shipment nationally and internationally of 10 million pounds of lobster each year. The weathervane atop the police and fire department building is a giant copper lobster.

Rockland is more year-round community than tourist town, which adds to its appeal. But visitors pour in during two big summer festivals—the North Atlantic Blues Festival in mid-July and the Maine Lobster Festival in early August. A highlight of the Lobster Festival is King Neptune's coronation of the Maine Sea Goddess—carefully selected from a bevy of local young women—who then sails off with him to his watery domain.

SIGHTS

★ The Farnsworth Art Museum and the Wyeth Center

Anchoring downtown Rockland is the nationally respected **Farnsworth Art Museum** (16 Museum St., 207/596-6457, www.farnsworthmuseum.org), established in 1948 through a trust fund set up by Rocklander Lucy Farnsworth. With an ample checkbook, the first curator, Robert Bellows, toured the country, accumulating a splendid collection of 19th- and 20th-century Maine-related American art, the basis for the permanent *Maine in America* exhibition.

The 15,000-piece collection today includes works by Fitz Henry Lane, Gilbert Stuart, Eastman Johnson, Childe Hassam, John Marin, Maurice Prendergast, Rockwell Kent, George Bellows, and Marsden Hartley. Best known are the paintings by three generations of the Wyeth family (local summer residents) and sculpture by Louise Nevelson, who grew up in Rockland. (The only larger Nevelson collection is in New York's Whitney Museum of American Art.) The **Wyeth Center,** across Union Street in a former church, contains the work of Andrew,

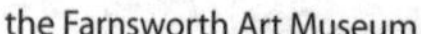
the Farnsworth Art Museum

N. C., and Jamie Wyeth. The 6,000-square-foot Jamien Morehouse Wing hosts rotating exhibits.

In the Farnsworth's library—a grand, high-ceilinged oasis akin to an English gentleman's reading room—browsers and researchers can explore an extensive collection of art books and magazines. The museum's education department annually sponsors hundreds of lectures, concerts, art classes for all ages, poetry readings, and field trips. Most are open to nonmembers; some require an extra fee. A glitzy gift shop stocks posters, prints, note cards, imported gift items, and art games for children.

The Farnsworth is open year-round, including summer holidays. Farnsworth hours are 10am-5pm Thursday-Tuesday, 10am-8pm Wednesday in summer; 10am-5pm Tuesday-Sunday in spring and fall, and 10am-5pm Wednesday-Sunday in winter.

Next door to the museum is the mid-19th-century Greek Revival **Farnsworth Homestead** ($10 adults, $5 under age 17), with original high-Victorian furnishings. Looking as though William Farnsworth's family just took off for the day, the house has been preserved rather than restored. Guided tours are offered at 11am, noon, and 1pm Thurs.-Sun., late May-mid Oct.

The Farnsworth also owns the Olson House, 14 miles away in nearby Cushing, where the whole landscape looks like a Wyeth diorama. Pick up a map at the museum to help you find the house; it's definitely worth the side trip.

Center for Maine Contemporary Art

In summer 2016, the **Center for Maine Contemporary Art** (21 Winter St., 207/236-2875, www.cmcanow.org) plans to move into its new home, a 12,143-square-foot building designed by Toshiko Mori, who made *Architectural Digest*'s 2014 list of the world's preeminent architects. The striking building provides 4,600 square feet of galleries to display works by some of Maine's best contemporary artists. Neither museum nor gallery, the nonprofit doesn't have a permanent collection or represent individual artists. It mounts temporary exhibitions, drawing from traditional and nontraditional artistic expressions from both established and emerging artists. It also offers educational programs, workshops, and special events, including a wildly popular art auction (early August). An exceptional gift shop carries high-end crafts.

★ Owls Head Transportation Museum

Don't miss this place, even if you're not an old-vehicle buff. A generous endowment has made the **Owls Head Transportation Museum** (Rte. 73, Owls Head, 207/594-4418, www.ohtm.org, 10am-5pm daily, $12 adults, $10 seniors, free under age 18; special events are $16 adults/seniors) a premier facility for celebrating wings and wheels; it draws more than 75,000 visitors per year. Scads of eager volunteers help restore the vehicles and keep them running. On weekends May-October, the museum sponsors air shows (often including aerobatic displays) and car and truck meets for hundreds of enthusiasts. The season highlight is the annual rally and aerobatic show (early Aug.), when more than 300 vehicles gather for two days of festivities. Want your own vintage vehicle? Attend the antique, classic, and special-interest auto auction (third Sun. in Aug.). The gift shop carries transportation-related items. If the kids get bored (unlikely), there's a play area outside with picnic tables. In winter, groomed cross-country skiing trails wind through the museum's 60-acre site; ask for a map at the information desk.

Maine Lighthouse Museum

The headliner at the **Maine Discovery Center** (1 Park Dr.) is the **Maine Lighthouse Museum** (207/594-3301, www.mainelighthousemuseum.org, 10am-5pm Mon.-Fri., 10am-4pm Sat.-Sun. in summer, by appt. in winter, $8 adults, $6 seniors, free under age 12), home to the nation's largest collection of Fresnel lenses, along with a boatload-plus of artifacts related to lighthouses, the Coast Guard, and the sea. On view are foghorns, ships' bells, nautical books and photographs, marine instruments, ship models, scrimshaw, and much more.

Project Puffin Visitor Center

If you can't manage a trip to see the puffins, Audubon's **Project Puffin Visitor Center** (311 Main St., 207/596-5566 or 877/478-3346, www.projectpuffin.org, 10am-5pm daily to 7pm Wed., June 1-Oct. 31, call for off-season hours) will bring them to you. Live videos of nesting puffins are just one of the features of the center, which also includes interactive exhibits, a gallery, and films, all highlighting successful efforts to restore and protect these clowns of the sea. Ask about children's programs and lecture series.

★ Rockland Breakwater

Protecting the harbor from wind-driven waves, the 4,346-foot-long **Rockland Breakwater** took 18 years to build with 697,000 tons of locally quarried granite. In the late 19th century it was piled up, chunk by chunk, from a base 175 feet wide on the harbor floor (60 feet below the surface) to the 43-foot-wide cap. The **Rockland Breakwater Light**—now automated—was built in 1902 and added to the National Register of Historic Places in 1981. The city of Rockland owns the keeper's house, but the Friends of the Rockland Harbor Lights (www.rocklandharborlights.org) maintain it. Volunteers usually open the lighthouse to the public 10am-5pm Saturday-Sunday late May-mid-October and for special events. The breakwater provides unique vantage points for photographers as well as a place to picnic or catch sea breezes or fish on a hot day, but it is extremely dangerous during storms. Anyone on the breakwater risks being washed into the sea or struck by lightning (ask the local hospital staff; it has happened). Do not take chances when the weather is iffy.

To reach the breakwater, take Route 1 North to Waldo Avenue and turn right. Take the next right onto Samoset Road and drive to the end to **Marie Reed Memorial Park** (with a tiny beach, benches, and limited parking). Or go to the Samoset Resort and walk the path to the breakwater from there.

Sail, Power & Steam Museum

Opened in 2009, the **Sail, Power & Steam Museum** (Sharp's Point South, 75 Mechanic

To reach the Rockland Breakwater Light, you have to walk nearly a mile along the Breakwater.

St., 207/701-7626, www.sailpowersteammuseum.org, 10am-3:30pm Wed.-Sat., 1pm-4pm Sun.) is Captain Jim Sharp's labor of love. Built on the grounds of the former Snow Shipyard, the museum highlights Rockland's maritime heritage and includes half-models of boats used by shipbuilders in the 19th century, vintage photos, tools of the trade, and other artifacts. Concerts are frequently held on the site. Free guided tours are offered 2pm-3pm Wednesday; musical jams take place 2pm-4pm Sunday.

Coastal Children's Museum

If you're traveling with wee ones, the **Coastal Children's Museum** (Sharp's Point South, 75 Mechanic St., 207/596-0300, www.coastalchildrensmuseum.org, 10am-4pm Wed.-Sat., 1pm-4pm Sun., $5) is just the ticket, with hands-on and educational play exhibits including a touch tank. It's located underneath the Sail, Power & Steam Museum.

Maine Coastal Islands National Wildlife Refuge Visitor Center

Seabird restoration is the focus of the **Maine Coastal Islands National Wildlife Refuge** (91 Water St., 207/594-0600, http://www.fws.gov/refuge/maine_coastal_islands, 8:30-4pm Mon.-Fri.), where Friends of Maine's Seabird Islands (www.maineseabirds.org) maintain a handful of exhibits, a theater screening a film about the refuge's work, and an art gallery, as well as run special events. Stop in, if only to view the map of the Maine coast in the lobby.

Main Street Historic District

Rocklanders are justly proud of their **Main Street Historic District,** lined with 19th- and early-20th-century Greek and Colonial Revival structures as well as examples of mansard and Italianate architecture. Most now house retail shops on the ground floor; upper floors have offices, artists' studios, and apartments. The chamber of commerce has a map and details.

ENTERTAINMENT AND EVENTS

The historic **Strand Theater** (339 Main St., 207/594-7266, www.rocklandstrand.com), opened in 1923, underwent an extensive restoration in 2005. Films as well as live entertainment are scheduled. It's also the venue for many **Bay Chamber Concerts** (207/236-2823 or 888/707-2770, www.baychamberconcerts.org) events.

The Historic Inns of Rockland coordinate the annual **January Pies on Parade,** when the inns and dozens of downtown businesses serve a variety of sweet and savory pies as a fundraiser for the local food pantry. It's always a sellout.

In mid-July the **North Atlantic Blues Festival** means a weekend of festivities featuring big names in blues. Thousands of fans jam Harbor Park for the nonstop music.

August's **Maine Lobster Festival** is a five-day lobster extravaganza with live entertainment, the Maine Sea Goddess pageant, a lobster-crate race, crafts booths, boat rides, a parade, lobster dinners, and megacrowds (the hotels are full for miles in either direction). Tons of lobsters bite the dust during the weekend despite annual protests by People for the Ethical Treatment of Animals.

SHOPPING

Galleries

Piggybacking on the fame of the Farnsworth Museum, or at least working symbiotically, art galleries line Rockland's main street and many side streets. Ask around and look around. During the summer, many of them coordinate monthly openings to coincide with **First Friday Art Walks** (5-8pm, www.artsinrockland.org), so you can meander, munch, and sip from one gallery to another.

Across from the Farnsworth's side entrance, the **Caldbeck Gallery** (12 Elm St., 207/594-5935, www.caldbeck.com) has gained a top-notch reputation as a must-see (and must-be-seen) space. Featuring the work of contemporary Maine artists, the gallery mounts more than half a dozen solo and group shows in May-September each year.

Archipelago (386 Main St., 207/596-0701), on the ground floor of the Island Institute, a nonprofit steward of Maine's 4,617 offshore islands, is an attractive retail outlet for talented craftspeople from 14 year-round islands.

Other eminently browsable downtown Rockland galleries are **Harbor Square Gallery** (374 Main St., 207/594-8700 or 877/594-8700, www.harborsquaregallery.com), **Dowling Walsh Gallery,** 365 Main St., 207/596-0084, www.dowlingwalsh.com), **Landing Gallery** (409 Main St., 207/239-1223, www.landingart.com), and **Playing with Fire! Glassworks & Gallery** (497 Main St., 207/594-7805, www.playingwithfireglassworks.com).

RECREATION

Parks

★ OWLS HEAD LIGHT STATE PARK

On Route 73, about 1.5 miles past the junction of Routes 1 and 73, you'll reach North Shore Road in the town of Owls Head. Turn left toward Owls Head Light State Park. Standing 3.6 miles from this turn, Owls Head Light occupies a dramatic promontory with panoramic views over Rockland Harbor and Penobscot Bay. The 1854 **Keeper's House Interpretive Center & Gift Shop** (10am-4pm Wed.-Sun., Mon.-Tues. by chance) doubles as headquarters for the American Lighthouse Foundation (www.lighthousefoundation.org). The light tower is usually open 11am-4pm Wednesday and 10am-4pm Saturday-Sunday. The park surrounding the tower has easy walking paths, picnic tables, and a pebbly beach where you can sunbathe or check out Rockland Harbor's boating traffic. If it's foggy or rainy, don't climb the steps toward the light tower: The view evaporates in the fog, the access ramp can be slippery, and the foghorn is dangerously deafening. Follow signs to reach the park. From North Shore Road, turn left onto Main Street, then left onto Lighthouse Road, and continue along Owls Head Harbor to the parking area. This is also a particularly pleasant bike route—about 10 miles round-trip from downtown Rockland—although the roadside shoulders are poor along the Owls Head stretch.

HARBOR PARK

If you're looking for a park with more commotion than quiet green space, spend some time at **Harbor Park.** Boats, cars, and delivery

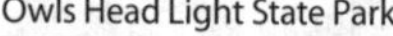
Owls Head Light State Park

vehicles come and go, and you can corner a picnic table, a bench, or a patch of grass and watch all the action. During the holidays, a lobster-trap Christmas tree presides over the park. Public restrooms (late May-mid-Oct.) are available. The park is just off Main Street.

Swimming

Lucia Beach is the local name for **Birch Point Beach State Park,** one of the best-kept secrets in the area. In Owls Head, just south of Rockland—and not far from Owls Head Light—the spruce-lined sand crescent (free) has rocks, shells, tidepools, and very chilly water. There are outhouses but no other facilities. There's ample room for a moderate-size crowd, although parking and turnaround space can get a bit tight on the access road. From downtown Rockland, take Route 73 one mile to North Shore Drive (on your left). Take the next right, Ash Point Drive, and continue past Knox County Regional Airport to Dublin Road. Turn right, go 0.8 mile, then turn left onto Ballyhac Road (opposite the airport landing lights). Go another 0.8 mile, fork left, and continue 0.4 mile to the parking area.

If frigid ocean water doesn't appeal, head for freshwater **Chickawaukee Lake,** on Route 17, two miles inland from downtown Rockland. Don't expect to be alone, though; on hot days, **Johnson Memorial Park**'s pocket-size sand patch is a major attraction. A lifeguard stands watch, and there are restrooms, picnic tables, a snack bar, and a boat-launch ramp. In winter, iceboats, snowmobiles, and ice-fishing shacks take over the lake. A signposted bicycle path runs alongside the busy highway, making the park an easy pedal from town.

Golf

The semiprivate **Rockland Golf Club** (606 Old County Rd., 207/594-9322, www.rocklandgolf.com, Apr.-Oct.) is an 18-hole course 0.2 mile northeast of Route 17.

For an 18-hole course in an unsurpassed waterfront setting (but with steep rental and greens fees), tee off at the **Samoset Resort** (220 Warrenton St., Rockport, 207/594-2511 or 800/341-1650).

Sea Kayaking

Veteran Maine Guide and naturalist Mark DiGirolamo is the spark plug behind **Breakwater Kayak** (Snow Marine Park, 69 Mechanic St., 207/542-3631, www.breakwaterkayak.com), which has a full range of tours, even multiday ones. A two-hour Rockland Harbor tour is $45, and the all-day Owls Head Lighthouse tour is $110, including lunch. Reservations are advisable. This outfit is particularly eco-sensitive—Mark has a degree in environmental science—and is definitely worth supporting. Maine Audubon often taps Mark to lead natural-history field trips. Dress warmly and bring a filled water bottle.

Boat Excursions

Marine biologist Captain Bob Pratt is the skipper of ***A Morning in Maine*** (207/594-1844 or 207/691-7245 seasonal boat phone, www.amorninginmaine.com), a classic 55-foot ketch designed by noted naval architect R. D. (Pete) Culler and built by Concordia Yachts. June-October, *Morning* departs from the middle pier at the Rockland Public Landing three times daily for two-hour sails ($40), with plenty of knowledgeable commentary from Captain Pratt. A 6pm sunset sail is available in July-August.

Watch Captain Steve Hale set and haul lobster traps during a 1.25-hour cruise ($30 adults, $18 under age 12) aboard the ***Captain Jack*** (Rockland Harbor, 207/42-6852, www.captainjacklobstertours.com), a 30-foot working lobster boat. Cruises depart up to six times daily Monday-Saturday May-October. Note that there are no toilets aboard. Captain Jack offers a lobster-roll lunch cruise for $45 pp. Reservations required; minimum two people for a trip.

Maine State Ferry Service

Car and passenger ferries service the islands of Vinalhaven, North Haven, and Matinicus. The Vinalhaven and North Haven routes

Windjamming

In 1936, Camden became the home of the "cruise schooner" (sometimes called "dude schooner") trade when Captain Frank Swift restored a creaky wooden vessel and offered sailing vacations to paying passengers. He kept at it for 25 years, gradually adding other boats to the fleet. Now, more than a dozen sail Penobscot Bay's waters. Rockland wrested the Windjammer Capital title from Camden in the mid-1990s and so far has held onto it.

Named for their ability to "jam" into the wind when they carried freight up and down the New England coast, windjammers trigger images of the Great Age of Sail. Most member vessels of the Maine Windjammer Association are rigged as schooners, with two or three soaring wooden masts; their lengths range 64-132 feet. Seven are National Historic Landmarks.

These windjammers head out for 2-6 days late May-mid-October, tucking into coves and harbors around Penobscot Bay and its islands. They set their itineraries by the wind, propelled by stiff breezes to Buck's Harbor, North Haven, and Deer Isle. Everything's totally informal and geared for relaxing.

You're aboard for the experience, not for luxury, so expect basic accommodations with few frills, although newer vessels were built with passenger trade in mind and tend to be a bit more comfy. Below deck, cabins typically are small and basic, with paper-thin walls—sort of a campground afloat (earplugs are often available for light sleepers). It may not sound romantic, but be aware that the captains keep track of postcruise marriages. Most boats have shared showers and toilets. If you're Type A, given to pacing, don't inflict yourself on the cruising crowd; if you're flexible, ready for whatever, go ahead and sign on. You can help with the sails, eat, curl up with a book, inhale salt air, snap photos, eat, sunbathe, bird-watch, chat up fellow passengers, sleep, eat, or just settle back and enjoy spectacular sailing you'll never forget.

When you book a cruise, you'll receive all the details and directions, but for a typical trip, you arrive at the boat by 7pm for the captain's call to meet your fellow passengers. You sleep aboard at the dock that night and then depart midmorning and spend the next nights and days cruising Penobscot Bay, following the wind, the weather, and the whims of the captain. (Many of the windjammers have no engines, only a motorized yawl boat used as a pusher and a water taxi.) You might anchor in a deserted cove and explore the shore, or you might pull into a harbor and hike, shop, and barhop. Then it's back to the boat for chow—windjammer cooks are legendary

make fantastic day trips (especially with a bike), or you can spend the night; the Matinicus ferry is much less predictable, and island services are few.

Bicycling

Rentals (from $25), sales, and repair are provided by **Sidecountry Sports** (481 Main St., 207/701-5100, www.sidecountrysports.com).

ACCOMMODATIONS

If you're planning an overnight stay in the Rockland area the first weekend in August—during the Maine Lobster Festival—make reservations well in advance. Festival attendance runs close to 100,000, so "No Vacancy" signs extend from Waldoboro to Belfast.

Samoset Resort

The 221-acre **Samoset Resort** (220 Warrenton St., Rockport, 207/594-2511 or 800/341-1650, www.samoset.com, from $359) commands a spectacular oceanfront site straddling the boundary between Rockland and Rockport, the next town to the north. Built on the ashes of a classic 19th-century summer hotel, the Samoset is a full-service, modern, family-oriented resort. Most of its 178 guest rooms and suites, all refurbished since 2007, and four cottages have knockout ocean views and all the expected bells and whistles. Facilities include a fitness center with an indoor heated pool, an outdoor zero-entry heated pool with a bar and food service, lighted tennis courts, a children's day camp

on board a Maine windjammer

for creating three hearty all-you-can-eat meals daily, including at least one lobster feast. When the cruise ends, most passengers find it hard to leave.

On the summer cruising schedule, several weeks coincide with special windjammer events, so you'll need to book a berth far in advance for these: mid-June (Boothbay Harbor's Windjammer Days), Fourth of July week (Great Schooner Race), Labor Day weekend (Camden's Windjammer Weekend), and the second week in September (WoodenBoat Sail-In).

Most windjammers offering sails out of Camden, Rockland, and Rockport are members of the **Maine Windjammer Association** (800/807-9463, www.sailmainecoast.com), a one-stop resource for vessel and schedule information. One that isn't but is renowned for its onboard cuisine is the ***Schooner J. & E. Riggin*** (207/594-1875, www.mainewindjammer.com), captained by the husband-wife team of Annie Mahle, author of two cookbooks, and Jon Finger.

(ages 5-12, morning and evening sessions), daily planned activities, access to the adjacent famed Rockland Breakwater, a fabulous 18-hole waterfront golf course, full-service spa, and casual restaurant and lounge with outdoor terrace seating. For a real treat, book the Flume cottage.

Inns and Bed-and-Breakfasts

These bed-and-breakfasts are in Rockland's historic district, within easy walking distance of downtown attractions and restaurants; the first three are members of the **Historic Inns of Rockland Maine** (www.historicinnsofrockland.com), which coordinates the January Pies on Parade event—a blast.

Most elegant—although that's tempered by a lighthearted attitude, evidenced by a toy hamster collection—is ★ **The Berry Manor Inn** (81 Talbot Ave., 207/596-7696 or 800/774-5692, www.berrymanorinn.com, $145-310), on a quiet side street a few blocks from downtown. Cheryl Michaelsen and Michael LaPosta have totally restored the manse built in 1898 by wealthy Rocklander Charles Berry as a wedding gift for his wife (thoughtful fellow). High ceilings and wonderful Victorian architectural touches are everywhere, especially in the enormous front hall and two parlors. Guest rooms and suites are spread between the main house and adjacent carriage house. Most have gas fireplaces and whirlpool tubs. All have air-conditioning, flat-screen TVs and video players, and Wi-Fi. A guest pantry is stocked with free soft drinks and juices and sweets—not that you'll be hungry after the extravagant breakfast.

The Limerock Inn (96 Limerock St., 207/594-2257 or 800/546-3762, www.limerockinn.com, $169-249) is a lovely painted lady. The 1890s Queen Anne mansion, with wraparound porch and turret, is listed on the National Register of Historic Places. Each of the eight guest rooms has its own distinctive flavor—such as the Turret Room, with a wedding canopy bed, and the Island Cottage Room, with a private deck overlooking the back gardens. All are elegantly furnished with an emphasis on guest comfort. Three have whirlpool tubs, and one has a fireplace; there's Wi-Fi and air-conditioning throughout. The inviting decor blends family antiques with mid-century modern furnishings and original art.

Traveling with Fido and the kiddos? Check into the kid- and pet-friendly **Granite Inn** (546 Main St., Rockland, 800/386-9036, www.oldgraniteinn.com, $95-215), where you can practically roll out of bed and onto an island ferry. Unlike most historical inns, the decor leans to contemporary and a bit artsy, blending mid-century modern with original artwork as well as antiques. Breakfast is full and satisfying, and might even include a seafood quiche. Front rooms have water views.

Opened in 1996, the The Lindsey Hotel (5 Lindsey St., 207/596-7950 or 800/523-2145, www.lindseyhouse.com, $180-250) is more like a boutique hotel than a bed-and-breakfast. The 1835 brick structure has been completely restored, adding such modernities as phones, air-conditioning, Wi-Fi, and TVs. The decor is casual contemporary with a nautical motif, and not at all fussy or frilly. Don't miss the hidden-from-the-street garden patio or the Maine art collection provided by Gleason Fine Art. It's right smack downtown, and a few rooms have glimpses of the water. Rates include an extensive hot-and-cold breakfast buffet and afternoon refreshments.

250 Main (207/594-5994, 250 Main St., www.250mainhotel.com, from $299), a chic and modern, 26-room boutique hotel overlooking Harbor Park, opened in early 2016. Owner Lyman Morse Boatbuilding custom-crafted many of the furnishings and interior finishes. Every room has a water view along with flat-screen TV and Wi-Fi. Afternoon refreshments are offered, and a continental breakfast is included.

FOOD

Rockland is gaining a reputation as a foodie town, with new options opening regularly.

Local Flavors

A great spot to grab breakfast before catching a ferry is **Home Kitchen Cafe** (650 Main St., 207/596-2449, www.homekitchencafe.com 7am-3pm Mon. and Wed.-Sat., 8am-3pm Sun., $4-10), where the huevos rancheros and lobster tacos earn raves. The menu is extensive and creative. Breakfast and lunch are served all day long.

Holding down the other end of Main Street is **The Brass Compass Café** (305 Main St., 207/596-5960, 5am-3pm Mon.-Sat., 6am-3pm Sun.), where the portions are big, the prices are small, and most of the ingredients are locally sourced. Sit indoors or on the dog-friendly patio. If you go for breakfast, the fish cakes are a real taste of Maine.

Lots of Rockland-watchers credit **Rock City Cafe** (252 Main St., 207/594-4123, www.rockcitycoffee.com) with sparking the designer-food renaissance in town. Lunch is served 11am-3pm daily.

Scratch-made bread, pastries, and grab-and-go sandwiches have made **Atlantic Baking Co.** (351 Main St., 207/596-0505, www.atlanticbakingco.com, 7am-6pm Mon.-Sat., 8am-4pm Sun.) a popular spot for a quick informal lunch. There are plenty of tables to enjoy your treats, or take them to the waterfront park.

If you're craving a decent breakfast or lunch and are up for a little foray "down the peninsula," head for the **Owls Head General Store** (2 S. Shore Dr., Owls Head, 207/596-6038, 7am-2:30pm Tues.-Thurs. and Sun.,

7am-6pm Fri.-Sat.), where the atmosphere is friendly and definitely contagious. If you get lost, the helpful staff will steer you the right way, and they will even take your photograph in front of the store. Despite all the competition from lobster-in-the-rough places, the lobster roll here is among the best around, and more than one critic has proclaimed the 7-Napkin Burger as the state's best.

The **Rockland Farmers Market** sets up 9am-1pm every Thursday June-September at Harbor Park on Rockland's Public Landing.

Fiore (503 Main St., 207/596-0276, www.fioreoliveoils.com), an artisan olive oil and vinegar tasting room and retail store, is a delicious addition to downtown Rockland.

Ethnic Fare

Ask local pooh-bah chefs where they go on their night off, and the answer often is Keiko Suzuki Steinberger's **Suzuki's Sushi Bar** (419 Main St., 207/596-7447, www.suzukisushi.com, from 5pm Tues.-Sat.). The food matches the decor: simple yet sophisticated. Sashimi, *nigiri, maki,* and *temaki* choices range $6-10; hot entrées are $14-28. Both hot and cold sake are served, or try a saketume, made with gin or vodka, sake, and an *ume* plum. Reservations are essential.

An avocado-and-gold dining room is the appropriate setting for the Cal-Mex food dished out at **Sunfire Mexican Grill** (488 Main St., 207/594-6196, 11am-3pm Tues.-Sat., and 5pm-8pm Wed.-Sat.). You'll find all the usuals, from tacos to seafood specialties; most choices run $8-17. Everything is prepared fresh on-site.

Authentic Italian cuisine draws repeat customers to **Rustica** (315 Main St., 207/594-0025, www.rusticamaine.com, 5pm-9pm Mon.-Sat., $13-24). The two dining areas are comfortable yet refined, with candles on the tables; the fare is fresh and plentiful.

Hard to say which is better, the views or the fare at the Samoset Resort's **La Bella Vita & The Enoteca Lounge** (220 Warrenton St., 207/594-2511, www.labellavitaristorante.com). Ocean Properties operates this restaurant at other locations, but this one really shines. The flavor is Italian, with pastas, pizzas from the wood-fired oven, and other specialties. Views from the restaurant and deck over the golf course to the ocean are terrific. It's open daily for breakfast, lunch, and dinner; Sunday brunch is served noon-2:30pm.

Casual Dining

Big flavors come out of the tiny kitchen at **Café Miranda** (15 Oak St., 207/594-2034, www.cafemiranda.com, 11:30am-2pm and 5pm-9pm Mon.-Sat., 10:30am-2pm and 5-9pm Sun.). The menu is overwhelming in size and hard to read; it's even harder to digest the flavor contrasts, which will make your brain spin. Entrées are $18-27, but many of the appetizers ($6.50-12.50) are enough for a meal. Fresh-from-the-brick-oven focaccia comes with everything. If you sit at the counter, you can watch chef-owner Kerry Altiero's creations emerging from the oven. Beer and wine only. Reservations are essential throughout the summer and on weekends off-season; there is patio dining in-season.

At the end of a day exploring Rockland, it's hard to beat ★ **In Good Company** (415 Main St., 207/593-9110, www.ingoodcompanymaine.com, 4:30-9pm daily), a chic and casual wine and tapas bar. Sit at the bar and watch chef-owner Melody Wolfertz, a Culinary Institute of America grad, concoct her creative tapas-style selection of small and large plates; entrées are $20-28.

Destination Dining

Arriving in Rockland trailing a James Beard Award-winning reputation, chef Melissa Kelly opened ★ **Primo** (2 S. Maine St./Rte. 73, 207/596-0770, www.primorestaurant.com) in 2000 and hasn't had time to breathe since. She has gone on to open two other restaurants, and in 2007 expanded this one, in an air-conditioned Victorian home. In 2013 she won her second Beard Award for Best Chef in the Northeast. Fresh local ingredients, many from the restaurant's gardens, are a high priority, and unusual fish specials appear every day; pork and chicken are raised on the premises. Primo is really three experiences under one roof: the intimate and elegant dining rooms downstairs; the upstairs bar, with a handful of tables; and an upstairs counter, with seating by an open kitchen as well as at tables. There are two menus, one for the dining room (entrées from $32) and the counter menu, which highlights cheeses and charcuterie and small plates, making it possible to mix and match a meal of tapas-size portions and stay within a budget. Upstairs you can dine from either menu. Kelly's partner, Price Kushner, produces an impressive range of breads and desserts. Reservations are essential for the dining rooms, usually at least a week ahead on midsummer weekends—and you still may have to wait when you get there; no reservations are taken for the upstairs bar or counter. Primo opens at 5pm Wed.-Mon. in July-August, with fewer days off-season.

INFORMATION AND SERVICES

For information, visit the **Penobscot Bay Regional Chamber of Commerce** (Gateway Center, 207/596-0376 or 800/223-5459, www.mainedreamvacation.com) or **Rockland Public Library** (80 Union St., 207/594-0310, www.rocklandlibrary.org).

Find **public restrooms** at the Gateway Center; the Knox County Courthouse (Union St. and Masonic St.); the Rockland Recreation Center (Union St. and Limerock St.), across from the courthouse, next to the playground; the Rockland Public Library; off Tillson Ave near the municipal parking lots; and the Maine State Ferry Service terminal.

GETTING THERE AND AROUND

Rockland is about five miles or 10 minutes via Route 1 from Thomaston. It's about eight miles or 15 minutes via Route 1 to Camden.

The Fox Islands

Vinalhaven (pop. 1,165) and neighboring **North Haven** (pop. 355) have been known as the Fox Islands since 1603, when English explorer Martin Pring sailed these waters and allegedly spotted gray foxes in his search for sustenance. Nowadays, you'll find reference to that name only on nautical charts, identifying the passage between the two islands as the Fox Islands Thorofare—and there's nary a fox in sight.

Each island has its own distinct personality. To generalize, Vinalhaven is bustling, whereas North Haven is sedate and exclusive.

VINALHAVEN

Five miles wide, 7.5 miles long, and covering 10,000 acres, Vinalhaven is 13 miles off the coast of Rockland—a 75-minute ferry trip. The shoreline has so many zigs and zags that no place on the island is more than a mile from the water.

The island is famed for its granite. The first blocks headed for Boston around 1826, and within a few decades quarrymen arrived from as far away as Britain and Finland to wrestle out and shape the incredibly resistant stone. Schooners, barges, and "stone sloops" left **Carver's Harbor** carrying mighty cargoes of granite destined for government and commercial buildings in Boston, New York, and Washington DC. In the 1880s, nearly 4,000 people lived on Vinalhaven, North Haven, and Hurricane Island. After World War I, demand declined, granite gave way to concrete and steel, and the industry petered out and died. But Vinalhaven has left its mark in ornate columns, paving blocks, and curbstones in communities as far west as Kansas City.

Vinalhaven is a serious working community, not primarily a playground. Lobster and fishing are the island's chief industries. Shopkeepers cater to locals as well as visitors,

Vinalhaven

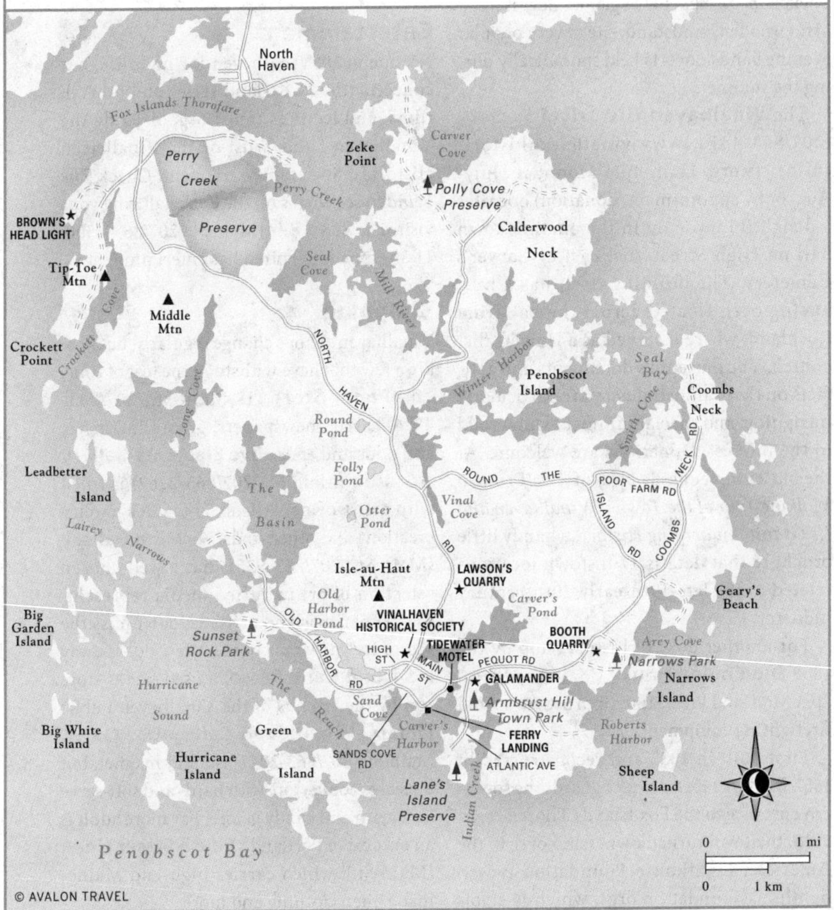

and increasing numbers of artists and artisans work away in their studios. For day-trippers, there's plenty to do—shopping, picnicking, hiking, biking, swimming—but an overnight stay provides a chance to sense the unique rhythm of life on a year-round island.

Sights

One Main Street landmark that's hard to miss is the three-story cupola-topped **Odd Fellows Hall,** a Victorian behemoth with American flag motifs on the lower windows and assorted gewgaws in the upper ones. Artist Robert Indiana, who first arrived as a visitor in 1969, owns the structure, built in 1885 for the Independent Order of Odd Fellows Star of Hope Lodge. It's not open to the public.

At the top of the hill just beyond Main Street (School St. and E. Main St.) is a greenish-blue replica **galamander,** a massive reminder of Vinalhaven's late-19th-century granite-quarrying era. Galamanders, hitched to oxen or horses, carried the stone from island quarries to the finishing shops. (By the way, the origin of the name remains unexplained.) Next to the galamander is a colorful wooden bandstand, site of very popular evening band concerts held sporadically during the summer.

The **Vinalhaven Historical Society** (207/863-4410, www.vinalhavenhistoricalsociety.org, 11am-4pm Mon.-Sat., July-Aug. or by appointment, donation) operates a delightful museum in the onetime town hall on High Street, just east of Carver's Cemetery. The building itself has a tale, having been floated across the bay from Rockland, where it served as a Universalist church. The museum's documents and artifacts on the granite industry are particularly intriguing, and special summer exhibits add to the interest. Donations are welcome. At the museum, request a copy of *A Self-guided Walking Tour of the Town of Vinalhaven and Its Granite-quarrying History*, a handy little brochure that details 17 in-town locations related to the late-19th-early-20th-century industry.

For another dose of history, stop by the 1888 **Old Engine House** (Main St., 10am-2pm Mon. and Wed., 1pm-3pm Sat.) to see old firefighting equipment.

First built in 1832 and reconstructed in 1857, **Brown's Head Light** guards the southern entrance to the Fox Islands Thorofare. In 2015, the town turned ownership over to the American Lighthouse Foundation (www.lighthousefoundation.org), which is stabilizing it and developing a five-year plan. To reach the grounds, take the North Haven Road about six miles, at which point you'll see a left-side view of the Camden Hills. Continue about another mile to the second road on the left, Crockett River Road. Turn and take the second road on the right, continuing past the Brown's Head Cemetery to the hill overlooking the lighthouse. Check with the foundation for its current status.

See **Vinalhaven by Boat** (207/248-1775, www.vinalhavenbyboat) with Capt. Mark Jackson aboard the *Ruth*, a small open wooden boat built for pleasure, not speed. The $75/hour rate covers four people.

Entertainment

No one visits Vinalhaven for nightlife, but concerts (the Fox Island series and others), films, and lectures (most organized by the Vinalhaven Land Trust or the Vinalhaven Historical Society) are frequent. Check *The Wind* to see what's on the docket during your visit. The **Sand Bar** (Main St., 207/863-4500, 11am-9pm daily) often has entertainment.

Shopping

Vinalhaven's shops change regularly, but here are a few that have withstood the test of time. **The Paper Store** (18 Main St., 207/863-4826) carries newspapers, gifts, film, maps, and odds and ends. **Five Elements Gallery + Studio** (Main St., 207/863-2262) is filled with artist-owner Alison Thibault's jewelry creations and other finds. **New Era Gallery** (Main St., 207/863-9351) has a well-chosen selection of art in varied media representing primarily island artisans; don't miss the sculpture garden or barn. A few doors away is **Second Hand Prose,** a used-books store run by the Friends of the Vinalhaven Public Library. **Vinalhaven Candy Co.** (35 W. Main St., 207/863-2041) is a kid magnet, but it pleases adults, too, with hard- and soft-serve ice cream and candy galore. Far more adult is an outpost of Portland's **South Street Linen** (Main St.), which carries high-end Maine-made linen clothing and more.

The Saturday-morning anything-goes **flea markets** are an island must, as much for the browsing and buying as for the gossip.

Recreation

PARKS AND PRESERVES

Vinalhaven is loaded with wonderful hikes and walks, some deliberately unpublicized. Since the mid-1980s, the **Vinalhaven Land Trust** (207/863-2543, www.vinalhavenlandtrust.org) has expanded the opportunities. When you reach the island, pick up maps at the land trust's kiosk at **Skoog Memorial**

Vinalhaven Candy Co. is a kid pleaser.

Park (12 Skoog Park Rd., off Sands Cove Rd., west of the ferry terminal) or inquire at the town office or the Paper Store. The trust also offers a seasonal series of educational walks and talks.

Some hiking options are the Perry Creek Preserve, which has a terrific loop trail; Middle Mountain Park; Tip-Toe Mountain; Isle au Haut Mountain; Huber Preserve; and Eleanor L. Campbell.

The Maine chapter of **The Nature Conservancy** (207/729-5181) owns or manages several islands and island clusters near Vinalhaven. **Big Garden** (formerly owned by Charles and Anne Morrow Lindbergh) and **Big White Islands** are easily accessible and great for shoreline picnics if you have your own boat. Other Nature Conservancy holdings in this area are fragile environments, mostly nesting islands off-limits mid-March-mid-August. Contact The Nature Conservancy for specifics.

No, you're not on the moors of Yorkshire, but you could be fooled in the 45-acre **Lane's Island Preserve,** one of The Nature Conservancy's most-used island preserves. Masses of low-lying ferns, rugosa roses, and berry bushes cover the granite outcrops of this sanctuary—and a foggy day makes it even more moorlike and mystical, like a setting for a Brontë novel. The best (albeit busiest) time to come is early August, when you can compete with the birds for blackberries, raspberries, and blueberries. Easy trails wind past old stone walls, an aged cemetery, and along the surf-pounded shore. The preserve is a 20-minute walk (or five-minute bike ride) from Vinalhaven's ferry landing. Set off to the right on Main Street, through the village. Turn right onto Water Street and then right on Atlantic Avenue. Continue across the causeway on Lane's Island Road and left over a salt marsh to the preserve. The large white house on the harbor side of Lane's Island is privately owned.

Next to the ferry landing in Carver's Harbor is **Grimes Park,** a wooded pocket retreat with a splendid view of the harbor. Owned by the American Legion, the 2.5-acre park is perfect for picnics or for hanging out between boats, especially in good weather.

Just behind the Island Community Medical Center, close to downtown, is 30-acre **Armbrust Hill Town Park,** once the site of granite-quarrying operations. Still pockmarked with quarry pits, the park has beautifully landscaped walking paths and native flowers, shrubs, and trees—much of it thanks to late island resident Betty Roberts, who made this a lifelong endeavor. From the back of the medical center, follow the trail to the summit for a southerly view of Matinicus and other offshore islands. If you're with children, be especially careful about straying onto side paths, which go perilously close to old quarry holes. Before the walk, lower the children's energy level at the large playground off to the left of the trail.

SWIMMING

Two town-owned quarries are easy to reach from the ferry landing. **Lawson's Quarry** is one mile from downtown on the North Haven Road; **Booth Quarry** is 1.6 miles from downtown via East Main Street. Both are signposted. You'll see plenty of sunbathers on the rocks and swimmers on a hot day, but there are no lifeguards, so swimming is at your own risk. There are no restrooms or changing rooms. Note that pets and soap are not allowed in the water; camping, fires, and alcohol are not allowed in the quarry areas.

Down the side road beyond Booth Quarry is **Narrows Park,** a town-owned space looking out toward Narrows Island, Isle au Haut, and, on a clear day, Mount Desert Island.

For saltwater swimming, take East Main Street 2.4 miles from downtown to a crossroads, where you'll see a whimsical bit of local folk art—the Coke lady sculpture. Turn right (east) and go 0.5 mile to **Geary's Beach** (also called **State Beach**), where you can picnic and scour the shoreline for shells and sea glass.

BICYCLING

Even though Vinalhaven's 40 or so miles of public roads are narrow, winding, and poorly shouldered, they're relatively level, so a bicycle is a fine way to tour the island. Bring your own, preferably a hybrid or mountain bike, or rent one ($15/day for a clunky one-speed) at the **Tidewater Motel** (207/863-4618) on Main Street. If you choose to bring a bike from the mainland, know that it costs extra to bring one on the ferry.

A 10-mile, 2.5-hour bicycle route begins on Main Street and goes clockwise out on the North Haven Road (rough pavement), past Lawson's Quarry, to Round the Island Road (some sections are dirt), then Poor Farm Road to Geary's Beach and back to Main Street via Pequot Road and School Street. Carry a picnic and enjoy it on Lane's Island, stop for a swim in one of the quarries, or detour down to Brown's Head Light. If you're here for the day, keep track of the time so you don't miss the ferry.

Far more rewarding view-wise, and far shorter, is the one-way-and-back pedal out along the Old Harbor Road to The Basin, which is rich in wildlife and serves as a seal nursery. There's also a nice trail at the road's end to The Basin's shorefront and across to an island; ask Phil at the Tidewater Motel for directions.

SEA KAYAKING

Sea-kayak rentals are available at the Tidewater Motel for $25/day, including delivery. A guide can be arranged, but it's not necessary to have one to poke around the harbor or, even better, paddle through The Basin, which is especially popular with birders and wildlife-watchers.

BIRDING AND WILDLIFE-WATCHING

Join ornithologist **John Drury** (207/596-1841, www.maineseabirdtours.com, $90/hour) aboard his 36-foot lobster boat on a birding and wildlife-watching cruise through the islands of Penobscot Bay. Sightings have included Arctic terns, guillemots, shearwaters, petrel, puffins, and eagles, along with seals, dolphins, minke whales, and perhaps even an albatross.

Accommodations

If you're planning on staying overnight, don't even consider arriving in summer without reservations. If you're coming for the day, pay attention to the ferry schedule and allow enough time to get back to the boat. The island has no campsites. Rates listed are for peak season.

Your feet practically touch the water when you spend the night at the ★ **Tidewater Motel and Gathering Space** (12 Main St., Carver's Harbor, 207/863-4618, www.tidewatermotel.com, year-round, $185-315), in two buildings cantilevered over the harbor. Owned by Phil and Elaine Crossman (she operates the New Era Gallery down the street), the 19-room motel was built by Phil's parents in 1970. It's the perfect place to sit on the deck and watch the lobster boats do their thing. Be aware, though, that commercial fishermen are early risers, and lobster-boat engines can rev up as early as 4:30am on a summer morning—all part of the pace of Vinalhaven. Phil can recommend hikes and other activities, and since he maintains the island's calendar of events, he always knows what's happening and when. Continental breakfast and use of bicycles (clunky one-speeds) are included in the rates; sea-kayak rentals are available. Kids 10 and under are free; seven units are efficiencies. If you want to get a better sense of island life, pick up a copy of Phil's book *Away Happens,* a collection of humorous essays about island living. You can see a sample from it on the motel's website.

Also convenient to downtown is **The Libby House** (Water St., 207/863-4696, www.libbyhouse1869.com, $110-150, no breakfast), an 1869 Victorian with a two-bedroom apartment and five guest rooms, some sharing a bath.

Food

Island restaurant hours change frequently; call for current schedules.

LOCAL FLAVORS

Vinalhaven Farmer's Market sets up 8am-noon Saturday in conjunction with the Flea Market. Look for Creelman Creamery Cheese made on the island.

Baked bean suppers are regularly held at a couple of island locations. Check the local newsletter *The Wind* for details.

The island's best breakfast place is **Surfside** (Harborside Wharf, Main St., 207/863-2767, 4-11am daily), a hole-in-the-wall on the wharf with tables inside and out. The fish cakes earn raves and are always available on Sunday.

If the weather's fine, look for **Greet's Eats** (207/863-2057, 11am-2:30pm Thurs.-Mon.), takeout on the wharf by the Co-op that has a stellar rep for its lobster rolls but has other options, too.

Our Daily Bread (Harborside Wharf, Main St., 207/864-2517, 5am-2pm Mon.-Sat.) is a must for freshly baked goods.

Pick up the fixings for a fancy picnic at **Island Spirits** (Main St., 207/863-2192), a small gourmet-foods store stocked with wines, beers, cheeses, breads, and other goodies.

For premade or made-to-order sandwiches, stop into **Carver's Harbor Market** (Main St., 207/863-4319).

FAMILY FAVORITES

The order-at-the-counter **Harbor Gawker** (Main St., 207/863-9365, 11am-8pm Mon.-Sat., $9-18), a local downtown landmark since 1975, has seating indoors and out; the crab biscuits (fritters) are awesome. **The Pizza Pit** (Harborside Wharf, Main St., 207/863-4311, 4pm-8pm Wed.-Sun.) is an easy-on-the-budget choice.

CASUAL DINING

For casual fine dining, book one of the white-clothed tables in the rustic Harborside room at **The Haven Restaurant** (Main St., 207/863-4969, Wed.-Sat., seatings at 6pm and 8:15pm, $17-25), where popular local caterer Torry Pratt offers a menu that changes daily but might include roasted pork rack, pan blackened local halibut, or broiled tenderloin.

Another choice for casual fine dining is **SALT Restaurant** (Main St., 27/863-4444, www.saltvh.com, 5:30-9:30pm Wed.-Sun. and 10am-1pm Sun., $18-30), owned by Chef John Feingold, whose culinary pedigree includes Michelin three-star restaurants. Options may include a rave-worthy lobster bisque, diver scallops, poached out-of-shell lobster, or a burger.

Information and Services

Vinalhaven Chamber of Commerce (www.vinalhaven.org) produces a handy flyer-map showing locations in the Carver's Harbor area. Also helpful for trip planning is a guidebook published by Phil Crossman at the Tidewater Motel (207/863-4618, $3.50). On the island, pick up a copy of Vinalhaven's weekly newsletter, *The Wind,* named after the island's original newspaper, first published in 1884. It's loaded with island flavor: news items, public-supper announcements, editorials, and ads. A year's subscription is $50; free single copies are available at most downtown locales.

Check out the **Vinalhaven Public Library** (E. Main St. and Chestnut St., 207/863-4401).

Public restrooms are at the ferry landing and in town at the chamber of commerce office in the big red fire barn.

Getting Around

Don't bring a car unless it is absolutely necessary. If you're day-tripping, you can get to parks and quarries, shops, restaurants, and the historical society museum on foot. If you want to explore farther, a bicycle is an excellent option, or you can rent a car ($55) or reserve a **taxi** through the Tidewater Motel (207/863-4618; call well ahead).

NORTH HAVEN

Eight miles long by three miles wide, **North Haven** (pop. 355) is 12 miles off the coast of Rockland—70 minutes by ferry. The island has sedate summer homes, open fields where hundreds of sheep once grazed, an organic farm, about 350 year-round residents, and a yacht club called the Casino.

Originally called North Island, North Haven had much the same settlement history as Vinalhaven, but being smaller (about 5,280 acres) and more fertile, it has developed—or not developed—differently. In 1846, North Haven was incorporated and severed politically from Vinalhaven, and by the late 1800s, the Boston summer crowd began buying traditional island homes, building tastefully unpretentious new ones, and settling in for a whole season of sailing and socializing. Several generations later, "summer folk" now come for weeks rather than months, often rotating the schedules among slews of siblings. Informality remains the key, though—now more than ever.

The island has two distinct hamlets—North Haven Village, on the Fox Islands Thorofare, where the state ferry arrives; and Pulpit Harbor, particularly popular with the yachting set. The village is easily explored on foot in a morning—if you take the 9:30am ferry and return on the same boat at 12:30, you qualify for the excursion fare.

North Haven doesn't offer a lot for the day visitor, and islanders tend not to welcome them with open arms.

Entertainment

Waterman's Community Center (Main St., 207/867-2100, www.watermans.org) provides a place for island residents and visitors to gather for entertainment, events, and even coffee and gossip. It's home to North Haven Arts & Enrichment. Check the schedule on the website to see what's planned.

Shopping

Fanning out from the ferry landing is a delightful cluster of substantial year-round clapboard homes—a marked contrast to the weathered-shingle cottages typical of so many island communities. It won't take long to stroll and visit the handful of shops and galleries, which include **Hopkins Wharf Gallery** on the waterfront and **North Haven Gallery** on Main Street.

Recreation

North Haven has about 25 miles of paved roads that are conducive to **bicycling**, but, just as on most other islands, they are narrow, winding, and nearly shoulderless. Starting near the ferry landing in North Haven Village, take South Shore Road eastward, perhaps stopping en route for a picnic at town-owned Mullin's Head Park (also spelled Mullen Head) on the southeast corner of the island. Then follow the road around, counterclockwise, to North Shore Road and Pulpit Harbor.

Rent an electronic bicycle from **Savin' the Haven Bike Rentals** (207/867-4946, $12/hour or $50/day), located at Windwollow East Gift Shop in the lower level of Calderwood Hall.

Accommodations and Food

Within walking distance of the ferry is **Nebo Lodge** (11 Mullins Lane, 207/867-2007, www.

nebolodge.com, $160-285). Nine rooms, some with shared baths, are decorated with island art, and many have rugs by Angela Adams. There's Wi-Fi throughout. Rates include a continental breakfast. Bicycles are available for $20/day. Dinner is available from 5pm Mon.-Sat., entrées $28-38. Nebo also runs a lobster-boat dinner shuttle from Rockland Moday-Saturday in July and August, and Saturdays in the spring and fall; call for schedule.

For soups, salads, sandwiches, lobster rolls, ice cream, and more, duck into **Cooper's Landing** (9 Main St., 207/867-2060, 6am-4pm Wed.-Mon.), an order-at-the-window joint within steps of the ferry.

Pizza dominates the menu at **Calderwood Hall** (2 Iron Point Rd., 207/867-4700, www.calderwoodhall.com, 5-9pm Wed.-Sun.). A market with prepared foods, baked goods, sandwiches, and more operates here 9am-6pm Tues.-Sat. **North Haven Brewing Company** plans to open in the basement in early 2016.

If you have wheels, head over to **Turner Farm** (73 Turner Farm Rd., 207/867-4962, www.turner-farm.com), an organic farm dating back 200 years. The location is spectacular, with fields rolling down to the Fox Island Thorofare, and the farmstand (10am-1pm Tues. and Thurs.) is a great place to pick up fresh meats, produce, and goat cheese. The farm is also the site of lobster bakes and barn suppers.

Information

The best source of information about North Haven is the **North Haven Town Office** (Upper Main St., 207/867-4433, www.northhavenmaine.org).

GETTING THERE

The Maine State Ferry Service (207/596-2202, www.exploremaine.org) operates six round-trips daily between Rockland and Vinalhaven (75-minute crossing) in summer and three round-trips between Rockland and North Haven (70-minute crossing). Round-trip tickets for either are $17.50 adults, $8.50 children. Both ferries take cars ($49.50 round-trip, plus $14 reservation fee), but a bicycle ($16.50 round-trip/adult bike, $9.50/child bike) will do fine unless you have the time or inclination to see every corner of the island. If you simply want a taste of the islands, purchase an excursion fare ticket ($10 round-trip on the same ferry). For the longest on-island stay, book the 10:30am from Rockland to Vinalhaven, which overlays for a lunch break,

Hopkins Wharf Gallery

allowing about an hour—enough time for a lobster roll from Greet's. For North Haven, take the 9:30am boat from Rockland, returning on the 12:30, which allows nearly two hours to explore the village.

Getting car space on the ferry during midsummer can be a frustrating—and complicated—experience, so *avoid taking a car to the island.* Give yourself time to find a parking space and perhaps to walk from it to the terminal. If you leave a car at the Rockland lot (space is limited and availability varies), it's $10/24 hours or $50/week. You can also park free on some of Rockland's side streets and at Oceanside High School (400 Broadway) and walk, or, for a day trip, park in the city lot between Main Street and the water or Harbor Park.

No official ferry service travels between Vinalhaven and North Haven, even though the two islands are almost within spitting distance. Fortunately, the **J. O. Brown and Sons boat shop** on North Haven provides shuttles 7am-5pm daily. Call the boat shop (207/867-4621) to arrange a pickup on the Vinalhaven side. The fee is $5 pp round-trip. Don't let anyone persuade you to return to Rockland for the ferry to North Haven.

Penobscot Island Air (207/596-7500, www.penobscotislandair.net) flies twice daily to Vinalhaven and North Haven, weather permitting, from Knox County Regional Airport in Owls Head, just south of Rockland. Seat availability is dependent on mail volume. Non-mail flights may be available.

Greater Camden

Camden (pop. 4,850), flanked by **Rockport** (pop. 3,330) to the south and **Lincolnville** (pop. 2,164) to the north, is one of the Mid-Coast's—even Maine's—prime destinations.

Camden is the better known of the three and typifies Maine nationwide, even worldwide, on calendars, postcards, and photo books. Much of its appeal is its drop-dead-gorgeous setting—a deeply indented harbor with parks, a waterfall, and a dramatic backdrop of low mountains. That harbor is a summer-long madhouse, jammed with dinghies, kayaks, windjammers, mega-yachts, minor yachts, and a handful of fishing craft.

Driven apart by a local squabble in 1891, Camden and Rockport have been separate towns for more than a century, but they're inextricably linked. They share school and sewer systems and an often-hyphenated partnership. On Union Street, just off Route 1, a white wooden arch reads Camden on one side and Rockport on the other. Rockport has a much lower profile, and its harbor is relatively peaceful—with yachts, lobster boats, and a single windjammer schooner.

Two distinct enclaves make up Lincolnville: oceanfront Lincolnville Beach ("the Beach") and, about five miles inland, Lincolnville Center ("the Center"). Lincolnville is laid-back and mostly rural; the major activity center is a short strip of shops and restaurants at the beach, and few visitors realize there's anything else.

SIGHTS

Self-Guided Historical Tour

Historic Downtown Camden is an illustrated map and brochure detailing historical sites and businesses in and around downtown. To cover it all, you'll want a car or bike; to really appreciate the architecture, don your walking shoes. Pick up a copy of the brochure at the chamber of commerce.

Old Conway Homestead and Cramer Museum

Just inside the Camden town line from Rockport, the **Old Conway Homestead and Cramer Museum** (Conway Rd., Camden, 207/236-2257, www.conwayhouse.org, $5 adults, $2 children) is a six-building complex owned and run by the Camden-Rockport Historical Society. The 18th-century Cape-style Conway House, on the National Register of Historic Places, contains fascinating construction details and period furnishings; in the barn are carriages and farm tools. Two other buildings—a blacksmith shop and an 1820 maple sugarhouse used for making maple syrup—have been moved to the grounds and restored. In the contemporary Mary Meeker Cramer Museum (named for its prime benefactor) are displays from the historical society's collection of ship models, old documents, and period clothing. Also here is an education center for workshops and seminars. For local color, don't miss the Victorian outhouse. The museum and sap house are also open for maple-syrup demonstrations on Maine Maple Sunday (fourth Sunday in March). Call for the current tour schedule.

Vesper Hill

Built and donated to the community by a local benefactor, the rustic open-air **Vesper Hill Children's Chapel** is dedicated to the world's children. Overlooking Penobscot Bay and surrounded by gardens and lawns, the nondenominational chapel is an almost mystical oasis in a busy tourist region. Except during weddings or memorial services, there's seldom a crowd, and if you're lucky, you might have the place to yourself. From Central Street in downtown Rockport, take Russell Avenue east to Calderwood Lane (the fourth street on the right). On Calderwood, take the second right (Chapel St.) after the private golf course. If the sign is down, look for a boulder with "Vesper Hill" carved in it. From downtown Camden, take Chestnut Street to just past Aldermere Farm; turn left at Calderwood Lane and take the second right after the golf course.

Aldermere Farm (20 Russell Ave., Rockport, 207/236-2739, www.aldermere.org), by the way, is the home of the first U.S. herd of Belted Galloway cattle—Angus-like beef cattle with a wide white midriff. First imported from Scotland in 1953, the breed now shows up in pastures all over the United States. The animals' startling "Oreo-cookie" hide pattern never fails to halt passersby—especially in spring and early summer, when the calves join their mothers in the pastures. Maine Coast Heritage Trust, a state conservation organization based in Brunswick, owns the 136-acre farm. Call for information on tours or other events.

Camden's picturesque harbor gets even prettier in autumn.

Greater Camden

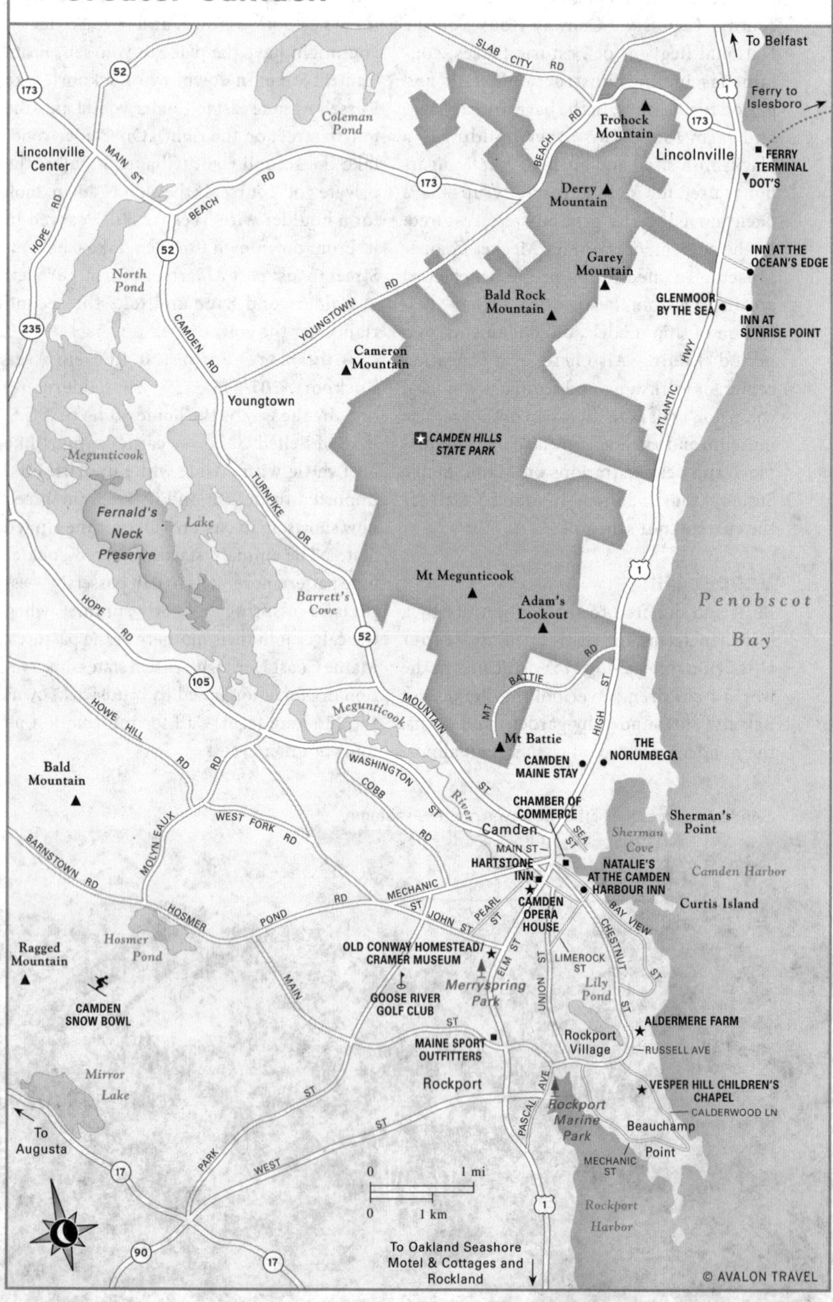

Wine Tasting

The number of wineries is increasing throughout Maine, and they're especially concentrated in this region. Tour on your own, armed with maps and a passport from **The Maine Winery Guild** (www.mainewinetrail.com), or sit back, relax, and enjoy the sipping experience at three wineries on a guided **Nap-Ah Valley Wine Tour** with All Aboard Trolley (207/691-9300, www.meetthefleet.com, $30).

Draft horses power Brian Smith's **Oyster River Winegrowers** (929 Oyster River Rd., Warren, 207/354-7177, www.oysterriverwine.com/ call for hours), a small farm with vineyard. Visit on pizza nights, held 5-8pm on the first and third Wednesdays of each month.

More than 3,000 vines are growing on 32 acres at **Breakwater Vineyards** (35 Ash Point Dr., Owls Head, 207/594-1721, www.breakwatervineyards.com, noon-5pm daily), which donates a portion of its profits to lighthouse restoration efforts. Tastings offer fruit and grape wines and mead. Tours are offered; call for details.

Head inland on Route 17 and then noodle off on the back roads to discover not one but two wineries. At **Sweetgrass Farm Winery and Distillery** (347 Carroll Rd., Union, 207/785-3024, www.sweetgrasswinery.com, 11am-5pm daily mid May-late Dec.), owner Keith Bodine uses Maine-grown fruits to produce both wines and spirits, and he is eager to show interested folks how. Bring a picnic to enjoy while hiking the winery's trails. Carroll Road is between Shepard Hill Road and North Union Road, both north of Route 17, west of Route 131.

Nearby is **Savage Oakes** (174 Barrett Hill Rd., Union, 207/785-5261, www.savageoakes.com, 11am-5pm daily mid-May-late Oct.), where Elmer and Holly Savage and their sons have added winemaking to their second-generation Belted Galloway cattle farm. They grow nine varieties of grapes, both red and white, and produce more than half a dozen wines. A free concert series is held during the summer. Guided farm tours are $7 and by appointment. Barrett Hill Road is off Route 17 directly opposite Route 131 South.

Gaze out the back door of the **Cellardoor Vineyard** (367 Youngtown Rd., Lincolnville, 207/763-44778, www.mainewine.com, call for hours) and it's possible to think you're in Sonoma Valley. Tucked in the folds of the rolling hills, just inland of Lincolnville Beach, Cellardoor occupies a 200-year-old farmhouse and barn overlooking six acres of grapes. During the summer, the retail shop offers free wine tastings daily and food and wine pairings on Sunday afternoons. Winery tours are also offered (call for the schedule), and cooking classes are often held in the commercial kitchen. You can pick up cheeses and other munchies for an impromptu picnic on the deck. The winery has another retail shop/tasting room, The Villa, at the intersection of Routes 1 and 90 in Rockport.

ENTERTAINMENT

Founded in the 1960s as a classical series, **Bay Chamber Concerts** (207/236-2823 or 888/707-2770, www.baychamberconcerts.org) has expanded to include world music, jazz, and dance. The summer concerts feature a resident quartet, prominent guest artists, and outstanding programs and draw sell-out audiences to venues in Camden, Rockland, and Rockport. Seats are reserved (from $30 adults, from $8 under 19, plus $5 processing fee per order, unless purchased online).

The beautifully renovated **Camden Opera House** (29 Elm St., Camden, 207/236-7963, box office 207/236-4884, www.camdenoperahouse.com) is the site of many performances by renowned performers.

The **Lincolnville Band,** one of the oldest town bands in the country, occasionally plays in the park's Bicentennial Bandstand, built to commemorate the town's 200th birthday.

FESTIVALS AND EVENTS

One weekend in February is given over to the **Camden Conference,** an annual three-day foreign-affairs conference with nationally and internationally known speakers.

Also in February, the **National Toboggan Championships** features two days of races and fun at the nation's only wooden toboggan chute at the Camden Snow Bowl.

The third Thursday of July is **House and Garden Day,** when you can take a self-guided tour (10am-4:30pm) of significant homes and gardens in Camden and Rockport. Proceeds benefit the Camden Garden Club. **HarborArts,** on the third weekend in July, draws dozens of artists and craftspeople displaying and selling their wares at the Camden Amphitheatre, Harbor Park.

Labor Day weekend is also known as **Windjammer Weekend,** with cruises, windjammer open houses, fireworks, and all kinds of live entertainment in and around Camden Harbor. Twenty top artisans open their studios for the annual **Country Roads Artists and Artisans Tour** in September.

Dozens of artists and craftspeople display and sell their wares at the **Fall Festival and Arts and Crafts Show,** the first weekend in October at the Camden Amphitheatre in Harbor Park.

A who's who of entrepreneurs show up for the annual **PopTech** conference in October.

Christmas by the Sea is a family-oriented early-December weekend featuring open houses, special sales, concerts, and a visit from Santa Claus.

SHOPPING

New and Old Books

The Owl and Turtle Bookshop (33 Bayview St., Camden, 207/230-7335), one of Maine's best independent new-books stores, has thousands of books and a wonderful children's selection.

Sherman's (14 Main St., Camden, 207/236-2223), part of a small Maine chain, is a source for books and a whole lot more.

If you want a good read at a great price, **Stone Soup Books** (33 Main St., Camden, no phone), a tiny second-floor shop across from the Lord Camden Inn, is Camden's best source for contemporary used fiction.

Art, Crafts, and Gifts

You'll need to wander the streets to take in all the gift and crafts shops, particularly in Camden. Some are obvious; others are tucked away on side streets and back alleys, so explore.

A downtown Camden landmark since 1940, **The Smiling Cow** (41 Main St., Camden, 207/236-3351) is as good a place as any to pick up Maine souvenirs—a few slightly kitschy, but most reasonably tasteful. Before or after shopping here, head for the rear balcony for coffee and a knockout view of the harbor and the Megunticook River waterfall.

Also downtown is **Ducktrap Bay Trading Co.** (20 Main St., Camden, 207/236-9568), source of decoys, wildlife, and marine art and other fine crafts.

At **Danica Candleworks** (Rte. 90, West Rockport, 207/236-3060), owner Erik Laustsen learned the hand-dipping trade from his Danish relatives.

The **Messler Gallery** (25 Mill St., Rockport, 207/594-5611), just off Route 90 and on the campus of the Center for Furniture Craftsmanship, presents rotating shows that focus on woodworking.

Handsome dark wood buildings 0.2 mile north of the Beach are home to **Windsor Chairmakers** (Rte. 1, Lincolnville, 207/789-5188 or 800/789-5188). You can observe the operation, browse the display area, or order some of the well-made chairs, cabinets, and tables.

Professional boatbuilder Walt Simmons has branched out into decoys and wildlife carvings, and they're just as outstanding as his boats. Walt and his wife, Karen, run **Duck Trap Decoys** (Duck Trap Rd., Lincolnville, 207/789-5363), a gallery-shop that features the work of more than 60 other woodcarvers.

It's a lot easier to get soft, wonderful handwoven and hand-dyed **Swans Island Blankets** (231 Rte. 1, Northport, 297/338-9691) since the company moved its sales operation off the island near Mount Desert to the mainland, just 2.7 miles north of Lincolnville Beach.

Islesboro

Lying three miles offshore from Lincolnville Beach, 20 minutes via car ferry, is 12-mile-long Islesboro, a year-round community with a population of about 600—beefed up annually by a sedate summer colony. Car ferries are frequent enough to make Islesboro an ideal day-trip destination—and that's the choice of most visitors, partly because food options are few and overnight lodging isn't available. The only camping is on nearby Warren Island State Park—and you have to have your own boat to get there.

The best way to get an island overview is to do an end-to-end auto or bike tour. Pick up an island map at the ferry terminal and explore, heading down to Dark Harbor and Town Beach at the island's bottom, then up to Pripet and Turtle Head at its top. You won't see all the huge "cottages" tucked down long driveways, and you won't absorb island life and its rhythms, but you'll scratch the surface of what Islesboro is about.

En route, you'll pass exclusive summer estates, workaday homes, spectacular seaside vistas, a smattering of shops, and the **Historical Society Museum** (388 Main St., 207/734-6733, www.islesborohistorical.org, 12:30pm-4:30pm Sat.-Wed. July-Aug. or by appointment, donation only). On the up-island circuit, watch for a tiny marker on the west side of the road (0.8 mile north of the Islesboro Historical Society building). It commemorates the 1780 total eclipse witnessed here—the first recorded in North America. At the time, British loyalists still held Islesboro, but they temporarily suspended hostilities, allowing Harvard astronomers to lug their instruments to the island and document the eclipse.

For nibbles and sips, duck into the **Dark Harbor Shop** (515 Pendleton Point Rd., 207/734-8878, 8am-5pm daily), **The Island Market** (113 Main Rd., 207/734-6672, 7am-5:30pm Mon.-Fri., 8am-5pm Sat.), or **Rabbit Corner Café** (103 Pendleton Point Rd., 207/734-8200, 7am-2p, Mon.-Thurs., 10am-2pm Sun.), at the Islesboro Community Center.

Allow time before the return ferry to visit the **Sailors' Memorial Museum,** a town-owned museum filled with seafaring memorabilia and allegedly home to a benevolent ghost or two. It's in the keeper's house adjacent to **Grindle Point Light** (207/734-2253, www.lighthouse.cc/grindle), built in 1850, rebuilt in 1875, and now automated.

The car ferry ***Margaret Chase Smith*** (207/789-5611, www.exploremaine.org) departs Lincolnville Beach almost every hour on the hour, 8 or 9am-5pm, and departs Islesboro on the half-hour, 7:30am-4:30pm. Round-trip fares are $27.50 for a car with driver, $10 adults, $4.75 kids, $8.50 adult bicycles, and $5.50 kids' bikes. Reservations are $5 extra. A slightly reduced schedule prevails late October-early May. The 20-minute trip crosses a stunning three-mile stretch of Penobscot Bay, with views of islands and the Camden Hills. In summer, avoid the biggest bottlenecks: Friday afternoon (to Islesboro), Sunday afternoon and Monday holiday afternoons (from Islesboro). The *Smith* remains on Islesboro overnight, so don't miss the last run to Lincolnville Beach.

Discount Shopping

How could anyone resist a thrift shop with the name **Heavenly Threads** (57 Elm St./Rte. 1, Camden, 207/236-3203)? Established by Camden's community-oriented First Congregational Church (next door to the shop), Heavenly Threads carries high-quality pre-owned clothing, books, and jewelry. It's staffed by volunteers, with proceeds going to such local ecumenical causes as Meals on Wheels.

RECREATION

Parks and Preserves

COASTAL MOUNTAINS LAND TRUST

Founded in 1986, the **Coastal Mountains Land Trust** (CMLT, 101 Mt. Battie St., Camden, 207/236-7091, www.coastalmountains.org) has preserved more than 9,100 acres. Maps and information about trails open to the public as well as information about guided hikes and other events are available on the website.

CMLT preserves more than 600 acres on 1,280-foot-high **Bald Mountain,** the fifth-highest peak on the eastern seaboard. The somewhat strenuous two-mile round-trip hike accesses the open summit ledges, with grand views over Penobscot Bay. Bald Mountain is home to rare subalpine plants and is a great spot to view migrating hawks in fall. From Route 1 at the southern end of town, take John Street for 0.8 mile. Turn left and go 0.2 mile to a fork. Continue on the left fork (Hosmer Pond Rd.) for two miles. Bear left onto Barnestown Road (passing the Camden Snow Bowl) and go 1.4 miles to the trailhead on the right, signposted Georges Highland Path Barnestown Access. Maps are available in the box; the parking lot holds half a dozen cars. The blue-blazed trail here is relatively easy, requiring just over an hour round-trip, and the summit views are spectacular, especially in fall. Carry a picnic and enjoy it at the top. Avoid this trail in late May-early June, when the blackflies take command, and dress appropriately during hunting season.

The views are almost as fine, but the hiking is easier on the 1.5-mile round-trip Summit Road Trail up the **Beech Hill Preserve,** in Rockport. The trailhead is on the Beech Hill Road about a mile off Route 1 (turn across from Hoboken Gardens).

FERNALD'S NECK

Three miles of Megunticook Lake shoreline, groves of conifers, and a large swamp ("the Great Bog") are features of 328-acre **Fernald's Neck Preserve,** on the Camden-Lincolnville line (and the Knox-Waldo County line). Shoreline and mountain views are stupendous, even more so during fall foliage season. The easiest trail is the 1.5-mile Blue Loop at the northern end of the preserve; from it, you can access the 1-mile Orange Loop. From the Blue Loop, take the 0.2-mile Yellow Trail offshoot to Balance Rock for a great view of the lake and hills. Some sections can be wet; wear boots or rubberized shoes, and use insect repellent. From Route 1 in Camden, take Route 52 (Mountain St.) about 4.5 miles to Fernald's Neck Road, about 0.2 mile beyond the Youngtown Inn. Turn left and then bear left at the next fork and continue to the parking lot at the road's end. Pick up a map-brochure at the trailhead register. A map is also available at the chamber of commerce office. Dogs are not allowed, and the preserve closes and the gate is locked at 7:30pm.

THE GEORGES RIVER LAND TRUST

A Rockland-based group, **The Georges River Land Trust** (207/594-5166, www.georgesriver.org), whose territory covers the Georges (St. George) River watershed, is the steward for **The Georges Highland Path,** a 40-mile low-impact footpath that reaches Rockport and Camden from the back side of the surrounding hills.

★ CAMDEN HILLS STATE PARK

A five-minute drive and a small fee gets you to the top of Mount Battie, centerpiece of 5,650-acre **Camden Hills State Park** (Belfast Rd./Rte. 1, 207/236-3109, www.parksandlands.com, $4.50 nonresident adults, $3 Maine resident adults, $1.50 nonresident seniors, free Maine resident seniors, $1 children 5-11) and the best place to understand why Camden is "where the mountains meet the sea." The summit panorama is breathtaking and reputedly the inspiration for Edna St. Vincent Millay's poem "Renascence" (a bronze plaque marks the spot); information boards identify the offshore islands. Climb the summit's stone tower for an even better view. The 20 miles of hiking trails (some for every ability) include two popular routes up Mount Battie—an easy hour-long hike from the base parking lot (Nature Trail) and a more strenuous 45-minute hike from the top of Mount Battie Street in Camden (Mount Battie Trail). Or drive up the paved Mount Battie Auto Road. The park has plenty of space for picnics. In winter, ice climbers use a rock wall near the Maiden's Cliff Trail, reached via Route 52 (Mountain St.). The park entrance is two miles north of downtown Camden. Request a free trail map. The park is open mid-May-mid-October, but hiking trails are accessible all year, weather permitting.

MERRYSPRING PARK

Straddling the Camden-Rockport boundary, 66-acre **Merryspring Park** (Conway Rd., Camden, 207/236-2239, www.merryspring.org) is a magnet for nature lovers. More than a dozen well-marked trails wind through woodlands, berry thickets, and wildflowers; near the preserve's parking area are lily, rose, and herb gardens. Admission is free, but donations are welcome. Also free are family programs. Special programs (fee charged) include lectures, workshops, and demonstrations. The entrance is on Conway Road, 0.3 mile off Route 1, at the southern end of Camden. Trails are open dawn-dusk daily.

IN-TOWN PARKS

Just behind the Camden Public Library is the **Camden Amphitheatre** (also called the Bok Amphitheatre, after a local benefactor), a sylvan spot resembling a set for *A Midsummer Night's Dream* (which has been performed here). Concerts, weddings, and all kinds of other events take place in the park. Across Atlantic Avenue, sloping to the harbor, is **Camden Harbor Park,** with benches, a couple of monuments, and some of the best waterfront views in town. The noted landscape firm of Frederick Law Olmsted designed the park in 1931, and it is listed on the National Register of Historic Places. Both the park and the amphitheater were restored to their original splendor in 2004.

Rockport's in-town parks include **Marine Park,** off Pascal Avenue, at the head of the harbor; **Walker Park,** on Sea Street, on the west side of the harbor; **Mary-Lea Park,** overlooking the harbor next to the Rockport Opera House; and **Cramer Park,** alongside the Goose River just west of Pascal Avenue. At Marine Park are the remnants of 19th-century lime kilns, an antique steam engine, picnic tables, a boat-launching ramp, and a polished granite sculpture of André, a harbor seal adopted by a local family in the early 1960s. André had been honorary harbormaster, ring bearer at weddings, and the subject of several books and a film—and even did the honors at the unveiling of his statue—before he was fatally wounded in a mating skirmish in 1986 at the age of 25.

CURTIS ISLAND

Marking the entrance to Camden Harbor is town-owned **Curtis Island,** with a 26-foot automated light tower and adjoining keeper's house facing into the bay. Once known as Negro Island, it's a sight made for photo ops; the views are stunning in every direction. A kayak or dinghy will get you out to the island, where you can picnic (take water; there are no facilities), wander around, gather berries, or just watch the passing fleet. Land on the Camden (west) end of the island, allowing for the tide change when you beach your boat. Respect the privacy of the keeper's house in summer; it's occupied by volunteer caretakers.

AVENA BOTANICALS MEDICINAL HERB GARDEN

Visitors are welcome to visit Deb Soule's one-acre **Avena Botanicals Medicinal Herb Garden** (219 Mill St., Rockport, 207/594-2403, www.avenabotanicals.com, noon-5pm Mon.-Fri., free), part of an herbal and healing-arts teaching center. Pick up a garden map and guide at the entrance, then stroll the paths. More than 125 species of common and medicinal herbs are planted, and everything is labeled. Mill Street is just shy of a mile south of the intersection of Routes 17 and 90 in West Rockport. Turn left on Mill Street and continue for almost a mile. Avena is on the right, down a long dirt driveway.

Camden Snow Bowl

More than an alpine ski area, the **Camden Snow Bowl** (207/236-3438, www.camden-snowbowl.com) is a four-season recreation area with tennis courts, public swimming in Hosmer Pond, and biking and hiking trails, as well as alpine trails for day and night skiing and riding, a tubing park, and Maine's only toboggan chute. The hill is small, but you get glimpses of island-studded Penobscot Bay when descending the trails.

Maine Sport Outfitters

Maine Sport Outfitters (Rte. 1, Rockport, 207/236-7120 or 888/236-8796, www.mainesport.com) is a major destination for anyone interested in outdoor recreation. The knowledgeable staff can lend a hand and steer you in almost any direction for almost any summer or winter sport. The store sells and rents canoes, kayaks, bikes, skis, and tents, plus all the relevant clothing and accessories. Bicycle rentals begin at $20/day, and calm-water canoes and kayaks are $30-40/day. Sea kayaks are $45/day single, $55/day tandem. Standup paddleboards are $55/day.

Maine Sport Outdoor School (207/236-8797 or 800/722-0826), a division of Maine Sport, has a full schedule of canoeing, kayaking, and camping trips. A two-hour guided Camden Harbor tour departs at least three times daily in summer and costs $40 adults, $35 ages 10-15. A four-hour guided harbor-to-harbor tour (Rockport to Camden) is offered three times weekly for $85 adults, $75 children, including a picnic lunch. Multiday instructional programs and tours are available. The store is 0.5 mile north of the junction of Routes 1 and 90.

Sea Kayaking

Ducktrap Kayak (2175 Rte. 1, Lincolnville Beach, 207/236-8608, www.ducktrapkayak.com) runs guided coastal tours, with rates beginning at $30 pp. Rentals are also available, beginning at $25-45, depending on the type and size; delivery can be arranged.

If you have your own boat, good saltwater launch sites include Eaton Point, at the end of Sea Street in Camden, and Marine Park in Rockport. For freshwater paddling, put in at Megunticook Lake, west and east sides; Bog Bridge on Route 105, about 3.5 miles from downtown Camden; Barrett's Cove on Route 52, also about 3.5 miles from Camden; or in Lincolnville's Norton Pond and Megunticook Lake. You can even paddle all the way from the head of Norton Pond to the foot of Megunticook Lake, but use care navigating the drainage culvert between the two.

Camden Snow Bowl offers a variety of winter activities.

Swimming

FRESHWATER

The Camden area is blessed with several locales for freshwater swimming—a real boon, since Penobscot Bay can be mighty chilly, even at summer's peak. **Shirttail Point,** with limited parking, is a small sandy area on the Megunticook River. It's shallow enough for young kids and has picnic tables and a play area. From Route 1 in Camden, take Route 105 (Washington Street) 1.4 miles; watch for a small sign on the right. **Barrett's Cove,** on Megunticook Lake, has more parking spaces, though usually more swimmers, and restrooms, picnic tables, and grills as well as a play area. Diagonally opposite the Camden Public Library, take Route 52 (Mountain St.) about three miles; watch for the sign on the left. To cope with the parking crunch on hot summer days, bike to the beaches. You'll be ready for a swim after the uphill stretches, and it's all downhill on the way back.

Lincolnville has several ponds (some would call them lakes). On Route 52 in Lincolnville Center is Breezemere Park, a small town-owned swimming and picnic area on **Norton Pond.** Other Lincolnville options are **Coleman Pond, Pitcher Pond,** and **Knight's Pond.**

SALTWATER

The region's best ocean swimming is at **Lincolnville Beach,** where Penobscot Bay flirts with Route 1 on a sandy stretch of shorefront in the congested hamlet of Lincolnville Beach. On a hot day, the sand is wall-to-wall people; during one of the coast's legendary nor-easters, it's quite a wild place.

Another place for an ocean dip is **Laite Beach Park,** on Bay View Street about 1.5 miles from downtown Camden. It edges Camden Harbor and has a strip of sand, picnic tables, a playground, a float, and a children's amphitheater.

In Rockport, dip your toes into the ocean at **Walker Park,** tucked away on the west side of the harbor. From Pascal Avenue, take Elm Street, which becomes Sea Street. Walker Park is on the left, with picnic tables, a play area, and a small pebbly beach.

Golf

On a back road straddling the Camden-Rockport line, the nine-hole **Goose River Golf Club** (50 Park St., Rockport, 207/236-8488) competes with the best for outstanding scenery.

Day Sails and Excursions

Most day sails and excursion boats operate late May-October, with fewer trips in the spring and fall than in July-August. You can't compare a two-hour day sail to a weeklong cruise on a Maine windjammer, but at least you get a hint of what could be—and it's a far better choice for kids, who aren't allowed on most windjammer cruises.

The classic wooden schooner ***Olad*** (207/236-2323, www.maineschooners.com, $41 adults, $29 under age 12) does several two-hour sails daily from Camden's Public Landing, weather permitting, late May-mid-October. Capt. Aaron Lincoln is a Rockland native, so he's got the local scoop on all the sights.

Another historic Camden day sailer is the 57-foot, 18-passenger schooner ***Surprise*** (207/236-4687, www.camdenmainesailing.com, $41 adult, $31 kids under 12), built in 1918 and skippered by congenial educator Jack Moore and his wife, Barbara. May-October they do daily two-hour sails departing from Camden's Public Landing; the minimum age is 12.

The 49-passenger ***Appledore*** (207/236-8353, www.appledore2.com), built in 1978 for round-the-world cruising, sails from Bay View Landing beginning around 10am three or four times daily June-October. Most cruises last two hours and cost $38 adults, $27 children. Cocktails, wine, and soft drinks are available.

Over in Rockport, the schooner ***Heron*** (207/236-8605 or 800/599-8605, www.woodenboatco.com) is a 65-foot John Alden-designed wooden yacht launched in 2003. Sailing options include a lobster-roll lunch sail, lighthouse sail, and sunset dinner sail ($50-75 adults, $25-37.50 under age 12).

If time is short, Camden Harbor Cruises (207/236-6672, www.camdenharborcruises.com, $28) offers one-hour cruises aboard the classic motor launch ***Lively Lady Too,*** operating from the Public Landing.

Climbing

Scale the cliffs rising above Camden with **Atlantic Climbing School** (207/288-2521, www.climbcamden.com), with half- and full-day options ($125-225) for all ability levels.

ACCOMMODATIONS

Many of Camden's most attractive accommodations (especially bed-and-breakfasts) are on Route 1 (variously disguised as Elm

Street, Main Street, and High Street), which is heavily trafficked in summer. If you're sensitive to noise, request a room facing away from the street.

Camden

BED-AND-BREAKFASTS AND INNS

A baker's dozen of Camden's finest bed-and-breakfasts have banded together in the **Camden Bed and Breakfast Association** (www.camdeninns.com), with an attractive brochure and website. Some of them are described here.

The 1874 **Camden Harbour Inn** (83 Bayview St., 207/236-4200 or 800/236-4200, www.camdenharbourinn.com, from $475) underwent a masterful renovation and restoration by new Dutch owners, partners Raymond Brunyanszki and Oscar Verest, reopening in 2007 as a boutique bed-and-breakfast complete with 21st-century amenities. It retains the bones of a 19th-century summer hotel, but the decor is contemporary European, with worldly accent pieces and velour furnishings in purples, reds, and silvers. Guest rooms, some with fireplaces, patios, decks, or balconies, have at least a glimpse of Camden's harbor or Penobscot Bay. All have air-conditioning, Wi-Fi, flat-screen TVs, refrigerators, and king beds. Service is five-star, right down to chocolates and slippers at turndown. At breakfast, which is included, the menu includes choices such as lobster Benedict as well as a buffet with fresh-baked items, smoked salmon, and other goodies. Snacks are always available. And the restaurant, Natalie's, is top-notch. The owners also speak Dutch, German, some French, and rudimentary Indonesian and Thai.

The ★ **Hartstone Inn** (41 Elm St., Rte. 1, 207/236-4259 or 800/788-4823, www.hartstoneinn.com, $135-304) is Michael and Mary Jo Salmon's imposing mansard-roofed Victorian close to the heart of downtown. Although some guest rooms face the street (and these are insulated with triple-pane windows), most do not, and all have air-conditioning. Once inside, you're away from it all. Even more removed are guest rooms in two other buildings under the Hartstone's umbrella. Suites in the Manor House, tucked behind the main inn, have contemporary decor. Guest rooms and suites in The Hideaway, in a residential neighborhood about a block away, have country French flair. All are elegant (Wi-Fi, air-conditioning); some have fireplaces and whirlpools. Make reservations for dinner. And then, there's the incredible breakfast.

Camden Harbour Inn is a destination for culinary travelers.

If you get hooked, the Salmons organize culinary classes during the winter, and you can even arrange for a one-on-one cooking experience with Michael.

After years of neglect, new owners Sue Walser and Phil Crispo have returned Camden's castle, **The Norumbega** (63 High St., 207/236-4646, www.norumbegainn.com, from $239) to its former opulence, but this time, they promise, there's no pretentiousness. Eleven spacious, air-conditioned guest rooms and two suites, some with balconies and terraces, many with panoramic ocean views, are on three floors of this turreted stone mansion by the sea. Phil, a former chef instructor at the Culinary Institute of America and winner on Chopped, makes the breakfasts. Seven-course tasting dinners ($55) are available to guests; call for details.

Opened to guests in 1901, the **Whitehall Inn** (52 High St./Rte. 1, 207/236-3391 or 800/789-6565, www.whitehall-inn.com, from $239) received a head-to-toe renovation and updating when it debuted as a member of the Lark Hotels group in 2015. Lovely gardens, rockers on the veranda, a tennis court, and attentive service all add to the appeal of this historic country inn, famed for its connection to local poet Edna St. Vincent Millay, who first recited her poem "Renascence" to Whitehall guests in 1912. The 36 guest rooms are decorated in neutrals with eye-popping color accents. All have flat-screen TVs, iPads, Internet access, and lovely linens; a few share baths. The dining room, Pig + Poet, is under the helm of celebrity chef Sam Talbot.

Claudio and Roberta Latanza, both natives of Italy, became the fourth innkeepers at the ★ **Camden Maine Stay** (22 High St./Rte. 1, 207/236-9636, www.mainestay.com, $175-295) in 2009. Like their predecessors, they do everything right, from the comfortable yet elegant decor to the delicious breakfasts and afternoon snacks to the welcoming window candles and garden retreats. The stunning residence, built in 1802, faces busy Route 1 and is just a bit uphill from downtown, but inside and out back, behind the carriage house and barn, you'll feel worlds away.

In the heart of downtown Camden, **The Lord Camden Inn** (24 Main St./Rte. 1, 207/236-4325 or 800/336-4325, www.lordcamdeninn.com, from $250) is a hotel alternative in a historic four-story downtown building (with an elevator). Top-floor rooms have harbor-view balconies. Rates include a breakfast buffet. Pooches are pampered in

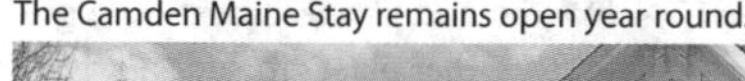

The Camden Maine Stay remains open year round.

pet-friendly rooms for $25/night, including a bed, biscuits, bowls, and local dog info.

New in 2010, the Shingle-style **Grand Harbor Inn** (14 Bay View Landing, 877/553/6997, www.grandharborinn.com, from $400), a luxury boutique hotel, provides a front-row seat on Camden's busy harbor. Each of the 10 guest rooms has a private balcony, gas fireplace, and a custom marble bathroom. Other perks include 24-hour concierge, evening turndown, and a room-service breakfast. Dog-friendly rooms are available for $35/night.

MOTEL

It's a short stroll into Merryspring Gardens from the **Cedar Crest Motel** (115 Elm St./Rte. 1, 207/236-4839, www.cedarcrestmotel.com, $134-154), a nicely maintained older property on 3.5 wooded and landscaped acres on the southern edge of downtown. Each of the 37 guest rooms has air-conditioning, Wi-Fi, a phone, and a TV. Some have mini-fridges. On the premises are an outdoor heated pool, playground, laundry, and restaurant serving all meals, with live music on Friday evenings.

Frills are few at the easy-on-the-budget, two-story **Towne Motel** (68 Elm St., Rte. 1, 207/236-3377, www.camdenmotel.com, $124-154), but it's just steps from downtown, all rooms are air-conditioned, and there's free Wi-Fi. A continental breakfast is provided. One studio is pet-friendly.

CAMPING

Camden Hills State Park (Belfast Rd./Rte. 1, 207/236-3109, $3 adults, $1 ages 5-11, camping $25 nonresidents, $15 Maine residents for basic site; $37.45 nonresidents, $26.75 Maine residents with water and electric) has a 112-site camping area and is wheelchair-accessible. Pets are allowed, showers are free, and the sites are large.

Rockport

MOTELS AND COTTAGE COLONIES

Step back in time at the oceanfront ★ **Oakland Seashore Motel & Cottages** (112 Dearborn Ln., 207/594-8104, www.oaklandseashorecabins.com, $80-140/night, $510-875/week), a low-key throwback on 70 mostly wooded acres that dates back more than a century. It was originally a recreational park operated by a trolley company, but its heyday passed with the arrival of the automobile. In the late 1940s, shorefront cabins were added, and in the 1950s, the dance pavilion was renovated into a motel. The rooms and cabins are simple, comfortable, clean, and right on the ocean's edge; some have kitchenettes, and a few have full kitchens. The bathrooms are tiny, and there are no phones or TVs, but the grounds are gorgeous, with big shade trees, grassy lawns, and well-placed benches and chairs, and there's a rocky beach that's ideal for launching a kayak. This place isn't for those who need attentive service or fluffy accommodations, but it's a gem for those who appreciate quiet simplicity with a big view. Pets are a possibility ($30/stay).

Clean rooms, a convenient location, lovely ocean views from most rooms, and reasonable prices have made the Beale family's **Ledges by the Bay** (930 Rte. 1, Glen Cove, 207/594-8944, www.ledgesbythebay.com, $89-199) a favorite motel among budget-conscious travelers. Guest rooms have air-conditioning, TVs, Wi-Fi, and phones; most have private balconies. Other pluses include a private shorefront, small heated pool, and light continental breakfast. Kids 13 and younger stay free in parents' room.

Family-owned and -operated, the all-suites **Country Inn** (8 Country Inn Way/Rte. 1, 207/236-2725 or 888/707-3945, www.countryinnmaine.com, $220-260) is an especially good choice for families, thanks to an indoor pool, play areas, a guest laundry, and a fitness room. Rooms are divided between a main inn and cottage suites. Some units have fireplaces, whirlpool tubs, and microwaves; all have air-conditioning, phones, fridges, Wi-Fi, and TVs. A breakfast buffet and evening cookies are included. On-site massage and yoga classes are available. Pet-friendly rooms are available.

Lincolnville

INNS

Private, secluded, and surrounded by 22 acres of woods and gardens, the renovated-in-2015, oceanfront shingle-style **Inn at the Ocean's Edge** (Rte. 1, Lincolnville Beach, 207/236-0945, www.innatoceansedge.com, from $329) is splurge-worthy. Every room has a fireplace, and some have whirlpool tubs. All have TV, air-conditioning, and Wi-Fi. Most have superb ocean views. The grounds are lovely, with lounge chairs placed just so to take in the views. Facilities include an outdoor heated pool that makes it seem as if you're almost in the ocean, a hot tub, massage service, a sauna, and a fitness room. Rates include a full breakfast and afternoon snacks.

Even more private and secluded is **The Inn at Sunrise Point** (Rte. 1, Lincolnville, Camden, 207/236-7716 or 800/435-6278, www.sunrisepoint.com, from $410), an elegant oceanfront retreat with all the bells and whistles you'd expect at these rates. The three handsome rooms in the main house, five separate cottages, and four rooms in the Garden House are all named after Maine authors or artists. Breakfast in the conservatory is divine.

MOTEL AND COTTAGES

The family-run **Mount Battie Motel** (2158 Atlantic Hwy./Rte. 1, Lincolnville, 207/236-3870 or 800/224-3870, www.mountbattie.com, $135-222) is an environmentally sensitive property with 22 charming motel-style guest rooms, some with water views, all with air-conditioning, TVs, phones, Wi-Fi, and fridges. The continental breakfast includes home-baked treats.

Another family-run gem, the **Ducktrap Motel** (12 Whitney Rd., Lincolnville, 207/789-5400 or 877/977-5400, www.ducktrapmotel.com, $100-115) is set back from Route 1 and screened by trees. Both the grounds and the rooms are meticulously maintained. All rooms have TVs, fridges, microwaves, coffeemakers; the cottage has an efficiency kitchen.

On 12 hillside acres rolling down to the oceanfront, **Glenmoor by the Sea** (2143 Atlantic Hwy./Rte. 1, 855/706-7905, www.glenmoorbythesea.com, $159-299) is a destination in itself, with 19 cottages and 14 rooms, all recently renovated, two heated outdoor pools, and a nice lawn for activities. Other plusses include Wi-Fi, an oceanfront deck, tennis court, exercise room, fire pit, and a guest laundry. The motel rooms are close to Route 1, and noise may be a problem; opt for a cottage near the water if you can. A continental breakfast is included. Dogs are allowed in some rooms for $20/night.

FOOD

Local Flavors

ROCKPORT

The best source for health foods, homeopathic remedies, and fresh seasonal produce is **Fresh Off the Farm** (495 Rte. 1, 207/236-3260, 8am-7pm Mon.-Sat., 9am-5:30pm Sun.), an inconspicuous red-painted roadside place that looks like an overgrown farm stand (which it is). Watch for one of those permanent-temporary signs highlighting the latest arrivals, which might include native blueberries or native corn. The shop is 1.3 miles south of the junction of Routes 1 and 90.

At the southern Rockport town line, a sprawling red building is the home of **The Rockport Marketplace and the State of Maine Cheese Company** (461 Commercial St./Rte. 1, 207/236-8895 or 800/762-8895, 9am-6pm Mon.-Sat., noon-4pm Sun.). Inside are locally made varieties of cows' milk hard cheeses, all named after Maine locations (Aroostook Jack, Allagash Caraway, St. Croix Black Pepper, and so on) as well as hundreds of Maine-made products, from food to crafts. **Maine Street Meats** (207/236-6328, 10am-6pm Mon.-Sat.), a separate business within the marketplace, is a full-service butcher shop and specialty food market, selling drool-worthy local and imported meats, cheeses, charcuterie, and prepared foods, including soups, sandwiches, and flatbread pizzas.

At the junction of Routes 1 and 90, a colorfully painted barn is the home of **The Market**

Basket (Rte. 1, 207/236-4371, 7am-6:30pm Mon.-Sat., 9am-4pm Sun.), the best take-out source for creative sandwiches, homemade soups, cheeses, exotic condiments, pastries, wine (large selection), beer, and entrées to go.

Locals know one of the area's best spots for lobster rolls and fried seafood is **Graffam Bros. Seafood Shack** (211 Union St., 207/236-8391, 8:30am-6pm Mon.-Sat.). There's some seating at picnic tables, but take it to Harbor Park for the oceanside setting.

CAMDEN

The **Camden Farmers Market** (3:30pm-6pm Wed. June-late Sept. and 9am-noon Sat. early May-late Oct.) holds forth at the Knox Mill Complex on Washington Street.

Made-to-order sandwiches and wraps, homemade soups, veggie burgers, and baked goods are the draws at the **Camden Deli** (37 Main St., 207/236-8343, 7am-10pm daily), in the heart of downtown, but its biggest asset is the windowed seating overlooking the Megunticook River waterfall. The view doesn't get much better than this (go upstairs for the best angle).

Since the early 1970s, **Scott's Place** (85 Elm St./Rte. 1, 207/236-8751, 10:30am-4pm Mon.-Fri., to 3pm Sat.), a roadside lunch stand near Renys at the Camden Marketplace, has been dishing up inexpensive ($3-12) burgers and dogs, nowadays adding veggie burgers and salads. Call ahead and it'll be ready.

Peek behind the old-fashioned facade at **Boynton-McKay Food Company** (30 Main St., 207/236-2465, 7am-2pm Tues.-Sat., 8am-1pm Sun.) and you'll see an old-fashioned soda fountain, early-20th-century tables, antique pharmacy accessories, and a thoroughly modern café menu. Restored and rehabbed in 1997, Boynton-McKay had been *the* local drugstore for more than a century. The new incarnation features bagels, creative salads, homemade soups, superb wrap sandwiches, an espresso bar, and the whole works from the soda fountain. It's open for breakfast and lunch.

Facing downtown Camden's five-way intersection, **French and Brawn** (1 Elm St., 207/236-3361, 6am-7pm Mon.-Sat., 8am-7pm Sun.) is an independent market that earns the description *super.* Ready-made sandwiches, soups, and other goodies complement the oven-ready take-out meals, high-cal frozen desserts, esoteric meats, and staff with a can-do attitude.

LINCOLNVILLE

Need a sandwich before heading for the hills or beach? **Dot's** (2457 Rte. 1, 207/706-7922, 7am-5:30pm Mon.-Sat., 8am-3pm Sun.) is the place. It also bakes breakfast goods and treats, makes salads and prepared meals, and sells cheeses and wines. There's seating inside.

Local chef Annemarie Ahearn's oceanfront **Salt Water Farm** (25 Woodward Hill Rd., 207/230-0966, www.saltwaterfarm.com) is a haven for serious foodies. Hands-on cooking classes (around $125 for a four-hour class) and multiday workshops are offered. During the summer months, four- to five-course full-moon suppers ($85) are offered by reservation.

Venture well off the beaten path to find **Dolce Vita Farm and Bakery** (488 Beach Rd., 207/323-1052), a working farm with a wood-fired brick oven that turns out excellent baked goods and, usually one night each week, pizzas; call for current hours.

Family Favorites

CAMDEN

With a menu ranging from burgers to pastas and pizzas, the **Elm Street Grille** (Cedar Crest Motel, 115 Elm St./Rte. 1, 207/236-4839, www.elmstreetgrille.com, 7am-11am Fri.-Sun. and 4pm-8pm Tues.-Sun.) is a popular spot for families seeking a good meal at a fair price. Breakfast also get high marks. Dinner choices range from pizzas to a broiled seafood platter ($10-22); a kids' menu is available. There's live music most Friday nights.

In 2016, Cappy's, a longtime institution in the heart of Camden, along with Cappy's Harborview, changed hands. Expected to open in Cappy's place is **Sea Dog Brewing Co.** (1 Main St., www.seadogbrewing.com,

$10-22), which started in Camden in 1993, but moved to Bangor in 1995. Since then, it's opened other locations in Maine, as well as Florida and New Hampshire. Sea Dog has a solid family friendly rep all over, and I would expect it to be the same here. The usual menu includes soups, salads, burgers, sandwiches, pastas, and pub classics such as fish and chips. See their website for more information.

Casual Dining

ROCKPORT

When **Shepherd's Pie** (18 Central St., 207/236-8500, www.shepherdspierockport.com, 5-10pm daily, $13-24), a sibling of chef-owner Brian Hill's successful Francine Bistro in Camden, occupies a historical building with high tin ceilings and beautiful dark wood walls. Expect pub- and home-style favorites updated with verve; think duck hot dogs, smoked alewife Caesar, fried clam tacos, and baked beans with candied bacon. It doesn't take reservations; expect to wait for a table.

CAMDEN

Chef-owner Brian Hill has created one of the region's hottest restaurants with **Francine Bistro** (55 Chestnut St., 207/230-0083, www.francinebistro.com, 5:30pm-10pm Tues.-Sat., entrées $24-30). The well-chosen menu is short and focused on whatever's fresh and (usually) locally available that day. In addition to the dining room, there's seating at the bar and, when the weather cooperates, on the front porch. Be forewarned, it can get quite noisy.

The Waterfront Restaurant (Bay View St., 207/236-3747, 11:30am-9pm daily, $18-30) has a huge waterside dining deck in town, but you'll need to arrive early to snag one of the tables. Lunches are the most fun, overlooking lots of harbor action; at high tide, you're eye to eye with the boats. Most folks rave about the place, but I've found it inconsistent.

The word is out about **Long Grain** (20 Washington St., 207/236-9001, 11:30am-3pm and 4:30pm-9pm Tues.-Sat.), a tiny restaurant that's earned kudos far and wide for its outstanding and authentic Pan-Asian cuisine. Flavors are fresh, complex, and layered, and presentation is gorgeous. In 2016, it moved from its original, tiny location to a much larger space. Most items are $10-18. Reservations are a good idea.

Celebrity chef Sam Talbot presides over **Pig + Poet** (52 High St./Rt. 1, 207/236-3391, www.pigandpoetmaine.com, 5-10pm Wed.-Mon., $16-28), located at the Whitehall Inn. The locally sourced menu ranges from burgers to squid.

The fish-and-chips alone are worth the mosey inland along Route 105 from Camden to find the **Hatchet Mountain Publick House** (42 Hatchet Mountain Rd., Hope, 207/763-4565, www.hatchetmountain.com, from 5pm Thurs.-Sat., $11-26), a combination tavern and antiques shop in a beautifully renovated barn.

Go for Happy Hour at **40 Paper** (40 Washington St., 207/230-0111, 5pm-9pm daily), located in the renovated Knox Mill, and then maybe stick around for the handmade pastas, flatbread pizzas, and other Italian fare. Food is generally quite good; service is mediocre at best.

LINCOLNVILLE

Maine fare with an unpretentious French accent paired with Penobscot Bay views have drawn diners to **Chez Michel** (2530 Rte. 1, 207/789-5600, 4pm-9pm Tues.-Sun.) for decades. Early-bird specials are served until 5:30pm; otherwise, most entrées top out around $22. This isn't a French restaurant, but there are French-inspired preparations, such as *coquille* St. Jacques and duck au poivre, as well as fried and broiled seafood, steak, and pastas. There's a children's menu too.

Fine Dining

CAMDEN

Reservations are a must for the intimate restaurant at the **Hartstone Inn** (41 Elm St., 207/236-4259 or 800/788-4823, www.

hartstoneinn.com, 5:30pm-8:30pm daily). Michael Salmon, named Caribbean chef of the year when he lived in Aruba, has cooked at the Beard House by invitation. Even Julia Child dined here. The menu changes weekly to use the freshest ingredients. The nightly chef's tasting menu is $55; entrées on the lighter, à la carte menu run $20-30.

Since opening in 2007 to rave reviews, ★ **Natalie's at the Camden Harbour Inn** (83 Bayview St., 207/236-4200, www.natalies-restaurant.com, 5pm-9:30pm daily in season, call off-season) has become one of the state's top tables. The dining room was designed to be reminiscent of the Left Bank in Paris a century ago. The ambience is fancy here, but casual attire is fine. Instead of looking out at the Seine, you're gazing over Camden Harbor. Dining options are a three-course à la carte menu with a vegetarian option ($76), a seven-course chef's tasting menu ($102), or a five-course lobster-tasting menu ($109). A more casual tapas menu ($20-28) is available at the bar or in the lounge.

LINCOLNVILLE

For a romantic, classic French experience, head a bit inland to **Youngtown Inn and Restaurant** (581 Youngtown Rd., 207/763-4290 or 800/291-8438, www.youngtowninn.com, 6pm-9pm Tues.-Sun., $28-34), where chef-owner Manuel Mercier draws on his Parisian heritage and European training. The best deal is the four-course $45 chef's menu. Upstairs are six guest rooms (from $170, includes breakfast).

Lobster

Lincolnville's best-known landmark is **The Lobster Pound Restaurant** (Rte. 1, Lincolnville Beach, 207/789-5550, www.lobsterpoundmaine.com, 11:30am-10pm daily, $12-35). About 300 people—some days, it looks like more than that—can pile into the restaurant and enclosed patio, so make reservations on summer weekends. Despite the crowds, food and service are reliably good. In 2014, it merged with Andrews Brewing Co. and turned half the space into a brewpub. Lobster, of course, is still king, but the huge menu will satisfy everyone.

Next door is **McLaughlins Lobster Shack** (Rte. 1, Lincolnville Beach, 207/789-5205, www.thelobshack.com, 11:30am-8pm daily), with inside and outdoor tables.

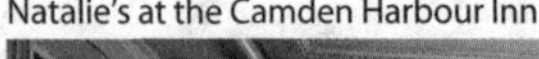
Natalie's at the Camden Harbour Inn

INFORMATION AND SERVICES

For planning, contact **Penobscot Bay Regional Chamber of Commerce** (207/236-4404 or 800/223-5459, www.mainedreamvacation.com). Also handy is a map and guide published by the **Lincolnville Business Group** (www.visitlincolnville.com).

Check out the **Camden Public Library** (Main St./Rte. 1, Camden, 207/236-3440, www.camden.lib.me.us) or **Rockport Public Library** (1 Limerock St., Rockport, 207/236-3642, www.rockport.lib.me.us).

Find **public restrooms** in Camden at the Public Landing, near the chamber of commerce, and at the Camden Public Library; in Rockport at Marine Park; and in Lincolnville, at the ferry terminal.

GETTING THERE AND AROUND

Camden is about eight miles or 15 minutes via Route 1 from Rockland. It's about six miles or 10 minutes via Route 1 from Lincolnville or about 20 miles or 30 minutes via Route 1 from Belfast.

Belfast

Belfast (pop. 6,668) is relatively small as cities go, but it's officially cool: *Budget Travel* magazine named it one of the top 10 coolest towns in the United States. Even before that, Belfast was one of those off-the-beaten-track destinations popular with tuned-in travelers. Chalk that up to its status as a magnet for leftover back-to-the-landers and enough artistic types to earn the city a nod for cultural cool. Belfast has a curling club, a food co-op, and a green store, meditation centers, an increasing number of art galleries and boutiques, dance and theater companies, the oldest shoe store in the country, and half a dozen different 12-step, self-help groups. There's a festival nearly every weekend during the summer. It even has a poet laureate.

This eclectic city is a work in progress, a study in Maine-style diversity. It's also a gold mine of Federal, Greek Revival, Italianate, and Victorian architecture. Take the time to stroll the well-planned backstreets, explore the shops, and hang out at the gussied-up waterfront.

Separating Belfast from East Belfast, the Passagassawakeag River (puh-sag-gus-uh-WAH-keg) fortunately is known more familiarly as "the Passy." The Indian name has been translated as both "place of many ghosts" and the rather different "place for spearing sturgeon by torchlight." You choose. No matter, you can cross it via a pedestrian bridge.

Many travelers make Belfast a day stop on their way between Camden and Bar Harbor. Truly, Belfast is worth more time than that. Spend a full day or two here and it's likely you'll be charmed, like many of the other urban refugees, into resettling here.

SIGHTS

Historic Walking Tour

No question, the best way to appreciate Belfast's fantastic architecture is to tour by ankle express. At the Belfast Area Chamber of Commerce, pick up the well-researched *Belfast Historic Walking Tour* map-brochure. Among more than 40 highlights on the mile-long self-guided route are the 1818 Federal-style **First Church,** handsome residences on **High Street** and **Church Street,** and the 1840 **James P. White House** (Church St. and Northport Ave.), now an elegant bed-and-breakfast and New England's finest Greek Revival residence. Amazingly for a community of this size, the city actually has three distinct listed districts on the National Register of Historic Places: Belfast Commercial Historic District (47 downtown buildings), Church Street Historic District (residential), and Primrose Hill Historic

District (also residential). Another walking tour is presented by the Belfast Historical Society's **Museum in the Streets,** comprising two large panels and 30 smaller ones highlighting historic buildings and people. Signs are in English and French.

Bayside

Continuing the focus on architecture, just south of Belfast in Northport is the Victorian enclave of Bayside, a neighborhood-y sort of place with small, well-kept gingerbread-trimmed cottages cheek-by-jowl on pint-size lots. Formerly known as the Northport Wesleyan Grove Campground, the village took shape in the mid-1800s as a summer retreat for Methodists. In the 1930s the retreat was disbanded and the main meeting hall was razed, creating the waterfront park at the heart of the village. Today, many of the colorfully painted homes are rented by the week, month, or summer season, and their tenants are more likely to indulge in athletic rather than religious pursuits. The camaraderie remains, though, and a stroll (or cycle or drive) through Bayside is like a visit to another era. Bayside is four miles south of Belfast, just east of Route 1. If you want to join the fun, try **Bayside Cottage Rentals** (539 Bluff Rd., Northport, 207/338-5355, www.baysidecottagerentals.com).

Temple Heights

Continue south on Shore Road from Bayside to **Temple Heights Spiritualist Camp** (Shore Rd., Northport, 207/338-3029, www.templeheightscamp.org), yet another religious enclave—this one still ongoing. Founded in 1882, Temple Heights has become a shadow of its former self, reduced primarily to the funky 12-room Nikawa Lodge on Shore Road ($45, shared bath, some with ocean views), but the summer program continues thanks to prominent mediums from all over the country. Even a temporary setback in 1996—when the camp president was suspended for allegedly putting a hex on Northport's town clerk—failed to derail the operation. Camp programs mid-June–early September are open to the public; a schedule is published each spring. Spiritualist church services and group healing circles are by donation; Saturday-morning workshops are $25. Better yet, sign up for a 1.5-hour or longer **group message circle** (7:30pm Wed., Fri. and Sat., $15), when you'll sit with a medium and a dozen or so others and receive insights—often uncannily on target—from departed relatives or friends; reservations are requested, and you should plan to arrive a half-hour early. Private half-hour readings can be arranged for $40.

Belfast & Moosehead Railroad

The nonprofit Brooks Preservation Society operates the **Belfast & Moosehead Railroad** (207/722-3899, www.brookspreservation.org), which rolls through the inland countryside west of Bethel. The one-hour trips ($14 adults, $5 ages 3-14) aboard vintage trains depart from the **City Point Station** (13 Oak Hill Rd., Belfast); call for the current schedule, which may include options such as pizza trains and a chocolate express.

ENTERTAINMENT

It's relatively easy to find nightlife in Belfast—not only are there theaters and a cinema, but there are usually a couple of bars open at least until midnight and sometimes later. Some spots also feature live music, particularly on weekends. A good source for listings is Belfast Creative Coalition (www.belfastcreativecoalition.org).

If you don't feel like searching out a newspaper to check the entertainment listings, just go to the **Belfast Co-op Store** (123 High St., 207/338-2532) and study the bulletin board. You'll find notices for more activities than you could ever squeeze into your schedule.

Open-mike nights, jazz jams, classes, and lectures pepper the calendar for **Waterfall Arts** (265 High St., 207/338-2222, www.waterfallarts.org).

Just south of Belfast, the funky **Blue Goose Dance Hall** (Rte. 1, Northport, 207/338-3003) is the site for folk concerts, contra dances, auctions, and other events. Check local papers or the Belfast Co-op Store bulletin board.

Street entertainers perform and about 20 galleries participate in Belfast Arts' **Fourth Friday Gallery Walk** (www.belfastartwalk.com), held 5:30pm-8pm the fourth Friday, May-December.

Two local theater groups stage productions in various venues, the **Belfast Maskers** (207/338-9668, www.belfastmaskers.com) and **Cold Comfort Theater** (207/930-7244, www.coldcomforttheater.com).

The Belfast Garden Club sponsors **Open Garden Days** (www.belfastgardenclub.org) once a week throughout the summer at the homes of club members and friends in and around Belfast. Gardens are usually open 10am-3pm rain or shine; a $5 pp donation is requested to benefit local beautification projects. Check local newspapers or ask at the chamber of commerce for the schedule.

EVENTS

Belfast is a hotbed of events, with a festival scheduled nearly every weekend during the summer.

In early July, soon after the Fourth of July, the **Arts in the Park** festival gets under way at Heritage Park, on the Belfast waterfront. It's a weekend event with two days of music, juried arts and crafts, children's activities, and lots of food booths.

Cheese-rolling, Highland games, and music are just a few of the activities at the midsummer **Maine Celtic Celebration.**

In October, the **Belfast Poetry Festival** pairs poets with artists for workshops and readings.

SHOPPING

It's easy and fun to shop in downtown Belfast, a town that has so far managed to keep the big boxes away, providing fertile ground for entrepreneurs. Downtown shops reflect the city's population, with galleries and boutiques, thrift and used-goods stores, and eclectic shops, including a number specializing in books: new, used, and antiquarian. During **Fourth Friday Art Walks** (www.belfastcreativecoalition.org), 5:30-8pm May-Nov., more than a dozen galleries welcome shoppers.

Specialty Shops

Even if shoes aren't on your shopping list, stop in at "the oldest shoe store in America." Founded in the 1830s, **Colburn Shoe Store** (81 Main St., 207/338-1934 or 877/338-1934) may be old, but it isn't old-fashioned, and it has a bargain basement.

Brambles (2 Cross St., 207/338-3448) is a gardener's delight, with fun, whimsical, and practical garden-themed merchandise.

Left Bank Books (109 Church St., 207/338-9009) is one of those wonderful bookstores that not only has a well-curated selection, but also presents readings and signings.

Seeking an out-of-print treasure or a focused tome? **Old Professor's Bookshop** (99 Main St., 207/338-2006) specializes in new, used, and rare books that answer the big questions: What is? And what matters?

Calling itself a "general store for the 21st century," **The Green Store** (71 Main St., 207/338-4045) carries a huge selection of environmentally friendly products. Whether you're thinking of going off the grid, need a composting toilet, or just want natural-fiber clothing or other natural-living products, this is the place. A very knowledgeable staff can answer nearly any question on environmentally sustainable lifestyles.

About two miles east of Belfast's bridge, on the right, is the small roadside shop of **Mainely Pottery** (181 Searsport Ave./Rte. 1, 207/338-1108). Since 1988, Jeannette Faunce and Jamie Oates have been marketing the work of more than two dozen Maine potters, each with different techniques, glazes, and styles. It's the perfect place to select from a wide range of reasonably priced work.

South of town, **Work of Hand** (371 Atlantic Hwy/Rte. 1, Northport, 207/383-3030) carries an intriguing and eclectic mix of fun and funky gifts and home décor.

Visiting Liberty

Seventeen miles west of Belfast, off Route 3, is **Liberty** (www.historicliberty.com), a tiny town with a funky tool store, a quirky museum, a bargain T-shirt shop, and a great state park. Everything is seasonal, running about mid-May-mid-October. Call before visiting if you want to be sure everything's open.

It's a store! It's a museum! It's amazing! More than 10,000 "useful" tools—plus used books and prints and other choice items—fill the three-story **Liberty Tool Company** (Main St., Liberty, 207/589-4771). Drawn by nostalgia and a compulsion for handmade adzes and chisels, thousands of vintage-tool buffs arrive at this eclectic emporium each year; few leave empty-handed. Nor do the thousands of everyday home hobbyists looking to pick up a hammer or find a missing wrench to fill out a set, or the antiques-seekers, who browse the trash and treasures on the upper floors. The collection is beyond amazing, especially in its organization. Owner Skip Brack brings back vanloads of finds almost every week, and after sorting and cleaning, many make it into this store.

The best-of-the-best make it into Brack's **Davistown Museum and Maine Artists Guild** (Main St., 207/589-4900, www.davistownmuseum.org, 11am-5pm Thurs.-Sun.), on the third floor of the building housing Liberty Graphics, across the street. The museum houses not only a history of Maine and New England hand tools but also local, regional, Native American, and environmental artifacts and information and an amazing collection of contemporary art, highlighted by works by artists such as Louise Nevelson (who used to buy tools across the street), Melitta Westerlund, and Phil Barter.

Downstairs is **Liberty Graphics Outlet Store** (1 Main St., 207/589-4035, www.lgtees.com), selling the eco-sensitive company's overstocks, seconds, and discontinued-design T-shirts. Outstanding silk-screened designs are done with water-based inks, and many of the shirts are organic cotton; prices begin at $7.

Just down Main Street is the old **Liberty Post Office,** a unique octagonal structure that looks like an oversize box. It was built in 1867 as a harness-maker's shop and later used as the town's post office.

A few miles south of downtown, off Route 220, is **Liberty Craft Brewing** (7 Coon Mountain Ln., 207-322-7663, www.libertycraftbrewing.com, 11:30am-9pm Wed.-Sat., noon-7pm Sun.), a family owned microbrewery serving pub fare, such as burgers, bratwurst, and sandwiches.

Two miles west of downtown, **Lake St. George State Park** (Rte. 3, 207/589-4255, $6 nonresident adults, $4 Maine resident adults, $1 ages 5-11) is a refreshing find. This 360-acre park has wooded picnic sites with grills along the lake, a beach, rental boats, a playground, volleyball and basketball courts, and five miles of hiking trails. Also available are campsites ($25 nonresidents, $15 Maine residents). Afterward, head to **John's Ice Cream** (510 Belfast Ave./Rte. 3, 207/589-3700) for amazing flavors handcrafted ("homemade" is too pedestrian to describe it) on the premises, or good country cooking at the **Olde Mill Diner** (143 Belfast Ave./Rte. 3, Searsmont, 207/342-2999).

If you're up for more inland exploring, weave your way along the **Georges River Scenic Byway,** a 50-mile auto route along the St. George River (a.k.a. Georges River) from its inland headwaters to the sea in Port Clyde. It's lovely anytime, but is especially pretty during foliage season. The official start is at the junction of Routes 3 and 220 in Liberty, but you can follow the trail in either direction or pick it up anywhere along the way. Road signs are posted, but it's far better to obtain a map-brochure at a chamber of commerce or other information locale. Or contact the architects of the route, **The Georges River Land Trust** (207/594-5166, www.georgesriver.org).

RECREATION

Parks

Belfast is rich in parks and picnic spots. One of the state's best municipal parks is just on the outskirts of downtown. Established in 1904, **Belfast City Park** (87 Northport Ave., 207/338-1661, free) has lighted tennis courts, an outdoor pool, a pebbly beach, plenty of picnic tables, an unusually creative playground, lots of green space for the kids, and fantastic views of Islesboro, Blue Hill, and Penobscot Bay. For more action right in the heart of Belfast, head for **Heritage Park,** at the bottom of Main Street, with front-row seats on waterfront happenings. Bring a picnic, grab a table, and watch the yachts, tugs, and lobster boats. Every street between the two parks that ends at the ocean is a public right of way.

Hiking

Here's an easy amble, with just enough rise and fall to make you think you got a bit of a workout: The blue-blazed **Little River Community Trail** parallels the east bank of the Little River, departing from a trailhead at the Water District complex on Route 1 and ebbing and flowing just shy of a mile to the Perkins Road. You can cross the road and continue for nearly another three miles to another trailhead near the YMCA on Route 52.

Pick up a brochure for the **Belfast In-Town Nature Trail** (belfastbaywatershed.org), with four segments totaling a 5-mile loop that meanders through the city's downtown. Segment 3, City Park to Kirby Lake, is especially good for birders.

The **Harbor Walk** follows the downtown shoreline from Steamboat Landing to the Armistice Bridge, the footbridge crossing the Passy.

The former Belfast & Moosehead Lake Railroad corridor is morphing into **The Passy Rail Trail,** a 2-mile non-motorized trail paralleling the Passagassawakeag River that will connect The Harbor Walk to City Point.

Golf

Just south of Belfast is the nine-hole **Northport Golf Club** (581 Bluff Rd., Northport, 207/338-2270), established in 1916.

Boat Excursions

Cruise Belfast Bay aboard the ***Clara K*** (207/323-1443, www.belfastbaycompany.com), based at the Belfast Public Landing, for a two-hour introduction to lobster fishing

Belfast's Harbor Walk

($45 pp) or for private charters (from $350). The classic sloop, built in 1901 in Friendship, was originally used for lobstering. Now beautifully restored, it carries up to six passengers.

Kayaking

If you don't have your own kayak, **Water Walker** (152 Lincolnville Ave., 207/338-6424, www.kayak-tour-maine.com) has a full range of options. Owner Ray Wirth, a Registered Maine Guide and American Canoe Association-certified open-water instructor, will arrange customized trips from a few hours to multiple days, as well as provide instruction. A twp-plus-hour evening harbor tour is $35 pp.

Curling

The Scottish national sport of curling has dozens of enthusiastic supporters at Maine's only curling rink, the **Belfast Curling Club** (211 Belmont Ave./Rte. 3, 207/338-9851, www.belfastcurlingclub.org), an institution here since the late 1950s. Leagues play regularly on weeknights, and the club holds bonspiels (tournaments) and open houses several times during the season, which runs early November-early April.

ACCOMMODATIONS

Bed-and-Breakfasts and Inns

On a quiet side street, **The Jeweled Turret** (40 Pearl St., 207/338-2304 or 800/696-2304, www.jeweledturret.com, $139-175) is one of Belfast's pioneer bed-and-breakfasts. Carl and Cathy Heffentrager understand the business, and they go out of their way to make guests comfortable. The 1898 inn is loaded with handsome woodwork and Victorian antiques—plus an astonishing stone fireplace, one of four in the house. The wraparound porches are a fine place to settle and view the gardens while enjoying afternoon tea.

Over three years, beginning in 2005, professional innkeepers Ed and Judy Hemmingsen renovated adjacent mid-19th-century row houses into an elegant boutique hotel, the ★ **Belfast Bay Inn** (72 Main St., 207/338-5600, www.belfastbayinn.com, from $300). The two guest rooms and six suites differ in size and design, some with fireplaces, others with balconies, but all have original art, expanded wet bars, and high-quality furnishings that invite relaxation. In-room spa services are available. A full breakfast is included. The Hemmingsens delight in surprising guests with unexpected extras.

Sea kayaking is a popular way to explore Belfast Bay.

It's an easy walk to downtown from the **Alden House Inn** (63 Church St., 207/338-2151, www.thealdenhouse.com, $150-340), a B&B in Belfast's Historic District. The 1840 house has distinct architectural features, including a gazebo porch, spiral stairway, two parlors and a library. Breakfast is a highlight, and afternoon tea with freshly baked goods is included.

Motels

Renovated in 2015, the 61 guest rooms at the oceanfront **Belfast Harbor Inn** (91 Searsport Ave., 207/338-2740 or 800/545-8576, www.

belfastharborinn.com, $115-169) have TVs, air-conditioning, and free Wi-Fi and local calls; there's an outdoor heated pool—a real plus for families, as is the laundry. Pets are allowed in some guest rooms for $20/night. Rates include a light continental breakfast buffet. If you can swing it, request an ocean-view room.

In 2012, new owners completely renovated the **Yankee Clipper Motel** (50 Searsport Ave./Rte. 1, 207/338-2353, www.yankeeclippermotelbelfast.com, $99-149), giving the vintage 1950s strip motel on Route 1 a boutique vibe. All rooms have laminated wood floors, contemporary decor, and neutral colors along with a microwave and mini-fridge. There's a guest laundry, too. All it lacks is green space and a view.

FOOD

Local Flavors

Wraps are fast food at **Bay Wrap** (20 Beaver St., 207/338-9757, www.thebaywrap.com, 8am-7pm Mon.-Sat.). There's no limit to what the staff can stuff into various flavors of tortillas. Eat here or get them to go.

Industrial chic, casual, and laid-back best describe **Three Tides** (2 Pinchy Lane, on Marshall Wharf, 207/338-1707, www.3tides.com, 4pm-9pm Tues.-Sun.), a brewpub with Marshall Wharf beers on tap. Grab a booth inside, a seat at the bar, or a table on the deck overlooking the working harbor, and then choose from the tapas-style menu ($3.50-14). You might even play a game of boccie while waiting. Beers and ales are brewed on the premises. Also part of the operation is **LB,** a lobster pound, so lobster is often on the menu. Before hitting the pub, visit the adjacent tasting room (11am-4pm Tues.-Sat.), which also fills and sells growlers to go.

Love cheese? You'll love **Eat More Cheese** (94 Main St., 207/358-9701), which carries a selection from around the world, along with charcuterie, chocolate, and specialty foods; go hungry!

The **Belfast Co-op Store** (123 High St., 207/338-2532, www.belfast.coop, 7:30am-8pm daily) is an experience in itself. You'll have a good impression of Belfast after one glance at the clientele and the bulletin board. Open to members and nonmembers alike (with a discount for members), the co-op is a full-service organic and natural foods grocery, with a deli-café serving breakfast, lunch, and take-out fare.

Food trucks arrived in Belfast with **Good N You** (parking lot behind Main St.,

Three Tides has a lovely harborfront location.

11:30am-3pm Tues.-Sat.), which dishes out tacos, falafel, burritos, and other street food ($3-7).

The **Chocolate Drop Candy Shop** (64 Main St., 207/338-0566) is a kid-pleasing, retro-themed ice cream parlor and candy shop.

Sinfully delicious scratch-made croissants, bagels, and pastries emerge from the ovens at **Moonbat City Baking Co.** (137 Main St., 207/218-1039, 7am-noon Thurs- Sun.).

The Belfast Farmers Market (Waterfall Arts, 256 High St., 9am-1pm Fri.) provides the perfect opportunity for stocking up for a picnic.

Ethnic and Vegetarian Fare

Excellent Thai food pairs with a fabulous view of Penobscot Bay at **Seng Thai** (139 Searsport Ave./Rte. 1, 207/338-0010, 11:30am-9pm daily, entrées $8-18).

Fresh food prepared in creative ways has earned **Chase's Daily** (96 Main St., 207/338-0555, 7am-5pm Tues.-Thurs. and Sat., 7am-8pm Fri., 8am-2pm Sun.) a devoted local following. The emphasis is on vegetarian fare, and most of the produce comes from the Chase family farm in nearby Freedom. Most choices are in the $7-12 range; dinner entrées range $15-22. The restaurant also serves as an art gallery, farmers market, and bakery. It's not the place for a quiet dinner, as the space is large and tends to be noisy.

Delvino's Grill and Pasta House (32 Main St., 207/338-4565, www.delvinos.com, 11:30am-8pm daily, entrées $10-26) satiates cravings for Italian fare with a menu that includes lasagna, mussels marinara, and even lobster.

Laan Xang Cafe (18 Main St., 207/338-6338, www.laanxangcafe.com, 11:30am-3pm and 5-7pm Mon.-Sat., $11-14), specializing in Thai, Laotian, and Vietnamese fare, is a tiny, mostly take-out spot with a handful of tables on a deck.

Vegans and vegetarians, rejoice! **The Gothic** (108 Main St., 207/338-4684, www.gothicrestaurant.com, 11:30am-3pm and 5-9pm Tues.-Sat., 10am-3pm Sun.), in the meticulously restored flatiron building at the head of Main Street, is all about you. Celebrity chef Matthew Kenney, who owns the restaurant, was a pioneer in the raw food movement, and the menus here reflect his passion for plant-based cuisine. The menu comprises small plates, such as almond gazpacho, seared radicchio, and nettle gnocchi, with most choices ranging $12-14.

A longtime standby for world cuisine, including vegetarian items, **Darby's Restaurant and Pub** (155 High St., 207/338-2339, www.darbysrestaurant.com, from 11:30am daily, entrées $12-25) served tofu before tofu was cool. This place has been providing food and drink since just after the Civil War; the tin ceilings and antique bar are reminders of that.

Mexico meets the Caribbean at **La Vida** (132 High St., 207-338-2211, from 11:30am daily, $16-18), serving entrees such as coconut fish, fish fajitas, and Mexican meatloaf.

For authentic Neapolitan pizza made by a certified Neapolitan Master Pizza Chef has earned **Meanwhile in Belfast** (2 Cross St., 207-218-1288, www.meanwhile-in-belfast.com, Thurs.-Mon., 11:30am-9:30pm, $10-20) a solid following for its scratch-made, wood-fired fare.

Destination Dining

Plan well in advance and make reservations to score a table Chef Erin French's aptly named **The Lost Kitchen** (22 Mill St., Freedom, 207/382-3333, 5-9pm Wed.-Sat., entrées $26-42), housed in the renovated Mill at Freedom Falls, located about a half-hour northwest of Belfast. French's bright takes on comfort foods have garnered her national kudos.

Lobster

Young's Lobster Pound (4 Mitchell St., 207/338-1160, 7:30am-8pm daily), a barn of a place just off Route 1 on the east side of the harbor, is the place to go for no-frills, fresh-from-the-sea lobster. BYOB.

INFORMATION AND SERVICES

The **Belfast Area Chamber of Commerce** (16 Main St., 207/338-5900, www.belfastmaine.org) produces a regional guide.

Check out the **Belfast Free Library** (106 High St., 207/338-3884, www.belfast.lib.me.us).

Find **public restrooms** at the waterfront Public Landing, in the railroad station, at the Waldo County Courthouse, and at the Waldo County General Hospital.

GETTING THERE AND AROUND

Belfast is about 20 miles or 30 minutes via Route 1 from Camden and about 45 miles or one hour from Augusta and I-95 via Route 3. It's about 6.5 miles or 10 minutes via Route 1 to Searsport.

Searsport Area

Searsport (pop. 2,615) is synonymous with the sea, thanks to an enduring oceangoing tradition that's appropriately commemorated here in the state's oldest maritime museum. The seafaring heyday occurred in the mid-19th century, but settlers from the Massachusetts Colony had already made inroads here 200 years earlier. By the 1750s, Fort Pownall, in nearby **Stockton Springs** (pop. 1,592) was a strategic site during the French and Indian War (the North American phase of Europe's Seven Years' War).

Shipbuilding was under way by 1791, reaching a crescendo 1845-1866, with six year-round shipyards and nearly a dozen more seasonal ones. Ten percent of all full-rigged American-flag ships on the high seas were under the command of Searsport and Stockton Springs captains by 1885—a significant number of them bearing the names Pendleton, Nichols, or Carver. Many of these ships were involved in the perilous China trade, rounding notorious Cape Horn with great regularity.

All this global contact shaped Searsport's culture, adding a veneer of cosmopolitan sophistication. Imposing mansions of seafaring families were filled with fabulous Oriental treasures, many of which eventually made their way to today's Penobscot Marine Museum. Brick-lined Main Street is more evidence of the mid-19th-century wealth, and local churches reaped the benefits of residents' generosity. The Second Congregational Church, known as the Safe Harbor Church and patronized by captains and shipbuilders (most ordinary seamen attended the Methodist church), is ornamented with recently restored Tiffany-style windows and a Christopher Wren steeple.

Another inkling of this area's oceangoing superiority comes from visits to local burial grounds: Check out the headstones at Gordon, Bowditch, and Sandy Point cemeteries. Many have fascinating tales to tell.

Today the Searsport area's major draws are the Penobscot Marine Museum, the still-handsome brick Historic District, a couple of special state parks, and plentiful antiques shops and flea markets.

The Maine Historic Preservation Commission considers the buildings in Searsport's Main Street Historic District the best examples of their type outside Portland—a frozen-in-time mid-19th-century cluster of brick-and-granite structures. The ground floors of most of the buildings are shops or restaurants; make time to stop in and admire their interiors.

SIGHTS

★ Penobscot Marine Museum

Exquisite marine paintings, historical photographs, ship models, boats, and unusual China-trade objets d'art are just a few of the 10,000 treasures at the **Penobscot Marine**

Museum (5 Church St. at Rte. 1, Searsport, 207/548-2529, www.penobscotmarinemuseum.org, 10am-5pm Mon.-Sat., noon-5pm Sun. late May-mid-Oct., $12 adults, $10 seniors, $8 ages 7-15, $30 family), Maine's oldest maritime museum, founded in 1936. Allow several hours to explore the exhibits, housed in five separate buildings on the museum's downtown campus. For a start, you'll see one of the nation's largest collections of paintings by marine artists James and Thomas Buttersworth. And the 1830s Fowler-True-Ross House is filled with exotic artifacts from foreign lands. Call or check the website for the schedule of lectures, concerts, and temporary exhibits. This isn't a very sophisticated museum, but it is a treasure.

Museum in the Streets

Walk through Searsport's history by visiting a dozen placards detailing historic sites with text in both French and English. Pick up a brochure at the downtown info booth, the Penobscot Maritime Museum, or other local businesses.

BlueJacket Shipcrafters

Complementing the collections at the museum are the classic and contemporary models built by **BlueJacket Shipcrafters** (160 E. Main St./Rte. 1, Searsport, 800/448-5567, www.bluejacketinc.com). Even if you're not a hobbyist, stop in to see the incredibly detailed models on display. Shipcrafters is renowned for building one-of-a-kind museum-quality custom models—it's the official model-maker for the U.S. Navy—but don't despair: There are kits here for all abilities and budgets. It's easy to find: Just look for the inland lighthouse on Route 1.

SHOPPING

Shopping in Searsport usually applies to antiques—from 25-cent flea-market collectibles to well-used tools to high-end china, furniture, and glassware.

More than two dozen dealers supply the juried inventory for the **Pumpkin Patch** (15 W. Main St./Rte. 1, Searsport, 207/548-6047), with a heavy emphasis on Maine antiques. Specialties include quilts (at least 80 are always on hand), silver, paint-decorated furniture, Victoriana, and nautical and Native American items.

In excess of 70 dealers sell their antiques and collectibles at the **Searsport Antique Mall** (149 E. Main St./Rte. 1, Searsport, 207/548-2640), making it another worthwhile stop for those seeking oldies but goodies.

Strewn along Route 1 are also a couple of flea markets.

RECREATION

Parks

MOOSE POINT STATE PARK

Here's a smallish park with a biggish view—183 acres wedged between Route 1 and a dramatic Penobscot Bay panorama. **Moose Point State Park** (Rte. 1, Searsport, 207/548-2882, $3 nonresident adults, $2 Maine resident adults, $1 ages 5-11) is 1.5 miles south of downtown Searsport. Bring a picnic, let the kids hang out and play (there's no swimming, but there's good tidepooling at low tide), or walk through the woods or along the meadow trail.

MOSMAN PARK

Southeast of busy Route 1, the four-acre town-owned **Mosman Park** has picnic tables, a traditional playground, lots of grassy space, a pocket-size pebbly beach, seasonal toilets, and fabulous views of the bay. Turn off Route 1 at Water Street and continue to the end.

SEARS ISLAND

After almost two decades of heavy-duty squabbling over a proposed cargo port on Searsport's 936-acre **Sears Island** (http://friendsofsearsisland.org), the state bought the island for $4 million in 1997. In 2009, a conservation easement was created, forever protecting 601 acres on one of the largest uninhabited islands on the East Coast. The island is a fine place for bird-watching, picnicking, walking, fishing, and cross-country skiing; pick up a brochure at the kiosk. It's linked to the mainland by a causeway. From downtown Searsport, continue northeast on Route 1 two miles to Sears Island Road (on the right). Turn and go 1.2 miles to the beginning of the island, where you can pull off and park before a gate; cars aren't allowed on the island. An easy 1.5-mile walk will take you to the other side of the island, overlooking Mack Point (a cargo port) and hills off to the left. Bring a picnic and binoculars—and a swimsuit if you're hardy enough to brave the water.

FORT POINT STATE PARK

Continuing northeast on Route 1 from Sears Island will get you to the turnoff for **Fort Point State Park** (Fort Point Rd., Stockton Springs, 207/567-3356, $3 nonresident adults, $2 Maine resident adults, $1 ages 5-11) on Cape Jellison's eastern tip. Within the 154-acre park are the earthworks of 18th-century **Fort Pownall,** a British fortress built during the French and Indian War; **Fort Point Light,** a square, 26-foot, 19th-century tower guarding the mouth of the Penobscot River, with an adjacent bell tower; shoreline trails; and a 200-foot pier where you can fish or watch birds or boats. Bird-watchers can spot waterfowl—especially ruddy ducks, but also eagles and ospreys. Bring picnic fixings, but stay clear of the keeper's house—it's private. At the Route 1 fork for Stockton Springs, bear right onto Main Street and continue to Mill Road, in the village center. Turn right and then left onto East Cape Road, and then take another left onto Fort Point Road, which leads to the parking area.

SANDY POINT BEACH

There's a nice swath of sand on **Sandy Point Beach,** a 104-acre town-managed preserve at the mouth of the Penobscot River with walking trails, osprey nests, and a beaver pond. It's at the end of Steamboat Wharf Road (off Route 1) in Stockton Springs.

Bicycling

Birgfeld's Bicycle Shop (184 E. Main St./Rte. 1, Searsport, 207/548-2916), in business since 1979, is a mandatory stop for any cyclist, novice or pro. Local information on about 15 biking loops, supplies, maps, weekly group rides, sales (also skateboards and scooters), and excellent repair services are all part of the Birgfeld's mix.

An especially good ride in this area is the **Cape Jellison** loop in Stockton Springs. Park at Stockton Springs Elementary School and do the loop from there. Including a detour to Fort Point, the ride totals less than 10 miles from downtown Stockton Springs.

The **Belfast Bicycle Club** (www.belfastbicycleclub.org) offers group rides for all abilities.

ACCOMMODATIONS

Inns

The **Captain A. V. Nickels Inn** (127 E. Main St./Rte. 1, Searsport, 207/548-1104, www.captainnickelsinn.com, $165-250) is an oceanside stunner. The cupola-topped mansion, built by the good captain in 1874 as a gift to his bride, is elegantly furnished with European and American antiques. Public rooms range from cozy to expansive. Guest rooms, some with shared or detached baths, are named after ports of call; two suites have decks overlooking the ocean; all have flat-screen TVs, Wi-Fi, and iPod docks. Rates include an extravagant breakfast. There's also an on-site restaurant and lounge.

Motels

The **Yardarm** (172 E. Main St./Rte. 1, Searsport, 207/548-2404, www.searsportmaine.com, $80-115), a small motel set back from the road, is next door to BlueJacket Shipcrafters. Each of the 18 pine-paneled units has a TV, air-conditioning, Wi-Fi, and a phone; suites (perfect for families) have a dinette, a microwave, and a small fridge. A continental breakfast is served in a cheery breakfast room in the adjacent farmhouse. Two rooms are pet-friendly.

Bait's Motel (215 E. Main St./Rte. 1, Searsport, 207/548-7299, http://www.

baitsmotel.anglersseafoodrestaurant.com, $79-119) doesn't look like much from the exterior, but inside, the recently renovated guest rooms are outfitted with high-quality, comfortable furniture, down duvets and pillows, and nice toiletries. Add fridges, cable TV, and individually controlled heat and air-conditioning. While not as nice, the standard rooms are dog-friendly ($20). It's adjacent to Angler's Restaurant, where guests check in (there is no dedicated office, nor is the restaurant open for breakfast).

Camping

How can you beat 1,100 feet of tidal oceanfront and unobstructed views of Islesboro, Castine, and Penobscot Bay? **Searsport Shores Camping Resort** (216 W. Main St./Rte. 1, Searsport, 207/548-6059, www.campocean.com) gets high marks for its fabulous setting. About 100 good-size sites (including walk-in oceanfront tenting sites) go for $42-88. Facilities include a private beach, a small store, free showers, laundry, play areas, a recreation hall, nature trails, and a volleyball court. Request a site away from organized-activity areas. Bring a sea kayak and launch it here. Leashed pets are allowed. In early September, the campground hosts Fiber Arts College, a weekend of classes, demonstrations, and camaraderie for spinners, hookers, weavers, and the like.

FOOD

Local Flavors

Good home cooking with an emphasis on fried food has made **Just Barb's** (Main St./Rte. 1, Stockton Springs, 207/567-3886, 6am-8pm Mon.-Sat., 7am-8pm Sun.) a dandy place for an unfussy meal at a low price. Fried clams and scallop stew are both winners; finish up with a slab of pie or shortcake. The all-you-can-eat fish fry, usually less than $10, is available daily after 11am.

Pick up sandwiches for a picnic at Fort Knox, along with soups, wine, cheeses, prepared entrées, baked goods, and homemade marmalades and chutneys at **The Good Kettle** (247 Rte. 1, Stockton Springs, 207/567-2035, 8:30am-4pm Sun.-Wed., 8:30am-7pm Thurs.-Sun.) There's also a dog-friendly indoor seating area and a fenced-in area for dogs out back.

Family Favorites

The **Anglers Restaurant** (215 E. Main St./Rte. 1, Searsport, 207/548-2405, www.anglersrestaurant.net, 11am-8pm daily, $7-20) is probably the least-assuming and yet one of the most popular restaurants around. Expect hearty New England cooking, hefty portions, local color, no frills, and a bill that won't dent your wallet. Big favorites are the chowders, stews, and lobster rolls. The "minnow menu" for smaller appetites runs $6-13. Desserts are a specialty: The gingerbread with whipped cream is divine, and kids love the "bucket o' worms." If it's not too busy and you've ordered a lobster, ask owner Buddy Hall if he'll demonstrate hypnotizing it. It's adjacent to the Bait's Motel, 1.5 miles northeast of downtown Searsport.

The menu at the casual **Mermaid Restaurant & Pub** (121 E. Main St., 207/548-0084, 11am-9pm Tues.-Sun., $8-22), in the Homeport Inn, ranges from burgers to lobster, and there's a kids' menu too. There's entertainment on weekends.

Casual and Fine Dining

Relax and savor the views over Penobscot Bay along with a fine wine and dinner at **The Captain's Table** (127 E. Main St./Rte. 1, Searsport, 207/548-1104, www.captainnickelsinn.com, 6pm-9pm Thurs.-Sun.), an elegant, white-tablecloth restaurant in the magnificently restored Capt. A. V. Nickels Inn. The four-course continental-inspired menu is $49; add $38 for wine pairings. For a lighter meal, dine in the less formal **Port of Call** tapas lounge (from 4pm Thurs.-Mon., entrées $16-24).

INFORMATION AND SERVICES

The **Searsport Business and Visitors Guide** publishes a visitors guide and maintains a small self-serve info center in a shed-like building on Route 1 (at Norris St.), across from the Pumpkin Patch antiques shop.

Check out the **Carver Memorial Library** (Mortland Rd. and Union St., Searsport, 207/548-2303, www.carver.lib.me.us).

GETTING HERE AND AROUND

Searsport is about six miles or 10 minutes via Route 1 from Belfast. It's about 13 miles or 18 minutes to Bucksport.

Bucksport Area

The new Penobscot Narrows Bridge provides an elegant entry to Bucksport, a longtime rough-and-ready river port and former papermaking town that's slowly gentrifying. Bucksport is no upstart. Native Americans first gravitated to these Penobscot River shores in summer, finding a rich source of salmon for food and grasses for basket making. In 1763, the area was officially settled by Colonel Jonathan Buck, a Massachusetts Bay Colony surveyor who modestly named it "Buckstown" and organized a booming shipping business here. His remains are interred in a local cemetery, where his tombstone bears the distinct outline of a woman's leg; this is allegedly the result of a curse by a witch Buck ordered executed, but in fact it's probably a flaw in the granite. Most townsfolk prefer not to discuss the matter, but the myth refuses to die—and it has immortalized a man whose name might otherwise have been consigned to musty history books. The monument is across Route 1 from the Hannaford supermarket, on the corner of Hinks Street. Bucksport's riverfront mill closed in 2014; dismantlement is in progress. The riverfront walkway provides great views of Fort Knox.

Just south of Bucksport, at the bend in the Penobscot River, Verona Island (pop. 544) is best known as the mile-long link between Prospect and Bucksport. Prospect is home to the Penobscot Narrows Bridge and Observatory and Fort Knox, guarding the mouth of the Penobscot River. Just before you cross the bridge from Verona to Bucksport, hang a left, then a quick right to a small municipal park with a boat launch and broad views of Bucksport Harbor (and the paper mill). Admiral Robert Peary's Arctic exploration vessel, the *Roosevelt,* was built on this site in 1905 and used in his final 1908 expedition to the North Pole. A scale model can be viewed in the Buck Memorial Library.

Route 1 east of Bucksport leads to Orland (pop. 2,225), whose idyllic setting on the banks of the Narramissic River makes it a magnet for shutterbugs. It's also the site of a unique service organization called H.O.M.E. (Homeworkers Organized for More Employment). East Orland (officially part of Orland) claims the Craig Brook National Fish Hatchery and Great Pond Mountain (you can't miss it, jutting from the landscape on the left as you drive east on Route 1).

SIGHTS

★ Fort Knox

Looming over Bucksport Harbor, the *other* **Fort Knox** (Rte. 174, Prospect, 207/469-7719, www.fortknox.maineguide.com, 9am-sunset May 1-Oct. 31, $4.50 nonresident adults, $3 Maine residents, $1 ages 5-11) is a 125-acre state historic site just off U.S. 1. Named for Major General Henry Knox, George Washington's first secretary of war, the sprawling granite fort was begun in 1844. Built to protect the upper Penobscot River from attack, it was never finished and never saw battle. Still, it was, as guide Kathy Williamson says, "very well thought out and planned, and that may have been its best defense." Begin your visit at the Visitor and Education Center, operated by the Friends of Fort Knox, a nonprofit group that has partnered with the state to preserve and interpret the fort. Guided tours are sometimes available. The fort's distinguishing features include two complete Rodman cannons. Wear rubberized shoes and bring a flashlight to explore the underground passages; you can set the kids loose. The fort hosts Civil War reenactments several times each summer as well as a Medieval Tournament, a paranormal-psychic fair, and other events (check the website). The Halloween Fright at the Fort is a ghoulish event for the brave. The grounds are accessible all year. Bring a picnic; views over the river to Bucksport are fabulous.

★ Penobscot Narrows Bridge and Observatory

On a clear day, do not miss the **Penobscot Narrows Bridge and Observatory** (9am-5pm daily late May-June and Sept.-Nov. 1, 9am-6pm daily July-Aug., $7 nonresident adults, $5 Maine resident adults, $3 ages 5-11, includes fort admission), accessible via Fort Knox. The three-deck observatory caps the bridge's 447-foot-high west tower, with the observatory's top floor sited at 420 feet above the Penobscot River. It's one of only three such structures in the world, and the only one in the United States. You'll zip up in an elevator, and when the doors open, you're facing a wall of glass—it's a bit of a shocker, and downright terrifying for anyone with a serious fear of heights. Ascend two more flights (an elevator is available) and you're in the glass-walled observatory; the views on a clear day extend from Mount Katahdin to Mount Desert Island. Even when it's hazy, it's still a neat experience.

Alamo Theatre

Phoenixlike, the 1916 **Alamo Theatre** (85 Main St., Bucksport, 207/469-0924 or 800/639-1636, event line 207/469-6910, www.oldfilm.org, 9am-4pm Mon.-Fri. year-round) has been digitally retrofitted for a new life. It shows not only contemporary films but also indie and local ones. Before each feature, it screens archival shorts about New England produced or revived by the unique **Northeast Historic Film,** which is headquartered here. NHF has more than 12 million feet of film in its archives, including rarities. Celebrities ranging from Ken Burns to Oprah Winfrey have requested footage for projects. Stop in,

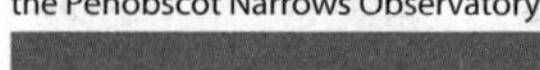
the Penobscot Narrows Observatory

Bucksport's waterfront walkway

survey the restoration, visit the displays (donation requested), and browse the Alamo Theatre Store for antique postcards, T-shirts, toys, and reasonably priced videos on ice harvesting, lumberjacks, maple sugaring, and other traditional New England topics.

H.O.M.E.

Adjacent to the flashing light on Route 1 in Orland, **H.O.M.E.** (207/469-7961, www.home-coop.net) is tough to categorize. Linked with the international Emmaus Movement founded by a French priest, H.O.M.E. (Homeworkers Organized for More Employment) was started in 1970 by Lucy Poulin, still the guiding force, and two nuns at a nearby convent. The quasi-religious organization shelters refugees and the homeless, operates a soup kitchen and a car-repair service, runs a day-care center, and teaches work skills in a variety of hands-on cooperative programs. Seventy percent of its income comes from sales of crafts, produce, and services. At the Route 1 store (Rte. 1 and Upper Falls Rd., 9am-4:30pm daily), you can buy handmade quilts, organic produce, maple syrup, and jams—and support a worthwhile effort. You can also tour the craft workshops on the property. For information about volunteering time in the workshops, store, or learning center, check the website.

Bucksport Waterfront Walkway

Stroll the one-mile paved walkway from the Bucksport-Verona Bridge to Webber Docks. Along the way are historical markers, picnic tables, a gazebo, restrooms, and expansive views of the harbor and Fort Knox.

SHOPPING

Locals come just as much for the coffee and conversation as the selection of new and used reads at **BookStacks** (71 Main St., Bucksport, 207/469-8992).

You'll find a smattering of antiques and curiosity shops dotting Route 1. Just south of Route 1 is **Wild Blueberry Patch Gift Shop** (Allen's Wild Maine Blueberries, Rte. 15, Orland, 207/469-7060), a tiny blue cottage next to the Allen family's blueberry processing building. Stop in for fresh, canned, frozen, or dried wild Maine blueberries and all manner of blueberry merchandise, from baking mixes to T-shirts.

RECREATION

Craig Brook National Fish Hatchery

For a day of hiking, picnicking, swimming, canoeing, and a bit of natural history, pack a lunch and head for 135-acre **Craig Brook National Fish Hatchery** (306 Hatchery Rd., East Orland, 207/469-6701), on Alamoosook Lake. Turn off Route 1 six miles east of Bucksport and continue 1.4 miles north to the parking area. The **visitors center** (8:30am-3:30pm Mon.-Fri., 8am-3:30pm Sat.-Sun. summer, free) offers interactive displays on Atlantic salmon (don't miss the downstairs viewing area), maps, and a restroom. The grounds are accessible 6am-sunset daily year-round. Established in 1889, the U.S.

Fish and Wildlife Service hatchery raises sea-run Atlantic salmon for stocking seven Maine rivers. The birch-lined shorefront has picnic tables, a boat-launching ramp, an Atlantic salmon display pool, additional parking, and a spectacular cross-lake view. Watch for eagles, ospreys, and loons. Also on the premises is the small **Atlantic Salmon Heritage Museum,** housed in a circa-1896 ice house and operated by the Friends of Craig Brook (call the hatchery for current hours). Inside are salmon and fly-fishing artifacts and memorabilia.

Great Pond Mountain Wildlands

Encompassing two parcels of land and roughly 4,300 acres, the Great Pond Mountain Wildlands is a jewel. Acquired by the **Great Pond Mountain Conservation Trust** (207/469-7190, www.greatpondtrust.org) in 2005 after a decade of negotiation, the Wildlands is divided into two areas. The larger parcel totals 3,420 acres and surrounds Hothole Valley, including Hothole Brook, prized for its trout, and shoreline on Hothole Pond. The smaller 875-acre tract includes two miles of frontage on the Dead River (not to be confused with the Dead River of rafting fame in northwestern Maine) and reaches up Great Pond Mountain and down to the ominously named Hellbottom Swamp. The land is rich with wildlife: black bears, moose, bobcats, and deer, to name just a few species; plus, with the pond, swamp, and river, it's ideal for bird-watching. With 14 miles of woods roads lacing the land, it's prime territory for walking, mountain biking, and snowshoeing, and the waterways invite fishing and paddling. Avoid the area during hunting season. Snowmobiling is permitted; ATVs are banned. Access to the Dead River tract is from the Craig Brook National Fish Hatchery; follow Don Fish Road to the Dead River Gate and Dead River Trail. The South Gate to Hothole Pond Tract is on Route 1 just southwest of Route 176. There's a parking lot at the gate, or, when it's open, you can drive in along Valley Road about 2.5 miles to another parking area.

The biggest rewards for the 1.8-mile easy-to-moderate hike up 1,038-foot **Great Pond Mountain** are 360-degree views and lots of space for panoramic picnics. On a clear day, Baxter State Park's Mount Katahdin is visible from the peak's north side. In fall, watch for migrating hawks. Access to the mountain is via gated private property beginning about a mile north of Craig Brook National Fish Hatchery on Dog Fish Rd in East Orland. Roadside parking is available near the trailhead, but during fall foliage season you may need to park at the hatchery. Pick up a brochure from the box at the trailhead, stay on the trail, and respect the surrounding private property. For a longer hike, access the Great Pond Mountain Trail via the Dead River Trail and Connector, a moderately difficult multi-use gravel trail, for a total distance of seven miles.

Canoeing

If you've brought a canoe, **Silver Lake,** just two miles north of downtown Bucksport, is a beautiful place for a paddle. There's no development along its shores, and the bird-watching is excellent. Swimming is not allowed and is punishable by a $500 fine; this is Bucksport's reservoir. To get to the public launch, take Route 15 north off Route 1. Go 0.5 mile and turn right on McDonald Road, which becomes Silver Lake Road, and follow it 2.1 miles to the launch site.

Golf

Bucksport Golf Club (Duck Cove Rd./Rte. 46, 1.5 miles north of Rte. 1, 207/469-7612, mid-Apr.-Sept.), running 3,397 yards, prides itself on having Maine's longest nine-hole course.

ACCOMMODATIONS

Inns and Bed-and-Breakfasts

Location, location, location: If only the six simple guest rooms at the old-timey **Alamoosook Lakeside Inn** (off Route 1, Orland, 207/469-6393 or 866/459-6393, www.alamoosooklakesideinn.com, year-round,

$150) actually overlooked the lake, it would be the perfect rustic lakeside lodge. The property is gorgeous, however, and the location is well suited for exploring the area. All guest rooms, decorated in country style, have windows and doors opening onto a long, enclosed sunporch overlooking the lake (so if the curtains are open, other guests passing by can see into the room). The upside: The lodge has 1,300 feet of lakefront and is great for bird-watching and fishing, especially for bass, trout, salmon, and pickerel, and guests may use the inn's canoes and kayaks. Paddle across the lake to the fish hatchery for a hike up Great Pond Mountain. If the weather doesn't cooperate, retreat to the basement rec room, with games, a fireplace, a library, and even a kitchenette. A full breakfast is served, and Wi-Fi is included. Do note, the inn often hosts events.

Bliss! Escape everything at **Williams Pond Lodge Bed and Breakfast** (327 Williams Pond Rd., Bucksport, 207/460-6064, www.williamspondlodge.com, $195), a secluded, solar-powered, eco-conscious, off-the-grid retreat on 20 wooded acres with 3,000 feet of frontage on spring-fed Williams Pond. Three guest rooms are decorated in cozy lodge style. Rates include a full breakfast and nightly dessert (the Scottish shortbread is so popular, it's now sold commercially). Wi-Fi is available. Canoes and kayaks are provided for guests. Innkeeper David Weeda plays his highland bagpipes most evenings at Hulls Cove and atop Cadillac in Acadia National Park. Access is via a long dirt road through the woods; if you're not accustomed to the locale, try to avoid arriving after dark.

Motels

On the edge of downtown and set back from Route 1, **The Bucksport Motor Inn** (70 Rte. 1, Bucksport, 207/469-3111 or 800/626-9734, www.bucksportmotorinn.com, late May-late Sept., $89-109) is a family-owned, vintage 1956 motel that's being updated; be sure to ask for one of the renovated rooms. Perks include Wi-Fi, TV, air-conditioning, refrigerators, and microwaves. Some rooms are dog-friendly ($15).

In downtown Bucksport, the **Fort Knox Inn** (64 Main St., Bucksport, 207/469-3113, www.fortknoxparkinn.com, $150-180) is a four-story motel right at the harbor's edge. It's a bit tired, but the 40 guest rooms have phones, air-conditioning, free Wi-Fi, and cable TV. Be sure to request a water view, preferably on an upper floor, or you'll be facing a parking lot.

Camping

The rivers, lakes, and ponds between Bucksport and Ellsworth make the area especially appealing for camping, and sites tend to be cheaper than in the Bar Harbor area. Six miles east of Bucksport, on the shores of 10-mile-long Toddy Pond, which reaches 100 feet in depth in some places, is **Balsam Cove Campground** (286 Back Ridge Rd., East Orland, 207/469-7771, www.balsamcove.com, late May-late Sept., $30-60), which leans toward bigger RVs. Facilities on the 50 acres include 60 wooded waterfront or water-view tent and RV sites, rental cabins ($75-80), on-site rental trailers ($95-105), a dump station, a store, laundry, free showers and Wi-Fi, boat rentals, and freshwater swimming. Dogs are welcome on camping sites for $2 per day. During July-August, especially on weekends, reservations are wise.

FOOD

MacLeod's (Main St., Bucksport, 207/469-3963, noon-9pm Tues.-Thurs., 4pm-9pm Fri.-Mon., $10-22) is Bucksport's most popular and enduring restaurant. Some tables in the pleasant dining room have glimpses of the river and Fort Knox. The wide-ranging menu has choices for all tastes and budgets. Reservations are wise for Saturday nights.

For generous portions of home-style breakfast and lunch fare, pull into **The Island Rise & Shine Restaurant** (Rte. 1, Verona Island, 207/469-1110, 6am-2pm Mon., Wed., Thurs.,

5am-2pm Tues. and Fri., 6:30am-2pm Sat., 7am-2pm Sun.).

Carrier's Mainely Lobster (corner Rtes. 1 and 46, 207/469-1011, www.carriersmainelylobster.com, 11am-9pm daily) doesn't look like much, but it's owned by a fishing family and is the best local spot for lobster or fried seafood. The large lobster roll (around $18) is filled with meat from about two of the tasty crustaceans. There's an indoor dining room out back as well as picnic tables. For cheap eats, the lunch specials, served 11am-3pm, are each less than $3.

Roughly 100 yards up the road is another local fave that's stood the test of time. **Crosby's Drive-In and Dairy Bar** (30 Rte. 46, Bucksport, 207/469-3640, www.crosbysdrivein.com, 10:30am-8pm daily) has been dishing out burgers, dogs, fried seafood, and ice cream since 1938. Thursday night is Cruise Night.

INFORMATION AND SERVICES

The best source for local info is the **Bucksport Bay Area Chamber of Commerce** (207/469-6818, www.bucksportchamber.org).

In Bucksport, **public restrooms** next to the town dock (behind the Bucksport Historical Society) are open spring-fall. Restrooms are open year-round in the Gateway gas station (at the Route 1 traffic light next to the Bucksport bridge) and in the Bucksport Municipal Office (Main St., Mon.-Fri.).

GETTING THERE AND AROUND

Bucksport is about 20 miles or 35 minutes via Route 15 from Bangor. It's about 17 miles or 25 minutes via Routes 1 and 15 to Blue Hill, about 22 miles or 30 minutes via Route 1 to Ellsworth, and about 18 miles or 30 minutes via Routes 175 and 166 to Castine.

Blue Hill Peninsula and Deer Isle

Look for ★ to find recommended sights, activities, dining, and lodging.

Highlights

★ **Parson Fisher House:** More than just another historic house, the Parson Fisher House is a remarkable testimony to one man's ingenuity (page 261).

★ **Blue Hill Mountain:** It's a relatively easy hike for fabulous 360-degree views from the summit of Blue Hill Mountain (page 264).

★ **Flash! In the Pans Community Steelband:** Close your eyes and you might think you're on a Caribbean island rather than in Maine when you hear this phenomenal steel-pan band (page 271).

★ **Holbrook Island Sanctuary State Park:** Varied hiking trails and great birding are the rewards for finding this off-the-beaten-path preserve (page 273).

★ **Castine Historic Tour:** A turbulent history detailed on signs throughout town makes Castine an irresistible place to tour on foot or by bike (page 277).

★ **Sea Kayaking:** Hook up with "Kayak Karen" in Castine for a tour (page 280).

★ **Haystack Mountain School of Crafts:** Don't miss an opportunity to visit this internationally renowned crafts school with an award-winning architectural design in a stunning setting (page 285).

★ **Nervous Nellie's:** Sculptor Peter Beerits's ever-expanding whimsical world captivates all ages—and it's free (page 285).

★ **Arts and Crafts Galleries:** Given Haystack's presence and the inspiring scenery, it's no surprise to find dozens of fabulously talented artisans on Deer Isle (page 289).

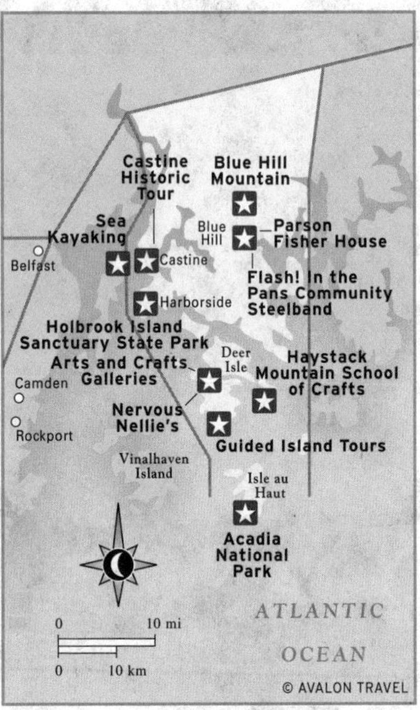

★ **Guided Island Tours:** Captain Walter Reed knows these waters and is an expert on the flora and fauna (page 293).

★ **Acadia National Park:** Isle au Haut's limited access makes this remote section of the park truly special. It's unlikely you'll have to share the trails—or the views—with more than a few other people (page 298).

The Blue Hill Peninsula, once dubbed "The Fertile Crescent," is unique. Few other locales harbor such a high concentration of artisans, musicians, and on-their-feet retirees juxtaposed with topflight wooden-boat builders, lobstermen, and umpteenth-generation Mainers. Perhaps surprisingly, the mix seems to work.

Anchored by the towns of Bucksport to the east and Ellsworth to the west, the peninsula comprises several enclaves with markedly distinct personalities. Blue Hill, Brooklin, Brooksville, Sedgwick, Castine, Deer Isle, and Stonington are stitched together by a network of narrow, winding country roads. Thanks to the mapmaker-challenging coastline and a handful of freshwater ponds and rivers, there's a view of water around nearly every bend.

You can watch the sun set from atop Blue Hill Mountain; tour the home of the fascinating Jonathan Fisher; stroll through the village of Castine (charming verging on precious), whose streets are lined with dowager-like homes; visit *WoodenBoat* magazine's world headquarters in tiny Brooklin; and browse top-notch studios and galleries throughout the peninsula. Venture a bit inland of Route 1, and you find lovely lakes for paddling and swimming and another hill to hike.

After weaving your way down the Blue Hill Peninsula and crossing the soaring pray-as-you-go bridge to Little Deer Isle, you've entered the realm of island living. Sure, bridges and causeways connect the points, but the farther down you drive, the more removed from civilization you'll feel. The pace slows; the population dwindles. Fishing and lobstering are the mainstays; lobster boats rest near many homes, and trap fences edge properties. If your ultimate destination is the section of Acadia National Park on Isle au Haut, the drive down Deer Isle to Stonington helps to disconnect you from the mainland. To reach the park's acreage on Isle au Haut, you'll board the Isle au Haut ferryboat for the trip down Merchant Row to the island.

PLANNING YOUR TIME

To truly enjoy this region, you'll want to spend at least 3-4 days here, perhaps splitting your

Previous: Isle au Haut; Stonington Harbor. **Above:** a beautiful view from the Haystack Mountain School of Crafts.

Blue Hill Peninsula and Deer Isle

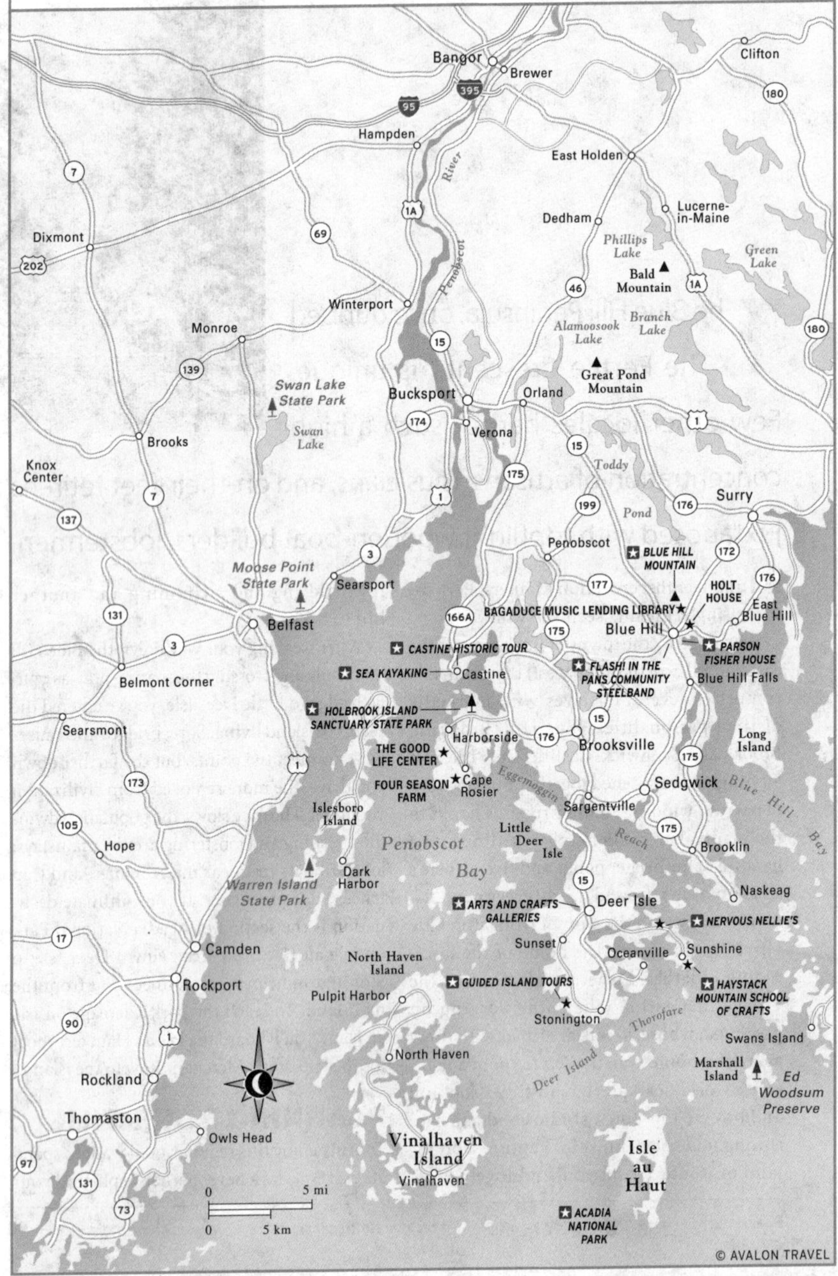

lodging between two or three locations. The region is designed for leisurely exploring; you won't be able to zip from one location to another. Traveling along the winding roads, discovering galleries and country stores, and lodging at traditional inns are all part of the experience.

Arts fans will want to concentrate their efforts in Blue Hill, Deer Isle, and Stonington. Outdoor-oriented folks should consider Deer Isle, Stonington, or Castine as a base for sea kayaking or exploring the area preserves. For architecture and history buffs, Castine is a must.

No visit to this region is complete without at least a cruise by, if not a visit to, Isle au Haut, an offshore island that's home to a remote section of Acadia National Park. Allow at least a few hours for a ride on the mail boat, but if you can afford the time, spend a full day hiking the park's trails. Don't forget to pack food and water.

Blue Hill

Twelve miles south of Route 1 is the hub of the peninsula, **Blue Hill** (pop. 2,686), exuding charm from its handsome old homes to its waterfront setting to the shops, restaurants, and galleries that boost its appeal.

Eons back, Native American summer folk gave the name Awanadjo (small, hazy mountain) to the mini-mountain that looms over the town and draws the eye for miles around. The first permanent settlers arrived in the late 18th century, after the French and Indian War, and established mills and shipyards. More than 100 ships were built here between Blue Hill's incorporation in 1789 and 1882—bringing prosperity to the entire peninsula.

Critical to the town's early expansion was its first clergyman, Jonathan Fisher, a remarkable fellow who has been likened to Leonardo da Vinci. In 1803, Fisher founded Blue Hill Academy (predecessor of today's George Stevens Academy), then built his home (now a museum), and eventually left an immense legacy of inventions, paintings, engravings, and poetry.

Throughout the 19th century and into the 20th, Blue Hill's granite industry boomed, reaching its peak in the 1880s. Scratch the Brooklyn Bridge and the New York Stock Exchange and you'll find granite from Blue Hill's quarries. Around 1879, the discovery of gold and silver brought a flurry of interest, but little came of it. Copper was also found here, but quantities of it, too, were limited.

At the height of industrial prosperity, tourism took hold, attracting steamboat-borne summer boarders. Many succumbed to the scenery, bought land, and built waterfront summer homes. Thank these summer folk and their offspring for the fact that music has long been a big deal in Blue Hill. The Kneisel Hall Chamber Music School, established in the late 19th century, continues to rank high among the nation's summer music colonies. New York City's Blue Hill Troupe, devoted to Gilbert and Sullivan operettas, was named for the longtime summer home of the troupe's founders.

SIGHTS

★ Parson Fisher House

Named for a brilliant Renaissance man who arrived in Blue Hill in 1794, the **Parson Fisher House** (44 Mines Rd./Rte. 15/176, 207/374-2459, www.jonathanfisherhouse.org, 1pm-4pm Thurs.-Sat. early July-early Sept., Fri.-Sat. to mid-Oct., $5) immerses visitors in period furnishings and Jonathan Fisher lore. And Fisher's feats are breathtaking: He was a Harvard-educated preacher who also managed to be an accomplished painter, poet, mathematician, naturalist, linguist, inventor, cabinetmaker, farmer, architect, and printmaker. In his spare time, he fathered nine children. Fisher also pitched in to help build the yellow house on Tenney Hill, which served as the Congregational church parsonage. Now it contains intriguing items created by Fisher, memorabilia that volunteer tour guides delight in explaining, including a camera obscura. Don't miss it.

Historic Houses

A few of Blue Hill's elegant houses have been converted to museums, inns, restaurants, and even some offices and shops, so you can see them from the inside out. To appreciate the private residences, you'll want to walk, bike, or drive around town. Also ask at the Holt House about village walking tours.

In downtown Blue Hill, a few steps off Main Street, stands the **Holt House** (3 Water St., www.bluehillhistory.org, 1pm-4pm Tues. and Fri., 11am-2pm Sat. July-mid-Sept., $3 adults, free under age 13), home of the Blue Hill Historical Society. Built in 1815 by Jeremiah Holt, the Federal-style building contains restored stenciling, period decor, and masses of memorabilia contributed by local residents. In the carriage house are even more goodies, including old tools, a sleigh, carriages, and more.

Walk or drive up Union Street (Rte. 177), past George Stevens Academy, and wander **The Old Cemetery,** established in 1794. If gnarled trees and ancient headstones intrigue you, there aren't many good-size Maine cemeteries older than this one.

Bagaduce Music Lending Library

At the foot of Greene's Hill in Blue Hill is one of Maine's more unusual institutions, the **Bagaduce Music Lending Library** (South Street, 207/374-5454, www.bagaducemusic.org, 10am-4pm Mon.-Fri. or by appointment), where you can borrow from a collection of more than 250,000 titles. Somehow this seems appropriate for a community that's a magnet for music lovers. Annual membership is $20 ($10 for students); fees range $1-4/piece.

Scenic Routes

Parker Point Road (turn off Rte. 15 at the Blue Hill Library) takes you from Blue Hill to Blue Hill Falls the back way, with vistas en route toward Acadia National Park. For other serene views, drive the length of **Newbury Neck** in nearby Surry, or head west on Route 15/176 toward Sedgwick, Brooksville, and beyond.

Parson Fisher House

ENTERTAINMENT AND EVENTS

Live Music

Since 1922, chamber-music students have been spending summers perfecting their skills and demonstrating their prowess at the **Kneisel Hall Chamber Music School** (Pleasant St./Rte. 15, 207/374-2811, www.kneisel.org). Faculty concerts run Friday evenings and Sunday afternoons late June-late August. The concert schedule is published in the spring, and reserved-seating tickets ($30 inside, $20 on the porch outside, nonrefundable) can be ordered online or by phone. Other opportunities to hear the students and faculty exist, including young-artist concerts, children's concerts, open rehearsals, and more. Kneisel Hall is about 0.5 mile from the center of town.

The Blue Hill Congregational Church is the site for the **Vanderkay Summer Music Series** (207/374-2891), whose offerings range from choral music from the Middle Ages to bluegrass. Suggested donation is $20.

Chamber music continues in winter thanks to the volunteer **Blue Hill Concert Association** (207/326-4666, www.bluehillconcertassociation.org), which presents five concerts January-March at the Congregational church. Recommended donation is $30.

Blue Hill Bach (207/590-2677, www.bluehillbach.org) was formed in 2011 to present Baroque music, and does so with its summer Bach Festival.

The **New Surry Theatre** (18 Union St., Blue Hill, 207/200-4720, www.newsurrytheatre.org) stages musicals and classics from November through August.

Home to the former Surry Opera Company, the Surry Concert Barn is being revitalized by **Surry Arts: At The Barn** (8 Cross Rd., Surry, 207/669-9216, surryartsatthebarn.com), which presents concerts, talks, and films.

Lectures

The **Marine Environmental Research Institute Center for Marine Studies** (55 Main St., 207/374-2135, www.meriresearch.org) sponsors an evening lecture series, which tackles subjects such as The State of Blue Hill Bay: A 10-Year Window on a Changing Ecosystem.

Events

WERU's annual **Full Circle Fair** is usually held in mid-August at the Blue Hill Fairgrounds (Rte. 172, north of downtown Blue Hill). Expect world music, good food, crafts, and socially and environmentally progressive talks.

On Labor Day weekend, the **Blue Hill Fair** (Blue Hill Fairgrounds, Rte. 172, 207/374-9976) is one of the state's best agricultural fairs.

The **Foliage, Food & Wine Festival** takes place in October.

SHOPPING

Perhaps it's Blue Hill's location near the renowned Haystack Mountain School of Crafts. Perhaps it's the way the light plays off the rolling countryside and onto the twisting coastline. Perhaps it's the inspirational landscape. Whatever the reason, numerous artists and artisans call Blue Hill home, and top-notch galleries are abundant.

The **Liros Gallery** (14 Parker Point Rd., Blue Hill, 207/374-5370 or 800/287-5370, www.lirosgallery.com) has been dealing in Russian icons since the mid-1960s. Prices are high, but the icons are fascinating. The gallery also carries Currier & Ives prints, antique maps, and 19th-century British and American paintings. Just up the street is the **Cynthia Winings Gallery** (24 Parker Point Rd., 917/204-4001, www.cynthiawiningsgallery.com), which shows contemporary works by local artists. From here it's a short walk to **Blue Hill Bay Gallery** (Main St., Blue Hill, 207/374-5773, www.bluehillbaygallery.com), which represents contemporary artists in various media.

Don't miss **Jud Hartmann** (79 Main St., at Rte. 15, Blue Hill, 207/374-9917, www.judhartmanngallery.com). The spacious, well-lighted, in-town gallery carries Hartmann's limited-edition bronze sculptures of the woodland Native Americans of the Northeast. Hartmann often can be seen working on his next model in the gallery—a real treat. He's a wealth of information about his subjects, and he loves sharing the mesmerizing stories he's uncovered during his meticulous research.

Also on Main Street are two other fun, artsy gallery-shops. **Handworks Gallery** (48 Main St., Blue Hill, 207/374-5613, www.handworksgallery.org) sells a range of fun, funky, utilitarian, and fine-art crafts, including jewelry, furniture, rugs, wall hangings, and clothing, by more than 50 Maine artists and craftspeople.

Pottery is abundant in Blue Hill. **Rackliffe Pottery** (Rte. 172, Blue Hill, 207/374-2297 or 888/631-3321, www.rackliffepottery.com), noted for its vivid blue wares, also makes its own glazes and has been producing lead-free pottery since 1969.

About two miles from downtown is another don't-miss: **Mark Bell Pottery** (Rte. 15, Blue Hill, 207/374-5881), in a tiny building signaled only by a small roadside sign, is the home of exquisite, award-winning porcelain by the eponymous potter. It's easy to understand why his wares have been displayed at the Smithsonian Institution's Craft Show as well as at other juried shows across the country. The delicacy of each vase, bowl, or piece is astonishing, and the glazes are gorgeous. Twice each summer he has kiln openings—must-go events for collectors and fans.

Outside of Blue Hill, but just a few miles from Bell's studio, is **Clay Forms** (189 Rope Ferry Rd., Sedgwick, 207/359-2320, www.clayformspottery.com), where Melody Lewis-Kane displays her handmade functional and decorative porcelain pottery. To find it, follow Route 15 to the T intersection with Route 176 and cross it, continuing straight onto Rope Ferry Road. Follow it to the bottom of the hill, then take the road marked Private and continue to the sixth driveway on the right. Drive slowly—the road is narrow and winding. It's wise to call first.

Blue Hill Books (26 Pleasant St./Rte. 15, 207/374-5632, www.bluehillbooks.com) is a wonderful independent bookstore that organizes an "authors series" during the summer.

RECREATION

Parks and Preserves

Blue Hill Heritage Trust (101 Union St., 207/374-5118, www.bluehillheritagetrust.org, 8am-5pm Mon.-Fri.) works hard at preserving the region's landscape. Trail maps for all sites can be downloaded from the website. It also presents a Walks and Talks series, with offerings such as a mushroom walk and talk, a full-moon hike up Blue Hill Mountain, and farm tours. Many include talks by knowledgeable folks on complementary topics.

★ BLUE HILL MOUNTAIN

Mountain seems a fancy label for a 943-footer, yet **Blue Hill Mountain** stands alone, visible from Camden and even beyond. On a clear day, head for the summit and take in the wraparound view encompassing Penobscot Bay, the hills of Mount Desert, and the Camden Hills. Climb the fire tower and you'll see even more. In mid-June the lupines along the way are breathtaking; in fall the colors are spectacular—with reddened blueberry barrens added to the variegated foliage. Go early in the day; it's a popular easy-to-moderate two-mile round-trip hike via the Osgood Trail. A short loop on the lower slopes takes only half an hour. Take Route 15 (Pleasant St.) to Mountain Road. Turn right and go 0.8 mile to the trailhead (on the left) and the small parking area (on the right). You can also walk (uphill) the mile from the village.

BLUE HILL TOWN PARK

At the end of Water Street is a small park with a terrific view, along with a small pebble beach, picnic tables, a portable toilet, and a playground.

Outfitters

The Activity Shop (139 Mines Rd., 207/374-3600, www.theactivityshop.com) rents

The Blue Hill Inn has been sheltering guests since 1840.

bicycles for $65/week and Old Town canoes and kayaks for $45 single, $55 double per day, including delivery within a reasonable area.

ACCOMMODATIONS

If you're trying to imagine a classic country inn, **The Blue Hill Inn** (Union St./Rte. 177, 207/374-2844 or 800/826-7415, www.bluehillinn.com, mid-May-late Oct., $190-250) would be it. The antiques-filled inn, open since 1840, is located steps from Main Street's shops and restaurants. Ten air-conditioned guest rooms and a suite have real chandeliers, four-poster beds, down comforters, fancy linens, and braided and Oriental rugs; three have wood-burning fireplaces. Rear rooms overlook the extensive cutting garden, with chairs and a hammock. The inn was expected to change hands in 2016, so call for details about breakfasts, afternoon hors d'oeuvres, and other meals, as well as rates.

What's old is new at **Barncastle** (125 South St., 207/374-2330, www.barn-castle.com, $145-195), a late 19th-century Shingle-style cottage that's listed on the National Register of Historic Places. It opens to a two-story foyer with a split stairway and balcony. Rooms and suites open off the balcony. All are spacious, minimally decorated, and offer contemporary accents, including flat-screen TVs, Wi-Fi, a fridge, and a microwave. Rates include a continental breakfast. The downstairs tavern serves pizza, salads, and sandwiches; noise can be a factor.

The ★ **Wave Walker Bed and Breakfast** (28 Wavewalker Ln., Surry, 207/667-5767, www.wavewalkerbedandbreakfast.com, $195-290) has a jaw-dropping location near the tip of Newbury Neck. It sits on 20 private acres with 1,000 feet of shorefront as well as woods and blueberry fields. The newly built inn is smack on the oceanfront, with views across the water to Mount Desert Island. Four spacious guest rooms have wowser views as well as Wi-Fi, DIRECTV, and a DVD player; some have fireplaces, oversized whirlpool tubs, or both. The first-floor room is a good choice for those with mobility problems. Guests also have use of a living room, sunroom, and oceanfront deck, which has a fire pit. A full, hot breakfast is served. Kayaks are available for guests. A separate two-bedroom-plus-loft cottage rents for $1,700 per week.

Just north of town, Bill and Ann Rioux opened **The Farmhouse Inn** (578 Pleasant St., 207/374-5286, www.thefarmhouseinnmaine.com, $150-300) in 2015 after completely renovating the house and barn. Nine cheery guest rooms are split between the main house and the barn, and rates include breakfast.

FOOD

Local Flavors

Picnic fare and pizza are available at **Merrill & Hinckley** (11 Union St., 207/374-2821, 6am-9pm Mon.-Fri., 7am-9pm Sat., 8am-8pm Sun.), a quirky, 150-year-old family-owned grocery and general store.

Craving chocolate? **Black Dinah**

Forever Farms

Despite popular perception, family farms are experiencing a resurgence in Maine. According to the **Maine Farmland Trust** (207/338-6575, www.mainefarmlandtrust.org), since 2002 Maine has gained more than 1,000 farms and it leads the nation in attracting young farmers. It leads the New England states in agricultural production, contributing $2 billion to the state's economy each year.

Maine is the world's largest producer of brown eggs and wild blueberries; it ranks eighth in the country in production of potatoes and second in production of maple syrup, and it ranks second in New England for both milk and livestock production. But much of the recent growth has been in smaller farms that grow vegetables and/or raise small livestock for local sale. Farm stands and farmers markets, community-supported agriculture programs, demand for fresh local fare in local restaurants, and growing public awareness of the importance of knowing where food originates all contribute to the strength of Maine's farms. Impressive statistics, yes, but there's a cloud on the horizon. The rising cost of land combined with the aging of the farmers who own much of the state's agricultural land threatens Maine's farming future.

Maine Farmland Trust is working to bridge that gap. The nonprofit organization's mission is to protect Maine's farmland and to support farmers and the future of farming in Maine. It does this in two primary ways: Forever Farms, which permanently protects farmland with conservation easements that ensure that the land will always be available for farming, and Farm Viability, which gives farmers support with business planning and market development to help them prosper. The seedbed of farmland preservation in Maine was on the Blue Hill Peninsula, where the **Blue Hill Heritage Trust** (207/374-5118, www.bluehillheritagetrust.org) has preserved more than 2,000 acres of farmland since 1989. One of the driving forces behind the BHHT's efforts is local farmer Paul Birdsall, who helped found the organization in 1985 and then went on to help found Maine Farmland Trust in 1999. Birdsall's 360-acre Horsepower Farm is one of 13 permanently preserved agricultural properties on the peninsula. Birdsall is the elder of four generations on the family farm in Penobscot. Back in the 1980s, when he recognized that development was pushing the cost of land higher than farmers could afford, he began to purchase available farmland, preserve it with easements, and then resell it to farmers, such as Philip and Heather Retberg of Quills End Farm, a 105-acre property in Penobscot.

The battle to preserve Maine's farmland is at a crucial stage. Over the next 10 years, ownership of as much as 400,000 acres of farmland is expected to change as aging farmers die or sell. Since its founding, the Maine Farmland Trust has supported more than 500 farm families and protected more than 45,000 acres of farmland. It is working to support 1,000 families and to protect 100,000 acres. Doing so is expected to cost $50 million, but it will help ensure Maine's food security, and the economic impact of that investment is projected to be more than $50 million annually.

Chocolatiers (5 Main St., 207/374-5621, www.blackdinahchocolatiers.com) has a mainland home, sharing space with Fairwinds Florist. Here you'll find the Isle au Haut confectioner's freshly made to-die-for chocolates, ice cream, and sorbet, as well as a coffee/tea/hot chocolate bar. Don't miss the Art Box, a vending machine with $10 works by 10 local artists—perfect gift for someone back home, perhaps?

The **Blue Hill Wine Shop** (138 Main St., 207/374-2161), tucked into a converted horse barn, carries more than 1,000 wines, plus teas, coffees, breads, and cheeses. Monthly wine tastings (usually 2:30pm-6pm last Sat. of the month) are always an adventure.

The **Blue Hill Co-op and Café** (4 Ellsworth Rd./Rte. 172, 207/374-2165, bluehill.coop, 7am-7pm daily) sells organic and natural foods. Breakfast items, sandwiches, salads, and soups—many with ethnic flavors—are available in the café.

Black Dinah Chocolatiers in downtown Blue Hill

Local gardeners, farmers, and craftspeople peddle their wares at the **Blue Hill Farmers Market** (9am-11am Sat. late May-mid-Oct.). It's a particularly enduring market, well worth a visit. Demonstrations by area chefs and artists are often on the agenda. Late May-late August the Saturday market is at the Blue Hill Fairgrounds; then it moves to the Blue Hill Congregational Church.

Every Thursday morning, the **Northern Bay Market** (177 Southern Bay Rd.,/Rte. 175, 207/326-8606) sells Toni Staples's homemade cake and yeast-raised doughnuts. Go early, or risk being disappointed; the market opens at 6am.

Blue Hill's first microbrewery, **Deep Water Brew Pub** (33 Tenney Hill Rd., 207/374-2441, 5pm-9pm Wed.-Sun.) serves pub-style fare such as ribs, burgers, and tacos ($10-18). Ask about tours of the brewery, located in a beautifully renovated historic barn behind the pub.

With a full bar, indoor and outdoor seating, and a boatyard location, the **Boatyard Grill** (13 E. Blue Hill Rd., 207/374-3533, from noon Tues.-Sat., from $8) attracts the sailing crowd, who appreciate its laid-back, Caribbean-esque style. The menu ranges from burgers to lobster. There's often live music on Saturdays.

Family Favorites

Marlintini's Grill (83 Mines St./Rte. 15, 207/374-2500, www.marlintinisgrill.com, from 11am daily, $10-20) is half-sports bar and half-restaurant. You can sit in either, but the bar side can get raucous. Best bet: the screened-in porch. The menu includes soups, salads, burgers, fried seafood, rib eye, and nightly home-style specials; there's a kids' menu, too. The portions are big, the service is good, and the food is decent.

Just south of town is **Barncastle** (125 South St., 207/374-2300, www.barn-castle.com, 3pm-8pm Sun.-Thurs., 3pm-9pm Fri.-Sat., entrées $8-20), serving a creative selection of wood-fired pizzas in three sizes as well as sandwiches, subs, panini, calzones, and salads in a lovely Shingle-style cottage. There are vegetarian options. Expect to wait for a table; this is one popular spot.

The wide-ranging menu comprising small plates ($6-10) pub favorites ($10-17), and entrees ($15-18) at **The Farmhouse Inn** (578 Pleasant St., 207/374-5286, 3-9pm Wed.-Sat.), makes it easy to find something to everyone's liking and in the right price range. The inn also has a few guestrooms and often offers live music.

Fine Dining

For a lovely dinner by candlelight, make reservations at ★ **Arborvine** (33 Upper Tenney Hill/Main St., 207/374-2119, www.arborvine.com, 5:30pm-9pm Tues.-Sun., entrées $28-35), a conscientiously renovated, two-century-old Cape-style house with four dining areas, each with a different feel and understated decor. Chef-owner John Hikade and his wife, Beth, prepare classic entrées such as crispy roasted duckling and roasted rack of lamb. Their mantra has been fresh and local for more than 30 years.

Seafood

For lobster, fried fish, and the area's best lobster roll, head to **The Fish Net** (163 Main St., 207/374-5240, 11am-8pm daily), an inexpensive, mostly take-out joint on the eastern end of town.

It's not easy to find ★ **Perry's Lobster Shack and Pier** (1076 Newbury Neck Rd., Surry, 207/667-1955, 10am-7pm daily), but for a classic lobster-shack experience, make the effort. The traditional Maine lobster shack is about five miles down Newbury Neck, just after the Causeway Place beach. Expect lobster, lobster and crab rolls, corn, chips, mussels, and clams. From the pier-top picnic tables, you're overlooking the water with Mount Desert Island as a backdrop. No credit cards.

INFORMATION AND SERVICES

The **Blue Hill Peninsula Chamber of Commerce** (207/374-3242, www.bluehillpeninsula.org) is the best source for information on Blue Hill and the surrounding area.

At the **Blue Hill Public Library** (5 Parker Point Rd., 207/374-5515, www.bluehill.lib.me.us), ask to see the suit of armor, which *may* have belonged to Magellan. The library sponsors a summer lecture series.

Public restrooms are in the Blue Hill Town Hall (Main St.), Blue Hill Public Library (Main St.), and Blue Hill Memorial Hospital (Water St.).

GETTING THERE AND AROUND

Blue Hill is about 17 miles or 25 minutes via Routes 1 and 15 from Bucksport. It's about 14 miles or 20 minutes via Route 172 to Ellsworth, about 8 miles or 15 minutes via Route 15 to Brooksville, and about 20 miles or 35 minutes via Routes 15, 175, 199, and 166 to Castine.

Enjoy the views from Perry's Lobster Shack and Pier.

Brooklin, Brooksville, and Sedgwick

I'm going to let you in on a secret, a part of Maine that seems right out of a time warp—a place with general stores and family farms, where family roots go back generations and summer rusticators have returned for decades. Nestled near the bottom of the Blue Hill Peninsula and surrounded by Castine, Blue Hill, and Deer Isle, this often-missed area offers superb hiking, kayaking, and sailing, plus historic homes and unique shops, studios, lodgings, and personalities.

The best-known town is **Brooklin** (pop. 824), thanks to two magazines: *The New Yorker* and *WoodenBoat.* Wordsmiths extraordinaire E. B. and Katharine White "dropped out" to Brooklin in the 1930s and forever afterward dispatched their splendid material for *The New Yorker* from here. (The Whites' former home, a handsome colonial not open to the public, is on Route 175 in North Brooklin, 6.5 miles from the Blue Hill Falls bridge.) In 1977, *WoodenBoat* magazine moved its headquarters to Brooklin, where its 60-acre shore-side estate attracts builders and dreamers from all over the globe.

Nearby **Brooksville** (pop. 934) drew the late Helen and Scott Nearing, whose book *Living the Good Life* made them role models for back-to-the-landers. Their compound now verges on must-see status. **Buck's Harbor,** a section of Brooksville, is the setting for *One Morning in Maine,* one of Robert McCloskey's beloved children's books.

Incorporated in 1789, the oldest of the three towns is **Sedgwick** (pop. 1,196), which once included all of Brooklin and part of Brooksville. Now wedged between Brooklin and Brooksville, it includes the hamlet of Sargentville, the Caterpillar Hill scenic overlook, and a well-preserved complex of historic buildings. The influx of pilgrims—many of them artists bent on capturing the spirit that has proved so enticing to creative types—continues in this area.

SIGHTS

WoodenBoat Publications

On Naskeag Point Road, 1.2 miles from Route 175 in downtown Brooklin, a small sign marks the turn to the world headquarters of ***WoodenBoat*** (Naskeag Point Rd., Brooklin, 207/359-4651, www.woodenboat.com). Buy magazines, books, clothing, and all manner of nautical merchandise at the handsome store, stroll the grounds, or sign up for one of the dozens of one- and two-week spring, summer, and fall courses in seamanship, navigation, boatbuilding, sail making, marine carving, and more; tuition varies by course and duration. Special courses are geared to kids, women, pros, and all-thumbs neophytes; the camaraderie is legendary, and so is the cuisine. School visiting hours are 8am-5pm Monday-Saturday June-October.

Historical Sights

Now used as the museum and headquarters of the Sedgwick-Brooklin Historical Society, the 1795 **Reverend Daniel Merrill House** (Rte. 172, Sedgwick, 2pm-4pm Sun. July-Aug. donation) was the parsonage for Sedgwick's first permanent minister. Inside the house are period furnishings, old photos, toys, and tools; a few steps away are a restored 1874 schoolhouse, an 1821 cattle pound (for corralling wandering bovines), and a hearse barn. Pick up a brochure during open hours and guide yourself around the buildings and grounds. The **Sedgwick Historic District,** crowning Town House Hill, comprises the Merrill House and its outbuildings, plus the imposing 1794 Town House and the 23-acre Rural Cemetery (the oldest headstone dates from 1798) across Route 172.

The **Brooksville Historical Society Museum** (150 Coastal Rd./Rte. 176, Brooksville, www.brooksvillehistoricalsociety.org, 1pm-4pm Wed. and Sun. July-Aug.) houses a collection of nautical doodads, farming implements, blacksmith tools, and quilts in a converted boathouse. The museum is restoring a local farmhouse for more exhibits.

The Good Life Center

Forest Farm, home of the late Helen and Scott Nearing, is now the site of **The Good Life Center** (372 Harborside Rd., Harborside, 207/326-8211, www.goodlife.org). Advocates of simple living and authors of 10 books on the subject, the Nearings created a trust to perpetuate their farm and philosophy. Resident stewards lead tours (usually 1pm-5pm Thurs.-Mon. mid-June-early Sept., Sat.-Sun. early Sept.-mid-Oct., $5 donation). Ask about the schedule for the traditional Monday-night meetings (7pm), featuring free programs by gardeners, philosophers, musicians, and other guest speakers. Occasional work parties, workshops, and conferences are also on the docket. The farm is on Harborside Road, just before it turns to dirt. From Route 176 in Brooksville, take Cape Rosier Road and go eight miles, passing Holbrook Island Sanctuary. At the Grange Hall, turn right and follow the road 1.9 miles to the end. Turn left onto Harborside Road and continue 1.8 miles to Forest Farm, across from Orrs Cove.

Four Season Farm

About a mile beyond the Nearings' place is **Four Season Farm** (609 Weir Cove Rd., Harborside, 207/326-4455, www.fourseasonfarm.com, 1pm-5pm Mon.-Sat. June-Sept.), the lush organic farm owned and operated by internationally renowned gardeners Eliot Coleman and Barbara Damrosch. Both have written numerous books and articles and starred in TV gardening shows. Coleman is a driving force behind the use of the word *authentic* to mean "beyond organic," demonstrating a commitment to food that is local, fresh, ripe, clean, safe, and nourishing. He's successfully pioneered a "winter harvest," developing environmentally sound and economically viable systems for extending fresh vegetable production October-May in cold-weather climates. Visitors are welcome to drive in and around the farm, but no produce is sold here in summer.

Scenic Routes

No one seems to know how **Caterpillar Hill** got its name, but its reputation comes from a panoramic vista of water, hills, and blueberry barrens—with a couple of convenient picnic tables where you can stop for

Get way off the beaten path with a loop around Cape Rosier.

lunch, photos, or a ringside view of sunset and fall foliage. From the 350-foot elevation, the views take in Walker Pond, Eggemoggin Reach, Deer Isle, Swans Island, and even the Camden Hills. The signposted rest area is on Route 175/15, between Brooksville and Sargentville; watch out for the blind curve when you pull off the road. If you want to explore on foot, the one-mile Cooper Farm Trail loops through the blueberry barrens and woods. From the scenic overlook, walk down to and out Cooper Farm Road to the trailhead.

Between Sargentville and Sedgwick, Route 175 offers nonstop views of Eggemoggin Reach, with shore access to the Benjamin River just before you reach Sedgwick village.

Two other scenic routes are **Naskeag Point** in Brooklin and **Cape Rosier,** the westernmost arm of the town of Brooksville. Naskeag Point Road begins off Route 175 in "downtown" Brooklin, heads down the peninsula for 3.7 miles past the entrance to WoodenBoat Publications, and ends at a small shingle beach (limited parking) on Eggemoggin Reach. Here you'll find picnic tables, a boat launch, a seasonal toilet, and a marker commemorating the 1778 Battle of Naskeag, when British sailors came ashore from the sloop *Gage,* burned several buildings, and were run off by a ragtag band of local settlers. Cape Rosier's roads are poorly marked, perhaps deliberately, so keep your DeLorme atlas handy. The Cape Rosier loop takes in Holbrook Island Sanctuary, Goose Falls, the hamlet of Harborside, and plenty of water and island views. Note that some roads are unpaved, but they usually are well maintained.

ENTERTAINMENT AND EVENTS

★ Flash! In the Pans Community Steelband

If you're a fan of steel-band music, the **Flash! In the Pans Community Steelband** (207/374-2172, www.flashinthepans.org) usually performs somewhere on the peninsula 7:30pm-9pm Monday mid-June-early September. Local papers carry the summer schedule for the nearly three-dozen-member band, which deserves its devoted following. Admission is usually a small donation to benefit a local cause.

Eggemoggin Reach Regatta

Wooden boats are big attractions hereabouts, so when a huge fleet sails in for the **Eggemoggin Reach Regatta** (usually the first Saturday in August, but the schedule can change), crowds gather. Don't miss the parade of wooden boats. The best locale for watching the regatta itself is on or near the bridge to Deer Isle or near the Eggemoggin Landing grounds on Little Deer Isle. For details, see www.erregatta.com.

SHOPPING

Most of these businesses are small, owner-operated shops, which means they're often catch-as-catch-can.

Antiques

When you need a slate sink, a claw-foot tub, brass fixtures, or a Palladian window, **Architectural Antiquities** (52 Indian Point Lane, Harborside, 207/326-4938, www.arch-antiquities.com), on Cape Rosier, is just the ticket—a restorer's delight. Prices are reasonable for what you get, and they'll ship your purchases. It's open all year by appointment; ask for directions when you call. Antiques dating from the Federal period through the turn of the 20th century are the specialties at **Sedgwick Antiques** (775 N. Sedgwick Rd./Rte. 172, Sedgwick, 207/359-8834). Early furniture, handmade furniture, and a full range of country accessories and antiques can be found at **Thomas Hinchcliffe Antiques** (26 Cradle Knolls Lane, off Rte. 176, West Sedgwick, 207/326-9411).

Artists' and Artisans' Galleries

Small studio-galleries pepper Route 175

E. B. White: Some Writer

Every child since the mid-1940s has heard of E. B. White—author of the memorable *Stuart Little, Charlotte's Web,* and *Trumpet of the Swan*—and every college kid for decades has been reminded to consult his copy of *The Elements of Style.* But how many realize that White and his wife, Katharine, were living not in the big city but in the hamlet of North Brooklin, Maine? It was Brooklin that inspired Charlotte and Wilbur and Stuart, and it was Brooklin where the Whites lived very full, creative lives.

Abandoning their desks at *The New Yorker* in 1938, Elwyn Brooks White and Katharine S. White bought an idyllic saltwater farm on the Blue Hill Peninsula and moved here with their young son, Joel, who became a noted naval architect and yacht builder in Brooklin before his untimely death in 1997. Andy (as E. B. had been dubbed since his college days at Cornell) produced 20 books, countless essays and letters to editors, and hundreds (maybe thousands?) of "newsbreaks"—those wry clipping-and-commentary items sprinkled through each issue of *The New Yorker.* Katharine continued wielding her pencil as the magazine's standout children's-book editor, donating many of her review copies to Brooklin's Friend Memorial Library, one of her favorite causes. (The library also has two original Garth Williams drawings from *Stuart Little,* courtesy of E. B., and a lovely garden dedicated to the Whites.) Katharine's book, *Onward and Upward in the Garden,* a collection of her *New Yorker* gardening pieces, was published in 1979, two years after her death.

Later in life, E. B. sagely addressed the young readers of his three award-winning children's books:

> *Are my stories true, you ask? No, they are imaginary tales, containing fantastic characters and events. In real life, a family doesn't have a child who looks like a mouse; in real life, a spider doesn't spin words in her web. In real life, a swan doesn't blow a trumpet. But real life is only one kind of life—there is also the life of the imagination. And although my stories are imaginary, I like to think that there is some truth in them, too—truth about the way people and animals feel and think and act.*

E. B. White died on October 1, 1985, at the age of 86. He and Katharine and Joel left large footprints on this earth, but perhaps nowhere more so than in Brooklin.

(Reach Rd.) in Sedgwick and Brooklin; most are marked only by small signs, so watch carefully. First up is **Eggemoggin Textile Studio** (off Rte. 175/Reach Rd., Sedgwick, 207/359-5083, www.chrisleithstudio.com), where the incredibly gifted Christine Leith weaves scarves, wraps, hangings, and pillows with hand-dyed silk and wool; the colors are magnificent. You might catch her at work on the big loom in her studio shop, a real treat.

Just down the road is **Mermaid Woolens** (Reach Rd., Sedgwick, 207/359-2747, www.mermaidwoolens.com), source of Elizabeth Coakley's wildly colorful hand knits—vests, socks, and sweaters. They're pricey but worth every nickel.

Continue over to Brooklin, where Virginia G. Sarsfield handcrafts paper products, including custom lampshades, calligraphy papers, books, and lamps, at **Handmade Papers** (113 Reach Rd., Brooklin, 207/359-8345, www.handmadepapersonline.com).

It's worth the mosey out Flye Point to find **Flye Point Sculpture & Art Gallery** (436 Flye Point Rd., Brooklin, 207/610-0350), where Peter Stremlau displays fine works in varied media by Maine-based and Maine-inspired artists. Wander through gardens and woodlands accented with sculptures. More sculptures, as well as paintings and accordion books, are inside the gallery. The waterfront location is spectacular.

It's also worth looking through Brooksville

to find **Weaving a Life Studio Gallery** (1643 Coastal Rd./Rte. 176, Brooksville, 207/326-9503, www.weavingalife.com) to view Susan Barrett Merrill's amazing fiber sculptures. She also offers weaving and spinning classes.

Wine, Books, and Gifts

Three varieties of English-style hard cider are specialties at **The Sow's Ear Winery** (Rte. 176 at Herrick Rd., Brooksville, 207/326-4649, no credit cards), a minuscule operation in a funky two-story shingled shack. Winemaker Tom Hoey also produces sulfite-free blueberry, chokecherry, and rhubarb wines; he'll let you sample it all.

Betsy's Sunflower (12 Reach Rd., 207/359-5030), in Brooklin village, is a browser's delight filled with garden and kitchen must-haves and books. Her motto: "It has to be affordable, useful, and fun."

Don't miss the "world's smallest bookstore," Bill Henderson's **Pushcart Press Bookstore** (Christy Hill, Sedgwick, 207/359-2427). It's a trove of literary fiction both used (paperbacks $2, hardbacks $5) and new, including editions of the *Pushcart Prize: Best of the Small Presses* annual series. Sales help support Pushcart fellowships.

RECREATION

★ Holbrook Island Sanctuary State Park

In the early 1970s, foresighted benefactor Anita Harris donated to the state 1,230 acres in Brooksville that would become the **Holbrook Island Sanctuary** (207/326-4012, www.parksandlands.com, free). From Route 176, between West Brooksville and South Brooksville, head west on Cape Rosier Road, following brown-and-white signs for the sanctuary. Trail maps and bird checklists are available in boxes at trailheads or at park headquarters. The easy Backshore Trail (about 30 minutes) starts here, or go back a mile and climb the steepish trail to **Backwoods Mountain** for the best vistas. Other attractions include shorefront picnic tables and grills, four old cemeteries, super birdwatching during spring and fall migrations, a pebble beach, and a stone beach. Leashed pets are allowed, but no bikes are allowed on the trails and camping is not permitted. The park is officially open May 15-October 15, but the access road and parking areas are plowed in winter for cross-country skiers.

Swimming

A small, relatively little-known beach is

Welcome to Flye Point Sculpture & Art Gallery.

Brooklin's **Pooduck Beach.** From the Brooklin General Store (Rte. 175), take Naskeag Point Road about 0.5 mile, watching for the Pooduck Road sign on the right. Turn right and drive to the end; parking is very limited. You can also launch a sea kayak here into Eggemoggin Reach.

Bicycling

Bicycling in this area is for confident, experienced cyclists. The roads are particularly narrow and winding, with poor shoulders. Best bets for casual pedal pushers are the **Naskeag scenic route** or around **Cape Rosier,** where traffic is light.

Picnicking

You can take a picnic to the **Bagaduce Ferry Landing,** in West Brooksville off Route 176, where there are picnic tables and cross-river vistas toward Castine. Another good spot is **Holbrook Island Sanctuary State Park** on Cape Rosier.

ACCOMMODATIONS

Bed-and-Breakfasts

The Brooklin Inn (Rte. 175, Brooklin, 207/359-2777, www.brooklininn.com, $105-125 with breakfast; add $10 for a one-night stay) has five comfortable—if tired—bedrooms; two share a bath. It's open year-round and often offers packages including meals.

Cottage Colonies

The two operations in this category feel much like informal family compounds—where you quickly become an adoptee. These are extremely popular spots, where successive generations of hosts have catered to successive generations of visitors, and reservations are usually essential for July-August. Many guests book for the following year before they leave. We're not talking fancy; the cottages are old-shoe rustic, of varying sizes and decor. Most have cooking facilities; one colony includes breakfast and dinner in July-August. Both have hiking trails, playgrounds, rowboats, and East Penobscot Bay on the doorstep.

The fourth generation manages the **Hiram Blake Camp** (220 Weir Cove Rd., Harborside, 207/326-4951, www.hiramblake.com, Memorial Day-late Sept., no credit cards), but other generations pitch in and help with gardening, lobstering, maintenance, and kibitzing. Fifteen cottages line the shore of this 100-acre property, which has been in family hands since before the Revolutionary War. The camp itself dates from 1916. Don't bother bringing reading material: The dining room has ingenious ceiling niches lined with countless books. Guests also have the use of rowboats, and kayak rentals are available. Home-cooked breakfasts and dinners are served family-style; lobster is always available at an additional charge. Much of the fare is grown in the expansive gardens. Other facilities include a dock, a recreation room, a pebble beach, and an outdoor chapel. There's a one-week minimum (beginning Sat. or Sun.) in July-August, when cottages go for $1,100-3,500 per week (including breakfast, dinner, and linens). Off-season rates (no meals or linens, but cottages have cooking facilities) are $650-1,100 per week. The best chances for getting a reservation are in June and September. Dogs are welcome.

Sally Littlefield is the hostess at ★ **Oakland House Seaside Resort** (435 Herrick Rd., Brooksville, 207/359-8521, www.oaklandhouse.com). Much of this rolling, wooded land, fronting on Eggemoggin Reach, was part of the original king's grant to her late husband Jim's ancestors, way back in 1765. Ten one- and two-bedroom nicely furnished and well-equipped cottages are tucked along the shoreline or in the trees. All but one have ocean views; five have kitchenettes, and four have full kitchens. One is pet-friendly ($10/night). Weekly rates begin around $900, varying with month and by cottage; nightly rates begin around $150. Other pluses are trails threading through the woods and providing access to viewpoints and a pocket beach.

Hostels

Sited on the lovely Oakland House Seaside

Resort grounds is **Hostel@Acorn by the Sea** (435 Herrick Rd., Brooksville, 207/359-8521, www.mainehostel.com), offering a mix of dorm-style, private, and semi-private rooms, with rates ranging from $30pp for a bunk to $75 for a private room with queen bed for two. Living spaces, bathrooms, and kitchen are shared. Linens and towels are provided.

Camping

With 730 feet of waterfront on Eggemoggin Reach and 16 wooded acres, **Oceanfront Camping @ Reach Knolls** (666 Reach Rd., Brooklin, 207/359-5555, www.reachknolls.com, $25-30, no credit cards) is a no-frills campground with 32 wooded sites. The camp office building has free Wi-Fi, free showers, and potable water; there is no water at the sites. The campground can accommodate RVs up to 35 feet in length, and electricity is available. There are privies and a dump station. A path leads to the pebbly beach, where you can launch a kayak.

FOOD

Local Flavors

The **Brooklin General Store** (1 Reach Rd., junction of Rte. 175 and Naskeag Point Rd., Brooklin, 207/359-8817), vintage 1872, carries groceries, beer and wine, newspapers, take-out sandwiches, and local chatter.

Millbrook Company bakery and restaurant (160 Snow's Cove. Rd./Rte. 15, 207/359-8344, www.millbrookcompany.com, Sedgwick, 7:30am-2pm Wed.-Sun.) is a good bet for reasonably priced breakfasts and lunches, as well as occasional dinners.

Lunch is the specialty at **Buck's Harbor Market** (Rte. 176, South Brooksville, 207/326-8683), a low-key, marginally gentrified general store popular with yachties in summer. Pick up sandwiches, cheeses, breads, and treats for a Holbrook Island adventure.

You often can find **Tinder Hearth's** (1452 Coastal Rd., Brooksville, 207/326-8381, http://tinderhearth.com) organic, wood-fired, European-style breads and croissants in local shops and at farmers markets, but you can buy it right at the bakery on Tuesday and Friday. In addition, call in advance to purchase thin-crust pizzas on Tuesday, Wednesday, and Friday evenings 5pm-8pm. It's on the western side of Route 176 north of the Cape Rosier Road. It's not well marked, so keep an eye out for the Open sign.

In North Brooksville, where Route 175/176 crosses the Bagaduce River, stands the

one of the cottages at the Oakland House Seaside Resort

Bagaduce Lunch (11am-7pm Thurs.-Tues, 11am-3pm Wed.), a take-out shack named an "American Classic" by the James Beard Foundation in 2008. Owners Judy and Mike Astbury buy local fish and clams. Check the tide calendar and go when the tide is changing; order a clam roll or a hamburger, settle in at a picnic table, and watch the reversing falls. If you're lucky, you might sight an eagle, osprey, or seal. The food is so-so, but the setting is tops.

Ethnic Fare

★ **El El Frijoles** (41 Caterpillar Rd./Rte. 15, Sargentville, 207/359-2486, www.elelfrijoles.com, 11am-7pm Wed.-Sat., $5-16)—that's *L. L. Beans* to you gringos—gets raves for its made-from-scratch California-style empanadas, burritos, and tacos, many of which have a Maine accent. Try the spicy lobster burritos or a daily special, such as ranchero shrimp tacos. Dine in the screen house or on picnic tables on the lawn; there's a play area for children.

El El Frijoles is a local favorite for Cal-Mex fare with a Maine accent.

Casual Dining

Behind the Buck's Harbor Market is ★ **Buck's Restaurant** (6 Cornfield Hill Rd., Brooksville, 207/326-8688, www.bucksrestaurant.weebly.com, 5:30pm-8:30pm Tues.-Sat., $22-32), where guests dine at white-clothed tables inside or on a screened porch. Chef Jonathan Chase's menu reflects what's locally available and changes nightly. Possibilities include Tuscan-style braised rabbit or Portuguese pork and clams. Service is excellent.

INFORMATION AND SERVICES

The best source of information about the region is the **Blue Hill Peninsula Chamber of Commerce** (207/374-2281, www.bluehillpeninsula.org).

Local **Penobscot Bay Press** (www.penobscotbaypress.com), which publishes a collection of local newspapers, also maintains an excellent site, with listings for area businesses as well as articles highlighting area happenings.

The **public libraries** in this area are small and welcoming, but hours are limited. Most have Wi-Fi and restrooms. **Friends Memorial Library** (Rte. 175, Brooklin, 207/359-2276) has a lovely Circle of Friends Garden, with benches and a brick patio. It's dedicated to the memory of longtime Brooklin residents E. B. and Katharine White. Also check out **Free Public Library** (1 Town House Rd./Rte. 176, Brooksville, 207/326-4560) and **Sedgwick Village Library** (Main St., Sedgwick, 207/359-2177).

GETTING THERE AND AROUND

Brooksville is about eight miles or 15 minutes via Route 15 from Castine. It's about 11 miles or 25 minutes to Deer Isle Village.

Castine

Castine (pop. 1,366) is a gem—a serene New England village with a tumultuous past. It tips a cape, surrounded by water on three sides, including the entrance to the Penobscot River, which made it a strategic defense point. Once beset by geopolitical squabbles, saluting the flags of three different nations (France, Britain, and Holland), its only crises now are local political skirmishes. This is an unusual community, a National Register of Historic Places enclave that many people never find. The town celebrated its bicentennial in 1996. Today a major presence is the Maine Maritime Academy, yet Castine remains the quietest college town imaginable. Students in search of a party school won't find it here; naval engineering is serious business.

What visitors discover is a year-round community with a busy waterfront, an easy-to-conquer layout, a handful of traditional inns, wooded trails on the outskirts of town, an astonishing collection of splendid Georgian and Federalist architecture, and water views nearly every which way you turn. If you're staying in Blue Hill or even Bar Harbor, spend a day here. Or book a room in one of the town's lovely inns, and use Castine as a base for exploring here and beyond. Either way, you won't regret it.

HISTORY

Originally known as Fort Pentagouet, Castine received its current name courtesy of Jean-Vincent d'Abbadie, Baron de St-Castin. A young French nobleman manqué who married a Wabanaki princess named Pidiwamiska, d'Abbadie ran the town in the second half of the 17th century and eventually returned to France.

A century later, in 1779, occupying British troops and their reinforcements scared off potential American seaborne attackers (including Col. Paul Revere), who turned tail up the Penobscot River and ended up scuttling their more than 40-vessel fleet—a humiliation known as the Penobscot Expedition and still regarded as one of the worst naval defeats for the United States.

When the boundaries for Maine were finally set in 1820, with the St. Croix River marking the east rather than the Penobscot River, the last British Loyalists departed, some floating their homes north to St. Andrews in New Brunswick, Canada, where they can still be seen today. For a while, peace and prosperity became the bywords for Castine—with lively commerce in fish and salt—but it all collapsed during the California gold rush and the Civil War trade embargo, leaving the town down on its luck.

Of the many historical landmarks scattered around town, one of the most intriguing must be the sign on "Wind Mill Hill," at the junction of Route 166 and State Street:

> On Hatch's Hill there stands a mill. Old Higgins he doth tend it. And every time he grinds a grist, he has to stop and mend it.

In smaller print, just below the rhyme, comes the drama:

> Here two British soldiers were shot for desertion.

Castine has quite a history indeed.

SIGHTS

★ Castine Historic Tour

To appreciate Castine fully, you need to arm yourself with the Castine Merchants Association's visitors brochure-map (all businesses and lodgings in town have copies) and follow the numbers on bike or on foot. With no stops, walking the route takes less than an hour, but you'll want to read dozens of historical plaques, peek into public buildings,

Maine Maritime Academy

the *State of Maine*, Maine Maritime Academy's training ship

The state's only merchant-marine college—one of only seven in the nation—occupies 35 acres in the middle of Castine. Founded in 1941, the academy awards undergraduate and graduate degrees in such areas as marine engineering, ocean studies, and marina management, preparing a student body of about 850 men and women for careers as ship captains, naval architects, and marine engineers.

The academy owns a fleet of 60 vessels, including the historic gaff-rigged research schooner *Bowdoin*, flagship of Arctic explorer Admiral Donald MacMillan, and the 499-foot training vessel *State of Maine*, berthed down the hill at the waterfront. In 1996-1997, the *State of Maine*, formerly the U.S. Navy hydrographic survey ship *Tanner*, underwent a $12 million conversion for use by the academy. It is still subject to deployment, and in 2005 the school quickly had to find alternate beds for students using the ship as a dormitory when it was called into service in support of rescue and rebuilding efforts after Hurricane Katrina in New Orleans. Midshipmen conduct free 30-minute **tours of the vessel** on weekdays in summer (mid-July-late Aug.). The schedule is posted at the dock, or call 207/326-4311 to check; photo ID is required.

Weekday **tours of the campus** can be arranged through the admissions office (207/326-2206 or 800/227-8465 outside Maine, www.mainemaritime.edu). Campus highlights include the three-story Nutting Memorial Library, in Platz Hall; the Henry A. Scheel Room, a cozy oasis in Leavitt Hall containing memorabilia from late naval architect Henry Scheel and his wife, Jeanne; and the well-stocked bookstore (Curtis Hall, 207/326-9333).

shoot some photos, and perhaps even do some shopping.

Highlights of the tour include the late-18th-century **John Perkins House,** moved to Perkins Street from Court Street in 1969 and restored with period furnishings. It's open in July-August for guided tours (2pm-5pm Sun. and Wed., $5).

Next door, **The Wilson Museum** (107 Perkins St., 207/326-8545, www.wilsonmuseum.org, 10am-5pm Mon.-Fri. and 2pm-5pm Sat.-Sun. late May-late Sept., free), founded in 1921, contains an intriguingly eclectic two-story collection of prehistoric artifacts, ship models, dioramas, baskets, tools, and minerals assembled over a lifetime by John Howard Wilson, a geologist-anthropologist who first visited Castine in 1891 (and died in 1936). Among the exhibits are Balinese masks, ancient oil lamps, cuneiform tablets,

Zulu artifacts, pre-Inca pottery, and assorted local findings.

Open the same days and hours as the Perkins House are the **Blacksmith Shop,** where a smith does demonstrations, and the **Hearse House,** containing Castine's 19th-century winter and summer funeral vehicles. Both have free admission.

At the end of Battle Avenue stands the 19th-century **Dyce's Head Lighthouse,** no longer operating; the keeper's house is owned by the town. Alongside it is a public path (signposted; pass at your own risk) leading via a wooden staircase to a tiny patch of rocky shoreline and the beacon that has replaced the lighthouse.

The highest point in town is **Fort George,** site of a 1779 British fortification. Nowadays, little remains except grassy earthworks, but there are interpretive displays and picnic tables.

Main Street, descending toward the water, is a feast for historic architecture fans. Artist Fitz Hugh Lane and author Mary McCarthy once lived in elegant houses along the elm-lined street (neither building is open to the public). On Court Street between Main and Green Streets stands turn-of-the-20th-century **Emerson Hall,** site of Castine's municipal offices. Since Castine has no official information booth, you may need to duck in here (it's open weekdays) for answers to questions.

Across Court Street, **Witherle Memorial Library,** a handsome early-19th-century building on the site of the 18th-century town jail, looks out on the Town Common. Also facing the Common are the Adams and Abbott Schools, the former still an elementary school. The **Abbott School** (10am-4pm Mon.-Sat., 1pm-4pm Sun. July-early Sept., reduced schedule spring and fall, donation), built in 1859, has been carefully restored for use as a museum and headquarters for the **Castine Historical Society** (207/326-4118, www.castinehistoricalsociety.org). A big draw at the volunteer-run museum is the 24-foot-long Bicentennial Quilt, assembled for Castine's 200th anniversary in 1996. The historical society, founded in 1966, organizes lectures, exhibits, and special events (some free) in various places around town.

On the outskirts of town, across the narrow neck between Wadsworth Cove and Hatch's Cove, stretches a rather overgrown canal (signposted British Canal) scooped out by the occupying British during the War of 1812. Effectively severing land access to the town of Castine, the Brits thus raised havoc, collected local revenues for eight months, then departed for Halifax with enough funds to establish Dalhousie College, now Dalhousie University. Wear waterproof boots to walk the canal route; the best time to go is at low tide.

If a waterfront picnic sounds appealing, settle in on the grassy earthworks along the harbor-front at **Fort Madison,** site of an 1808 garrison (then Fort Porter) near the corner of Perkins and Madockawando Streets. The views from here are fabulous, and it's accessible all year. A set of stairs leads down to the rocky waterfront.

ENTERTAINMENT AND EVENTS

Possibilities for live music include **Dennett's Wharf** (15 Sea St., 207/326-9045), where some performances require a ticket, and **Danny Murphy's Pub** (on the wharf, tucked underneath the bank and facing the parking area and harbor).

The **Castine Town Band** often performs free concerts on the Common; check www.castine.org for its schedule.

A different band performs on the Town Dock every Wednesday evening for free **Waterfront Wednesdays.**

The Wilson Museum (107 Perkins St., 207/326-8545, www.wilsonmuseum.org) frequently schedules concerts, lectures, and demonstrations.

The **Trinitarian Church** often brings in high-caliber musical entertainment.

Castine sponsors the intellectual side of the early August Wooden Boat Regatta, The **Castine Yacht Club** brings in a who's who of big-name sail-related designers and racers for this annual lecture series. Other events include on-the-dock boat tours and limited sailing opportunities.

Another source of intellectual stimulation is the **Castine Library,** which presents lectures and other programs.

Gardening fans should ask about **kitchen and garden tours,** which take place every few years.

SHOPPING

Clustered downtown along Castine's Main Street are **Gallery B** (5 Main St., 213/839-0851, www.gallerybgallery.com), showing fine art and crafts; **Lucky Hill** (15 Main St., 207/326-1066), a combination gallery and home-goods boutique; and the **Compass Rose Bookstore** (3 Main St., 207/326-8526.

Oil paintings by local artists Joshua and Susan Adam are on view at **Adam Gallery** (140 Battle Ave., 207/326-8272).

RECREATION

Witherle Woods

The 185-acre **Witherle Woods,** owned by the Maine Coast Heritage Trust (www.mcht.org), is a popular walking area with a 4.2-mile maze of trails and old woods roads leading to the water. Many Revolutionary War-era relics have been found here; if you see any, do not remove them. Access to the preserve is via a dirt road off of Battle Avenue, between the water district property (at the end of the wire fence) and the Manor's exit driveway and diagonally across from La Tour Street. You can download a map from the website.

★ Sea Kayaking

Right near Dennett's Wharf is **Castine Kayak Adventures** (17 Sea St., Castine, 207/866-3506, www.castinekayak.com), spearheaded by Maine Guide Karen Francoeur. All skill levels are accommodated; "Kayak Karen," as she's known locally, is particularly adept with beginners, delivering wise advice from beginning to end. Three-hour half-day trips are $55; six-hour full-day tours are around $105 and include lunch. Two-hour sunset tours are $45; the sunrise tour includes a light breakfast for $55. Friday and Saturday nights, there are special two-hour phosphorescence tours under the stars (weather permitting) for $55 per person. Longer trips are available for $150 per day. If you have your own boat, call Karen; she knows these waters. She offers instruction for all levels as well as a Maine Sea Kayak Guide course. Karen also rents bikes for $20 per day.

Swimming

Backshore Beach, a crescent of sand and gravel on Wadsworth Cove Road (turn off Battle Ave. at the Castine Golf Club), is a favorite saltwater swimming spot, with views across the bay to Stockton Springs. Be forewarned, though, that ocean swimming in this part of Maine is not for the timid. The best time to try it is on the incoming tide, after the sun has had time to heat up the mud. At mid- to high tide, it's also the best place to put in a sea kayak.

Golf

The nine-hole **Castine Golf Club** (200 Battle Ave., 207/326-8844, www.castinegolfclub.com) dates to 1897, when the first tee required a drive from a 30-step-high mound. Willie Park Jr. redesigned it in 1921.

Boat Excursions

Glide over Penobscot Bay aboard the handsome and quite comfortable wooden motor-sailer ***Guildive*** (207/701-1421, www.guildivecruises.com), constructed in 1934 and captained by Kate Kana and Zander Parker. Two-hour sails, departing up to three times daily from Dennett's Wharf, cost $45; sunset sails, which include a light appetizer, are $60.

ACCOMMODATIONS

Inns

Castine is not the place to come if you require in-room phones, air-conditioning, or fancy bathrooms. The pace is relaxed and the accommodations reflect the easy elegance of a bygone era.

The three-story Queen Anne-style ★ **Pentagöet Inn** (26 Main St., Castine, 207/326-8616 or 800/845-1701, www.pentagoet.com, May-late Oct., $135-295) is the perfect Maine summer inn, right down to the lace curtains billowing in the breeze, the soft floral wallpapers, and the intriguing curiosities that accent but don't clutter the guest rooms. Congenial innkeepers Jack Burke, previously with the U.S. Foreign Service, and Julie Van de Graaf, a pastry chef, took over the century-old inn in 2000 and have given it new life, upgrading rooms and furnishing them with Victorian antiques, adding handsome gardens, and carving out a niche as a dining destination. Their enthusiasm for the area is contagious. The inn's 16 guest rooms are spread between the main house (with Wi-Fi service) and the adjoining 1791 Federal-style Perkins House (newly renovated, with marble baths, Wi-Fi, and in-room TVs; pet-friendly). A hot buffet breakfast, afternoon refreshments, and evening hors d'oeuvres are provided. Jack holds court in the pub (chock-full of vintage photos and prints as well as exotic antiques), advising guests on activities and opportunities. Borrow one of the inn's bikes and explore around town or simply walk—the Main Street location is convenient to everything Castine offers. Better yet, just sit on the wraparound porch and take it all in.

In 2010, a group of local residents purchased the venerable **Castine Inn** (41 Main St., Castine, 207/326-4365, www.castineinn.com, $150-235), with 19 second- and third-floor guest rooms and suites; some have water views; a few are air-conditioned. Public space includes a formal living room as well as a wraparound porch overlooking the gardens. Wi-Fi is available in public areas, as is a TV. Breakfast ($9 guests, $10 public) is served in the dining room, which features a wraparound mural of Castine.

Rental Properties

Several Castine real estate agents have listings for summer cottage rentals; start with **Saltmeadow Properties** (7 Main St., Castine, 207/326-9116, www.saltmeadowproperties.com).

FOOD

Local Flavors

The **Castine Farmers Market** takes place on the Town Common 9am-11:30am Thursday.

Dudley's Refresher (Town Dock, 207/812-3800, www.dudleysrefresher.com), a waterfront take-out stand, is an excellent bet

the Pentagöet Inn

for summer classics such as fish-and-chips and lobster rolls. You can't beat the location or the view, and much of the menu is locally sourced and made from scratch.

Your best bet for late-night eats is **Danny Murphy's Pub** (2 Sea St., on the wharf, tucked underneath the bank facing the parking area and harbor, 207/326-1004, 11am-1am daily), a sports bar, with video games, a pool table, and frequent live entertainment. Opt for the pizza.

On a warm summer day, it's hard to find a better place to while away a few hours than **Dennett's Wharf** (15 Sea St., 207/326-9045, www.dennettswharf.net, 11am-11pm daily May-mid-Oct., $10-30), and that's likely what you'll do here, as service can be slow. Next to the town dock, it's a colorful barn of a place with an outside deck and front-row windjammer-watching seats in summer. The best advice is to keep your order simple.

MarKel's Bakehouse (26 Water St., Castine, 207/326-9510, www.markelsbakehouse.com, 7am-3pm daily), a higgledy-piggledy eatery of three rooms and a deck at the end of an alleyway tucked between Main and Water Streets, is a delicious find for breakfast, lunch, or sweets. Stop here for coffee, cold juices, pastries, interesting snacks and salads, homemade soups, specials, and delicious sandwiches.

Former pig farmer and barbecue aficionado Eric Gingerella combines his knowledge and passion at **Gingerella's Bar B Q** (14 Water St., 207/326-2350, from 11am Tues.-Sun.). Eat in or walk the half-block to waterfront picnic tables.

Casual Dining

Jazz music plays softly and dinner is by candlelight at the ★ **Pentagöet** (26 Main St., Castine, 207/326-8616 or 800/845-1701, www.pentagoet.com, from 6pm Tues.-Sat., entrées $16-30). In fine weather you can dine on the porch. Choices vary from pan-roasted halibut to port-braised lamb shanks, or simply make a meal of bistro plates, such as lamb lollipops and crab cakes and a salad. Don't miss the lobster bouillabaisse or the chocolate *budino*, a scrumptious warm Italian pudding that melts in your mouth (a must for chocoholics). On Tuesday nights, there's live jazz on the porch during dinner as well as porch specials menu from 5-6:30pm.

Snag a seat on the waterfront deck at Dennett's Wharf.

INFORMATION AND SERVICES

Castine has no local information office, but all businesses and lodgings in town have copies of the Castine Merchants Association's visitor's brochure-map. For additional information, go to the **Castine Town Office** (Emerson Hall, 67 Court St., 207/326-4502, www.castine.me.us, 8am-3:30pm Mon.-Fri.).

Check out **Witherle Memorial Library** (41 School St., 207/326-4375, www.witherle.lib.me.us). Also accessible to the public is the Nutting Memorial Library, in Platz Hall on the Maine Maritime Academy campus.

Find **public restrooms** by the dock, at the foot of Main Street.

GETTING THERE AND AROUND

Castine is about 16 miles or 25 minutes via Routes 1, 175, and 166 from Bucksport. It's about 20 miles or 35 minutes via Routes 166, 199, and 175 from Blue Hill.

Deer Isle

"Deer Isle is like Avalon," wrote John Steinbeck in *Travels with Charley*—"it must disappear when you are not there." **Deer Isle,** the name of both the island and its midpoint town, has been romancing authors and artisans for decades, but it is unmistakably real to the quarrymen and fishermen who've been here for centuries. These longtimers are a sturdy lot, as Steinbeck recognized: "I would hate to try to force them to do anything they didn't want to do."

Early-18th-century maps show no name for the island, but by the late 1800s nearly 100 families lived here, supporting themselves first by farming, then by fishing. In 1789, when Deer Isle was incorporated, 80 local sailing vessels were scouring the Gulf of Maine in pursuit of mackerel and cod, and Deer Isle men were circling the globe as yachting skippers and merchant seamen. At the same time, in the once-quiet village of Green's Landing (now called Stonington), the shipbuilding and granite industries boomed, spurring development, prosperity, and the kinds of rough high jinks typical of commercial ports the world over.

Green's Landing became the "big city" for an international crowd of quarrymen carving out the terrain on Deer Isle and nearby Crotch Island, source of high-quality granite for Boston's Museum of Fine Arts, the Smithsonian Institution, a humongous fountain for John D. Rockefeller's New York estate, and less showy projects all along the eastern seaboard. The heyday is long past, but the industry did extend into the 20th century (including a contract for the pink granite at President John F. Kennedy's Arlington National Cemetery gravesite). Today, Crotch Island is the site

lobster boats in Stonington Harbor

Deer Isle

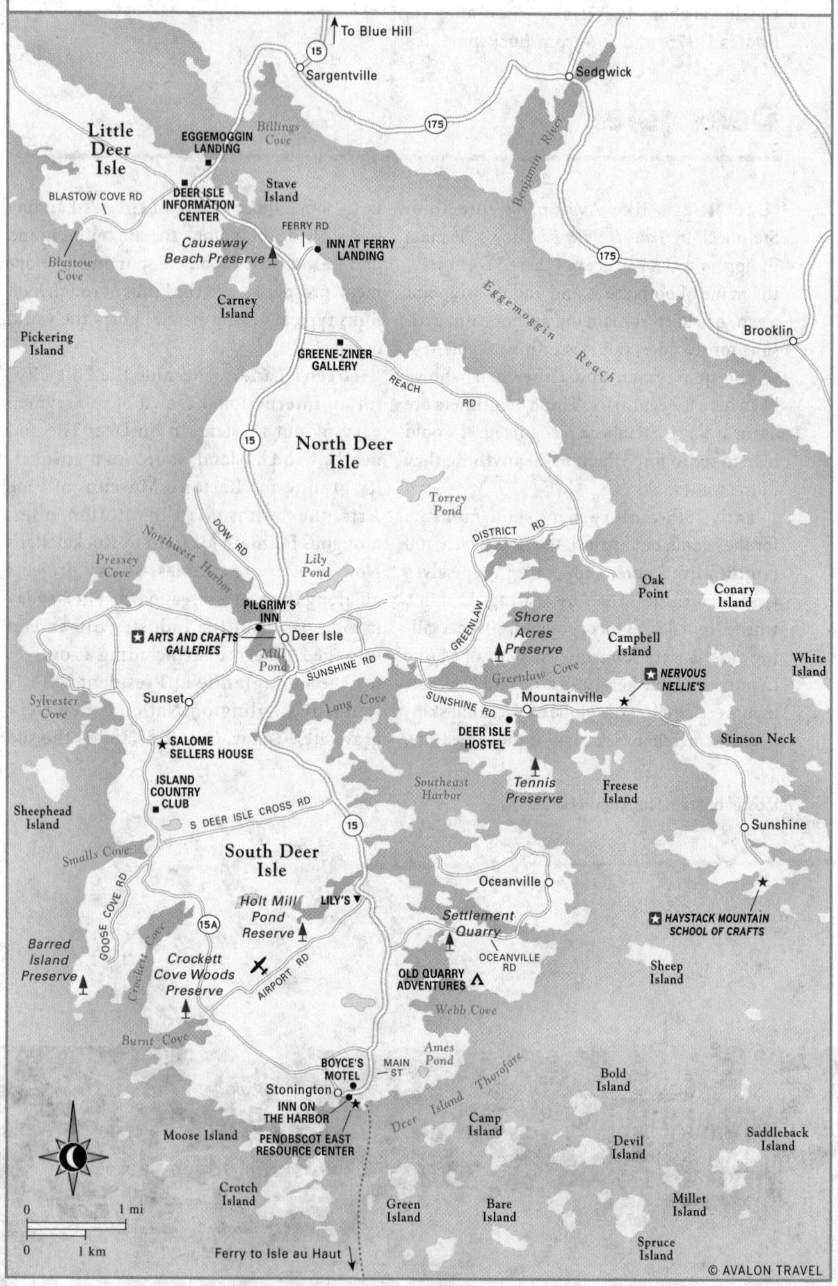
To Blue Hill
15
Sargentville
Sedgwick
175
Benjamin River
Little Deer Isle
EGGEMOGGIN LANDING
Billings Cove
DEER ISLE INFORMATION CENTER
Stave Island
BLASTOW COVE RD
Blastow Cove
FERRY RD
Causeway Beach Preserve
INN AT FERRY LANDING
Carney Island
Pickering Island
Eggemoggin Reach
Brooklin
GREENE-ZINER GALLERY
REACH RD
North Deer Isle
Torrey Pond
DOW RD
DISTRICT RD
Northwest Harbor
Pressey Cove
Lily Pond
Oak Point
Conary Island
PILGRIM'S INN
ARTS AND CRAFTS GALLERIES
Deer Isle
Mill Pond
GREENLAW
Shore Acres Preserve
Campbell Island
White Island
SUNSHINE RD
Greenlaw Cove
NERVOUS NELLIE'S
Sylvester Cove
Sunset
Long Cove
Mountainville
DEER ISLE HOSTEL
SALOME SELLERS HOUSE
Stinson Neck
ISLAND COUNTRY CLUB
Southeast Harbor
Tennis Preserve
Freese Island
Sheephead Island
S DEER ISLE CROSS RD
Sunshine
Smalls Cove
South Deer Isle
GOOSE COVE RD
Oceanville
Holt Mill Pond Reserve
LILY'S
15A
Settlement Quarry
HAYSTACK MOUNTAIN SCHOOL OF CRAFTS
Barred Island Preserve
Crockett Cove
Crockett Cove Woods Preserve
AIRPORT RD
OCEANVILLE RD
OLD QUARRY ADVENTURES
Sheep Island
Webb Cove
Burnt Cove
Ames Pond
BOYCE'S MOTEL
MAIN ST
Deer Island Thorofare
Bold Island
Stonington
INN ON THE HARBOR
Camp Island
Moose Island
PENOBSCOT EAST RESOURCE CENTER
Devil Island
Saddleback Island
Crotch Island
Green Island
Bare Island
Millet Island
0
1 mi
0
1 km
Ferry to Isle au Haut
Spruce Island
© AVALON TRAVEL

one of sculptor Peter Beerits's creations at Nervous Nellie's

of Maine's only operating island granite quarry.

Measuring about nine miles north to south (plus another three miles for Little Deer Isle), the island of Deer Isle today has a handful of hamlets (including **Sunshine, Sunset, Mountainville,** and **Oceanville**) and two towns—**Stonington** (pop. 1,043) and **Deer Isle** (pop. 1,975). Road access is via Route 15 on the Blue Hill Peninsula. A huge suspension bridge, built in 1939 over Eggemoggin Reach, links the Sargentville section of Sedgwick with Little Deer Isle; from there, a sinuous 0.4-mile causeway connects to the northern tip of Deer Isle.

Deer Isle remains an artisans' enclave, anchored by the Haystack Mountain School of Crafts. Studios and galleries are plentiful, although many require tooling along back roads to find them. Stonington, a rough-and-tumble fishing port with an idyllic setting, is slowly being gentrified, as each season more and more galleries and upscale shops open for the summer. Locals are holding their collective breaths, hoping that any improvements don't change the town too much (although most visitors could do without the car racing on Main Street at night). Already, real-estate prices and accompanying taxes have escalated way past the point where many a local fisherman can hope to buy, and in some cases maintain, a home.

SIGHTS

Sightseeing on Deer Isle means exploring back roads, browsing the galleries, walking the trails, hanging out on the docks, and soaking in the ambience.

★ Haystack Mountain School of Crafts

The renowned **Haystack Mountain School of Crafts** (Sunshine Rd., Deer Isle, 207/348-2306, www.haystack-mtn.org) in Sunshine is open to the public on a limited basis, but if it fits into your schedule, go. Anyone can visit the school store or walk down the central stairs to the water; to see more of the campus, take a tour (1pm Wed., $5), which includes a video, viewing works on display, and the opportunity to visit some studios. Beyond that, there are slide programs, lectures, demonstrations, and concerts presented by faculty and visiting artists on varying weeknights early June-late August. Perhaps the best opportunities are the end-of-session auctions, held on Thursday night every 2-3 weeks, when you can tour the studios for free at 7pm before the auction at 8pm. It's a great opportunity to buy craftwork at often very reasonable prices.

★ Nervous Nellie's

Part museum, part gallery, part jelly kitchen, and part tearoom: **Nervous Nellie's** (600 Sunshine Rd., Deer Isle, 800/777-6845, www.nervousnellies.com, free) is all that and more. Most visitors come to purchase the hand-produced jams and jellies and, perhaps, watch them being made. Once here, they discover sculptor Peter Beerits's "natural history museum of the imagination." Beerits, who has an MFA in sculpture, has built a fantasy world

The Maine Island Trail

In the early 1980s, a "trail" of coastal Maine islands was only the germ of an idea. By the end of the millennium, the **Maine Island Trail Association** (MITA) counted some 4,000 members dedicated to conscientious (i.e., low- or no-impact) recreational use of more than 180 public and private islands along 375 miles of Maine coastline from the New Hampshire border to Machias Bay. Access to the trail is only by private boat, and the best choice is a sea kayak, to navigate shallow or rock-strewn coves.

The trail's publicly owned islands—supervised by the state Bureau of Public Lands—are open to anyone; the private islands are restricted to MITA members, who pay $45/individual or $65/family/year for the privilege (and, it's important to add, the responsibility). With the fee comes the **Maine Island Trail Guidebook,** providing directions and information for each of the islands. With membership comes the expectation of care and concern. "Low impact" means different things to different people, so MITA experienced acute growing pains when enthusiasm began leading to "tent sprawl."

To cope with and reverse the overuse, MITA has created an "adopt-an-island" program, in which volunteers become stewards for specific islands and keep track of their use and condition. MITA members are urged to pick up trash, use tent platforms where they exist, and continue elsewhere if an island has reached its assigned capacity (stipulated on a shoreline sign and/or in the guidebook).

Membership information is available from the **Maine Island Trail Association** (207/761-8225, www.mita.org).

that's rooted in his boyhood and complements *The Nervous Nellie Story,* his comic-book-format illustrated series. "Ten years ago, I was primarily an artist who exhibited works in galleries. Now I'm primarily a museum curator," he says.

The buildings, fields, gardens, and woods are filled with interactive scenes and whimsical wood and metal sculptures Beerits has created from the flotsam and jetsam of everyday island life—farming implements, household furnishings, and industrial whatnots—what Beerits calls "good junk from the dump." Take a closer look at that dragon frolicking in the meadow. Its tail and legs are culled from four pianos, the scales are backhoe teeth, the claws are roof-ladder hooks, the neck is a potato harvester, and the head is a radar dish.

There's an interactive Western Town complete with a hotel, a Chinese laundry, a jail, a fortune-teller, a sheriff's office, blacksmith shop, and the Silver Dollar Saloon. Inside the saloon, Wild Bill Hickok is playing his last hand of cards, his back to a gunman sneaking through the back door. "Hickok made the mistake one time of sitting with his back to a door, not the wall," Beerits says, adding that the hand he holds, two aces and two eights, is now known as a dead man's hand in poker. It's that kind of detail that adds a touch of reality to the scenes, and it's the opportunity to grab a seat at the table that engages visitors and keeps the cameras clicking. The West fades into the Mississippi Delta, where blues music draws visitors into Red's Lounge, where a pianist and guitarist crank out the blues, while a couple flirts in a corner booth.

Beerits moved the original Hardy's Store here. Like a living-history museum, it provides a glimpse into island life decades ago. No detail is overlooked, from the red hot dogs and buns in the steamer to the pickled eggs on the counter, from Neville Hardy at the register to the women seated out front eyeing the gas pump. As in every exhibit, fans have left notes, often illustrated, sharing their thoughts and impressions.

Many visitors take in these sights and then settle into the café for a snack, not realizing that there's more to see. In the woods behind, King Arthur's knights in shining armor, some larger than life, guard and inhabit the Grail

Castle. A feast is in progress, and the Grail maidens are parading through the hall bearing holy objects. Continue down the path, and you'll arrive at a woodlands church, another of Beerits' projects.

You can easily spend an hour here, and there's no admission; wander freely. Beerits will gladly explain his creations, if he's free. The property is also home to **Nervous Nellie's Jams and Jellies,** known for outstanding, creative condiments. You can peek into the kitchen to see the jams being made. The best time to come is 9am-5pm daily May-early October, when the shop operates the casual **Mountainville Café,** serving tea, coffee, and delicious scones—with, of course, delicious Nervous Nellie's products; sampling is encouraged. Stock up, because they're sold in only a few shops. Also sold is a small, well-chosen selection of Maine products. Really, trust me, you must visit this place.

Historic Houses and Museums

There's more to the 1830 **Salome Sellers House** (416 Sunset Rd./Rte. 15A, Sunset Village, 207/348-6400, www.dis-historical-society.org, 1pm-4pm Wed., Thurs., Fri., mid-June-mid-Sept., donation) than first meets the eye. A repository of local memorabilia, archives, and intriguing artifacts, it's also the headquarters of the **Deer Isle-Stonington Historical Society.** Sellers, matriarch of an island family, was a direct descendant of *Mayflower* settlers. She lived to be 108, a lifetime spanning 1800-1908, earning the record for oldest recorded Maine resident. The house contains Sellers's furnishings, and in a small exhibit space in the rear is a fine exhibit of baskets made by Maine Native Americans. Behind the house are the archives, heritage gardens, and an exhibit hall filled with nautical artifacts. Bringing all this to life are enthusiastic volunteer guides, many of them island natives. They love to provide tidbits about various items; seafarers' logs and ship models are particularly intriguing, and don't miss the 1920s peapod, the original lobster boat on the island. The house is just north of the Island Country Club and across from Eaton's Plumbing. Hours vary season to season; call for current schedule.

Close to the Stonington waterfront, the **Deer Isle Granite Museum** (51 Main St., Stonington, 207/367-6331, www.deerisle-granitemuseum.org, 9am-5pm Sat.-Tues. and Thurs. July-Aug.) was established to commemorate the centennial of the quarrying business hereabouts. The best feature of the small museum is a 15-foot-long working model of Crotch Island, center of the industry, as it appeared at the turn of the 20th century. Flatcars roll, boats glide, and derricks move—it all looks very real. Donations are welcome.

Another downtown Stonington attraction is a Lilliputian complex known as the **Miniature Village.** Beginning in 1947, the late Everett Knowlton created a dozen and a half replicas of local buildings and displayed them on granite blocks in his yard. Since his death, they've been restored and put on display each summer in town—along with a donation box to support the upkeep. The village is set up on East Main Street (Rte. 15), below Hoy Gallery.

Pumpkin Island Light

A fine view of Pumpkin Island Light can be had from the cul-de-sac at the end of the Eggemoggin Road on Little Deer Isle. If heading south on Route 15, bear right at the information booth after crossing the bridge and continue to the end.

Penobscot East Resource Center

The purpose of the **Penobscot East Resource Center** (13 Atlantic Ave., Stonington, 207/367-2708, www.penobscoteast.org, 10am-4pm Mon.-Fri.) is "to energize and facilitate responsible community-based fishery management, collaborative marine science, and sustainable economic development to benefit the fishermen and the communities of Penobscot Bay and the Eastern Gulf of Maine." Bravo to that! At the center are educational displays and interactive exhibits, including a touch tank, highlighting Maine fisheries and the Gulf of Maine ecosystem. One of the driving forces behind the venture is Ted Ames, who won a $500,000 MacArthur Fellowship "genius grant" in 2005.

ENTERTAINMENT AND EVENTS

Stonington's National Historic Landmark, the 1912 **Opera House** (207/367-2788, www.operahousearts.org), is home to Opera House Arts, which hosts films, plays, lectures, concerts, family programs, and workshops year-round.

Bird-watchers flock to Deer Isle in mid-May for the annual **Wings, Waves & Woods Weekend** (www.deerisle.com).

Mid-June, when lupines in various shades of pink and purple seem to be blooming everywhere, brings the **Lupine Festival** (www.deerisle.com), a weekend event that includes art openings and shows, boat rides, a private garden tour, and entertainment ranging from a contra dance to movies.

Early July-September is the season for **First Friday,** an open-house night held on the first Friday evening of each month, with demonstrations, music, and refreshments sponsored by the Stonington Galleries (www.stoningtongalleries.com).

Mid-July brings the **Stonington Lobsterboat Races** (207/348-2804), very popular competitions held in the harbor, with lots of possible vantage points. Stonington is one of the major locales in the lobster-boat race circuit.

The **Peninsula Potters Studio Tour and Sale** (www.peninsulapotters.com) is held in October, when more than a dozen potters from Blue Hill to Stonington welcome visitors.

Want to meet locals and learn more about the area? **Island Heritage Trust** (www.islandheritagetrust.org) sponsors a series of walks, talks, and tours late May-mid-September. For information and reservations, call 207/348-2455.

SHOPPING

The greatest concentration of shops is in Stonington, where galleries, clothing boutiques, and eclectic shops line Main Street.

In "downtown" Deer Isle Village, Candy and Jim Eaton now operate **The Periwinkle** (8 Main St., Deer Isle, 207/348-2256), stocking it with a fun mix of books, handcrafts, and niceties.

Just beyond the Opera House, **Dockside**

the Opera House in Stonington

Books & Gifts (62 W. Main St., Stonington, 207/367-2652) carries just what its name promises, with a specialty in marine and Maine books. The rustic two-room shop has spectacular harbor views.

Shoppers need to be cautious going into **The Dry Dock** (24 Main St., Stonington, 207/367-5528), where the merchandise instantly sells itself. Imported women's clothing from Nigerian, Tibetan, and Indian cottage industries; unique jewelry; and unusual notecards are just some of the options in one large room and a smaller back room.

★ Arts and Crafts Galleries

Thanks to the presence and influence of Haystack Mountain School of Crafts, supertalented artists and artisans lurk in every corner of the island. Most galleries are tucked away on back roads, so watch for roadside signs. Many have studios open to the public where you can watch the artists at work. **Deer Isle Galleries and Studios** (deerislegalleriesandstudios.com) usually present monthly art openings; check the site for details. Here is a sampling of galleries.

LITTLE DEER ISLE

Alfred's Roost (360 Eggemoggin Rd., 207/348-6699) is a fun gallery and working glass studio in an old schoolhouse. Ask Dusty Eagen to share mascot Alfred Peabody's life story.

DEER ISLE

The **Greene-Ziner Gallery** (73 Reach Rd., 207/348-2601, www.melissagreene.com) is a double treat. Melissa Greene turns out incredible painted and incised pottery—she's represented in the Smithsonian's Renwick Gallery—and Eric Ziner works magic in metal sculpture and furnishings. Your budget may not allow for one of Melissa's pots (in the four-digit range), but I guarantee you'll covet them. The gallery also displays the work of several other local artists.

The **Hutton Gallery** (89 N. Deer Isle Rd./Rte. 15, 207/348-6171, www.huttongallery.com) offers a nice range of fine art and craft work, including prints, jewelry, paintings, basketry, glass, and fiber art.

The **Frederica Marshall Gallery** (81 N. Deer Isle Rd., 207/348-2782, www.fredericamarshall.com) is a multifaceted find. Marshall is a master brush painter who delights in explaining Japanese sumi-e work and demonstrating the brushes that vary from a cat's whisker to four horsetails in size. She also has a classroom and offers workshops ranging from two hours to four days in length. Her husband, Herman Kidder, operates **Kidder Forge** on the same property. His knives forged from old tools are available in the gallery.

One of the island's premier galleries is Elena Kubler's **The Turtle Gallery** (61 N. Deer Isle Rd./Rte. 15, 207/348-9977, www.turtlegallery.com), in a handsome space formerly known as the Old Centennial House Barn (owned by the late Haystack director Francis Merritt) and the adjacent farmhouse. Group and solo shows of contemporary paintings, prints, and crafts are hung upstairs and down in the barn; works by gallery artists are in the farmhouse; and there's usually sculpture in the gardens both in front and in back. It's just north of Deer Isle Village, across from the Shakespeare School.

The **Dowstudio Gallery** (19 Dow Rd., 207/348-6498, www.dowstudiodeerisle.com) shows pottery, metalwork, jewelry, prints, and drawings by Ellen Wieske, Carole Ann Fer, and other artists and artisans.

In the village, **Deer Isle Artists Association** (5 Main St., 207/348-2330, www.deerisleartists.com) features two-week exhibits of paintings, prints, drawings, and photos by member artists.

Just a bit south is **John Wilkinson Sculpture** (41 Church St., 207/348-2363, www.sculptor1.com), open by chance or appointment. Wilkinson works in concrete, wood, and plaster.

Detour down Sunshine Road to view sculptor **Peter Beerits Sculpture at Nervous Nellie's** (600 Sunshine Rd.,

800/777-6845, www.nervousnellies.com), a world of whimsy that will entertain all ages, and if the timing works, catch the Wednesday tour at Haystack.

STONINGTON

Cabinetmaker Geoffrey Warner features his work at **Geoffrey Warner Studio** (431 N. Main St., 207/367-6555, www.geoffreywarner-studio.com). Warner mixes classic techniques with contemporary styles and Eastern, nature-based, and arts and crafts accents to create some unusual and rather striking pieces. He also crafts the budget-friendly ergonomic Owl stool as well as offers kits and workshops.

The **Watson Gallery** (68 Main St., 207/367-2900, www.gwatsongallery.com) is a fine-art gallery representing a number of top-notch painters and printmakers. Occasionally it hosts live performances.

More paintings, many in bold, bright colors, can be found at Jill Hoy's **Hoy Gallery** (80 Main St., 207/367-2368, www.jillhoy.com).

On the other end of Main Street, **Marlinespike Chandlery** (58 W. Main St., 207/348-2521, www.marlinespike.com) specializes in rope work, both practical and fancy.

A bit off the beaten path but worth seeking out is the **Siri Beckman Studio** (115 Airport Rd., 207/367-5037, www.siribeckman.com), Beckman's home studio-gallery featuring her woodcuts, prints, and watercolors.

RECREATION

Parks and Preserves

Foresighted benefactors have managed to set aside precious acreage for respectful public use on Deer Isle. The Nature Conservancy (207/729-5181, www.nature.org) owns two properties: **Crockett Cove Woods Preserve** and **Barred Island Preserve.** The conscientious steward of other local properties is the **Island Heritage Trust** (420 Sunset Rd., Sunset, 207/348-2455, www.islandheritagetrust.org, 8am-4pm Mon.-Fri.). At the office you can pick up notecards, photos, T-shirts, and helpful maps and information on hiking trails and nature preserves. Proceeds benefit the Island Heritage Trust's efforts; donations are appreciated.

SETTLEMENT QUARRY

Here's one of the easiest, shortest walks in the area, leading to an impressive vista. From the parking lot on Oceanville Road (just under one mile off Rte. 15), marked by a carved granite sign, it's about five minutes to the top of the old **Settlement Quarry,** where the viewing platform (a.k.a. the "throne room") takes in the panorama—all the way to the Camden Hills on a good day. In early August, wild raspberries are an additional enticement. Three short loop trails lead into the surrounding woods from here. A map is available in the trailhead box.

EDGAR TENNIS PRESERVE

The 145-acre **Edgar Tennis Preserve,** off Sunshine Road, has very limited parking, so don't try to squeeze in if there isn't room; schedule your visit for another hour or day. But do go, and bring at least a snack if not a full picnic to enjoy on one of the convenient rocky outcroppings (carry out what you carry in). Allow at least 90 minutes to enjoy the walking trails, one of which skirts Pickering Cove, providing sigh-producing views. Another trail leads to an old cemetery. Parts of the trails can be wet, so wear appropriate footwear. Bring binoculars for bird-watching. The preserve is open sunrise-sunset. To find it, take Sunshine Road 2.5 miles to Tennis Road and follow it to the preserve.

SHORE ACRES PRESERVE

The 38-acre **Shore Acres Preserve,** a gift in 2000 from Judy Hill to the Island Heritage Trust, comprises old farmland, woodlands, clam flats, a salt marsh, and granite shorefront. Three walking trails connect in a 1.5-mile loop, with the Shore Trail section edging Greenlaw Cove. As you walk along the waterfront, look for the islands of Mount Desert rising in the distance and seals basking on offshore ledges. Do not walk across the salt marsh, and try to avoid stepping on beach plants. To find the preserve, take Sunshine Road 1.2 miles and then bear left at the fork onto Greenlaw District Road. The preserve's parking area is just shy of one mile down the road. Park only in the parking area, not on the paved road.

CROCKETT COVE WOODS PRESERVE

Donated to The Nature Conservancy by benevolent eco-conscious local artist Emily Muir, 98-acre **Crockett Cove Woods Preserve** is Deer Isle's natural gem—a coastal fog forest laden with lichens and mosses. Four interlinked walking trails cover the whole preserve, starting with a short nature trail. Pick up the helpful map-brochure at the registration box. Wear rubberized shoes or boots, and respect adjacent private property. The preserve is open sunrise-sunset daily year-round. From Deer Isle Village, take Route 15A to Sunset Village. Go 2.5 miles to Whitman Road and then to Fire Lane 88.

BARRED ISLAND PRESERVE

Owned by The Nature Conservancy but managed by the Island Heritage Trust, **Barred Island Preserve** was donated by Carolyn Olmsted, grandniece of noted landscape architect Frederick Law Olmsted, who summered nearby. A former owner of adjacent Goose Cove Lodge donated an additional 48 acres of maritime boreal fog forest. A single walking trail, one mile long, leads from the parking lot to the point. At low tide, and when eagles aren't nesting, you can continue out to Barred Island. Another trail skirts the shoreline of Goose Cove, before retreating inland and rejoining the main trail. From a high point on the main trail, you can see more than a dozen islands, many of which are protected from development, as well as Saddleback Ledge Light, 14 miles distant. To get to the preserve, follow Route 15A to Goose Cove Road and then continue to the parking area on the right. If it's full, return another day.

HOLT MILL POND PRESERVE

The Stonington Conservation Commission administers the town-owned **Holt Mill Pond Preserve,** where more than 47 bird species have been identified (bring binoculars). It comprises four habitats: upland spruce forest, lowland spruce-mixed forest, freshwater marsh, and saltwater marsh. A self-guiding nature trail is accessible off the Airport Road (off Route 15 at the intersection with Lily's Café). Look for the Nature Trail sign just beyond the medical center. The detailed self-guiding trail brochure, available at the trailhead registration kiosk, is accented with drawings by noted artist Siri Beckman.

AMES POND

Ames Pond is neither park nor preserve, but it might as well be. On a back road close to Stonington, it's a mandatory stop in July-August, when the pond wears a blanket of pink and white water lilies. From downtown Stonington, take Indian Point Road just under a mile east to the pond.

CAUSEWAY BEACH AND SCOTT'S LANDING

If you're itching to dip your toes into the water, stop by **Causeway Beach** along the causeway linking Little Deer Isle to Deer Isle. It's popular for swimming and is also a significant habitat for birds and other wildlife. On the other side of Route 15 is **Scott's Landing,** with more than 20 acres of fields, trails, and shorefront.

ED WOODSUM PRESERVE AT MARSHALL ISLAND

The Maine Coast Heritage Trust (www.mcht.org) owns 985-acre **Marshall Island,** the largest undeveloped island on the eastern seaboard. Since acquiring it in 2003, the trust has added 10 miles of hiking trails. After exploring, picnic on Sand Cove beach on the southeastern shore. **Old Quarry Ocean Adventures** (Stonington, 207/367-8977, mobile 207/266-7778, www.oldquarry.com) offers full-day trips on select dates for $50/

person. Or, charter a trip aboard Captain Steve Johnson's **Bert & I** (207/460-8679). Johnson will transport you to Marshall on weekends for about $140 pp round-trip plus $35 pp for each additional person or hour. Primitive camping is available by **reservation** (207/729-7366) at designated sites; fires require a **permit** (207/827-1800).

Sporting Outfitters and Guided Trips

The biggest operation is **Old Quarry Ocean Adventures** (Stonington, 207/367-8977, www.oldquarry.com), with a broad range of outdoor adventure choices. Bill Baker's ever-expanding enterprise rents canoes, kayaks, sailboats, bikes, moorings, platform tent sites, and cabins. Bicycle rentals are $23 per day or $113 per week. Sea-kayak rentals are $72 per day for a single, $90 for a tandem. Half-day rates (based on a four-hour rental) are $52 and $70, respectively. Overnight 24-hour rental is available for a 10 percent surcharge. Other options include canoes, rowboats, and sailboats; check the website for details. For all boat rentals, you must demonstrate competency in the vessel. They'll deliver and pick up anywhere on the island for a fee of $31 each way. All-day guided sea-kayaking tours are $135 per person; half-day is $68 per person. Plenty of other options are available, including sunset tours and family trips.

A Registered Maine Guide leads overnight kayaking camping trips on nearby islands. Rates, for kayak rental and guide, begin around $300 per adult for one night, with a three-person minimum; add meals for $8 per person. If you're bringing your own kayak, you can park your car ($7/night up to 2 nights, $6/night for 3 or more nights) and launch from here ($5/boat for launching); they'll take your trash and any trash you find. Old Quarry is off the Oceanville Road, less than a mile from Route 15, just before you reach the Settlement Quarry preserve. It's well signposted.

Guided Walks

The **Island Heritage Trust** (402 Sunset Rd., Sunset, 207/348-2455, www.islandheritagetrust.org), along with the Stonington and Deer Isle Conservation Commissions, sponsors a Walks and Talks series. Guided walks cover topics such as "Bird Calls for Beginners," "Salt Marsh Ecology," and "Butterflies, Bees, and Biodiversity." Call for information and reservations.

The nooks and crannies along Deer Isle's coastline are best explored by sea kayak.

Sea Kayaking

The waters around Deer Isle, with lots of islets and protected coves, are extremely popular for sea kayaking, especially off Stonington.

If you sign up with the **Maine Island Trail Association** (207/761-8225, www.mita.org, $45/year), you'll receive a handy manual that steers you to more than a dozen islands in the Deer Isle archipelago where you can camp, hike, and picnic—eco-sensitively, please. Boat traffic can be a bit heavy at the height of summer, so to best appreciate the tranquility of this area, try this in September after the Labor Day holiday. Nights can be cool, but days are likely to be brilliant. Remember that this is a working harbor.

The six-mile paddle from Stonington to Isle au Haut is best left to experienced paddlers, especially since fishing folks refer to kayakers as "speed bumps."

Swimming

The island's only major freshwater swimming hole is the **Lily Pond,** northeast of Deer Isle Village. Just north of the Shakespeare School, turn into the Deer Run Apartments complex. Park and take the path to the pond, which has a shallow area for small children.

Golf and Tennis

About two miles south of Deer Isle Village, watch for the large sign (on the left) for the **Island Country Club** (Rte. 15A, Sunset, 207/348-2379, early June-late Sept.), a nine-hole public course that has been here since 1928. Also at the club are three Har-Tru tennis courts. The club's cheeseburgers and salads are among the island's best bargain lunches.

Excursion Boats

ISLE AU HAUT BOAT COMPANY

The *Miss Lizzie* departs at 2pm Monday-Saturday mid-June-mid September from the **Isle au Haut Boat Company** (Seabreeze Ave., Stonington, 207/367-5193 or 207/367-6516, www.isleauhaut.com) dock in Stonington for a narrated 1.25-hour Lobster Fishing Scenic Cruise, during which the crew hauls a string of lobster traps. Cost is $22 adults, $8 under age 12. Special puffin and lighthouse cruises are offered on a limited basis. Another option is to cruise over and back to Isle au Haut without stepping foot off the boat ($22 adults). Reservations are advisable, especially in July-August. Dockside parking is around $10, or find a spot in town and save the surcharge.

★ GUIDED ISLAND TOURS

Captain Walter Reed's **Guided Island Tours** (207/348-6789, www.guidedislandtours.com) aboard the *Gael* are custom designed for a maximum of four passengers. Walt is a Registered Maine Guide and professional biologist who also is a steward for Mark Island Lighthouse and several uninhabited islands in the area. He provides in-depth perspective and the local scoop. The cost is $35 pp for the first hour plus $25 pp for each additional hour (no credit cards); kids under 12 are half-price. Reservations are required; box lunches are available for an additional fee. No credit cards.

OLD QUARRY OCEAN ADVENTURES

Yet another aspect of the **Old Quarry Ocean Adventures** (Stonington, 207/367-8977, www.oldquarry.com) empire are sightseeing tours on the *Nigh Duck*. The three-hour trips, one in the morning (9am-noon) and one in the afternoon (1pm-4pm), are $48 adults and $36 under age 12. Both highlight the natural history of the area as Captain Bill navigates the boat through the archipelago. Lobster traps are hauled on both trips (but not on Sunday); the morning trip visits Isle au Haut. The afternoon excursion features an island swimming break in a freshwater quarry. Also available is a 1.5-hour sunset cruise, departing half an hour before sunset, for $41 adults and $31 under age 12. And if that's not enough, Old Quarry also offers puffin-watching, lighthouse, and island cruises, with rates beginning around $75 adults, $55 children. Of course, if none of this floats your boat, you can also arrange for a custom charter for $205 per hour.

Old Quarry also offers a number of special trips in conjunction with Island Heritage Trust. Most are noted on Old Quarry's website, but for reservations or more info, call 207/348-2455.

SUNSET BAY CO.

Cruise through East Penobscot Bay aboard the mail boat ***Katherine*** (207/701-9316, $24 adults, $12 under age 12), which departs the Deer Isle Yacht Club at 9am, Mon.-Sat., for a two-hour excursion taking in Eagle, Butter, Barred, and Great Spruce Head islands.

ACCOMMODATIONS

Inns and Bed-and-Breakfasts

Pilgrim's Inn (20 Main St., Deer Isle, 207/348-6615, www.pilgrimsinn.com, early May-mid-Oct., $149-259) comprises a beautifully restored colonial building with 12 rooms and three newer cottages overlooking the peaceful Mill Pond. The inn, on the National Register of Historic Places, began life in 1793 as a boardinghouse named The Ark. Rates include a full breakfast, snacks, and Wi-Fi. The Whale's Rib Tavern serves dinner.

★ **The Inn on the Harbor** (45 Main St., Stonington, 207/367-2420 or 800/942-2420, www.innontheharbor.com, $150-240) is exactly as its name proclaims—its expansive deck hangs right over the harbor. Although recently updated, the 1880s complex still has an air of unpretentiousness. Most of the 14 guest rooms and suites, each named after a windjammer, have fantastic harbor views and private or shared decks where you can keep an eye on lobster boats, small ferries, windjammers, and pleasure craft; binoculars are provided. All have a small fridge, Wi-Fi, and flat-screen TV and DVD. Street-side rooms can be noisy at night. Rates include a continental buffet breakfast. An espresso bar is open 11am-4:30pm daily. Nearby are antiques, gift, and crafts shops; guest moorings are available. The inn is open all year, but call ahead in the off-season, when rates are lower.

Eggemoggin Reach is almost on the doorstep at **The Inn at Ferry Landing** (77 Old Ferry Rd., Deer Isle, 207/348-7760, www.ferrylanding.com, $130-185), overlooking the abandoned Sargentville-Deer Isle ferry wharf. The view is wide open from the inn's great room, where guests gather to read, play games, talk, and watch passing windjammers. Professional musician Gerald Wheeler has installed two grand pianos in the room; it's a treat when he plays. His wife, Jean, is the hospitable innkeeper, managing three water-view guest rooms and a suite. A harpsichord and a great view are big pluses in the suite. The Mooring, an annex that sleeps five, is rented by the week ($1,200 without breakfast). The inn is open year-round except Thanksgiving and Christmas; Wi-Fi is available throughout.

Penny's B&B (41 Main St., Stonington, 949/494-7747, www.pennys-bnb.com, $90-$150), an art-filled, shingled and turreted Victorian sited on the edge of downtown, is a laid-back, low-key spot to kick back and relax. Not a place for fussbudgets, this is more of a homestay, with three bedrooms (and an overflow single room) sharing two baths, a tiny one upstairs and a spacious one downstairs. Owner Penny Parkinson, an artist, is a great resource about the area, but don't expect handholding or even a hot breakfast—it's a simple self-serve continental available whenever you desire. The best room is the queen-bedded one opening to a huge private deck with harbor views; if you're day-tripping to Isle au Haut, you can simply wake up and roll down the hill to the dock.

Motels

Right in downtown Stonington, just across the street from the harbor, is **Boyce's Motel** (44 Main St., Stonington, 207/367-2421 or 800/224-2421, www.boycesmotel.com, year-round, $75-160). Eleven units all have TVs, phones, Wi-Fi, and refrigerators; some have kitchens and living rooms, and one has two bedrooms. Across the street, Boyce's has a private harbor-front deck for its guests. Ask for rooms well back from Main Street to lessen the noise of locals cruising the street at night.

Hostels

In 2009, the rustic bordering on primitive **Deer Isle Hostel** (65 Tennis Rd., Deer Isle, 207/348-2308, www.deerislehostel.com, $25 adults, $30 pp private room, no credit cards) opened near the Tennis Preserve. Owner Dennis Carter, a Surry, Maine, native and local stoneworker and carpenter, modeled it on The Hostel in the Forest in Brunswick, Georgia. It's completely off the grid, with a pump in the kitchen for water, an outhouse, watering-can shower, and wood-fired hot tub. Carter expects guests to work in the extensive organic gardens, using produce for shared meals prepared on a woodstove, the sole source of heat. The three-story timber-frame design is taken from a late 17th-century home in Massachusetts. Carter hand-cut the granite for the basement, and the timbers in the nail-free frame are hand-hewn from local blown-down spruce. The goal is sustainability, not profit. Communal dinners are available nightly.

Old Quarry Ocean Adventures Bunkhouse (130 Settlement Rd., Stonington, 207/367-8977, www.oldquarry.com) sleeps up to eight in three private rooms for $65-85 double; weekly rates as well as whole-building rates are available. Guests use the campground bathhouse facilities. Bring your own sleeping bag or linens, or rent them for $4.

Camping

Plan ahead if you want to camp at **Old Quarry Ocean Adventures Campground** (130 Settlement Rd., Stonington, 207/367-8977, www.oldquarry.com), with both oceanfront and secluded platform sites for tents and just three RV sites. Rates range $42-56 for two people, plus $19 for each additional adult, varying with location and hookups. Children ages 5-11 are $6.50. Leashed pets are permitted ($2/stay); Wi-Fi is $3 per stay. Parking is designed so that vehicles are kept away from most campsites, but you can use a garden cart to transport your equipment between your car and your site. The campground is adjacent to the Settlement Quarry preserve.

FOOD

Local Flavors

Craving sweets? Head to **Susie Q's Sweets and Curiosities** (40 School St., Stonington, 207/367-2415, 8am-3pm Wed.-Sun.). Susan Scott bakes a fine selection of cookies and pies, offers breakfast and lunch choices (including homemade doughnuts, blueberry pancakes, and often crabmeat quiche), and also carries antiques, books, quilts, toys, and other fun items. It's a Wi-Fi hotspot.

Water's Edge Wines (6 Thurlow's Hill Rd., Stonington, 207/367-6348, 11am-5pm Tues-Fri., 11am-4pm Sat.) sells wine, beer, baked goods, and specialty food, as well as pizzas and sandwiches.

Coffee zealots praise **44 North Coffee,** which has two locations: The Café (70 Main St., Stonington) and the roastery (11 Church St./Rte. 15, Deer Isle, 207/348-5208, www.44northcoffee.com).

On a fine afternoon, there's no better place to hang out and sip coffee than the **Espresso Bar at the Inn on the Harbor** (45 Main St., Stonington, 800/942-2420).

Burnt Cove Market (Rte. 15, Stonington, 207/367-2681, 6am-8pm Mon.-Thurs., 6am-9pm Fri.-Sat., 7am-8pm Sun.) sells pizza, fried chicken, and sandwiches, plus beer and wine.

The Fairway Café (442 Sunset Rd., Deer Isle, 207/348-2379, www.islandcountryclub.net, 11am-2pm daily), located at the country club, is a good bet for a reasonably priced lunch.

Fried seafood, lobsters, burgers, ice cream, and other usuals are available at **Madelyn's Drive In & Takeout** (495 N. Deer Isle Rd./Rte. 15, 207/348-9444, 11am-7pm daily), a popular family spot with picnic tables and a playground.

The Island Community Center (6 Memorial Ln., just off School St., Stonington) is the locale for the lively **Island Farmers Market** (10am-noon Fri. late May-late Sept.), with more than 50 vendors selling smoked and organic meats, fresh herbs and flowers, produce, gelato and yogurt, maple syrup, jams and jellies, fabulous breads and baked goods, chocolates, ethnic foods, crafts, and so much more. Go early; items sell out quickly.

The **Island Culinary & Ecological Center** (www.edibleisland.org), comprising area chefs, aims to create a high-level cooking school and also supports the region as a culinary destination. It offers occasional workshops and programs, as well as an annual fund-raiser featuring a five-course dinner prepared by renowned chefs.

Family Favorites

Harbor Café (36 Main St., Stonington, 207/367-5099, 6am-8pm Mon.-Sat., 6am-2pm Sun., $5-20) is *the* place to go for breakfast (you can eavesdrop on the local fisherfolk if you're early enough), but it's also open for lunch and dinner (especially popular on Friday night for the seafood fry, with free seconds). Food varies, as does the service; best advice is to stick to the basics.

The views are top-notch from the harborfront **Fisherman's Friend Restaurant** (5 Atlantic Ave., Stonington, 207/367-2442 www.fishermansfriendrestaurant.com, from 11am Thurs.-Tues., $10-25). The restaurant turns out decent fried food, generous portions, fresh seafood, and outstanding desserts, but it seems to have lost its soul since it moved from its old digs to this larger and more modern space. Prices are reasonable—the Friday-night fish fry, with free seconds, is around $11.

Casual Dining

The **Whale's Rib Tavern** (20 Main St./Sunset Rd., Deer Isle Village, 207/348-5222, 5pm-8:30pm Wed.-Sun., $18-30) is a comfy, white-tablecloth tavern with a rustic feel in the lower level of the Pilgrim's Inn. Well-prepared entrées may include seared halibut with lobster risotto, rack of lamb, and vegetarian fare.

Views! Views! Views! Gaze over lobster boats toing-and-froing around spruce-and-granite-fringed islands and out to Isle au Haut from ★ **Aragosta** (27 Main St., Stonington, 207/367-5500, www.aragostamaine.com, 5pm-9pm Thurs.-Tues.), a culinary bright spot fronting on the harbor in downtown Stonington. The emphasis is on seafood—the lobster ravioli earns raves—but Chef Devin Finigan's six-plus-course chef's tasting menu ($75), served in the unpretentiously elegant dining room, draws from what's currently available from local farms. She also makes her own charcuterie, flavored salts, and ice cream. For lighter fare, opt for the Happy Hour Menu (5-8pm Thurs.-Sun., $10-28) or lunch (11am-3pm Thurs-Sun.), both served on the harbor-hugging deck. Reservations are wise.

INFORMATION AND SERVICES

The **Deer Isle-Stonington Chamber of Commerce** (207/348-6124, www.deerislemaine.com) has a summer information booth on a grassy triangle on Route 15 in Little Deer Isle, 0.25 mile after crossing the bridge from Sargentville (Sedgwick).

Across from the Pilgrim's Inn is the **Chase Emerson Memorial Library** (Main St., Deer Isle Village, 207/348-2899). At the tip of the island is the **Stonington Public Library** (Main St., Stonington, 207/367-5926).

Find **public restrooms** at the Atlantic Avenue Hardware pier and the Stonington Town Hall on Main Street, Chase Emerson Library in Deer Isle Village, and behind the information booth on Little Deer Isle.

GETTING THERE AND AROUND

Deer Isle Village is about 12 miles or 25 minutes via Route 15 from Brooksville. Stonington is about six miles or 15 minutes via Route 15 from Deer Isle Village.

Isle au Haut

Eight miles off Stonington lies 4,700-acre **Isle au Haut,** roughly half of which belongs to Acadia National Park. Pronounced variously as "I'll-a-HO" or "I'LL-a-ho," the island has nearly 20 miles of hiking trails, excellent birding, and a tiny village.

Around 50 souls call Isle au Haut home year-round, and most of them eke out a living from the sea. Each summer, the population temporarily swells with day-trippers, campers, and cottagers—then settles back in fall to the measured pace of life on an offshore island.

Samuel de Champlain, threading his way through this archipelago in 1605 and noting the island's prominent central ridge, named it Isle au Haut (High Island). Appropriately, the tallest peak (543 feet) is now named Mount Champlain.

First settled in 1792, then incorporated in 1874, Isle au Haut earned a world record during World War I, when all residents were members of the Red Cross. Electricity came in 1970, and phone service in 1988.

More recent fame has come to the island thanks to island-based authors Linda Greenlaw, of *Perfect Storm* fame, who wrote *The Lobster Chronicles,* and more recently Kate Shaffer, of Black Dinah Chocolatiers, who shared her recipes along with island tales, in *Desserted.* Although both books piqued interest in the island, Isle au Haut remains uncrowded and well off the beaten tourist track.

Most of the southern half of the six-mile-long island belongs to Acadia National Park, thanks to the wealthy summer visitors who began arriving in the 1880s. It was their heirs who, in the 1940s, donated valuable acreage to the federal government. Today, this offshore division of the national park has a well-managed 19-mile network of trails, a few lean-tos, several miles of unpaved road, a lighthouse inn, and summertime passenger-ferry service to the park entrance. The National Park Service has a no-promote policy regarding Isle au Haut; unless you ask about it, you won't be told about it.

In the island's northern half are the private residences of fishing families and summer folk, a minuscule village (including a market,

Plan a day trip to Isle au Haut.

chocolate shop café, gift shop, and post office), and a five-mile stretch of paved road. The only vehicles on the island are owned by residents.

If spending the night on Isle au Haut sounds appealing (it is), you'll need to plan well ahead; it's no place for spur-of-the-moment sleepovers. (Even spontaneous day trips aren't always possible.) The best part about staying on Isle au Haut is that you'll have much more than seven hours to enjoy this idyllic island.

Folk singer Gordon Bok penned the lyrics to *The Hills of Isle au Haut:*

> The winters drive you crazy
> And the fishin's hard and slow
> You're a damn fool if you stay
> But there's no better place to go

★ ACADIA NATIONAL PARK

Mention **Acadia National Park** and most people think of Bar Harbor and Mount Desert Island, where more than three million visitors arrive each year. The Isle au Haut section of the park sees maybe 5,000-7,500 visitors annually, with a daily cap of 128. The limited boat service, the remoteness of the island, and the scarcity of campsites contribute to the low count, leaving the trails and views for only a few hardy souls.

About a third of a mile from the town landing, where the year-round mail boat and another boat dock, is the **Park Ranger Station** (207/335-5551), where you can pick up trail maps and park information—and use the island's only public facilities. (Do yourself a favor, though: Plan ahead by downloading Isle au Haut maps and information from the Acadia National Park website, www.nps.gov/acad and instead opt for the boat to the park's dock.)

ENTERTAINMENT AND EVENTS

Although Isle au Haut is pretty much a make-your-own-fun place, summer events usually include a Fourth of July parade, which all islanders participate in, so there are few spectators, and an island talent show in August. Look also for signs at the town landing dock about themed cook-offs, which might include such gourmet items as Spam.

RECREATION

Hiking

Hiking on Acadia National Park trails is the major recreation on Isle au Haut, and even in the densest fog you'll see valiant hikers going for it. A loop road circles the whole island; an unpaved section goes through the park, connecting with the mostly paved nonpark section. Walking on that is easy. Beyond the road, none of the park's 18 miles of trails could be labeled "easy"; the footing is rocky, rooty, and often squishy. But the park trails are well marked, and the views—of islets, distant hills, and the ocean—make the effort worthwhile. Go prepared with proper footwear. If you're day-tripping, consult with the ranger who meets the park boat about the best options for your ability, as most first-time visitors overestimate the amount of terrain they can cover.

The most-used park trail is the four-mile one-way **Duck Harbor Trail,** connecting the town landing with Duck Harbor. You can either use this trail or follow the island road—mostly unpaved in this stretch—to get to the campground when the summer ferry ends its Duck Harbor runs.

Even though the summit is only 314 feet, **Duck Harbor Mountain** is the island's toughest trail. Still, it's worth the 1.2-mile one-way effort for the stunning 360-degree views from the summit. Option: Rather than return via the trail's steep, bouldery sections, cut off at the Goat Trail and return to the trailhead that way.

For terrific shoreline scenery, take **Western Head Trail** and **Cliff Trail** at the island's southwestern corner. They form a nice loop around Western Head. The route follows the coastline, ascending to ridges and cliffs and descending to rocky beaches, with some forested sections. Options: Close the loop by returning via the Western Head Road. If the tide is out (and only if it's out), you can walk across the tidal flats to the quaintly named Western Ear for views back toward the island. Western Ear is privately owned, so don't linger. The **Goat Trail** adds another four miles (round-trip) of moderate coastline hiking east of the Cliff Trail; views are fabulous and birdwatching is good, but if you're here only for a day, you'll need to decide whether there's time to do this and still catch the return mail boat. If you do have the time and the energy, you can connect from the Goat Trail to the **Duck Harbor Mountain Trail.**

Bicycling

Pedaling is limited to the 12 or so miles of mostly unpaved, hilly roads, and although it is a way to get around, frankly, the terrain is neither exciting, fun, nor view-worthy. Mountain bikes are not allowed on the park's hiking trails, and rangers try to discourage park visitors from bringing them to the island. You can rent a bike (about $25/day) on the island from the Isle au Haut Ferry Service or Old Quarry Ocean Adventures. It costs $22 round-trip to bring your own bike aboard the Isle au Haut ferry. Both boats carry bikes *only* to the town landing, not to Duck Harbor.

Swimming

For freshwater swimming, head for **Long Pond,** a skinny, 1.5-mile-long swimming hole running north-south on the east side of the island, abutting national park land. You can bike over there, clockwise along the road, almost five miles, from the town landing. Or bum a ride from an island resident. There's a minuscule beach-like area on the southern end with a picnic table and a float. If you're here only for the day, though, there's not enough time to do this *and* get in a long hike. Opt for the hiking—or do a short hike and then go for a swim (the shallowest part is at the southern tip).

ACCOMMODATIONS AND FOOD

Options for food are extremely limited on Isle au Haut, so if you're coming for a day trip, bring sufficient food and water. If you want to stay overnight, plan well in advance.

Inns

Escape to ★ **The Keeper's House** (P.O. Box 26, Lighthouse Point, Isle au Haut 04645, 207/335-2990, www.keepershouse.com, from $325), a lighthouse inn. Connected by boardwalk to the Robinson Point Light and

The Keeper's House, a lighthouse inn

situated in view of three other lighthouses at night, the inn and outlying rustic cottages are a truly special, all-inclusive, rustic retreat. The spacious top-floor Garret Room, tucked under the eaves—perhaps not the best choice for tall folks—has a bath across from it. The three other rooms in the main building share a bath on the 2nd floor. Although guests have access to both bathrooms, most use the one on their floor. The best view is from The Keeper's Room, overlooking the light tower and Isle au Haut Thorofare. Detached from the main house are the rustic Oil House, with a private outhouse, and The Woodshed, with two bedrooms, kitchenette, and bath. Guests relax outdoors or gather in the small living room. Rates include breakfast, lunch, and candlelight dinners as well as use of mountain bicycles and a rowboat. Adding to the yesteryear ambience are a 1924 Model T Doctor's Coupe and a 1928 AA Ford commercial vehicle, both parked at the inn. Guests may have the opportunity to cruise aboard the inn's restored 1949 Isle au Haut lobster boat or Friendship sloop. In season, the Isle au Haut Boat Company stops at the inn's dock. BYOB and pack a light. Battery-powered electricity, no phones, no TV, no Internet, no smoking, no credit cards, no pets, no stress. Nirvana.

Camping

You'll need to get your bid in early to reserve one of the five six-person lean-tos at **Duck Harbor Campground,** open May 15-October 15. Before April 1, contact the park for a reservation request form (207/288-3338, www.nps.gov/acad). From April 1 on *(not before, or the park people will send it back to you),* return the completed form, along with a check for $25, covering camping for up to six people for a maximum of five nights May 15-June 14, three nights June 15-September 15, and five nights again September 16-October 15. Competition is stiff in the height of summer, so list alternative dates. The park refunds the check if there's no space; otherwise, it's nonrefundable and you'll receive a

the Isle au Haut General Store

"special-use permit" (*do not* forget to bring it along). There's no additional camping fee.

Note: Campers must carry all gear on/off the boat, which means navigating ramps and docks, and lean-to access is via a trail ascending through rocky and rooty terrain. The distance from boat to dock is roughly one-quarter mile.

Unless you don't mind backpacking nearly five miles to reach the campground, try to plan your visit between mid-June and late September, when the mail boat makes a stop in Duck Harbor. It's wise to call the **Isle au Haut Company** (207/367-5193) for the current ferry schedule before choosing dates for a lean-to reservation.

Trash policy is carry-in/carry-out, so pack a trash bag or two. Also bring a container for carting water from the campground pump, since it's 0.3 mile from the lean-tos. It's a longish walk to the general store for food—when you could be off hiking the island's trails—so bring enough to cover your stay.

The three-sided lean-tos are big enough

The Isle au Haut Boat Company ferries passengers to the village and the park.

(8-by-12 feet, 8 feet high) to hold a small (two-person) tent, so bring one along if you prefer being fully enclosed. A tarp will also do the trick. (Also bring mosquito repellent—some years, the critters show up here en masse.) No camping is permitted outside of the lean-tos, and nothing can be attached to trees.

Food

Isle au Haut is pretty much a BYO place—and for the most part, that means BYO food.

Thanks to the **Isle au Haut General Store** (207/335-5211, www.theislandstore.net), less than a five-minute walk from the town landing, you won't starve. The summer inventory includes all the makings for a great picnic.

Black Dinah Chocolatiers (207/335-5010, www.blackdinahchocolatiers.com, call or check website for current hours) is located half a mile west of the Town Landing dock. Steve and Kate Shaffer's little shop doubles as a café, serving pastries, organic coffees and teas, a few lunch-type offerings, exquisite ice cream, and, of course, decadent handmade chocolates. Eat inside or on the deck. The café has free Wi-Fi.

And then there's **The Maine Lobster Lady** (207/669-2751), a seasonal takeout serving lobster, fried seafood, blueberry pie, and ice cream, of course.

GETTING THERE

Two companies offer transportation to Isle au Haut's town landing. Use Isle au Haut Boat Company if your destination is the park, as it lands right at Duck Harbor twice daily during peak season. If money's no object, you can always arrange a private charter.

Isle au Haut Boat Company

The **Isle au Haut Boat Company** (Seabreeze Ave., Stonington, 207/367-5193, www.isleauhaut.com) generally operates five daily trips Monday-Saturday, plus two on Sunday from mid-June to early September. Other months, there are two or three trips Monday-Saturday. The best advice is to request a copy of the current schedule, covering dates, variables, fares, and extras.

Round-trips April-mid-October are $38 adults, $19.50 kids under 12 (two bags per adult, one bag per child). Round-trip surcharges include bikes ($23), kayaks/canoes ($46 minimum), and pets ($10.50). If you're considering using a bike, inquire about on-island bike rentals ($25/day). Weather seldom affects the schedule, but be aware that heavy seas could cancel a trip.

There is twice-daily ferry service, from mid-June to Labor Day, from Stonington to Duck Harbor, at the edge of Isle au Haut's Acadia National Park campground. For a day trip, the schedule allows you 6.5 hours on the island Monday-Saturday and 4.5 hours on Sunday. No boats or bikes are allowed on this route, and no dogs are allowed in the campground. A ranger boards the boat at the town landing and goes along to Duck Harbor to answer questions and distribute maps. Before mid-June and after Labor Day, you'll be off-loaded at the Isle au Haut town landing, about five miles from Duck Harbor. The six-mile passage from Stonington to the Isle au Haut town landing takes 45 minutes; the trip to Duck Harbor is 1.25 hours.

Ferries depart from the Isle au Haut Boat Company dock (Seabreeze Ave., off E. Main St. in downtown Stonington). Parking around $10 is available next to the ferry landing. Arrive at least an hour early to get all this settled so you don't miss the boat. Better yet, spend the night on Deer Isle before heading to Isle au Haut.

Old Quarry Ocean Adventures

Also offering seasonal service to Isle au Haut is **Old Quarry Ocean Adventures** (Stonington, 207/367-8977, www.oldquarry.com) which transports passengers on the *Nigh Duck*. The boat usually leaves Old Quarry at 9am and arrives at the island's town landing at 10am, returning from the same point at 5pm. The fee is $38 round-trip for adults, $20 for children under 12. You can add an island bike rental for an additional $22 or a kayak for $20. Old Quarry also offers a taxi service to Isle au Haut for $175/hour for up to six people.

INFORMATION AND SERVICES

Information about the section of Acadia National Park on Isle au Haut is available both online (www.nps.gov/acad) and at the Ranger Station (207/335-5551), about one-third of a mile from the town landing boat dock. General information on the island is available online from **Isle au Haut Boat Company** (www.isleauhaut.com).

Acadia Region

Look for ★ to find recommended sights, activities, dining, and lodging.

Highlights

★ **Park Loop Road:** If you do nothing else on Mount Desert, drive this magnificent road that takes in many of Acadia National Park's highlights (page 317).

★ **The Carriage Roads:** Whether you walk, bike, or ride in a horse-drawn carriage, make a point of seeing Mr. Rockefeller's roads and bridges (page 318).

★ **Abbe Museum:** The downtown Abbe Museum and its seasonal museum at Sieur de Monts Spring are fascinating places to learn about Maine's Native American heritage (page 328).

★ **Oceanarium:** A fabulous introduction to the coastal ecology is provided at this low-tech, kid-friendly site (page 329).

★ **Dive-In Theater Boat Cruise:** Got kids? Don't miss this tour, where Diver Ed brings the undersea world aboard (page 335).

★ **Asticou Azalea Garden and Thuya Garden:** "Magical and enchanting" best describes these two peaceful gardens. Whereas Zen-like Asticou is best seen in spring, Thuya delivers color through summer (page 347).

★ **Wendell Gilley Museum:** Gilley's intricately carved birds, from miniature shorebirds to life-size birds of prey, are a marvel to behold (page 353).

★ **Island Cruises:** Kim Strauss shares his deep knowledge of island ways and waters on the lunchtime cruise that allows time to explore Frenchboro (page 357).

★ **Schoodic Loop:** A scenic six-mile road edges the pink-granite shores of Acadia National Park's only mainland section and accesses hiking trails and picnic spots (page 370).

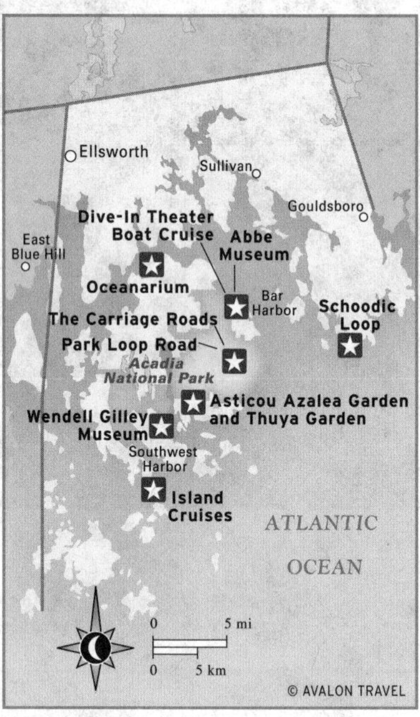

Summer folk have been visiting Mount Desert Island (MDI) for millennia. The earliest Native Americans discovered fabulous fishing and clamming, good hunting and camping, and invigorating salt air. Today's arrivals find variations on the same theme: thousands of lodgings and campsites, hundreds of restaurant seats, dozens of shops, plus 40,000 acres of Acadia National Park.

It's no coincidence that artists were a large part of the 19th-century vanguard here: The dramatic landscape, with both bare and wooded mountains descending to the sea, still inspires all who see it. Once the word got out, painterly images began confirming the reports, and the surge began. Even today, no saltwater locale on the entire eastern seaboard can compete with the variety of scenery on Mount Desert Island.

Those pioneering artists brilliantly portrayed this area, adding romantic touches to landscapes that really need no enhancement. From the 1,530-foot summit of Cadillac Mountain, preferably at an off hour, you'll sense the grandeur of it all—the slopes careening toward the bay and the handful of islands below looking like the last footholds between Bar Harbor and Bordeaux.

For nearly four centuries, controversy has raged about the pronunciation of the island's name, and we won't resolve it here. French explorer Samuel de Champlain apparently gets credit for naming it l'Ile des Monts Deserts (island of bare mountains) when he sailed by in 1604. The accent in French would be on the second syllable, but today "De-SERT" and "DES-ert" both have their advocates, although the former gets the accuracy nod. In any case, the island is anything but deserted today. Even as you approach it, via the shire town of **Ellsworth** and especially in **Trenton,** you'll run the gauntlet of big-box stores, amusements, and enough high-cholesterol eateries to stun the surgeon general. Don't panic: Acadia National Park lies ahead, and amid the thick of consumer congestion there are glimpses of the prize. Even on the most crowded days, if you venture more than

Previous: hikers enjoying views of Jordan Pond; at low tide, you can walk to Bar Island. **Above:** lobstering is big business on the Schoodic Peninsula.

a few steps into the park, you'll find you have it nearly to yourself.

As you drive or bike around Mount Desert—vaguely shaped like a lobster claw and indented by Somes Sound (the only fjord on the U.S. East Coast)—you'll cross and recross the national-park boundaries, reminders that Acadia National Park, covering a third of the island, is indeed the major presence here. It affects traffic, indoor and outdoor pursuits, and, in a way, even the climate.

The other major presence is **Bar Harbor,** largest and best known of the island's communities. It's the source of just about anything you could want, from T-shirts to tacos, books to bike rentals. The contrast with Acadia is astonishing, as the park struggles to maintain its image and character. And yet, even in Bar Harbor, the park's presence is felt.

Bar Harbor shares the island with **Southwest Harbor, Tremont,** and a number of small villages: **Bass Harbor, Bernard, Northeast Harbor, Seal Harbor, Otter Creek, Somesville,** and **Hall Quarry.** From Bass, Northeast, and Southwest Harbors, private and state ferries shuttle bike and foot traffic to offshore **Swans Island, Frenchboro** (Long Island), and the **Cranberry Isles** (and cars to Swans Island).

Stay on Route 1 instead of taking Route 3 to the island, and the congestion disappears. The towns lining the eastern shore of Frenchman Bay—**Hancock, Sullivan, Winter Harbor,** and **Gouldsboro**—have some of the best views of all: front-row seats facing the peaks of Mount Desert Island. It's no wonder many artists and artisans make their homes here. And at the tip of the **Schoodic Peninsula,** a stunning pocket of Acadia National Park sees only a fraction of the visitors who descend on the main part of the park.

PLANNING YOUR TIME

So much to do, so little time—that's the lament of most visitors. You can circumnavigate Mount Desert Island in a day, hitting the highlights along the Park Loop with just enough time to *ooh* and *aah* at each, but to appreciate Acadia, you need time to hike the trails, ride the carriage roads, get afloat on a whale-watching cruise or a sea kayak, visit museums, and explore an offshore island or two. A week or longer is best, but you can get a taste of Acadia in 3-4 days.

The region is very seasonal, with most restaurants, accommodations, and shops open mid-May-mid-October. May and June bring the new greens of spring and blooming rhododendrons and azaleas in Northeast Harbor's Asticou Garden, but mosquitoes and blackflies are at their worst and weather is temperamental—perhaps sunny and hot one day, damp and cold the next; a packing nightmare. July and August bring summer at its best, along with the biggest crowds. September is a gem of a time to visit: few bugs, fewer people, less fog, and autumn's golden light. Foliage usually begins turning in early October, making it an especially beautiful time to visit (the Columbus Day holiday weekend brings a spike in visitors). Winter is Acadia's silent season, best left for independent travelers who don't mind making do or perhaps making a meal of peanut-butter crackers if an open restaurant can't be found.

The only way onto Mount Desert Island is Route 3. Unless you're traveling in the wee hours of the morning or late at night, expect traffic. Avoid it during shift changes on-island, 8am-9am and 3pm-4pm weekdays, when traffic slows to a crawl. On the island, use the Island Explorer bus system to avoid parking hassles.

Acadia Region

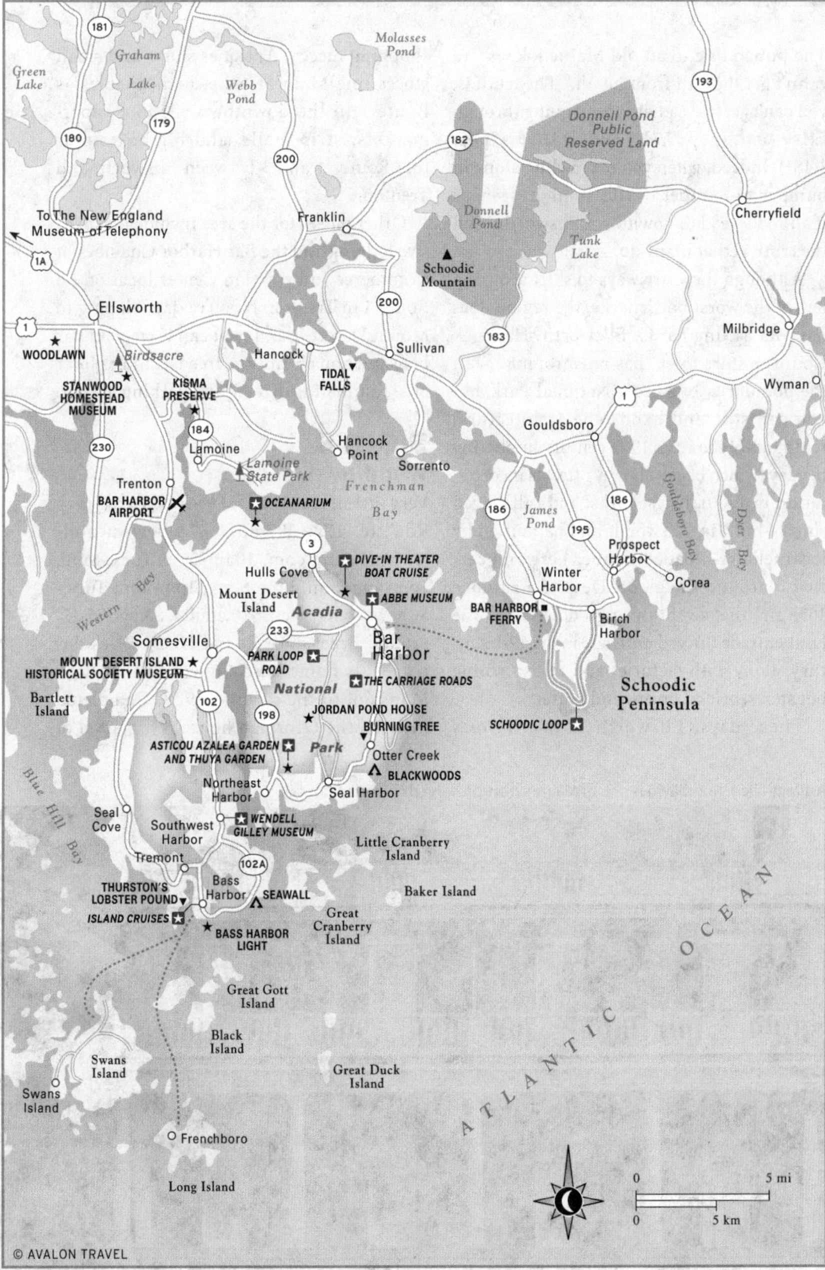

Ellsworth

The punch line to an old Maine joke is "Ya cahn't get they-ah from he-ah." The truth is, you can't get to Acadia without going through **Ellsworth** (pop. 7,741) and **Trenton** (pop. 1,481). Indeed, when you're crawling along in bumper-to-bumper traffic, it might seem as if all roads lead to downtown Ellsworth. And the truth is that many do.

Although there are ways to skirt around a few of the worst bottlenecks, the region does have its calling cards. Ellsworth, Hancock County's shire town, has mushroomed with the popularity of Acadia National Park, but you can still find handsome architectural remnants of the city's 19th-century lumbering heyday (which began shortly after its incorporation in 1800). Brigs, barks, and full-rigged ships—built in Ellsworth and captained by local fellows—loaded lumber here and carried it around the globe. Despite a ruinous 1855 fire that swept through downtown, the lumber trade thrived until late in the 19th century, along with factories and mills turning out shoes, bricks, boxes, and butter.

These days, Ellsworth is the region's shopping mecca. Antiques shops and small stores line Main Street, which doubles as Route 1 in the downtown section; supermarkets, strip malls, and big-box stores line Routes 1 and 3 between Ellsworth and Trenton.

Other pluses for the area include inexpensive lodging and the Bar Harbor Chamber of Commerce Information Center location on Route 3 in Trenton. If you're day-tripping to Mount Desert Island, you can leave your car here and hop aboard the free Island Explorer bus, eliminating driving and parking hassles.

SIGHTS

Woodlawn

Very little has changed at **Woodlawn** (Surry Rd./Rte. 172, 207/667-8671, www.woodlawnmuseum.com, 10am-5pm Tues.-Sun., 1pm-4pm Sun. June-Sept., 1pm-4pm Tues.-Sun. May and Oct., $10 adults, $3 ages 5-12, grounds free) since George Nixon Black donated his home, also known as the Black Mansion, to the town in 1928. Completed in 1828, the Georgian house is a marvel of

Artifact-filled Woodlawn is one of Maine's best-preserved Georgian houses.

preservation—one of Maine's best—filled with Black family antiques and artifacts. House highlights include a circular staircase, rare books and artifacts, canopied beds, a barrel organ, and lots more. After taking an audio tour, plan to picnic on the manicured grounds, and then explore two sleigh-filled barns, the Memorial Garden, and the two miles of mostly level trails in the woods up beyond the house. Consider timing a visit with one of the frequent events: On several Wednesday afternoons in July-August there are elegant teas ($25 pp) in the garden (or in the carriage house if it's raining), with china, silver, linens, special-blend tea, sandwiches, pastries, and live music; reservations are required. On Route 172, watch for the small sign 0.25 mile southwest of U.S. 1, and turn into the winding uphill driveway.

Birdsacre

En route to Bar Harbor, watch carefully on the right for the sign that marks **Birdsacre** (Rte. 3/Bar Harbor Rd., 207/667-8460, www.birdsacre.com, sunrise-sunset daily, donation), a 200-acre urban sanctuary. Wander the trails in this peaceful preserve, spotting wildflowers, birds, and well-labeled shrubs and trees, and you'll have trouble believing you're surrounded by prime tourist territory. One trail, a boardwalk loop through woods behind the nature center, is accessible for wheelchairs and strollers.

At the sanctuary entrance is the 1850 **Stanwood Homestead Museum** once owned by noted ornithologist Cordelia Stanwood. Previously open to the public, the home, with period furnishings and wildlife exhibits, was badly damaged in 2014 by arson. Restoration is in progress. Birdsacre is also a wildlife rehabilitation center, so expect to see all kinds of winged creatures, especially hawks and owls, in various stages of recuperation. Some will be returned to the wild, and others remain here for educational purposes. Stop by the **nature center** (10am-4pm daily June through Sept., volunteer dependent) for even more exhibits.

Kisma Preserve

I can't stress this enough: **Kisma Preserve** (446 Bar Harbor Rd./Rte. 3, 207/667-3244, www.kismapreserve.org, 10am-6pm daily mid-May-late fall) is not a zoo; it's a nonprofit educational facility, and everything revolves around preserving and protecting the animals, most of which are either rescues or retirees. Rules are strictly enforced—no running,

Birdsacre, a 200-acre urban sanctuary

loud voices, or disruptive behavior is permitted. The easiest way to view the animals is on a one-hour guided tour ($14). Guides educate visitors about the biology of the animals, how they came to be here, and whether they'll be returned to the wild. For serious animal lovers, the preserve offers behind-the-scenes tours and close-ups; there are even options for staying in the preserve overnight. It truly is a special place, home to more than 100 exotic and not-so-exotic creatures, with an emphasis on wolves and bears. Donations are essential to Kisma's survival, and yes, it's pricey, but so is feeding and caring for these animals.

Kisma Preserve is a sanctuary for retired or relocated exotic animals.

Downeast Scenic Railroad

All aboard! The all-volunteer **Downeast Rail Heritage Preservation Trust** (245 Main St., 866/449-7245, www.downeastscenicrail.org) has restored a 1948 diesel engine and rehabilitated the Calais Branch Line from Ellsworth to Ellsworth Falls, and then back and on to Washington Junction. Saturday-Sunday (late May-mid-Oct.) you can board the two vintage coaches, an open flatcar, or the caboose for a roughly 10-mile, 90-minute scenic excursion ($15 adults, $8 ages 3-12). Work continues on the track to Green Lake, which will allow a 24-mile round-trip. Boarding takes place behind the Maine Community Foundation (245 Main St.). If you're a train buff, ask about volunteer opportunities.

Telephone Museum

What was life like before cell phones? Find out at the **Telephone Museum** (166 Winkumpaugh Rd., 207/667-9491, www.thetelephonemuseum.org, $10 adults, $5 children), a hands-on museum with the largest collection of old-fashioned switching systems in the East. To find the museum, head 10 miles north on Route 1A toward Bangor, then go left on Winkumpaugh Road for one mile. Call for schedule.

Flightseeing

Two businesses provide options for getting an eagle's-eye view of the area. Both are based on the Route 3 side of Hancock County/Bar Harbor Airport, just north of Mount Desert Island.

Scenic Flights of Acadia (Bar Harbor Rd./Rte. 3, 207/667-6527, www.scenicflightsofacadia.com) offers low-level flightseeing services in the Mount Desert Island region. Flights range 15-75 minutes, with prices beginning around $50 per person with a two-passenger minimum.

Scenic Biplane and Glider Rides (968 Bar Harbor Rd./Rte. 3, 207/667-7627, www.acadiaairtours.com) lets you soar in silence with daily glider flights. The one- or two-passenger gliders are towed to an altitude of at least 2,500 feet and then released. An FAA-certified pilot guides the glider. Rates begin at $220 for a 15-minute flight for one or two. Or ride in a biplane: A 20-minute ride in an open-cockpit plane is $250 for two. Or, for a different twist, consider experiencing a World War II-era T-6 fighter plane, with flights beginning at $275 for 15 minutes. All flights are subject to an airport fee.

ENTERTAINMENT

Ellsworth has three free summer series (www.downtownellsworth.com). The **Ellsworth Concert Band** performs Wednesday evening in the plaza outside Ellsworth City Hall (City Hall Ave.). If it rains, it's held inside City Hall. Practice begins at 6:30pm, concerts start at 8pm, and the 30-member community band even welcomes visitors with talent and instruments—just show up at practice time. **Outdoor family movies** are shown at sunset Thursday at the Knowlton Playground on State Street (donations appreciated). **Concerts** are staged at Waterfront Park at 6pm on Friday.

Ace lumberjack "Timber" Tina Scheer has been competing around the world since she was seven, and she shows her prowess at **The Great Maine Lumberjack Show** (Rte. 3, 207/667-0067, www.mainelumberjack.com, 7pm daily mid-June-early Sept., 4pm Sat. and 2pm Sun. early Sept.-mid-Oct., $12 adults, $11 over age 62, $7.50 ages 4-11). During the 75-minute "Olympics of the Forest," you'll watch two teams compete in 12 events, including ax throwing, crosscut sawing, log rolling, speed climbing, and more. Some events are open to participation. (Kids can learn some skills by appointment.) Performances are held rain or shine. Seating is under a roof, but dress for the weather if it's inclement. The ticket office opens at 6pm.

The carefully restored art deco **Grand Auditorium of Hancock County** (100 Main St., 207/667-9500, www.grandonline.org) is the year-round site of films, concerts, plays, and art exhibits.

SHOPPING

Specialty Shops

You're unlikely to meet a single person who has left **Big Chicken Barn Books and Antiques** (1768 Bucksport Rd./U.S. 1, 207/667-7308, www.bigchickenbarn.com) without buying something. You'll find every kind of collectible on the vast first floor, courtesy of more than four-dozen dealers. Climb the stairs for books, magazines, old music, and more. With free coffee, restrooms, and 21,000 square feet of floor space, this place is addictive. The Big Chicken is 11 miles east of Bucksport, 8.5 miles west of Ellsworth.

Just south of downtown, in a property listed on the National Register of Historic Places, the 1838 courthouse at the corner of Court Street and Route 1 is **Courthouse Gallery Fine Art** (6 Court St., 207/667-6611, www.

Downtown Ellsworth is lined with independently owned shops.

courthousegallery.com), showcasing works by some of Maine's top contemporary artists.

The 40-plus-dealer **Old Creamery Antique Mall** (13 Hancock St., 207/667-0522) fills 6,000 square feet on two jam-packed floors.

Around the corner is **Atlantic Art Glass** (25 Pine St., 207/664-0222, www.atlanticart-glass.com), where you can watch Linda and Ken Perrin demonstrate glassblowing and buy their contemporary creations.

Don't miss **Rooster Brother** (29 Main St./Rte. 1, 800/866-0054, www.roosterbrother.com) for gourmet cookware, cards, and books on the main floor; coffee, tea, candy, cheeses, a huge array of exotic condiments, fresh breads, and other gourmet items on the lower level; and discounted merchandise on the second floor, open seasonally. You can easily pick up all the fixings for a fancy picnic here.

It's hard to categorize **J&B Atlantic Company** (142 Main St./Rte. 1, 207/667-2082). It takes up a good part of the block, with room after room filled with furniture, home accessories, gifts, books, and antiques.

John Edwards Market (158 Main St., 207/667-9377) is a twofold find: Upstairs is a natural-foods store; downstairs is the Wine Cellar Gallery, a terrific space showcasing Maine artists throughout the year.

Union River Book & Toy Co. (100 Main St., 207/667-6604, www.unionrivertoys.com) is filled with books, toys, games, puzzles, dolls, stuffed animals, puppets, and more to keep the kiddos happy should the weather turn gloomy. Out back are Karen's Café, a great spot for lunch, as well as a couple of other little shops.

Stock up on Maine-made jams, syrups, honeys, and other specialty foods at **Maine's Own Treats** (68 Rte. 3/Bar Harbor Rd., 207/667-8888).

Discount Shopping

The **L. L. Bean Factory Store** (150 High St./Rte. 1, 207/667-7753) carries everything from clothing to sporting equipment, but don't expect a full range of sizes or designs. That said, I've never left empty-handed.

Across the road is **Renys Department Store** (Ellsworth Shopping Center, 175 High St./Rte. 1, 207/667-5166, www.renys.com), a Maine-based discount operation with a "you never know what you'll find" philosophy. Trust me, though, you'll find something here.

Marden's (461 High St./Rte. 3, 207/669-6035, www.mardenssurplus.com) is another Maine "bit of this, bit of that" enterprise with the catchy slogan "I shoulda bought it when I saw it." Good advice.

ACCOMMODATIONS

These updated motels and cottage colonies along Routes 1 and 3 provide cheap sleeps with a few frills, but fussbudgets should look elsewhere.

If all you want is a good bed in a clean room, the family-owned and operated **Sunset Motor Court** (210 Twin Hill Rd., 207/667-8390, www.sunsetmotorcourtmotel.com, $78-135), a pet-friendly tourist court facing Route 1 south of town, fits the bill. It's also well situated for exploring the Blue Hill Peninsula region. Each of the comfortably renovated, rainbow-colored, one- and two-bedroom cabins has heat, air-conditioning, a TV, a microwave, a refrigerator, and in-room coffee with prepackaged pastries. There's even a coin-op laundry.

The Kelley family's **Isleview Motel** (1169 Bar Harbor Rd./Rte. 3, Trenton, 207/667-5661 or 866/475-3843, www.isleviewmoteland-cottages.com, $60-99) comprises a motel, one- and two-bedroom cottages, and a few "sleep-and-go" rooms above the office, all decorated in country style. At these prices and with this location—eight miles from the park entrance, on the Island Explorer shuttle route, across from a lobster restaurant, and just 0.5 mile from the Thompson Island Picnic Area—don't go looking for fancy, but wallet-conscious travelers will be pleased. Although small, most guest rooms are equipped with a mini-refrigerator, a microwave, Wi-Fi, a coffeemaker, air-conditioning, and a TV. Outside are picnic tables and grills. Rates include breakfast pastries, juice, and coffee.

Clean, cheap, convenient, and charming describe the family-owned **Open Hearth Inn** (Bar Harbor Rd./Rte. 3, Trenton, 207/667-2930 or 800/655-0234, www.openhearthinn.com, year-round, $80-150). Choose an inn room or opt for a tourist court-style cottage or motel room, or an apartment with a kitchen. All have TVs, fridges, air-conditioning, and Wi-Fi. Also on the premises are an enclosed family hot tub and a putting green. Kids under 12 stay free, and free pickup at Bar Harbor Airport is offered during business hours. On most mornings, until they run out, homemade muffins are available in the office, along with tea and coffee. It's on the Island Explorer bus route, less than 0.25 mile from the bridge connecting Trenton to Mount Desert Island and within walking distance of four lobster restaurants.

The pet-friendly ($10) **Acadia Sunrise Motel** (952 Bar Harbor Rd./Rte. 3, Trenton, 207/667-8452, www.acadiasunrisemotel.com, $85-125) has undergone a sea change since originally built in 1985 as a strip mall. All guest rooms have air-conditioning, cable TV, phones, refrigerators, microwaves, and coffeemakers; efficiency units have kitchenettes with stoves. Perks include an outdoor heated pool, playground, and a guest laundry. Ask for a room at the back, away from the street noise and overlooking the airport with the ocean and Acadia's mountains in the distance.

The **Chocolate Chip Bed & Breakfast** (720 Lamoine Beach Rd., Lamoine, 207/610-1691, www.chocolatechipbb.com, $135-160) treats guests to all kinds of chocolate treats, from muffins in the morning to cookies at night. Eric and Sue Hahn's lovingly rebuilt, early 19th-century, pond-side farmhouse has four comfy guest rooms decorated in country style, all with hardwood floors, handmade quilts, free Wi-Fi, and cable TV.

Camping

Here's a prize. Equally convenient to the Schoodic region and Mount Desert Island is the 55-acre, oceanfront **Lamoine State Park** (23 State Park Rd./Rte. 184, Lamoine, 207/667-4778, www.parksandlands.com, day-use $4.50 nonresident adults, $3 Maine resident adults, $1 ages 5-11). Park facilities include a picnic area with a spectacular view, a boat-launch ramp, a children's play area, a treehouse, and a dumping station. Camping (mid-May-mid-Oct., $25 nonresidents, $15 Maine residents, reservations $2/night) is available at 62 sites. Most are wooded and several are oceanfront. No hookups are available (except for one site designated for the disabled), and the minimum stay in July and August is two nights, with a 14-night maximum. The campground has a modern bathhouse with free hot showers. Reserve online with a credit card, or call 207/624-9950 or 800/332-1501 weekdays within Maine. Leashed pets are allowed; cleanup is required.

FOOD

Local Flavors

Order breakfast anytime at **The Riverside Café** (151 Main St., Ellsworth 207/667-7220, 7am-2pm daily). Lunch service begins at 11am. And the café's name? It used to be down the street, overlooking the Union River.

Less creative but no less delicious are the home-style breakfasts at **Martha's Diner** (Renys Plaza, 151 High St., Ellsworth, 207/664-2495, www.marthasdiner.com, 6am-2pm Tues.-Fri., 6am-1pm Sat., 7am-1pm Sun., under $10), where lunch is also served 11am-2pm Tuesday-Friday. Booths are red leatherette and Formica, and the waitresses may call you "doll."

Big flavors come out of tiny **86 This** (125 Main St., Ellsworth, 207/610-1777, 11am-8pm Tues.-Sat.), a wrap and burrito joint. The flavors are rich, the portions are generous, and wraps are named after the owners' favorite indie bands.

Hidden in the back of Union River Book & Toy Co. is **Karen's Café** (100 Main St., 207/412-0102, 8am-3pm Mon.-Sat.), a local secret for hearty sandwiches (gluten-free bread is available) and seafood chowder. On the upper end of Main Street, **Flexit Café and Bakery** (192 Main St., 207/412-0484, 7am-5pm daily) serves breakfast and lunch daily, with vegan and gluten-free options available.

Jordan's Snack Bar (200 Down East Hwy./U.S. 1, 207/667-2174, www.jordanssnackbar.com, 10:30am-8pm daily) has an almost cult following for its crabmeat rolls and fried clams. Wednesday Cruise-Ins, beginning at 6pm, usually feature live entertainment and draw up to 50 vintage cars.

Ice cream doesn't get much finer than that sold at **Morton's Moo** (9 School St., 207/266-9671), a family-run spot with a deservedly giant reputation for homemade Italian gelato, *sorbetto,* and ice cream in creative flavors. It's half a block off Main Street behind The Maine Grind.

Mighty fine pizza is served at **Finelli Pizzeria** (12 U.S. 1, 207/664-0230, www.finellipizzeria.com, 11am-9pm daily daily) where the pizza dough and focaccia bread are made fresh daily. The specialty is New York-style thin-crust pizza, but other options include calzones, pastas, subs, and salads.

Mosey through Lamoine to **Seal Cove Farm** (202 Partridge Cove Rd./Rte. 204, Lamoine, 207/667-7127, www.mainegoatcheese.com, noon-5pm Fri.-Sun.), a working goat farm best known for its handcrafted artisan cheeses. Adjacent to the small post-and-beam farm stand is an outdoor wood-burning oven. Ten-inch handcrafted pizzas ($11) are made not only with Seal Cove's fresh goat and mixed-milk cheeses, but also with seasonal, farm-fresh produce. For dessert, don't miss the goat gelato. There's a small picnic pavilion. Human kids will get a kick out of watching the goat kids romping in the pasture.

The **Ellsworth Farmers Market** gets under way in the parking lot behind the Maine Community Foundation (245 Main St., 2pm-5:30pm Mon. and Thurs. mid-June-late Oct.), and in the Hancock Oil parking lot (190 Main St., 9:30am-noon Sat. mid-June-late Oct.). It features fresh produce as well as jams, pickles, maple syrup, homemade breads, and homespun yarns.

Seal Cove Farm bakes their handmade goat cheese pizzas in an outdoor oven.

Casual Dining

Down East meets Far East at **Shinbashi** (139 High St., 207/667-6561, www.myshinbashi.com, 11:30am-9:30pm daily, $8-24), serving an extensive menu of Japanese, Chinese, Vietnamese, and Thai specialties, including sushi and Peking duck; there's also a children's menu.

Lobster

It's hard to say which is better—the serene views or the tasty lobster—at Brian and Jane Langley's **Union River Lobster Pot** (8 South St., 207/667-5077, www.lobsterpot.com, 4pm-9pm daily June-mid-Oct., $15-24). It's tucked behind Rooster Brother, right on the banks of the Union River. The menu includes far more than lobster, with chicken, fish, meat, and pasta dishes, and a kids' menu is available. Remember to save room for the pie, especially the blueberry.

Far more touristy is **Trenton Bridge Lobster Pound** (Bar Harbor Rd./Rte. 3, 207/667-2977, www.trentonbridgelobster.com, 11am-7:30pm Mon.-Sat. late May-mid-Oct.),

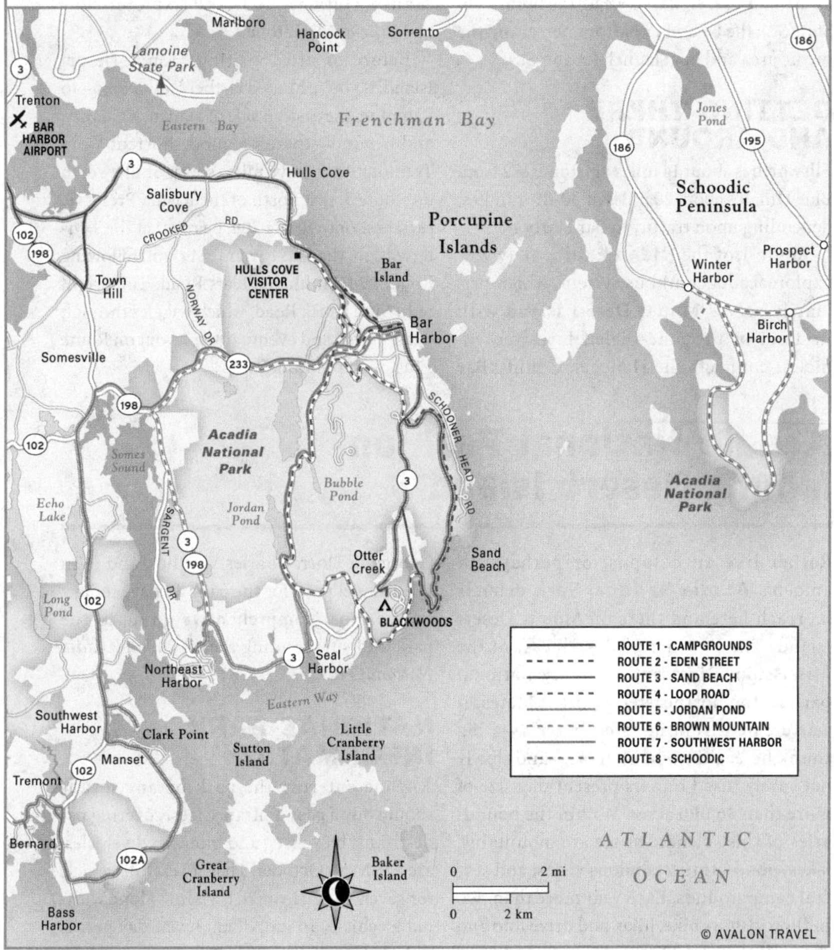

on the right next to the bridge leading to Mount Desert Island. Watch for the "smoke signals"—steam billowing from the huge vats.

INFORMATION AND SERVICES

The **Ellsworth Area Chamber of Commerce** (207/667-5584, www.ellsworthchamber.org) also covers Trenton.

The **Thompson Island Visitors Center** (Rte. 3, Thompson Island, 207/288-3411) represents the Mount Desert Island Regional Chambers of Commerce, which includes the Trenton Chamber of Commerce. An Acadia National Park ranger is usually stationed here, and park passes are available.

George Nixon Black, grandson of the builder of the Woodlawn Museum, donated the Federalist **Ellsworth Public Library** (46 State St., 207/667-6363, www.ellsworth.lib.me.us), listed on the National Register of Historic Places, to the city in 1897.

Find **public restrooms** in City Hall (City Hall Ave.) in downtown Ellsworth, open 24 hours daily, seven days a week; the library (46 State St.); the Chamber of Commerce; and the picnic area and boat launch (Water St.).

GETTING THERE AND AROUND

Ellsworth is about 14 miles via Route 172 from Blue Hill. It's about 20 miles or 30-45 minutes, depending upon traffic, to Bar Harbor.

Route 1 of the **Island Explorer** (www.exploreacadia.com) bus system, which primarily serves Mount Desert Island with its fleet of propane-fueled fare-free vehicles, connects the Hancock County/Bar Harbor Airport in Trenton with downtown Bar Harbor. Operated by Downeast Transportation, the Island Explorer runs late June-mid-October.

Before or after visiting Mount Desert Island, if you're headed farther Down East—to Lamoine, the eastern side of Hancock County, and beyond—there's a good shortcut from Trenton. About five miles south of Ellsworth on Route 3, just north of the Kisma Preserve, turn east onto Route 204, bear left at the T intersection, then take your first right, following Route 204/Pinkhams Flats Road. Turn right onto Mud Creek Road, which wiggles through a salt marsh and eventually spits out on Route 1 just west of Franklin.

Acadia National Park on Mount Desert Island

Rather like an octopus, or perhaps an amoeba, **Acadia National Park** extends its reach here and there on Mount Desert Island. The first national park east of the Mississippi River and the only national park in the northeastern United States, it was created from donated parcels—a big chunk here, a tiny chunk there—and slowly but surely fused into its present-day size of more than 46,000 acres. Within the boundaries of this splendid space are mountains, lakes, ponds, trails, fabulous vistas, and several campgrounds. Each year more than two million visitors bike, hike, and drive into and through the park. Yet even at the height of summer, when the whole world seems to have arrived, it's possible to find peaceful niches and less-trodden paths.

Acadia's history is unique among national parks and is indeed fascinating. Several books have been written about some of the high-minded (in the positive sense) and high-profile personalities who provided the impetus and wherewithal for the park's inception and never flagged in their interest and support. Just to spotlight a few, we can thank George B. Dorr, Charles W. Eliot, and John D. Rockefeller Jr. for the park we have today.

The most comprehensive guide to the park and surrounding area is *Moon Acadia National Park*.

NATIONAL PARK INFORMATION

Anyone entering the park by any means should buy a pass. Entrance fees, covering pedestrians, bicyclists, and motorized vehicles, are $25 May- October. That covers one vehicle for seven days. If you're traveling alone without a vehicle, an individual seven-day pass is $12. A motorcycle pass is $20. An annual pass to Acadia is $50, the Interagency annual pass covering all federal recreation sites is $80, a lifetime senior pass (age 62 and older) is $10, and an access pass for citizens with disabilities is free. Passes are available at the visitors centers.

Hulls Cove Visitor Center

The modern **Hulls Cove Visitor Center** (Rte. 3, Hulls Cove, 207/288-3338, 8am-4:30pm daily Apr.-June and Sept.-Oct., 8am-6pm daily July-Aug.) is eight miles southeast of the head of Mount Desert Island and well signposted. Here you can buy your park pass, make reservations for ranger-guided natural- and cultural-history programs, watch a 15-minute film about Acadia, study a relief map of the park, and buy books, park souvenirs, and guides. Pick up a copy of the ***Beaver Log,*** the tabloid-format park newspaper, with a schedule of park activities plus tide calendars and the entire schedule for the excellent **Island Explorer** shuttle-bus system, which operates late June-early October. The Island Explorer is supported by entrance fees (park pass required), as well as by Friends of Acadia and L. L. Bean. If you have children, enroll them in the park's **Junior Ranger Program** (a nominal fee may be charged). They'll receive a booklet. To earn a Junior Ranger Patch, they must complete the activities and join one or two ranger-led programs or walks.

Thompson Island Visitor Center

As you cross the bridge from Trenton toward Mount Desert Island, you might not even notice that you arrive first on tiny **Thompson Island,** site of a visitors center (8am-6pm daily mid-May-mid-Oct.) established jointly by the chambers of commerce of Mount Desert Island's towns and Acadia National Park. In season, a park ranger is usually posted here to answer questions and provide basic advice on hiking trails and other park activities, but consider this a stopgap—be sure to continue to the park's main visitors center.

Acadia National Park Headquarters

November-April, information is available at **Acadia National Park Headquarters** (Eagle Lake Rd./Rte. 233, 8am-4:30pm Mon.-Fri.), about 3.5 miles west of downtown Bar Harbor.

SIGHTS

★ Park Loop Road

The 27-mile **Park Loop Road** takes in most of the park's big-ticket sites. It begins at the visitor center, winds past several of the park's scenic highlights (with parking areas), ascends to the summit of **Cadillac Mountain,** and provides overlooks to magnificent vistas. Along the route are trailheads and overlooks as well as **Sieur de Monts Spring** (Acadia Nature Center, Wild Gardens of Acadia, Abbe Museum summer site, and the convergence of several spectacular trails), **Sand Beach,**

Hulls Cove Visitor Center

Thunder Hole, Otter Cliffs, Fabbri picnic area (there's one wheelchair-accessible picnic table), **Jordan Pond House, Bubble Pond, Eagle Lake,** and the summit of **Cadillac Mountain.** Just before you get to Sand Beach, you'll see the Park Entrance Station, where you'll need to buy a pass if you haven't already done so. If you're here during nesting and fledging season—April-mid-August—be sure to stop in the Precipice Trailhead parking area.

Start at the parking lot below the Hulls Cove Visitor Center and follow the signs; part of the loop is one-way, so you'll be doing the loop clockwise. Traffic gets heavy at midday in midsummer, so aim for an early-morning start if you can. Maximum speed is 35 mph, but be alert for gawkers and photographers stopping without warning, and pedestrians dashing across the road from stopped cars or tour buses. If you're out here at midday in midsummer, don't be surprised to see cars and RVs parked in the right lane in the one-way sections; it's permitted.

Allow a couple of hours so you can stop along the way. You can rent an audio tour on cassette or CD for $13 (including directions, an instruction sheet, and a map) at the Hulls Cove Visitor Center. Another option is to pick up the drive-it-yourself tour booklet ***Motorist Guide: Park Loop Road*** ($1.50), available at the Thompson Island and Hulls Cove Visitor Centers.

★ The Carriage Roads

In 1913, John D. Rockefeller Jr. began laying out what eventually became a 57-mile carriage-road system, and he oversaw the project through the 1940s. Motorized vehicles have never been allowed on these lovely graded byways, making them real escapes from the auto world. Devoted now to multiple uses, the "Rockefeller roads" see hikers, bikers, baby strollers, wheelchairs, and even horse-drawn carriages. Fortunately, a $6 million restoration campaign, undertaken during the 1990s, has done a remarkable job of upgrading surfaces, opening overgrown panoramas, and returning the roads to their original 16-foot width.

Pick up a free copy of the carriage-road map at any of the centers selling park passes. The busiest times are 10am-2pm.

The most crowded carriage roads are those closest to the visitors center—the Witch Hole Pond Loop, Duck Brook, and Eagle Lake. Avoid these, opting instead for roads west of Jordan Pond, or go early in the morning or

Take Park Loop Road by vehicle or bicycle.

Park Loop Road and Carriage Roads

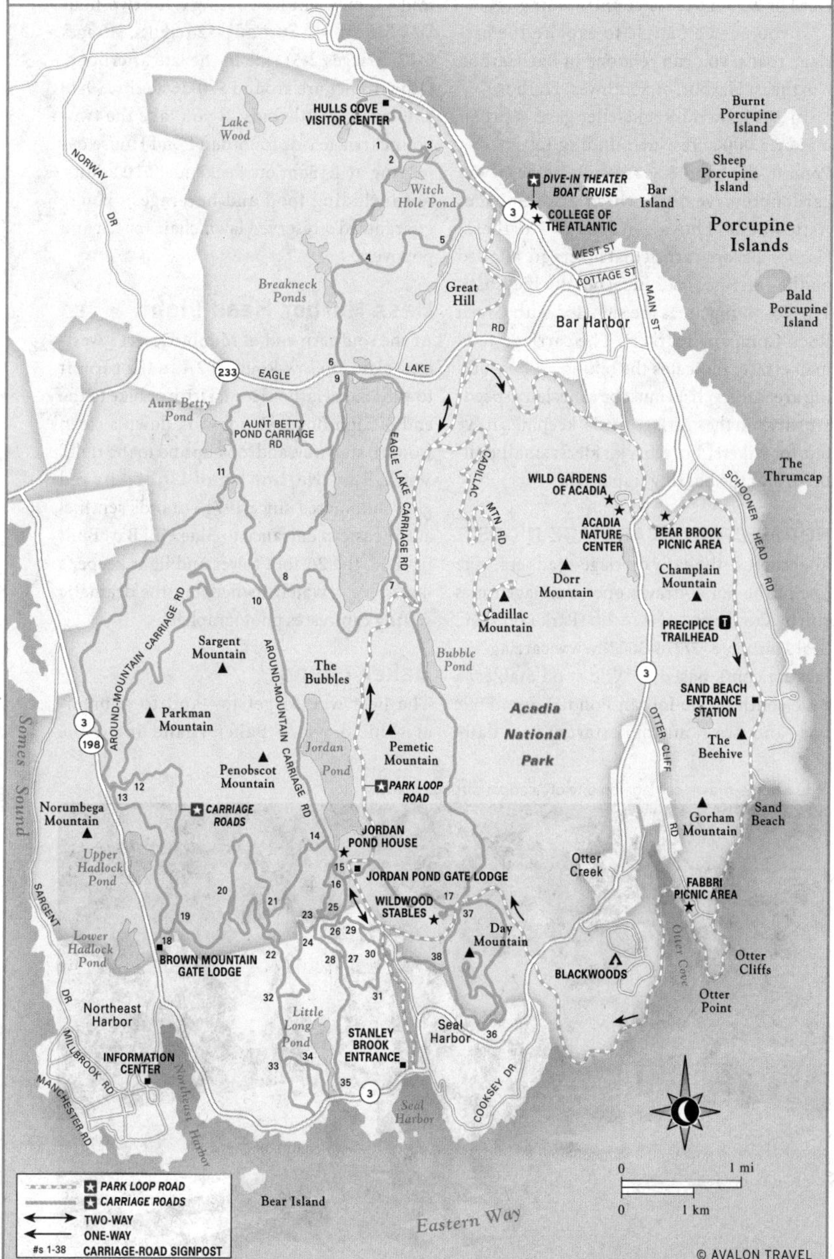

late in the day. Better still, go off-season, when you can enjoy the fall foliage (late Sept.-mid-Oct.) or winter's cross-country skiing.

If you need a bicycle to explore the carriage roads, you can rent one in Bar Harbor, Northeast Harbor, or Southwest Harbor.

In 2015, David Rockefeller gave approximately 1,000 acres surrounding Little Long Pond to the Land & Garden Preserve (www.gardenpreserve.org), which also manages Asticou and Thuya Gardens in Northeast Harbor. Be forewarned that hikers are allowed on the carriage roads here, but not bicyclists. The no-biking areas are signaled with Green Rock Company markers. The carriage-road map clearly indicates the biking and no-biking areas. Bicyclists must be especially speed-sensitive on the carriage roads, keeping an eye out for hikers, horseback riders, small children, and the hearing impaired.

HORSE-DRAWN CARRIAGE RIDES

To recapture the early carriage-roads era, take one of the horse-drawn open-carriage tours run by **Carriages of Acadia** (Park Loop Rd., Seal Harbor, 877/276-3622, www.carriagesofacadia.com), based at Wildwood Stables, a mile south of the Jordan Pond House. Four one- and two-hour tours start at 9am daily mid-June-mid-October. Reservations are not required, but they're encouraged, especially in midsummer. The best outing is the two-hour **Day Mountain Summit** ($26 adults, $10 ages 6-12, $7 ages 2-5) ride in the late afternoon. Other routes are around $20-26 adults, $9-10 children, $7 little kids. If you take the two-hour carriage ride to Jordan Pond House departing at 1:15pm on weekends ($20 adults, not including food and beverages), you're guaranteed a reserved lawn chair for tea and popovers.

Bass Harbor Head Light

At the southern end of Mount Desert's western "claw," follow Route 102A to the turnoff toward Bass Harbor Head. Drive or bike to the end of Lighthouse Road, walk down a steep wooden stairway, and look up and to the right. Voilà! **Bass Harbor Head Light**—its red glow automated since 1974—stands sentinel at the eastern entrance to Blue Hill Bay. Built in 1858, the 26-foot tower and light keeper's house are privately owned, but the dramatic setting captivates photographers.

Baker Island

The best way to get to—and to appreciate—history-rich Baker Island is on the

Ride a horse-drawn carriage on one of Acadia's carriage roads.

ranger-narrated Acadia National Park Baker Island Tour aboard the *Miss Samantha*, booked through **Bar Harbor Whale Watch Co.** (1 West St., Bar Harbor, 207/288-2386 or 888/942-5374, www.barharborwhales.com, $46 adults, $27 ages 6-14, $9 under age 6). The half-day tours are offered mid-June-mid-September and include access via skiff to the 130-acre island with a farmstead, a lighthouse, and intriguing rock formations. The return trip provides a view from the water of Otter Cliffs (bring binoculars and look for climbers), Thunder Hole, Sand Beach, and Great Head. Call for the current schedule.

RECREATION

Hikes

If you're spending more than a day on Mount Desert Island, plan to buy a copy of *A Walk in the Park: Acadia's Hiking Guide*, by Tom St. Germain, which details more than 60 hikes, including some outside the park. Remember that pets are allowed on park trails, but only on leashes no longer than six feet. Four of the Island Explorer bus routes are particularly useful for hikers, alleviating the problems of backtracking and car-jammed parking lots. Here's a handful of favorite Acadia hikes, from easy to rugged.

These three easy trails are ideal for young families. **Jordan Pond Nature Trail** starts at the Jordan Pond parking area. This is an easy, wheelchair-accessible, one-mile wooded loop trail; pick up a brochure at the beginning of the trail. Include Jordan Pond House (for tea and popovers) in your schedule. **Ship Harbor Nature Trail** starts at the Ship Harbor parking area, on Route 102A between Bass Harbor and Seawall Campground, in the southwestern corner of the island. The easy 1.3-mile loop trail leads to the shore; pick up a brochure at the trailhead. Ship Harbor is particularly popular among bird-watchers seeking warblers, and you just might spot an eagle while you picnic on the rocks. An even easier trail, with its parking area just east of the Ship Harbor parking area, **Wonderland** is 1.4 miles round-trip—a great hike that delivers a microcosm of the island's eco systems.

A moderate 1.4-mile loop, the **Great Head Trail** starts at the eastern end of Sand Beach, off the Park Loop Road. Park in the Sand Beach parking area, and cross the beach to the trailhead. Or take Schooner Head Road from downtown Bar Harbor and park in the small area where the road dead-ends. There are actually two trail loops here, both of which have enough elevation to provide terrific views.

hikers enjoying views from Jordan Pond to the Cranberry Isles

With a Little Help from Our Friends

As we watch federal funding for national parks lose headway year after year, every park in the United States needs a safety net like **Friends of Acadia** (FOA, 207/288-3340 or 800/625-0321, www.friendsofacadia.org), a dynamic organization headquartered in Bar Harbor. Propane-powered shuttle-bus service needs expanding? FOA finds a multi-million-dollar donor. Well-used trails need maintenance? FOA organizes volunteer work parties. New connector trails needed? FOA gets them done. No need seems to go unfilled.

FOA—one of Acadia National Park's greatest assets—is both reactive and proactive. It's an amazingly symbiotic relationship. When informed of a need, the Friends stand ready to help; when they themselves perceive a need, they propose solutions to park management and jointly figure out ways to make them happen. It's hard to avoid sounding like a media flack when describing this organization.

Friends of Acadia was founded in 1986 to preserve and protect the park for resource-sensitive tourism and myriad recreational uses. Since then, FOA has contributed more than $20 million to the park and surrounding communities for trail upkeep, carriage-road maintenance, seasonal park staff funding, and conservation projects. FOA also cofounded the Island Explorer bus system and instigated the Acadia Trails Forever program, a joint park-FOA partnership for trail rehabilitation. In 2003, for instance, FOA and the park announced the reopening (after considerable planning and rebuilding) of the Homans Path, on the east side of Dorr Mountain. The trail, built around 1916 and named after Eliza Homans, a generous benefactor, fell into disuse in the 1940s. It ascends via a granite stairway to a ledge with a commanding view of the Great Meadow and Frenchman Bay. More recently, the Kebo Connector, the wheelchair-accessible Jesup Path, and the Asticou and Jordan Pond Path have been reconstructed through Acadia Trails Forever; altogether, more than 40 trails have been rehabilitated or built through the program.

As part of its efforts to reduce traffic congestion on Mount Desert Island, FOA purchased land in Trenton for an off-island transit and welcome center and sold approximately 150 acres to the

Another moderate hike with great views is the 1.8-mile round-trip **Gorham Mountain Trail.** It's a great family hike, as kids especially love the Cadillac Cliffs section. Access is off the Park Loop Road, just beyond Thunder Hole.

The moderate hike to **Beech Mountain**'s summit has an abandoned fire tower, from which you can look out toward Long Pond and the Blue Hill Peninsula. A knob near the top is a prime viewing site for the migration of hawks and other raptors in September. Round-trip on the wooded route is about 1.2 miles, although a couple of side trails can extend it. You'll have less competition here in a quieter part of the park. Take Route 102 south from Somesville, heading toward Pretty Marsh. Turn left onto Beech Hill Road and follow it to the parking area at the end.

Beehive Trail and **Precipice Trail** are the park's toughest routes, with sheer faces and iron ladders; Precipice is often closed (usually mid-Apr.-late July) to protect nesting peregrine falcons. If challenges are your thing and these trails are open (check beforehand at the visitors center), go ahead. But a fine alternative in the difficult category is the **Beachcroft Trail** on Huguenot Head. Also called the Beachcroft Path, the trail is best known for its 1,500 beautifully engineered granite steps. Round-trip is 2.4 miles, or you can continue a loop at the top, taking in the **Bear Brook Trail** on Champlain Mountain, for about 4.4 miles. The parking area is just north of Route 3, near Sieur de Monts Spring.

Rock Climbing

Acadia has a number of splendid sites prized by climbers: the sea cliffs at Otter Cliffs and Great Head; South Bubble Mountain;

Maine Department of Transportation for the facility. The organization constructed a community trail on the remaining land. The Acadia Land Legacy Partnership between FOA, Acadia National Park, Maine Coast Heritage Trust, and conservation donors, purchases or protects privately held lands in or adjacent to Acadia's borders; recent achievements include the purchase of 37 acres on Lower Hadlock Pond and a conservation easement that will protect 1,400 acres of intact woods and wetland bordering Acadia's Schoodic District. FOA also funds more than 130 seasonal staff serving the park.

You can join FOA and its 4,000 members and support this worthy cause; memberships start at $35/year. You can also lend a hand while you're here: FOA and the park organize volunteer work parties for Acadia trail, carriage-road, and other outdoor maintenance three times weekly (8:20am-12:30pm Tues., Thurs., and Sat.) between June and Columbus Day. Call the recorded information line (207/288-3934) for the work locations, or call the FOA office for answers to questions. The meeting point is Park Headquarters (Eagle Lake Rd./Rte. 233, Bar Harbor), about three miles west of town. This is a terrific way to give something back to the park, and the camaraderie is contagious. Take your own water, lunch, and bug repellent. Dress in layers and wear closed-toe shoes. More than 10,000 volunteer hours go toward this effort each year.

Each summer, Friends of Acadia also sponsors a handful of **Ridge Runners,** who work under park supervision and spend their days out and about on the trails repairing cairns, watching for lost hikers, and handing out Leave No Trace information. FOA also hires more than a dozen area teens each summer for the Acadia Youth Conservation Corps, which does trail and carriage-road work, and Cadillac Summit Stewards, who work atop Acadia's highest mountain to protect the fragile alpine environment and the visitor's experience there.

If you happen to be in the region on the first Saturday in November, call the FOA office to register for the annual carriage-road cleanup, which usually draws up to 500 or so volunteers. Bring water and gloves; there's a free hot lunch at midday for everyone who participates. It's dubbed Take Pride in Acadia Day—indeed an apt label.

Canada Cliff (on the island's western side); and the South Wall and the Central Slabs on Champlain Mountain. If you haven't tried climbing, never do it yourself without instruction. **Acadia Mountain Guides Climbing School** (228 Main St., Bar Harbor, 207/288-8186 or 888/232-9559, www.acadiamountainguides.com) and **Atlantic Climbing School** (ACS, 24 Cottage St., 2nd fl., Bar Harbor, 207/288-2521, www.acadiaclimbing.com) both provide instruction and guided climbs. Costs vary on the site, experience, session length, and number of climbers.

Swimming

Slightly below the Park Loop Road (take Island Explorer Route No. 3—Sand Beach), **Sand Beach** is the park's and the island's biggest sandy beach. Lifeguards are on duty during the summer, and even then, the biggest threat can be hypothermia. The saltwater is terminally glacial—in mid-July it still might not reach 60°F. The best solution is to walk to the far end of the beach, where a warmer shallow stream meets the ocean. Avoid the parking lot scramble by taking the Explorer bus.

The park's most popular freshwater swimming site, staffed with a lifeguard and inevitably crowded on hot days, is **Echo Lake,** south of Somesville on Route 102 and well signposted (take Island Explorer Route No. 7—Southwest Harbor).

If you have a canoe, kayak, or rowboat, you can reach swimming holes in **Seal Cove Pond** and **Round Pond,** both on the western side of Mount Desert. The eastern shore of **Hodgdon Pond** (also on the western side of the island) is accessible by car via Hodgdon Road and Long Pond Fire Road. **Lake Wood,** at the northern end of Mount Desert, has a

Mount Desert Island with Kids

Acadia National Park is a great place to introduce kids to the great outdoors. Between park visits, you'll find plenty of other activities with real kid appeal. Here are a few sure bets.

IN THE PARK

Before arriving, register either by phone or online for **Acadia Quest,** an experiential scavenger hunt in the park. At park headquarters, sign kids up as **Junior Rangers.** Then pick and choose from the **ranger-led activities** that appeal to your family's interests and abilities. Good choices for **easy family hikes** include the Ocean Path, Jordan Pond Nature Trail, Ship Harbor Nature Trail, and Wonderland. If you're into **geocaching,** ask about the park's EarthCache Program (www.nps.gov/acad/earthcache.htm).

SLIMY SEA CREATURES

You can't beat the wow appeal of **Diver Ed's Dive-in Theater Boat Cruise** (207/288-3483 or 800/979-3370, www.divered.com). Ed dives to the depths with an underwater camera while you wait onboard and watch the action. When he resurfaces, he brings along with him a variety of creatures from the depths for passengers to see, feel, and learn about.

LOBSTER LORE

Even if the kids won't eat lobster, they'll be fascinated by Captain John Nicolai, who tells all during two-hour cruises aboard the ***Lulu*** (56 West St., Bar Harbor, 207/963-2341 or 866/235-2341, www.lululobsterboat.com).

HANDS-ON NATURE

"Please touch" is the philosophy at the **George B. Dorr Museum of Natural History** (105 Eden St./Rte. 3, Bar Harbor, 207/288-5015, www.coa.edu, 10am-5pm Tues.-Sat., donation), a small museum on the College of the Atlantic campus in Bar Harbor. Kids have the opportunity to touch fur, skulls, and even whale baleen.

FERRY HOPPING

Spend the better part of a day on the **Cranberry Isles,** visiting both Big and Little Cranberry and either walking or biking around, or take the passenger ferry to **Winter Harbor,** and hop on the Island Explorer bus to visit the Schoodic section of Acadia National Park. En route, watch for seals, seabirds, and lobster boats hauling traps.

NATIVE AMERICAN CULTURE

Check with the **Abbe Museum** (26 Mt. Desert St., Bar Harbor, 207/288-3519, www.abbemuseum.

tiny beach, restrooms, and auto access. To get to Lake Wood from Route 3, head west on Crooked Road to unpaved Park Road. Turn left and continue to the parking area, which will be crowded on a hot day, so arrive early.

Park Ranger Programs

Pick up a copy of ***Acadia Weekly,*** which details the ranger programs available. Don't miss these possibilities for learning more about the park's natural and cultural history.

The park ranger programs, lasting 1-3 hours, are great—and most are free. During July-August there are dozens of weekly programs, all listed in the *Beaver Log.* Included are early-morning (7am) bird-watching walks; moderate-level mountain hikes; tours of the historic Carroll Homestead, a 19th-century farm; Cadillac summit natural-history tours; children's expeditions to learn about tidepools and geology (an adult must accompany kids); trips for those in wheelchairs; and even org, 10am-5pm daily late May-early Nov., call for off-season hours, $6 adults, $2 ages 6-15) about scheduled special programs for kids, and time your visit to take advantage of them. There's a resource room for children downstairs and a few other kid-friendly exhibits at this Native American history museum, but the events bring it all to life.

NATURALIST'S NOTEBOOK

Bookstore? Museum? Arts space? Exploratorium? **The Naturalist's Notebook** (16 Main St., Seal Harbor, 207/801-2777, www.thenaturalistsnotebook.com) is all that and more, with three floors of kid-friendly engaging exhibits, books, and treasures.

LAUGH FEST

Improv Acadia (15 Cottage St., Bar Harbor, 207/288-2503, www.improvacadia.com, $15 adults, $10 under age 13) stages a family-friendly show every evening.

I SCREAM, YOU SCREAM

The ultimate kid-in-a-candy-store experience is at **Ben & Bill's** (66 Main St., Bar Harbor, 207/288-3281 or 800/806-3281), where you can buy not only chocolates made on-site but also to-die-for ice cream in both adult- and kid-pleasing flavors.

OLYMPICS OF THE FOREST

Expert lumberjack Tina Scheer and her crew perform the most amazing skills at **The Great Maine Lumberjack Show** (Rte. 3, Trenton, 207/667-0067, www.mainelumberjack.com, 7pm daily mid-June-early Sept., 4pm Sat. and 2pm Sun. early Sept.-mid-Oct., $12 adults, $11 over age 62, $7.50 ages 4-11). During the 75-minute performance, two teams compete in 12 events, including ax throwing and log rolling. You can participate in some and even arrange for your youngster to learn how to log roll. Talk about a great story for that "What I did on my summer vacation" assignment.

FAMILY NATURE CAMP

Explore tidepools, learn about animal tracks, discover the diversity of bats, go whale-watching, and take a hike and learn about the natural world in the process at College of the Atlantic's **Family Nature Camp** (800/597-9500, www.coa.edu/summer). This **hands-on, participatory, naturalist-led program** provides plenty of fodder for those "What I Did on My Summer Vacation" essays. The minimum age is five; extended family is welcome. Camp includes campus lodging, meals, field trips, and some boat tours.

a couple of tours a week in French. Some tours require reservations, but most do not; a few, including boat tours, have fees.

Park rangers also give the evening lectures during the summer in the amphitheaters at Blackwoods and Seawall Campgrounds.

CAMPING

Mount Desert Island has at least a dozen commercial campgrounds, but there are only two—Blackwoods and Seawall—within park boundaries on the island; neither has hookups. Both have seasonal restrooms with no showers, dumping stations, and seasonal amphitheaters, where rangers present evening programs.

Blackwoods Campground

Year-round **Blackwoods,** just off Route 3, five miles south of Bar Harbor, has 306 sites. Because of its location on the east side of the island, it's also the more popular of the two campgrounds. **Reservations** (877/444-6777, www.recreation.gov, credit card required) are suggested May 1-October 31, when the fee is $30/site/night. Reservations can be made up to six months ahead. In April and November, camping is $10; December-March it's free. A trail connects the campground to the Ocean Drive trail system.

Seawall Campground

Reservations (877/444-6777, www.recreation.gov, credit card required) are accepted for half of the 214 sites at **Seawall Campground,** on Route 102A in the Seawall district, four miles south of Southwest Harbor, but the rest are first-come, first-served. In midsummer you'll need to arrive as early as 8:30am (when the ranger station opens) to secure one of the 200 or so sites. Seawall is open late May-September. The cost is $30/night for drive-up sites and $22/night for walk-in tent sites.

RV length at Seawall is limited to 35 feet, with the width limited to an awning extended no more than 12 feet. Generators are not allowed in the campground.

FOOD

Jordan Pond House

The only restaurant within the park is the **Jordan Pond House** (Park Loop Rd., 207/276-3316, www.acadiajordanpondhouse.com, 11am-9pm daily), a modern facility in a spectacular waterside setting. Jordan Pond House began life as a rustic 19th-century teahouse; wonderful old photos still line the walls of the current incarnation, which went up after a disastrous fire in 1979. Afternoon tea is still a tradition, with tea, popovers, and strawberry jam served on the lawn until 5 daily in summer, weather permitting. Jordan Pond is far from a secret, so expect to wait for seats at the height of summer. Jordan Pond House is on the Island Explorer's Route No. 5. The locally based Acadia Corporation managed Jordan Pond House for 80 years, but in a controversial 2014 decision, the park service awarded the contract to an out-of-state concessionaire. Unfortunately, the overall experience has declined, while the prices have risen.

Bar Harbor and Vicinity

In 1996, **Bar Harbor** (pop. 5,235) celebrated the bicentennial of its founding (as the town of Eden). In the late 19th century and well into the 20th, the town grew to become one of the East Coast's fanciest summer watering holes.

In those days, ferries and steam yachts arrived from points south, large and small resort hotels sprang up, and exclusive mansions (quaintly dubbed "cottages") were the venues of parties thrown by summer-resident Drexels, DuPonts, Vanderbilts, and prominent academics, journalists, and lawyers. The "rusticators" came for the season with huge entourages of servants, children, pets, and horses. The area's renown was such that by the 1890s, even the staffs of the British, Austrian, and Ottoman embassies retreated here for the summer from Washington DC.

The establishment of the national park in 1919 and the arrival of the automobile changed the character of Bar Harbor and Mount Desert Island; two World Wars and the Great Depression took an additional toll in myriad ways; but the coup de grâce for Bar Harbor's era of elegance came with the Great Fire of 1947, a wind-whipped conflagration that devastated more than 17,000 acres on the eastern half of the island and leveled gorgeous mansions, humble homes, and more trees than anyone could ever count. Only three people died, but property damage was estimated at $2 million. Whole books have been written about the October inferno; fascinating scrapbooks in Bar Harbor's Jesup Memorial Library dramatically relate the gripping details of the story. Even though some of the elegant cottages have survived, the fire altered life here forever.

Bar Harbor and Vicinity

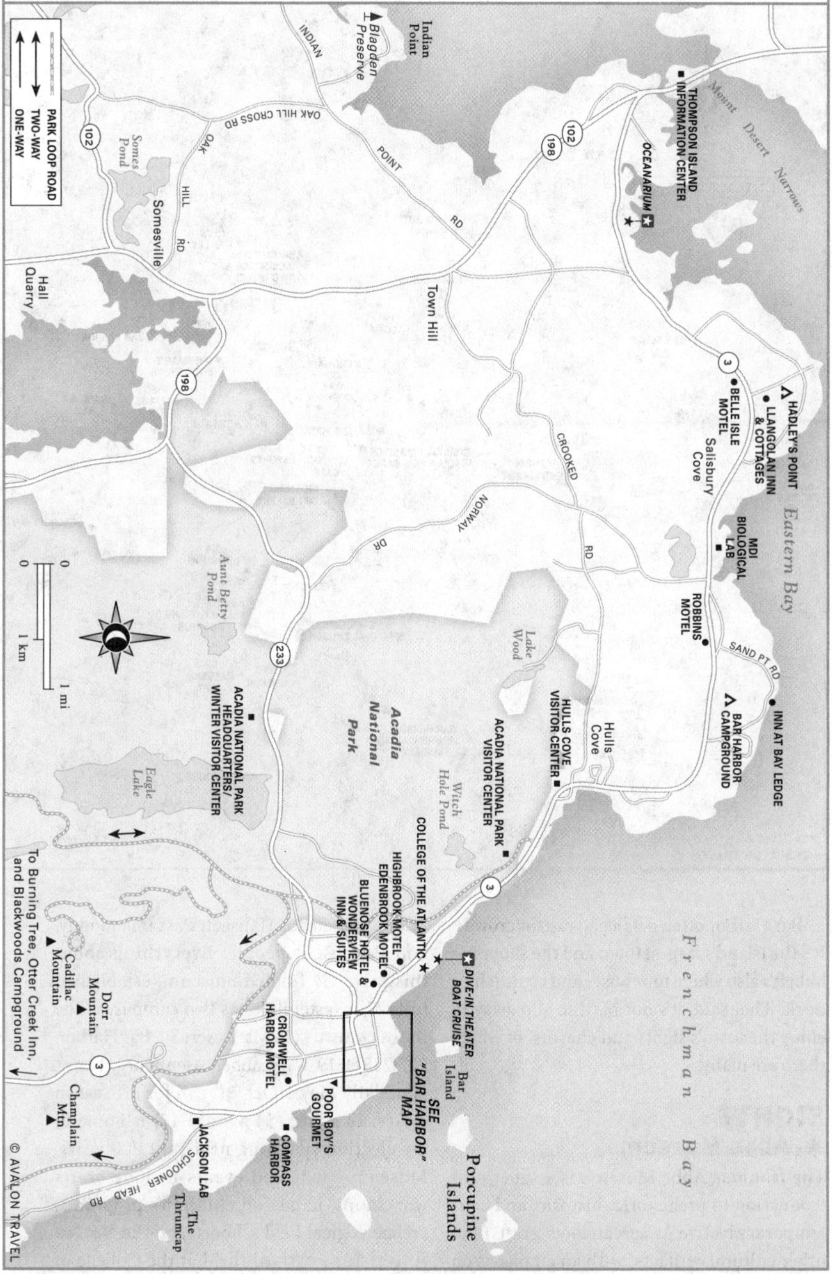

PARK LOOP ROAD
TWO-WAY
ONE-WAY

Indian Point
Blagden Preserve
INDIAN POINT RD
OAK HILL CROSS RD
OAK HILL RD
Somes Pond
Somesville
Hall Quarry
Town Hill
THOMPSON ISLAND INFORMATION CENTER
OCEANARIUM
Mount Desert Narrows
HADLEY'S POINT
LLANGOLAN INN & COTTAGES
BELLE ISLE MOTEL
Salisbury Cove
CROOKED RD
NORWAY DR
MDI BIOLOGICAL LAB
Eastern Bay
ROBBINS MOTEL
SAND PT RD
INN AT BAY LEDGE
BAR HARBOR CAMPGROUND
Hulls Cove
HULLS COVE VISITOR CENTER
Lake Wood
ACADIA NATIONAL PARK VISITOR CENTER
Witch Hole Pond
Acadia National Park
Aunt Betty Pond
ACADIA NATIONAL PARK HEADQUARTERS/ WINTER VISITOR CENTER
Eagle Lake
0 1 mi
0 1 km
COLLEGE OF THE ATLANTIC
HIGHBROOK MOTEL
EDENBROOK MOTEL
BLUENOSE HOTEL & WONDERVIEW INN & SUITES
DIVE-IN THEATER BOAT CRUISE
Frenchman Bay
Bar Island
SEE "BAR HARBOR" MAP
CROMWELL HARBOR MOTEL
POOR BOY'S GOURMET
COMPASS HARBOR
Porcupine Islands
Dorr Mountain
Cadillac Mountain
Champlain Mtn
JACKSON LAB
SCHOONER HEAD RD
The Thrumcap
To Burning Tree, Otter Creek Inn, and Blackwoods Campground
102
198
3
233

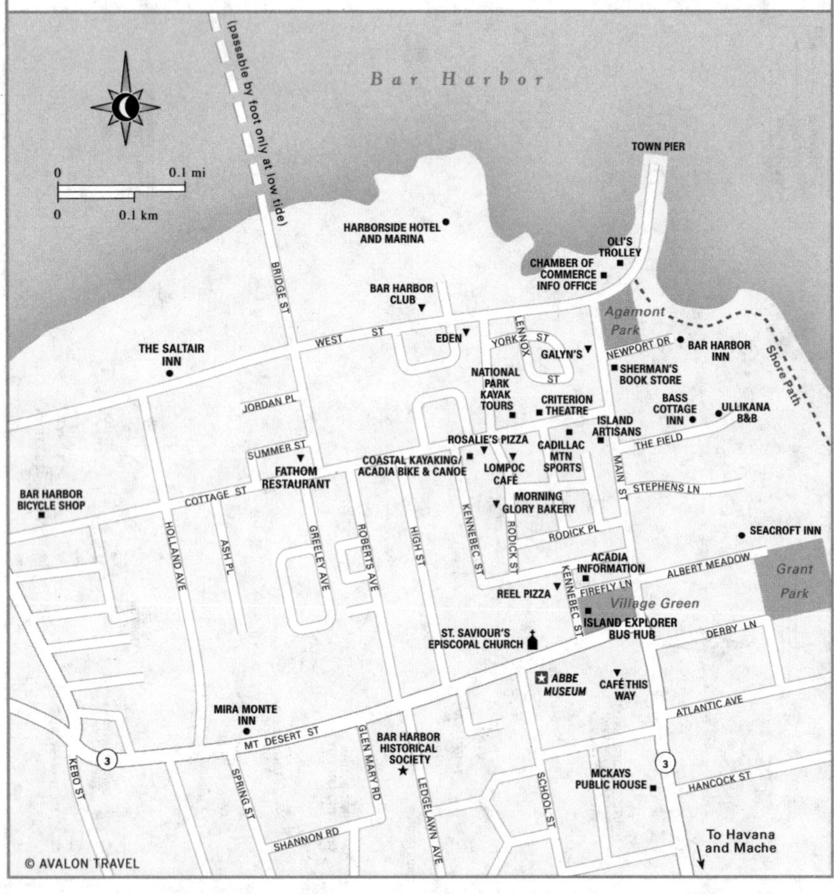

Bar Harbor often gets a bad rap for crowds. It's the island's largest town and the shopping hub; it's also where tour buses and cruise ships dock. That said, it's not hard to slip away to enjoy the town's sights and charms, of which there are many.

SIGHTS

★ Abbe Museum

The fabulous Abbe Museum is a superb introduction to prehistoric, historic, and contemporary Native American tools, crafts, and other cultural artifacts, with an emphasis on Maine's Micmac, Maliseet, Passamaquoddy, and Penobscot people. Everything about this privately funded museum, established in 1927, is tasteful. It has two campuses: The **main campus** (26 Mt. Desert St., Bar Harbor, 207/288-3519, www.abbemuseum.org, 10am-5pm daily May 1-Oct. 31, call for off-season hours, \$8 adults, \$4 ages 11-17) is home to a collection spanning nearly 12,000 years. Museum-sponsored events include crafts workshops, hands-on children's programs, archaeological field schools, and the **Native American Festival** (held at the College of the Atlantic, usually the first Sat. after the Fourth of July).

Admission to the in-town Abbe also includes admission to the **museum's original site** (9am-4pm daily mid-May-mid-Oct.), in the park about 2.5 miles south of Bar Harbor at Sieur de Monts Spring, where Route 3 meets the Park Loop Road. Inside a small but handsome building listed on the National Register of Historic Places are displays from a 50,000-item collection. Admission to only the Sieur de Monts Spring Abbe is $3 adults, $1 ages 11-17, and admission paid here can be credited to admission to the main museum.

While you're at the original Abbe Museum site, take the time to wander the paths in the adjacent **Wild Gardens of Acadia,** a 0.75-acre microcosm of more than 400 plant species native to Mount Desert Island. Twelve separate display areas, carefully maintained and labeled by the Bar Harbor Garden Club, represent native plant habitats; pick up the map-brochure that explains each.

★ Oceanarium

At the northern edge of Mount Desert Island, 8.5 miles northwest of downtown Bar Harbor, is this understated but fascinating spot, also called the **Maine Lobster Museum and Hatchery** (1351 Rte. 3, Bar Harbor, 207/288-5005, www.theoceanarium.com, 9am-5pm Mon.-Sat. mid-May-late Oct.). This low-tech, high-interest operation awes the kids, and it's pretty darn interesting for adults too. David and Audrey Mills have been at it since 1972 and are determined to educate visitors while showing them a good time. Visitors on tour view thousands of tiny lobster hatchlings, enjoy a museum, greet sea life in a touch tank, and meander along a salt marsh walk, where you can check out tidal creatures and vegetation. All tours begin on the hour and half-hour. Allow 1-2 hours to see everything. Tickets are $15 adults, $10 ages 4-12, covering admission to the lobster hatchery, lobster museum, and touch tank; an expanded program includes a 45-minute marsh walk for $17 adults, $11 children.

St. Saviour's Episcopal Church

St. Saviour's (41 Mt. Desert St., Bar Harbor, 207/288-4215, 7am-dusk daily), close to downtown Bar Harbor, boasts Maine's largest collection of Tiffany stained-glass windows. Ten originals are here; an 11th was stolen in 1988 and replaced by a locally made window. Of the 32 non-Tiffany windows, the most intriguing is a memorial to Clarence Little, founder of The Jackson Laboratory and a descendant of Paul Revere. Images in the window include the laboratory, DNA, and mice. In July-August, volunteers regularly conduct free tours of the Victorian-era church, completed in 1878; call for the schedule or make an appointment for an off-season tour. The church is open for self-guided tours 8am-8pm daily—pick up a brochure in the back. If old cemeteries intrigue you, spend time wandering the 18th-century town graveyard next to the church.

The Bar Harbor Historical Society

The Bar Harbor Historical Society (33 Ledgelawn Ave., Bar Harbor, 207/288-0000, www.barharborhistorical.org, 1pm-4pm Mon.-Sat. mid-June-mid-Oct., free), in a Jacobean Revival-style building listed on the National Register of Historic Places, has fascinating displays, stereopticon images, and a scrapbook about the 1947 fire that devastated the island. The photographs alone are worth the visit. Also here are antique maps, Victorian-era hotel registers, and other local memorabilia. In winter, it's open by appointment.

For a sample of Bar Harbor before the great fire, wander over to upper West Street, which is on the National Register of Historic Places thanks to the remaining grand cottages that line it.

College of the Atlantic

A museum, a gallery, and a pleasant campus for walking are reasons to visit the **College of the Atlantic** (COA, 105 Eden St./Rte. 3,

Bar Harbor, 207/288-5015, www.coa.edu), which specializes in human ecology, or humans' interrelationship with the environment. In a handsome renovated building that originally served as the first Acadia National Park headquarters, the **George B. Dorr Museum of Natural History** (10am-5pm Tues.-Sat., donation) showcases regional birds and mammals in realistic dioramas made by COA students. The biggest attraction for children is the please-touch philosophy, allowing them to reach into a touch tank and to feel fur, skulls, and even whale baleen. The museum gift shop has a particularly good collection of books and gifts for budding naturalists.

Across the way is the **Ethel H. Blum Gallery** (207/288-5015, ext. 254, 11am-4pm Mon.-Sat. summer, Mon.-Fri. during the academic year), a small space that hosts some intriguing exhibits.

Also on campus is the **Beatrix Farrand Garden,** behind Kaelber Hall. The garden, designed in 1928, contained more than 50 varieties of roses and was the prototype for the rose garden at Dumbarton Oaks in Washington DC. Both are known for Farrand's use of garden rooms, such as the walled terraces in this garden.

The 1st floor of **The Turrets,** a magnificent 1895 seaside cottage that's now an administration building, can be explored. Don't miss **Turrets Sea Side Garden,** fronting on the ocean, which was restored by a student in 2005. The central fountain, created by alumnus Dan Farrenkopf of Lunaform Pottery, was installed in 2009. Adjacent to The Turrets is a **sunken garden,** created in a foundation and restored in 2009 by two students.

The college also offers excellent and very popular weeklong sessions of **Family Nature Camp** (800/597-9500, www.coa.edu/summer, July-early Aug., $940 adults, $480 ages 15 and younger covers almost everything). It's essential to register well in advance; ask about early-season discounts. Families are housed and fed on the campus, and explore Acadia National Park with expert naturalist guides.

The George B. Dorr Museum of Natural History is a must for kids.

Check the college's calendar of events for lectures, conversations, and other events.

The college and its museum are 0.5 mile northwest of downtown Bar Harbor; take Island Explorer Route 2/Eden Street.

Garland Farm

Fans of landscape architect Beatrix Farrand will want to visit **Garland Farm** (475 Bayview Dr., Bar Harbor, 207/288-0237, www.beatrixfarrandsociety.org), the ancestral home of Lewis Garland, who managed her Reef Point property. When Farrand dismantled that property in 1955, she moved here with the Garlands, engaging an architect to build an addition to the original farmhouse and barn using architectural elements from Reef Point. The property was sold a few times, and greatly reduced in size, until the Beatrix Farrand Society was formed in 2002 and purchased it in 2004. The society's goal is to restore Garland Farm to its Farrand-era design and condition and to create a center for the study of design and horticulture. The property, now listed on the National Register of Historic Places, hosts special events and programs. Garland Farm is open for visits one or two days per week and tours by appointment; call for current schedule. Horticulture-related programs fill the summer calendar.

Research Laboratories

Some of the world's top scientists live year-round or come to Bar Harbor in summer to work at two prominent scientific laboratories.

World renowned in genetic research, scientists at **The Jackson Laboratory for Mammalian Research** (600 Main St./Rte. 3, Bar Harbor, 207/288-1429, www.jax.org) study cancer, diabetes, muscular dystrophy, heart disease, and Alzheimer's disease, among others—with considerable success. The non-profit research institution, locally called JAX or just "the lab," is also renowned for its genetics databases and for producing genetically defined laboratory mice, which are shipped to research labs worldwide. Free summer public tours (limited to 15 people; preregistration required) begin in the lab's visitors lobby and visit the lab's three main research wings. These show the evolution of facilities over the decades, beginning with the 1980s, and the guide discusses the genetic research occurring in each. The lab is 1.5 miles south of downtown Bar Harbor. If this is on your must-do list, plan ahead. Tours often sell out well in advance. JAX also offers a weekly 45-minute general introduction, featuring a lab scientist discussing research. As with the tours, preregistration is required.

No less impressive is the **Mount Desert Island Biological Laboratory** (159 Old Bar Harbor Rd., Salisbury Cove, 207/288-3605, www.mdibl.org), one of the few scientific research institutions in the world dedicated to studying marine animals to learn more about human health and environmental health. It is the only comprehensive effort in the country to sequence genomes. Tours are offered by advance reservation, with at least one week's notice. **Science Café** is a comfortable community science forum offered every other week at an off-site location. **Family Science Night,** held once or twice each summer, is an interactive program of performances, demonstrations, and hands-on science; reservations are recommended. In 2012, the lab won a $250,000 grant to work with the National Park Service and the Schoodic Education and Research Center to create **BioTrails,** a hands-on program to involve park visitors in scientific research. The program monitors park flora and fauna using a genetic technique called DNA barcoding. Ultimately, the program will offer a range of citizen science projects organized around hiking, cycling, and sea-kayaking trails, allowing visitors, research scientists, and park staff to work together to assess the effect of environmental changes. The lab is six miles north of Bar Harbor off Route 3.

Bar Harbor and Park Tours

The veteran of the Bar Harbor-based bus tours is **Acadia National Park Tours** (tickets at Testa's Restaurant, Bayside Landing, 53 Main St., Bar Harbor, 207/288-0300, www.acadiatours.com, $30 adults, $17.50 under age 13), operating May-October. A 2.5-3-hour naturalist-led tour of Bar Harbor and Acadia departs at 10am and 2pm daily from downtown Bar Harbor (Testa's is across from Agamont Park, near the Bar Harbor Inn). Reservations are advised in midsummer and during fall-foliage season (late Sept.-early Oct.); pick up reserved tickets 30 minutes before departure.

If you have a time crunch, take the one-hour trolley-bus tour operated by **Oli's Trolley** (ticket office at 1 West St., Bar Harbor, 207/288-9899 or 866/987-6553, www.acadiaislandtours.com), which departs from the West Street boardwalk five times daily in July-August, and includes Bar Harbor mansion drive-bys and the Cadillac summit. Purchase tickets at Harbor Place (1 West St.), next to the town pier on the waterfront. Dress warmly if the air is at all cool; it's an open-air trolley. Cost is $16 adults, $11 under age 12. Reservations are advisable. The trolley also does 2.5-hour park tours two or three times daily May-October. Tickets are $30 adults, $16 ages 5-12, $6 younger than 5. The bus and trolley routes both include potty stops.

Clip clop through downtown Bar Harbor in the same manner of those during the gilded age on a half-hour horse-drawn carriage ride with **Wild Iris Farm** ($25 adults, $12.50 children, departing from 55 West St.).

Although the Island Explorer buses do reach a number of key park sights, they are not tour buses. There is no narration, the bus cuts off the Park Loop at Otter Cliffs, and it excludes the summit of Cadillac Mountain.

Bird-Watching and Nature Tours

For private tours of the park and other parts of the island, contact Michael Good at **Down East Nature Tours** (150 Knox Rd., Bar Harbor, 207/288-8128, www.downeastnaturetours.com). A biologist and Maine Guide, Good is simply batty about birds. He has spent more than 25 years studying the birds of North America, and he has even turned his home property on Mount Desert Island into a bird sanctuary. Good specializes in avian ecology in the Gulf of Maine, giving special attention to native and migrating birds. Whether you're a first-timer wanting to spot eagles, peregrine falcons, shorebirds, and warblers, or a serious birdwatcher seeking to add to your life list, perhaps with a Nelson's sharp-tailed sparrow, Good's your man. Prices begin at $75 pp for four hours and include transportation from your lodging; kids are half-price. Bring your own binoculars, but Good supplies a spotting scope. A two-hour wetland ecology tour is $40 adults, $20 kids.

ENTERTAINMENT

The **Bar Harbor Town Band** performs for free at 8pm Monday and Thursday evenings July-mid-August in the bandstand on the Village Green (Main St. and Mt. Desert St., Bar Harbor).

You never know quite what's going to happen at **Improv Acadia** (15 Cottage St., Bar Harbor, 207/288-2503, www.improvacadia.com, $17 adults, $12 under age 11). Every show is different, as actors use audience suggestions to create comedy sketches. Shows are staged once or twice nightly; in summer, the 8pm show is child-friendly. Dessert, snacks, and drinks are available.

The **Bar Harbor Music Festival** (207/288-5744 in July-Aug., 212/222-1026 off-season, www.barharbormusicfestival.org), a summer tradition since 1967, emphasizes up-and-coming musical talent in a series of classical, jazz, and pop concerts and even an opera, usually Friday and Sunday early July-early August, at various island locations that include local inns and an annual outdoor concert in Acadia National Park. Tickets are $25-40 adults, $15 students, and can be purchased at the festival office building (59 Cottage St., Bar Harbor). Reservations are advised.

The nonprofit, community-based **Harborside Shakespeare Company** (207/939-6929, www.harborsideshakespeare.org) performs one of the bard's works each summer.

Every evening, 7pm-11pm, **pianist Bill Trowell** plays in the Great Room Piano Lounge at The Bluenose Hotel (90 Eden St., Bar Harbor, 207/288-3348, www.barharborhotel.com).

Theaters

Built in 1932 and listed on the National Register of Historic Places, the **Criterion Theatre** (35 Cottage St., Bar Harbor, 207/288-0829, www.criteriontheatre.org) is an 877-seat art deco classic with an elegant floating balcony. Its recent history is a roller coaster of openings and closings, but with the help of an anonymous donor, the nonprofit Bar Harbor Jazz Festival (www.bhjf.org) purchased it late in 2014 and reopened it as a year-round venue for movies and live performances.

Combine pizza with your picture show at **Reel Pizza Cinerama** (33 Kennebec Pl., Bar Harbor, 207/288-3811 for films, 207/288-3828 for food, www.reelpizza.net). Two films are screened nightly on each of two screens. All tickets are $6; pizzas start at $9. Doors open at 4:30pm; get there early for the best seats.

EVENTS

Bar Harbor is home to numerous special events; here's just a sampling. For more, call 800/345-4617 or visit www.barharbormaine.com.

In early June, the annual **Acadia Birding Festival** (www.acadiabirdingfestival.com) attracts bird-watchers with guided walks, boating excursions, tours, talks, and meals.

In late June, **Legacy of the Arts** is a weeklong celebration of music, art, theater, dance, and history, with tours, exhibits, workshops, concerts, lectures, demonstrations, and more.

The **Fourth of July** is always a big deal in Bar Harbor, celebrated with a 6am blueberry-pancake breakfast, a 10am parade, an 11am seafood festival, a band concert, and fireworks. A highlight is the Lobster Race, a crustacean competition drawing contestants such as Lobzilla and Larry the Lobster in a four-lane saltwater tank on the Village Green. Independence Day celebrations in the island's smaller villages always evoke a bygone era.

The Abbe Museum, the College of the Atlantic, and the Maine Indian Basketmakers Alliance sponsor the annual **Native American Festival** (10am-4pm first Sat. after July 4, free), featuring baskets, beadwork, and other handicrafts for sale as well as Indian drumming and dancing, held at College of the Atlantic.

In even-numbered years, the **Mount Desert Garden Club Tour** (www.gcmdgardenday.com) presents a rare chance to visit some of Maine's most spectacular private gardens on a Saturday in late July.

The **Directions Craft Show** fills a weekend in late July or early August with extraordinary displays and sales of crafts by members of the Maine Crafts Guild. You'll find it at Mount Desert Island High School (Rte. 233/Eagle Lake Rd., Bar Harbor).

The September **Acadia Night Sky Festival** (www.acadianightskyfestival.com) celebrates Acadia's stellar stargazing with arts and science events, presentations, and activities.

SHOPPING

Bar Harbor's boutiques—running the gamut from attractive to kitschy—are indisputably visitor-oriented; most shut down for the winter.

Downtown Bar Harbor's best fine crafts gallery is **Island Artisans** (99 Main St., Bar Harbor, 207/288-4214, www.islandartisans.com). More than 100 Maine artists are represented here, and the quality is outstanding. You'll find basketwork, handmade paper, wood carvings, blown glass, jewelry, weaving, metalwork, ceramics, and more.

Gallery? Funky gift store? Museum? It's hard to categorize the **Rock & Art Shop** (13 Cottage St., Bar Harbor, 207/288-4800). Fossils, gems, minerals, bug-filled marbles, and preserved sea horses are part of the intriguing mix, most of which carries educational signs.

Bark Harbor (150 Main St., Bar Harbor, 207/288-0404) is the place to pick up the perfect souvenir for your cat or dog.

Toys, cards, and newspapers blend in with the new-book inventory at **Sherman's Book Store** (56 Main St., Bar Harbor, 207/288-3161). It's just the place to pick up maps and trail guides for fine days and puzzles for foggy days.

Find field guides, books, nature-based games and toys, binoculars, and other must-haves for exploring the wild side of Acadia at **The Natural History Center** (6 Firefly Ln., Bar Harbor, 207/801-2617, www.thenaturalhistorycenter.com), which also offers naturalist-led tours.

RECREATION

Walks

A real treat is a stroll along downtown Bar Harbor's **Shore Path,** a well-trodden granite-edged byway built around 1880. Along the craggy shoreline are granite-and-wood benches, town-owned **Grant Park** (great for picnics), birch trees, and several handsome mansions that escaped the 1947 fire. Offshore are the four Porcupine Islands. The path is open 6:30am-dusk, and leashed pets are allowed. Allow about 30 minutes for the mile loop, beginning next to the town pier and the Bar Harbor Inn and returning via Wayman Lane.

Check local newspapers or the Bar Harbor Chamber of Commerce visitor booklet for the times of low tide, then walk across the gravel bar to wooded **Bar Island** (formerly Rodick's Island) from the foot of Bridge Street in downtown Bar Harbor. Shell heaps recorded on the eastern end of the island indicate that Native Americans enjoyed this turf in the distant past. You'll have the most time to explore the island during new-moon or full-moon low tides, but no more than four hours—about 1.5 hours before and after low tide. Be sure to wear a watch so you don't get trapped (for up to 10 hours). The foot of Bridge Street is also an excellent kayak-launching site.

Bar Harbor's Shore Path

About a mile from downtown along Main Street (Rte. 3) is **Compass Harbor,** a section of the park where you can stroll through woods to the water's edge and explore the overgrown ruins of Acadia National Park cofounder George Dorr's home.

Five trails wind through The Nature Conservancy's forested 110-acre **Indian Point-Blagden Preserve**, a rectangular parcel with island, hill, and bay vistas. Seal-watching and bird-watching are popular, and there are harbor seals on offshore rocks as well as woodpeckers and 130 other species in blowdown areas. To spot the seals, plan your hike around low tide, when they'll be sprawled on the rocks close to shore. Wear rubberized shoes. Bring binoculars or use the telescope installed here for the purpose. To keep from disturbing the seals, watch quietly and avoid jerky movements. Park near the preserve entrance and follow the Big Woods Trail, which runs the length of the preserve. A second parking area is farther in, but then you'll miss much of the preserve. When you reach the second parking area, just past an old field, bear left along the Shore Trail to see the seals. Register at the caretaker's house (just beyond the first parking lot, where you can pick up bird and flora checklists), and respect private property on either side of the preserve. It's open dawn-6pm daily year-round. From the junction of Routes 3 and 102/198, continue 1.8 miles to Indian Point Road and turn right. Go 1.7 miles to a fork and turn right. Watch for the preserve entrance on the right, marked by a Nature Conservancy oak leaf.

Bicycling

With all the great biking options, including 33 miles of carriage roads open to bicycles and some of the best roadside bike routes in Maine, you'll want to bring a bike or rent one here.

The Minutolo family's **Bar Harbor Bicycle Shop** (141 Cottage St., Bar Harbor, 207/288-3886, www.barharborbike.com), on the corner of Route 3, has been in business since 1977. If you have your own bike, stop here for advice on routes—the Minutolos have cycled everywhere on the island and can suggest the perfect mountain-bike or road-bike loop based on your ability and schedule. The shop has rentals varying from standard mountain bikes to full-suspension models and even tandems as well as all the accessories and gear you might need; rates begin at about $25/day. Hours in summer are 8am-6pm daily, 9am-5pm spring and fall. The shop also can give you the schedule for local rides organized by the **Downeast Bicycle Club** (www.downeastbicycleclub.ning.com).

Sea Kayaking

National Park Kayak Tours (39 Cottage St., Bar Harbor, 207/288-0342 or 800/347-0940, www.acadiakayak.com) limits its Registered Maine Guide-led tours to a maximum of six tandem kayaks per trip. Four-hour morning, midday, afternoon, or sunset paddles are offered, including shuttle service, a paddle and safety lesson, and a brief stop, for $52 pp in July-August, $48 off-season. Trips cover about six miles on the western side of the island and include transportation. Multiday camping trips also are offered. Try to make reservations at least one day in advance.

Half-day, full-day, and multiday sea-kayak tours are on the schedule organized by **Coastal Kayaking Tours** (48 Cottage St., Bar Harbor, 207/288-9605 or 800/526-8615, www.acadiafun.com). The best option for beginners is the 2.5-hour morning harbor tour ($39 pp). A half-day family tour, departing at 1pm, can handle kids age eight and over ($49 pp). A 2.5-hour sunset cruise ($39 pp) begins around 5pm, depending on season; a full-day tour ($74 pp, lunch not included) covers about 10 miles; and a three-day island-camping adventure is $429 per person, including equipment and meals. All trips are weather-dependent, and reservations are essential.

Golf

Duffers first teed off at **Kebo Valley Golf Club** in 1888 (100 Eagle Lake Rd./Rte. 233, Bar Harbor, 207/288-5000, www.kebovalleyclub.com, May-Oct.), Maine's oldest club and the eighth-oldest in the nation. The 17th hole became legendary when it took President William Howard Taft 27 strokes to sink a ball in 1911.

Boat Excursions

★ DIVE-IN THEATER BOAT CRUISE

You don't have to go diving in these frigid waters; others will do it for you. When the kids are clamoring to touch slimy sea cucumbers and starfish at various touch tanks

Excursion boats depart from Bar Harbor's waterfront.

in the area, they're likely to be primed for Diver Ed's **Dive-In Theater Boat Cruise** (207/288-3483 or 800/979-3370, www.divered.com), departing from the College of the Atlantic pier (105 Eden St., Bar Harbor). Ed Monat, former Bar Harbor harbormaster and College of the Atlantic grad, heads the crew aboard the 46-passenger *Starfish Enterprise,* which goes a mile or two offshore, where Ed, a professional diver, goes overboard with a video camera and a mini-Ed, who helps put things in proportion. You and the kids stay on deck, all warm and dry, along with Captain Evil, who explains the action on a TV screen. There's communication back and forth, so the kids can ask questions as the divers pick up urchins, starfish, crabs, lobsters, and other sea life. When Ed resurfaces, he brings a bag of touchable specimens—another chance to pet some slimy creatures (which go back into the water after show-and-tell). It's a great concept. Watch the kids' expressions—this is a big hit. The two-hour trips depart three times daily Monday-Friday, twice daily Saturday, and once on Sunday early July-early September; fewer trips are made in spring and fall. The cost is $40 adults, $35 seniors, $30 ages 5-12, $15 under age 5. Advance reservations are strongly recommended.

WHALE-WATCHING AND PUFFIN-WATCHING

Whale-watching boats go as far as 20 miles offshore, so no matter what the weather in Bar Harbor, dress warmly and bring more clothing than you think you'll need—even gloves, if you're especially sensitive to cold. I've been out on days when it's close to 90°F on the island but feels more like 30°F in a moving boat on the open ocean. Motion-sensitive children and adults should plan in advance for appropriate medication, such as seasickness pills or patches. Adults are required to show a photo ID when boarding the boat.

Whale-watching, puffin-watching, and combo excursions are offered by **Bar Harbor Whale Watch Company** (1 West St., Bar Harbor, 207/288-2386 or 800/942-5374, www.barharborwhales.com), sailing from the town pier (1 West St.) in downtown Bar Harbor. The company operates under various names, including Acadian Whale Watcher, and has a number of boats. Most trips are accompanied by a naturalist (often from Allied Whale at the College of the Atlantic), who regales passengers with all sorts of interesting trivia about the whales, porpoises, seabirds, and other marine life spotted along the way. In season, some trips go out as far as the puffin colony on Petit Manan Light. Trips depart daily late May-late October, but with so many options it's impossible to list the schedule—call for the latest details. Tickets are around $60 adults, $35 ages 6-14, $9 under age 6. A portion of the ticket price benefits Allied Whale, which researches and protects marine animals in the Gulf of Maine. Trips may extend longer than the time advertised, so don't plan anything else too tightly around the trip.

Scenic Nature Cruises (1.5-2 hours) and kid-friendly **Lobster** and **Seal Watch Cruises** (1.5 hours) are also offered. Rates for these are around $30 adults, $18 ages 6-14, and $5 or less for little kids.

SAILING

Captain Steve Pagels, under the umbrella of **Downeast Windjammer Cruises** (207/288-4585 or 207/288-2373, www.downeastwindjammer.com), offers 1.5-2-hour day sails on the 151-foot steel-hulled *Margaret Todd,* a gorgeous four-masted schooner with tanbark sails that he designed and launched in 1998; the Halie & Matthew, or the Bailey Louise Todd. Trips depart at 10am, 2pm, and around sunset daily mid-May-mid-October (weather permitting) from the Bar Harbor Inn pier, just east of the town pier in downtown Bar Harbor. You'll get the best wildlife sightings on the morning trip, but better sailing on the afternoon trip; there's live music on the sunset one. A park ranger narrates some sails, which adds to the experience. Buy tickets either at the pier, at

Adopt-a-Whale

Here's a trump card: When everyone else is flashing photos of kids or grandkids, you can whip out images of your very own adopted whale. And for that, you can thank Allied Whale's **Adopt-a-Whale** program at College of the Atlantic (COA) in Bar Harbor.

In 1972, COA established Allied Whale, a marine-mammal laboratory designed to collect, interpret, and apply research on the world's largest mammal. Although Allied Whale's primary focus is the Gulf of Maine, its projects span the globe and involve international scientific collaboration. Since 1981, part of the research has involved assembling an enormous photo collection (more than 25,000 images) for identification of specific humpback and finback whales (with names such as Quartz and Elvis) and tracking of their migration routes. The photo catalog of finbacks already numbers more than 1,000.

And here's where the adoption program comes in—it's a way to support the important research being done by Allied Whale and its colleagues. If you sign up as an adoptive "parent" for a year, you'll receive a Certificate of Adoption, a large color photo and a biography of your whale, its sighting history, an informational booklet, and an Adopt a Whale-Allied Whale bumper sticker. It's a superb gift for budding scientists. The adoption fee is $30 for a single whale or $40 for a mother and calf.

For further information, contact **Allied Whale** (207/288-5644, www.barharborwhalemuseum.org/adopt2.php).

27 Main St., or online with a credit card; plan to arrive at least half an hour early. The cost is $40 adults, $37 seniors, $30 ages 6-11, $5 ages 2-5. Dogs are welcome on all sails.

SEA VENTURE

Captain Winston Shaw's custom boat tour by **Sea Venture** (207/288-3355, www.svboattours.com) lets you design the perfect trip aboard *Reflection*, a 20-foot motor launch. Captain Shaw, a Registered Maine Guide and committed environmentalist, specializes in nature-oriented tours. He's the founder and director of the Coastal Maine Bald Eagle Project, and he was involved in the inaugural Earth Day celebration in 1970. He's been studying coastal birds for more than 25 years. You can pick from 10 recommended cruises lasting 1-8 hours, or design your own. In any case, the boat is yours. The boat charter rate is $120/hour for up to two people, $140 for three or four, and $180 for five or six. Captain Shaw can also arrange for picnic lunches. On longer trips, restroom stops are available. The boat departs from the Atlantic Oakes Motel pier, off Route 3 in Bar Harbor.

LOBSTER CRUISE

When you're ready to learn *the truth* about lobsters, sign up for a two-hour cruise aboard **Captain John Nicolai's *Lulu*** (55 West St., Bar Harbor, 207/963-2341 or 866/235-2341, www.lululobsterboat.com), a traditional Maine lobster boat that departs up to four times daily from the Harborside Hotel and Marina. Captain Nicolai provides an entertaining commentary on anything and everything, but especially about lobsters and lobstering. He hauls a lobster trap and explains intimate details of the hapless critters. This is a real kid-pleaser, but adults are equally entertained. Reservations are required. Cost is $33 adults, $30 seniors and active U.S. military, $20 ages 2-12.

ACCOMMODATIONS

Unless otherwise noted, these properties operate seasonally; most are open May-October. Rates listed are for peak season.

Hotels and Motels

One of the town's best-known, most visible, and best-situated hotels is the **Bar Harbor Inn** (Newport Dr., Bar Harbor, 207/288-3351 or 800/248-3351, www.barharborinn.com, from $229), a sprawling complex on eight acres overlooking the harbor and islands. The 153 rooms and suites vary considerably in style, from traditional inn to motel, and are in three different buildings. Continental breakfast is included, and special packages, with meals and activities, are available—an advantage if you have children. The kids will appreciate the heated outdoor pool; adults might enjoy the full-service spa. Also under the same management and ownership (www.bar-harbor-hotels.com) is the family-oriented **Acadia Inn** (98 Eden St., Bar Harbor, 207/288-3500, www.acadiainn.com, $180-210), located between the park entrance and downtown Bar Harbor. Facilities include an outdoor heated pool, whirlpool tub, and laundry. Rates include continental breakfast, Wi-Fi, and in-room fridge.

The appropriately named **Harborside Hotel & Marina** (55 West St., Bar Harbor, 207/288-5033 or 800/238-5033, www.theharborsidehotel.com, from $429) fronts the water in downtown Bar Harbor. Most of the guest rooms, studios, and suites have a water view and semiprivate balcony. Some have large outdoor hot tubs. The $25 resort fee allows access to the beautifully restored Bar Harbor Club, with a full-service spa, fitness center, tennis courts, and oceanfront heated pool. Also on the premises are a second outdoor pool, an Italian restaurant, a pier, and a marina. Sharing use of those facilities is a sister property, the **West Street Hotel** (50 West St., 877/905-4498, www.theweststreethotel.com, from $499), a new and tony spot with a rooftop pool (ages 18 and older, only) overlooking downtown, harbor, islands, and ocean. Rooms have a nautical vibe, and those on the West Street-side have harbor views. All have Wi-Fi, flat-screen TVs, and in-room fridge.

On the edge of downtown, across from College of the Atlantic, are two adjacent sister properties tiered up a hillside: **Wonder View Inn & Suites** (55 Eden St., Bar Harbor, 888/439-8439, www.wonderviewinn.com, $129-279) and **The Bluenose Hotel** (90 Eden St., Bar Harbor, 207/288-3348 or 800/445-4077, www.barharborhotel.com, from $249). The pet-friendly ($20/pet/night) Wonder View comprises four older motels on 14 acres of estate-like grounds with grassy lawns and mature shade trees, an outdoor pool, and a restaurant. The estate was the home of famed mystery writer Mary Roberts Rinehart, who coined the phrase "The butler did it." Guest rooms vary widely, and rates reflect both style of accommodation and views; all have refrigerator, TV, Wi-Fi, and air-conditioning. The Bluenose, one of the island's top properties, comprises two buildings. Mizzentop is newest, and its guest rooms and suites are quite elegant, many with fireplaces, and all with fabulous views and balconies. The property also includes a spa, fitness center, indoor and outdoor pools, and a lounge with live music every evening. Stenna Nordica guest rooms, accessed from outdoor corridors, are more modest, but still have views.

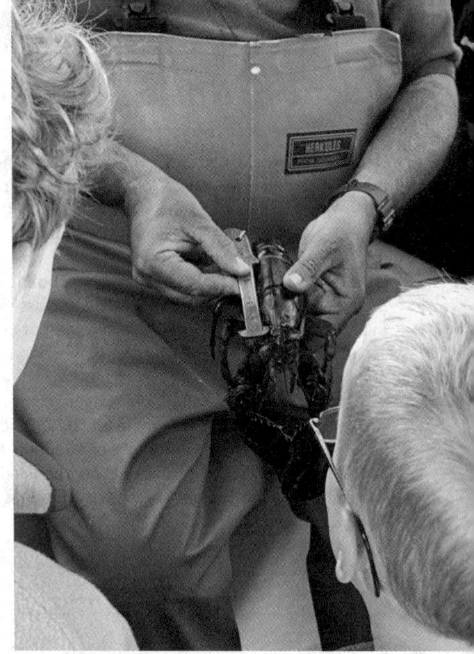

Tours on Captain John Nicolai's *Lulu* are an excellent introduction to lobster fishing.

On the edge of town, the **Cromwell Harbor Motel** (359 Main St., Bar Harbor,

207/288-3201 or 800/544-3201, www.cromwellharbor.com, $130-180) is set back from the road on nicely landscaped grounds with an outdoor pool. All guest rooms have air-conditioning, phones, TVs, microwaves, and refrigerators. The location puts all of downtown's sights within walking distance.

On the lower end of the budgetary scale are two neighboring motels: **Edenbrook Motel** (96 Eden St./Rte. 3, Bar Harbor, 207/288-4975 or 800/323-7819, www.edenbrookmotelbh.com, $80-130), with panoramic views of Frenchman Bay from some rooms, and the wee bit fancier **Highbrook Motel** (94 Eden St./Rte. 3, Bar Harbor, 207/288-3591 or 800/338-9688, www.highbrookmotel.com, $119-179), with Wi-Fi, in-room mini-fridge, and continental breakfast. Both are about 1.5 miles from Acadia's main entrance, one mile from downtown.

Clean and affordable, the **Belle Isle Motel** (910 Rte. 3, Bar Harbor, 207/288-5726, www.belleislemotel.net, $82-95) is a vintage mom-and-pop roadside motel. Darren and Camille Taylor purchased the Belle in 2011 and have spruced it up. The rooms are small, but all have air-conditioning, TV, free local calls, Wi-Fi, and refrigerators; deluxe rooms are more spacious, but closer to the road. Also on the premises are a heated pool, playground, picnic area, and guest laundry.

If all you want is a room with a bed, **Robbins Motel** (396 Rte. 3, Bar Harbor, 207/288-4659, www.robbinsmotel.com, $65), an older motel, has 30 small, unadorned (some might call them dismal) but clean, pine-paneled, queen-bed guest rooms. All have air-conditioning and TV; some have Wi-Fi. There is no charm and it's not quiet, but it's cheap. Off-season rates are as low as $36.

Inns and Bed-and-Breakfasts

Few innkeepers have mastered the art of hospitality as well as Roy Kasindorf and Hélène Harton, owners of ★ **The Ullikana** (16 The Field, Bar Harbor, 207/288-9552, www.ullikana.com, $205-385), located in a quiet downtown location close to Bar Harbor's Shore Path. Roy and Hélène genuinely enjoy their guests. Hélène is a whiz in the kitchen; after one of her multicourse breakfasts, usually served on the water-view patio, you won't be needing lunch. She's also a decorating genius, blending antiques and modern art, vibrant color with soothing hues, and folk art with fine art. Roy excels at helping guests select just the right hike, bike route, or other activity. Afternoon refreshments provide a time for guests to gather and share experiences. Alpheus Hardy, Bar Harbor's first cottager, built the 10-room Victorian Tudor inn in 1885. The comfortable rooms all have private baths (although one is detached); many have working fireplaces, and some have private terraces with water views. The innkeepers also speak French.

Right next door is the gorgeously renovated and rejuvenated ★ **Bass Cottage** (14 The Field, Bar Harbor, 207/288-1234 or 866/782-9224, www.basscottage.com, from $260). Corporate refugees Teri and Jeff Anderholm purchased the 26-room 1885 cottage in 2003 and spent a year gutting it, salvaging the best of the old, and blending in the new to turn it into a luxurious and stylish 10-room inn. It retains its Victorian bones, yet is most un-Victorian in style. Guest rooms are soothingly decorated with cream- and pastel-colored walls and have phones, Wi-Fi, and flat-screen TVs with DVD players (a DVD library is available—valuable on a stormy day); many rooms have fireplaces and whirlpool tubs. The spacious and elegant public rooms—expansive living rooms, a cozy library, porches—flow from one to another. Teri puts her culinary degree to use preparing baked goods, fruits, and savory and sweet entrées for breakfast and evening refreshments. A guest pantry is stocked with tea, coffee, and snacks.

Completing the trio of inns sited in The Field is the **Yellow House Bed & Breakfast** (207/288-5100, 15 The Field, www.yellowhousemaine.com, from $285), a lovely 1875 summer cottage with an inviting wraparound porch overlooking a sculpture garden that blends gentle ease with contemporary comforts, such as TVs and air-conditioning.

Situated on one oceanfront acre in the West Street Historical District, **The Saltair Inn** (121 West St., Bar Harbor, 207/288-2882, www.saltairinn.com, $195-370) was originally built in 1887 as a guesthouse. Innkeepers Kristi and Matt Losquadro and their young family now welcome guests in eight guest rooms, most of which are quite spacious, and five of which face Frenchman Bay. Frills vary by room but might include whirlpool tubs, fireplaces, and balconies. All have TVs and Wi-Fi. A full breakfast is served either in the dining room or on the water-view deck. It's steps from downtown but, really, with a location like this, why leave?

Outside of town, in a serene location with fabulous views of Frenchman Bay, is the ★ **Inn at Bay Ledge** (150 Sand Point Rd., Bar Harbor, summer 207/288-4204, www.innatbayledge.com, $175-400), an elegant, casual retreat tucked under towering pines atop an 80-foot cliff. Built in 1800 as a minister's home, it's been expanded and updated in the intervening years. Terraced decks descend to a pool and onto the lawn, which stretches to the cliff's edge. Stairs descend to a private stone beach below. Almost all guest rooms have water views; some have whirlpool tubs and/or private decks. A sauna and a steam shower are available. In the woods across the street are cottages, which lack the view but have use of the inn's facilities. Also on the premises is the Summer House ($475), a shingled cottage with a deck 25 feet from the edge of Frenchman Bay.

Much less pricey and a find for families is the **Seacroft Inn** (18 Albert Meadow, Bar Harbor, 207/288-4669 or 800/824-9694, www.seacroftinn.com, $109-149), well-situated just off Main Street and near the Shore Path. All rooms in Bunny and Dave Brown's white multigabled cottage have air-conditioning, phones, TVs, refrigerators, and microwaves; a continental breakfast is available for $5 pp. Housekeeping is $10/day. Some rooms can be joined as family suites.

Marian Burns, a former math and science teacher, is the reason everything runs smoothly at **Mira Monte Inn** (69 Mount Desert St., Bar Harbor, 207/288-4263 or 800/553-5109, www.miramonte.com, $200-300), close (but not too close) to downtown. Born and raised here and an avid gardener, Marian's a terrific resource for island exploring. Try to capture her during wine and cheese (5pm-7pm), and ask about her experience

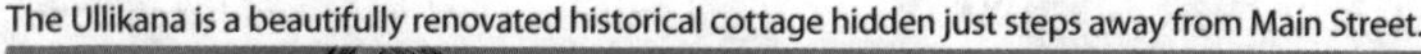
The Ullikana is a beautifully renovated historical cottage hidden just steps away from Main Street.

Mount Desert Island Ice Cream

during the 1947 Bar Harbor fire. And don't miss her collection of antique Bar Harbor hotel photos. The 13 Victorian-style rooms have air-conditioning, cable TV, and either a balcony or a fireplace, and some have whirlpool tubs. Also available are four suites, some with kitchen or kitchenette. Rates include an extensive hot-and-cold breakfast buffet. Open year-round.

Hostels

Not officially a hostel, but with a hostel-style atmosphere, and only for women, the **MDI YWCA** (36 Mount Desert St., Bar Harbor, 207/288-5008, $30-40/night; $75-100/week) has second- and third-floor single and double rooms, as well as a seven-bed solarium (dorm). Located in a historic downtown building next to the library and across from the Island Explorer bus hub, "the Y" has bathrooms on each floor, as well as a laundry room (coin-operated machines), a TV room, and shared kitchen facilities. There's zero tolerance for smoking, alcohol, and drugs (you'll need to sign an agreement). For summer and fall reservations, call way ahead, as the Y is popular with the island's young summer workers.

FOOD

You won't go hungry in Bar Harbor. The island's best collection of good, inexpensive restaurants are along Rodick Street, from Reel Pizza down to Rosalie's, which actually fronts on Cottage Street. For sit-down restaurants, make reservations as far in advance as possible. Expect reduced operations during spring and fall; few places are open in winter.

Mount Desert Island is a seasonal community, and restaurant days and hours change frequently, so always call ahead. Also note that staffing is always a challenge in the region, and many businesses import workers from overseas. By the time waiters and waitresses have been fully trained, the season is almost over.

Local Flavors

Free tastings are offered daily at **Bar Harbor Cellars** (854 Rte. 3, Bar Harbor, 207/288-3907, www.barharborcellars.com). The winery is in the early stages of using organic techniques to grow hybrid grapes. In the meantime, it's making wines from European and California grapes. Also here is a Maine chocolate room and a small selection of complementary foods, such as olives, cheese, and crackers.

Only a masochist could bypass **Ben and Bill's Chocolate Emporium** (66 Main St., Bar Harbor, 207/288-3281 or 800/806-3281), which makes homemade candies and more than 50 ice cream flavors (including a dubious lobster flavor); the whole place smells like the inside of a chocolate truffle. It opens daily at 10am, with closing dependent on the season and crowds, but usually late in the evening.

That said, the most creative flavors come from **Mount Desert Island Ice Cream** (7 Firefly Ln., Bar Harbor, 207/288-0999, and 325 Main St., Bar Harbor, 207/288-5664, www.mdiic.com). It's made in small batches, just five gallons at a time, using the finest ingredients. We're talking creamy, rich, delicious, and wild flavors.

Probably the least-expensive lunch or ice cream option in town is **West End Drug Co.** (105 Main St., Bar Harbor, 207/288-3318), where you can get grilled-cheese sandwiches, PBJ, and other white-bread basics as well as shakes, egg creams, and sundaes at the fountain.

Equally inexpensive, but with a healthful menu, is the **Take-A-Break Cafe** (105 Eden St., Bar Harbor, 207/288-5015, www.coa.edu) in Blair Dining Hall, at College of the Atlantic. If you find yourself on the college campus, perhaps for a boat tour or museum visit, consider eating here. The cafeteria-style café serves breakfast, lunch, and dinner on most weekdays, and although there are individual choices, the best deals are the all-you-can eat meals ($5-10). There are always vegetarian, vegan, gluten-free, and meat choices, and the selection is organic and local whenever possible. Even better, the food is excellent.

When it comes to pub-grub favorites, such as burgers and fish sandwiches, **The Thirsty Whale Tavern** (40 Cottage St., Bar Harbor, 207/288-9335, www.thirstywhaletavern.com, 11am-9pm daily, $7-16) does it right.

Combine a pizza with a first-run or art flick at **Reel Pizza Cinerama** (33 Kennebec Pl., Bar Harbor, 207/288-3811 for films, 207/288-3828 for food, www.reelpizza.net), where you order your pizza, grab an easy chair, and watch for your number to come up on the bingo board. Most films are screened twice nightly. Pizzas ($12-20 or by the slice) have cinematic names—Zorba the Greek, The Godfather, Manchurian Candidate. Then there's Mussel Beach Party—broccoli, tomatoes, goat cheese, and smoked mussels. You get the idea. Reel Pizza opens daily at 4:30pm and has occasional Saturday matinees; closed Monday in winter. Arrive early; the best seats go quickly.

For breakfast or brunch, you can't beat **2 Cats** (130 Cottage St., Bar Harbor, 207/288-2808 or 800/355-2828, www.2catsbarharbor.com, 7am-1pm daily). Fun, funky, and fresh best describe both the restaurant and the food ($8-12). Dine inside or on the patio. Dinner is also served at 2 Cats—call for nights and hours. Three upstairs guest rooms are available for $165-195, less in winter—with breakfast, of course.

Escape the downtown madness at **Tea House 278** (278 Main St., Bar Harbor, 207/288-2781, www.teahouse278.com, 11am-7pm Wed.-Sun.), a traditional Chinese teahouse offering Gaiwan service, along with light fare (don't miss the tea-steeped eggs) and even Mahjong. The owners source all teas from small farms in China and Taiwan. Sit inside or in the tea garden, with dwarf trees and waterfall. Upstairs is a gallery.

Choco-Latte (240 Main St., Bar Harbor, 207-801-9179, www.choco-lattecafe.com, 7am-9pm daily) aims to make all of its chocolates in house from organic Criollo cacao sourced from women-owned co-ops in Chiapas and Veracruz, Mexico. Pair it with an organic coffee or a hot chocolate.

Between Mother's Day and late October, the **Eden Farmers Market** operates out of the YMCA parking lot off Lower Main Street in Bar Harbor, 9am-noon each Sunday. You'll find fresh meats and produce, local cheeses and maple syrup, yogurt and ice cream, bread, honey, preserves, and even prepared Asian foods.

Picnic Fare

Although a few of these places have some seating, most are for the grab-and-go crowd.

For a light, inexpensive meal, you can't go wrong at **Morning Glory Bakery** (39 Rodick St., Bar Harbor, 207/288-3041, www.morningglorybakery.com, 7am-5pm Mon.-Fri., 8am-5pm Sat.-Sun.). Fresh-baked goodies, breakfast and regular sandwiches, soups, and salads are all made from scratch.

Another good choice for take-out fare is **Downeast Deli** (65 Main St., Bar Harbor, 207/288-1001, 7am-4pm daily). You can get both hot and cold fresh lobster rolls as well as other sandwiches, soups, and salads.

At **Adelmann's Deli** (224 Main St., Bar

Harbor, 207/288-0455, 11am-7pm daily), build-your-own lunch sandwiches are $9. Choose from a variety of breads, Boar's Head-brand meats and cheeses, veggies, condiments, and more.

If you happen to be on Route 102 in the Town Hill area around lunchtime, plan to pick up picnic fare at **Mother's Kitchen** (Rte. 102, Town Hill, Bar Harbor, 207/288-4403, www.motherskitchenfoods.com, 9am-2pm Mon.-Fri.). The plain, minuscule building next to Salsbury's (look for the Real Good Food sign) is deceiving—it has been operating since 1995 and turns out 20 different sandwiches as well as deli salads, scones, breakfast sandwiches, great cookies, and pies.

Brewpubs and Microbreweries

Bar Harbor's longest-lived brewpub is the **Lompoc Cafe** (36 Rodick St., Bar Harbor, 207/288-9392, www.lompoccafe.com, from 4:30pmdaily late Apr.-mid-Dec.), with brews on tap. Go for pizzas, salads, and entrées ($10-21), along with boccie in the beer garden and live entertainment on weekends. After 9pm there's just beer and thin-crust pizza until about 1am.

Lompoc's signature Bar Harbor Real Ale and five or six others are brewed by the **Atlantic Brewing Company** (15 Knox Rd., Town Hill, in the upper section of the island, 207/288-2337, www.atlanticbrewing.com). Free brewery tours, including tastings, are given daily at 2pm, 3pm, and 4pm late May-mid-October. Also operating here in summer is **Mainely-Meat Bar-B-Q** (207/288-9200, 11:30am-7pm daily, $8-16), offering pulled pork, chicken, ribs, and similar fare for lunch and dinner.

Bar Harbor Brewing Company (8 Mt. Desert St., Bar Harbor, 207/288-4592, www.barharborbrewing.com), a sister of Atlantic Brewing, produces Thunder Hole Ale, Cadillac Mountain Stout, and True Blue. The microbrewery is located downtown in a spacious shop, where tours and tastings are held most afternoons; stop by or call for the schedule.

Family Favorites

An unscientific but reliable local survey gives the best-pizza ribbon to **Rosalie's Pizza & Italian Restaurant** (46 Cottage St., Bar Harbor, 207/288-5666, www.rosaliespizza.com, 4pm-10pm daily), where the Wurlitzer jukebox churns out tunes from the 1950s. Rosalie's earns high marks for consistency with its homemade pizza, in four sizes or by the slice, along with calzones and subs; there are lots of vegetarian options. If you need something a bit heartier, try the Italian dinners—spaghetti, eggplant parmigiana, and others—all less than $10, including a garlic roll. Beer and wine are available. Avoid the downstairs lines by heading upstairs and ordering at that counter, or call in your order.

Efficient, friendly cafeteria-style service makes **EPI's Pizza** (8 Cottage St., Bar Harbor, 207/288-5853, 11am-7pm daily Sept.-June, to 9pm daily July-Aug.) an excellent choice for subs, salads, pizzas, and even spaghetti. If the weather closes in, there are always the pinball machines in the back room.

Route 66 Restaurant (21 Cottage St., Bar Harbor, 207/288-3708, www.barharbor-route66.com, 7am-about 8pm daily, $9-25), filled with 1950s memorabilia and old toys, is a fun restaurant that's a real hit with kids (check out the Lionel train running around just below the ceiling). The wide-ranging menu includes sandwiches, burgers, pizza, steak, chicken, seafood, and kids' choices. No raves here, just okay food in a fun atmosphere.

Savor the panoramic views over Bar Harbor, Frenchman Bay, and the Porcupine Islands along with breakfast or dinner at the **Looking Glass Restaurant** (Wonder View Inn, 50 Eden St., Bar Harbor, 207/288-5663, www.wonderviewinn.com, 7am-10:30am and 5:30pm-9pm daily, $11-38). It's quite casual, there's a children's menu, and the deck is pet-friendly.

Most folks come to **Sweet Pea's Café** (854 Rte. 3, Bar Harbor, 207/801-9078, 8am-8pm daily, $9-16) for the wood-oven sourdough pizzas, topped with fresh greens, veggies, and local seafood, but the mussels and the oyster starters earn raves, as does the local cheese plate. Other options include sandwiches, salads, and sweets. Atlantic Brewing Company ales and Bar Harbor Cellars' wines are available. People love the breakfast popovers.

Casual Dining

You can't go wrong at **Galyn's Galley** (17 Main St., Bar Harbor, 207/288-9706, www.galynsbarharbor.com, 11am-9pm daily Mar.-Nov., dinner entrées $3-35). Once a Victorian boardinghouse and later a 1920s speakeasy, Galyn's has been a popular restaurant since 1986. Lots of plants, modern decor, reliable service, a great downtown location, and several indoor and outdoor dining areas contribute to the loyalty of the clientele. Reservations are advisable in midsummer.

When you're craving fresh and delicious fare but not a heavy meal, the **Side Street Café** (49 Rodick St., Bar Harbor, 207/801-2591, www.sidestreetbarharbor.com, 11am-midnight daily, $8-26) delivers. It's a cheerful place with a relaxed demeanor combined with good service and a friendly attitude. The lobster roll and the crab melt earn high fives, as do the burgers.

Set back from the road behind a garden is the very popular **McKays Public House** (231 Main St., Bar Harbor, 207/288-2002, www.mckayspublichouse.com, from 4:30pm daily, $11-26), a comfortable pub with seating indoors in small dining rooms or at the bar, or outdoors in the garden. The best bet is the classic pub fare, which includes shepherd's pie, burgers, and fish-and-chips. Fancier entrées, such as seafood risotto, are also available.

Casual, friendly, creative, and reliable defines **Cafe This Way** (14 Mt. Desert St., Bar Harbor, 207/288-4483, www.cafethisway.com, 7am-11:30am Mon.-Sat., 8am-1pm Sun., and 5:30pm-9:30pm daily, $16-25), where it's easy to make a meal out of the appetizers alone. Vegetarians will be happy here, and there's a gluten-free menu, too. The breakfast menu is a genuine wake-up call ($5-9). It's not a choice for quiet dining.

Chef-owner Karl Yarborough is putting ★ **Mache Bistro** (321 Main St., Bar Harbor, 207/288-0447, www.machebistro.com, from 5:30pm Tues.-Sat., $20-28) on the must-dine list. His interpretations of "French flavors with local flair" are creative without being over the top. This place is justifiably popular, so do make reservations.

Ethnic Fare

For Thai food, **Siam Orchid** (30 Rodick St., Bar Harbor, 207/288-9669, www.siamorchidrestaurant.net, 11am-11pm daily) gets the locals' nod, although it's a bit pricey. House specials run $14-20; curries and noodle dishes, such as pad thai, are $12-17. There are plenty of choices for vegetarians. Siam Orchid serves beer and wine only.

Sharing the same building is **Gringo's** (30 Rodick St., Bar Harbor, 207/288-2326, 11am-10pm daily), a Mexican hole-in-the-wall specializing in take-out burritos, wraps, homemade salsas, and smoothies, with almost everything—margaritas and beer included—less than $8. For a real kick, don't miss the jalapeño brownies.

For "American fine dining with Latin flair," head to ★ **Havana** (318 Main St., Bar Harbor, 207/288-2822, www.havanamaine.com, 5pm-10pm daily May-Nov., call for off-season hours, entrées $24-35), where the innovative Cuban-esque menu changes frequently to take advantage of what's locally available. Inside, bright orange walls and white tablecloths set a tone that's equally festive and accomplished. Out back, a wood-fired grill and open-air bar offer a tapas menu. Also part of Havana is **Parrilla** (from 3pm Sun.-Thurs., from 4pm Fri.-Sat., $8-33), a street-side outdoor bar with Argentinian-style wood-fired grill serving a selection of small and large plates.

Fine Dining

Five miles south of Bar Harbor, in the village of Otter Creek, which itself is in the town of Mount Desert, is the inauspicious-looking **Burning Tree** (Rte. 3, Otter Creek, 207/288-9331, 5pm-10pm Wed.-Mon. late June-early

Oct., closed Mon. after Labor Day, $19-30), which is anything but nondescript inside. Chef-owners Allison Martin and Elmer Beal Jr. have created one of Mount Desert Island's better restaurants, but it can get quite noisy when busy, which it usually is. Reservations are essential in summer. Specialties are imaginative seafood entrées and vegetarian dishes. The homemade breads and desserts are delicious. At the height of summer, service can be a bit rushed, and the kitchen runs out of popular entrées. Solution: Plan to eat early; it's worth it.

At **Fathom** (6 Summer St., 207/288-9664, www.fathombarharbor.com, from 5:30pm daily), the menu might include lobster with gnocchi, seared long island duck breast, or vegan pasta. Most entrées run $26-32.

Lobster

Nearly every restaurant in town serves some form of lobster (my top choice for a lobster roll is the Side Street Café).

Dine inside or on the dock at **Stewman's Lobster Pound** (35 West St., 207/288-0346, www.stewmanslobsterpound.com, 11am-10pm, daily), where the menu ranges from burgers to lobster.

Although it lacks the oceanfront location, **West Street Café** (76 West St., Bar Harbor, 207/288-5242, www.weststreetcafe.com, 11am-8pm daily) is a fine spot for a lobster dinner at a fair price. Dine before 6pm for the best price. There are other items on the menu, but the reason to go here is for the lobster (market price). A kids' menu is available.

INFORMATION AND SERVICES

The **Bar Harbor Chamber of Commerce** (1201 Bar Harbor Rd./Rte. 3, Trenton, 207/288-5103, www.barharbormaine.com) operates a seasonal info center at the corner of Main and Cottage Streets.

Once you're on Mount Desert, if you manage to bestir yourself early enough to catch sunrise on the Cadillac summit (you won't be alone—it's a popular activity), stop in at the chamber of commerce office later and request an official membership card for the **Cadillac Mountain Sunrise Club** (they'll take your word for it).

Jesup Memorial Library (34 Mount Desert St., Bar Harbor, 207/288-4245, www.jesup.lib.me.us) is open all year. The library holds its annual book sale on the third Saturday in August.

Find **public restrooms** at the park visitors centers, and in downtown Bar Harbor in Agamont Park, Harbor Place at the town pier, adjacent to the Village Green, and on the School Street side of the athletic field.

GETTING THERE AND AROUND

Bar Harbor is about 20 miles or 30-45 minutes, depending upon traffic, via Route 3 from Ellsworth; about 45 miles or 75 minutes via Routes 1A and 3 from Bangor; and about 275 miles or five hours via Routes 195 and 3 from Boston. It's about 12 miles or 20 minutes via Routes 233 and 198 or 20 miles/35 minutes via Route 3 to Northeast Harbor.

Make it easy on yourself and help improve the air quality by leaving your car at your lodging (or if day-tripping, at the Bar Harbor Chamber of Commerce on Route 3 in Trenton) and taking the Island Explorer bus.

RVs are not allowed to park near the town pier; designated RV parking is alongside the athletic field, on Lower Main and Park Streets, about eight blocks from the center of town.

Northeast Harbor

Ever since the late 19th century, the upper crust from Philadelphia has been summering in and around Northeast Harbor. Sure, they also show up in other parts of Maine, but it's hard not to notice the preponderance of Pennsylvania license plates surrounding Northeast Harbor's elegant "cottages" mid-July-mid-August.

Actually, even though Northeast Harbor is a well-known name with special cachet, it isn't even an official township; it's a zip-coded village within the town of **Mount Desert** (pop. 2,053), which collects the breathtaking property taxes and doles out the municipal services.

The attractive boutiques and eateries in Northeast Harbor's small downtown area cater to a casually posh clientele, and the well-protected harbor attracts a tony crowd of yachties. For their convenience, a palm-sized annual directory, *The Redbook*, discreetly lists owners' summer residences and winter addresses—but no phone numbers.

Except for two spectacular public gardens and two specialized museums, not much here is geared to budget-sensitive visitors—but there's no charge for admiring the spectacular scenery.

Although all of Mount Desert Island is seasonal, Northeast Harbor is especially so, and it has a tiny and decreasing year-round population. Many businesses don't open until early July and close in early September.

SIGHTS

Somes Sound

As you head toward Northeast Harbor on Route 198 from the northern end of Mount Desert Island, you'll begin seeing cliff-lined Somes Sound, on your right. The glacier-sculpted fjard (not as deep or as steeply walled as a fjord) juts five miles into the interior of Mount Desert Island from its mouth between Northeast Harbor and Southwest Harbor. Watch for the right-hand turn for Sargent Drive (no RVs allowed), and follow the lovely, granite-lined route along the east side of the sound. Halfway along, a marker explains the geology of this spectacular natural inlet. There aren't many pullouts en route,

yacht-filled Northeast Harbor

The Japanese-inspired Asticou Azalea Garden is especially lovely in spring.

and traffic can be fairly thick in midsummer, but don't miss it. **Suminsby Park,** located off Sargent Drive, 400 feet from Route 3, is a fine place for a picnic. The park has rocky shore access, a hand-carry boat launch, picnic tables, grills, and a pit toilet. An ideal way to appreciate Somes Sound is from the water—sign up for an excursion out of Northeast Harbor or Southwest Harbor.

Gardens

★ ASTICOU AZALEA GARDEN AND THUYA GARDEN

If you have the slightest interest in gardens, allow time for Northeast Harbor's two marvelous public gardens, both operated by the nonprofit **Mount Desert Land and Garden Preserve** (207/276-3727, www.gardenpreserve.org).

One of Maine's best spring showcases is the **Asticou Azalea Garden,** a 2.3-acre pocket where about 70 varieties of azaleas, rhododendrons, and laurels—many from the classic Reef Point garden of famed landscape designer Beatrix Farrand—burst into bloom. When Charles K. Savage, beloved former innkeeper of the Asticou Inn, learned the Reef Point garden was being undone in 1956, he went into high gear to find funding and managed to rescue the azaleas and provide them with the gorgeous setting they have today, across the road and around the corner from the inn. Serenity is the key—with a Japanese sand garden that's mesmerizing in any season, stone lanterns, granite outcrops, pink gravel paths, and a tranquil pond. Try to visit early in the season and early in the morning to savor the effect. Blossoming occurs May-August, but the prime time for azaleas is roughly mid-May-mid-June. The garden is on Route 198, at the northern edge of Northeast Harbor, immediately north of the junction with Peabody Drive (Rte. 3). Watch for a tiny sign on the left (if you're coming from the north), marking access to the parking area. A small box suggests a $5 donation, and another box contains a garden guide ($2). Pets are not allowed in the garden. Take Island Explorer Route No. 5 (Jordan Pond) or Route No. 6 (Brown Mountain) and request a stop. Note: The Asticou Stream Trail, a lovely meander through fields and woods and down to the shoreline, connects the garden to the town. Look for a small signpost just north of the Asticou Inn and across from the Route 3 entrance to the garden.

Behind a carved wooden gate on a forested hillside not far from Asticou lies an enchanted garden also designed by Charles K. Savage as a semi-formal English herbaceous garden, inspired by Beatrix Farrand and interpreted for coastal Maine. Special features of **Thuya Garden** are perennial borders and sculpted shrubbery. On a misty summer day, when few visitors appear, the colors are brilliant. Adjacent to the garden is **Thuya Lodge** (207/276-5130), former summer cottage of Joseph Curtis, donor of this awesome municipal park. The lodge, with an extensive botanical and horticultural library and quiet rooms for reading, is open 10am-4:30pm daily late June-Labor Day. The garden is open 7am-7pm daily. A collection box next to the front gate requests a $5 donation per adult. To reach Thuya, continue on Route 3 beyond Asticou Azalea Garden and watch for the Asticou Terraces parking area (no RVs; two-hour limit) on the right. Cross the road and climb the Asticou Terraces Trail (0.4 mile) to the garden. Allow time to hang out at the three lookouts en route. Alternatively, drive 0.2 mile beyond the Route 3 parking area, watching for a minuscule Thuya Garden sign on the left. Go 0.5 mile up the steep, narrow, and curving driveway to the parking area (but walking up reaps higher rewards). Or take Island Explorer Route No. 5 (Jordan Pond) and request a stop.

Note: It's possible to connect Asticou and Thuya Gardens by walking the Asticou Hill Trail, which follows an old road, or hiking the moderately difficult (lots of exposed roots) Eliot Mountain Trail. From the Asticou, the Asticou Hill Trail road across from the Asticou Inn provides access to both; it's a private road, but foot traffic has a right of way.

ABBY ALDRICH ROCKEFELLER GARDEN

The private **Abby Aldrich Rockefeller Garden** (207/276-3330 in season, www.rockgardenmaine.wordpress.com, free) was created in 1921, when the Rockefellers turned to renowned garden designer Beatrix Farrand to create a garden using treasures they'd brought back from Asia. The enclosed garden is a knockout, accented with secret passages, a sunken garden, English floral beds, Korean tombstone figures, a moon gate, and even yellow roof tiles from Beijing. It's open only one day a week from late July to early September, and admission is limited, so reservations are vital; check the website for current details. A garden guide with map is provided, but you're free to explore at your own pace. Note: The Rockefeller family has indicated it will donate this garden to Garden Preserve, which may mean increased days and hours.

Petite Plaisance

On Northeast Harbor's quiet South Shore Road, **Petite Plaisance** (35 South Shore Rd., Northeast Harbor, 207/276-3940, www.petiteplaisanceconservationfund.org, Tues.-Sat. June 15-Aug. 31, donation) is a special-interest museum commemorating noted Belgian-born author and college professor Marguerite Yourcenar (pen name of Marguerite de Crayencour), the first woman elected to the prestigious Académie Française. From 1950 to 1987, Petite Plaisance was her home, and it's hard to believe she's no longer here; her intriguing possessions and presence fill the two-story house, of particular interest to Yourcenar devotees. In 2014 the French Ministry of Culture added Petite Plaisance to its registry of illustrious houses. Free hour-long tours of the 1st floor are given, by advance appointment only. Tours are offered in French or English, depending on visitors' preferences; French-speaking visitors often make pilgrimages here. No children under 12 are allowed. Call at least a day ahead, between 9am and 4pm, to schedule an appointment. Yourcenar admirers should request directions to Brookside Cemetery in Somesville, seven miles away, where she is buried. Tours are free, but donations are much appreciated.

Great Harbor Maritime Museum

Annual exhibits focusing on the maritime heritage of the Mount Desert Island area are held in the small, eclectic **Great Harbor Maritime Museum** (124 Main St., Northeast Harbor, 207/276-5262, 10am-5pm Tues.-Sat. late June-Labor Day, donation), housed in the old village fire station and municipal building. ("Great Harbor" refers to the Somes Sound area—Northeast, Southwest, and Seal Harbors, as well as the Cranberry Isles.) Yachting, coastal trade, and fishing receive special emphasis. Look for the canvas rowing canoe, built in Veazie, Maine, between 1917 and 1920; it's the only one of its kind known to exist today.

ENTERTAINMENT

The **Mount Desert Festival of Chamber Music** (207/276-3988, www.mtdesertfestival.

The Maine Sea Coast Mission

the Maine Sea Coast Mission's *Sunbeam V*

Remote islands and other isolated communities along Maine's rugged coastline may still have a church, but few have a full-time minister; fewer yet have a health-care provider. Yet these communities aren't entirely shut off from either preaching or medical assistance.

Since 1905, the **Maine Sea Coast Mission** (127 West St., Bar Harbor, 207/288-5097, www.seacoastmission.org), a nondenominational, nonprofit organization rooted in a Christian ministry, has offered a lifeline to these communities. The mission, based in Bar Harbor, serves nearly 2,800 people on eight different islands, including Frenchboro, the Cranberries, Swans, and Isle au Haut, as well as others living in remote coastal locations on the mainland. Its numerous, much-needed services include a Christmas program; in-school, after-school, and summer school programs; emergency financial assistance; food assistance; a thrift shop; ministers for island and coastal communities; scholarships; and health services.

Many of these services are delivered via the mission's ***Sunbeam V,*** a 75-foot diesel boat that has no limitations on when, and few on where, it can travel. In winter, it even serves as an icebreaker, clearing harbors and protecting boats from ice damage. During your travels in the Acadia region, you might see the *Sunbeam V* homeported in Northeast Harbor or on its rounds.

A nurse and a minister usually travel on the ship. The minister may conduct services on the island or on the boat, which also functions as a gathering place for fellowship, meals, and meetings. The minister also reaches out to those in need, marginalized, or ill, and often helps with island funerals. Onboard telemedicine equipment enables the nurse to provide much-needed health care, including screening clinics for diabetes, cholesterol, and prostate and skin cancer; flu and pneumonia vaccines; and tetanus shots.

The mission welcomes donations and volunteers. You can make a difference.

org) presents concerts in the century-old Neighborhood House on Main Street at 8:15pm Tuesday mid-July-mid-August. Tickets ($25 general admission, $10 students) are available at the Neighborhood House box office Monday-Tuesday during the concert season or by phone reservation.

SHOPPING

Upscale shops, galleries, and boutiques with clothing, artworks, housewares, antiques, and antiquarian books line both sides of Main Street, making for intriguing browsing and expensive buying (check the sale rooms of the clothing shops for bona fide bargains). The season is short, though, with some shops open only in July-August.

One must-visit is **Shaw Contemporary Jewelry** (100 Main St., 207/276-5000 or 877/276-5001, www.shawjewelry.com, year-round). Besides the spectacular silver and gold beachstone jewelry created by Rhode Island School of Design alumnus Sam Shaw, the work of more than 100 other jewelers is displayed exquisitely. Plus there are sculptures, Asian art, and rotating art exhibits. It all leads back toward a lovely light-filled garden. Prices are in the stratosphere, but appropriately so. As one well-dressed customer was overheard sighing to her companion: "If I had only one jewelry store to go to in my entire life, this would be it."

If you're traveling with children or if you have any interest in art, science, or nature, don't miss **The Naturalist's Notebook** (16 Main St., Seal Harbor, 207/801-2777, www.thenaturalistsnotebook.com) a shop and exploratorium. Owned by artist-photographer Pamelia Markwood and her *Sports Illustrated* writer/editor husband, Craig Neff, the shop has three stories full of engaging exhibits, books, and treasures. A branch operates at 15 Main St. in Northeast Harbor.

RECREATION

Boat Excursions

Northeast Harbor is the starting point for a couple of boat services headed for the **Cranberry Isles.** The vessels leave from the commercial floats at the end of the concrete municipal pier on Sea Street.

The 75-foot ***Sea Princess*** (207/276-5352, www.barharborcruises.com) carries visitors as well as an Acadia National Park naturalist on a 2.75-hour morning trip around the mouth of Somes Sound and out to Little Cranberry Island (Islesford) for a 50-minute stopover. The boat leaves Northeast Harbor at 10am daily mid-May-mid-October. A narrated afternoon trip departs at 1pm on the same route. Other trips operate, but not daily. These include a scenic 1.5-hour day cruise and a 1.5-hour sunset cruise of Somes Sound. Fees range $25-29 adults, $16 ages 5-12, $5 under age 5. Reservations are advisable for all trips, although even that provides no guarantee, since the cruises require a 15-passenger minimum.

The *Helen Brooks,* built in 1970, is one of two traditional Friendship sloops operated by **Downeast Friendship Sloop Charters** (Northeast Harbor Municipal Marina, 41 Harbor Dr., 207/266-5210, www.

The *Sea Princess* cruises around the mouth of Somes Sound and out to Little Cranberry Island.

downeastfriendshipsloop.com); the other one sails out of Southwest Harbor. Private charters start at $250 for a two-hour sail, covering up to six passengers and including an appetizer and soft drinks; shared trips are $50 per person for two hours, $75 per person for three hours. A sunset sail is a lovely way to end a day.

ACCOMMODATIONS

Inns

For more than 100 years, the genteel **Asticou Inn** (Rte. 3, Northeast Harbor, 207/276-3344 or 800/258-3373, www.asticou.com, from $200) has catered to the whims and weddings of Northeast Harbor's well-heeled summer rusticators. She's an elegant, if faded, old gal that seems right out of a Hollywood romance movie set in the 1950s: Hardwood floors are topped with Asian and braided rugs, rooms are papered with floral or plaid wallpapers, and gauzy ruffled curtains blow in the breeze. It's all delightfully old-fashioned, and most guests would have it no other way. But it's not for everybody. The one nod to modern times is free Wi-Fi. There's no air-conditioning, no in-room phone or TV, and no soundproofing. The inn tops a lawn that slopes down to the yacht-filled harbor, and cocktails and lunch are served daily on the porch overlooking the heated pool, tennis court, and water. Accommodations are spread out between the main inn, three cottages, and four funky Topsiders, which seem inspired by the old *Jetsons* TV show. The nicest accommodations, a mix of rooms and suites, face the harbor. The inn's restaurant serves breakfast, lunch, and dinner daily. Try to plan a late-May or early-June visit; you're practically on top of the Asticou Azalea Garden, Thuya Garden is a short walk away (or hike via the Eliot Mountain Trail), and the rates are lowest. Asticou is a popular wedding venue, so if you're looking for a quiet weekend, check the inn's event schedule before booking a room. Note: The Acadia Corp., which lost its contract to operate the Jordan Pond House in a controversial 2014 decision, was managing the inn as of 2015.

Bed-and-Breakfasts

In 1888, architect Fred Savage designed the two Shingle-style buildings that make up the three-story **Harbourside Inn** (Main St., Northeast Harbor, 207/276-3272, www.harboursideinn.com, mid-June-mid-Sept., $160-260). The Sweet family has preserved the old-fashioned feel by decorating the 11 spacious guest rooms and three suites with antiques, yet modern amenities include some kitchenettes and phones. Most rooms have working fireplaces. A continental breakfast is served. Trails to Norumbega Mountain and Upper Hadlock Pond leave from the back of the property.

The new in 2009 **Colonel's Suites** (143 Main St., Northeast Harbor, 207/288-4775, www.colonelssuites.com, $179-219), above the bakery/restaurant of the same name, provide comfortable accommodations with modern amenities. Every suite has a separate seating area, refrigerator, and flat-screen TV. Rates include a full breakfast in the restaurant.

Three miles from Northeast Harbor, in equally tony Seal Harbor, is a true bargain, the **Lighthouse Inn and Restaurant** (12 Main St./Rte. 3, Seal Harbor, 207/276-3958, www.lighthouseinnandrestaurant.com, $75-125). Sure, the three guest rooms (one small, one very large with a kitchenette, one two-room suite with a kitchenette) are a bit dated and dowdy, but at these prices, who cares? Downstairs is a restaurant (11am-8pm daily) with equally reasonable prices. It's a short walk to Seal Harbor Beach and the Seal Harbor entrance to the Park Loop Road.

Motels

Although it's long overdue for an overhaul—every guest room has two double beds, towels are tiny, and the decor is uninspired—you can't beat the location of the **Kimball Terrace Inn** (10 Huntington Rd., Northeast Harbor, 207/276-3383 or 800/454-6225, www.kimballterraceinn.com, $190-265). The three-story motel faces the harbor, and every guest room has a patio or private balcony (ask for a harbor-facing room). Bring binoculars for yacht-spotting. The motel has a small pool, a restaurant, and a lounge, and is a short walk from Northeast Harbor's downtown. It is a popular wedding venue, so if that's a concern, ask if there are any groups in-house before you book.

FOOD

Hours listed are for peak season, early July-early September. At other times, call, most restaurants are open fewer days and hours.

Local Flavors

In the **Pine Tree Market** (121 Main St., Northeast Harbor, 207/276-3335), you'll find gourmet goodies, a huge wine selection, a resident butcher, fresh fish, a deli, homemade breads, pastries, sandwiches, and salads. The market offers free delivery to homes and boats.

Tasteful Tides (102 Main St., Northeast Harbor, 207/276-0746, www.tastefultides.com, 10am-6pm Mon.-Sat.) sells specialty foods, including Fiore olive oils, along with house-made to-go soups, salads, and entrées.

Pop into **Milk & Honey** (3 Old Firehouse Ln., Northeast Harbor, 207/276-4003, 10am-4pm Mon.-Sat.) for soups, sandwiches, and sweets.

Mrs. Brown's (104 Main St., Northeast Harbor, 207/276-5066, 10am-5pm Mon.-Fri.) sells farm-fresh produce and eggs, goat cheese, baked goods, and local crafts.

Rising Tide Partners, created to help Northeast Harbor recover from its devastating 2008 Main Street fires, expects to open **The Creamery** (123 Main St.), an old fashioned soda fountain and café, in 2016.

From June well into October, the **Northeast Harbor Farmers Market** is set up each Thursday, 9am-noon, across from the Kimball Terrace Inn on Huntington Road.

Family Favorites

The homemade doughnuts are reason enough to visit **The Colonel's Restaurant and Bakery** (143 Main St., Northeast Harbor, 207/288-4775, www.colonelsrestaurant.com, 7am-9pm daily), but tucked behind the bakery is a full-service restaurant, serving everything from burgers to prime rib, as well as the usual seafood musts ($10-20). It draws families, thanks to a kids' menu and a casual atmosphere, and can be quite boisterous inside. There's also a deck out back and a separate bar area, which often is the quietest spot with the fastest service.

The **Docksider** (14 Sea St., Northeast Harbor, 207/276-3965, 11am-9pm daily summer) is a low-key, family-friendly, unassuming hole-in-the-wall. Located just up the hill from the chamber office, it has an outside deck, no view, and a reputation that's fading. Prices are on the high side, with burgers and sandwiches beginning around $7, and more popular options in the $15-28 range. The saving grace is Morton's Moo ice cream. Early-bird specials and a 10 percent discount are offered 4:30pm-6pm. If you're smitten, buy one of the T-shirts, featuring an upright lobster announcing, "Frankly, I don't give a clam."

Casual Dining

Nonguests are welcome at the **Asticou Inn** (Rte. 3, 207/276-3344 or 800/258-3373, 7:30am-10am, 11:30am-9pm daily), now operated by the Acadia Corp, which ran the Jordan Pond House for 60 years. It's toned down the prices and brought some favorites (popovers!) to its new home. Go for breakfast ($10-18), lunch and afternoon tea with popovers ($9-18), or dinner ($12-28). When the weather cooperates, the best seats in the house are on the deck with serene views over Northeast Harbor. A lighter menu is served in the lounge.

Lobster

Abel's Lobster Pound (Rte. 198, Mount Desert, 2078/276-5827, www.abelslobsterpound.com, noon-9pm) tends to be a little pricier than other island pounds, but it does have a location overlooking Somes Sound as well as indoor dining with wait service (reservations required, with seatings at 6pm, 6:30pm, 8pm, and 8:30pm) and outdoor picnic tables.

INFORMATION AND SERVICES

The harbor-front information bureau of the **Mount Desert Chamber of Commerce** (18 Harbor Rd., Northeast Harbor, 207/276-5040, www.mountdesertchamber.org) covers the villages of Somesville, Northeast Harbor, Seal Harbor, Otter Creek, Pretty Marsh, Hall Quarry, and Beech Hill.

Find **public restrooms** at the end of the building housing the Great Harbor Maritime Museum, in the town office on Sea Street, and at the harbor.

GETTING THERE AND AROUND

Northeast Harbor is about 12 miles or 20 minutes via Routes 233 and 198 or 20 miles/35 minutes via Route 3 from Bar Harbor. It's about 13 miles or 25 minutes to Southwest Harbor.

Northeast Harbor is served by Route No. 5 (Jordan Pond) and Route No. 6 (Brown Mountain) of the Island Explorer bus system.

Southwest Harbor and Vicinity

Southwest Harbor (pop. 1,764) is the hub of Mount Desert Island's "quiet side." In summer, its tiny downtown district is probably the busiest spot on the whole western side of the island (west of Somes Sound), but that's not saying a great deal. "Southwest" has the feel of a settled community, a year-round flavor that Bar Harbor sometimes lacks. And it competes with the best in the scenery department. The Southwest Harbor area serves as a very convenient base for exploring Acadia National Park, as well as the island's less-crowded villages and offshore Swans Island, Frenchboro, and the Cranberry Isles.

The quirky nature of the island's four town boundaries creates complications in trying to categorize various island segments. Officially, the town of Southwest Harbor includes only the villages of **Manset** and **Seawall,** but nearby is the precious hamlet of **Somesville.** The Somesville National Historic District, with its distinctive arched white footbridge, is especially appealing, but traffic gets congested here along Route 102, so rather than just rubbernecking, plan to stop and walk around.

The "quiet side" of the island becomes even quieter as you round the southwestern edge into **Tremont** (pop. 1,563), which includes the villages of **Bernard; Bass Harbor,** home of Bass Harbor Head Light and ferry services to offshore islands; and **Seal Cove.** Tremont occupies the southwesternmost corner of Mount Desert Island. It's about as far as you can get from Bar Harbor, but the free Island Explorer bus service's Route No. 7 (Southwest Harbor) comes through here regularly.

Be sure to visit these small villages. Views are fabulous, the pace is slow, and you'll feel as if you've stumbled upon "the real Maine."

SIGHTS

★ Wendell Gilley Museum

In the center of Southwest Harbor, the **Wendell Gilley Museum** (Herrick Rd. and Rte. 102, Southwest Harbor, 207/244-7555, www.wendellgilleymuseum.org, 10am-4pm Tues.-Sat., noon-4pm Sun. June-mid Oct., call for off-season hour, $5 adults, $2 ages 5-12) was established in 1981 to display the life work of local woodcarver Wendell Gilley (1904-1983), a onetime plumber who had gained a national reputation for his carvings by the time of his death. The modern, energy-efficient museum houses more than 200 of his astonishingly realistic bird specimens carved over more than 50 years. Summer exhibits also feature other wildlife artists. Many days, a local artist gives woodcarving demonstrations, and members of the local carving club often can be seen whittling away. The gift shop carries an ornithological potpourri, including books, binoculars, and carving tools. Kids over eight appreciate this more than younger ones. If you're bitten by the carving bug, workshops are available, ranging from 90-minute introductory lessons for adults and children ($25, includes kit and admission), offered most weekdays during the summer, to multiday classes on specific birds.

Somesville Historical Museum and Gardens

The tiny **Somesville Historical Museum and Gardens** (Rte. 102, Somesville, 207/276-9323, www.mdihistory.org, 1pm-4pm Tues.-Sat. June 1-late Sept., donation) is adjacent to the gently curving white bridge in Somesville, so there's a good chance you're going to stop nearby, if just for a photo. In season, the heirloom garden, filled with flowering plants and herbs of the 19th and early 20th centuries, is worth a photo or two. The one-room museum has local artifacts and memorabilia displayed in a themed exhibit that changes annually. You can purchase a walking-tour guide to Somesville in the museum. If you're especially interested in history, ask about the museum's programs, which include speakers, demonstrations, and workshops.

Charlotte Rhoades Park and Butterfly Garden

It's easy to miss the **Charlotte Rhoades Park and Butterfly Garden** (Rte. 102, Southwest Harbor, 207/244-5405, www.rhoadesbutterflygarden.org), but that would be a mistake. This tiny seaside park was donated to the town in 1973, and the butterfly garden was established in 1998 to promote conservation education. The park is seldom busy, and it's a delightful place for a picnic. A kiosk is stocked with butterfly observation sheets, and there's usually a volunteer docent on duty on Thursday mornings. Time a visit with the annual butterfly release in July, if you can. The park is on the waterside of Route 102 between the Causeway Golf Club and the Seal Cove Road.

Country Store Museum

Stepping inside the former general store that's now headquarters for the **Tremont Historical Society** (Shore Rd., Bass Harbor, 207/244-9753, www.tremontmainehistory.us,

Bass Harbor Head Light

1pm-4pm Mon., Wed., Fri. July-mid-Oct.) is like stepping into the 1800s. Displays highlight the local heritage. If you're lucky, seventh-generation islander Muriel Davisson might be on duty and regale you with stories about her aunt, author Ruth Moore. You can buy copies of Moore's books here—good reads all. The museum is across from the Seafood Ketch.

Seal Cove Auto Museum

The late Richard C. Paine Jr.'s Brass Era (late 19th to early 20th centuries) car collection, one of the largest in the country, is nicely displayed and identified in the **Seal Cove Auto Museum** (1414 Tremont Rd./Rte. 102, Seal Cove, 207/244-9242, www.sealcoveautomuseum.org, 10am-5pm daily May 1-Oct. 31, $6 adults, $5 seniors and teens, $2 ages 5-12). All vehicles are in as-found condition; this ranges from fresh-from-the-barn to meticulously restored. It's easy for kids of any age to spend an hour here, reminiscing or fantasizing. Among the highlights are a 1913 Peugeot with mahogany skiff body; a 1915 F.R.P., the only one still in existence; an original 1903 Ford Model A, the first car commercially produced by the Ford Motor Co.; and a 1909 Ford Model T "Tin Lizzie," from the first year of production. The oldest car in the collection is an 1899 DeDion-Bouton, one of the earliest cars produced in the world. The museum is about six miles southwest of Somesville. Or, if you're coming from Southwest Harbor, take Route 102 north to Seal Cove Road (partly unpaved) west to the other side of Route 102 (it makes a giant loop) and go north about 1.5 miles. This is not on the Island Explorer route.

The Maine Granite Industry Historical Society Museum

Delve into the history of Maine granite at the **Maine Granite Industry Historical Society Museum** (62 Beech Hill Cross Rd., Mount Desert, 207/244-7299, www.mainegraniteindustry.org, 10am-5pm Tues.-Sun. Apr. 1-Nov. 31, winter by appt., donation). Founder and curator Steven Haynes oversees a collection comprising hundreds of tools, photographs, ledgers, books, and other artifacts related to quarry workers, blacksmiths, stone cutters, and stone carvers. Immigrants from countries including Italy, Finland, Sweden, Norway, and Portugal worked quarries in nine Maine counties, and the granite can still be seen in public buildings, including churches, courthouses, and libraries, as well as bridges throughout the country. Displays show the

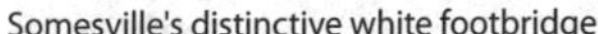

Somesville's distinctive white footbridge

difference between granite from different quarries. Haynes is a wealth of information, and he loves to share his passion. He's often carving and polishing at the site.

Harding Wharf Lighthouse

Drive to the end of the road, and you can't miss the faux lighthouse Harding Wharf. The attached fishing shack was built in 1891 by the Murphy family, who lived in the house, now called Centennial House, across the road. They sold it to Charles Harding in 1927, and it remained in the family until Charles's brother Clarence sold it to Nancy and Irving Silverman in 1981. Later that year, the Silverman's attached their colorful collection of 29 historical wooden lobster buoys to the seaward side of the shack. The lighthouse is now a wedding chapel. Visitors are welcome to take photos for private use, but commercial use requires a permit.

ENTERTAINMENT

Acadia Repertory Theatre

Somesville is home to the **Acadia Repertory Theatre** (Rte. 102, Somesville, 207/244-7260, www.acadiarep.com, $25 adults; $20 seniors, students, and military; $12 under age 16), which has been providing first-rate professional summer stock on the stage of Somesville's antique Masonic Hall since 1973. Classic plays by Oscar Wilde, Neil Simon, and even Molière have been staples, as has the annual Agatha Christie mystery. Performances in the 148-seat hall run at 8:15pm Tuesday-Sunday late June-late August, with 2pm matinees on the last Sunday of each play's run. Special children's plays are performed at 10:30am Wednesday and Saturday in July-August. Tickets for children's theater programs are $9 adults, $6 children.

Lecture and Concert Series

During July-August, the Claremont Hotel (22 Claremont Rd., Southwest Harbor, 207/244-5036 or 800/244-5036, www.theclaremonthotel.com) sponsors a **free weekly lecture series** at 8pm on Thursday evening. Past topics have ranged from John Marin and Maine Modernism to Understanding Climate Change and the Climate Change Debate. It also offers a Saturday Evening Concert series ($10), with music ranging from bluegrass to classical.

Somesville Historical Museum and Gardens

EVENTS

During July-August, the Wednesday **Pie Sale** at the Somesville Union Meeting House is always a sellout.

In early August, the annual **Claremont Croquet Classic,** held on the grounds of the classic Claremont Hotel, is open to all ages.

In September, Smuggler's Den Campground, on Route 102 in Southwest Harbor, is home to the annual **MDI Garlic Festival,** with entertainment and opportunities to savor the stinking rose, and in October the campground hosts the annual **Oktoberfest and Food Festival** (207/244-9264 or 800/423-9264, www.acadiachamber.com), a one-day celebration with crafts, food, games, music, and about two dozen Maine microbrewers presenting about 80 different brews.

The **Acadia Night Sky Festival** (www.acadianightskyfestival.com), in September, includes lectures, movies, sky-viewing opportunities, and other activities.

SHOPPING

Southwest Harbor

Fine art of the 19th and early 20th centuries is the specialty at **Clark Point Gallery** (46 Clark Point Rd., Southwest Harbor, 207/244-0920). Most works depict Maine and Mount Desert Island.

Jewelry approaches fine art at **Aylen & Son Jewelers** (332 Main St./Rte. 102, Southwest Harbor, 207/244-7369). For more than 25 years Peter and Judy Aylen have been crafting and selling jewelry in 18-karat gold and sterling silver and augmenting it with fine gemstones or intriguing beads.

Bernard and Seal Cove

It's fun to poke around **Ravenswood** (McMullen Ave., Bass Harbor, 207/669-4287), a musty shop filled with old books, nautical gifts, model ship kits, and marvelous birds carved on-site.

Linda Fernandez Handknits (Bernard Rd., Bernard, 207/244-7224) sells beautiful hand-knit sweaters, mittens, hats, socks, Christmas stockings, and embroidered pillowcases all handcrafted by the talented and extended Fernandez family. The kids' lobster sweaters are especially cute.

Potters Lisbeth Faulkner and Edwin Davis can often be seen working in their studio at **Seal Cove Pottery & Gallery** (Kelleytown Rd., Seal Cove, 207/244-3602). In addition to their functional hand-thrown or hand-built pottery, they exhibit Davis's paintings as well as crafts by other island artisans.

RECREATION

Hiking

At the Southwest Harbor/Tremont Chamber of Commerce office, or at any of the area's stores, lodgings, and restaurants, pick up a free copy of the *Trail Map/Hiking Guide,* a very handy foldout map showing more than 20 hikes on the west side of Mount Desert Island. Trail descriptions include distances, time required, and skill levels (easy to strenuous).

Bicycle Rentals

A veteran business with a first-rate reputation, **Southwest Cycle** (370 Main St., Southwest Harbor, 207/244-5856 or 800/649-5856, www.southwestcycle.com) is open all year (8:30am-5:30pm Mon.-Sat. and 9:30am-4pm Sun. July-Aug.; 9am-5pm Mon.-Sat. and 9:30am-4pm Sun.). The staff will fix you up with maps and lots of good advice for three loops (10-30 miles) on the western side of Mount Desert. Rentals begin around $18 for an afternoon and $24 for a full day, with multiday discounts available. The shop also rents every imaginable accessory, from baby seats to jogging strollers.

Golf

The nine-hole **Causeway Club** (Fernald Point Rd., 207/244-3780), which edges the ocean, is more challenging than it looks.

Excursion Boats

★ ISLAND CRUISES

High praise goes to **Island Cruises** (Little Island Marine, Shore Rd., Bass Harbor,

207/244-5785, www.bassharborcruises.com), owned and operated by Captains Kim Strauss and his son Eli, for its narrated 3.5-hour lunch cruise to Frenchboro. The 49-passenger *R. L. Gott,* which Kim built, departs at 11am daily during the summer. Kim has been navigating these waters for more than 55 years, and his experience shows not only in his boat handling but also in his narration. Expect to pick up lots of local heritage and lore about once-thriving and now abandoned granite-quarrying and fishing communities, the sardine industry, and lobstering; and to see seals, cormorants, guillemots, and often eagles. The trip allows enough time on Frenchboro for a picnic (or lunch at the summertime deli on the dock) and a short village stroll, then a return through the sprinkling of islands along the 8.3-mile route. Kim also hauls a few traps and explains lobstering. He earns major points for maneuvering the boat so that passengers on both sides get an up-close view of key sights. It's an excellent, enthralling tour for all ages. Round-trip cost is $30 adults, $15 children 11 and younger. Make reservations; if the weather looks iffy, call ahead to confirm. Most of the trip is in sheltered water, but rough seas can put the kibosh on it. Island Cruises also does a two-hour **afternoon nature cruise** among the islands that covers the same topics but spends a bit more time at seal ledges and other spots ($25 adults, $15 children). On either trip, don't forget to bring binoculars. You'll find the Island Cruises dock by following signs to the Swans Island ferry and turning right at the sign shortly before the state ferry dock.

FRIENDSHIP SLOOP CHARTERS

Sail Acadia (Dysert's Great Harbor Marina, 11 Apple Ln., Southwest Harbor, 207/266-5210, www.downeastfriendshipsloop.com) is the umbrella for Downeast Friendship Sloop Charters and Quietside Cruises. The former sails the *Alice E.,* built in 1899 and the oldest Friendship Sloop sailing today. Private charters start at $250 for a two-hour sail, covering up to six passengers and including an appetizer and soft drinks; shared trips are $50 per person for two hours, $75 per person for three hours. The latter offers scenic Somes Sound cruises that include baiting and hauling a lobster trap and visiting a seal colony ($30 adults, $20 under age 12) aboard the *Elizabeth T,* a wooden lobster boat.

DEEP SEA FISHING

Go fishing with **Vagabond Deep Sea Fishing** (Beal's Wharf, Clark Point Rd., Southwest Harbor, 207/244-5385, www.vagabondfishing.com, half-day from $59 adults, $39 ages 5-12) aboard the 43-foot *Vagabond,* and you might return with a lobster. The boat goes 8-20 miles offshore for mackerel, bluefish, codfish, and more. All equipment is included; dress warmly and come prepared with seasickness medications.

BOAT RENTALS AND LESSONS

Mansell Boat Rental Co. (135 Shore Rd., Manset, next to Hinckley, 207/244-5625, www.mansellboatrentals.com) rents sailboats and powerboats by the day or week, including a keel day-sailer for $195/day and a 13.6-foot Boston Whaler for $175/day. Also available are sailing lessons: $295 for a two-plus-hour sail lesson cruise for two, which includes rigging and unrigging the boat; $100/hour for private lessons, minimum two hours.

Paddling

SEA KAYAKING

On the outskirts of Southwest Harbor's downtown is **Maine State Kayak** (254 Main St., Southwest Harbor, 207/244-9500 or 877/481-9500, www.mainestatekayak.com). Staffed with experienced, environmentally sensitive kayakers (all are Registered Maine Guides), the company offers four-hour guided trips departing at 8:30am, 10am, and 2pm along with a sunset tour, with a choice of half a dozen routes that depend on tides, visibility, and wind conditions. The rate is $48 pp, $44 in June and September. Most trips include island or beach breaks. Maximum group size is six tandems; minimum age is 12. Neophytes are welcome.

CALM-WATER PADDLING

Just west of Somesville (take Pretty Marsh Rd.) and across the road from Long Pond, the largest lake on Mount Desert Island, **National Park Canoe & Kayak Rental** (145 Pretty Marsh Rd./Rte. 102, Mount Desert, 207/244-5854, www.nationalparkcanoerental.com, mid-May-mid-Oct.) makes canoeing and kayaking a snap. Just rent the boat, carry it across the road to Pond's End, and launch it. Be sure to pack a picnic. Rates begin at $34 for a three-hour canoe or solo kayak rental, $37 for a tandem kayak, and $36 for a paddleboard. A do-it-yourself sunset canoe or kayak tour (5pm-sunset) is $20 per person. The late fee is $10 per half-hour. Reservations are essential in July-August.

If you've brought your own canoe or kayak, launch it at Pond's End and head off. It's four miles to the southern end of the lake. If the wind kicks up, skirt the shore; if it really kicks up from the north, don't paddle too far down the lake, because you'll have a difficult time getting back.

Another option is to launch your canoe on the quieter, cliff-lined southern end of the lake, much of which is in the park. To find the put-in, take the Seal Cove Road (on the east end of downtown Southwest Harbor). Go right on Long Cove Road to the small parking area at the end near the pumping station. You can also put in from the Long Pond Fire Road, off Route 102, in Pretty Marsh.

Almost the entire west side of **Long Pond** is Acadia National Park property, so plan to picnic and swim along here; tuck into the sheltered area west of Southern Neck, a crooked finger of land that points northward from the western shore. Stay clear of private property on the east side of the lake.

ACCOMMODATIONS

Inns

If you're pining for the "old Maine," stay at **The Claremont** (22 Claremont Rd., Southwest Harbor, 207/244-5036 or 800/244-5036, www.theclaremonthotel.com), an elegant, oceanfront grande dame dressed in mustard-yellow clapboard with a spectacular six-acre hilltop setting overlooking Somes Sound. Dating from 1884, the main building has 24 guest rooms, most of them refurbished yet pleasantly old-fashioned and neither fussy nor fancy; if you want techie frills, go elsewhere. Additional guest rooms are in

Launch a canoe or kayak to explore Long Pond.

the Phillips House, Rowse House, and Cole Cottage. Rates for guestrooms begin around $145 in spring and fall and rise to as high as $335 in August and include a buffet breakfast. Also on the premises are 14 cottages ($180-370). Guests have access to croquet courts, a clay tennis court, one-speed cruiser bikes, rowboats, and a library. The boathouse bar is especially popular. The most popular time here is the first week in August, during the annual Claremont Croquet Classic. Children are welcome. The hotel and dining room are open mid-June-mid-October; cottages are open late May-mid-October.

Bed-and-Breakfasts

Many of Southwest Harbor's bed-and-breakfasts are clustered downtown, along Main Street and the Clark Point Road.

Set on a corner, well back from Clark Point Road, is ★ **Harbour Cottage Inn** (9 Dirigo Rd., Southwest Harbor, 207/244-5738 or 888/843-3022, www.harbourcottageinn.com, $225-290), appealingly revamped in 2002 when Javier Montesinos and Don Jalbert took over the reins. Built in 1870, it was the annex for the island's first hotel and housed the increasing numbers of rusticators who patronized this part of the island. It has evolved into a lovely bed-and-breakfast with eight guest rooms and three suites decorated in a colorful and fun cottage style. Some guest rooms have whirlpool baths and/or fireplaces, and all have TVs and Wi-Fi. Rates include a multicourse breakfast. Also part of Harbour Cottage is **Pier One,** which offers five truly waterfront suites ($1,540-1,825 weekly), including a studio cottage. All were renovated in 2009 in a comfortable cottage style; all have kitchens and TVs.

The linden-blossom fragrance can be intoxicating in summer at the **Lindenwood Inn** (118 Clark Point Rd., Southwest Harbor, 207/244-5335 or 800/307-5335, www.lindenwoodinn.com, $189-349). The inn's 15 guest rooms, split between two buildings, and poolside bungalow are decorated in a sophisticated yet comfortable style. After you hike Acadia's trails, the heated pool and hot tub are especially welcome, and after that, perhaps enjoy a drink while shooting pool or playing darts. Some guest rooms have harbor views.

Even glimpsed through the trees from the road, ★ **The Birches** (46 Fernald Point Rd., Southwest Harbor, 207/244-5182, www.thebirchesbnb.com, from $289) is appealing. A wooded drive winds down to the large home fronting the ocean, near the mouth of Somes

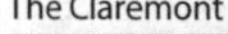
The Claremont

Sound. It's just 350 yards to the Causeway Golf Club and a short walk to the Flying Mountain trailhead and Valley Cove fire road with access to the Acadia and St. Sauveur trails. Built as a summer cottage in 1916, The Birches retains that casual summer ease, right down to the stone fireplace in the living room and the croquet court on the lawn. Guest rooms are especially large and comfortably decorated; most have water views, and one has a sleeping porch. Innkeeper Susi Homer, whose grandfather built this magical home, and her daughter Kate treat guests like family. Her breakfasts are legendary. A pet-friendly cottage also is available. Open year-round, by reservation.

In Manset, adjacent to the Hinckley Yacht complex and with jaw-dropping views down Somes Sound, is **The Moorings** (133 Shore Rd., Manset, 207/244-5523, www.mooringsinn.com, $150-260), where fourth-generation innkeeper Leslie Watson is now owner. The oceanfront complex is part motel, part cottage rental, and part old-fashioned bed-and-breakfast. Rooms are named after locally built sailing vessels. The motel-style rooms in the Lighthouse View Wing have refrigerators, microwaves, Wi-Fi, waterfront decks, and incredible views (spend the afternoon counting the Hinckley yachts). A continental breakfast is available each morning. Also on the property or nearby are cottage units ($160-270). This is an older complex, and soundproofing is minimal. Bikes, canoes, and kayaks are available for guests, so you can paddle around the harbor; Mansell Boat Rental Co. is also on the premises. Dogs are permitted with prior approval.

Built in 1884 as the Freeman Cottage, the mansard-roofed Victorian **Inn at Southwest** (371 Main St./Rte. 102, Southwest Harbor, 207/244-3835, www.innatsouthwest.com, $175-215) has 13 dormers and a wraparound veranda furnished with wicker. Seven second- and third-floor guest rooms—named for Maine lighthouses and full of character—are decorated with a mix of contemporary and antique furnishings. Some have gas stoves or limited water views; all have Wi-Fi. Breakfast is a feast, with such treats as cheesecake crepes and eggs Florentine served indoors or on the patio. In the afternoon, cookies are available.

Across the lane is the elegant Queen Anne **Kingsleigh Inn 1904** (373 Main St., Southwest Harbor, 207/244-5302, www.kingsleighinn.com, $170-315), with eight air-conditioned rooms, some with private harbor-facing decks, on three floors; all have Wi-Fi. The best splurge is the turret suite, with a fireplace, TV, private deck, and a telescope trained on the harbor. Breakfast is an elegant, three-course affair, served on the water-view porch, weather permitting. Afternoon refreshments are served, and chocolate truffles or chocolate-raspberry rum balls and port wine are replenished daily in guest rooms.

Smack dab in the middle of town, **Penury Hall** (374 Main St., Southwest Harbor, 207/244-7102, www.penuryhall.com, $165) offers three bedrooms with private, detached bathrooms, and an unfussy, relaxed atmosphere that leans toward homestay. The living rooms are bright and cheerful and filled with games, puzzles, music, and books, and there are laundry facilities. A full breakfast is included. Penury Hall is open year-round.

When price is no object and you really want pampering, check into ★ **Ann's Point Inn** (79 Anns Point Rd., Bass Harbor, 207/244-9595, www.annspointinn.com, $325-360), on a private waterfront at the tip of Ann's Point. Each of four guest rooms has a king bed covered in luxurious linens, a gas fireplace, and all the amenities you might expect, including robes and slippers, in-room TVs and DVD players, phones, Wi-Fi, CD players, and air-conditioning. The guest rooms are huge, and all have ocean views. If that's not enough, there's an indoor pool, a hot tub, and a sauna, plus afternoon hors d'oeuvres and evening sweets. Even better, the inn's green and sustainable practices include solar-powered electricity and hot water and garden-fresh fare at breakfast. All this is on two acres with 690 feet of shorefront, from which you can watch eagles soar and lobster boats at work.

On a low rung of the luxury scale but also

on the water is **Bass Harbor Cottages and Country Inn** (95 Harbor Dr./Rte. 102A, Bass Harbor, 207/244-3460, www.bassharborcottages.com). All accommodations are housekeeping; there's no maid service. The sturdy white home has three air-conditioned guest rooms ($135-180), some with gas fireplaces, kitchens, or TVs. Breakfast is not served. Also on the premises are a number of cottages and suites with a wide range of amenities ($1,600-2,800 weekly). A staircase descends to a rocky beach.

Simple guest rooms, nice views, and an included continental breakfast draw guests to the **Bass Harbor Inn** (28 Shore Rd., Bass Harbor, 207/244-5157, www.bassharborinn.com, $95-140), a restored 1870 home with four guest rooms (two with private half-baths and a shared shower) and a studio with a kitchen and harbor-view deck. Most rooms require navigating at least one if not two flights of steep stairs. You can walk to local restaurants, the ferry dock, and the museum.

Motels and Cottages

Smack on the harbor and just a two-minute walk from downtown is the appropriately named **Harbor View Motel & Cottages** (11 Ocean Way, Southwest Harbor, 207/244-5031 or 800/538-6463, www.harborviewmotelandcottages.com). The family-owned complex comprises motel rooms ($90-136/night, $560-845/week) spread out in two older, somewhat dowdy, one-story buildings and a newer, three-story structure fronting on the harbor. A meager continental breakfast is served to motel guests July 1-early September. Also on the premises are seven housekeeping cottages with kitchenettes (weekly rentals only, $775-1,225), ranging from studios to two-bedrooms. Pets are welcome in some units ($10/day or $60/week).

Directly across from the famed seawall and adjacent to the park is the **Seawall Motel** (566 Seawall Rd./Rte. 102A, Southwest Harbor, 207/244-9250 or 800/248-9250, www.seawallmotel.com, $120), a budget-friendly find. The no-surprises-but-dated two-story motel (upstairs guest rooms have the best views) has free Wi-Fi, in-room phones, cable TV, a communal microwave and fridge, a coin-op laundry, and service-oriented owners. Kids 12 and younger stay free. The location is excellent for bird-watchers. A continental breakfast is served.

Cottage Rentals

L. S. Robinson Co. (337 Main St., Southwest Harbor, 207/244-5563, www.lsrobinson.com) has an extensive list of cottage rentals in the area. The Southwest Harbor/Tremont Chamber of Commerce (329 Main St., Southwest Harbor, 207/244-9264 or 800/423-9264, www.acadiachamber.com) also keeps a helpful listing of privately owned homes and cottages available for rent.

Camping

Acadia National Park's Seawall Campground is on this side of the island.

On the eastern edge of Somesville, just off Route 198, at the head of Somes Sound, the Craighead family's ★ **Mount Desert Campground** (516 Somes Sound Dr./Rte. 198, Somesville, 207/244-3710, www.mountdesertcampground.com) is especially centrally located for visiting Bar Harbor, Acadia, and the whole western side of Mount Desert Island. The campground has 152 wooded tent sites, about 45 on the water, spread out on 58 acres. Reservations are essential in midsummer—one-week minimum for waterfront sites, three days for off-water sites in July-August. (Campers book a year ahead for waterfront sites here.) This deservedly popular and low-key campground gets high marks for maintenance, noise control, and convenient tent platforms. Another plus is The Gathering Place, where campers can relax, play games, use free Wi-Fi, and purchase coffee and fresh-baked treats or ice cream. Summer rates are $40-60 per night for two adults and two children younger than 18. Electrical hookups are $2 per night. No pets are allowed July-early September, and no trailers over 20 feet are permitted.

Kayak, canoe, and standup paddleboard rentals are available.

Built on the site of an old quarry, on a hillside descending to rocky frontage on Somes Sound, **Somes Sound View Campground** (86 Hall Quarry Rd., Mount Desert, 207/244-3890, off-season 207/244-7452, www.ssvc.info, late May-mid-Oct., $30-60) is among the smallest campgrounds on the island, with fewer than 60 sites, all geared to tents and vans. Rustic camping cabins are $70 per night. Facilities include hot showers (if you're camping on the lowest levels, it's a good hike up to the bathhouse), a heated pool, a boat launch, kayak, canoe, and paddleboat rentals, and a fishing dock. All sites have a faucet, fire pit, and picnic table. You can swim in the sound from a rocky beach. Leashed pets are allowed. It's two miles south and east of Somesville and a mile east of Route 102.

The Worcester family's **Smuggler's Den Campground** (Rte. 102, Southwest Harbor, 207/244-3944, www.smugglersdencampground.com, $34-60) is a midsized, pet-friendly campground between Echo Lake and downtown Southwest Harbor. It's also the site of the annual Oktoberfest. Trails access back roads to Echo Lake (1.25 miles) and Long Pond (1 mile) as well as 25 miles of Acadia National Park trails. Big-rig sites are grouped in the top third, pop-ups and small campers are in the middle third, and tenting sites are in the lower third and in the woods rimming the large recreation field. Also available are cabins ($575 camping, $1,200 with kitchen and bath, per week). Facilities include Wi-Fi, a heated pool and kiddie pool, a four-acre recreation field with horseshoe pit, half-court basketball, and lawn games, a laundry, free hot showers, lobster.

FOOD

Local Flavors

Lots of goodies for picnics can be found at **Sawyer's Market** (344 Main St., Southwest Harbor, 207/244-3315, 7:30am-8:30pm daily); for wine, cheese, and gourmet goodies, head across the street to **Sawyer's Specialties** (353 Main St., Southwest Harbor, 207/244-3317, open daily).

Here's a breakfast you can feel good about. ★ **Common Good Café** (19 Clark Point Rd., Southwest Harbor, 207/2664-2733, www.commongoodsoupkitchen.org, 7:30am-11:30am daily, donation) offers a self-serve buffet comprising hot popovers, slow-simmered steel-cut oatmeal, tea, and coffee, along with accompaniments including maple syrup and plain and flavored butters. The volunteer-run program is a fundraiser by the Common Good Soup Kitchen Community, which distributes free soup to shut-ins, offers a winter community meal, and stocks a winter community-clothing program, among other things. Be as generous as you can in your donation: remember just one popover with tea is about $12 at the Jordan Pond House; here you can eat as many as you like. That said, no one monitors it, and if you're on a tight budget, just give what you can. Every penny is appreciated. You might also consider picking up a package of the popover mix.

Good chowders, sandwiches, fried clams, lobster rolls, and even pizza are served at the cozy **Quietside Café** (360 Main St., Southwest Harbor, 207/244-9444, 11am-10pm Mon.-Sat., 11am-8pm Sun., $6-18). Do save room for Frances's sky-high homemade blueberry and key lime pies.

Some of the island's most creative sandwiches and pizza toppings emerge from **Little Notch Café** (340 Main St., Southwest Harbor, 207/244-3357, 7:30am-8:30pm daily, $8-16), next to the library in Southwest Harbor's downtown. Also available are Little Notch Bakery's famed breads, a couple of pasta choices, and homemade soups, stews, and chowders.

Good food, good coffee, and good wine mix with a Mediterranean-influenced menu at **Sips** (4 Clark Point Rd., Southwest Harbor, 207/244-4550, www.sipsmdi.com, 7am-9pm Mon.-Sat., 7am-noon sun.), a congenial place. Small- and large-plate and tapas-style choices range $8-28; the risottos are especially good. A children's menu is available. On Wednesday nights during the summer season, there usually is live music.

Treat yourself to lunch overlooking Somes Sound at the **Boat House** at the Claremont Hotel (22 Claremont Rd., Southwest Harbor, 207/244-5036 or 800/244-5036, noon-2pm daily July-Aug., $7-18). It's also a popular spot for cocktails, served 5:30pm-9pm, when you can watch the sun set behind Cadillac Mountain.

Yes, the cookies and bars that Maureen McDonald bakes at **Manset Little Farm** (281 Rte. 102A, Manset, 207/244-7013) are pricey at $4 each, but they're big and scratch-made, and after one bite, you'll be wishing you'd purchased more.

College of the Atlantic students run **Beech Hill Farm** (171 Beech Hill Rd., Mount Desert, 207/244-5204, 9am-4pm Tues.-Sat.), a five-acre farm certified organic by the Maine Organic Farmers and Gardeners Association. Also here are acres of heirloom apple trees and 65 acres of forestland. Visit the farm stand for fresh produce as well as other organic or natural foods such as cheeses and baked goods.

Ethnic Fare

Craving a taste of Mexico? **XYZ Restaurant** (80 Seawall Rd./Rte. 102A, Manset, 207/244-5221, www.xyzmaine.com, entrées $26) specializes in the flavors of interior Mexico: Xalapa, Yucatán, and Zacatecas (hence "XYZ"). The most popular dish is *cochinita*—citrus-marinated pork rubbed with achiote paste, worthy of its reputation. For dessert, try the XYZ pie. Dine inside or on the porch. The food is great, but it's pricey and served with a dose of attitude. Hours vary, often by week, so call for the current schedule.

Casual Dining

By day, **Eat-a-Pita** (326 Main St., Southwest Harbor, 207/244-4344, 8am-4pm daily, dinner 5pm-9pm Tues.-Sun.) is a casual, order-at-the-counter restaurant serving breakfast and lunch. At night it morphs into **Café 2,** a full-service restaurant. The dining room, furnished with old oak tables and chairs, has a funky, artsy attitude; there's also patio seating outside and an outdoor bar (think pink flamingos). Start the day with a Greek or Acapulco omelet. Lunch emphasizes pita sandwiches, burgers, panini, and salads (delicious—call in advance for takeout); dinner choices ($10-26) include salads, light meals, a half-dozen pastas, and entrées.

Earning high praise for its internationally accented fare, good service, harbor views, and specialty cocktails is ★ **Fiddlers' Green** (411 Main St., Southwest Harbor, 207/244-9416, www.fiddlersgreenrestaurant.com, 5:30pm-10pm Tues.-Sun.). House specialties, such as Asian vegetable hot pot, trout livorese, and farm-to-table roast pig, range $16-38, but you can also make a meal of small plates, soups, sandwiches, and salads.

Rogue Café (Rte. 102, Southwest Harbor, 207/244-7101, 5:30-9:30 Tues.-Sun., $10-28) made its debut midsummer 2015 to raves. The farm-to-table menu comprises small plates ($7-12) as well as entrees ($21-24), such as gnocchi, line-caught halibut, or grilled rump sirloin. The unpretentious setting takes a backstage to the well prepared food.

If you have a penchant for puns—or can tune them out—head for the family-run **Seafood Ketch Restaurant** (McMullin Ave., Bass Harbor, 207/244-7463, www.seafoodketch.com, 11am-9pm daily). The corny humor begins with "Please, no fishing from dining room windows or the deck" and "What foods these morsels be," and goes up (or down, depending on your perspective) from there. But there's nothing corny about the seafood roll, an interesting change from the usual lobster or crab roll. There are a few "landlubber delights," but mostly the menu has fresh seafood dishes—including the baked lobster-seafood casserole, a recipe requested by *Gourmet* magazine. Most entrées run $19-24, but sandwiches and lighter fare are available. Sunday omelets are the specialty, served 11am-2pm along with the full menu. This is a prime family spot, with a kids' menu, where the best tables are on the flagstone patio overlooking Bass Harbor (bring bug repellent). Follow signs for the Swans Island ferry terminal.

Fine Dining

The dreamy views from **Xanthus** (22 Claremont Rd., 207/244-5036 or 800/244-5036, 6pm-9pm daily), at the Claremont Hotel, descend over the lawns and croquet courts, boathouse, and dock to the water backed by mountains. It's truly a special place for an elegant meal complemented by an old-fashioned grace. Collared shirts are required for men, but not jackets, although you won't feel out of place wearing one. Entrées range $24-30; a three-course fixed-price dinner is $30. Dining-room reservations are advised in midsummer.

Red sky at night, diners delight: Gold walls, artwork, wood floors, and a giant hearth set a chic tone for **Red Sky** (14 Clark Point Rd., 207/244-0476, www.redskyrestaurant.com, 5:30pm-9pm daily, entrées $22-35), one of the island's tonier restaurants. Owners James and Elizabeth Geffen Lindquist's creative fare emphasizes fresh seafood, hand-cut meats, and local organic produce; there's always a vegetarian choice. The restaurant is open Valentine's Day-New Year's Eve.

Seafood and Lobster in the Rough

Few restaurants have as idyllic a setting as ★ **Thurston's Lobster Pound** (Steamboat Wharf Rd., Bernard, 207/244-7600, 11am-8:30pm daily, market rates), which overlooks lobster boat-filled Bass Harbor. The screened dining room practically sits in the water. Family-oriented Thurston's also has chowders, sandwiches, and terrific desserts. Beer and wine are available. Read the directions at the entrance and order before you find a table on one of two levels.

Eat, drink, and be messy is the slogan at **Beal's Lobster Pier** (182 Clark Point Rd., Southwest Harbor, 207/244-3202, www.bealslobster.com, 11am-9pm daily), which only serves lobster that comes from boats unloading at the pier. Go for the lobster, but if you're traveling with landlubbers, there are burgers, fried fish, salads, sandwiches, and even veggie burgers on the menu.

Vintage burger-joint-style takeout meets lobster shack at **Charlotte's Legendary Lobster Pound** (465 Seawall Rd./Rte. 102A, Southwest Harbor, 207/244-8021, 4pm-8:30pm Mon., 11am-8:30pm Tues.-Sun.), an order-at-the-window, eat-on-picnic-tables spot that earns raves for its lobster and lobster rolls.

INFORMATION AND SERVICES

The **Southwest Harbor/Tremont Chamber of Commerce** (329 Main St., Southwest Harbor, 207/244-9264 or 800/423-9264, www.acadiachamber.com) stocks brochures, maps, menus, and other local info.

Check out **Southwest Harbor Public Library** (338 Main St., Southwest Harbor, 207/244-7065, www.swhplibrary.org).

In downtown Southwest Harbor, **public restrooms** at the southern end of the parking lot behind the Main Street park and near the fire station. There are portable toilets at the town docks and at the Swans Island ferry terminal in Bass Harbor.

GETTING THERE AND AROUND

Southwest Harbor is about 13 miles or 25 minutes via Routes 198 and 102 from Northeast Harbor. It's about 14 miles or 25 minutes to Bar Harbor.

Southwest Harbor, Tremont, and Bass Harbor are serviced by Route No. 7 (Southwest Harbor) of the Island Explorer bus system.

Islands Near Mount Desert

Sure, Mount Desert is an island, but for a sampling of real island life, you'll want to make a day trip to one of the offshore islands. Most popular are the **Cranberry Isles** and **Swans Island,** but don't overlook **Frenchboro,** an off-the-radar gem.

CRANBERRY ISLES

The **Cranberry Isles** (pop. 141), south of Northeast and Seal Harbors, comprise Great Cranberry, Little Cranberry (called Islesford), Sutton, Baker, and Bear Islands. Islesford and Baker include property belonging to Acadia National Park. Bring a bike and explore the narrow, mostly level roads on the two largest islands, Great Cranberry and Islesford, but remember to respect private property. Unless you've asked permission, do not cut across private land to reach the shore.

The Cranberry name has been attributed to 18th-century loyalist governor Francis Bernard, who received these islands along with all of Mount Desert as a king's grant in 1762. Cranberry bogs (now long gone) on the two largest islands evidently caught his attention. Permanent European settlers arrived in the 1760s, and there was even steamboat service by the 1820s.

Lobstering and other fishing industries are the commercial mainstays, boosted in summer by the various visitor-related pursuits. Artists and writers come for a week, a month, or longer; day-trippers spend time on Great Cranberry and Islesford. There are no inns on either.

Largest of the islands is **Great Cranberry,** with a general store, a small historical museum with a café, and a gift shop, but not much else except pretty views. Public restrooms are located near the dock and at the museum.

The second-largest island is **Little Cranberry,** locally known as Islesford. It's easy to spend the better part of a day here exploring. Begin at **The Islesford Historical Museum** (207/288-3338, www.nps.gov/acad, free), operated by the National Park Service. The exhibits focus on local history, much of it maritime, so displays include ship models, household goods, fishing gear, and other memorabilia. Also on Islesford are a handful of galleries, and a general store. For lunch, bring a picnic or head to the **Islesford Dock** (207/244-7494, www.islesford.com, 11am-3pm and 5pm-9pm Wed.-Sat., 10am-2pm and 5pm-9pm Sun. late June-Labor Day, $6-29), where prices are moderate, the food is home-cooked, and the views across to Acadia's mountains are incredible, especially at sunset. Public restrooms are near the museum.

Getting There

Do call to confirm current ferry schedules, as online versions aren't always accurate.

Decades-old, family-run **Beal and Bunker** (207/244-3575, www.bealandbunker.com) provides year-round mail and passenger boat service to the Cranberries from Northeast Harbor. The schedule makes it possible to do both islands in one day. The summer season, with more frequent trips, runs late June-Labor Day. The boats make a variety of stops on the three-island route (including Sutton in summer), so be patient as they make the circuit. It's a people-watching treat. If you just did a round-trip and stayed aboard, the loop would take about 1.5 hours. Round-trip tickets (covering the whole loop, including intraisland trips if you want to visit both Great Cranberry and Islesford) are $32 adults, $14 ages 3-11, free under age 3. Bicycles are $8 round-trip. The off-season schedule operates early May-mid-June and early September-mid-October; the winter schedule runs mid-October-April. In winter, the boat company advises phoning ahead on what Mainers quaintly call "weather days."

The **Cranberry Cove Ferry** (upper

Day Trip to Frenchboro, Long Island

Since Maine has more Long Islands than anyone cares to count, most of them have other labels for easy identification. Here's a case in point—a Long Island known universally as Frenchboro, the name of the village that wraps around Lunts Harbor. With a year-round population hovering around 50, Frenchboro has had ferry service only since 1960. Since then, the island has acquired phone service, electricity, and satellite TV, but don't expect to notice much of that when you get here. One of only 15 Maine coastal islands that still support a year-round population, Frenchboro is a very quiet place, where islanders live as islanders always have—making a living from the sea and being proud of it.

In 1999, when roughly half of the island (914 acres, including 5.5 miles of shorefront) went up for sale by a private owner, an incredible fundraising effort collected nearly $3 million, allowing purchase of the land in 2000 by the Maine Coast Heritage Trust. Some of the funding helped restore the village's church and one-room schoolhouse. Since then, thanks to a gift from David Rockefeller, it's expanded to include Rich's Head, adding 192 acres and three miles of shoreline. Visitors now have more than 10 miles of hiking trails, though take heed: most are rustic and unmarked. Today the preserve comprises 1,159 acres—more than 80 percent of the island, including about 10 miles of shoreline. Frenchboro is the subject of *Hauling by Hand*, a fascinating, well-researched "biography" published in 1999 by eighth-generation islander Dean Lunt.

Frenchboro is a delightful day trip. A good way to get a sense of the place is to take the 3.5-hour lunch cruise run by Captain Kim Strauss of **Island Cruises** (Little Island Marine, Shore Rd., Bass Harbor, 207/244-5785, www.bassharborcruises.com). For an even longer day trip to Frenchboro, plan to take the passenger ferry *R. L. Gott* during her weekly run for the Maine State Ferry Service. Each Friday early April-late October, the *R. L. Gott* departs Bass Harbor at 8am, arriving in Frenchboro at 9am. The return trip to Bass Harbor is at 6pm, allowing nine hours on the island. The **Maine State Ferry Service** (207/244-3254, daily recorded info 800/491-4883, www.exploremaine.org) uses the ferry *Captain Henry Lee,* the same vessel used on the Swans Island route, for service to Frenchboro on Wednesday, Thursday, and Sunday. On some days, the schedule allows five hours on the island, but the days and times are limited, so it's best to check the current schedule online.

When you go, take a picnic with you, or stop at **Lunt's Dockside Deli** (207/334-2902, www.luntlobsters.com, 11am-7:30pm), open only in July-August. It's a very casual establishment—order at the window, grab a picnic table, and wait for your name to be called. Lobster rolls and fish chowder are the specialties, but there are plenty of other choices, including sandwiches, hot dogs, and even vegetable wraps. Of course, you can get lobster too. Prices are low, the view is wonderful, and you might even get to watch lobsters being unloaded from a boat.

The **Frenchboro Historical Society Museum** (207/334-2924, www.frenchboro.lib.me.us, free), just up from the dock, has interesting old tools, other local artifacts, and a small gift shop. It's usually open afternoons Memorial Day-Labor Day. The island has a network of easy and not-so-easy maintained trails through the woods and along the shore; some can be squishy, and some are along boulder-strewn beachfront. The trails are rustic, and most are unmarked, so proceed carefully. In the center of the island is a beaver pond. (You'll get a sketchy map on the boat, but you can also get one at the historical society.)

There's a restroom above the Dockside Deli and two others near the museum.

Every year since 1961, on the second Saturday of August, Frenchboro hosts its annual **Lobster Festival** (www.frenchboro-dinner.org), a midday meal comprising lobster, chicken salad, hot dogs, coleslaw, homemade pies, and more, served rain or shine, with proceeds benefiting a local cause. Islanders and hundreds of visitors gather in the village for the occasion. The Maine State Ferry makes a special run that day.

There are no inns on the island, but beginning in 2016, the Maine Coast Heritage Trust planned to open two wilderness, leave-no-trace (including human waste) campsites.

town dock, Clark Point Rd., Southwest Harbor, 207/244-5882, cell 207/460-1981, www.downeastwindjammer.com) operates a summertime service to the Cranberries mid-May-mid-October. The ferry route begins at the upper town dock (Clark Point Rd.) in Southwest Harbor (free parking, but be sure to park in one of the marked eight-hour slots; or take the Island Explorer), with stops in Manset and Great Cranberry before reaching Islesford an hour later and reversing the itinerary; two hours total, if you stay on the boat. (Stops at Sutton can be arranged.) In summer (mid-June-mid-Sept.) there are six daily round-trips, with two additional evening trips Wednesday-Saturday. Round-trip fares are $28 adults, $20 children, $6 bicycles.

Captain John Dwelley (207/244-5724) also operates a water-taxi service to the Cranberries. His six-passenger ***Delight*** makes the run from Northeast, Southwest, or Seal Harbor. Reservations are required for trips 6am-8am and 6pm-11pm. Round-trip rates range $80-110. Custom cruises are available, including excursions to Baker's Island. Consider the sunset cruise to The Islesford Dock for dinner ($110 round-trip covering up to 6 passengers).

SWANS ISLAND

Six miles off Mount Desert Island lies scenic, roughly 7,000-acre **Swans Island** (pop. 332; www.swansisland.org/), named after Col. James Swan, who bought it and two dozen other islands as an investment in 1786. As with the Cranberries, fishing is the year-round way of life here, with lobstering being the primary occupation. In summer the population practically triples with the arrival of artists, writers, and other seasonal visitors. The island has no campsites, few public restrooms, and only a handful of guest rooms. Visitors who want to spend more than a day tend to rent cottages by the week.

You'll need either a bicycle or a car to get around on the island, as the ferry comes in on one side and the village center is on the other. Should you choose to bring a car, it's wise to make reservations for the ferry, especially for the return trip. Bicycling is a good way to get around, but be forewarned that the roads are narrow, lack shoulders, and are hilly in spots.

A Swans Island summer highlight is the **Sweet Chariot Music Festival,** a three-night midweek extravaganza in early August geared to boaters.

Overnight accommodations are available at **The Harbor Watch Inn** (111 Minturn Rd.,

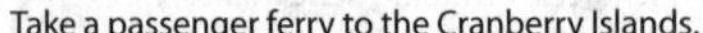

Take a passenger ferry to the Cranberry Islands.

207/526-4563 or 800/532-7928, www.swansisland.com, $95-155) and the **Carter House** (207/266-0958 or 207/526-4198, $90). For sustenance, try **TIMS, The Island Market & Supply** (40 North Rd., 207/526-4043, www.tims-swans-island.com).

Getting There and Around

Swans Island is a six-mile, 40-minute trip on the state-operated car ferry *Captain Henry Lee,* operated by the **Maine State Ferry Service** (207/244-3254, daily recorded info 800/491-4883, www.exploremaine.org). The ferry makes up to six round-trips a day, the first from Bass Harbor at 7:30am Monday-Saturday, 9am Sunday, and the last from Swans Island at 4:30pm. Round-trip fares are around $17.50 adults, $8.50 ages 5-11; bikes are $16.50 adults, $9.50 children; vehicles are $49.50. Reservations are accepted only for vehicles; be in line at least 15 minutes before departure or you risk forfeiting your space.

To reach the Bass Harbor ferry terminal on Mount Desert Island, follow the distinctive blue signs, marked Swans Island Ferry, along Routes 102 and 102A.

Southwest Cycle (Main St., Southwest Harbor, 207/244-5856 or 800/649-5856) rents bikes by the day and week and is open year-round. It also has ferry schedules and Swans Island maps. For the early-morning ferry, you'll need to pick up bikes the day before; be sure to reserve them if you're doing this in July-August.

Schoodic Peninsula

Slightly more than 2,366 of Acadia National Park's acres are on the mainland Schoodic Peninsula; the rest are all on islands, including Mount Desert. World-class scenery and the relative lack of congestion, even at the height of summer, are just two reasons to sneak around to the eastern side of Frenchman Bay. Other reasons are abundant opportunities for outdoor recreation, two scenic byways, and dozens of artists' and artisans' studios tucked throughout this region.

Still, the biggest attractions in this area are the spectacular vignettes and vistas—of offshore lighthouses, distant mountains, and close-in islands—and the unchanged villages. **Winter Harbor** (pop. 516) known best as the gateway to Schoodic, shares the area with an old-money, low-profile Philadelphia-linked summer colony on exclusive Grindstone Neck.

Gouldsboro (pop. 1,737) including the not-to-be-missed villages of **Birch Harbor, Corea,** and **Prospect Harbor,** earned its own minor fame from Louise Dickinson Rich's 1958 book *The Peninsula,* a tribute to her summers on Corea's Cranberry Point, "a place that has stood still in time." Since 1958, change has crept into Corea, but not so as you'd notice. It's still the same quintessential lobster-fishing community, perfect for photo ops. A new section of the Maine Coastal Islands National Wildlife Reserve, the 431-acre **Corea Heath Unit,** has taken over former navy lands along Route 195 in Corea. In another initiative, the Frenchman Bay Conservancy acquired the 600-acre Northern Corea Heath, across the highway, home to Grand Marsh and Grand Marsh Bay.

Between Ellsworth and Gouldsboro are **Hancock** (pop. 2,394), **Sullivan** (pop. 1,236), and **Sorrento** (pop. 274). Venture down the oceanside back roads and you'll discover an old-timey summer colony at Hancock Point, complete with a library, a post office, a yacht club, and tennis courts.

Meander inland to find the **Donnell Pond Public Reserved Lands,** a spectacular chunk of mostly undeveloped lakes for boating and fishing, peaks for hiking, and even a beach for camping.

Scenic Byways

The Schoodic region boasts not one but two designated scenic byways: the **Schoodic National Scenic Byway,** which wraps around the peninsula, and the **Black Woods Scenic Byway,** an inland blue highway cutting through the Donnell Pond Public Reserved Land. If time permits, drive at least one of these routes. Ideally you'd do both, because the scenery differs greatly. Best idea yet: Connect the two via Route 1, creating a loop that includes lakes and forests, mountains and fields, ocean and rocky coast. If you have only one day to explore this region, this route takes in the best of it. In early to mid-October, when the fall foliage is at its peak colors, the vistas are especially stunning.

The 29-mile Schoodic National Scenic Byway stretches from Sullivan on Route 1 to Gouldsboro and then south on Route 186 and around the Schoodic Peninsula, ending in Prospect Harbor. A detailed guide is available at www.schoodicbyway.org. Other information is available at www.byways.org. There is interpretive signage, explaining sights and history, along the route.

The 12.5-mile Black Woods Scenic Byway meanders along Route 182 inland of Route 1, from Franklin to Cherryfield, edging lakes and passing through small villages. You'll find access to trailheads and boat launches at Donnell Pond and Tunk Lake. Although Cherryfield is beyond the Schoodic region, it's a beautiful town to visit, filled with stately Victorian homes. It's also the self-proclaimed wild blueberry capital of the world. Maps and information are available at www.blackwoodsbyway.org.

SCHOODIC SECTION OF ACADIA NATIONAL PARK

The smaller and far-less-touristed Schoodic section of Acadia isn't as overpowering as that on Mount Desert, but it's no less powerful. Even though it's on the mainland, it feels more remote, and the landscape has a raw edge, with too-frequent fog shrouding the stunted and scraggly spruce clinging to its pink granite shores. The autumn 2015 opening of an approximately 100-site campground with visitor center here, along with eight miles of carriage roads, made it easier to explore much of the park on foot or a bicycle without hitting the main roads.

As with so much of Acadia's acreage on Mount Desert Island, the Schoodic section became part of the park largely because of the deft diplomacy and perseverance of George B. Dorr. No obstacle ever seemed too daunting to Dorr. In 1928, when the owners objected to donating their land to a national park tagged with the Lafayette name (geopolitics being involved at the time), Dorr even managed to obtain congressional approval for the 1929 name change to Acadia National Park—and Schoodic was part of the deal.

To reach the park boundary from Route 1 in Gouldsboro, take Route 186 south to Winter Harbor. Continue through town, heading east, and then turn right and continue to the park entrance sign, just before the bridge over Mosquito Harbor.

You can also tour the park using the free Island Explorer bus, which circulates through Winter Harbor, around the Schoodic Loop, and on to Prospect Harbor, with stops along the way. It's an efficient and environmentally friendly way to go.

★ Schoodic Loop

The major sights of Acadia's Schoodic section lie along the six-mile one-way road that meanders counterclockwise around the tip of the Schoodic Peninsula. You'll discover official and unofficial picnic areas, hiking trailheads, offshore lighthouses, a welcome center with exhibits, and turnouts with scenic vistas. Also named the Park Loop Road, it's best referred to as the Schoodic Loop, to distinguish it from the one on Mount Desert Island. Begin at the new **Schoodic Woods Campground,**

where you can pick up information and, should you choose, leave your car to explore via bicycle or the Island Explorer bus.

The first landmark is **Frazer Point Picnic Area,** with lovely vistas, picnic tables, and wheelchair-accessible restrooms. Other spots are fine for picnics, but this is the only official one. The area takes its name from Thomas Frazer, a free African American and the first recorded nonnative resident of Winter Harbor, who operated a saltworks here and was listed in the 1790 census. If you've brought bikes, leave your car here and do a counterclockwise 12.2-mile loop through the park and back to your car via Birch Harbor and Route 186. It's a fine day trip. Or, if there's room in the rack for your bike, skip Route 186 and pedal only the park loop.

From the picnic area, the road becomes one-way. Unlike the Park Loop Road on Mount Desert Island, no parking is allowed in the right lane. There are periodic pullouts, but not many cars can squeeze in. Despite the fact that this is far from the busiest section of Acadia, it can still be frustrating not to be able to find a space in the summer months. The best advice is to stay in the area and do this loop early in the morning or later in the afternoon. The late September-early October foliage is gorgeous, but traffic does increase then. While you're driving, if you see a viewpoint you like with room to pull off, stop; it's a long way around to return.

From this side of Frenchman Bay, the views of Mount Desert Island's summits are gorgeous, rising beyond islands sprinkled here and there.

Drive 1.5 miles from the picnic area to **Raven's Head,** an unmarked, Thunder Hole-type cliff with sheer drops to the churning surf below and fabulous views. There are no fences, and the cliffs are eroded, so it's not a good place for little ones. The trail is unsigned, but there's a small pullout on the left side of the road opposite it. Be extremely careful here, stay on the path (the environment is very fragile and erosion is a major problem), and stay well away from the cliff's edge.

At 2.2 miles past the picnic area, watch for a narrow, unpaved road on the left, across from an open beach vista. It winds for one mile (keep left at the fork) up to a tiny parking circle, from which you can follow the trail (signposted Schoodic Trails) to the open ledges on 440-foot **Schoodic Head.** From the circle, there's already a glimpse of the view, but it gets much better. If you bear right at the fork, you'll come to a grassy parking area with

While you can drive the Schoodic Loop without getting out of your car, close-up views are worth the extra effort.

access to the Alder Trail (over to the Blueberry Hill parking lot) and the Schoodic Head Trail.

Continue on the Schoodic Loop Road and hang a right onto a short, two-way spur to **Schoodic Point.** On your right is the **Schoodic Institute** campus (207/288-1310, www.sercinstitute.org), on the site of a former top-secret U.S. Navy base that became part of the park in 2002. At the entrance is a small info center (with ADA-accessible restroom), staffed by volunteers and park rangers. Continue up the road to the restored **Rockefeller Hall,** which opened in 2013 as a welcome center. Inside are exhibits highlighting Schoodic's ecology and history, the former Navy base's radio and cryptologic operations, and current research programs. The Schoodic Institute also offers ranger-led activities, lectures by researchers or nationally known experts addressing environmental topics related to the park and its surroundings, and other programs and events. Check the online calendar for current opportunities.

After touring SERC, continue out to **Schoodic Point,** the highlight of the drive, with surf crashing onto big slabs of pink granite. Be extremely cautious here; chances of rescue are slim if a rogue wave sweeps someone offshore.

From Schoodic Point, return to the Loop Road. Look to the right and you'll see Little Moose Island, which can be accessed at low tide. Be careful, though, not to get stranded here—ask at the info center for safe crossing times. Continue about one mile past the Schoodic Point/Loop Road intersection to the **Blueberry Hill** parking area, a moorlike setting where the low growth allows almost 180-degree views of the bay and islands. There are a few trails in this area—all eventually converging on **Schoodic Head,** the highest point on the peninsula. (Don't confuse this with Schoodic Mountain, which is well north of here.) Across and up the road a bit is the trailhead for the 180-foot-high **Anvil headland.**

As you continue along this stretch of road, keep your eyes peeled for eagles, which frequently soar here. There's a nest on the northern end of Rolling Island; you can see it with binoculars from some of the roadside pullouts.

From Blueberry Hill, continue 1.2 miles to a pullout for the East Trail, the shortest and most direct route to Schoodic Head. From here, it's about another mile to the park exit, in Wonsqueak Harbor. It's another two miles to the intersection with Route 186 in Birch Harbor.

ENTERTAINMENT AND EVENTS

Winter Harbor's biggest wingding is the annual **Lobster Festival** (www.acadia-schoodic.org), the second Saturday in August. The daylong gala includes a parade, live entertainment, lobster-boat races (a serious competition in these parts), crafts fair, games, and more crustaceans than you could ever consume.

Concerts, art classes, coffeehouses, workshops, and related activities are presented year-round by **Schoodic Arts for All** (207/963-2569, www.schoodicarts.org). Many are held at historic Hammond Hall in downtown Winter Harbor. A summer series presents monthly concerts on Friday evenings May-October. In early August the two-week **Schoodic Arts Festival** is jam-packed with daily workshops and nightly performances for all ages.

The **Pierre Monteux School for Conductors and Orchestra Musicians** (Rte. 1, Hancock, 207/422-3280, www.monteuxschool.org), a prestigious summer program founded in 1943, has achieved international renown for training dozens of national and international classical musicians. It presents two well-attended concert series late June-July. The Wednesday series (7:30pm, $12 adults, $5 kids/students) features chamber music; the Sunday concerts (5pm, $22 adults, $5 students/kids) feature symphonies. An annual free children's concert usually is held on a Monday (1pm) in early to mid-July. All

Educating for the Future

The Schoodic section of Acadia National Park is well on the way to becoming a world-class center for the study of science and nature, thanks to a history of benefactors dating back to the early 19th century. Maine native and Wall Street tycoon John G. Moore once owned most of Schoodic Point. In 1927, George Dorr persuaded Moore's heirs to donate the land to the Hancock County Trustees of Public Reservations, with the stipulation that the land be used as a public park and for the "promotion of biological and other scientific research." Seven years later, more than 2,000 acres of the peninsula were donated to Acadia National Park.

The timing was perfect. John D. Rockefeller Jr. was working with the National Park Service to construct the Park Loop Road on Mount Desert Island. The U.S. Naval Radio Station on Otter Point was in the way, so Rockefeller, working with Dorr, helped the National Park Service work with the U.S. Navy to relocate the station to Schoodic Point. Six buildings were constructed. Most noteworthy is Rockefeller Hall, a French Norman Revival-style mansion designed by New York architect Grosvenor Atterbury, who used a similar design for the park's carriage road gatehouses on Mount Desert Island.

In 1935, the U.S. Naval Radio Station at Schoodic Point was commissioned, and by the late 20th century, the 100-acre campus comprised more than 35 buildings and was home to 350 Navy employees. When the station closed in 2002, the land was returned to the park for use as a research and education center.

It took 10 years and millions of dollars to transform the former Navy base. The campus now offers housing and meals for individual researchers, groups, and conferences, classrooms, laboratories, and a modern 124-seat auditorium, all in the inspirational setting of Schoodic Point. A renovated Rockefeller Hall, listed on the National Register of Historic Places, now serves as Schoodic's welcome center, with exhibits highlighting Schoodic's ecology and history, the former navy base's radio and cryptologic operations, and current research programs. Credit for the renovations goes to local benefactor Edith Robb Dixon, who donated $1 million in the name of her late husband, Fitz Eugene Dixon Jr.

Schoodic Institute at Acadia National Park (207/288-1310, www.schoodicinstitute.org) is the nonprofit that partners with Acadia to manage the campus and advance science and education throughout the park and the region. Schoodic Institute connects education with research, while managers at Acadia National Park rely on the research to restore Acadia's ecosystems and improve their resiliency in the face of rapid environmental changes.

The Schoodic Institute offers education and research programs aimed not only at scientists and researchers but also at students and teachers. The institute also hosts Acadia National Park's artist-in-residence program and works with the park to present programs, lectures, special events, and ranger-led activities; check the online calendar for current offerings. Among these are "bio blitzes," in which teams of specialists and volunteers research the park's flora and fauna in minute detail. In 2013-2014, a two-year blitz focused on beetles found more than 100 species never previously identified in the park.

concerts are held in the school's Forest Studio; payment via cash or checks only.

Seeking to add more vibrancy and diversity to the peninsula's entertainment offerings and to indulge their own interests in music and the sciences, the owners of Oceanside Meadows Inn created the **Institute for the Arts and Sciences** (207/963-5557), which presents a series of Thursday-night events late June-late September, with a break during the Schoodic Arts Festival. The wide-ranging calendar includes lectures and concerts as well as art shows. Some are free; others are $10-12 in advance or $12-15 at the door.

On Monday evenings in July-August, weather permitting, the **Frenchman Bay Conservancy** (207/422-2328, www.frenchmanbay.org) presents a concert series at its Tidal Falls Preserve. Pack a picnic supper or purchase lobster rolls or other fare from

Gallery Hopping in Hancock and Sullivan

From Route 1 take Eastside Road, just before the Hancock-Sullivan Bridge, and drive 1.6 miles south to the Wray family's **Gull Rock Pottery** (103 Gull Rock Rd., Hancock, 207/422-3990, www.gullrockpottery.com). Torj and Kurt Wray created this gallery, which daughter-in-law Akemi now runs. She's continued crafting their wheel-thrown, hand-painted, dishwasher-safe pottery decorated with cobalt blue and white Japanese-style motifs, but has added some of her own designs. Complementing the indoor gallery is an outdoor, oceanfront sculpture gallery with views to Mount Desert Island.

Cross the Hancock-Sullivan Bridge, then take your first left off Route 1 onto Taunton Drive to find the next four galleries, beginning with Dan Farrenkopf's and Phid Lawless's **Lunaform** (66 Cedar Ln., Sullivan, 207/422-0923, www.lunaform.com), set amid beautifully landscaped grounds surrounding an old quarry. At first glance, it appears that many of the wonderfully aesthetic garden ornaments created here are hand-turned pottery, when in fact they're hand-turned steel-reinforced concrete. Take the first right off Taunton Drive onto Track Road, proceed 0.5 mile, then turn left onto Cedar Lane.

Return to Taunton Drive and take the next right onto Quarry Road, then left on Whales Back Drive, a rough dirt lane, to find granite sculptor Obadiah Bourne Buell's **Stone Designs Studio and Granite Garden Gallery** (124 Whales Back Rd., Sullivan, 207/422-3111, www.stonedesignsmaine.com). Bourne displays his home accents and garden features in a self-serve gallery adjacent to a quarry and in the surrounding gardens. This really is a magical spot, and if you time it right, you might be able to see the sculptor at work.

Continue north on Taunton Road as it changes its name to South Bay Road. Bet you can't keep from smiling at the whimsical animal sculptures and fun furniture of talented sculptor-painter Philip Barter. His work is the cornerstone of the eclectic **Barter Gallery** (South Bay Rd., Sul-

a local food truck. Music might include jazz, steel pan drums, ukuleles, or an orchestra.

SHOPPING

You can find just about anything at the **Winter Harbor 5 and 10** (Main St., Winter Harbor, 207/963-7927). It's the genuine article, an old-fashioned five-and-dime that's somehow still surviving in the age of Walmart.

Prospect Harbor Soap Co. (4 Duck Pond Rd. at Rte. 186, Winter Harbor, 207/963-7598, www.prospectharborsoapco.com) maintains an outlet where you can purchase lotions, handmade soaps, and other skin-care products.

Galleries

From Route 1, loop down to Winter Harbor and back up on Route 186 through Prospect Harbor to find these galleries.

An old post office houses **Lee Art Glass** (679 S. Gouldsboro Rd./Rte. 186, Gouldsboro, 207/963-7280). The fused-glass tableware is created by taking two pieces of window glass and firing them on terra-cotta or bisque molds at 1,500°F. What makes the result so appealing are the colors and the patterns—crocheted doilies or stencils—impressed into the glass. The almost magical results are beautiful and delicate-looking, yet functional.

In the village center is **Artisans & Antiques** (357 Main St., Winter Harbor, 207/963-2400), a 15-member group shop with a nice mix of craftwork and treasures.

Winter Harbor Antiques and Works of Hand (424-426 Main St., Winter Harbor, 207/963-2547) is a double treat: Antiques fill one building, and a well-chosen selection of distinctive works by local craftspeople and artists fills the other. It's across from Hammond Hall and set behind colorful, well-tended gardens.

Works by contemporary Maine artists, including noted painters and sculptors associated with the Schoodic International livan, 207/422-3190, www.bartergallery.com). But there's more: Barter's wife and seven children, especially son Matt, along with son-in-law Brian Emerson, have put their considerable skills to work producing hooked and braided rugs, jewelry, and paintings as well as wood sculptures. The gallery is 2.5 miles off Route 1.

Continue on South Bay Road (note that it becomes dirt for a roughly 0.5-mile section) and turn left, heading north, when it meets Route 200/Hog Bay Road. Almost immediately on your left is Charles and Susanne Grosjean's **Hog Bay Pottery** (245 Hog Bay Rd./Rte. 200, Franklin, 207/565-2282), in operation since 1974. Inside the casual, laid-back showroom are Charles's functional, nature-themed pottery and Susanne's stunning handwoven wool rugs. Pottery seconds are often available.

Next, head south on Route 200/Bert Gray Road. Handwoven textiles are the specialty at **Moosetrack Studio** (388 Bert Gray Rd./Rte. 200, Sullivan, 207/422-9017, www.moosetrack-handweaving.com), where the selections range from handwoven area rugs to shawls of merino wool and silk. Camilla Stege has been weaving since 1969, and her exquisite work reflects her experience and expertise. The gallery is 1.8 miles north of Route 1.

Continue south. Just before the intersection with U.S. 1 is a double hit. Artist Paul Breeden, best known for the remarkable illustrations, calligraphy, and maps he's done for *National Geographic*, Time-Life Books, and other national and international publications, displays and sells his paintings at the **Spring Woods Gallery and Willowbrook Garden** (19 Willowbrook Ln., Sullivan, 207/422-3007, www.springwoodsgallery.com or www.willowbrook-garden.com). Also filling the handsome modern gallery space are paintings by Ann Breeden. Be sure to allow time to meander through the shady sculpture garden, where there's even a playhouse for kids.

Sculpture Symposium, are shown in rotating shows at **Littlefield Gallery** (145 Main St., Winter Harbor, 207/963-6005, www.littlefieldgallery.com).

The folk-art funk begins on the exterior of the **Salty Dog Gallery/Hurdy Gurdy Man Antiques** (173 Main St., Prospect Harbor, 207/963-7575), a twofold find. The lower level is filled with fun folk-arts vintage goods. Upstairs, owner Dean Kotula displays his fine art, documentary-style photographic prints.

Visiting the **U.S. Bells Foundry and Watering Cove Pottery** (56 W. Bay Rd./Rte. 186, Prospect Harbor, 207/963-7184, www.usbells.com) is a treat for the ears, as browsers try out the many varieties of cast-bronze bells made in the adjacent foundry by Richard Fisher. If you're lucky, he may have time to explain the process—particularly intriguing for children and a distraction from their instinctive urge to test every bell in the shop. The store also carries quilts by Dick's wife, Cindy, and wood-fired stoneware and porcelain by their daughter-in-law Liza Fisher. U.S. Bells is 0.25 mile up the hill from Prospect Harbor's post office.

Here's a nifty place: **Chapter Two** (611 Corea Rd., Corea, 207/963-7269, www.chaptertwocorea.com) is home to Spurling House Gallery, Corea Rug Hooking Company, and Accumulated Books Gallery. Spread out in three buildings is a nice selection of used and antiquarian books, fine crafts, and Rosemary's hand-hooked rugs. Yarn, rug-hooking supplies, and lessons are available.

Down the first dirt lane after the Corea Post Office is **The Corea Wharf Gallery** (13 Gibbs Ln., 207/963-2633, www.coreawharfgallery.com). Inside a humble wharf-top fishing shack are displayed historic photographs of Corea, taken in the 1940s-1960s by Louise Z. Young, born in Corea in 1919. She was a friend of painter Marsden Hartley, and took many candid photographs of him around the area. Young also worked with noted photographer Berenice Abbott. Also here are artifacts from

Corea's history, especially ones connected to fishing. The gallery doubles as a food stand selling lobster, lobster rolls, hot dogs, and ice cream.

RECREATION

Preserves

The very active **Frenchman Bay Conservancy** (FBC, 207/422-2328, www.frenchmanbay.org) manages a number of small preserves dotting the region, and most have at least one trail providing access. The conservancy publishes a free *Short Hikes* map, available locally, that provides directions to seven of these.

TIDAL FALLS PRESERVE

FBC's four-acre **Tidal Falls Preserve** (off Eastside Rd., Hancock) overlooks Frenchman Bay's only reversing falls (roiling water when the tide turns). There's no longer a lobster pound, but there are still picnic tables on the lawn overlooking the falls and ledges where seals often slumber. It's an idyllic spot. A summer concert series takes place here on Mondays during the summer, and Thyme Traveler, a local food truck, usually sells lobster rolls and other dinner options at the event. No dogs are permitted.

COREA HEATH

In 2008, FBC purchased 600 acres of land known as the Corea Heath, and volunteers began cutting trails that summer. *Heath* is a local word for peat land or bog, and this one is a rare coastal plateau bog, distinguished because it rises above the surrounding landscape. It's a spectacular property, with divergent ecosystems including bogs, ledges, and mixed-wood forest. Natural features include pitcher plants, sphagnum mosses, rare vascular plants, and jack pines. It's a fabulous place for bird-watching too, and the preserve borders a section of the Maine Coastal Islands National Wildlife Refuge. A one-mile trail loops through the preserve. Trail access is signed on the Corea Road, 1.9 miles from the Route 195 intersection.

DONNELL POND PUBLIC RESERVED LAND

More than 15,000 acres of remote forests, ponds, lakes, and mountains have been preserved for public access in **Donnell Pond Public Reserved Land** (Maine Bureau of Parks and Lands, 207/827-1818, www.parksandlands.com), north and east of Sullivan. The reserve includes five peaks taller than 900 feet, a 1,940-acre wetland, and 35 miles

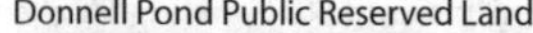

Donnell Pond Public Reserved Land

of freshwater shoreline, making it especially rich in sightings for bird-watchers. Hikers can climb Schoodic, Black, Caribou, and Tunk Mountains for expansive views taking in Frenchman Bay and Mount Desert Island; paddlers and anglers have Donnell Pond, Tunk Lake, Spring River Lake, Long Pond, Round Pond, and Little Pond, among others. Route 182, an official Scenic Highway, snakes through the Donnell Pond preserve. Hunting is permitted, so take special care during hunting season.

The hiking isn't easy here, but it isn't technical, and the options are many. The interconnecting trail system takes in Schoodic Mountain, Black Mountain, and Caribou Mountain. Follow the Schoodic Mountain Loop clockwise, heading westward first. To make a day of it, pack a picnic and take a swimsuit (and don't forget a camera and binoculars for the summit views). On a brilliantly clear day, you'll see Baxter State Park's Mount Katahdin, the peaks of Acadia National Park, and the ocean beyond. And in late July-early August, blueberries are abundant on the summit. For such rewards, this is a popular hike, so don't expect to be alone, especially on fall weekends, when the foliage colors are spectacular.

The Black Mountain ascent begins easily enough and then climbs steadily through the woods, easing off a bit before reaching bald ledges. Continue to the true summit by taking the trail past Wizard Pond. Views take in the forested lands, nearby lakes and peaks, and out to Acadia's peaks. You can piggyback it with Schoodic Mountain, using that trailhead base for both climbs. Another possibility is to add Caribou Mountain. That loop exceeds seven miles, making a full day of hiking.

Trailheads are accessible by either boat or vehicle. To reach the vehicle-access trailhead for Schoodic Mountain from Route 1 in East Sullivan, drive just over four miles northeast on Route 183 (Tunk Lake Rd.). Cross the Maine Central Railroad tracks and turn left at the Donnell Pond sign onto an unpaved road (marked as a jeep track on the USGS map). Go about 0.25 mile and then turn left for the parking area and trailhead for Schoodic Mountain, Black Mountain, Caribou Mountain, and a trail to Schoodic Beach. If you continue straight, you'll come to another trailhead for Black and Caribou Mountains. Water-access trailheads are at Schoodic Beach and Redman's Beach.

Down East Sunrise Trail

Hike, mountain bike, snowshoe, cross-country ski, or ride an ATV, snowmobile, or horse on the **Down East Sunrise Trail** (www.sunrisetrail.org). The gravel-surfaced trail, a joint effort by the Maine Department of Transportation and Maine Department of Conservation, stretches 85 miles along a rehabilitated discontinued railroad bed between Washington Junction, in Hancock, and Ayers Junction, south of Calais. Maps, available to download from the website, show trailheads, highlights, and parking lots along the route. The 30-mile section between Washington Junction and Cherryfield roughly follows the Down East coastline of the Schoodic region. Additional access points include Franklin and Sullivan; see the map for details and directions.

The seven-mile Franklin Crossing to Tunk Lake Road section edges Schoodic Bog and the southwest corner of the Donnell Pond Public Reserved Land and offers fine views of Schoodic Mountain. There's limited parking on both ends: the Franklin Crossing intersection with Route 182 and the Tunk Lake Road intersection on Route 183.

Bicycling

The Maine Department of Transportation has mapped and provides info on area bicycle routes. These include the Schoodic Peninsula, with 10-, 12-, and 24-mile loops, and the Downeast Route/East Coast Greenway Trail, a 140-mile trail stretching from Ellsworth to Calais. PDF maps with tour details are available at www.exploremaine.org, or you can pick up a copy of *Explore Maine by Bike: 33 Loop Bicycle Tours* at any of the Maine Visitor

Centers. Do be extremely careful pedaling in this region, because, as in much of Maine, shoulders are few and traffic moves swiftly.

The best choices for cycling are the **Schoodic Loop,** the **carriage roads** in the park, and the quiet roads of **Grindstone Neck** and **Corea.** The Down East Sunrise Trail (www.sunrisetrail.org) is also open to bicyclists.

SeaScape Kayak and Bike (8 Duck Pond Rd., Winter Harbor, 207/963-5806, www.seascapekayaking.com) rents bicycles for $18/day.

Canoeing and Kayaking

Experienced sea kayakers can explore the coastline throughout this region. Canoeists can paddle the placid waters of Jones Pond on the Schoodic Peninsula. In Donnell Pond Public Reserved Land, the major water bodies are **Donnell Pond** (big enough by most gauges to be called a lake) along with **Tunk Lake, Spring River Lake,** and **Long Pond;** all are accessible for boats (even, alas, powerboats). In early August, Round Mountain, rising a few hundred feet from Long Pond's eastern shore, is a great spot for gathering blueberries and huckleberries.

To reach the boat-launching area for Donnell Pond from Route 1 in Sullivan, take Route 200 north to Route 182. Turn right and go about 1.5 miles to a right turn just before Swan Brook. Turn and go not quite two miles to the put-in; the road is poor in spots but adequate for a regular vehicle. The Narrows, where you'll put in, is lined with summer cottages ("camps" in the Maine vernacular); keep paddling east to the more open part of the lake. Continue on Route 182 to find the boat launches for Tunk Lake and Spring River Lake (hand-carry only). Canoeists and kayakers can access Tunk Stream from Spring River Lake.

Also accessed from Route 182 is Flanders Pond, 2.9 miles off Route 1 on the Flanders Pond Road. It's a beautiful pond, with islands and mountain views. The public park has a parking area and an offshore float, as the pond is also a local swimming spot.

OUTFITTERS AND TRIPS

Paddle around the waters of Schoodic or Flanders Bay with **SeaScape Kayak and Bike** (8 Duck Pond Rd., Winter Harbor, 207/963-5806, www.seascapekayaking.com). Guided three-hour tours are $55 pp, including homemade blueberry snacks. SeaScape also has rental kayaks ($45 double, $35 single) stashed on Jones Pond. Visit the shop for directions, key, PFDs, and paddles.

Antonio Blasi, a Master Maine Sea Kayak and Recreational Guide, leads guided tours of Frenchman or Taunton Bay and hiking and camping expeditions through **Hancock Point Kayak Tours** (58 Point Rd., Hancock, 207/422-6854, www.hancockpointkayak.com). A three-hour paddle, including all equipment, safety and paddling demonstrations, and usually an island break, is $45. Overnight kayak camping trips are $150 pp.

Swimming

The best freshwater swimming in the area is at **Jones Beach** (sunrise-sunset daily), a community-owned recreation area on Jones Pond in West Gouldsboro. Here you'll find restrooms, a nice playground, picnic facilities, a boat launch, a swim area with a float, and a small beach. The beach is located at the end of Recreation Road, off Route 195, which is 0.3 mile south of Route 1. No unleashed pets are permitted.

Two beach areas on Donnell Pond are also popular for swimming, **Schoodic Beach** and **Redman's Beach,** and both have picnic tables, fire rings, and pit toilets. It's a 0.5-mile hike to Schoodic Beach from the parking lot. Redman's Beach is only accessible by boat. Other pocket beaches are also accessible by boat or via roadside pullouts.

A sand beach on a remote freshwater pond is the reward for a 0.25-mile hike into the Frenchman Bay Conservancy's **Little Tunk Pond Preserve.** From Route 1 in Sullivan, take Route 183 about five miles, then look for the parking area on the left. Just east of that is the **Spring River Lake Beach Day Use Area,** with parking and toilets.

Golf

Play the nine-hole **Grindstone Neck Golf Course** (Grindstone Ave., Winter Harbor, 207/963-7760, www.grindstonegolf.com) just for the dynamite scenery and for a glimpse of this exclusive late-19th-century summer enclave.

ACCOMMODATIONS

There's a campground in the Schoodic section of the park, and within 15 minutes are pleasant inns and bed-and-breakfasts.

Country Inns and Bed-and-Breakfasts

Follow Hancock Point Road 4.8 miles south of Route 1 to the three-story, gray-blue **Crocker House Country Inn** (967 Point Rd., Hancock, 207/422-6806, www.crockerhouse.com, $125-165), Rich and Liz Malaby's antidote to Bar Harbor's summer traffic. Built as a summer hotel in 1884, the inn underwent rehabbing a century later, but it retains a delightfully old-fashioned air despite now offering Wi-Fi and having air-conditioning. Breakfast is included. A few bicycles are available; clay tennis courts are nearby. If you're arriving by boat, request a mooring. The inn's dining room, open nightly for dinner in season, is a draw in itself. Some rooms are pet-friendly.

Overlooking the Gouldsboro Peninsula's only sandy saltwater beach, ★ **Oceanside Meadows Inn** (Rte. 195, Corea Rd., Prospect Harbor, 207/963-5557, www.oceaninn.com, May-mid-Oct., $169-209) is an eco-conscious retreat on 200 acres with organic gardens, wildlife habitat, and walking trails. Fourteen guest rooms are split between the 1860s captain's house and the 1820 Shaw farmhouse next door. Rooms have a comfy, old-fashioned shabby-chic decor. Note that there are no TVs or air-conditioning, and many of the bathrooms are tiny. Breakfast is a multicourse vegetarian event, usually featuring herbs and flowers from the inn's gardens. The husband-and-wife team Ben Walter and Sonja Sundaram, assisted by a loyal staff, seem to have thought of everything—hot drinks available all day, a guest fridge, beach toys, even detailed guides to the property's trails and habitats (great for entertaining kids). As if all that weren't enough, Sonja and Ben have totally restored the 1820 timber-frame barn out back—creating the **Oceanside Meadows Institute for the Arts and Sciences.** Local art hangs on the walls, and the 125-seat barn has a full schedule of concerts and lectures June-September on natural history, Native American traditions, and more, usually on Thursday night. Some are free, some require tickets; all require reservations. Oceanside Meadows is six miles off Route 1. There are no nearby restaurants, so expect to head out for lunch or dinner.

Watch lobster boats unload their catch at the dock opposite **Elsa's Inn on the Harbor** (179 Main St., Prospect Harbor, 207/963-7571, www.elsasinn.com, $125-175). Every room has an ocean view, and a few have separate entrances. Innkeepers Scott and Cherrie Markwood pamper their guests with nice linens, down duvets, terry robes, Wi-Fi, a hearty hot breakfast, and afternoon refreshments. After a day of exploring, settle into a rocker on the veranda and gaze over the boat-filled harbor out to Prospect Harbor Light. One room is ADA-accessible.

Something of a categorical anomaly, **The Bluff House Inn** (57 Bluff House Rd., Gouldsboro, 207/963-7805, www.bluffinn.com, year-round, $95-150) is part motel, part hotel, part bed-and-breakfast. The 1980s post-and-beam building overlooks Frenchman Bay. Verandas wrap around the first and second floors, so bring binoculars for sighting ospreys and bald eagles. Pine walls and flooring give a lodge feeling to the open first floor. Settle by the stone fireplace or grab a seat by the window. Breakfast is continental buffet, usually with one hot entrée. The eight second-floor rooms are decorated "country" fashion, with quilts on the very comfortable beds. (In hot weather, request a corner room.) Pet-friendly rooms are available for $15/stay. Also available is a two-bedroom apartment ($175).

Just off the peninsula, and set well back from Route 1, **Acadia View Bed and Breakfast** (175 Rte. 1, Gouldsboro, 866/963-7457, www.acadiaview.com, $145-175) tops a bluff with views across Frenchman Bay to the peaks of Mount Desert and a path down to the shorefront. Pat and Jim Close built the oceanfront house as a bed-and-breakfast that opened in 2005. It's filled with antique treasures from the Closes' former life in Connecticut. Each of the four guest rooms has a private deck. The Route 1 location is convenient to everything. It's open year-round.

Machias native Dottie Mace operated a bed-and-breakfast in Virginia before returning to Maine to open **Taunton River Bed & Breakfast** (19 Taunton Dr., Sullivan, 207/422-2070, www.tauntonriverbandb.com, $115-125) in a 19th-century farmhouse with river views. Rooms are carefully decorated; they're warm and inviting, formal without being stuffy. Two of the three guest rooms share a bath. It would be easy to spend the day just sitting on the porch swing, but it's an easy pedal or drive to local art galleries. The inn is just a stone's throw off Route 1, so traffic noise might bother the noise sensitive.

Sustainable living is the focus of Karen and Ed Curtis's peaceful **Three Pines Bed and Breakfast** (274 East Side Rd., Hancock, 207/460-7595, www.threepinesbandb.com, year-round, $125), fronting on Sullivan Harbor, just below the Reversing Falls. Their quiet off-the-grid 40-acre oceanfront organic farm faces Sullivan Harbor and is home to a llama, rare-breed chickens and sheep, ducks, and bees as well as a large organic garden, berry bushes, an orchard, and greenhouses. Photovoltaic cells provide electricity, and appliances are primarily propane powered; satellite technology operates the phone, TV, and Wi-Fi systems. Two inviting guest rooms have private entrances and water views. A full vegetarian breakfast (with fresh eggs from the farm) is served. Bicycles and a canoe are available. You can walk or pedal along an abandoned railway line down to the point, and you can launch a canoe or kayak from the yard. Children are welcome; pets are a possibility.

Although **Ironbound** (1513 U.S. 1, Hancock, 207/422-3395 www.ironbound-inn.com, from $145), a four-room inn located above the restaurant of the same name, is right on Route 1, when you're on the garden-view balconies, or on the lawn out back, you're oblivious to the traffic whizzing by. Rooms are bright and airy and have Wi-Fi, Bose Wave radios, and air-conditioning, but no TV. Continental breakfast, including bagels with Sullivan Harbor Farms smoked salmon, is included. Guests have use of a comfy sitting area downstairs, adjacent to the restaurant. The inn adjoins Crabtree Neck Conservation Trust lands, laced with trails and a pond.

Cottages

Roger and Pearl Barto, whose family roots in this region go back five generations, have four rental accommodations on their Henry Cove oceanfront property, **Main Stay Cottages** (66 Sargent St., Winter Harbor, 207/963-2601, www.mainstaycottages-rvpark.com, $90-125). Most unusual is the small, one-bedroom Boat House, which has stood since the 1880s. It hangs over the harbor, with views to Mark Island Light, and you can hear the water gurgling below at high tide (but it is cramped, be forewarned). Other options include a very comfortable efficiency cottage, a one-bedroom cottage, a 2nd-floor suite with a private entrance, and a four-bedroom house ($250/night). All have big decks and fabulous views over the lobster boat-filled harbor; watch for the eagles that frequently soar overhead. Main Stay is on the Island Explorer bus route and just a short walk from where the Bar Harbor Ferry docks.

Simple and rustic, but charming in a sweet old-fashioned way, **Albee's Shorehouse Cottages** (Rte. 186, Prospect Harbor, 207/963-2336 or 800/963-2336, www.theshorehouse.com, May-mid-Oct., $95-150) is a cluster of 10 vintage cottages decorated with braided rugs, fresh flowers, and other homey touches. They're spaced out along the shoreline and in on the lawns amid gorgeous gardens and mature shade trees. Two things make this place special: the waterfront location—and it's truly waterfront; many of the cottages are just a couple of feet from the high-tide mark—and the management. Owner Richard Rieth goes out of his way to make guests feel welcome. If you're staying a week, pick up lobsters and say what time you want dinner, and they'll be cooked and delivered to your cottage. He's slowly fixing up the cottages, but these will never be fancy; if you're fussy or bothered by water stains or spring-coil beds, go elsewhere. In peak season, preference is given to Saturday-Saturday rentals, but shorter stays are often available. Wi-Fi is available throughout, and dogs are welcome. No credit cards.

The views to Mount Desert are dreamy from **Edgewater Cabins** (25 Benvenuto Ave., Sullivan, 207/422-6414 May 15-Oct. 15, 603/472-8644 rest of year, www.edgewatercabins.com, $595-995/week), a colony of seven housekeeping cottages on a spit of land jutting into Frenchman Bay. The well-tended four-acre property has both sunrise and sunset water views, big trees for shade, and lawns rolling to the shorefront. Stays of at least three nights ($95-175/night) are possible, when there's availability.

Camping

Acadia National Park's new 96-site ★ **Schoodic Woods Campground** (Park Loop Rd., Schoodic Peninsula, 877/444-6777 or 518/885-3639 international, www.recreation.gov, credit or debit card required $22-$40) opened in 2015 on an approximately 1,400-acre property over which Acadia National Park holds a conservation easement. It's located about a mile south of Route 186, north of the Frazer Point Picnic Area. Sites include remote walk-in tenting, drive-in tenting, and RV with water and electricity. There is also a welcome center and an amphitheater with National Park Service programming. Hiking trails connect it to Schoodic Head, and nonmotorized paths link the east and west sides of the peninsula. Note: There are no showers.

The Bartos, owners of **Main Stay Cottages** (66 Sargent St., Winter Harbor, 207/963-2601, www.mainstaycottages-rvpark.com, $50), have added a 10-site campground overlooking Henry Cove. It's designed for self-contained RVs, as there are no restrooms

Albee's Shorehouse Cottages are simple and rustic.

or showers on-site; sewer, water, electric, and Wi-Fi are available.

A handful of authorized primitive campsites can be found on **Tunk Lake** (southwestern corner) and **Donnell Pond** (at Schoodic Beach and Redman's Beach), all accessible on foot or by boat. Each has a table, a fire ring, and a nearby pit toilet. Many of the sites are on the lakefront. All are first-come, first-served with no fees or permits required; they are snapped up quickly on midsummer weekends. You can camp elsewhere within this public land, except in day-use areas, but fires are not permitted at unofficial sites.

FOOD

Local Flavors

There's no food in the park's Schoodic section, so if you're planning a picnic, you'll need to stock up along the way—in Winter Harbor or Prospect Harbor—if you haven't done so earlier. Nor are there a lot of restaurant options on the Schoodic Peninsula itself. You won't go hungry, but a little advance planning can go a long way.

Make a point to attend one of the many **public suppers** held throughout the summer in this area and in so many other rural corners of Maine. Typically benefiting a worthy cause, these usually feature beans or spaghetti or the serendipity of potluck. Everyone saves room for the homemade pies. Notices of such suppers are usually posted on public bulletin boards in country stores and in libraries, on signs in front of churches, and at other places that people gather. Local newspapers also often detail such events.

The **Winter Harbor Farmers Market** takes place in the parking lot at the corner of Newman Street and Route 186, Winter Harbor, on Tuesday morning, late June-early September.

This area has two excellent smokehouses. Stock up on gourmet goodies at **Grindstone Neck of Maine** (311 Newman St./Rte. 186, just north of downtown Winter Harbor, 207/963-7347 or 866/831-8734, www.grindstoneneck.com), which earns high marks for its smoked salmon, shellfish, spreads and pâtés, and smoked cheeses, all made without preservatives or artificial ingredients. Also available are fresh fish, wine, and frozen foods for campers. Defying its name, **Sullivan Harbor Smokehouse** (Rte. 1, Hancock, 207/422-3735 or 800/422-4014, www.sullivanharborfarm.com) is in spacious modern digs in Hancock. Big interior windows allow visitors to see into the production facility.

Have a hankering for Korean? Sonye Carroll and family serve *bi-bim-bahp, boulkoh-kee,* barbecued ribs, and kimchee, along with burgers and dogs, homemade doughnuts, and Gifford's ice cream at **YU Takeout** (674 Rte. 1, Hancock, 207/667-0711, www.yutakeout.com).

Hikers, especially, frequent **182 Pizza** (138 Blackwoods Rd./Rte. 182, Franklin, 207/565-2068), a hole-in-the-wall on the edge of in-town Franklin serving pizzas, subs, calzones, and sandwiches using family recipes rooted in the old country.

Two Sisters Café & Deli (Corner Rtes. 186 & 195, Prospect Harbor, 207/963-2000, 11am-8pm daily) is the latest incarnation of this local go-to for pizza, subs, and fried foods.

Go early for the best selection at **Seanna's Sweets** (Rte. 182, 207/479-8004, Birch Harbor), a phone booth-sized self-serve honor bakery with cookies, pies, bread, and other treats, is run by adorable tyke Seanna and her mom.

Take Route 182 to Route 200 (Eastbrook Rd.) and go 1.6 miles to family-operated **Shalom Orchard Organic Winery** (158 Eastbrook Rd., Franklin, 207/565-2312, www.shalomorchard.com). The certified-organic farm is well off the beaten path but worth a visit for its organic fruit and wines as well as for its yarns, pelts, fleece, and especially the views of Frenchman Bay from the hilltop.

German and Italian presses, Portuguese corks, and Maine fruit all contribute to the creation of Bob and Kathe Bartlett's award-winning dinner and dessert wines at **Bartlett Maine Estate Winery** (175 Chicken Mill Pond Rd., Gouldsboro, 207/546-2408, www.

bartlettwinery.com, 10am-5pm Mon.-Sat. June-Oct., or by appointment), just north of the Schoodic Peninsula. Founded in 1982, the winery produces more than 20,000 gallons annually in a handsome wood-and-stone building designed by the Bartletts. Not ones to rest on their many laurels, in 2008 the Bartletts introduced grape wines, and more recently, the **Spirits of Maine Distillery.** There are no tours, but you're welcome to sample for a small tasting fee. Reserve wines and others of limited vintage are sold only on-site. A sculpture garden patio makes a nice spot to relax. Bartlett's is 0.5 mile south of Route 1 in Gouldsboro.

Family Favorites

J. M. Gerrish (352 Main St., Winter Harbor, 207/963-7000, 8am-4pm) has had its ups and downs, but locals are confident that the century-old store is now back in local, reliable hands. It's open for breakfast and lunch, and has a classic ice cream counter along with a small penny candy section.

The best place for grub and gossip in Winter Harbor is **Chase's Restaurant** (193 Main St., Winter Harbor, 207/963-7171, 7am-8pm daily, to 2pm Sun.), a seasoned no-frills booth-and-counter operation.

Shoot pool, play darts or horseshoes, watch the game on TV, sip a cold drink, and savor a burger or fried seafood at the family-friendly **The Pickled Wrinkle** (9 E. Schoodic Dr., at the intersection with Rte. 186, Birch Harbor, 207/963-7916, www.thepickledwrinkle.com, from 11am daily, $9-20). Don't be fooled by the humble appearance; new owners here know their way around the kitchen and opt for local and organic whenever possible. That said, the overall atmosphere is more tavern than restaurant. There's often live music.

Don't be put off by "Wilbur," the lobster *sculpture* outside **Ruth & Wimpy's Kitchen** (792 Rte. 1, Hancock, 207/422-3723, www.ruthandwimpys.com, 11am-9pm Mon.-Sat.); you'll probably see a crowd as well. This family-fare standby serves hefty sandwiches, lobster prepared 30 ways, pizza, pasta, and steak. Prices begin around $3.25 for a cheeseburger and climb to about $35 for a twin lobster shore dinner. Antique license plates and collections of miniature cars and trucks accent the interior. It's five miles east of Ellsworth, close to the Hancock Point turnoff.

Good food served by friendly folks is what pulls the locals into ★ **Chester Pike's Galley** (2336 U.S. 1, Sullivan, 207/422-8200, 6am-2pm Tues.-Sat., 7am-2pm Sun., and 4:30pm-8:30pm Fri. $6-18). The prices are low, and the portions are big. If you're on a diet, don't even *look* at the glass case filled with fresh-baked pies, cakes, and cookies. Go early if you want to snag one of the homemade doughnuts (and order dessert first). It's also open Friday nights for a fish fry with free seconds.

Casual Dining

In 2016, The Fisherman's Inn became **The Fisherman's Galley** (7 Newman St./Rte. 186, Winter Harbor, 207/963-5585, www.fishermansgalleymaine.com, 3pm-9pm daily mid-May-mid-Oct.), a cool, rustic, earth-friendly, and somewhat tech-y lobster pound. Not to worry, Chef Carl Johnson is still in the kitchen, but now guests order at the counter, and the food is delivered to their tables. Expect hearty stews and chowders, lobster and crab rolls, hard- and soft-shelled lobster, steamers, oyster shooters, and fried seafood, along with options for landlubbers and a full bar with Maine craft beers on tap. The menu makes it easy to cobble together a meal that fits your appetite and budget. Don't miss the lobster Bloody Mary, made with the meat of a full crustacean; it's a meal itself, served in a souvenir 16-ounce shaker glass. Dine inside where it's air-conditioned, outside under a tent, or get a lobster boil in a bucket to go. No tipping. Carl's daughter-in-law Nui operates a food cart out front, serving meat-packed lobster rolls and gourmet hot dogs for lunch (11am-3pm).

In 2013, chef Mike Poirier and baker Alice Letcher opened **The Salt Box** (1161 Rte. 1, 207/422-9900, www.saltboxmaine.com, 5pm-9pm Wed.-Sat., 9am-1pm Sun., $22-28), in a log building set back from the road, and they quickly earned a following. The decor is gently rustic, the food is sophisticated yet approachable and focused on fresh seasonal ingredients, and the service is excellent. Wednesday night, a seven-course tasting menu is offered by reservation at 6:30pm. Reservations are advised. No credit cards.

Ironbound (1513 U.S. 1, 207/422-3395, www.ironboundinn.com, from 5pm daily mid-June-mid-Oct., $10-35), opened in 2014 by the owners of Sullivan Harbor Farm, welcomes guests with a menu that ranges from sandwiches and burgers to duck breast and rib eye steak. A huge brick hearth adorned with copper pots anchors one end of the main dining room. The atmosphere is casual, with wood floors and undressed tables. The fare complements the setting, with ingredients sourced locally whenever possible. The adjacent bar is popular with locals, who come for the happy hour on the back porch and garden, 5pm-6:30pm daily, and for live entertainment Thursday-Saturday.

Ask locally about **Bunker's Wharf,** located overlooking Wonsqueak Harbor on the two-way section of East Schoodic Drive. It closed in 2014, but locals are hopeful it will reopen. Also ask about **Ravens Nest** (10 Newman St., 207/963-2234, www.ravensnestrestaurant.com, 12-3pm Mon.-Fri., 11:30am-2pm Sat.-Sun., and from 5:30pm nightly, $15-32), which opened in 2015 in downtown Winter Harbor. The building is striking, but the chef and concept seem to change frequently.

Fine Dining

The unpretentious dining rooms at the **Crocker House Country Inn** (967 Point Rd., Hancock Point, 207/422-6806, www.crockerhouse.com, 5:30pm-9pm daily May 1-Oct. 31, 5:30pm-8:30pm Fri.-Sun. Apr. and Nov.-Dec., entrées $25-33) provide a setting for well-prepared continental fare with flair, crafted from fresh and local ingredients; reservations are essential as this is one of the area's most consistent and popular dining spots. On Friday nights, a jazz trio provides background music.

One of the more dependable dining experiences in the area is **Chipper's** (1239 U.S. 1, 207/422-8238, www.chippersrestaurant.com, 5pm-9pm Wed.-Sun.). Owner Chipper Butterwick opened his popular restaurant in 1995 and expanded the simple cape-style building in 2010, adding a pub. The restaurant's wide-ranging menu includes rack of lamb and even chateaubriand, but the emphasis is on seafood; the crab cakes earn rave reviews. Meals include a sampling of tasty haddock chowder and a salad, but save room for the homemade ice cream for dessert. Entrées are in the $17-33 range, but some appetizer-salad combos provide budget options, and burgers and subs are available in the pub.

Lobster

You'd be hard-pressed to find a better place to enjoy a lobster than the ★ **Wharf Gallery & Grill** (13 Gibbs Ln., Corea, 207/963-2633, www.coreawharfgallery.com), an eat-on-the-wharf food stand overlooking dreamy, lobster boat-filled Corea Harbor. The menu includes lobster rolls, lobster grilled cheese (trust me, try it), crab claws, hot dogs, sausages, and ice cream.

Tracey's Seafood (2719 Rte. 1, Sullivan, 207/422-9072) doesn't look like much from the road, but don't be fooled. The Tracey family harvests the clams and catches the lobsters, shucks and picks, and dishes out ultra-fresh lobster, chowders, and fried seafood. There's a takeout window and picnic tables on the lawn as well as a dining room with waitress service. Portions are big, prices are low—$4 burgers, two-fer lobster rolls (usually around $12-15, but I've seen them as low as $10), and weekend fish fries and clam fries with free seconds for $10.95. Don't miss the homemade pies. For inside dining, BYOB.

INFORMATION

For advance information about eastern Hancock County, contact the **Schoodic Peninsula Chamber of Commerce** (207/963-7658, www.acadia-schoodic.org). Another source for advance information is **Downeast & Acadia Regional Tourism**

(207/546-3600 or 888/665-3278, www.downeastacadia.com). Also covering the area is the **Ellsworth Area Chamber of Commerce** (207/667-5584, www.ellsworthchamber.org).

To plan ahead, see the Acadia website (www.nps.gov/acad), where you can download a Schoodic map.

For information on the National and Maine Scenic Byways in this region, visit www.byways.org or www.exploremaine.org/byways.

Check out **Dorcas Library** (Rte. 186, Prospect Harbor, 207/963-4027, www.dorcas.lib.me.us) or **Winter Harbor Public Library** (18 Chapel Ln., Winter Harbor, 207/963-7556, www.winterharbor.lib.me.us), in the 1888 beach-stone and fieldstone Channing Chapel.

The inviting octagonal **Hancock Point Library** (Hancock Point Rd., Hancock Point, 207/422-6400, summer only) was formed in 1899. More than a library, it's a center for village activities. Check the bulletin boards by the entrance to find out what's happening when.

GETTING THERE AND AROUND

Winter Harbor is about 25 miles via Routes 1 and 186 from Ellsworth. It's about 20 miles or 30 minutes to Milbridge, on the Down East Coast. Although Winter Harbor is roughly 43 miles or 1.15 hours from Bar Harbor by car, it's only about 7 miles by water. You can get here by passenger ferry from Bar Harbor or bus from Ellsworth, but you'll need a vehicle or bicycle to explore beyond the part of the Schoodic Peninsula that's served by the Island Explorer bus.

The free **Island Explorer** (www.exploreacadia.com), Route 8, covers the lower part of the peninsula, from Winter Harbor through Prospect Harbor, late June-mid October. The bus circulates roughly once an hour, with a schedule that coordinates with the ferry.

The seasonal passenger-only **Bar Harbor Ferry** (207/288-2984, www.barharborferry.com, round-trip $32 adults, $22 children, $7 bicycle) operates at least four times daily mid-June-late September between Bar Harbor and Winter Harbor, and coordinates with the free **Island Explorer** (www.exploreacadia.com) bus's Schoodic Route 8.

Since the ferry's summer schedule is coordinated with the Island Explorer's Schoodic route, you can board the ferry in Bar Harbor, pick up the bus at the dock in Winter Harbor, and be shuttled along the Schoodic Loop. Stop where you like for a picnic or a hike, and then board a later bus. Take the last bus back to the ferry and return to Bar Harbor. It makes for a super car-free excursion.

A ferry alternative is **Winter Harbor Water Taxi & Tours** (207/963-7007, www.winterharborwatertaxiandtours.com). Captain Wes Shaw will squire you around Schoodic's waters or over to Bar Harbor for $75 per hour, covering up to six passengers.

The Down East Coast

The term *Down East* is rooted in the direction the wind blows; the prevailing southwest wind powered 19th-century sailing vessels along this rugged coastline. But to be truly Down East, in the minds of most Mainers, you have to be physically here in Washington County—a stunning landscape of waterways, forests, blueberry barrens, rocky shoreline dotted with islands and lighthouses, and independent pocket-size communities, many still dependent upon fishing or lobstering for their economies.

At one time, most of the Maine Coast used to be as underdeveloped as this part of it. You can set your clock back a generation or two while you're here; you'll find no giant malls, only a couple of fast-food joints, and two—count 'em—traffic lights. Although there are a handful of restaurants offering fine dining, for the most part your choices are limited to family-style restaurants specializing in home cooking with an emphasis on fresh (usually fried) seafood and lobster rolls. Nor will you find grand resorts or even not-so-grand hotels. Motels, tourist cabins, and small inns and bed-and-breakfasts dot the region. The upside is that prices too are a generation removed. If you're searching for the Maine of your memories or your imagination, this is it.

When eastern Hancock County flows into western Washington County, you're on the Down East Coast (sometimes called the Sunrise Coast). From Steuben eastward to Jonesport, Machias, and Lubec—then "around the corner" to Eastport, and Calais—Washington County is twice the size of Rhode Island, covers 2,528 square miles, has about 30,000 residents, and stakes a claim as the first U.S. real estate to see the morning sun. The region also includes handfuls of offshore islands—some accessible by ferry, charter boat, or private vessels. (Some, with sensitive bird-nesting sites, are off-limits during the summer.) At the uppermost point of the coast, and conveniently linked to Lubec by a bridge, New Brunswick's Campobello Island is a popular day-trip destination—the locale of Franklin D. Roosevelt's summer retreat. Other attractions in this area include festivals, concert series, art and antiques galleries, lighthouses,

Previous: Head Harbour Wharf; Head Harbour Lightstation. **Above:** fishing shack in Jonesport.

Look for ★ to find recommended sights, activities, dining, and lodging.

Highlights

★ **Maine Coastal Islands National Wildlife Refuge:** More than 300 birds have been sighted at Petit Manan Point. Even if you're not a bird-watcher, come for the hiking and, in August, the blueberries (page 393).

★ **Great Wass Island Preserve:** The finest natural treasure in this part of Maine is the Great Wass Archipelago, partly owned by The Nature Conservancy, with opportunities for hiking and bird-watching (page 398).

★ **Machias Seal Island Puffin Tour:** An excursion boat departs from Cutler for Machias Seal Island, home to Atlantic puffins, as well as razorbill auks, Arctic terns, and common murres (page 405).

★ **West Quoddy Head State Park:** This park features the iconic candy-striped West Quoddy Head Light, as well as recreational opportunities like cliff-side hiking trails, beach-combing, and bird-watching (page 408).

★ **Roosevelt Campobello International Park:** Make it an international vacation by venturing over to this New Brunswick park, home to the Roosevelt Cottage and miles of hiking trails (page 416).

★ **Whale-Watching:** Sail with Island Cruises into Passamaquoddy Bay, pass the Old Sow whirlpool, and ogle seabirds and whales (page 418).

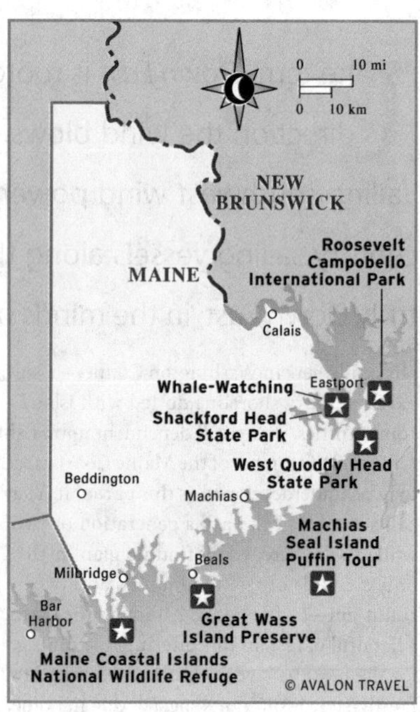

★ **Shackford Head State Park:** The rewards for this easy hike are panoramic views over Cobscook Bay from Eastport to Campobello (page 422).

historical homes, and the great outdoors for hiking, biking, birding, sea kayaking, whale-watching, camping, swimming, and fishing.

One of the Down East Coast's millennial buzzwords has been ecotourism, and local conservation organizations and chambers of commerce have targeted and welcomed visitors willing to be careful of the fragile ecosystems here—visitors who will contribute to the economy while respecting the natural resources and leaving them untrammeled, who don't cross the fine line between light use and overuse. Low-impact tourism is essential for this area. However, outfitters and canoe-, kayak-, and bicycle-rental outlets are few and far between.

One natural phenomenon no visitor can affect is the tide—the inexorable ebb and flow, predictably in and predictably out. If you're not used to it, even the 6-10-foot tidal ranges of southern Maine may surprise you. But along this coastline, the tides are astonishing—as much as 28 feet difference in water level within six hours. Old-timers tell stories of big money lost betting on horses racing the fast-moving tides.

Another surprise to visitors may be how early the sun rises—and sets—on the Sunrise Coast. Keep in mind that if you cross into Canada from either Lubec or Calais, you enter the Atlantic time zone, and you'll need to set your clock ahead one hour.

Yet another distinctive natural feature of Washington County is its blueberry barrens (fields). Depending on the time of year, the fields will be black (torched by growers to jump-start the crop), blue (ready for harvest), or maroon (fall foliage, fabulous for photography). In early summer, a million rented bees set to work pollinating the blossoms. By August, when a blue haze forms over the knee-high shrubs, bent-over bodies use old-fashioned wooden rakes to harvest the ripe berries. It's backbreaking work, but the employment lines usually form quickly when newspaper ads announce the start of the annual harvest.

Warm clothing is essential in this corner of Maine. It may be nicknamed the Sunrise Coast, but it also gets plenty of fog, rain, and cool temperatures. Temperatures tend to be warmer, and the fog diminishes, as you head toward the inland parts of the county, but you can never count on that. Mother Nature is an accomplished curveball pitcher, and El Niño and La Niña periodically provide an assist.

PLANNING YOUR TIME

Down East Maine is not for those in a hurry. Traffic ambles along, and towns are few and far between. Nature is the biggest calling card here, and to appreciate it you'll need time to hike, bike, canoe, sea kayak, or take an excursion boat. Although Route 1 follows the coast in general, it's often miles from the water. You'll want to ramble down the peninsulas to explore the seaside villages, see lighthouses, or hike in parks and preserves, and perhaps wander inland to the unspoiled lakes. You'll need at least three days to begin to cover the territory, ideally five days or longer if you want to really explore it.

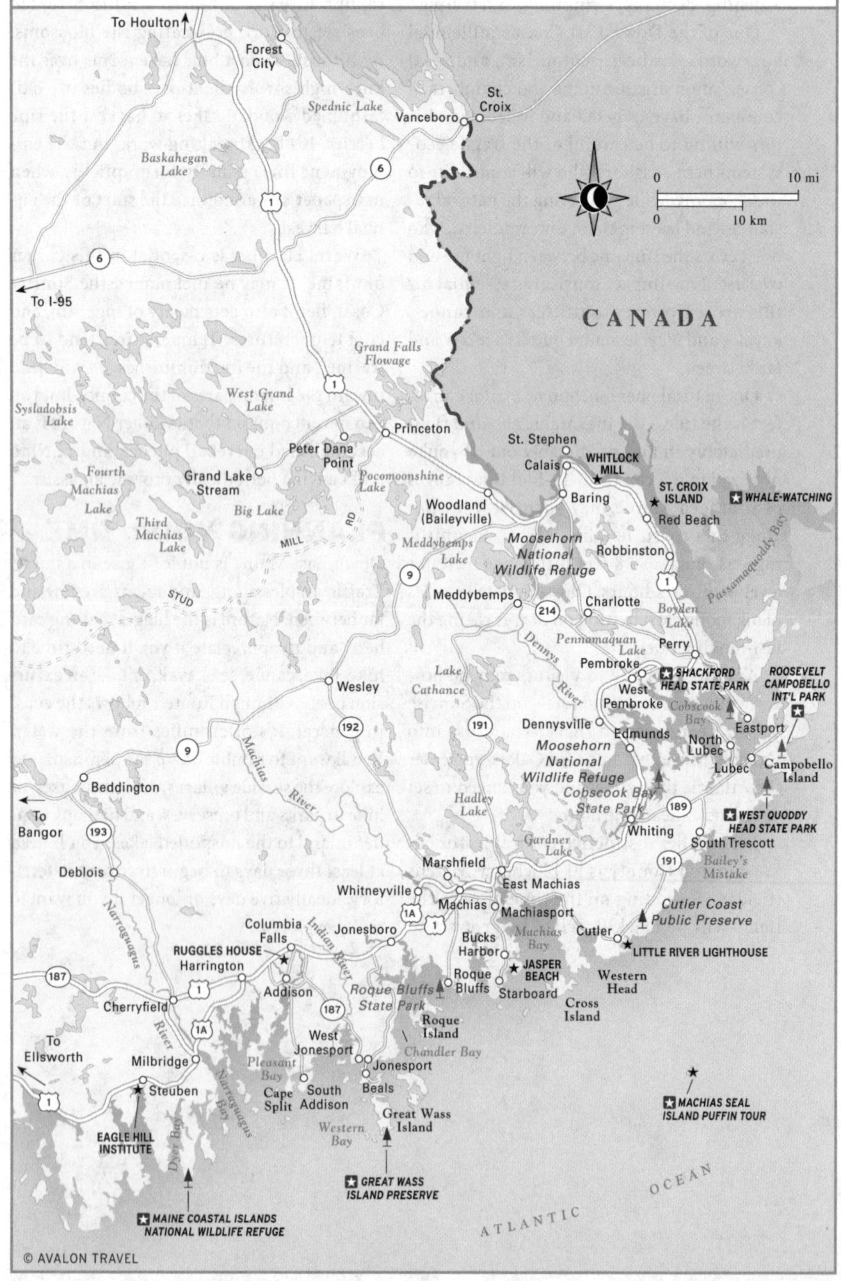
The Down East Coast
To Houlton
Forest City
Spednic Lake
Vanceboro
St. Croix
Baskahegan Lake
0
10 mi
0
10 km
To I-95
CANADA
Grand Falls Flowage
West Grand Lake
Sysladobsis Lake
Princeton
Peter Dana Point
St. Stephen
Calais
WHITLOCK MILL
Fourth Machias Lake
Grand Lake Stream
Pocomoonshine Lake
Woodland (Baileyville)
Baring
ST. CROIX ISLAND
WHALE-WATCHING
Big Lake
Third Machias Lake
Red Beach
MILL RD
Meddybemps Lake
Moosehorn National Wildlife Refuge
Robbinston
Passamaquoddy Bay
STUD
Meddybemps
Charlotte
Boyden Lake
Pennamaquan Lake
Perry
Dennys River
Pembroke
Lake Cathance
Wesley
SHACKFORD HEAD STATE PARK
ROOSEVELT CAMPOBELLO INT'L PARK
West Pembroke
Cobscook Bay
Eastport
Dennysville
Edmunds
Machias River
Moosehorn National Wildlife Refuge
North Lubec
Lubec
Campobello Island
Beddington
Cobscook Bay State Park
Hadley Lake
To Bangor
WEST QUODDY HEAD STATE PARK
Whiting
South Trescott
Gardner Lake
Bailey's Mistake
Deblois
Marshfield
East Machias
Whitneyville
Narraguagus River
Machias
Machiasport
Cutler Coast Public Preserve
Columbia Falls
Indian River
Jonesboro
Cutler
Machias Bay
RUGGLES HOUSE
Bucks Harbor
LITTLE RIVER LIGHTHOUSE
Harrington
Roque Bluffs
JASPER BEACH
Western Head
Addison
Roque Bluffs State Park
Starboard
Cherryfield
Cross Island
Roque Island
To Ellsworth
Milbridge
West Jonesport
Chandler Bay
Jonesport
Pleasant Bay
Steuben
Cape Split
South Addison
Beals
MACHIAS SEAL ISLAND PUFFIN TOUR
Narraguagus Bay
Great Wass Island
Western Bay
Dyer Bay
EAGLE HILL INSTITUTE
GREAT WASS ISLAND PRESERVE
OCEAN
ATLANTIC
MAINE COASTAL ISLANDS NATIONAL WILDLIFE REFUGE
© AVALON TRAVEL

Milbridge

The pace begins to slow by the time you've left Hancock County and entered western Washington County, the beginning of the Down East Coast. In this little pocket are the towns of Steuben, Milbridge, Cherryfield, and Harrington.

Nowadays life can be tough here. Once, great wooden ships slid down the ways and brought prosperity and trade to shippers, builders, and barons of the timber industry, of which Cherryfield's stunning houses are evidence enough. Now the barons control the wild blueberry barrens, covering much of the inland area of western Washington County and annually shipping millions of pounds of blueberries out of headquarters in Milbridge and Cherryfield, named for the wild cherries that once were abundant here. The big names here are Jasper Wyman and Sons and Cherryfield Foods.

Milbridge (pop. 1,353) straddles Route 1 and the Narraguagus River (Nar-ra-GWAY-gus, a Native American name meaning "above the boggy place"), once the state's premier source of Atlantic salmon. **Cherryfield** (pop. 1,232) is at the tidal limit of the Narraguagus. Even though Route 1A trims maybe three miles off the trip from Milbridge to Harrington, resist the urge to take it. Take Route 1 from Milbridge to Cherryfield—the Narraguagus Highway—and then continue to Harrington. You shouldn't miss Cherryfield.

Steuben's (pop. 1,131) claim to fame is the Petit Manan section of the Maine Coastal Islands National Wildlife Refuge.

SIGHTS

Milbridge Historical Society Museum

A group of energetic residents worked tirelessly to establish the **Milbridge Historical Society Museum** (83 Main St., Milbridge, 207/546-4471, www.milbridgehistoricalsociety.org, 1pm-4pm Sat.-Sun. June-Sept. and also Tues. July-Aug., donation). Displays in the large exhibit room focus on Milbridge's essential role in the shipbuilding trade, but kids will enjoy such oddities as an amputation knife used by a local doctor and a re-created country kitchen. The museum also sponsors a monthly lecture series June-October.

Scenic Fall Foliage Routes

In fall—roughly early September-early October in this part of Maine—the postharvest blueberry fields take on brilliant scarlet hues. They're gorgeous. The best barren-viewing road is Route 193 between Cherryfield and Beddington, via Deblois, the link between Routes 1 and 9—a 21-mile stretch of granite outcrops, pine windscreens, and fiery-red fields.

Cherryfield Historic District

Imagine a little town this far Down East having a 75-acre National Register Historic District with 52 architecturally significant buildings. If architecture appeals to you, don't miss Cherryfield. The **Cherryfield-Narraguagus Historical Society** (88 River Rd., Cherryfield, 207/546-2076, www.cherryfieldhistorical.com, 1pm-4pm Sat. summer) has produced a free brochure-map, *Walking Tour of the Cherryfield Historic District*. Architectural styles included on the route are Greek Revival, Italianate, Queen Anne, Colonial Revival, Second Empire, Federal, and Gothic Revival—dating 1803-1940, with most from the late 19th century. Especially impressive for such a small town are the Second Empire-style homes.

ENTERTAINMENT AND EVENTS

The biggest event in this end of Washington County is **Milbridge Days,** in late July, drawing hundreds of visitors. The Saturday-afternoon highlight is the codfish relay

Maine Fisheries Trail

According to the National Marine Fisheries Service, the proportion of Maine workers employed in commercial fishing is more than 10 times the percentage nationwide. Maine's **Downeast Fisheries Trail** (www.downeastfisheriestrail.org) stretches along Route 1 from Penobscot Bay to Cobscook Bay, but here in Washington County, where the percentage of fishing folks is even higher, you're in the thick of it.

Of the hundreds of sardine canneries that peppered coastal Maine's waterfront, none remain. Once, groundfish such as cod were a major fishery for boats heading to sea from ports such as Jonesport, Lubec, and Eastport, but now they're all but gone. These days, commercial fishermen harvest clams, elvers, crabs, alewives, scallops, urchins, shrimp, marine worms, and even seaweed, in addition to fish and lobster; hatcheries seek to replenish species such as sea-run salmon; and farms raise Atlantic salmon, oysters, and mussels.

The mapped trail comprises 45 sites celebrating Maine's maritime heritage and marine resources, from the Penobscot Marine Museum in Searsport to the Cobscook Bay Resource Center in Eastport. Marked sites allow you to delve into Maine's fishing and maritime heritage by visiting fish hatcheries, aquaculture facilities, active fishing harbors, processing plants, working wharves and piers, and related historical sites. You can request a printed copy of the map by calling 207/581-1435.

race—hilarious enough to have been featured in *Sports Illustrated* magazine and on national television. The four-member teams, clad in slickers and hip boots, really do hand off a greased cod instead of the usual baton. Race rules specify that runners must be "reasonably sober" and not carry the codfish between their teeth or legs. Also on the schedule are blueberry pancake breakfasts, a fun parade, kids' games, an auction, a dance, beano and cribbage tournaments, crafts booths, and a lobster bake. You have to be there. The relay race has been going since the mid-1980s; the festival has been going for a century and a half.

The **Eagle Hill Institute** (59 Eagle Hill Rd., Steuben, 207/546-2821, www.eaglehill.us) presents advanced natural history seminars and scientific illustration workshops and publishes peer-reviewed scientific journals. It also sponsors various opportunities to meet and mingle with scientists and others. If you're especially interested in natural history and the arts, the institute offers longer programs as well. The institute is located four miles off Route 1. Take Dyer Bay Road off Route 1, bearing left at the fork on Mogador Road, for a total of 3.6 miles, then left on Schooner Point Road, then right on Eagle Hill Road. Programs take place in the Dining Hall lecture room.

Public **lectures,** by recognized experts on often fascinating topics, are offered two or three times each week. Subjects have included Maine Poets and the Natural World: A Different Lens; the Existential Problem of the Whale in the Sagas of the Vikings; Maine's Best Edible Mushrooms; Foraging and Cooking Tips across the Season; and Songbird Superhighway: Understanding Migration in the Gulf of Maine. The onsite restaurant, Christopher's, is open for dinner on program nights.

SHOPPING

Arthur Smith (Rogers Point Rd., Steuben, 207/546-3462) is the real thing when it comes to chain-saw carvings. He's an extremely talented folk artist who looks at a piece of wood and sees an animal in it. His carvings of great blue herons, eagles, wolves, porcupines, flamingoes, and other creatures are incredibly detailed, and his wife, Marie, paints them in lifelike colors. Don't expect a fancy studio; much of the work can be viewed roadside.

Also in Steuben, but on the other end of the spectrum, is **Ray Carbone** (460 Pigeon Hill Rd., Steuben, 207/546-2170, www.raycarbonesculptor.com), whose masterful wood, stone, and bronze sculptures and fine furniture are definitely worth stopping to see or buy. Don't miss the granite sculptures and birdbaths in the garden.

Contemporary Maine art by local artists and artisans is shown in rotating shows at **Schooner Gallery** (59 Main St., Milbridge, 207/546-3179, www.schoonergallery.com), where you can also preorder a handsome wreath for the holidays.

Just across the bridge from downtown Cherryfield, **Riverlily** (2 Wilson Hill Rd., Cherryfield, 207/546-7666) carries a little bit of everything, from lotions and potions to jewelry and scarves.

Stop by **4 Main Street Antiques** (4 Main St., Cherryfield, 207/546-2664) for European and American furniture and decorative works.

Tunk Mountain Arts & Crafts (639 Blackswoods Rd./Rt. 182, Cherryfield, 207/546-8948) shows works in varied media by local and regional artists.

RECREATION

★ Maine Coastal Islands National Wildlife Refuge

Restoring and managing colonies of nesting seabirds is the focus of the **Maine Coastal Islands National Wildlife Refuge,** which spans 250 coastal miles and comprises 55 offshore islands and four mainland parcels totaling more than 8,200 acres spread out in five refuges. Occupying a 2,195-acre peninsula in Steuben with 10 miles of rocky shoreline and three offshore islands is the refuge's outstandingly scenic **Petit Manan Point Division** (Pigeon Hill Rd., Steuben, 207/546-2124, www.fws.gov/refuge/maine_coastal_islands, sunrise-sunset daily year-round). The remote location means it sees only about 15,000 visitors per year, and most of those are likely birders, as more than 300 different bird species have been sighted here. Among the other natural highlights are stands of jack pine, coastal raised peat lands, blueberry barrens, freshwater and saltwater marshes, granite shores, and cobble beaches. When asking directions locally, you'll hear it called "'tit Manan." Note: There is no visitors center.

The moderately easy, four-mile round-trip Birch Point Trail and the slightly more difficult, 1.8-mile round-trip Hollingsworth

Take a tour of the architecture in Cherryfield.

Trail loop provide splendid views and opportunities to spot wildlife along the shore and in the fields, forests, and marshlands. The Hollingsworth Trail, leading to the shoreline, is the best. This is foggy territory, but on clear days you can see the 123-foot lighthouse on Petit Manan Island, 2.5 miles offshore (for a closer look at the puffin colony there, book a trip on an excursion boat from Milbridge). The Birch Point Trail heads through blueberry fields to Dyer Bay and loops by the waterfront, with much of the trail passing through woods. Family-friendly interpretive signage explains flora and fauna along the route.

From Route 1, on the east side of Steuben, take Pigeon Hill Road. Six miles down is the first parking lot, for the Birch Point Trail; another 0.5 mile takes you to the parking area for the Hollingsworth Trail; space is limited. If you arrive in August, help yourself to blueberries. Cross-country skiing is permitted in winter.

Pigeon Hill

It doesn't require too much effort to hike Pigeon Hill and reap views taking in Cadillac Mountain, Petit Manan Light, and the island-studded Bold Coast from its 317-foot summit, the highest point on Washington County's coastline. Since acquiring this 172-acre preserve, **Downeast Coastal Conservancy** (207/255-4500, www.downeastcoastalconservancy.org) has been enhancing the original trail and adding new ones. It now has 1.6 miles of linked trails to the summit ledges; the shortest route, 0.8 mile round-trip, ascends steeply but swiftly. For the best views on the descent, take the Summit Loop and Silver Mine Trails; the latter passes an abandoned silver mine (not much to see but a pile of rocks). The trailhead is on the western side of Pigeon Hill Road, 4.5 miles south of Route 1. If you continue on the road, you'll end up at the Petit Manan Point Division of the Maine Coastal Islands National Wildlife Refuge.

McClellan Park

You can picnic, hike, and camp at this 10-acre oceanfront park in Milbridge. Go tidepooling, clamber over rocks, or just admire the views over the rugged islands offshore. From Route 1, take Wyman Road approximately 4.5 miles.

Boat Excursions

Captain Jamie Robertson's **Robertson Sea Tours and Adventures** (Milbridge Marina, Fickett's Point Rd., 207/483-6110 or 207/461-7439, www.robertsonseatours.com, May 15-Oct. 1) offers cruises from the Milbridge Marina aboard the *Kandi Leigh*, a classic Maine lobster boat. Options include puffins and seabirds, whale-watching, and lobstering. Prices range $60-95 adults, $25-75 children for the 1.5-4-hour cruises. Boat minimums may apply.

ACCOMMODATIONS

One of Cherryfield's 52 buildings on the National Register of Historic Places, the 1793 Archibald-Adams House is now the **Englishman's Bed and Breakfast** (122 Main St., Cherryfield, 207/546-2337, www.englishmansbandb.com, $125-150). The magnificently restored, Federal-style home borders the Narraguagus River and makes a superb base for exploring inland and Down East Maine. The lovely grounds have gardens and a screened-in gazebo. Owners Peter (the Englishman) and Kathy Winham are archaeologists and serious tea drinkers—they also sell fine teas online (www.teasofcherryfield.com) and in area specialty stores. Two guest rooms in the main house have river views. One has a private half-bath but shares a full bath. A riverside guesthouse, built in the 1990s, melds beautifully with the inn's architecture and is self-catering; pets are allowed here for $7/night.

Camping

Since 1958 the Ayr family has welcomed campers at its quiet, well-off-the-beaten-path property on Joy Cove. With a convenient location 15 minutes from Petit Manan National Wildlife Refuge and 20 minutes from Schoodic Point, **Mainayr Campground** (321

Village Rd., Steuben, 207/546-2690, www.mainayr.com, late May-mid-Oct., $30-33) has 32 mostly wooded tenting and RV sites (five with full hookups). Also on the premises are a playground, a laundry, a beach for tidal swimming, clamming flats, a grassy launch area for kayaks and canoes, a camp store, berries for picking, and fresh lobsters.

Town-owned **McClellan Park** (Wayman Rd., Milbridge, 207/542-2422, $10/site), a gift to the town in 1925 from George B. McClellan, son of a Civil War general, has 14 primitive wooded campsites, each with picnic table and fire ring. The 10-acre park, sited on Tom Leighton Point at the mouth of Narraguagus Bay, a picnic area, and excellent views of undeveloped islands.

FOOD

Local Flavors

The **Milbridge Farmers Market** (9am-noon Sat. early June-mid-Oct.) sets up on Main Street.

Although it's cultivating a small vineyard out front, **Catherine Hill Winery** (661 Blackswoods Rd., Cherryfield, 207/546-3426, www.cathillwinery.com) is currently making small-batch wines from grapes sourced elsewhere. Stop by the tasting room (12-5pm Wed.-Fri. and Sun.) to learn more.

Thank the migrant community who arrive here in summer to pick blueberries for ★ **Vazquez Mexican Takeout** (38 Main St., Milbridge, 207/598-8141, 10am-7pm Mon.-Sat., $3-8). What began as a food truck serving authentic Mexican fare to blueberry pickers has evolved into a family operated permanent take-out spot, with picnic tables on a covered porch, open patio, and lawn. The food is excellent, the portions are generous, and the Mexican fare is delicious and authentic, with house-made tortillas and salsas.

Family Favorites

Cheery waitresses serve big portions of home-cooked fare at **44 Degrees North** (17 Main St., Milbridge, 207/546-4440, www.44-degrees-north.com, 11am-8pm Mon.- Sat.). The front room is family oriented, with booths, tables, and cheerful decor. The back room doubles as a bar and has a big-screen TV. As is usually the case in this part of Maine, there's a case full of mouthwatering desserts. Most heartier choices are less than $17.

More home cooking, from shepherd's pie to fried fish, comes out of the kitchen at **Scovils Millside Dining** (1276 Main St./Rte. 1, Harrington, 207/483-6544, 7am-7pm Tues.-Sat., 7am-2pm Sun.), a family-run restaurant near the intersections of Routes 1 and 1A. The Friday all-you-can-eat fish fry is $10. Dinner choices run $8-22.

Casual Dining

Long before farm-to-table became mainstream, Jessie King and Alva Lowe had earned a reputation for garden-fresh fare at ★ **Kitchen Garden Restaurant** (35 Village Rd., 207/546-4269, www.thekitchengarden-restaurant.com, $22-30, no credit cards), based in their 1860s Cape-style home. When they closed in 2003, locals mourned, but in 2011 the talented duo reopened it, again drawing from their gardens as well as local, mostly organic sources to create authentic Jamaican fare, such as jerk chicken and curried goat, as well as seafood and vegetarian entrées. Reservations are required, and guests are requested to order their meals in advance. Bring your own wine or beer ($5 bottle fee); call for current days of operation.

Chef Christopher Meyell's ★ **Christopher's at Eagle Hill** (59 Eagle Hill Rd., 207/546-1219, www.eaglehill.us/christophers, 5pm-8pm Tues.-Sat., 10am-1pm Sun., $15-32) is an unexpected find: French-American fusion cuisine in a remote fine-dining restaurant in a woodland setting at the Eagle Hill Institute. You might begin with lobster ravioli or duck terrine and move on to entrées such as grilled lamb chops, roasted salmon, or vegetarian cannelloni. Pair dinner with attending an Eagle Hill lecture.

INFORMATION

Info on the area is available from the **Milbridge Area Merchants Association** (www.milbridge.org) or **Destination Cherryfield** (www.destinationcherry-field.org).

GETTING THERE AND AROUND

Milbridge is about 20 miles or 25 minutes via Routes 186 and 1 from Winter Harbor. It's about 25 miles or 30 minutes via Routes 1 and 187 to Jonesport.

Jonesport and Beals Area

Between western Washington County and the Machias Bay area is the molar-shaped Jonesport Peninsula, reached from the west via the attractive little town of **Columbia Falls,** bordering Route 1. Rounding the peninsula are the picturesque towns of Addison, Jonesport, and Beals Island. First settled around 1762, Columbia Falls still has a handful of houses dating from the late 18th century, but its best-known structure is the early-19th-century Ruggles House.

On the banks of the Pleasant River, just south of Columbia Falls, **Addison** (pop. 1,266) once had four huge shipyards cranking out wooden cargo vessels that circled the world. Since that 19th-century heyday, little seems to have changed, and the town today may be best known as the haunt of painter John Marin, who first came to Maine in 1914.

Jonesport (pop. 1,370) and **Beals Island** (pop. 508) are traditional hardworking fishing communities—old-fashioned, friendly, and photogenic. Beals, connected to Jonesport via an arched bridge over Moosabec Reach, is named for Manwarren Beal Jr. and his wife, Lydia, who arrived around 1773 and quickly threw themselves into the Revolutionary War effort. But that's not all they did—the current phone book covering Jonesport and Beals Island lists dozens of Beal descendants (as well as dozens of Alleys and Carvers, other early names).

Even more memorable than Manwarren Beal was his six-foot, seven-inch descendant Barnabas, dubbed "Tall Barney" for obvious reasons. The larger-than-life fellow became the stuff of legend all along the Maine Coast.

Also legendary here is the lobster-boat design known as the Jonesport hull. People "from away" won't recognize its distinctive shape, but count on the fishing pros to know it. The harbor here is jam-packed with Jonesport lobster boats, and souped-up versions are consistent winners in the summertime lobster-boat race series.

There's not all that much here in terms of attractions, never mind lodging or dining, but self-sufficient, outdoor-oriented visitors and history buffs should enjoy the simple pleasures and beauty of the area.

SIGHTS

Ruggles House

Behind a picket fence on a quiet street in Columbia Falls stands the remarkable **Ruggles House** (146 Main St., Columbia Falls, 207/483-4637, www.ruggleshouse.org, 10am-4pm Mon.-Sat., noon-4pm Sun. mid June-mid Oct., $5 adults, $2 ages 6-12). Built in 1818 for Judge Thomas Ruggles—lumber baron, militia captain, even postmaster—the tiny house on a grand scale boasts a famous flying (unsupported) staircase, intricately carved moldings, a Palladian window, and unusual period furnishings. Rescued in the mid-20th century and maintained by the Ruggles House Society, this gem has become a magnet for savvy preservationists. A quarter mile east of Route 1, it's open for hour-long guided tours.

Jonesport Historical Society

In 2012, the **Jonesport Historical Society** (Sawyer Sq., Jonesport, www.peabody.lib.

me.us, 11am-3pm Tues., Thurs., Sat.) began moving into a permanent home inside an 1896 building that had remained in the Sawyer family and retained original ledgers, daybooks, letters, and receipts dating back to the building's construction. Society members have delighted in finding artifacts in the basement and the original safe in a shipping clerk's office, which appears as it did circa 1900.

Downeast Institute for Applied Marine Research and Education

University of Maine at Machias professor Brian Beal founded the Beals Island Regional Shellfish Hatchery, now the **Downeast Institute** (Black Duck Cove, Great Wass Island, 207/497-5769, www.downeastinstitute.org), a marine field station for the University of Maine at Machias. Learn everything there is to know about shellfish, especially soft-shell clams, on this eight-acre property with two natural coves. Tours are by appointment.

Wreaths Across America Museum

Wreaths Across America has earned international fame for its annual wreath-laying at Arlington National Cemetery. This **museum** (4 Point St., Columbia Falls, 877/385-9504, www.wreathsacrossamerica.org, 9am-4pm daily, free), located at its headquarters, shows films and showcases items donated to the company over the years by veterans and their families. You can tour this heart-tugging memorial to American soldiers on your own or with a guide.

Wild Salmon Resource Center

Established in 1922, the **Wild Salmon Resource Center** (Columbia Falls, 207/483-4336, www.mainesalmonrivers.org, 9am-4pm Mon.-Fri., free), on the Pleasant River, has educational displays and a library. The basement-level, volunteer-run fish hatchery raises 50,000 Atlantic salmon fry annually. Staff welcome visitors and explain the efforts to save Maine's endangered salmon.

Moosabec Mussels

Family-owned **Moosabec Mussels** (Jonesport, 207/497-2500) processes wild harvested mussels, clams, and periwinkles. At the plant, mussels are purged, decluped, graded, washed, and inspected before being packaged for sale. Free tours are available by appointment; call plant manager Roger Dame at 207/399-4783.

The Ruggles House in Columbia Falls is an architectural marvel.

ENTERTAINMENT AND EVENTS

For a taste of real Maine, don't miss the Downeast Salmon Federation's April **Smelt Fry** (207/483-4336), held under a riverside tent in Columbia Falls.

The biggest annual wingding hereabouts is Jonesport's **Fourth of July** celebration, with several days of special activities, including barbecues, a beauty pageant, kids' games, fireworks, and the famed **Jonesport Lobster Boat Races** in Moosabec Reach.

Peabody Memorial Library (207/497-3003, www.peabody.lib.me.us) in Jonesport presents bimonthly art shows and sponsors a summer music series.

SHOPPING

You can't miss the humongous blueberry housing **Wild Blueberry Land** (1067 Rte. 1, Columbia Falls, 207/483-2583, www.wildblueberryland-maine.com). Step inside to find blueberry everything, from baked goods—including pies—to blueberry-themed merchandise ranging from scented candles to condiments.

Flower-design majolica pottery and whimsical terra-cotta items are April Adams's specialties at **Columbia Falls Pottery** (150 Main St., Columbia Falls, 207/483-4075 or 800/235-2512, www.columbiafallspottery.com), an appealing shop in a rehabbed country store next to the Ruggles House.

Nelson Decoys Downeast Gallery (13 Cranberry Lane, Jonesport, 207/497-3488) is equal parts shop, gallery, and museum. Inside are not only hand-carved decoys but also creations by other area artists and artisans. It's in an old schoolhouse, just off Main Street downtown.

RECREATION

★ Great Wass Island Preserve

Allow a whole day to explore 1,576-acre Great Wass Island, an extraordinary preserve, even when it's drenched in fog—a not-infrequent event. Owned by **The Nature Conservancy** (207/729-5181, www.nature.org), the preserve is at the tip of Jonesport's peninsula. Best hiking routes are the wooded 2.2-mile Little Cape Point and 2.3-mile Mud Hole Trails, retracing your path for each. Note that neither is flat, the terrain is often uneven, and the exposed bedrock can be slippery. Making a loop by connecting the two along the rocky shoreline adds considerably to the time and difficulty, but do it if you have time; allow about six hours, and wear waterproof footwear. Expect

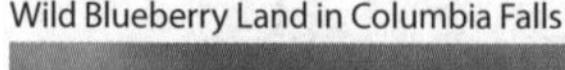

Wild Blueberry Land in Columbia Falls

to see beach-head irises (like a blue flag) and orchids, jack pines, a rare coastal peat bog, seals, pink granite, pitcher plants, lots of warblers, and maybe some grouse. Carry water and a picnic; wear bug repellent. No camping, fires, or pets are allowed, and there are no toilet facilities; access is during daytime only. To reach the preserve from Route 1, take Route 187 to Jonesport (12 miles) and then cross the arched bridge to Beals Island. Continue across Beals to the Great Wass causeway (locally called "the Flying Place") and then go three miles on Black Duck Cove Road to the parking area (on the left). Watch for The Nature Conservancy oak-leaf symbol. At the parking area, pick up a trail map and a bird checklist.

Also owned by The Nature Conservancy is 21-acre **Mistake Island,** accessible only by boat. Low and shrubby, Mistake has a Coast Guard-built boardwalk from the landing at the northwest corner to **Moose Peak Light,** standing 72 feet above the water at the eastern end of the island. The only eyesore on this lovely island is rubble left behind when the government leveled the keeper's house.

Scenic Cruises

Operating as **Coastal Cruises** (Kelley Point Rd., Jonesport, 207/497-3064 or 207/497-2699, www.cruisedowneast.com), Captain Laura Fish, her brother Harry Fish and her son Aaron Fish Herzon, both PADI-certified dive masters, offer three-hour Moosabec Reach cruises in the 23-foot powerboat *Aaron Thomas.* Among the sights are Great Wass Island and Mistake Island. Rates begin at $200 covering up to six passengers. Custom dive trips and instruction are available. Reservations are required. Trips depart from Jonesport and operate May-mid-October.

Captain Paul Ferriero's **Pleasant River Boat Tours** (280 Water St., Addison, 207/483-6567 or 207/598-6993, www.pleasantriverboattours.com) offers lobster, puffin, and river cruises aboard his 34-foot lobster boat, *Honey B,* for $50-60/person; boat minimums apply.

ACCOMMODATIONS

Bed-and-Breakfasts

How about staying in a beautiful modern farmhouse overlooking the water—with llamas lolling outside? At **Pleasant Bay Bed and Breakfast** (386 West Side Rd., Addison, 207/483-4490, www.pleasantbay.com, year-round, $55-160), Joan Yeaton and Jerry Metz manage to pamper llamas as well as their two-legged guests. Three miles of trails wind through the 110 acres, and a canoe is available for guests. Three lovely guest rooms (private and shared baths) and one suite, with a microwave and a refrigerator, all have water views. Rates include a delicious breakfast. The farm borders Pleasant Bay, 3.9 miles southwest of Route 1.

Cottages and Apartments

Proprietor Dorothy Higgins's **Cranberry Cove Cottages** (56 Kelley Point Rd., Jonesport, 207/497-2139, cranberry-cove@hotmail.com, $125) comprise two coveside efficiency lofts, each distinctively furnished in cottage style and with TVs, phones, fireplaces, and harbor views. Kayaks are provided. Pets are welcome. Rates decrease with the length of stay.

Camping

The town of Jonesport operates the low-key, no-frills **Henry Point Campground** (Henry Point, Kelley Point Rd., Jonesport, early May-Labor Day) on two acres with fabulous views over Sawyer Cove and Moosabec Reach. Basic facilities include outhouses, picnic tables, and fire rings; three power poles provide hookups. Showers and washing machines are available across the cove at Jonesport Shipyard (207/497-2701). The campground is exposed to wind off the water, so expect nights to be cool. Sites are allocated on a first-come, first-served basis for a small fee. Avoid the campground during Fourth of July festivities; it's jam-packed. From Route 187 at the northeastern edge of Jonesport, turn right onto Kelley Point Road and then right again to Henry Point.

FOOD

Say hi to **American Pie** (20 Route 1, Columbia, 207-483-2227, 11am-8pm. Tues.-Sat.), which makes lobster rolls, subs, and burgers, but is best loved for its hand-tossed, New York-style fresh-dough pizzas in 8- to 24-inch sizes.

The choices are slim in the Jonesport/Beals area. **Bayview Takeout** (42 Bayview Dr., Beals, 207/497-3301, 11am-8pm daily) delivers on its slogan "Wicked Good Food." Burgers, subs, salads, and fried seafood run $4-16, with a few combo specials nearly doubling that.

INFORMATION AND SERVICES

The town maintains a website with listings of area businesses: www.townofjonesport.com.

GETTING THERE AND AROUND

Jonesport is about 25 miles or 30 minutes via Routes 1 and 187 from Milbridge. It's about 22 miles or 30 minutes via Routes 187 and 1 to Machias.

Machias Bay Area

The only negative thing about **Machias** (muh-CHAI-us, pop. 1,221) is its Micmac Indian name, meaning "bad little falls" (even though it's accurate—the midtown waterfall here is treacherous). A contagious local esprit pervades this shire town of Washington County thanks to antique homes, a splendid river-valley setting, Revolutionary War monuments, and a small university campus.

If you regard crowds as fun, an ideal time to land here is during the renowned annual Machias Wild Blueberry Festival, the third weekend in August, when harvesting is under way in Washington County's blueberry fields and you can stuff your face with blueberry everything—muffins, jam, pancakes, ice cream, and pies. You can also collect blueberry-logo napkins, T-shirts, magnets, pottery, and jewelry. Biggest highlight: the annual summer musical parody.

Among the other summer draws are a chamber-music series, art shows, and semiprofessional theater performances. Within a few miles are day trips galore—options for hiking, biking, golfing, swimming, and sea kayaking.

Also included within the Machias sphere are the towns of **Roque Bluffs, Jonesboro, Whitneyville, Marshfield, East Machias,** and **Machiasport.** Just to the east, between Machias and Lubec, are the towns of **Whiting** and **Cutler.**

HISTORICAL SIGHTS

History is a big deal in this area, and since Machias was the first settled Maine town east of the Penobscot River, lots of enthusiastic amateur historians have helped rescue homes and sites dating from as far back as the Revolutionary War.

English settlers, uprooted from communities farther west on the Maine Coast, put down permanent roots here in 1763, harvesting timber to ensure their survival. Stirrings of revolutionary discontent surfaced even at this remote outpost, and when British loyalists in Boston began usurping some of the valuable harvest, Machias patriots plotted revenge. By 1775, when the armed British schooner *Margaretta* arrived as a cargo escort, local residents aboard the sloop *Unity,* in a real David-and-Goliath episode, chased and captured the *Margaretta.* On June 12, 1775, two months after the famed Battles of Lexington and Concord (and five days before the Battle of Bunker Hill), Machias Bay was the site of what author James Fenimore Cooper called "The Lexington of the Sea"—the first naval battle of the American Revolution. The name of patriot leader Jeremiah O'Brien today appears throughout

Two Scenic Routes

The drives described below can also be bike routes (easy to moderately difficult), but be forewarned that the roads are narrow and shoulderless, so caution is essential. Heed biking etiquette.

ROUTE 191, THE CUTLER ROAD

Never mind that Route 191, between East Machias and West Lubec, is one of Maine's most stunning coastal drives—you can still follow the entire 27-mile stretch and meet only a handful of cars. **East Machias** even has its own historic district, with architectural gems dating from the late 18th century along High and Water Streets. Farther along Route 191, you'll find fishing wharves, low moorlands, a hamlet or two, and islands popping over the horizon. The only peculiarly jarring note is the 26-tower forest of North Cutler's Naval Computer and Telecommunications Station, nearly 1,000 feet high—monitoring global communications—but you'll see this only briefly. (At night, the skyscraping red lights are really eerie, especially if you're offshore aboard a boat.) Off Route 191 are minor roads and hiking trails worth exploring, especially the coastal trails of the Cutler Coast Public Preserve. About three miles south of the Route 191 terminus, you can also check out **Bailey's Mistake,** a hamlet with a black-sand (volcanic) beach. The name? Allegedly it stems from one Captain Bailey who, misplotting his course and thinking he was in Lubec, drove his vessel ashore here one night in the late 19th century. Unwilling to face the consequences of his lapse, he and his crew off-loaded their cargo of lumber and built themselves dwellings. Whether true or not, it makes a great saga. Even though it's in the town of **Trescott,** and the hamlet is really South Trescott, everyone knows this section as Bailey's Mistake.

ROUTE 92, STARBOARD PENINSULA

Pack a picnic and set out on Route 92 (beginning at Elm Street in downtown Machias) down the 10-mile length of the Starboard Peninsula to a stunning spot known as the Point of Maine. Along the way are the villages of Larrabee, Bucks Harbor, and Starboard, all part of the town of Machiasport. In Bucks Harbor is the turnoff (a short detour to the right) to **Yoho Head,** a controversial upscale development overlooking Little Kennebec Bay.

South of the Yoho Head turnoff is the sign for **Jasper Beach.** From the Jasper Beach sign, continue 1.4 miles to two red buildings (the old Starboard School House and the volunteer fire department). Turn left onto a dirt road and continue to a sign reading Driveway. Go around the right side of a shed and park on the beach. (Keep track of the tide level, though.) You're at **Point of Maine,** a quintessential Down East panorama of sea and islands. On a clear day, you can see offshore **Libby Island Light,** the focus of Philmore Wass's entertaining narrative *Lighthouse in My Life: The Story of a Maine Lightkeeper's Family.*

the Machias area—on a school, a street, a cemetery, and a state park. In 1784, Machias was incorporated; it became the shire town in 1790.

Museums

One-hour guided tours vividly convey the atmosphere of the 1770 **Burnham Tavern** (Main St./Rte. 192, Machias, 207/255-6930, www.burnhamtavern.com, 9:30am-3:30pm Mon.-Fri. mid-June-late Sept. or by appointment, $5 adults, $1-2 kids), one of 21 homes in the entire country designated as most significant to the American Revolution. Upstart local patriots met here in 1775 to plot revolution against the British. Job and Mary Burnham's tavern-home next served as an infirmary for casualties from the Revolution's first naval battle, just offshore. Lots of fascinating history lies in this National Historic Site, maintained by the Daughters of the American Revolution. Hanging outside is a sign reading "Drink for the thirsty, food for the hungry, lodging for the weary, and good keeping for horses, by Job Burnham."

Headquarters for the Machiasport

Historical Society and one of the area's three oldest residences, the 1810 **Gates House** (344 Port Rd., Machiasport, 207/255-8461, www.machiasporthistoricalsociety.org, 12:30pm-4:30pm Tues.-Fri. July-Aug., or by appointment, free) was snatched from ruin and restored in 1966. The building, on the National Register of Historic Places, overlooks Machias Bay and contains fascinating period furnishings and artifacts, many related to the lumbering and shipbuilding era. The museum, four miles southeast of Route 1, has limited parking on a hazardous curve.

O'Brien Cemetery

Old-cemetery buffs will want to stop at **O'Brien Cemetery,** resting place of the town's earliest settlers. It's next to Bad Little Falls Park, close to downtown, off Route 92 toward Machiasport. A big plus here is the view, especially in autumn, of blueberry barrens, the waterfall, and the bay.

Fort O'Brien State Historic Site

The American Revolution's first naval battle was fought just offshore from **Fort O'Brien** (207/942-4014, www.parksandlands.com, free) in June 1775. Now a State Historic Site, the fort was built and rebuilt several times—originally to guard Machias during the Revolutionary War. Only Civil War-era earthworks now remain, plus well-maintained lawns overlooking the Machias River. Steep banks lead down to the water; keep small children well back from the edge. There are no restrooms or other facilities, but there's a playground at the Fort O'Brien School next door. Officially the park is open Memorial Day weekend-Labor Day, but it's accessible all year. Take Route 92 from Machias about five miles toward Machiasport; the parking area is on the left.

OTHER SIGHTS

Maine Sea Salt Company

Season your visit with a tour of the **Maine Sea Salt Company** (11 Church Ln., Marshfield, 207/255-3310, www.maineseasalt.com), which produces sea salt in its solar greenhouses and shallow pools using evaporation and reduction of seawater. Free tours (available most days 9am-5pm, call first) explain the process and include tastings of natural, seasoned, and smoked salts.

University of Maine at Machias

Founded in 1909 as Washington State Normal School, the **University of Maine at Machias** (UMM, 116 O'Brien Ave., Machias, 207/255-1200, www.machias.edu) is part of the state university system. **The Art Gallery** (Powers Hall, afternoon Mon.-Fri. during school terms or by appointment) features works from the university's expanding permanent collection of Maine painters—including John Marin, William Zorach, Lyonel Feininger, and Reuben Tam. Rotating exhibits occur throughout the school year.

UMM's **Center for Lifelong Learning** has a fitness center and a six-lane heated pool. The pool and fitness room are open to the public ($5); call for the current schedule.

Also open to the public is **Merrill Library** (207/255-1284).

Little River Lighthouse

Friends of the **Little River Lighthouse** (207/259-3833, www.littleriverlight.org) usually open the restored lighthouse and tower for tours a couple of times each summer. Transportation is provided to the island from Cutler Harbor. Donations benefit care and maintenance of the 1876 beacon.

East Machias Aquatic Research Center

The **Downeast Salmon Federation** (13 Willow St., East Machias, 207/263-7072, www.mainesalmonrivers.org) operates this Atlantic salmon restoration facility, home to an aquarium stocked with fish native to local rivers and a hatchery with more than 300,000 juvenile Atlantic salmon. Free tours are offered (call or check the website for current hours).

ENTERTAINMENT AND EVENTS

The **University of Maine at Machias** (207/255-1384, www.machias.edu) is the cultural focus in this area, particularly during the school year.

If the **Machias Ukulele Club** is performing anywhere, don't miss them.

Machias Bay Chamber Concerts (207/255-3849, www.machiasbaychamberconcerts.com, $20 adults, $8 students, free under age 13) are held at 7:30pm on Tuesday evenings in July at the Centre Street Congregational Church. Art exhibits accompany concerts.

The **Machias Wild Blueberry Festival** (www.machiasblueberry.com) is the summer highlight, running Friday-Saturday the third weekend in August and featuring a pancake breakfast, road races, concerts, crafts booths, a baked-bean supper, a homegrown musical, and more. The blueberry motif is everywhere. It's organized by Centre Street Congregational Church, United Church of Christ, in downtown Machias.

SHOPPING

Influenced by traditional Japanese designs, Connie Harter-Bagley markets her dramatic raku ceramics at **Connie's Clay of Fundy** (Rte. 1, East Machias, 207/255-4574, www.clayoffundy.com), on the East Machias River, four miles east of Machias. If she's at the wheel, you can also watch her work.

Need a read? **Jim's Books, Etc.** (8 Elm St., Machias, 207/255-9058), at the third house on the left on Route 92, just beyond the university campus, is open by chance or by appointment. Jim's a great source of info about the region.

Fine wines, craft beers, and a nice selection of cheeses are sold at **The French Cellar** (7 Water St., Machias, 207/255-4977).

RECREATION

Parks, Preserves, and Beaches

BAD LITTLE FALLS PARK

At Bad Little Falls Park, alongside the Machias River, stop to catch the view from the footbridge overlooking the roiling falls (especially in spring). Bring a picnic and enjoy this midtown oasis tucked between Routes 1 and 92.

JASPER BEACH

Thanks to a handful of foresighted year-round and summer residents, spectacular crescent-shaped **Jasper Beach**—piled high with ocean-polished stones—has been preserved by the town of Machiasport. There is no sand here, just rocks in intriguing shapes and colors. According to the Maine Geological Survey, although the beach is named for jasper, a form of iron-enriched silica, the disc-shaped red volcanic stone here is rhyolite; the rounder ones are granites and quartzites. Resist the urge to fill your pockets with souvenirs. Parking is limited, and there are no facilities. From Route 1 in downtown Machias, take Route 92 (Elm Street) 9.5 miles southeast, past the village of Bucks Harbor. Watch for a large sign on your left. The beach is on Howard's Cove, 0.2 mile off the road and accessible year-round.

ROQUE BLUFFS STATE PARK

Southwest of Machias, six miles south of Route 1, is **Roque Bluffs State Park** (Roque Bluffs Rd., Roque Bluffs, 207/255-3475, www.parksandlands.com). Saltwater swimming this far north is for the young and brave, but this 274-acre park also comprises 60-acre Simpson Pond, with freshwater warm and shallow enough for toddlers and the old and timid. Facilities include primitive changing rooms, outhouses, hiking trails, a play area, and picnic tables; there is no food and there are no lifeguards. Views go on forever from the wide-open mile-long sweep of sand-and-pebble beach. Keep an eye out for eagles and sea ducks. Admission is $4.50 nonresident adults, $3 Maine resident adults, $1 ages 5-11 (the fee box relies on the honor system). The park is open daily May 15-September 15, but the beach is accessible year-round.

CUTLER COAST PUBLIC RESERVE

On Route 191, about 4.5 miles northeast of the center of Cutler, watch for the parking area (on the right) for the **Cutler Coast Public Reserve,** a spectacular 12,234-acre preserve with nearly a dozen miles of beautifully engineered hiking trails on the seaward side of Route 191. It's popular with wildlife-watchers: Birding is great, and you might spot whales (humpback, finback, northern right, and minke), seals, and porpoises. Easiest is the 2.8-mile round-trip Coastal Trail through a cedar swamp and spruce-fir forest to an ocean promontory and back. Allow 5-6 hours to continue with the 5.5-mile Black Point Brook Loop, which progresses along a stretch of moderately rugged hiking southward along dramatic tree-fringed shoreline cliffs. Then head back via the Black Point Brook cutoff and connect with the Inland Trail to return to the parking area. Bring binoculars and a camera; the views from this wild coastline are fabulous. Also bring insect repellent—inland boggy stretches are buggy. Carry a picnic and commandeer a granite ledge overlooking the surf. Precipitous cliffs and narrow stretches can make the shoreline section of this trail perilous for small children or insecure adults, so use extreme caution and common sense. There are no facilities in the preserve. If you're here in August, you can stock up on blueberries and even some wild raspberries. Another option, the 9.2-mile Fairy Head Loop, starts the same way as the Black Point Brook Loop but continues southward along the coast, leading to three primitive campsites (stoves only, no fires), available on a first-come, first-served basis. There's no way to reserve these, so you take your chances. Unless you have gazelle genes, the longer loop almost demands an overnight trip. Information on the preserve, including a helpful map, is available from the **Maine Bureau of Parks and Lands** (207/287-3821, www.parksandlands.com). Originally about 2,100 acres, this preserve expanded fivefold in 1997 when several donors, primarily the Richard King Mellon Foundation, deeded to the state 10,055 acres of fields and forests across Route 191 from the trail area, creating a phenomenal tract that now runs from the ocean all the way back to Route 1. Mostly in Cutler but also in Whiting, it is Maine's second-largest public-land gift after Baxter State Park.

BOG BROOK COVE PRESERVE

Adjacent to the Cutler Coast Public Preserve, on Route 191, is Maine Coast Heritage Trust's (www.mcht.org) 1,770-acre **Bog Brook Cove Preserve.** Between the two preserves, this is the largest contiguous area of conservation land in the state outside of Acadia National Park. Bog Brook Cove's lands flow from Cutler into neighboring Trescott and include nearly three miles of ocean frontage with headlands, smashing views of Grand Manan Island, gravel beaches, coastal peat lands, and 10-acre Norse Pond. The Norse Pond Trail takes in the pond and rises to a headland, with views over the Grand Manan Channel, before descending to Bog Brook Cove and a rocky beach. The northern access, via Moose River Road, begins with a 1,100-foot wheelchair/stroller-accessible trail to an overlook, before continuing as a footpath to Moose Cove.

Golf

With lovely water views and tidal inlets serving as obstacles, the nine-hole **Great Cove Golf Course** (387 Great Cove Rd., off Roque Bluffs Rd., Jonesboro, 207/434-7200) is a good challenge. You can also play a quick nine at **Barren View Golf Course** (Rte. 1, Jonesboro, 207/434-6531, www.barrenview.com).

Water Sports

If you've brought your own sea kayak, there are public launching ramps in Bucks Harbor (east of Rte. 92, the main Machiasport road) and at Roque Bluffs State Park. You can also put in at Sanborn Cove, beyond the O'Brien School on Route 92, about five miles south of Machias, where there's a small parking area. Before setting out, check the tide calendar and plan your strategy so you don't have to slog through acres of muck when you return.

Sunrise Canoe and Kayak (68 Hoytown Rd., Machias, 207/255-3375 or 877/980-2300, www.sunrisecanoeandkayak.com) rents canoes and kayaks for $25-45/day and offers sea-kayak excursions ($65 half-day, $110 full day) on Machias Bay, including one to a petroglyph site. It also offers guided day trips and fully outfitted multiday canoeing and kayaking excursions on the Machias and St. Croix Rivers and along the Bold Coast.

The **Machias River,** one of Maine's most technically demanding canoeing rivers, is a dynamite trip mid-May-mid-June, but no beginner should attempt it. The best advice is to sign on with an outfitter or guide. The run lasts from four days up to six days if you start from Fifth Machias Lake. Expect to see wildlife such as ospreys, eagles, ducks, loons, moose, deer, beavers, and snapping turtles. Be aware, though, that the Machias is probably the buggiest river in the state, and blackflies will form a welcoming party. In addition to Sunrise Canoe and Kayak, Bangor-based **Sunrise Expeditions** (207/942-9300 or 800/748-3730, www.sunrise-exp.com) also offers fully outfitted trips.

Boat Excursions

★ MACHIAS SEAL ISLAND PUFFIN TOUR

Andy Patterson, skipper of the 40-foot *Barbara Frost,* operates the **Bold Coast Charter Company** (207/259-4484, www.boldcoast.com), homeported in Cutler Harbor. Andy provides knowledgeable narration, answers questions in depth, and shares his considerable enthusiasm for this pristine corner of Maine. He is best known for his five-hour puffin-sighting trips to Machias Seal Island (departing between 7am and 8am daily mid-May-Aug., $120, no credit cards); the trip is unsuitable for small children or adults who are susceptible to seasickness. Daily access to the island is restricted and swells can roll in, so passengers occasionally cannot disembark, but the curious puffins often surround the boat, providing plenty of photo opportunities. No matter what the air temperature on the mainland, dress warmly and wear sturdy shoes. The *Barbara Frost*'s wharf is on Cutler Harbor, just off Route 191. Look for the Little River Lobster Company sign; you'll depart from the boat-launching ramp. All trips are dependent on weather and tide conditions, and reservations are required. Note: Reserve early, because trips can sell out a month or more in advance.

ACCOMMODATIONS

Bed-and-Breakfasts and Inns

The barn-red **Inn at Schoppee Farm** (Rte. 1, Machias, 207/255-4648, www.schoppeefarm.com, $110-135) fronts on the tidal Machias River. The 19th-century farm operated as a dairy for three generations before Machias natives David and Julie Barker returned home to operate it as a bed-and-breakfast. They welcome guests with three guest rooms, each furnished with antiques and such niceties as air-conditioning, Wi-Fi, whirlpool baths, satellite TV, and soft down comforters in addition to river views and a full breakfast. Just east of the causeway, it's a healthy walk to downtown diversions.

After a meticulous restoration, Michael and Liz Henry opened **The Talbot House Inn** (509 Main St., E. Machias, 207/259-1103, www.thetalbothouseinn.com, $105-115) in a Mansard-roofed mansion that served as a stop on the Underground Railroad. The house is rife with architectural riches, but the bathrooms (some shared) are modern.

Victoriana rules at the **Riverside Inn** (Rte. 1, East Machias, 888/255-4344 or 207/255-4134, www.riversideinn-maine.com, $110-145), a restored early-19th-century sea captain's home with four guest rooms (one with a kitchenette). Sit on the deck overlooking the East Machias River or in the lovely terraced perennial gardens and you'll forget you're a few steps from a busy highway. Rates include a full breakfast. On Fridays and Saturdays from 3pm to dusk, hors d'ocuvres and cocktails are available on the riverside terrace.

The second generation now operates

Puffins

The chickadee is the Maine state bird, and the bald eagle is our national emblem, but probably the best-loved bird along the Maine Coast is the Atlantic puffin *(Fratercula arctica)*, a member of the auk (Alcidae) family. Photographs show an imposing-looking creature with a quizzical mien; amazingly, this larger-than-life seabird is only about 12 inches long. Black-backed and white-chested, the puffin has bright orange legs, "clown-makeup" eyes, and a distinctive, rather outlandish red-and-yellow beak. Its diet is fish and shellfish.

Almost nonexistent in this part of the world as recently as the 1970s, the puffin (or "sea parrot") has recovered dramatically thanks to the unstinting efforts of Cornell University ornithologist Stephen Kress and his Project Puffin (www.projectpuffin.org). Starting with an orphan colony of two on remote Matinicus Rock, Kress painstakingly transferred nearly a thousand puffin chicks (also known fondly as "pufflings") from Newfoundland and used artificial nests and decoys to entice the birds to adapt to and reproduce on Eastern Egg Rock in Muscongus Bay.

In 1981, thanks to the assistance and persistence of hundreds of interns and volunteers, and despite the predations of great black-backed gulls, puffins finally were fledged on Eastern Egg, and the rest, as they say, is history. Within 20 years, more than three dozen puffin couples were nesting on Eastern Egg Rock, and still more had established nests on other islands in the area. Kress's methods have received international attention, and his proven techniques have been used to reintroduce bird populations in remote parts of the globe. In 2001, *Down East* magazine singled out Kress to receive its prestigious annual Environmental Award.

HOW AND WHERE TO SEE PUFFINS

Puffin-watching, like whale-watching, involves heading offshore, so be prepared with warm clothing, rubber-soled shoes, a hat, sunscreen, binoculars, and, if you're motion-sensitive, appropriate medication.

Maine Audubon naturalists accompany tours aboard Hardy Boat Cruises, out of New Harbor, and Cap'n Fish's, out of Boothbay Harbor, and excursion boats depart from Bar Harbor and Milridge. The best daily up-close-and-personal opportunities for puffin-watching along the Down East Coast—specifically, on Machias Seal Island—is with **Bold Coast Charters** (207/259-4484, www.boldcoast.com), which departs from Cutler May-August and costs about $120 pp. Weather permitting, you'll be allowed to disembark on the 20-acre island.

If you can't get afloat to see puffins, the next best thing is a visit to the **Project Puffin Visitor Center** (311 Main St., Rockland, 877/478-3346), where you can view exhibits, a film, and live video feeds of nesting puffins.

ADOPT-A-PUFFIN PROGRAM

Stephen Kress's Project Puffin has devised a clever way to enlist supporters via the Adopt-a-Puffin program (www.projectpuffin.org). For a $100 donation, you'll receive a certificate of adoption, vital statistics on your adoptee, annual updates, and a color photo.

Micmac Farm Guesthouses (47 Micmac Ln., Machiasport, 207/255-3008, www.micmacfarm.com, $95/night, $595/week). Stay in one of Anthony and Bonnie Dunn's three rustic but comfortable and well-equipped cottages and you'll find yourself on the deck over the tidal Machias River and watching for seabirds, seals, and eagles. (Note: Mosquitoes can be pesky.) No breakfast is provided, but each wood-paneled cottage has a kitchenette and dining area. Pets and children are welcome. There's also a river-view room in the restored 18th-century Gardner House, with a private bath with whirlpool tub ($125). Guests have use of the farmhouse, including a library. A light breakfast is provided for Gardner House guests.

Motels

The best feature of the two-story **Machias**

Motor Inn (109 Main St./Rte. 1, Machias, 207/255-4861, www.machiasmotorinn.com, year-round, $124-129) is its location overlooking the tidal Machias River; sliding doors open onto decks with a view. Twenty-eight guest rooms and six efficiencies have extralong beds as well as cable TV, air-conditioning, Wi-Fi, refrigerators, and microwaves. Next door is Helen's Restaurant—famed for seasonal fruit pies and an all-you-can-eat weekend breakfast buffet. Well-behaved dogs ($10/dog/night) are welcome. The motel is within easy walking distance of downtown, which makes it perfect if you're here for the Blueberry Festival.

Completely renovated in 2014, the vintage 1960's **Margaretta Inn** (330 Main St., Machias, 207/255-6671, www.margarettainn.com, $130) offers a lot of bang for your buck. Rooms have flat-screen TVs, Wi-Fi, air-conditioning, mini fridges, microwaves, Keurig brewers, and beds dressed in white and topped with duvets. A hefty, buffet-style continental breakfast is offered in a pleasant breakfast room.

For inexpensive digs, you can't beat the ★ **Blueberry Patch** (550 Rte. 1, Jonesboro, 207/434-5411, www.blueberrypatchmotel.com, $65-85), a clean and bright motel and tourist cabins, with three efficiency units. Robert and Tammie Alley provide homespun hospitality with a few extras. All rooms have satellite TV, air-conditioning, Wi-Fi, and phones, and there's even a pool and a small playground. If you're taller than six feet, choose a motel room rather than a cabin; the cabin bathrooms are tiny. A light continental breakfast is provided.

Lighthouse

Yes, you can spend a night or more at **Little River Lighthouse** (Cutler, 877/276-4682, www.littleriverlight.org, $150-225), thanks to the Friends of Little River Lighthouse. Three guest rooms sharing two baths are available, but you have to bring food, bottled water, towels, bed linens or sleeping bags, and all personal items (soap, shampoo) and clean up after yourself. Guests have use of a kitchen. Transportation to the lighthouse is provided, but you have to coordinate your arrival with the tide.

FOOD

Watch the local papers for listings of **public suppers, spaghetti suppers,** or **baked bean suppers,** a terrific way to sample the culinary talents of local cooks. Most begin at 5pm, and it's wise to arrive early to get near the head of the line. The suppers often benefit needy individuals or struggling nonprofits, and where else can you eat nonstop for less than $10?

Local Flavors

Craving something healthful? The **Whole Life Natural Market** (4 Colonial Way, Machias, 207/255-8855, www.wholelifemarket.com, 9am-6pm Mon.-Fri., 9am-2pm Sat., 10am-noon Sun.) is home to the **Saltwater Café** (9am-2pm Mon.-Sat.), serving salads, soups, sandwiches, and baked goods made from organic fruits, vegetables, and grains as well as hormone-free dairy products. When the café isn't open, grab-and-go foods are usually available in the store.

Another source for fresh, healthful foods is the **Machias Valley Farmers Market** (3pm-6pm Wed., 10am-4pm Fri., and 9am-1pm Sat. May-Oct.). It's held on "the dike," a low causeway next to the Machias River. It's usually a good source for blueberries in late July-August.

Riverside Take-Out (Rte. 1, Machias, 207/263-7676), a traileresque shack in a dirt lot wedged between road and river, doesn't look like much, but road-food cognoscenti heap praise on the monster haddock burger, house-made onion rings, and sweet potato fries as reasons alone to stop.

Family Favorites

Family-owned and very popular all day long is **The Blue Bird Ranch Family Restaurant** (78 Main St./Rte. 1, Machias, 207/255-3351, www.bluebirdranchrestaurant.com, 6am-8pm daily, $7-30), named for the Prout family's other enterprise, the Blue Bird Ranch Trucking Company. Service is efficient, the food is hearty, the desserts are homemade, and the portions are ample in the three dining rooms.

In 2015, **Helen's** (111 Main St./Rte. 1, Machias, 207/255-8423, 6am-8:30pm Mon.-Sat., 7am-3pm Sun., $5-20), an institution in these parts since 1950, rose anew from the ashes of a disastrous 2014 fire. It's located on the banks of the Machias River, with great views, especially from the deck, where cocktails and apps are served. Do save room for the blueberry pie.

INFORMATION AND SERVICES

The **Machias Bay Area Chamber of Commerce** (85 E. Main St., Machias, 207/255-4402, www.machiaschamber.org) stocks brochures, maps, and information on area hiking trails.

GETTING THERE AND AROUND

Machias is about 22 miles or 30 minutes via Routes 1 and 187 from Jonesport. It's about 28 miles or 40 minutes via Routes 1 and 189 to Lubec.

Lubec

As the nation's easternmost point, **Lubec** (pop. 1,359) is literally the beginning of the United States. Lubec residents love to point out that the closest traffic light is 50 miles away.

Settled in 1780 as part of Eastport, it split off in 1811 and was named for the German port of Lübeck (for convoluted reasons still not totally clear). The town's most famous resident was Hopley Yeaton, first captain in the U.S. Revenue-Marine (now the U.S. Coast Guard), who retired here in 1809.

With appealing homes and more than 90 miles of meandering waterfront, Lubec conveys the aura of realness: a hardscrabble fishing community that extends a wary welcome to visitors. Along the main drag, Water Street, a number of shuttered buildings, many undergoing restoration, reflect the town's roller-coaster history. Once the world's sardine capital, Lubec no longer has a packing plant, but new businesses are slowly arriving, and each year the town looks a bit spiffier. No longer primarily a fishing town, these days the summer residents far outnumber year-rounders. In 2010 the community reluctantly closed its high school, which will likely accelerate the transition.

Arrive here on a fine summer day and it's easy to understand why so many visitors are smitten and, seduced by the views and the real estate prices, purchase a piece of a dream.

SIGHTS

★ West Quoddy Head State Park

Beachcombing, bird-watching, hiking, picnicking, and an up-close look at Maine's only red-and-white-striped lighthouse are the big draws at 541-acre **West Quoddy Head State Park** (West Quoddy Head Rd., Lubec, 207/733-0911, www.parksandlands.com, 9am-sunset May 15-Oct. 15, $3 nonresident adults, $2 Maine resident adults, $1 children), the easternmost point of U.S. land. Begin with a visit to the **visitor center** (207/733-2180, www.westquoddy.com, 10am-4pm daily late May-early July and early Sept.-mid-Oct., 10am-5pm daily July-Aug., free), located in the 1858 keeper's house and operated by the enthusiastic all-volunteer West Quoddy Head Light Keepers Association. Inside are exhibits on lighthouse memorabilia, local flora and fauna, and area heritage; a gallery displaying local works; and a staffed information desk.

The current **West Quoddy Head Light,** towering 83 feet above mean high water, was built in 1857. (Its counterpart, Head Harbour

Lightstation, a.k.a. East Quoddy Head Light, is on New Brunswick's Campobello Island.) Views from the lighthouse grounds are fabulous, and whale sightings are common in summer. The lighthouse tower is open the Saturday after July 4; during Maine Open Lighthouse Day, usually held in September; and other times when Coast Guard personnel are on site and available.

The cliffs of Canada's Grand Manan Island are visible from the park's grounds. The four-mile round-trip, moderately difficult Coastal Trail follows the 90-foot cliffs to Carrying Place Cove. An easy mile-long boardwalk winds through a unique moss and heath bog; a second bog is designated as a National Natural Landmark. The one-mile Coast Guard Trail loops out to an observation point. Be forewarned that the park gate is locked at sunset. In winter the park is accessible for snowshoeing. From Route 189 on the outskirts of Lubec, take South Lubec Road (well signposted) to West Quoddy Head Road. Turn left and continue to the parking area.

Mulholland Market and McCurdy's Herring Smokehouse

Lubec Landmarks (207/733-2197, www.lubeclandmarks.org) is working to preserve these two local landmarks. The **smokehouse complex** (10am-4pm daily, $3 donation), one of the last herring-smoking operations in the country (closed in 1991 and now a National Historic Landmark), can be seen on the water side of Water Street. In 2007, after years of effort, it reopened to the public. You can tour it on your own, or volunteer guides will explain the exhibits, which include hands-on ones for kids. Next door, **Mulholland Market Gallery** (50 Water St., 10am-4pm daily), which now doubles as a community center, is the organization's headquarters. Inside are displays about the smokehouses, exhibits of local art, and a small gift shop. It is volunteer-operated, so hours aren't set in stone.

Robert S. Peacock Fire Museum

Worth a look-see for fans of old fire equipment, the small **museum at the fire station** (40 School St., Lubec, 207/733-2341) is open by request at the adjacent town office.

Lubec Breakwater

Even the humongous tides and dramatic sunsets over Johnson Bay can get your attention if you hang out at the breakwater. A

West Quoddy Head Light is officially the easternmost point in the U.S.

Lost Fishermen's Memorial Park, honoring regional fishermen lost at sea, is planned here. Across the channel on Campobello Island is red-capped **Mulholland Point Lighthouse,** an abandoned beacon built in 1885 and now part of Roosevelt-Campobello International Park. As the tide goes out—18 or so feet—you'll see hungry harbor seals dunking for dinner. And if you're lucky, you might spot the eagles that nest nearby (bring binoculars).

ENTERTAINMENT AND EVENTS

Classical music is the focus (for the most part) at **SummerKeys** (207/733-2316 or 973/316-6220 off-season, www.summerkeys.com), a music camp for adults, no prior experience required, with weeklong programs in piano, voice, oboe, flute, clarinet, guitar, violin, and cello. Free concerts by visiting artists, faculty, and students are held at 7:30pm Wednesday evening late June-early September in the Congregational Christian Church on Church Street.

Live music is usually on tap on weekends at Cohill's Inn and Annabell's Pub, both on Water Street.

The **Masonic Summer Music Series,** held most Thursday evenings at the town bandstand on Main Street, include an all-you-can-eat cookout ($8 adults, $4 children) and a free concert.

Timber-frame buildings built by the **Cobscook Community Learning Center** (Timber Cove Rd., Trescott, 207/733-2233, www.thecclc.org) house an open pottery studio, a fiber-arts studio, and multipurpose classrooms. The year-round programs offered include open-jam music nights, workshops, talks, adult education, indigenous education, sustainable and value-added eco-ventures, youth programs, and more.

Birders flock to the Cobscook Bay area for **The Down East Spring Birding Festival** (207/733-2233, www.downeastbirdfest.org), held annually in late May. Guided and self-guided explorations, presentations, and tours fill the schedule, and participation is limited, so register early.

Downeast Coastal Conservancy (www.downeastcoastalconservancy.org) offers workshops, guided walks, boat trips, and other events throughout the summer.

SHOPPING

Most of Lubec's shops are along Water Street.

Northern Tides (24 Water St., Lubec,

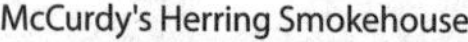

McCurdy's Herring Smokehouse

Tides

Nowhere in Maine is the adage "Time and tide wait for no man" truer than along the Washington County coastline. The nation's most extreme tidal ranges occur in this area, so the hundreds of miles of tidal shore frontage between Steuben and Calais provide countless opportunities for observing tidal phenomena. Every six hours or so, the tide begins either ebbing or flowing. The farther Down East you go, the higher (and lower) the tides. Although tides in Canada's Bay of Fundy are far higher, the highest tides in New England occur along the St. Croix River at Calais.

Tides govern coastal life—particularly Down East, where average tidal ranges may be 10-20 feet and extremes approach 28 feet. Everyone is a slave to the tide calendar, which coastal-community newspapers diligently publish. Boats tie up with extralong lines, clammers and worm diggers schedule their days by the tides, hikers have to plan for shoreline exploring, and kayakers need to plan their routes to avoid getting stuck in the muck.

Tides, as we learned in school, are lunar phenomena, created by the gravitational pull of the moon; the tidal range depends on the lunar phase. Tides are most extreme at new and full moons—when the sun, moon, and Earth are aligned. These are spring tides, supposedly because the water springs upward (the term has nothing to do with the season). And tides are smallest during the moon's first and third quarters—when the sun, Earth, and moon have a right-angle configuration. These are neap tides (*neap* comes from an Old English word meaning "scanty"). Other lunar and solar phenomena, such as the equinoxes and solstices, can also affect tidal ranges.

The best time for shoreline exploration is on a new-moon or full-moon day, when low tide exposes mussels, sea urchins, sea cucumbers, starfish, periwinkles, hermit crabs, rockweed, and assorted nonbiodegradable trash. Rubber boots or waterproof, treaded shoes are essential on the wet, slippery terrain.

Caution is also essential in tidal areas. Unless you've carefully plotted tide times and heights, don't park a car, bike, or boat trailer on a beach. Make sure your sea kayak is lashed securely to a tree or bollard, don't take a long nap on shoreline granite, and don't cross a low-tide land spit without an eye on your watch.

A perhaps apocryphal but almost believable story goes that one flatlander stormed up to a ranger at Cobscook Bay State Park one bright summer morning and demanded indignantly to know why they had had the nerve to drain the water from her shorefront campsite during the night. When it comes to tides...you have to go with the flow.

207/733-2500) carries intriguing works by local artisans such as sea-glass creations, pottery crafted with finds from the sea, felt work, and weaving.

Wags and Wool (83 Water St., Lubec, 207/733-4714) caters to knitters and dog lovers, with natural fibers, local yarns, hand-knit sweaters, socks, and gloves, and dog accessories.

Lighthouse buffs must stop at **West Quoddy Gifts** (Quoddy Head Rd., one mile before the lighthouse, 207/733-2457). It's stocked with souvenirs and gift items, most with a lighthouse theme.

Fred and Patty Hartman's **DownEast Drawings and Wildlife Art Gallery** (Rte. 189, Whiting, 207/733-0988) is filled with award-winning artwork featuring the flora and fauna of the region.

Shanna Wheelock's **Cobscook Pottery and Fiber Arts** (162 N. Lubec Rd., 207/733-2010) is worth the short detour off Route 1. Wheelock's been featured in *American Craft* magazine.

RECREATION

Boat Excursions

Explore Cobscook, Fundy, and Passamaquoddy Bays on a tour with **Downeast Charter Boat Tours** (31 Johnson St., Lubec, 207/733-2009, www.downeastcharterboattours.com) aboard the 25-foot lobster boat *Lorna Doone*. You'll pass lighthouses and likely also spy whales.

Jet-boat whale-watching tours are offered aboard the *Tarquin* from **The Inn on the Wharf** (60 Johnson St., Lubec, 207/733-4400, www.theinnonthewharf.com). The 2.5-3-hour tours are $50 adults, $25 kids under 12.

Hiking and Walking

Two preserves run by the Maine Coast Heritage Trust (www.mcht.org) are fine places for a walk. The 1,225-acre **Hamilton Cove Preserve**'s 1.5 miles of ocean frontage are highlighted by cobble beaches, rocky cliffs, and jaw-dropping views (on a clear day) of Grand Manan. To find it, take Route 189 to South Lubec Road toward Quoddy Head, but bear right at the fork on Boot Cove Road and continue 2.4 miles to a small parking lot on the left. There's a kiosk with maps about 100 feet down the trail. It's 0.8 mile to an observation platform and another 0.5 mile to the bench at the trail's end. For more expansive views, hike 1.2 miles to the summit of Benny's Mountain.

Continue on Boot Cove Road another 1.5 miles to find 700-acre **Boot Head Preserve,** with dramatic cliffs and ravines that epitomize Maine's Bold Coast reputation. The trail passes through a rare coastal raised peat land before continuing to a viewing platform on the coast. From the parking lot to Boot Cove via the Coastal Trail, it's 1.25 miles; return via the Interior Trail for another 0.75 mile.

For information on other hikes in the area, pick up a copy of *Cobscook Trail Guide,* with maps and trail details. It's available for about $7 at local stores or from the Quoddy Regional Land Trust Office on Route 1 in Whiting. Another resource available locally is *Self-Guided Birding Explorations, Washington County, Maine,* published in conjunction with the Down East Spring Birding Festival. It lists and maps walks and hikes, and notes habitats and bird species.

A 20-mile network of trails and gravel roads wind through the 8,800-acre Edmunds Unit of the **Moosehorn National Wildlife Refuge** (207/454-7161, http://www.fws.gov/refuge/moosehorn, sunrise-sunset daily, free), which straddles Rte. 1 between Whiting and Dennysville and also fronts on Cobscook Bay adjacent to the state park. The refuge, the northernmost in the United States along the Atlantic Flyway for migratory birds, is a favorite among birders.

In 2010, *Travel + Leisure* magazine named Lubec one of the best beach towns in the country. Where's the beach, you ask? **Mowry Beach,** owned by the Downeast Coastal Conservancy (www.downeastcoastalconservancy.org), is at the end of Pleasant Street; continue past the wastewater treatment plant to a parking lot. Follow the path over the dunes to the beach. When the tide rolls out, remnants of a drowned Ice Age forest are revealed. Also here is a wheelchair-accessible 0.4-mile boardwalk designed for sighting nesting, migrating, and wintering birds, including warblers, finches, waxwings, hawks, and northern shrikes.

Biking and Kayaking

The Wharf (60 Johnson St., Lubec, 207/733-4400) rents bikes for $18/day as well as kayaks for $25-35.

ACCOMMODATIONS

Many visitors use Lubec as a base for day trips to Campobello Island (passport or passport card necessary), so it's essential to make reservations at the height of summer. Several lodgings are also available on Campobello.

Bed-and-Breakfasts and Inns

Built in 1860 by a British sea captain, **Peacock House Bed and Breakfast** (27 Summer St., Lubec, 207/733-2403 or 888/305-0036, www.peacockhouse.com, $105-150) has long been one of Lubec's most prestigious residences. Among the notables who have stayed here are Donald MacMillan, the famous Arctic explorer, as well as U.S. senators Margaret Chase Smith and Edmund Muskie. It has three guest rooms and four suites, which have TVs and sitting areas; one has a gas fireplace and a refrigerator. One guest room is wheelchair-accessible.

Unusual antiques fill the guest rooms and sitting room of the 19th-century **Home Port Inn** (45 Main St., Lubec, 207/733-2077 or 800/457-2077 outside Maine, www.homeportinn.com, $99-135), ensconced on a Lubec hilltop. Each of the seven guest rooms has a private bath, although some are detached; some have water views. Rates include a full breakfast.

Ellen and Jack Gearrin extend a warm Irish welcome to guests at **Cohill's Inn** (7 Water St., 207/733-4300, www.cohillsinn.com, $95-140), which overlooks the Bay of Fundy on one side and the Narrows on the other. There are no frills or fuss in the simply but nicely furnished guest rooms; each has a fan and a TV, beds are covered with comforters and quilts, and a continental breakfast is included in the rates. Wi-Fi is available. Downstairs is a popular and reliable pub, but service ends at 8pm, so it's quiet at night.

Purpose-built **Whiting Bay Bed & Breakfast** (1 Cobscook Way, Whiting, 207/733-2402, www.whitingbaybb.com, $139-149) sits on 7.5 acres with water on three sides. It's a heavenly retreat, decorated with a light touch. Rates include a full breakfast.

The waterfront **Water Street Tavern & Inn** (12 Water St., Lubec, 207/733-2477, www.watersttavernandinn.com, $99-175) has three nicely appointed rooms and two suites, all with Wi-Fi, TV, and phone. All guests have access to a gathering room with comfy seating, big views, and a kitchenette. Also available is a two-bedroom waterview cottage for $850 per week.

Motels

The updated **Eastland Motel** (385 County Rd./Rte. 189, Lubec, 207/733-5501, www.eastlandmotel.com, $90) has 20 guest rooms with cable TV, Wi-Fi, refrigerator, microwave and air-conditioning. A homemade continental breakfast is included in the rates. One room is dog-friendly ($10 per dog).

Apartments, Suites, and Houses

Bill Clark has rescued the former Coast Guard station at West Quoddy Head and restored, renovated, and reopened it as ★ **West Quoddy Station** (S. Lubec Rd., Lubec, 207/733-4452 or 877/535-4714, www.quoddyvacation.com). The blufftop complex comprises six one-bedroom or studio units (four in the lodge and two separate cabins); the two-bedroom Keeper's Cottage; plus the five-bedroom, 2.5-bath Station House. All have

Enjoy spectacular views at The Inn on the Wharf.

kitchens, Wi-Fi, and satellite TV. Views are stupendous and extend to East Quoddy Head on Campobello; you can walk to West Quoddy Head, about 0.5 mile away. Rates begin at $120/night, when available, but weekly rentals ($800-$2,000) get first preference.

Another restoration project is the former Lubec Sardine Company's Factory B, where Judy and Victor Trafford have renovated the truly waterfront complex into ★ **The Inn on the Wharf** (60 Johnson St., Lubec, 207/733-4400, www.theinnonthewharf.com, $100-180), comprising lodging and a restaurant, while preserving the working waterfront. Guest rooms have use of a common kitchen and dining area and a laundry. Two-bedroom, two-bathroom apartments have full kitchens and laundry facilities. All have incredible views and Wi-Fi. Also on the premises are a yoga studio and bike and kayak rentals. A whale-watching boat and water taxi to Eastport departs from the wharf. That's all great, but what really distinguishes this property is that hidden on the basement level are huge tanks holding lobsters, crabs, and eels; an area for processing the periwinkle harvest; and other intriguing spots where you might catch local fishing folks bringing in their catches. Of course, a side effect of that is that there's a briny scent permeating the entire property. Also available are three rental houses, with varying configurations; call for details.

Camping

A 3.5-mile network of nature trails, picnic spots, great bird-watching and berry picking, hot showers, a boat launch, and wooded shorefront campsites make ★ **Cobscook Bay State Park** (Rte. 1, Edmunds Township, 207/726-4412, www.parksandlands.com), on the 888-acre Moosehorn Reserve, one of Maine's most spectacular state parks. It's even entertaining just to watch the 24-foot tides surging in and out of this area at five or so feet per hour; there's no swimming because of the undertow. Reserve well ahead to get a place on the shore. There are no hookups, but there's a dump station for RVs. To guarantee a site in July-August, using MasterCard or Visa, call 207/624-9950 (800/332-1501 in Maine) or visit www.campwithme.com; the reservation fee is $2/site/night with a two-night minimum. The park is open daily mid-May-mid-October; trails are groomed in winter for cross-country skiing, and one section goes right along the shore. Summer day-use fees are $4.50 nonresident adults, $3 Maine resident adults, $1.50 nonresident seniors, free Maine resident seniors, $1 ages 5-11. The nonresident camping fee is $24/site/night; the fee for Maine residents is $14.

FOOD

Local Flavors

Monica's Chocolates (100 County Rd./Rte. 189, Lubec, 866/952-4500, www.monicaschocolates.com, 8am-8pm daily) gives meaning to the term *sinfully delicious.* Monica Elliott creates sumptuous handmade gourmet chocolates using family recipes from her native Peru. Her hot chocolate, not always available, is swoon-worthy.

Stave off a midday hunger attack with home-baked goodies with an organic twist from **Sun Porch Industries** (99 Johnson St., Lubec, 207/733-7587, 11am-5pm Thurs.-Sun.), a tiny natural and organic foods store.

Baked goods, pizzas, freshly made sandwiches, and other light fare is served at **Atlantic House Coffee & Deli** (52 Water St., Lubec, 207/733-0906, 6am-2pm daily). Take it to one of two back decks overlooking the water.

Lubec Brewing Company (41 Water St., 207/733-4555, from 2pm daily) serves craft beer and organic, locally sourced pub fare in a living room-style lounge and adjacent tap room. It doubles as a live music venue.

It's a treat to visit the Bell family's 200-year-old, 1,600-acre organic saltwater farm, **Tide Mill Organic Farm** (91 Tide Mill Rd., Edmunds, 207/733-4756 or 207/733-2551, www.tidemillorganicfarm.com), now operated by the eighth generation on this land.

Tours ($5 age 7 and older or $20/family) are available; call for times.

Up for an adventure? Check out **The Most Absurd Bar in the World: A Sculpture** (45 Main St., Dennsyville, 207/726-4466). Melinda and Jonathan Jaques spent six years restoring and, ahem, decorating the wood shed and great room of the former Lincoln House tavern. The flotsam and jetsam of everyday life fills every available ceiling and wall space and much of that in between. It's occasionally open for light fare, such as chowders, chili, and crabmeat rolls ($10-14), along with beer and wine; call for current schedule.

Baker Jeremy Towne, a.k.a the **Towne Fryer** (Rte. 1, Whiting, 207/733-2066) sells divine doughnuts from his doughnut mobile, parked out front of his home (or sometimes on the dike in Machias). Go early if you want the raised honey glazed, as that sells out quickly.

Family Favorites

Good burgers, chowders, and other choices from the daily chalkboard menu as well as Guinness, Smithwick's, and microbrews have earned **Cohill's Inn** (7 Water St., Lubec, 207/733-4300, www.cohillsinn.com, 11am-8pm daily, $12-29) an enthusiastic two thumbs up from locals and visitors alike. The dining room has excellent water views, and there's often entertainment on Saturday afternoon.

Uncle Kippy's (County Rd./Rte. 189, Lubec, 207/733-2400, www.unclekippys.com, 11am-8pm Tues.-Sun., $8-25) gets high marks in Lubec for wholesome cooking. Go for the fried seafood and chowder—at unfancy prices—but there's steak and pizza, too. The motto: "Stop in, or we'll both starve."

Casual Dining

If the weather's nice, aim for a seat on the back deck at the **Water Street Tavern & Inn** (12 Water St., Lubec, 207/733-2477, from 7am daily, $12-28). The menu ranges from pizza to duck, but seafood is the specialty.

Craving Italian? Dine inside or on the waterside deck at **Frank's Dockside Deli** (20 Water St., Lubec, 11am-7pm Thurs.-Tues., 3pm-7pm Wed., $12-25).

Lobster

Fisherman's Restaurant on the Wharf (69 Johnson St., Lubec, 207/733-4400, www.theinnonthewharf.com, 7am-8pm daily $12-28), at the Inn on the Wharf, is in a renovated oceanfront sardine factory. There's seating inside and on a small deck, with panoramic views over Cobscook Bay to Eastport's Shackford Head. Seafood is the specialty, but there are landlubber choices and a full bar too.

Fresh seafood takeout is available at **Becky's Seafood** (145 Main St., 207/733-2228, 11am-8pm daily); nothing fancy, nothing fussy, but cheap and good.

INFORMATION AND SERVICES

The **Association to Promote and Protect the Lubec Environment** (888/347-9302, www.visitlubecmaine.com) is the best source for local information. The **Cobscook Bay Area Chamber of Commerce** (www.cobscookbay.com) also covers the Cobscook Bay region, including Lubec.

Lubec Memorial Library (Water St. and School St., Lubec, 207/733-2491) has a public restroom.

GETTING THERE AND AROUND

The Inn on the Wharf (60 Johnson St., Lubec, 207/733-4400, www.theinnonthewharf.com) operates a water taxi that's available for charter to Eastport. Expect fares of around $20 pp; boat minimums apply.

The **Franklin D. Roosevelt Memorial Bridge** connects Lubec to Campobello Island (passport, passport card, or enhanced driver's license required for return).

Lubec is approximately 28 miles or 40 minutes via Routes 1 and 189 from Machias. It's about 40 miles or one hour via Routes 189, 1, and 190 to Eastport.

Campobello Island

Just over the Franklin D. Roosevelt Memorial Bridge from Lubec lies nine-mile-long, unspoiled **Campobello Island** (pop. 1,000), in Canada's New Brunswick province. Most visitors come to see the place where President Franklin D. Roosevelt, along with other wealthy Americans, summered, but few take the time to explore the charms of Roosevelt's "beloved island." Those who do find a striking lighthouse that's open for tours, hiking trails, carriage roads for biking, whale-watching excursions, and spectacular vistas.

It's interesting to note that before becoming a summer retreat for wealthy Americans, Campobello was the feudal fiefdom of a Welsh family. King George III awarded the grant to Captain William Owen in 1767, and he arrived in 1770.

SIGHTS

★ Roosevelt Campobello International Park

Since 1964, **Roosevelt Campobello International Park**'s 2,800 acres of the island have been under joint U.S. and Canadian jurisdiction, commemorating U.S. president Franklin D. Roosevelt. FDR summered here as a youth, and it was here that he came down with infantile paralysis (polio) in 1921. The park, covering most of the island's southern end, has well-maintained trails and carriage roads, picnic sites, and dramatic vistas, but its centerpiece is the imposing Roosevelt Cottage, one mile northeast of the bridge.

Stop first at the park's **visitor centre** (459 Rte. 774, Welshpool, 506/752-2922 in season, www.fdr.net), where you can pick up brochures (including a trail map, bird-watching guide, and bog guide), sign up for Tea with Eleanor, and see a short video setting the stage for the cottage visit.

ROOSEVELT COTTAGE

It's a short walk from the visitor centre to the **Roosevelt Cottage** (10am-6pm Atlantic time, 9am-5pm eastern time, mid-May-mid-Oct., free). Little seems to have changed in the 34-room red-shingled Roosevelt "Cottage"

an observation deck in Roosevelt Campobello International Park

overlooking Passamaquoddy Bay since President Roosevelt last visited in 1939. The Roosevelt Cottage grounds are beautifully landscaped, and the many family mementos—especially those in the late president's den—bring history alive. It all feels very personal and far less stuffy than most presidential memorials. You tour on your own, but guides are stationed in various rooms to explain and answer questions.

TEA WITH ELEANOR

Don't miss the engaging one-hour **Tea with Eleanor** program, during which park interpreters tell stories about the remarkable Eleanor, highlighting her history and her many feats, while guests enjoy tea and cookies. Two programs are available. The free tea in the Hubbard Cottage is first come/first served, with tickets available each day from the visitor centre. Because it fills so quickly, the park has added a Reserved Tea in the Wells-Shober Cottage daily for $14 pp. The reserved tea also includes a booklet of cookie recipes complied by Eleanor's granddaughter.

THE PARK BY BICYCLE OR CAR

Carriage roads lace the park, and although you can drive them, a bike, if you have one, is far more fun. Options include **Cranberry Point Drive,** 5.4 miles round-trip from the visitor centre; **Liberty Point Drive,** 12.4 miles round-trip, via Glensevern Road, from the visitor centre; and **Fox Hill Drive,** a 2.2-mile link between the other two main routes. En route, you'll have access to beaches, picnic sites, spruce and fir forests, and great views of lighthouses, islands, and the Bay of Fundy.

Just west of the main access road from the bridge is the **Mulholland Point picnic area,** where you can spread out your lunch next to the distinctive red-capped lighthouse overlooking Lubec Narrows. A marine biology exhibit in the red shed adjacent to it highlights seals, whale rescue, tides, and other related topics.

HIKING AND PICNICKING

Within the international park are 8.5 miles of walking-hiking trails, varying from dead easy to moderately difficult. Easiest is the 1.2-mile (round-trip) walk from the visitor centre to **Friar's Head picnic area,** named for its distinctive promontory jutting into the bay. For the best angle, climb up to the observation deck on the "head." Grills and tables are here for picnickers. Pick up a brochure at the visitor centre detailing natural sights along the route.

The most difficult—and most dramatic—trail is a 2.4-mile stretch from **Liberty Point to Raccoon Beach,** along the southeastern shore of the island. Precipitous cliffs can make parts of this trail risky for small children or insecure adults, so use caution. Liberty Point is incredibly rugged, but observation platforms make it easy to see the tortured rocks and wide-open Bay of Fundy. Along the way is the SunSweep Sculpture, an international art project by David Barr. At broad Raccoon Beach, you can walk the sands, have a picnic, or watch for whales, porpoises, and ospreys. To avoid returning via the same route, park at Liberty Point and walk back along Liberty Point Drive from Raccoon Beach. If you're traveling with nonhikers, arrange for them to meet you with a vehicle at Con Robinson's Point.

You can also walk the park's perimeter, including just more than six miles of shoreline, but only if you're in good shape, have waterproof hiking boots, and can spend an entire day on the trails. Before attempting this, however, inquire at the visitor centre about trail conditions and tide levels.

Herring Cove Provincial Park

What a sleeper! Far too few people visit 1,049-acre **Herring Cove Provincial Park** (506/752-7010 or 800/561-0123), with picnic areas, 88 campsites, a four-mile trail system, a mile-long sandy beach, freshwater Glensevern Lake, a restaurant with fabulous views, and the nine-hole championship-level **Herring Cove Golf Course** (506/752-2467). The park is open early June-September. Admission is free.

Head Harbour Lightstation/ East Quoddy Head

Consult the tide calendar before planning your assault on **Head Harbour Lightstation** (also called East Quoddy Head Light), at Campobello's northernmost tip. The 51-foot-tall light, built in 1829, is on an islet accessible only at low tide. The distinctive white light tower bears a huge red cross. (You're likely to pass near it on whale-watching trips out of Eastport or Lubec.) From the Roosevelt Cottage, follow Route 774 through the village of Wilson's Beach and continue to the parking area. A stern Canadian Coast Guard warning sign tells the story: Extreme Hazard. Beach exposed only at low tide. Incoming tide rises 5 feet per hour and may leave you stranded for 8 hours. Wading or swimming are extremely dangerous due to swift currents and cold water. Proceed at your own risk.

It's definitely worth the effort for the bay and island views from the lighthouse grounds, often including whales and eagles. You can walk out to the lighthouse during a four-hour window around dead low tide (be sure your watch coincides with the Atlantic-time tide calendar).

In 2005 the **Friends of the Head Harbour Lightstation** (916 Rte. 774, Welshpool, www.campobello.com/lighthouse), a local nonprofit, took over maintenance of the station to restore it. It now charges access fees to support the efforts, which have included painting and furnishing the station. You can see the light from the nearby grounds at no charge, but if you want to hike out to the island or visit the light, the suggested donation is $5. Add a tour of the lighthouse, including climbing the tower, for $10; the family maximum for the walk or the tour is $25 (cash only). You can support the efforts with a membership, available for US$15 individual or US$25 family.

Campobello Island Public Library and Museum

A museum within Campobello's **library** (306 Welshpool St., 506/752-7082) houses a small collection of artifacts and memorabilia related to island life as well as birch bark items crafted by Tomah Joseph.

Herring Cove Golf Course

RECREATION

★ Whale-Watching

Island Cruises (506/752-1107 or 888/249-4400, www.bayoffundywhales.com, $50 adults, $40 children, $160 two adults and two children, $45 seniors) depart three or four times daily from Head Harbour Wharf for scenic whale-watching cruises aboard the *Mister Matthew*, a 37-foot traditional Bay of Fundy fishing boat that carries 20 passengers. Captain Mac Greene is a member of the Fundy Whale Rescue Team, so he has great insights and stories to share. Sightings might include minke, finback, humpback, and perhaps even northern right whales.

ACCOMMODATIONS AND FOOD

In midsummer, if you'd like to overnight on the island, reserve lodgings well in advance;

Campobello is a popular destination. The nearest backup beds are in Lubec, and those fill up too.

The Owen House (11 Welshpool St., Welshpool, 506/752-2977, www.owenhouse.ca, late May-mid-Oct., $104-210 Canadian) is the island's best address, an old-shore, comfortable, early-19th-century inn on 10 acres on Deer Point overlooking Passamaquoddy Bay and Eastport in the distance. Nine guest rooms (two with shared baths) on three floors are decorated with antiques and family treasures along with owner Joyce Morrel's paintings (Joyce grew up in this house) and assorted handmade quilts. There's a first-floor guest room that's ideal for those with mobility problems. Don't expect fancy or techy amenities; there are no phones, and there are no TVs, other than one for playing movies. Joyce and innkeeper Jan Meiners are very active in the lighthouse preservation efforts. Just north of the inn is the Deer Island ferry landing.

Check into **An Island Chalet** (115 Narrows Rd., Welshpool, 506/752-2971, www.anislandchalet.com, $125-180), a colony of waterfront housekeeping cabins overlooking the Lubec Narrows, and you might never leave. Each cabin has a loft suite with queen bed, twins downstairs, a full kitchen, and a front porch.

The campground at **Herring Cove Provincial Park** (506/752-7010, $25-40 Canadian) is a gem. It's underused, so crowds are rare. Sites are tucked in the woods near Herring Cove Beach. On the premises are a restaurant, nine-hole golf course, picnic grounds, and hiking trails that lead into adjacent Campobello International Park. Sites are available for tents to RVs.

Don't expect culinary creativity on Campobello, but you won't starve—at least during the summer season. The best choice is **Family Fisheries** (1977 Rte. 774, Wilson's Beach, 506/752-2470, www.familyfisheries.com, 11am-7:30pm daily, $8-32 Canadian), a seafood restaurant and fish market toward the northern end of the island. Portions are huge, service is friendly, the fish is superfresh, and the homemade desserts are decadent. BYOB—wine only.

Herring Cove (136 Herring Cove Rd., Welshpool, 506/752-1092, 8am-8pm daily, $8-25), at the golf course, has a full bar and serves a full menu.

Roosevelt Campobello International Park operates **The Fireside** (506/752-6055, noon-5pm Sun.-Wed., noon-9pm Thurs.-Sat.) in the restored and renovated Adams Cottage. Constructed in 1917 with logs cut on the island, the cottage once belonged to a cousin of FDR. If the weather's fine, aim for a seat on the deck and enjoy views of Friar's Bay. Dinner entrees such as cider-brined pork chop and maple sesame salmon range $19-28.

Owner Robert Calder roasts beans daily at **Jocie's Porch** (724 Rte. 774, Welshpool, 506/752-9816, 7am-7pm daily), which serves the island's best coffee as well as light fare, all overlooking Friar's Bay. There's also free Wi-Fi, often live entertainment, and it's always a great place to mingle with the locals.

INFORMATION AND SERVICES

Be aware that there's a one-hour time difference between Lubec and Campobello. Lubec, like the rest of Maine, is on eastern time; Campobello, like the rest of New Brunswick, is on Atlantic time, an hour later. As soon as you reach the island, set your clock ahead an hour.

There is no need to convert U.S. currency to Canadian money for use on Campobello; U.S. dollars are accepted everywhere on the island, but prices tend to be quoted in Canadian dollars.

Off the bridge, stop at the **Tourist Information Centre** (44 Rte. 774, Welshpool, 506/752-7043, May-Oct.) on your right for an island map, trail maps of the international park, tide info for lighthouse visits, and New Brunswick visitor information.

The best source of information on Campobello Island is **www.visitcampobello.com.**

Public restrooms are at the Tourist Information Centre near the bridge and the park's visitor centre.

GETTING THERE AND AROUND

Campobello is connected by bridge to Lubec. From Campobello you can also continue by ferry to New Brunswick's Deer Island and on to Eastport or make the Quoddy Loop and continue to Letete, N.B., and visit St. Andrews, before crossing the border at Calais and returning south to Eastport.

To visit the island, you'll have to pass immigration checkpoints on the U.S. and Canadian ends of the **Franklin D. Roosevelt Memorial Bridge** (U.S. Customs, Lubec, 207/733-4331; Canada Border Services, Campobello, 506/752-1130). Be sure to have the required identification: a passport or a passport card.

The funky two-stage boat-and-barge **East Coast Ferries** (877/747-2159, www.eastcoastferriesltd.com, no credit cards, passport or passport card required) departs Campobello for Deer Island on the hour 9am-7pm Atlantic time late June-early September; the fare is $16/car plus $3/passenger over age 11, $23 maximum per car. It connects with the ferry from Deer Island to Eastport, which departs on the hour 9am-6pm Atlantic time, $13/car and driver plus $3/passenger over age 11, $28 maximum per car. Motorcycles on each ferry are $8. All fares are subject to a fuel surcharge. A separate free ferry connects Deer Isle to Letete, near St. Andrews. It departs Deer Isle on the hour 6am-10pm Atlantic time, and on the half-hour 7:30am-6:30pm.

Eastport and Vicinity

When you leave Whiting, the gateway to Lubec and Campobello, and continue north on Route 1 around Cobscook Bay, it's hard to believe that life could slow down any more than it already has, but it does. The landscape's raw beauty is occasionally punctuated by farmhouses or a convenience store, but little else.

Edmunds Township's claims to fame are its splendid public lands—Cobscook Bay State Park and a unit of Moosehorn National Wildlife Refuge. Just past the state park, loop along the scenic shoreline before returning to Route 1.

Pembroke (pop. 840), once part of adjoining **Dennysville** (pop. 342), is home to Reversing Falls Park, where you can watch and hear ebbing and flowing tides draining and filling Cobscook Bay.

If time allows a short scenic detour, especially in fall, turn left (northwest) on Route 214 and drive 10 miles to quaintly named **Meddybemps** (pop. 157), allegedly a Passamaquoddy word meaning "plenty of alewives [herring]." Views over Meddybemps Lake, on the north side of the road, are spectacular, and you can launch a canoe or kayak into the lake here, less than a mile beyond the junction with Route 191 (take the dead-end unpaved road toward the water).

Backtracking to Route 1, heading east from Pembroke, you'll come to **Perry** (pop. 889), best known for the Sipayik Indian Reservation at Pleasant Point, a Passamaquoddy settlement two miles east of Route 1, that has been here since 1822. Route 191 cuts through the heart of the reservation.

The city (yes, it's officially a city) of **Eastport** (pop. 1,331) is on Moose Island, connected by a causeway to the mainland at Sipayik (Pleasant Point). Views are terrific on both sides, especially at sunset, as you hopscotch from one dollop of land to another and finally reach this mini-city, where the sardine industry was introduced as long ago as 1875. Five sardine canneries once operated here, employing hundreds of local residents, who snipped the heads off herring and stuffed them into cans.

Settled in 1772, Eastport has had its ups and downs, mostly mirroring the fishing industry. It's now on an upswing as people "from away" have arrived to soak up the vibe of a small town with a heavy Down East accent. Artists, artisans, and antiques shops are leading the town's rejuvenation as a tourist destination, with the Tides Institute at the forefront. A big push came in 2001 when the Fox Network reality-TV series *Murder in Small Town X* was filmed here; the city morphed into the village of Sunrise, Maine, and local residents happily filled in as extras. The huge waterfront statue of a fisherman is a remnant of the filming.

Until 1811 the town also included Lubec, which is about 2.5 miles across the water via boat but more than 40 miles in a car. A passenger ferry connects the two.

SIGHTS

Historic Walking Tour

The best way to appreciate Eastport's history is to pick up and follow the route in *A Walking Guide to Eastport*, available locally for $2.75. The handy map-brochure spotlights the city's 18th-, 19th-, and early-20th-century homes, businesses, and monuments, many now on the National Register of Historic Places. Among the highlights are historic homes converted to bed-and-breakfasts, two museums, and a large chunk of downtown Water Street, with many handsome brick buildings erected after a disastrous fire swept through in 1886.

Raye's Mustard Mill Museum

How often do you have a chance to watch mustard being made in a turn-of-the-20th-century mustard mill? Drive by **J. W. Raye and Co.** (83 Washington St./Rte. 190, Eastport, 207/853-4451 or 800/853-1903, www.rayes-mustard.com, 8am-5pm Mon.-Fri., 10am-5pm Sat.-Sun.) at the edge of Eastport and stop in for a free 15-minute tour (offered as schedules permit; call first) of North America's last traditional stone-ground mustard mill. You'll get to see the granite millstones, the mustard seeds being winnowed, and enormous vats of future mustard. Raye's sells mustard under its own label and produces it for major customers under their labels. The shop stocks all of Raye's mustard varieties (samples available), other Maine-made food, and gift items, and it also has a small café where you can buy coffee, tea, and light fare. Both Martha Stewart and Rachael Ray have discovered Raye's, which

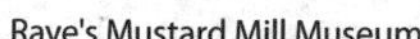
Raye's Mustard Mill Museum

has won both gold and bronze medals at the World-Wide Mustard Competition.

The Tides Institute and Museum of Art

One of the most promising additions to Eastport's downtown is the **Tides Institute** (43 Water St., 207/853-4047, www.tidesinstitute.org, 10am-4pm Tues.-Sun., donation appreciated), housed in a former bank that's being restored. The institute's ambitious goals are to build significant cultural collections and to produce new culturally important works employing printmaking, letterpress, photography, bookmaking, oral history, and other media. For its collection, the institute is focusing on works by artists associated with the U.S.-Canada northeast coast but with an eye to the broader world. It already has significant works by artists such as Martin Johnson Heade and photographers such as Paul Caponigro, a fine selection of baskets by Native Americans, and two organs made by the local Pembroke organ company in the 1880s. A series of rotating shows during the summer highlights both the permanent collections and loaned works. The research and reference library has more than 4,000 volumes. The institute also offers programs on a range of topics and workshops by visiting artists. These are open to the public by reservation; definitely stop in for a visit. In 2013, the institute opened **Studio Works,** a studio space with demonstrations and a resident artist program, across the street. In 2015, it began transforming the North Church (corner of Washington and High Streets) into a site for alternative arts programming.

Pleasant Point Reservation

To get to Eastport, you pass through the Passamaquoddy's Sipayik or **Pleasant Point Reservation** (www.wabanaki.com). Ask locally or check the website to find basket makers and other traditional artists who might sell from their homes. The decorative and work baskets are treasures that constantly escalate in price. It's a real treat to be able to buy one from the maker. For a more in-depth understanding of the culture, visit the **Waponahki Museum** (59 Passamaquoddy Rd., Perry, 207/853-4400, 1-4pm Mon.-Thurs. and the second Saturday of each month, when there are demonstrations).

Downeast Observatory

The **Downeast Amateur Astronomers' Downeast Observatory** (356 Old County Rd., Pembroke, 207/214-5706, www.downeastaa.com), with an eight-inch DE8 reflector and 3-5-inch refractors, is open to the public for free by appointment, but donations are greatly appreciated. Contact Charlie Sawyer at the observatory for details.

PARKS AND PRESERVES

★ Shackford Head State Park

Ninety-acre **Shackford Head** (off Deep Cove Rd., Eastport, www.parksandlands.com, free) is on a peninsula that juts into Cobscook Bay. The trailhead and parking area are just east of the Washington County Community College Marine Technology Center at the southern end of Eastport. The park has 3.2 miles of wooded trails. Easiest is the 1.2-mile round-trip to Shackford Head Overlook and its continuation onto the steeper Ship Point Trail, which adds another 0.4 mile. The trail rises gently to a 175-foot-high headland with wide-open views of Eastport and, depending on weather, Campobello Island, Lubec, Pembroke, and even Grand Manan. This state preserve is a particularly good family hike. There's a toilet near the parking area, but no other facilities. Also here is a memorial with plaques detailing the history of five Civil War ships that were decommissioned and burned on Cony Beach by the U.S. government between 1901 and 1920. Eastport's huge tides allowed the ships to be brought in and beached and then taken apart as the tide receded. Fourteen Eastport men served on four of the ships.

Reversing Falls Park

There's plenty of room for adults to relax

and kids to play at the 140-acre Reversing Falls Park in West Pembroke—plus shorefront ledges and a front-row seat overlooking a fascinating tidal phenomenon. It's connected via hiking trails to the Downeast Coastal Conservancy's **Reversing Falls Conservation Area** (www.downeastcoastalconservancy.org), a nearly 200-acre property with 1.5 miles of shorefront and 70 acres of coastal wetlands. Pack a picnic and then check newspapers or information offices for the tide times so that you can watch the saltwater surging through a 300-yard-wide passage at about 25 knots, creating a whirlpool and churning "falls." The park is at Mahar Point in West Pembroke, 7.2 miles south of Route 1. Coming from the south (Dennysville), bear right off Route 1 onto Old County in West Pembroke and continue to Leighton Point Road. Turn right on Young's Cove Road and continue to the park.

Gleason Cove

This quiet park and boat launch is a delightful place to walk along the shorefront or to grab a table and spread out a picnic while drinking in the dreamy views over fishing weirs and islands in Passamaquoddy Bay. To get here, take Shore Road (opposite the New Friendly Restaurant) and then take a right on Gleason Cove Road.

ENTERTAINMENT

The **Eastport Arts Center** (36 Washington St., Eastport, 207/853-4650, www.eastportartscenter.com) is an umbrella organization for local arts groups, with headquarters and performance space in a former church. You can pick up a brochure with a complete schedule, which usually includes concerts, workshops, films, puppet shows, productions by local theater group **Stage East,** and other cultural events. Also based here is the **Passamaquoddy Bay Symphony Orchestra,** formed in 2007 by conductor Trond Saeverud, who doubles as concertmaster of the Bangor Symphony Orchestra.

Concerts and other programs are sometimes held in the waterfront amphitheater between Water Street and the waterfront walkway. It's marked by *Nature's Grace,* a granite sculpture carved by New Brunswick artist Jim Boyd.

FESTIVALS AND EVENTS

For a small community, Eastport manages to pull together and put on plenty of successful events during the year.

Eastport's annual four-day **Fourth of July—Old Home Week** extravaganza includes a parade, pancake breakfasts, barbecues, a flea market, an auction, races, live entertainment, and fireworks. This is one of Maine's best Fourth of July celebrations and attracts a crowd of more than 10,000. Lodgings are booked months in advance, so plan ahead.

Indian Ceremonial Days, a three-day Native American celebration, includes children's games, canoe races, craft demos, talking circles, fireworks, and traditional food and dancing at Sipayik, the Pleasant Point Reservation in Perry, the second weekend in August.

The three-day **Eastport Pirate Festival** (www.eastportpiratefestival.com) in September features live music, parades, children's activities, reenactments, and races.

A great resource for area happenings is **CulturePass** (www.culturepass.net), which covers the entire Passamaquoddy Bay region. Pair it with the **Artsipelago Two Countries One Bay Passport** (www.artsipelago.net), a cultural guide to the international Passamaquoddy Bay region.

SHOPPING

Eastport has long been a magnet for artists and craftspeople yearning to work in a supportive environment, but the influx has increased in recent years. Nearly two dozen galleries line Water Street and overflow on side streets and throughout the area.

The Eastport Gallery (74 Water St., Eastport, 207/853-4166) is a cooperative with works in varied media. The gallery also sponsors the annual **Paint Eastport Day,** usually held the second Saturday in September, when anyone is invited to paint a local scene; a reception and "wet paint" auction follow.

A group of energetic women with local ties renovated a waterfront building, turning it into **The Commons** (51 Water St., Eastport, 207/853-4123), a fabulous gallery displaying works by artisans from the region and farther afield.

More than 20 artists from the region are represented at **Eastport Breakwater Gallery** (93 Water St., Eastport, 207/853-4773).

Woodworker Roland LaVallee's gallery **Crow Tracks** (11 Water St., Eastport, 207/853-2336) is filled with his intricate carvings of birds and local fauna. The tiny garden entryway doubles the pleasure of a visit.

Indulge your sweet tooth at **Sweeties Downeast** (80 Water St., 207/853-3120), where candy, nuts, fancy popcorn, and homemade fudge are sold by the pound.

Stop in, if only for a few minutes, at **S. L. Wadsworth and Son** (42 Water St., Eastport, 207/853-4343), the oldest ship chandlery in the country and the oldest retail business in Maine. In addition to hardware and marine gear, you'll find nautical gifts, souvenirs, and copies of Eastport-set mysteries penned by local author Sarah Graves.

Mary Creighton's **Native American Arts** (55 Bayview Drive, Pleasant Point, Perry, 207/853-4779) sells a nice selection of baskets, dream catchers, moccasins, jewelry, and other goods crafted by Maine Native Americans.

A number of very talented artists and artisans are tucked along the back roads of the area. You might get lucky and find them open, but it's wise to call before making a special trip. These include **Wrenovations** (6 Steam Mill Rd., Robbinston, 207/454-2382), with stained art creations by Mark Wren; **The Red Sleigh** (Rte. 1, Perry, 207/854-6688), filled with locally made treasures, from jewelry to pies; and **Susan Designs** (behind Loring's Body Shop, 416 Gin Cove Rd., Perry, 207/853-4315), where gifted quilt artist Susan Plachy sells her creations.

RECREATION

Boat Excursions

Eastport Windjammers (207/853-2500 or 207/853-4303, www.eastportwindjammers.com) offers a 2.5- to 3-hour whale-watching and lobster cruise ($45 adults, $38 ages 5-12, $15 under age 5) departing at 1:30pm daily

The Red Sleigh in Perry

Kilby House Inn B&B

and heading out into the prime whale-feeding grounds of Passamaquoddy Bay—passing the Old Sow whirlpool (the largest tidal whirlpool in the Northern Hemisphere), salmon aquaculture pens, and Campobello Island. En route you'll see bald eagles, porpoises, possibly puffins and ospreys, and a lighthouse. En route back, lobster traps are hauled, with specimen placed in a touch tank. The best months are July and August, but Butch is a skilled spotter, so if they're there, he'll find them. A two-hour sunset cruise ($35 adults, $25 children) departs the Eastport Pier (call for times). Note: The company's windjammer was badly damaged in the 2015 Eastport Pier collapse, so trips are aboard a new 49-passenger lobster boat. Also available are 3-hour fishing trips aboard the *Lady H* ($45 adults, $38 ages 5-12, $15 under age 5).

Fish for shark, tuna, cod, pollock, and haddock aboard the *Vonnie and Val*, a 33-foot sport-fishing boat, with **Fundy Breeze Charters** (109 Water St., Eastport, 207/853-4660, www.fundybreeze.com). A full day is $125 pp with a $600 boat minimum; half-day is $65 pp with a $300 minimum.

ACCOMMODATIONS

Bed-and-Breakfasts

Although musician and retired teacher Greg Noyes, innkeeper at the ★ **Kilby House Inn B&B** (122 Water St., Eastport, 800/853-4557, www.kilbyhouseinn.com, $95-115), grew up closer to Ellsworth, his great-great-grandfather was born in Eastport. Greg bought the Kilby House in 1992 and has masterfully updated and renovated the 1887 Victorian into a lovely four-bedroom inn filled with antiques (some original to the house), clocks, a grand piano, and an organ. Some bathrooms are small, but the hospitality and location, just one block off the ocean and two blocks from downtown, make up for that. Breakfast is served at 8am in the formal dining room. Tucked behind the inn is an adorable, self-catering air-conditioned carriage-house studio, with a private deck, TV, full kitchen, and laundry ($130/day or $850/week).

The old-shoe-comfortable **Milliken House Bed and Breakfast** (29 Washington St., Eastport, 207/853-2955 or 888/507-9370, www.eastport-inn.com, $90-100), an 1846 Victorian, is fine, but be forewarned that it's more homestay than inn. The six guestrooms are furnished with antiques and country pieces. Hosts Mary Williams and her son Greg welcome children and pets to their in-town home, an easy walk to shops and restaurants. Breakfasts are generous and served family-style in the very-Victorian dining room. There's a big TV in the double parlor downstairs, Wi-Fi throughout, and a phone is available. Call ahead in winter.

Apartments

On the second floor of **The Commons** (51 Water St., Eastport, 207/853-4123, www.thecommonseastport.com), a newly renovated downtown building on the waterfront, are two nicely appointed two-bedroom apartments with decks and spectacular harbor views. Tide Watcher has two baths and rents for $1,150/

week; Water's Edge has one bath and rents for $1,050/week; shorter stays may be possible.

FOOD

Local Flavors

Drool-worthy pastries, breads, and sweets fill the cases at **Moose Island Bakery** (75 Water St., Eastport, 207/853-3111, from 7am daily). The **Sunrise County Farmers Market** is held at Eastport's downtown waterfront park 11am-2pm Saturday. It's worth the slight detour off Route 1 to purchase hot- and cold-smoked salmon as well as smoked salmon sticks, and smoked haddock at **Maine-ly Smoked Salmon** (555 South Meadow Rd., Perry, 207/853-4794, 9am-5pm daily).

Family Favorites

The aptly named **New Friendly Restaurant** (1014 Rte. 1, Perry, 207/853-6610, 11am-8pm daily, $5-20) lays on home-cooked offerings for "dinnah" (a Maine-ism meaning "lunch").

Seafood, natch, is the specialty, at the bi-level **Eastport Chowder House** (167 Water St., Eastport, 207/853-4700, 11am-9pm daily), where most entrées are in the $13-21 range. There's a bar downstairs and a harbor-front deck too.

A downtown Eastport institution since 1924, the **WaCo Diner** (Bank Square, 207/853-9226, from 6am-8pm daily), pronounced WHACK-o, is short for Washington County or, the story goes, for Nelson Watts and Ralph Colwell, who started it as a lunch cart. Expect diner fare with an emphasis on seafood and prices in the $8-20 range. If the weather's fine, aim for a seat on the waterside deck.

A cut above the other dining options in town, **Landmark 1887 Grill & Ale House** (32 Water St., Eastport, 207/853-7074, 4-9pm daily) serves a menu ranging from burgers and pizza to pork tenderloin and prime rib.

Lobster

When the weather's clear, there's nothing better than lobster at ★ **Quoddy Bay Lobster** (7 Sea St., Eastport, 207/853-6640, 10am-6pm Mon.-Thurs., 10am-7pm Fri-Sat.). Lobster is the headliner—watch boats unload their catch, it's that fresh—and I think the lobster rolls are the state's best; each is topped with the meat from one claw. Other options include wraps, salads, and chowders. There's even a kids' menu. Eat indoors or head to the covered outside tables on the harbor's edge.

Quoddy Bay Lobster is the real deal when it comes to lobster shacks.

INFORMATION AND SERVICES

One of the best resources is the free *Artsipelago: Two Countries One Bay* (www.artsipelago.net) guidebook and map, available locally and online, which details the arts and culture of the Passamaquoddy Bay region on both sides of the border, sorted by town. Listings include artists, cultural institutions, galleries, farmers markets, farms, local foods, ferries, festivals, film, historic sites, lighthouses, music, parks/natural sites, and theater.

Brochures are available at the **Quoddy Maritime Museum and Visitor Center** (70 Water St., Eastport, 10am-6pm daily June-Sept.). In the museum section of the center is a huge model of the failed 1936 Passamaquoddy Tidal Power Project, an idea whose time hadn't come when it was proposed.

Information is also available from the **Eastport Chamber of Commerce** (207/853-4644, www.eastportchamber.net) as well as online at www.cobscookbay.com.

The handsome stone **Peavey Memorial Library** (26 Water St., Eastport, 207/853-4021), built in 1893, is named after the inventor of the Peavey grain elevator.

Public restrooms are available in the Port Authority building on the waterfront and the library.

GETTING THERE AND AROUND

Eastport is about 40 miles or one hour via Routes 189, 1, and 190 from Lubec. It's about 28 miles or 40 minutes to Calais via Routes 190 and 1. Ask locally about ferry service between Eastport and Lubec, which was suspended with the 2015 pier's collapse.

If your next stop is New Brunswick, Canada, consider taking the funky two-stage boat-and-barge **East Coast Ferries** (877/747-2159, www.eastcoastferries.nb.ca, no credit cards, passport or passport card required) that connect through Deer Island to Campobello Island. It departs Eastport for Deer Island on the half-hour 9:30am-6:30pm Atlantic time late June-early September; fares top out around $20 per car. It connects with the ferry from Deer Island to Campobello, which departs on the half-hour 8:30am-6:30pm Atlantic time, with fares maxing around $25/car. Motorcycles on each ferry are around $10. All fares are subject to additional fuel surcharges. A separate free ferry connects Deer Isle to Letete, near St. Andrews. It departs Deer Isle on the hour 6am-10pm Atlantic time, and on the half-hour 7:30am-6:30pm. Note: The ferry suspended its Eastport/Deer Isle route in 2015, but it was expected to return to service.

Calais and Vicinity

Calais (CAL-us, pop. 3,123) is as far as you'll get on the coast of Maine; from here on, you're headed inland. Europeans showed up in this area as early as 1604, when French adventurers established an ill-fated colony—the root of Acadian/Cajun civilization in the New World—on St. Croix Island in the St. Croix River, 16 whole years before the Pilgrims even thought about Massachusetts. After a winter-long debacle, all became relatively quiet until 1779, when the first permanent settler arrived.

Southeast of Calais is tiny **Robbinston** (pop. 574), a booming shipbuilding community in the 19th century but today little more than a blip on the map.

Calais is both a river town and a major border crossing into New Brunswick, Canada, so you'd think it would be a lively spot, but the economy struggles here, with many of the downtown storefronts empty.

SIGHTS

Walking Tour

Pick up a copy of the *Walking Tour Guide to Calais Residential Historic District* at the Maine Tourism Information Center (39 Union St., Calais). The guide, produced by the St. Croix Historical Society, briefly covers the town's history and maps and describes the architecture and early owners of 23 historic houses, four of which are listed on the National Register of Historic Places.

St. Croix Island International Historic Site

Acadian/Cajun civilization in North America has its roots on 6.5-acre **St. Croix Island,** an International Historic Site under joint U.S. and Canadian jurisdiction (Rte. 1, Red Beach Cove, eight miles south of Calais, 207/454-3871, www.nps.gov/sacr, free). The island is the site of the pioneering colony, the earliest European settlement in North America north of Florida, established by French explorers Samuel de Champlain and Pierre du Gua de Monts in 1604. Doomed by disease, mosquitoes, lack of food, and a grueling winter, 35 settlers died; in spring the emaciated survivors abandoned their effort and moved on to Nova Scotia. In 1969, archaeologists found the graves of 23 victims, but the only monument on the island is a commemorative plaque dating from 1904.

Unless you have your own boat, you can't get over to the island, but you can stop at the mainland **visitors center** (9am-4:30 pm mid May-mid June, 9am-4:30pm daily July-mid Oct.), partake in interpretation programs, and enjoy the heritage trail, with bronze statues depicting various key personae or cultures in the development of the colony. The trail ends on the point with views of the island. Also here are picnic tables, restrooms, a gravel beach, and a boat launch.

Whitlock Mill Lighthouse

From the lovely Pikewoods Rest Area, beside Route 1 about four miles southeast of Calais, there's a prime view of 32-foot-high **Whitlock Mill Lighthouse** on the southern shore of the St. Croix River. Built in 1892, the green flashing light is accessible only over private land, so check it out from this vantage point. You can also have a picnic break here.

Calais-Robbinston Milestones

A quirky little local feature, the **Calais-Robbinston milestones** are a dozen red-granite chunks marking each of the 12 miles between Robbinston and Calais. Presaging today's highway mile markers, late-19th-century entrepreneur and journalist James S. Pike had the stones installed on the north side of Route 1 to keep track of the distance while training his pacing horses.

RECREATION

Parks and Preserves

DEVIL'S HEAD

About six miles south of Calais, watch for signs pointing to Devil's Head, and take the dirt road on the river side. The 318-acre site has a mile of frontage on the St. Croix River estuary and views to St. Croix Island. A road with two parking areas descends to the shoreline, and there are pit toilets and a marked hiking trail, approximately 1.5 miles looping from the road, leading to the highest point of coastal land north of Cadillac Mountain. (The headland was originally called d'Orville Head, which morphed into Devil's Head.)

PIKE'S PARK

Calais has a lovely riverfront park at the foot of North Street. Pike's is the perfect place for a picnic. From here you have access to the **Calais Waterfront Walk,** which edges the river, running for 0.9 mile upriver and 0.6 mile downriver.

Golf

At the nine-hole **St. Croix Country Club** (River Rd./Rte. 1, Calais, 207/454-8875, late Apr.-late Oct.), the toughest and most scenic hole is the seventh, one of five holes on the river side of Route 1.

ACCOMMODATIONS

The same family has owned and operated the **International Motel** (626 Main St., Calais, 207/454-7515 or 800/336-7515, www.theinternationalmotel.com, $65-85) since 1955. The nicest guest rooms are in the newer Riverview building. Some rooms have refrigerators; all have air-conditioning, TVs, and Wi-Fi. Pet-friendly rooms are available.

The Gothic-styled, gingerbread-trimmed **Redclyffe Shore Motel and Dining Room** (Rte. 1, Robbinston, 207/454-3270, www.redclyffeshoremotorinn.com, $85-95) sits on a bluff jutting into the St. Croix River where it widens into Passamaquoddy Bay. The 16 motel units have cable TV, phones, and sunset-facing river views. Redclyffe is locally popular for its greenhouse-style dining room with ocean views; dinner is served nightly from 5pm ($11-26). It's 12 miles south of Calais.

FOOD

A bright spot downtown, **Crumbs Café & Bake Shoppe** (257 Main St., 207/454-8995, 7:30am-7pm Mon.-Fri., 10:30 am-6pm Sat.) opened in 2015 with a menu comprising sandwiches, soups, chowders, and sweets.

If you're near downtown Calais, order picnic sandwiches to go at **Border Town Subz** (311 Main St., Calais, 207/454-8562, 10am-6pm Tues.-Sun.), a reliable local favorite.

Fried foods, burgers, pizza, and reasonably priced dinner plates have earned **Yancy's** (332 North St., Calais, 207/454-8200, 11am-8pm daily, entrées $5-15) a solid reputation with families.

The **Calais Farmers Market** (11am-2pm Tues. mid June-mid Oct.) takes place in the downtown park.

INFORMATION AND SERVICES

The **Maine Visitor Information Center** (39 Union St., Calais, 207/454-2211) has free Wi-Fi, clean restrooms, and scads of brochures, including those produced by the **St. Croix Valley Chamber of Commerce** (207/454-2308 or 888/422-3112, www.visitstcroixvalley.com). The information center is open 8am-6pm daily mid-May-mid-October, 9am-5:30pm daily the rest of the year.

Check out **Calais Free Library** (Union St., Calais, 207/454-2758, www.calais.lib.me.us).

Public restrooms are available at the Maine Visitor Information Center and at the St. Croix International Heritage Site in Red Beach.

GETTING THERE AND AROUND

Calais is about 28 miles or 40 minutes from Eastport via Routes 190 and 1. It's about 95 miles or two hours and 15 minutes to Bangor via Routes 1 and 9.

If you plan to cross into Canada, you'll have to pass immigration checkpoints on both the U.S. (Calais, 207/454-3621) and Canadian (St. Stephen, 506/466-2363) ends of the bridges. Be sure to have the required identification (passport or passport card) and paperwork.

Pay attention to your watch too—Calais is on eastern time, whereas St. Stephen and the rest of New Brunswick is on Atlantic time, one hour later.

Background

The Landscape

Maine is an outdoor classroom for Geology 101, a living lesson in what the glaciers did and how they did it. Geologically, Maine is something of a youngster; the oldest rocks, found in the Chain of Ponds area in the western part of the state, are only 1.6 billion years old—more than two billion years younger than the world's oldest rocks.

Most significant is the great ice sheet that began to spread over Maine about 25,000 years ago, during the late Wisconsin Ice Age. As it moved southward from Canada, this continental glacier scraped, gouged, pulverized, and depressed the bedrock in its path. On it continued, charging up the north faces of mountains, clipping off their tops and moving southward, leaving behind jagged cliffs on the mountains' southern faces and odd deposits of stone and clay. By about 21,000 years ago, glacial ice extended well over the Gulf of Maine, perhaps as far as the Georges Bank fishing grounds.

But all that began to change with meltdown, beginning about 18,000 years ago. As the glacier melted and receded, ocean water moved in, covering much of the coastal plain and working its way inland up the rivers. By 11,000 years ago, glaciation had pulled back from all but a few minor corners at the top of Maine, revealing the south coast's beaches and the unusual geologic traits—eskers and erratics, kettleholes and moraines, even a fjord—that make the rest of the state such a fascinating natural laboratory.

TODAY'S LANDSCAPE

Three distinct looks make up the contemporary Maine coastal landscape. (Inland are even more distinct biomes: serious woodlands and mountains as well as lakes and ponds and rolling fields.)

Along the **Southern Coast,** from Kittery to Portland, are fine-sand beaches, marshlands, and only the occasional rocky headland. The **Mid-Coast** and **Penobscot Bay,** from Portland to the Penobscot River, feature one finger of rocky land after another, all jutting into the Gulf of Maine and all incredibly scenic. **Acadia** and the **Down East Coast,** from the Penobscot River to Eastport and including fantastic Acadia National Park, have many similarities to the Mid-Coast (gorgeous rocky peninsulas, offshore islands, granite everywhere), but, except on Mount Desert Island, takes on a different look and feel by virtue of its slower pace, higher tides, and quieter villages.

GEOGRAPHY

Bounded by the Gulf of Maine (Atlantic Ocean), the St. Croix River, New Brunswick Province, the St. John River, Québec Province, and the state of New Hampshire (and the only state in the Union bordered by only one other state), Maine is the largest of the six New England states, roughly equivalent in size to the five others combined—offering plenty of space to hike, bike, camp, sail, swim, or just hang out. The state—and the coastline—extends from 43° 05' to 47° 28' north latitude and 66° 56' to 80° 50' west longitude. (Technically, Maine dips even farther southeast to take in five islands in the offshore Isles of Shoals archipelago.) It's all stitched together by 22,574 miles of highways and 3,561 bridges.

Maine's more than 5,000 rivers and streams provide nearly half of the watershed for the Gulf of Maine. The major rivers are the Penobscot (350 miles), the St. John (211 miles),

Previous: osprey nest atop rocky cliffs; Maine's coast is often foggy.

Estuaries and Mudflats

Maine's estuaries, where freshwater and salt water meet, are ecosystems of outstanding biological importance. South of Cape Elizabeth, where the Maine coast is low and sandy, estuaries harbor large salt marshes of spartina grasses that can tolerate the frequent variations in salinity as runoff and tides fluctuate. Producing an estimated four times more plant material than an equivalent area of wheat, these spartina marshes provide abundant nutrients and shelter for a host of marine organisms that ultimately account for as much as 60 percent of the value of the state's commercial fisheries.

The tidal range along the Maine coast varies 9-26 vertical feet, southwest to northeast. Where the tide inundates sheltered estuaries for more than a few hours at a time, spartina grasses cannot take hold and mudflats dominate. Although it may look like a barren wasteland at low tide, a mudflat is also a highly productive environment and home to abundant marine life. Several species of tiny primitive worms called nematodes can inhabit the mud in densities of 2,000 or more per square inch. Larger worm species are also very common. One, the bloodworm, grows up to a foot long and is harvested in quantity for use as sportfishing bait.

More highly savored among mudflat residents is the soft-shell clam, famous for its outstanding flavor and an essential ingredient of an authentic Maine lobster bake. But because clams are suspension feeders—filtering phytoplankton through their long siphon, or "neck"—they can accumulate pollutants that cause illness, including hepatitis. Many Maine mudflats are closed to clam harvesting because of leaking septic systems, so it's best to check with the state's Department of Marine Resources or the local municipal office before digging a mess of clams yourself.

For birds—and bird-watchers—salt marshes and mudflats are an unparalleled attraction. Long-legged wading birds such as glossy ibis, snowy egret, little blue heron, great blue heron, tricolored heron, green heron, and black-crowned night heron frequent the marshes in great numbers throughout the summer, hunting the shallow waters for mummichogs and other small salt-marsh fish, crustaceans, and invertebrates. Mid-May-early June, and then again mid-July-mid-September, migrating shorebirds pass through Maine to and from their subarctic breeding grounds. On a good day, a discerning bird-watcher can find 17 or more species of shorebirds probing the mudflats and marshes with pointed bills in search of their preferred foods. In turn, the large flocks of shorebirds don't escape the notice of their own predators—merlins and peregrine falcons dash in to catch a meal.

the Androscoggin (175 miles), the Kennebec (150 miles), the Saco (104 miles), and the St. Croix (75 miles). The St. John and its tributaries flow northeast; all the others flow more or less south or southeast.

CLIMATE

Whoever invented the state's oldest cliché—"If you don't like the weather, wait a minute"—must have spent at least several minutes in Maine. The good news, though, is that it's true—if the weather is lousy, it's bound to change before too long, and when it does, it's intoxicating. Brilliant, cloud-free Maine weather has lured many a visitor to put down roots and buy a retirement home, or at least invest in a summer retreat.

The serendipity of it all necessitates two caveats: *Always pack warmer clothing than you think you'll need.* And *never arrive without a sweater or jacket—even at the height of summer.*

The National Weather Service assigns Maine's coastline a climatological category distinct from climatic types found in the interior.

The coastal category, which includes Portland, runs from Kittery northeast to Eastport and about 20 miles inland. Here, the ocean moderates the climate, making coastal winters warmer and summers cooler than in the interior (relatively speaking, of course). From early June through August, the Portland area—fairly typical of coastal weather—may have three to eight days of temperatures over 90°F, 25-40 days over 80°, 14-24 days of fog, and 5-10 inches of rain. Normal annual precipitation for the Portland area is 44 inches of rain and 71 inches of snow (the snow total is misleading, though, since intermittent thaws clear away much of the base).

The Seasons

Maine has four distinct seasons: summer, fall, winter, and mud. Lovers of spring need to look elsewhere in March, the lowest month on the popularity scale with its mud-caked vehicles, soggy everything, irritable temperaments, tank-trap roads, and often the worst snowstorm of the year.

Summer can be idyllic—with moderate temperatures, clear air, and wispy breezes—but it can also close in with fog, rain, and chills. Prevailing winds are from the southwest. Officially, summer runs June 20 or 21-September 20 or 21, but June, July, and August is more like it, with temperatures in the Portland area averaging 70°F during the day and in the 50s at night. The normal growing season is 148 days.

A poll of Mainers might well show autumn as the favorite season—days are still warmish, nights are cool, winds are optimum for sailors, and the foliage is brilliant. Fall colors usually begin appearing far to the north about mid-September, reaching their peak in that region by the end of the month. The last of the color begins in late September in the southernmost part of the state and fades by mid-October. Early autumn, however, is also the height of hurricane season, the only potential flaw this time of year.

Winter, officially December 20 or 21-March 20 or 21, means deep snow and cold inland and an unpredictable potpourri along the coastline. When the cold and snow hit the coast, it's time for cross-country skiing, ice fishing, snowshoeing, ice skating, ice climbing, and winter trekking and camping.

Spring, officially March 20 or 21-June 20 or 21, is the frequent butt of jokes. It's an ill-defined season that arrives much too late and departs all too quickly. Ice floes dot inland lakes and ponds until "ice-out" in early-mid-May. Spring planting can't occur until well into May, but lilacs explode in late May and disappear by mid-June. And just when you finally can enjoy being outside, blackflies stretch their wings and satisfy their hunger pangs. Along the coast, onshore breezes often keep the pesky creatures to a minimum.

In winter, snow blankets much of Maine.

The Environment of the Rocky Shoreline

On Maine's more exposed rocky shores—the dominant shoreline from Cape Elizabeth all the way Down East to Lubec—where currents and waves keep mud and sand from accumulating, the plant and animal communities are entirely different from those in the inland aquatic areas. The most important requirement for life in this impenetrable, rockbound environment is probably the ability to hang on tight. Barnacles, the calcium-armored crustaceans that attach themselves to the rocks immediately below the high-tide line, have developed a fascinating battery of adaptations to survive not only pounding waves but also prolonged exposure to air, solar heat, and extreme winter cold. Glued in place, however, they cannot escape being eaten by dog whelks, the predatory snails that also inhabit this intertidal zone. Whelks are larger and more elongate than the more numerous and ubiquitous periwinkle, accidentally transplanted from Europe in the mid-19th century.

Also hanging onto these rocks, but at a lower level, are the brown algae—seaweeds. Like a marine forest, the four species of rockweed provide shelter for a wide variety of life beneath their fronds. A world of discovery awaits those who make the effort to go out onto the rocks at low tide and look under the clumps of seaweed and into the tidepools they shelter. Venture into these chilly waters with mask, fins, and wetsuit and still another world opens for natural-history exploration. Beds of blue mussels, sea urchins, sea stars, and sea cucumbers dot the bottom close to shore. In crevices between and beneath the rocks lurk rock crabs and lobsters. Now a symbol of the Maine coast and the delicious seafood it provides, the lobster was once considered a "poor man's food"—so plentiful that it was spread on fields as fertilizer. Although lobsters are far less common than they once were, they are one of Maine's most closely monitored species, and their population continues to support a large and thriving commercial fishing industry.

The same cannot be said for most of Maine's other commercially harvested marine fish. When Europeans first came to these shores four centuries ago, cod, haddock, halibut, hake, flounder, herring, and tuna were abundant. No longer. Overharvested, their seabed habitat torn up by relentless dragging, these groundfish have all but disappeared. It will be decades before these species can recover—and then only if effective regulations can be put in place soon.

The familiar doglike face of the harbor seal, often seen peering alertly from the surface just offshore, provides a reminder that wildlife populations are resilient—if given a chance. A century ago, there was a bounty on harbor seals because it was thought they ate too many lobsters and fish. Needless to say, neither fish nor lobsters increased when the seals all but disappeared. With the bounty's repeal and the advent of legal protection, Maine's harbor seal population has bounced back to an estimated 15,000-20,000. Scores of them can regularly be seen basking on offshore ledges, drying their tan, brown, black, silver, or reddish coats in the sun. Though it's tempting to approach for a closer look, avoid bringing a boat too near these haul-out ledges, as it causes the seals to flush into the water and imposes an unnecessary stress on the pups, which already face a first-year mortality rate of 30 percent.

Positive changes in our relationships with wildlife are even more apparent with the return of birds to the Maine coast. Watching the numerous herring gulls and great black-backed gulls soaring on a fresh ocean breeze today, it's hard to imagine that a century ago egg collecting had so reduced their numbers that they were a rare sight. In 1903, there were just three pairs of common eiders left in Maine; today, 25,000 pairs nest along the coast. With creative help from dedicated researchers using sound recordings, decoys, and prepared burrows, Atlantic puffins are recolonizing historic offshore nesting islands. Osprey and bald eagles, almost free of the lingering vestiges of DDT and other pesticides, now range the length of the coast and up Maine's major rivers.

Northeasters and Hurricanes

A northeaster is a counterclockwise, swirling storm that brings wild winds out of—you guessed it—the northeast. These storms can occur any time of year, whenever the conditions brew them up. Depending on the season, the winds are accompanied by rain, sleet, snow, or all of them together.

Hurricane season officially runs June-November but is most prevalent late August-September. Some years, the Maine coast remains out of harm's way; other years, head-on hurricanes and even glancing blows have eroded beaches, flooded roads, splintered boats, downed trees, knocked out power, and inflicted major residential and commercial damage.

Sea Smoke and Fog

Sea smoke and fog, two atmospheric phenomena resulting from opposing conditions, are only distantly related, but both can radically affect visibility and therefore be hazardous. In winter, when the ocean is at least 40°F warmer than the air, billowy sea smoke rises from the water, creating great photo ops for camera buffs but especially dangerous conditions for mariners.

In any season, when the ocean (or lake or land) is colder than the air, fog sets in, creating perilous conditions for drivers, mariners, and pilots. Romantics, however, see it otherwise, reveling in the womblike ambience and the muffled moans of foghorns. Between April and October, Portland averages about 31 days with heavy fog, when visibility may be a quarter-mile or less.

Storm Warnings

The National Weather Service's official daytime signal system for wind velocity consists of a series of flags representing specific wind speeds and sea conditions. Beachgoers and anyone planning to venture out in a kayak, canoe, sailboat, or powerboat should heed these signals. The flags are posted on all public beaches, and warnings are announced on TV and radio weather broadcasts, as well as on cable TV's Weather Channel and the NOAA broadcast network.

History

PREHISTORIC MAINERS: THE PALEOINDIANS

As the great continental glacier receded northwestward out of Maine about 11,000 years ago, some prehistoric grapevine must have alerted small bands of hunter-gatherers—fur-clad Paleoindians—to the scrub sprouting in the tundra, burgeoning mammal populations, and the ocean's bountiful food supply. Because come they did—at first seasonally, and then year-round. Anyone who thinks tourism is a recent Maine phenomenon needs only to explore the shoreline in Damariscotta, Boothbay Harbor, and Bar Harbor, where heaps of cast-off oyster shells and clamshells document the migration of early Native Americans from woodlands to waterfront. "The shore" has been a summertime magnet for millennia.

Archaeological evidence from the Archaic period in Maine—roughly 8000-1000 BC—is fairly scant, but paleontologists have unearthed stone tools and weapons and small campsites attesting to a nomadic lifestyle supported by fishing and hunting (with fishing becoming more extensive as time went on). Toward the end of the tradition, during the late Archaic period, emerged a rather anomalous Indian culture known officially as the Moorehead phase but informally called the Red Paint People; the name is because of their curious trait of using a distinctive red ocher (pulverized hematite) in burials. Dark red puddles and stone artifacts have led excavators to burial pits as far north as the St. John River. Just as mysteriously as they had arrived, the Red Paint

People disappeared abruptly and inexplicably around 1800 BC.

Following them almost immediately—and almost as suddenly—hunter-gatherers of the Susquehanna Tradition arrived from well to the south, moved across Maine's interior as far as the St. John River, and remained until about 1600 BC, when they, too, enigmatically vanished. Excavations have turned up relatively sophisticated stone tools and evidence that they cremated their dead. It was nearly 1,000 years before a major new cultural phase appeared.

The next great leap forward was marked by the advent of pottery making, introduced about 700 BC. The Ceramic period stretched to the 16th century, and cone-shaped pots (initially stamped, later incised with coiled-rope motifs) survived until the introduction of metals from Europe. Houses of sorts—seasonal wigwam-style dwellings for fishermen and their families—appeared along the coast and on offshore islands.

THE EUROPEANS ARRIVE

The identity of the first Europeans to set foot in Maine is a matter of debate. Historians dispute the romantically popular notion that Norse explorers checked out this part of the New World as early as AD 1000. Even an 11th-century Norse coin found in 1961 in Brooklin (on the Blue Hill Peninsula) probably was carried there from farther north.

Not until the late 15th century, the onset of the great Age of Discovery, did credible reports of the New World (including what's now Maine) filter back to Europe's courts and universities. Thanks to innovations in naval architecture, shipbuilding, and navigation, astonishingly courageous fellows crossed the Atlantic in search of rumored treasure and new routes for reaching it.

John Cabot, sailing from England aboard the ship *Mathew*, may have been the first European to reach Maine, in 1498, but historians have never confirmed a landing site. No question remains, however, about the account of Giovanni da Verrazzano, an Italian explorer commanding *La Dauphine* under the French flag, who reached the Maine coast in May 1524, probably at the tip of the Phippsburg Peninsula. Encountering less-than-friendly Indians, Verrazzano did a minimum of business and sailed onward. His brother's map of the site labels it "The Land of Bad People." Esteban Gomez and John Rut followed in Verrazzano's wake, but nothing came of their exploits.

Nearly half a century passed before the Maine coast turned up again on European explorers' itineraries. This time, interest was fueled by reports of a Brigadoon-like area called Norumbega (or Oranbega, as one map had it), a myth that arose, gathered steam, and took on a life of its own in the decades after Verrazzano's voyage.

By the early 17th century, when Europeans began arriving in more than twos and threes and getting serious about colonization, Native American agriculture was already under way at the mouths of the Saco and Kennebec Rivers, the cod fishery was thriving on offshore islands, Indians far to the north were hot to trade furs for European goodies, and the birch-bark canoe was the transport of choice on inland waterways.

In mid-May 1602, Bartholomew Gosnold, en route to a settlement off Cape Cod aboard the *Concord*, landed along Maine's southern coast. The following year, merchant trader Martin Pring and his boats *Speedwell* and *Discoverer* explored farther Down East, backtracked to Cape Cod, and returned to England with tales that inflamed curiosity and enough sassafras to satisfy royal appetites. Pring produced a detailed survey of the Maine coast from Kittery to Bucksport, including offshore islands.

On May 18, 1605, George Waymouth, skippering the *Archangel*, reached Monhegan Island, 11 miles off the Maine coast, and moored for the night in Monhegan Harbor. (It's still treacherous even today, exposed to the weather from the southwest and northeast and subject to meteorological beatings and heaving swells; yachting guides urge sailors not to expect to anchor, moor, or tie up there.) The next day, Waymouth crossed the bay and scouted the mainland. He took five Indians hostage and sailed up the St. George River, near present-day Thomaston. Maritime historian Roger Duncan put it this way:

Waymouth returned to England and awarded his hostages to officials Sir John Popham and Sir Ferdinando Gorges, who, their curiosity piqued, quickly agreed to subsidize the colonization effort. In 1607, the *Gift of God* and the *Mary and John* sailed for the New World carrying two of Waymouth's captives. After returning them to their native Pemaquid area, Captains George Popham and Raleigh Gilbert continued westward, establishing a colony (St. George or Fort George) at the tip of the Phippsburg Peninsula in mid-August 1607 and exploring the shoreline between Portland and Pemaquid. Frigid weather, untimely deaths (including Popham's), and a storehouse fire doomed what's called the Popham Colony, but not before the 100 or so settlers built the 30-ton pinnace **Virginia**, the New World's first such vessel. When Gilbert received word of an inheritance waiting in England, he and the remaining colonists returned to the Old World.

Settlers in the Popham Colony built the *Virginia*.

In 1614, swashbuckling Captain John Smith, exploring from the Penobscot River westward to Cape Cod, reached Monhegan Island nine years after Waymouth's visit. Smith's meticulous map of the region was the first to use the "New England" appellation, and the 1616 publication of his *Description of New-England* became the catalyst for permanent settlements.

THE FRENCH AND THE ENGLISH SQUARE OFF

English dominance of exploration west of the Penobscot River in the early 17th century coincided roughly with French activity east of the river.

In 1604, French nobleman Pierre du Gua, Sieur de Monts, set out with cartographer Samuel de Champlain to map the coastline, first reaching Nova Scotia's Bay of Fundy and then sailing up the St. Croix River. In midriver, just west of present-day Calais, a crew planted gardens and erected buildings on today's St. Croix Island while de Monts and Champlain went off exploring. The two men reached the island Champlain named l'Isle des Monts Deserts (Mount Desert Island) and present-day Bangor before returning to face the winter with their ill-fated compatriots. Scurvy, lack of fuel and water, and a ferocious winter wiped out nearly half of the 79 men. In spring 1605, de Monts, Champlain, and other survivors headed southwest, exploring the coastline all the way to Cape Cod before heading northeast again and settling permanently at Nova Scotia's Port Royal (now Annapolis Royal).

Eight years later, French Jesuit missionaries en route to the Kennebec River ended up on Mount Desert Island and, with a band of French laymen, set about establishing the St. Sauveur settlement. But leadership squabbles led to building delays, and English marauder Samuel Argall—assigned to reclaim English territory—arrived to find them easy prey. The colony was leveled, the settlers were set adrift in small boats, the priests were carted off to Virginia, and Argall moved on to destroy Port Royal.

By the 1620s, more than four dozen English fishing vessels were combing New England waters in search of cod, and year-round fishing depots had sprung up along the coast between Pemaquid and Portland. At the same time, English trappers and dealers began usurping the Indians' fur trade—a valuable income source.

The Massachusetts Bay Colony was established in 1630 and England's Council of New England, headed by Sir Ferdinando Gorges, began making vast land grants throughout Maine, giving rise to permanent coastal settlements, many dependent on agriculture. Among the earliest communities were Kittery, York, Wells, Saco, Scarborough, Falmouth, and Pemaquid—places where recent transplants tilled the acidic soil, fished the waters, eked out a barely-above-subsistence living, coped with predators and endless winters, bartered goods and services, and set up local governments and courts.

By the late 17th century, as these communities expanded, so did their requirements and responsibilities. Roads and bridges were built, preachers and teachers were hired, and militias were organized to deal with internecine and Indian skirmishes.

Even though England yearned to control the entire Maine coastline, her turf, realistically, was primarily south and west of the Penobscot River. The French had expanded from their Canadian colony of Acadia, for the most part north and east of the Penobscot. Unlike the absentee bosses who controlled the English territory, French merchants actually showed up, forming good relationships with the Indians and cornering the market in fishing, lumbering, and fur trading. And French Jesuit priests converted many a Native American to Catholicism. Intermittently, overlapping Anglo-French land claims sparked locally messy conflicts.

In the mid-17th century, the strategic heart of French administration and activity in Maine was Fort Pentagöet, a sturdy stone outpost built in 1635 in what is now Castine. From here, the French controlled coastal trade between the St. George River and Mount Desert Island and well up the Penobscot River. In 1654, England captured and occupied the fort and much of French Acadia, but, thanks to the 1667 Treaty of Breda, title returned to the French in 1670, and Pentagöet briefly became Acadia's capital.

A short but nasty Dutch foray against Acadia in 1674 resulted in Pentagöet's destruction ("levell'd with ye ground," by one account) and the raising of a third national flag over Castine.

THE INDIAN WARS (1675-1760)

Caught in the middle of 17th- and 18th-century Anglo-French disputes throughout Maine were the Wabanaki (People of the Dawn), the collective name for the state's major Native American tribal groups, all of whom spoke Algonquian languages. Modern ethnographers label these groups the Micmacs, Maliseets, Passamaquoddies, and Penobscots.

In the early 17th century, exposure to European diseases took its toll, wiping out three-quarters of the Wabanaki in the years 1616-1619. Opportunistic English and French traders quickly moved into the breach, and the Indians struggled to survive and regroup.

But regroup they did. Less than three generations later, a series of six Indian wars began, lasting nearly a century and pitting the Wabanaki most often against the English but occasionally against other Wabanaki. The conflicts, largely provoked by Anglo-French tensions in Europe, were King Philip's War (1675-1678), King William's War (1688-1699), Queen Anne's War (1703-1713), Dummer's War (1721-1726), King George's War (1744-1748), and the French and Indian War

(1754-1760). Not until a get-together in 1762 at Fort Pownall (now Stockton Springs) did peace effectively return to the region—just in time for the heating up of the revolutionary movement.

COMES THE REVOLUTION

Near the end of the last Indian War, just beyond Maine's eastern border, a watershed event led to more than a century of cultural and political fallout. During the so-called Acadian Dispersal, in 1755, the English expelled from Nova Scotia 10,000 French-speaking Acadians who refused to pledge allegiance to the British Crown. Scattered as far south as Louisiana and west toward New Brunswick and Québec, the Acadians lost farms, homes, and possessions in this *grand dérangement.* Not until 1785 was land allocated for resettlement of Acadians along both sides of the Upper St. John River, where thousands of their descendants remain today. Henry Wadsworth Longfellow's epic poem *Evangeline* dramatically relates the sorry Acadian saga.

In the District of Maine, on the other hand, with relative peace following a century of intermittent warfare, settlement again exploded, particularly in the southernmost counties. The 1764 census tallied Maine's population at just under 25,000; a decade later, the number had doubled. New towns emerged almost overnight, often heavily subsidized by wealthy investors from the parent Massachusetts Bay Colony. With almost 4,000 residents, the largest town in the district was Falmouth (later renamed Portland).

In 1770, 27 Maine towns became eligible, based on population, to send representatives to the Massachusetts General Court, the colony's legislative body. But only six coastal towns could actually afford to send anyone, sowing seeds of resentment among settlers who were thus saddled with taxes without representation. Sporadic mob action accompanied unrest in southern Maine, but the flashpoint occurred in the Boston area.

On April 18, 1775, Paul Revere set out on America's most famous horseback ride—from Lexington to Concord, Massachusetts—to announce the onset of what became the American Revolution. Most of the Revolution's action occurred south of Maine, but not all of it.

In June, the Down East outpost of Machias was the site of the war's first naval engagement. The well-armed but unsuspecting British vessel HMS *Margaretta* sailed into the bay and was besieged by local residents angry about a Machias merchant's sweetheart deal with the British. Before celebrating their David-and-Goliath victory, the rebels captured the *Margaretta,* killed her captain, and then captured two more British ships sent to the rescue.

In the fall of 1775, Colonel Benedict Arnold—better known to history as a notorious turncoat—assembled 1,100 sturdy men for a flawed and futile "March on Québec" to dislodge the English. From Newburyport, Massachusetts, they sailed to the mouth of the Kennebec River, near Bath, and then headed inland with the tide. In Pittston, six miles south of Augusta and close to the head of navigation, they transferred to a fleet of 220 locally made bateaux and laid over three nights at Fort Western in Augusta. Then they set off, poling, paddling, and portaging their way upriver. Skowhegan, Norridgewock, and Chain of Ponds were among the landmarks along the grueling route. The men endured cold, hunger, swamps, disease, dense underbrush, and the loss of nearly 600 of their comrades before reaching Québec in late 1775. In the Kennebec River Valley, Arnold Trail historical signposts today mark highlights (or, more aptly, lowlights) of the expedition.

Four years later, another futile attempt to dislodge the British, this time in the District of Maine, resulted in America's worst naval defeat until World War II—a little-publicized debacle called the Penobscot Expedition. On August 14, 1779, as more than 40 American warships and transports carrying more than 2,000 Massachusetts men blockaded Castine to flush out a relatively small enclave of leftover Brits, a seven-vessel Royal Navy fleet appeared. Despite their own greater numbers, about 30 of the American ships turned tail up the Penobscot River. The captains torched their vessels, exploding the ammunition and leaving the survivors to walk in disgrace to Augusta or even Boston. Each side took close to 100 casualties, three commanders—including Paul Revere—were court-martialed, and Massachusetts was about $7 million poorer.

The American Revolution officially came to a close on September 3, 1783, with the signing of the Treaty of Paris between the United States and Great Britain. The U.S.-Canada border was set at the St. Croix River, but, in a massive oversight, boundary lines were left unresolved for thousands of square miles in the northern District of Maine.

TRADE TROUBLES AND THE WAR OF 1812

In 1807, President Thomas Jefferson imposed the Embargo Act, banning trade with foreign entities—specifically, France and Britain. With thousands of miles of coastline and harbor villages dependent on trade for revenue and basic necessities, Maine reeled. By the time the act was repealed, under president James Madison in 1809, France and Britain were almost unscathed, but the bottom had dropped out of New England's economy.

An active smuggling operation based in Eastport kept Mainers from utter despair, but the economy still had continued its downslide. In 1812, the fledgling United States declared war on Great Britain, again disrupting coastal trade. In the fall of 1814, the situation reached its nadir when the British invaded the Maine coast and occupied all the shoreline between the St. Croix and Penobscot Rivers. Later that same year, the Treaty of Ghent finally halted the squabble, forced the British to withdraw from Maine, and allowed the locals to get on with economic recovery.

STATEHOOD

In October 1819, Mainers held a constitutional convention at the First Parish Church on Congress Street in Portland. (Known affectionately as "Old Jerusalem," the church was later replaced by the present-day structure.) The convention crafted a constitution modeled on that of Massachusetts, with two notable differences: Maine would have no official church (Massachusetts had the Puritans' Congregational Church), and Maine would place no religious requirements or restrictions on its gubernatorial candidates. When votes came in from 241 Maine towns, only nine voted against ratification.

For Maine, March 15, 1820, was one of those good news/bad news days: After 35 years of separatist agitation, the District of Maine broke from Massachusetts (signing the separation allegedly, and disputedly, at the Jameson Tavern in Freeport) and became the 23rd state in the Union. However, the Missouri Compromise, enacted by Congress only 12 days earlier to balance admission of slave and free states, mandated that the slave state of Missouri be admitted on the same day. Maine had abolished slavery in 1788, and there was deep resentment over the linkage.

Portland became the new state's capital (albeit only briefly; it switched to Augusta in 1832), and William King, one of statehood's most outspoken advocates, became the first governor.

TROUBLE IN THE NORTH COUNTRY

Without an official boundary established on Maine's far northern frontier, turf battles were always simmering just under the surface. Timber was the sticking point—everyone wanted the vast wooded acreage. Finally, in early 1839, militia reinforcements descended on the disputed area, heating up what has come to be known as the Aroostook War, a border confrontation with no battles and no casualties (except a farmer who was shot by friendly militia). It's a blip in the historical time line, but remnants of fortifications in Houlton, Fort Fairfield, and Fort Kent keep the story alive today. By March 1839, a truce was negotiated, and the 1842 Webster-Ashburton Treaty established the border once and for all.

MAINE IN THE CIVIL WAR

In the 1860s, with the state's population slightly more than 600,000, more than 70,000 Mainers suited up and went off to fight in the Civil War—the greatest per-capita show of force of any northern state. About 18,000 of them died in the conflict. Thirty-one Mainers were Union Army generals, the best known being Joshua L. Chamberlain, a Bowdoin College professor, who commanded the Twentieth Maine regiment and later became president of the college and governor of Maine.

During the war, young battlefield artist Winslow Homer, who later settled in Prouts Neck, south of Portland, created wartime sketches regularly for such publications as *Harper's Weekly*. In Washington, Maine senator Hannibal Hamlin was elected vice president under Abraham Lincoln in 1860 (he was removed from the ticket in favor of Andrew Johnson when Lincoln came up for reelection in 1864).

MAINE COMES INTO ITS OWN

After the Civil War, Maine's influence in Republican-dominated Washington far outweighed the size of its population. In the late 1880s, Mainers held the federal offices of acting vice president, Speaker of the House, secretary of state, Senate majority leader, Supreme Court justice, and several important committee chairmanships. Best known of the notables were James G. Blaine (journalist, presidential aspirant, and secretary of state) and Portland native Thomas Brackett Reed, presidential aspirant and Speaker of the House.

In Maine itself, traditional industries fell into decline after the Civil War, dealing the economy a body blow. Steel ships began replacing Maine's wooden clippers, refrigeration techniques made the block-ice industry obsolete, concrete threatened the granite-quarrying trade, and the output from Southern textile mills began to supplant that from Maine's mills.

Despite Maine's economic difficulties, however, wealthy urbanites began turning their sights toward the state, accumulating land (including islands) and building enormous summer "cottages" for their families, servants, and hangers-on. Bar Harbor was a prime example of the elegant summer colonies that sprang up, but others include Grindstone Neck (Winter Harbor), Prouts Neck (Scarborough), and Dark Harbor (on Islesboro in Penobscot Bay). Vacationers who preferred fancy hotel-type digs reserved rooms for the summer at such sprawling complexes as Kineo House (on Moosehead Lake), Poland Spring House (west of Portland), or the Samoset Hotel (in Rockland). Built of wood and catering to long-term visitors, these and many others all eventually succumbed to altered vacation patterns and the ravages of fire.

As the 19th century spilled into the 20th, the state broadened its appeal beyond the well-to-do who had snared prime turf in the Victorian era. It launched an active promotion of Maine as "The Nation's Playground," successfully spurring an influx of visitors from all economic levels. By steamboat, train, and soon by car, people came to enjoy the ocean beaches, the woods, the mountains, the lakes, and the quaintness of it all. (Not that these features didn't really exist, but the state's aggressive public relations campaign at the turn of the 20th century stacks up against anything Madison Avenue puts out today.) The only major hiatus in the tourism explosion in the century's first two decades was 1914-1918, when 35,062 Mainers joined many thousands of other Americans in going off to the European front to fight in World War I. Two years after the war ended, in 1920 (the centennial of its statehood), Maine women were the first in the nation to troop to the polls after ratification of the 19th Amendment granted universal suffrage.

Maine was slow to feel the repercussions of the Great Depression, but eventually they came, with bank failures all over the state. Federally subsidized programs, such as the Civilian Conservation Corps (CCC) and the Works Progress Administration (WPA), left lasting legacies in Maine.

Politically, the state has contributed notables on both sides of the aisle. In 1954, Maine elected as its governor Edmund S. Muskie, only the fifth Democrat in the job since 1854. In 1958, Muskie ran for and won a seat in the Senate, and in 1980 he became secretary of state under president Jimmy Carter. Muskie died in 1996.

Elected in 1980, Waterville's George J. Mitchell made a respected name for himself as a Democratic senator and Senate majority leader before retiring in 1996, when Maine became only the second state in the union to have two women senators (Olympia Snowe and Susan Collins, both Republicans). After his 1996 reelection, president Bill Clinton appointed Mitchell's distinguished congressional colleague and three-term senator, Republican William Cohen of Bangor, as secretary of defense, a position he held through the rest of the Clinton administration. Mitchell spent considerable time during the Clinton years as the U.S. mediator for Northern Ireland's "troubles" and subsequently headed an international fact-finding team in the Middle East.

Government

Politics in Maine isn't quite as variable and unpredictable as the weather, but pundits are almost as wary as weather forecasters about making predictions. Despite a long tradition of Republicanism dating from the late 19th century, Maine's voters and politicians have a national reputation for being independent-minded—electing Democrats, Republicans, or independents more for their character than their political persuasions.

Four of the most notable recent examples are Margaret Chase Smith, Edmund S. Muskie, George J. Mitchell, and William Cohen—two Republicans and two Democrats, all Maine natives. Republican senator Margaret Chase Smith proved her flintiness when she spoke out against McCarthyism in the 1950s. Ed Muskie, the first prominent Democrat to come out of Maine, won every race he entered except an aborted bid for the presidency in 1972. George Mitchell, as mentioned, has gained a stellar reputation, as has William Cohen. In a manifestation of Maine's strong tradition of bipartisanship, Mitchell and Cohen worked together closely on many issues to benefit the state and the nation (they even wrote a book together).

In the 1970s, Maine elected an independent governor, James Longley, whose memory is still respected (Longley's son was later elected to Congress as a Republican, and his daughter to the state senate as a Democrat). In 1994, Maine voted in another independent, Angus King (now a Senator), a relatively young veteran of careers in business, broadcasting, and law. The governor serves a term of four years, limited to two terms.

The state's Supreme Judicial Court has a chief justice and six associate justices.

Maine is governed by a bicameral, biennial citizen legislature comprising 151 members in the House of Representatives and 35 members in the state senate, including a relatively high percentage of women and a fairly high proportion of retirees. Members of both houses serve two-year terms. In 1993, voters passed a statewide term-limits referendum restricting legislators to four terms. In general, Greater Portland and southern Maine are more liberal, while inland and northern Maine lean more conservatively.

Whereas nearly two dozen Maine cities are ruled by city councils, about 450 smaller towns and plantations retain the traditional form of rule: annual town meetings. Town meetings generally are held in March, when newspaper pages bulge with reports containing classic quotes from citizens exercising their rights to vote and vent. A few examples: "I believe in the pursuit of happiness until that pursuit infringes on the happiness of others"; "I don't know of anyone's dog running loose except my own, and I've arrested her several times"; and "Don't listen to him; he's from New Jersey."

Economy

When the subject of the economy comes up, you'll often hear reference to the "two Maines," as if an east-west line bisected the state in half. There's much truth to the image. Southern Maine is prosperous, with good jobs (although never enough), lots of small businesses, and a highly competitive real-estate market. Northern Maine struggles along, suffering from its immensity and lack of infrastructure as much as from its low population density.

The coast follows that same pattern. The Southern Coast reaps the benefit of its proximity to Boston. Not only is it a favorite weekend getaway for Boston-area residents, but it's increasingly becoming part of Boston's suburbs as more and more people move there and commute to the city. Tourism thrives here seasonally. Retail is strong, thanks to Kittery. And traditional maritime-related businesses continue, although real-estate pressures have contributed to their weakening, as fishermen struggle to hold on to wharves and to live near where they work.

According to state economists, Maine faces three challenges. First, slow job growth: Over the past two decades, Maine's has been about half of the national average. Second, changing employment patterns: Once famed for producing textiles and shoes and for its woods-based industries, now health care and tourism provide the most jobs. Third, an aging population: Economic forecasters predict that more than one in five residents will be older than 65 by 2020, which poses a challenge for finding workers in the future.

Portland is the state's largest city and has a strong economy, supported by tourism and maritime-related businesses. Years ago, Portland made the wise decision to preserve its waterfront for maritime use, so it's still very much a working waterfront. Not surprisingly, Freeport's economy is retail-based. Brunswick, Bath, and the surrounding towns are supported by Bowdoin College and Bath Iron Works.

Mid-Coast and Penobscot Bay and increasingly the Blue Hill Peninsula have strong maritime-related businesses, including lobstering, fishing, clamming, marine-worm digging, and their support services. Also driving this region is a vital creative economy of artists and artisans, boatbuilders and cabinetmakers, and entrepreneurial professionals such as architects and designers. Small businesses, technology-based companies, and telemarketing provide employment, as does tourism. These three regions are also extremely popular with retirees, who often take up second careers or are active in the local community as mentors and volunteers.

The farther Down East you travel, the harder it is to eke out a living. In Washington County, many folks cobble together some semblance of year-round employment in wreath making, fishing, clamming, guiding, logging, blueberry raking, and whatever else is available. As one local official told me, "Everyone complains that there are no jobs, but whenever an opportunity comes along, no one wants to risk changing the lifestyle." And that's a conundrum that's bound to continue for at least the foreseeable future.

People and Culture

THE PEOPLE

Maine's population didn't top the one-million mark until 1970. Forty years later, according to the 2010 census, the state had 1,318,301 residents. Along the coast, Cumberland County, comprising the Greater Portland area, has the highest head count.

Despite the longstanding presence of several substantial ethnic groups, plus four Native American tribes (about 1 percent of the population), diversity is a relatively recent phenomenon in Maine, and the population is about 95 percent Caucasian. A steady influx of refugees, beginning after the Vietnam War, has forced the state to address diversity issues, and it continues to do so today.

Natives and "People from Away"

People who weren't born in Maine aren't natives. Even people who *were* born here may experience close scrutiny of their credentials. In Maine, there are natives and *natives.* Every day, the obituary pages describe Mainers who have barely left the houses in which they were born—even in which their grandparents were born. We're talking roots!

Along with this kind of heritage comes a whole vocabulary all its own—lingo distinctive to Maine, or at least New England. (For help in translation, see the Glossary.)

Part of the "native" picture is the matter of "native" produce. Hand-lettered signs sprout everywhere during the summer advertising native corn, native peas, even—believe it or not—native ice. In Maine, homegrown is well grown.

"People from away," on the other hand, are those whose families haven't lived here year-round for a generation or more. But people from away (also called flatlanders) exist all over Maine, and they have come to stay, putting down roots of their own and altering the way the state is run, looks, and *will* look. Senators Snowe and Collins are natives, but Senator King came from away, as did most of his cabinet members. You'll find other flatlanders as teachers, corporate executives, artists, retirees, writers, town selectmen, and even lobstermen.

In the 19th century, arriving flatlanders were mostly "rusticators" or "summer complaints"—summer residents who lived well, often in enclaves, and never set foot in the state off-season. They did, however, pay property taxes, contribute to causes, and provide employment for local residents. Another 19th-century wave of people from away came from the bottom of the economic ladder: Irish escaping the potato famine and French Canadians fleeing poverty in Québec. Both groups experienced subtle and overt anti-Catholicism but rather quickly assimilated into the mainstream, taking jobs in mills and factories and becoming staunch American patriots.

The late 1960s and early 1970s brought bunches of "back-to-the-landers," who scorned plumbing and electricity and adopted retro ways of life. Although a few pockets of diehards still exist, most have changed with the times and adopted contemporary mores (and conveniences).

Today, technocrats arrive from away with computers, faxes, cell phones, and other high-tech gear and "commute" via the Internet and modern electronics. Maine has played a national leadership role in telecommunications reform—thanks to the university system's early push for installation of state-of-the-art fiber optics.

Native Americans

In Maine, the *real* natives are the Wabanaki (People of the Dawn)—the Micmac, Maliseet, Penobscot, and Passamaquoddy tribes of the eastern woodlands. Many live in or near three reservations, near the headquarters for their tribal governors. The Passamaquoddies are at Pleasant Point, in Perry, near Eastport, and at Indian Township, in Princeton, near Calais. The Penobscots are based on Indian Island, in Old Town, near Bangor. Other Native American population clusters—known as "off-reservation Indians"—are the Aroostook Band of Micmacs, based in Presque Isle, and the Houlton Band of Maliseets, in Littleton, near Houlton.

In 1965, Maine became the first state to establish a Department of Indian Affairs, but just five years later the Passamaquoddy and Penobscot tribes initiated a 10-year-long land-claims case involving 12.5 million Maine acres (about two-thirds of the state) weaseled from the Indians by Massachusetts in 1794. In late 1980, a landmark agreement, signed by President Jimmy Carter, awarded the tribes $80.6 million in reparations. Despite this, the tribes still struggle to provide jobs on the reservations and to increase the overall standard of living. A 2003 and 2011 referenda to allow the tribes to build a casino were defeated. The latest attempt to increase jobs and money is a controversial plan to bring a liquefied natural gas port to tribal lands in Perry.

One of the true success stories of the tribes is the revival of traditional arts as businesses. The Maine Indian Basketmakers Association has an active apprenticeship program, and Maine basket makers are getting national recognition. Several well-attended annual summer festivals—in Bar Harbor, Grand Lake Stream, and Perry—highlight Indian traditions and heighten awareness of Native American culture. Basket making, canoe building, and traditional dancing are all parts of the scene. The splendid Abbe Museum in Bar Harbor features Indian artifacts, interactive displays, historic photographs, and special programs.

Acadians and Franco-Americans

Within about three decades of their 1755 expulsion from Nova Scotia in *le grand dérangement,* Acadians had established new communities and new lives in northern Maine's St. John Valley. Gradually, they explored farther into central and southern coastal Maine and west into New Hampshire. The Acadian diaspora has profoundly influenced Maine and its culture, and it continues to do so today. Along the coast, French is spoken on the streets of Biddeford, where

The Abbe Museum shares the heritage of Maine's Native Americans.

there's an annual Franco-American festival and an extensive Franco-American research collection.

African Americans

Although Maine's African-American population is small, the state has had an African-American community since the 17th century; by the 1764 census, there were 322 slaves and free blacks in the District of Maine. Segregation remained the rule, however, so in the 19th century, blacks established their own parish, the Abyssinian Church in Portland. Efforts are under way to restore the long-closed church as an African-American cultural center and gathering place for Greater Portland's black community. Maine's African Americans have earned places in history books that far exceed their small population. In 1826, Bowdoin's John Brown Russworm became America's first black college graduate; in 1844, Macon B. Allen became the first African American to gain admission to a state bar; and in 1875, James A. Heay became America's first African American Roman Catholic Bishop, when he was ordained for the Diocese of Portland. For researchers delving into "Maine's black experience," the University of Southern Maine in Portland houses the African-American Archive of Maine, a significant collection of historic books, letters, and artifacts donated by Gerald Talbot, the first African American to serve in the Maine legislature.

Finns

Finns came to Maine in several 19th-century waves, primarily to work the granite quarries on the coast and on offshore islands and the slate quarries in Monson, near Greenville. Finnish families clustered near the quarries in St. George and on Vinalhaven and Hurricane Islands—all with landscapes similar to those of their homeland. Today, names such as Laukka, Lehtinen, Hamalainen, and Harjula are interspersed among the Yankee names in the Mid-Coast region.

Russians, Ukrainians, and Byelorussians

Arriving after World War II, Slavic immigrants established a unique community in Richmond, just inland from Bath. Only a tiny nucleus remains today, along with an onion-domed church, but a stroll through the local cemetery hints at the extent of the original colony.

The Newest Arrivals: Refugees from War

War has been the impetus for the more recent arrival of Asians, Africans, Central Americans, and Eastern Europeans. Most have settled in the Portland area, making that city the state's center of diversity. Vietnamese and Cambodians began settling in Maine in the mid-1970s. A handful of Afghanis who fled the Soviet-Afghan conflict also ended up in Portland. Somalis, Ethiopians, and Sudanese fled their war-torn countries in the early to mid-1990s, and Bosnians and Kosovars arrived in the last half of the 1990s. With every new conflict comes a new stream of immigrants—world citizens are becoming Mainers, and Mainers are becoming world citizens.

CULTURE

Mainers are an independent lot, many exhibiting the classic Yankee characteristics of dry humor, thrift, and ingenuity. Those who can trace their roots back at least a generation or two in the state and have lived here through the duration can call themselves natives; everyone else, no matter how long they've lived here, is "from away."

Mainers react to outsiders depending upon how those outsiders treat them. Treat a Mainer with a condescending attitude, and you'll receive a cold shoulder at best. Treat a Mainer with respect, and you'll be welcome, perhaps even invited in to share a mug of coffee. Mainers are wary of outsiders, and often with good reason. Many outsiders move to Maine because they fall in love with its independence and rural simplicity, and then they demand that the farmer stop spreading that stinky manure on his farmlands, or they insist that the town initiate garbage pickup, or they build a glass-and-timber McMansion in the midst of white clapboard historical homes.

In most of Maine, money doesn't impress folks. The truth is, that lobsterman in the old truck and the well-worn work clothes might be sitting on a small fortune. Or living on it. Perhaps nothing has caused more troubles between natives and newcomers than the rapidly increasing value of land and the taxes that go with that. For many visitors, Maine real estate is a bargain they can't resist.

If you want real insight into Maine character, listen to a CD or watch a video by one Maine master humorist, Tim Sample. As he often says, "Wait a minute; it'll sneak up on you."

THE ARTS

Fine Art

In 1850, in a watershed moment for Maine landscape painting, Frederic Edwin Church (1826-1900), Hudson River School artist par excellence, vacationed on Mount Desert Island. Influenced by the luminist tradition of such contemporaries as Fitz Hugh Lane (1804-1865), who summered in nearby Castine, Church accurately but romantically depicted the dramatic tableaux of Maine's coast and woodlands that continues to attract slews of admirers today.

By the 1880s, however, impressionism had become the style du jour and was being practiced by a coterie of artists who collected around Charles Herbert Woodbury (1864-1940) in Ogunquit. His program made Ogunquit the best-known summer art school in New England. After Hamilton Easter Field established another art school in town, modernism soon asserted itself. Among the artists who took up summertime Ogunquit residence was Walt Kuhn (1877-1949), a key organizer of New York's 1913 landmark Armory Show of modern art.

Meanwhile, a bit farther south, impressionist Childe Hassam (1859-1935), part of writer Celia Thaxter's circle, produced several hundred works on Maine's remote Appledore Island, in the Isles of Shoals off Kittery, and illustrated Thaxter's *An Island Garden*.

Another artistic summer colony found its niche in 1903, when Robert Henri (born Robert Henry Cozad, 1865-1929), charismatic leader of the Ashcan School of realist/modernists, visited Monhegan Island, about 11 miles offshore. Artists who followed him there included Rockwell Kent (1882-1971), Edward Hopper (1882-1967), George Bellows (1882-1925), and Randall Davey (1887-1964). Among the many other artists associated with Monhegan images are William Kienbusch (1914-1980), Reuben Tam (1916-1991), and printmakers Leo Meissner (1895-1977) and Stow Wengenroth (1906-1978).

But colonies were of scant interest to other notables, who chose to derive their inspiration from Maine's stark natural beauty and work mostly in their own orbits. Among these are genre painter Eastman Johnson (1824-1906); romantic realist Winslow Homer (1836-1910), who lived in Maine for 27 years and whose studio in Prouts Neck (Scarborough) still overlooks the surf-tossed scenery he so often depicted; pointillist watercolorist Maurice Prendergast (1858-1924); John Marin (1870-1953), a cubist who painted Down East subjects, mostly around Deer Isle and Addison (Cape Split); Lewiston native Marsden Hartley (1877-1943), who first showed his abstractionist work in New York in 1909 and later worked in Berlin; Fairfield Porter (1907-1975), whose family summered on Great Spruce Head Island, in East Penobscot Bay; and Andrew Wyeth (1917-2009), whose reputation as a romantic realist in the late 20th century surpassed that of his illustrator father, N. C. Wyeth (1882-1945).

On a parallel track was sculptor Louise Nevelson (1899-1988), raised in a poor Russian-immigrant family in Rockland and far better known outside her home state for her monumental wood sculptures slathered in black or gold. Two other noted sculptors with Maine connections were William Zorach

(1887-1966) and Gaston Lachaise (1882-1935), both of whom lived in Georgetown, near Bath.

Contemporary year-round or seasonal Maine residents with national (and international) reputations include Vinalhaven's Robert Indiana, Lincolnville's Alex Katz, North Haven's Eric Hopkins, Deer Isle's Karl Schrag, Tenants Harbor's Jamie Wyeth (third generation of the famous family), Kennebunk's Edward Betts, and Cushing's Lois Dodd and Alan Magee.

The two best collections of Maine art are at the **Portland Museum of Art** (7 Congress Sq., Portland, 207/775-6148) and the **Farnsworth Art Museum** (16 Museum St., Rockland, 207/596-6457). The Farnsworth, in fact, focuses only on Maine art, primarily from the 20th century. The Farnsworth is the home of the Wyeth Center, featuring the works of the family's three generations.

The **Ogunquit Museum of American Art,** appropriately, also has a very respectable Maine collection (in a spectacular setting), as does the Monhegan Museum. Other Maine paintings, not always on exhibit, are at the Bowdoin College Museum of Art in Brunswick.

All three are part of the **Maine Art Museum Trail** (www.maineartmuseums.org), comprising eight museums housing 73,000 works of art, statewide.

Crafts

Any survey of Maine art, however brief, must include the significant role of crafts in the state's artistic tradition. As with painters, sculptors, and writers, craftspeople have gravitated to Maine—most notably since the establishment in 1950 of the Haystack Mountain School of Crafts. Started in the Belfast area, the school put down roots on Deer Isle in 1960. Craft studios are abundant in Maine, and many festivals include craft displays.

Down East Literature

Maine's first big-name writer was probably the early 17th-century French explorer Samuel de Champlain (1570-1635), who scouted the Maine coast, established a colony in 1604 near present-day Calais, and lived to describe in detail his experiences. Several decades after Champlain's forays, English naturalist John Josselyn visited Scarborough and in the 1670s published the first two books accurately describing Maine's flora and fauna (aptly describing, for example, blackflies as "not only a pesterment but a plague to the country").

Today, Maine's best-known author lives not on the coast but just inland in Bangor—Stephen King (b. 1947), wizard of the weird.

CHRONICLERS OF THE GREAT OUTDOORS

John Josselyn was perhaps the first practitioner of Maine's strong naturalist tradition in American letters, but the Pine Tree State's rugged scenic beauty and largely unspoiled environment have given rise to many ecologically and environmentally concerned writers.

The 20th century saw the arrival in Maine of crusader Rachel Carson (1907-1964), whose 1962 wake-up call, *Silent Spring,* was based partly on Maine observations and research. The Rachel Carson National Wildlife Refuge, headquartered in Wells and comprising 10 chunks of environmentally sensitive coastal real estate, covers nearly 3,500 acres between Kittery Point and the Mid-Coast region.

The tiny town of Nobleboro, near Damariscotta, drew nature writer Henry Beston (1888-1968); his *Northern Farm* lyrically chronicles a year in Maine. Beston's wife, Elizabeth Coatsworth (1893-1986), wrote more than 90 books—including *Chimney Farm,* about their life in Nobleboro.

Fannie Hardy Eckstorm (1865-1946), born in Brewer to Maine's most prosperous fur trader, graduated from Smith College and became a noted expert on Maine (and specifically Native American) folklore. Among her extensive writings, *Indian Place-Names of the Penobscot Valley and the Maine Coast,* published in 1941, remains a sine qua non for researchers.

The out-of-doors and inner spirits shaped Cape Rosier adoptees Helen and Scott

Maine Food Specialties

Everyone knows Maine is *the* place for lobster, but there are quite a few other foods that you should sample before you leave.

For a few weeks in May, right around Mother's Day (the second Sunday in May), a wonderful delicacy starts sprouting along Maine woodland streams: **fiddleheads,** the still-furled tops of the ostrich fern *(Matteuccia struthiopteris).* Tasting vaguely like asparagus, fiddleheads have been on May menus ever since Native Americans taught the colonists to forage for the tasty vegetable. Don't go fiddleheading unless you're with a pro, though; the lookalikes are best left to the woods critters. If you find them on a restaurant menu, indulge.

As with fiddleheads, we owe thanks to Native Americans for introducing us to **maple syrup,** one of Maine's major agricultural exports. The annual crop averages 110,000 gallons. The syrup comes in four different colors/flavors (from light amber to extra dark amber), and inspectors strictly monitor syrup quality. The best syrup comes from the sugar or rock maple, *Acer saccharum.* On Maine Maple Sunday (usually the fourth Sunday in March), several dozen syrup producers open their rustic sugarhouses to the public for "sugaring-off" parties—to celebrate the sap harvest and share the final phase in the production process. Wood smoke billows from the sugarhouse chimney while everyone inside gathers around huge kettles used to boil down the watery sap. (A single gallon of syrup starts with 30-40 gallons of sap.) Finally, it's time to sample the syrup every which way—on pancakes and waffles, in tea, on ice cream, in puddings, in muffins, even just drizzled over snow. Most producers also have containers of syrup for sale.

The best place for Maine maple syrup is atop pancakes made with Maine **wild blueberries.** Packed with antioxidants and all kinds of good-for-you stuff, these flavorful berries are prized by bakers because they retain their form and flavor when cooked. Much smaller than the cultivated versions, wild blueberries are also raked, not picked. Although most of the Down East barren barons harvest their crops for the lucrative wholesale market, a few growers let you pick your own blueberries in mid-August. Contact the Wild Blueberry Commission (207/581-1475, www.wildblueberries.maine.edu) or the state Department of Agriculture (207/287-3491, www.getrealmaine.com) for locations, recipes, and other wild-blueberry information, or log on to the website of the Wild Blueberry Association of North America (207/570-3535, www.wildblueberries.com).

The best place to simply *appreciate* blueberries is Machias, site of the renowned annual Machias Wild Blueberry Festival, held the third weekend in August. While harvesting is under way in the surrounding fields, you can stuff your face with blueberry everything—muffins, jam, pancakes, ice cream, pies. Plus you can collect blueberry-logo napkins, T-shirts, fridge magnets, pottery, and jewelry.

Another don't-miss while in Maine is Maine-made **ice cream.** Skip the overpriced Ben and Jerry's outlets. Locally made ice cream and gelato are fresher and better and often come in an astounding range of flavors. The big name in the state is Gifford's, with regional companies being Shain's and Round Top. All beat the out-of-state competition by a long shot. Even better are some of the one-of-a-kind dairy bars and farmstands. Good bets are John's, in Liberty; Morton's, in Ellsworth; and Mt. Desert Ice Cream, in Bar Harbor and Portland.

Finally, whenever you get a chance, shop at a **farmers market.** Their biggest asset is serendipity—you never know what you'll find. Everything is locally grown and often organic. Herbs, unusual vegetables, seedlings, baked goods, meat, free-range chicken, goat cheese, herb vinegars, berries, exotic condiments, smoked salmon, maple syrup, honey, and jams are just a few of the possibilities. The Maine Department of Agriculture (207/287-3491, www.getrealmaine.com) provides info on markets.

Other must-try Maine favorites are **Moxie,** a carbonated beverage; **whoopie pies,** the state's official snack; and, especially in downeast Maine, **periwinkles,** a sea snail familiarly called wrinkles, and smelts, a small fish.

Nearing, whose 1954 *Living the Good Life* became the bible of Maine's back-to-the-landers.

CLASSIC WRITINGS ON THE STATE

Historical novels, such as *Arundel,* were the specialty of Kennebunk native Kenneth Roberts (1885-1957), but Roberts also wrote *Trending into Maine,* a potpourri of Maine observations and experiences (the original edition was illustrated by N. C. Wyeth). Kennebunkport's Booth Tarkington (1869-1946), author of the *Penrod* novels and *The Magnificent Ambersons,* described 1920s Kennebunkport in *Mary's Neck,* published in 1932.

A subgenre of sociological literary classics comprises astute observations, mostly by women, of daily life in various parts of the state. Some are fiction, some nonfiction, some barely disguised romans à clef. Probably the best-known chronicler of such observations is Sarah Orne Jewett (1849-1909), author of *The Country of the Pointed Firs,* a fictional 1896 account of "Dunnet's Landing" (actually Tenants Harbor); her ties, however, were in the South Berwick area, where she spent most of her life. Also in South Berwick, Gladys Hasty Carroll (1904-1999) scrutinized everyday life in her hamlet, Dunnybrook, in *As the Earth Turns* (a title later "borrowed" and tweaked by a soap-opera producer). Lura Beam (1887-1978) focused on her childhood in the Washington County village of Marshfield in *A Maine Hamlet,* published in 1957, and Louise Dickinson Rich (1903-1972) entertainingly described her coastal Corea experiences in *The Peninsula,* after first having chronicled her rugged wilderness existence in *We Took to the Woods.* Ruth Moore (1903-1989), born on Gott's Island, near Acadia National Park, published her first book at the age of 40. Her tales, recently brought back into print, have earned her a whole new appreciative audience. Elisabeth Ogilvie (b. 1917-2006) came to Maine in 1944 and lived for many years on remote Ragged Island, transformed into "Bennett's Island" in her fascinating "tide trilogy": *High Tide at Noon, Storm Tide,* and *The Ebbing Tide.* Ben Ames Williams (1887-1953), the token male in this roundup of perceptive observers, in 1940 produced *Come Spring,* an epic tale of hardy pioneers founding the town of Union, just inland from Rockland.

In the mid-19th century antislavery crusader Harriet Beecher Stowe (1811-1896), seldom recognized for her Maine connection, lived in Brunswick, where she wrote *The Pearl*

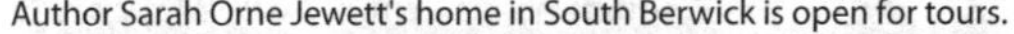
Author Sarah Orne Jewett's home in South Berwick is open for tours.

of Orr's Island, a folkloric novel about a tiny nearby fishing community.

Mary Ellen Chase was a Maine native, born in Blue Hill in 1887. She became an English professor at Smith College in 1926 and wrote about 30 books, including some about the Bible as literature. She died in 1973.

Two books do a creditable job of excerpting literature from throughout Maine—something of a daunting task. The most comprehensive is *Maine Speaks: An Anthology of Maine Literature*, published in 1989 by the Maine Writers and Publishers Alliance. *The Quotable Moose: A Contemporary Maine Reader*, edited by Wesley McNair and published in 1994 by the University Press of New England, focuses on 20th-century authors.

A WORLD OF HER OWN

For Marguerite Yourcenar (1903-1987), Maine provided solitude and inspiration for subjects ranging far beyond the state's borders. Yourcenar was a longtime Northeast Harbor resident and the first woman elected to the prestigious Académie Française. Her house, now a shrine to her work, is open to the public by appointment in summer.

ESSAYISTS, CRITICS, AND HUMORISTS NATIVE AND TRANSPLANTED

Maine's best-known essayist is and was E. B. White (1899-1985), who bought a farm in tiny Brooklin in 1933 and continued writing for *The New Yorker*. *One Man's Meat*, published in 1944, is one of the best collections of his wry, perceptive writings. His legions of admirers also include two generations raised on his classic children's stories *Stuart Little, Charlotte's Web*, and *The Trumpet of the Swan.*

Writer and critic Doris Grumbach (b. 1918), who settled in Sargentville, not far from Brooklin but far from her New York ties, wrote two particularly wise works from the perspective of a Maine transplant: *Fifty Days of Solitude* and *Coming into the End Zone.*

Maine's best contemporary exemplar of humorous writing is the late John Gould (1908-2003), whose life in rural Friendship has provided grist for many a tale. Gould's hilarious columns in the *Christian Science Monitor* and his steady book output made him an icon of Maine humor.

PINE TREE POETS

Born in Portland, Henry Wadsworth Longfellow (1807-1882) is Maine's most famous poet; his marine themes clearly stem from his seashore childhood (in "My Lost Youth," he wistfully rhapsodized, "Often I think of the beautiful town/That is seated by the sea...").

Widely recognized in her own era, poet Celia Thaxter (1835-1894) held court on Appledore Island in the Isles of Shoals, welcoming artists, authors, and musicians to her summer salon. Today, she's best known for *An Island Garden*, published in 1894 and detailing her attempts at horticultural TLC in a hostile environment.

Edna St. Vincent Millay (1892-1950) had connections to Camden, Rockland, and Union and described a stunning Camden panorama in "Renascence."

Whitehead Island, near Rockland, was the birthplace of Wilbert Snow (1883-1977), who went on to become president of Connecticut's Wesleyan University. His 1968 memoir, *Codline's Child*, makes fascinating reading.

A longtime resident of York, May Sarton (1912-1995) approached cult status as a guru of feminist poetry and prose—and as an articulate analyst of death and dying during her terminal illness.

Among respected Maine poets today are William Carpenter (b. 1940), of Stockton Springs; and Appleton's Kate Barnes (1932-1913), named Maine's Poet Laureate from 1996 to 1999. Although she comes by her acclaim legitimately, Barnes is also genetically disposed, being the daughter of writers Henry Beston and Elizabeth Coatsworth.

MAINE LIT FOR LITTLE ONES

Besides E. B. White's children's classics, *Stuart Little, Charlotte's Web*, and *The Trumpet of the Swan*, America's kids were also weaned on books written and illustrated by Maine island summer resident Robert McCloskey (1914-2003)—notably *Time of Wonder, One Morning in Maine,* and *Blueberries for Sal.* Neck-and-neck in popularity is prolific Walpole illustrator-writer Barbara Cooney (1917-1999), whose award-winning titles included *Miss Rumphius, Island Boy,* and *Hattie and the Wild Waves.* Cooney produced more than 100 books, and it seems as if everyone has a different favorite.

C. A. (Charles Asbury) Stephens (1844-1931) for 60 years wrote for the magazine *Youth's Companion.* In 1995, a collection of his vivid children's stories was reissued as *Stories from the Old Squire's Farm.*

Maine can also lay partial claim to Kate Douglas Wiggin (1856-1923), author of the eternally popular *Rebecca of Sunnybrook Farm;* she spent summers at Quillcote in Hollis, west of Portland.

Essentials

Transportation

GETTING THERE

Coastal Maine has two major airports, two major bus networks, a toll highway, limited Amtrak service, and some ad hoc local transportation systems that fill in the gaps.

Air

Maine's primary airline gateway is **Portland International Jetport** (PWM, 207/774-7301, www.portlandjetport.org), although visitors headed farther north sometimes prefer **Bangor International Airport** (BGR, 207/947-0384, www.flybangor.com). The "international" in their names is a bit misleading. Military and charter flights from Europe often stop at Bangor for refueling and customs clearance, and Portland has a few flights connecting to Canada, but Boston's Logan Airport is the nearest airport with direct flights from worldwide destinations.

PORTLAND JETPORT FACILITIES

Portland's airport is small and easy to navigate. Food options are few, but you won't starve. Visitor information is dispensed from a desk (not always staffed, unfortunately) between the gates and the baggage-claim area. Note: Since Portland is the terminus of most flights, baggage service isn't a priority; expect to hang around for a while. If you have an emergency, contact the airport manager (207/773-8462).

Ground Transportation: The Greater Portland Transportation District's **Metro** (207/774-0351, www.gpmetrobus.com) bus route 5 connects the airport with downtown Portland Monday through Saturday. **Taxis** are available outside baggage claim.

Mid-Coast Limo (207/236-2424 or 800/937-2424, www.midcoastlimo.com) provides car service, by reservation, between Portland and the Mid-coast and Penobscot Bay regions. **Mermaid Transportation Co.** (207/885-5630, www.gomermaid.com) services southern Maine.

Car rentals at the airport include **Alamo** (207/775-0855 or 877/222-9075, www.alamo.com), **Avis** (207/874-7500 or 800/230-4898, www.avis.com), **Budget** (207/874-7500 or 800/527-0700, www.drivebudget.com), **Hertz** (207/774-4544 or 800/654-3131, www.hertz.com), and **National** (207/773-0036 or 877/222-9058, www.nationalcar.com).

BANGOR AIRPORT FACILITIES

Bangor's airport has scaled-down versions of Portland's facilities but all the necessary amenities. If you need help, contact the airport manager (207/947-0384).

Ground Transportation: Community Connector (207/992-4670, www.bangormaine.gov) buses connect the airport to downtown Bangor. Buses run Monday-Saturday. **West's Coastal Connection** (207/546-2823 or 800/596-2823, www.westbusservice.com) has scheduled service along Route 1 to Calais, with stops en route. **Taxis** are available outside baggage claim.

Bar Harbor-Bangor Shuttle (207/479-5911, www.barharborbangorshuttle.com) operates between the airport, Greyhound and Concord Coachlines bus terminals, the Bangor Mall, Hollywood Slots, and Bar Harbor.

Car rentals at the airport include **Alamo** (207/947-0158 or 800/462-5266, www.alamo.com), **Avis** (207/947-8383 or 800/831-2847, www.avis.com), **Budget** (207/945-9429 or 800/527-0700, www.drivebudget.com), **Hertz** (207/942-5519 or 800/654-3131, www.hertz.com), and **National** (207/947-0158 or 800/227-7368, www.nationalcar.com).

Previous: Casco Bay Lines ferries; Island Explorer on Mount Desert Island.

REGIONAL AIRPORTS

JetBlue partner **Cape Air** (866/227-3247, www.flycapeair.com) flies from Boston to **Hancock County Airport** (BHB, 207/667-7329, www.bhbairport.com) near Bar Harbor, **Knox County Regional Airport** (RKD, 207/594-4131, www.knoxcountymaine.gov) at Owls Head, near Rockland and Camden, and **Augusta State Airport** (AUG, 207/626-2306, www.augustaairport.org). Alaska Air partner **PenAir** (800/448-4226, www.penair.com) provides summer service to Bar Harbor from Boston. Hancock County Airport has rental-car offices for Hertz and Enterprise and is also serviced by the Island Explorer bus late June-Columbus Day. Knox County has car rentals from Budget and Enterprise. Augusta has Hertz rentals.

BOSTON LOGAN AIRPORT

If you fly into Boston (BOS), you easily can get to Maine via rental car (all major rental companies are at the airport, but it's not pleasant to navigate Logan in a rental car) or Concord Coachlines bus (easiest and least-expensive option). You'll need to connect to North Station to take Amtrak's *Downeaster* train.

Car

The major highway access to Maine from the south is **I-95,** which roughly parallels the coast until Bangor before shooting up to Houlton. Other busy access points are **Route 1,** also from New Hampshire, departing the coast in Calais at the New Brunswick province border; **Route 302,** from North Conway, New Hampshire, entering Maine at Fryeburg; **Route 2,** from Gorham, New Hampshire, to Bethel; **Route 201,** entering from Québec province, just north of Jackman, and a couple of crossing points from New Brunswick into Aroostook and Washington Counties in northeastern Maine.

Bus

Concord Coachlines (800/639-3317, www.concordcoachlines.com) departs downtown Boston (South Station Transportation Center) and Logan Airport for Portland almost hourly from the wee hours of the morning until late at night, making pickups at all Logan airline terminals (lower level). Most of the buses continue directly to Bangor; three daily nonexpress buses continue along the coast, stopping in Brunswick, Bath, Wiscasset, Damariscotta, Waldoboro, Rockland, Camden, Belfast, and Searsport, before turning inland to Bangor. The Portland bus terminal is the Portland Transportation Center, Thompson Point Road, just west of I-295. Buses are clean, movies are shown, and there's free Wi-Fi on most.

Also servicing Coastal Maine but with far less frequent service is **Greyhound** (800/231-2222, www.greyhound.com).

Once-a-day buses to and from Calais coordinate with the Bangor bus schedules. The Calais line, stopping in Ellsworth, Gouldsboro, Machias, and Perry (near Eastport), is operated by **West's Coastal Connection** (207/546-2823 or 800/596-2823, www.westbusservice.com). Flag stops along the route are permitted.

Portland and South Portland have **city bus service,** with some wheelchair-accessible vehicles. A number of smaller communities have established **local shuttle vans** or **trolley-buses,** but most of the latter are seasonal. Trolley-buses operate (for a fee) in Ogunquit, Wells, the Kennebunks, Biddeford, Saco, Old Orchard Beach, Portland, Bath, and Boothbay. Mount Desert Island and the Schoodic Peninsula have the **Island Explorer,** an excellent free bus service operating late June-early October.

Rail

Amtrak's *Downeaster* (800/872-7245, www.thedowneaster.com) makes daily round-trip runs between Boston's North Station and Brunswick, with stops in Wells, Saco, Old Orchard Beach (May 1-Oct. 31), Portland, and Freeport. From the Portland station, Portland's Metro municipal bus service will take you gratis to downtown Portland; just show your Amtrak ticket stub. Amtrak trains from Washington via New York arrive in

Boston at South Station, not North Station, and there's no direct link between the two. While you can connect via the T (Boston's subway), it's a real hassle with baggage. Instead, splurge on a taxi or take the bus north from South Station.

GETTING AROUND

Getting to Maine is easy; getting around isn't. Two major **airports** service the state: Portland (convenient for the Southern Coast through Penobscot Bay regions) and Bangor (convenient for Penobscot Bay through the Down East regions). **Buses** and **Amtrak trains** connect Boston to Portland, stopping at various locations en route, with buses continuing to Bangor. Once here, unless you're visiting a destination with bus service, such as Portland, Bangor, or Bar Harbor, or are content with the trolley system serving the Southern Coast, you'll want a **car.**

The Maine Department of Transportation (800/877-9171) operates the Explore Maine site (www.exploremaine.org), which has information on all forms of transportation in Maine.

Car

No matter how much time and resourcefulness you summon, you'll never really be able to appreciate Maine without a car. Down every little peninsula jutting into the Atlantic lies a picturesque village or park or ocean view.

Two lanes wide from Kittery in the south to Fort Kent at the top, U.S. Route 1 is the state's most congested road, particularly in July and August. Mileage distances can be extremely deceptive, since it will take you much longer than anticipated to get from point A to point B. If you ask anyone about distances, chances are good that you'll receive an answer in hours rather than miles. If you're trying to make time, it's best to take the Maine Turnpike or I-95; if you want to see Maine, take U.S. 1 and lots of little offshoots. That said, bear in mind that even I-95 becomes megacongested on summer weekends, and especially summer *holiday* weekends.

Note that the interstate can be a bit confusing to motorists. Between York and Augusta, I-95 is the same as the Maine Turnpike, a toll highway regulated by the Maine Turnpike Authority (877/682-9433 or 800/675-7453 travel conditions, www.maineturnpike.com). All exit numbers along I-95 reflect distance in miles from the New Hampshire border. I-295 splits from I-95 in Portland and follows the coast to Brunswick before veering inland and rejoining I-95 in Gardiner. Exits on I-295 reflect distance from where it splits from I-95 just south of Portland at Exit 44.

ROAD CONDITIONS

For real-time information on road conditions, weather, construction, and major delays, dial 511 in Maine, 866/282-7578 from out of state, or visit www.511maine.gov. Information is available in both English and French.

DRIVING REGULATIONS

Seat belts are mandatory in Maine. Unless posted otherwise, Maine allows right turns at red lights after you stop and check for oncoming traffic. *Never* pass a stopped school bus in either direction. Maine law also requires drivers to turn on their car's headlights any time the windshield wipers are operating.

ROADSIDE ASSISTANCE

Since Maine is enslaved to the automobile and you may be driving in remote areas, it's not a bad idea for vacationers to carry membership in AAA in case of breakdowns, flat tires, and other car crises. Contact your nearest AAA office or AAA Northern New England (425 Marginal Way, Portland 04101, 207/780-6800 or 800/482-7497, www.aaanne.com). The emergency road service number is 800/222-4357.

Hitchhiking

Even though Maine's public transportation network is woefully inadequate and the crime rate is one of the lowest in the nation, it's still risky to hitchhike or pick up hitchhikers.

Say It Like a Native

Countless names for Maine cities, towns, villages, rivers, lakes, and streams have Native American origins; some are variations on French; and a few have German derivations. Below are some pronunciations to give you a leg up when requesting directions along the Maine coast.

- **Arundel**—Uh-RUN-d'l
- **Bangor**—BANG-gore
- **Bremen**—BREE-m'n
- **Calais**—CAL-us
- **Castine**—Kass-TEEN
- **Damariscotta**—dam-uh-riss-COTT-uh
- **Harraseeket**—Hare-uh-SEEK-it
- **Isle au Haut**—i'll-a-HO, I'LL-a-ho (subject to plenty of dispute, depending on whether or not you live in the vicinity)
- **Katahdin**—Kuh-TA-din
- **Lubec**—Loo-BECK
- **Machias**—Muh-CHIGH-us
- **Matinicus**—Muh-TIN-i-cuss
- **Medomak**—Muh-DOM-ick
- **Megunticook**—Muh-GUN-tuh-cook
- **Monhegan**—Mun-HE-gun
- **Mount Desert**—Mount Duh-ZERT
- **Narraguagus**—Nare-uh-GWAY-gus
- **Naskeag**—NASS-keg
- **Passagassawakeag**—Puh-sag-gus-uh-WAH-keg
- **Passamaquoddy**—Pass-uh-muh-QUAD-dee
- **Pemaquid**—PEM-a-kwid
- **Saco**—SOCK-oh
- **Schoodic**—SKOO-dick
- **Steuben**—Stew-BEN
- **Topsham**—TOPS-'m
- **Wiscasset**—Wiss-CASS-it
- **Woolwich**—WOOL-itch

Travel Tips

WHAT TO TAKE

Weather can be unpredictable in Maine, with fog, rain, and temperatures ranging from the low 30s on a cold spring day to the 90s on a hot summer one. But even summer sees days when a **fleece pullover** or jacket and a **lightweight, weatherproof jacket** are quite welcome. A hat and mittens are a plus when venturing far off shore on a windjammer or whale-watching boat or climbing inland peaks in spring or fall. Other handy items are **binoculars;** a small **backpack** for day trips or light hiking; and a small or collapsible **cooler** for picnics or storing food.

Unless you're dining at the White Barn Inn, you won't need fancy clothing. Resort casual is the dress code in most good restaurants and in downtown Portland, with nice T-shirts and shorts being acceptable almost everywhere in beach communities.

In winter and spring, add warm waterproof boots, gloves, hat, and winter-weight clothing to your list.

FOREIGN TRAVELERS

Since 9/11, security has been excruciatingly tight for foreign visitors, with immigration and customs procedures in flux. For current rules, visit www.usa.gov/visitors/arriving.shtml. It's wise to make two sets of copies of all paperwork, one to carry separately on your trip and another left with a trusted friend or relative at home.

For information on what can be brought into the United States, check the website of the Customs and Border Protection division of the Department of Homeland Security (www.cbp.gov).

SMOKING

Maine now has laws banning smoking in restaurants, bars, and lounges as well as enclosed areas of public places, such as shopping malls. Few accommodations permit smoking, and if they do, it's only in limited areas or rooms. Many have instituted high fines for smoking in a nonsmoking room. If you're a smoker, motels with direct outdoor access make it easiest to satisfy a craving.

ACCOMMODATIONS

For all accommodations listings, rates are quoted for peak season, which is usually July-August but may extend through foliage season in mid-October. Rates drop, often dramatically, in the shoulder seasons and off-season at many accommodations that remain open. Especially during peak season, many accommodations require a 2-3-night minimum.

For the best rates, be sure to check Internet specials and ask about packages. Many accommodations also provide discounts for members of travel clubs such as AAA and to seniors, members of the military, and other such groups.

Unless otherwise noted, accommodations listed have private baths.

A note about B&Bs: If you've never stayed at a B&B, begin by putting aside any ideas you may have about them. No two are alike, but all are built on the premise that your experience will be richer if it's easy to meet other travelers. That said, many provide private tables for breakfast—ask before booking—if you're just not up to being sociable first thing in the morning. The shared breakfast table does provide an opportunity to trade experiences with other guests. Some also provide afternoon refreshments, another opportunity to chat. Many B&Bs are quite exquisite and decorated with antiques and fine art, which means they're often inappropriate for young children. Others are equipped with in-room TVs, CD players, VCRs or DVD players, air-conditioning, phones, and other modern conveniences. Most B&Bs are operated by folks who live here year-round (some for generations), so they are able to provide recommendations based on their

Budget Tips

At first glance, Maine might seem pricey, but take another look. It is possible to keep a vacation within a reasonable budget; here are a few tips for doing so.

For starters, **avoid the big-name towns** and seek out accommodations in smaller, nearby ones instead. For example, instead of Damariscotta, consider Waldoboro; instead of Camden, try Belfast or Searsport; in place of Bar Harbor, check Trenton or Southwest Harbor. Or simply explore the Down East Coast, where rates are generally far lower than in other coastal regions.

Small, family-owned motels tend to have the lowest rates. Better yet, **book a cabin or cottage for a week,** rather than a room by the night. Not only can you find reasonable weekly rentals—especially if you plan well in advance—but you'll also have cooking facilities, allowing you to avoid eating all meals out.

Speaking of food, **buy or bring a small cooler** so you can stock up at supermarkets and farmers markets for picnic meals. Most Hannaford and Shaw's supermarkets have large selections of prepared foods and big salad bars and bakeries, and many local groceries have pizza and sandwich counters.

Do check local papers and bulletin boards for **Public Supper notices.** Most are very inexpensive, raise money for a good cause, and provide an opportunity not only for a good meal, but also to meet locals and glean a few insider tips.

Of course, sometimes you want to have a nice meal in a nice place. Consider **going out for lunch instead of dinner,** or take advantage of early-bird specials or of the Friday-night all-you-can-eat fish fries offered at quite a few home-cooking restaurants.

Take advantage of Maine's vast **outdoor-recreation** opportunities; many are free. Even Acadia, with its miles and miles of trails and carriage roads, and its Island Explorer bus service, is a bargain: buy a park pass and it's all yours to use and explore.

Take advantage of **free events:** concerts, lectures, farmers markets, art shows and openings, and family events. Most are usually listed in local papers.

Avoid parking hassles and fees and save gas by using **local transportation services** when available, such as the trolley network on the Southern Coast and the Island Explorer bus system on Mount Desert Island.

Finally, before making reservations for anything, check to see if there's a **special Internet rate** or ask about any **discounts** that might apply to you: AAA, senior, military, government, family rate, and so forth. If you don't ask, you won't get.

in-depth knowledge. B&Bs, especially, reflect their owners, so expect any of them to be different than described if ownership has changed.

FOOD

Days and hours of operation listed for places serving food are for peak season. These do change often, sometimes even within a season, and it's not uncommon for a restaurant to close early on a quiet night. To avoid disappointment, call before making a special trip.

ALCOHOL

As in the rest of the country, Maine's minimum drinking age is 21 years—and bar owners, bartenders, and serving staff can be held legally accountable for serving underage imbibers. If your blood alcohol level is 0.08 percent or higher, you are legally considered to be operating under the influence.

TIME ZONE

All of Maine is in the eastern time zone—the same as New York, Washington DC, Philadelphia, and Orlando. Eastern standard time (EST) runs from the first Sunday in November to the second Sunday in March; eastern daylight time (EDT), one hour later, prevails otherwise. Surprising to many first-time visitors, especially when visiting coastal areas, is how early the sun rises in the morning and how early it sets at night.

If your itinerary also includes Canada, remember that the provinces of New Brunswick and Nova Scotia are on Atlantic time—one hour later than eastern time—so if it's noon in Maine, it's 1pm in these provinces.

Health and Safety

There's too much to do in Maine, and too much to see, to spend even a few hours laid low by illness or mishap. Be sensible—be sure to get enough sleep, wear sunscreen and appropriate clothing, know your limits and don't take foolhardy risks, heed weather and warning signs, carry water and snacks while hiking, don't overindulge in food or alcohol, always tell someone where you're going, and watch your step. If you're traveling with children, you should quadruple your caution.

MEDICAL CARE

In an emergency, dial 911. For non-life-threatening issues, call the closest hospital and ask for the nearest walk-in services.

Southern Coast

York Hospital (15 Hospital Dr., York, emergency 207/351-2157); **York Hospital in Wells** (112/114 Sanford Rd., Wells, 207/646-5211); **Southern Maine Medical Center** (Rte. 111, Biddeford, 207/283-7000, emergency 207/294-5000).

Greater Portland

Maine Medical Center (22 Bramhall St., Portland, 207/662-0111, emergency 207/662-2381); **Mercy Hospital** (144 State St., Portland, 207/879-3000, emergency 207/879-3265).

Mid-Coast

Mid Coast Hospital (Bath Rd., Cooks Corner, Brunswick, 207/729-0181); **St. Andrews Hospital and Healthcare Center** (3 St. Andrews La., Boothbay Harbor, 207/633-2121); **Miles Memorial Hospital** (Bristol Rd., Rte. 130, Damariscotta, 207/563-1234).

Penobscot Bay

Penobscot Bay Medical Center (Rte. 1, Rockport, 207/596-8000, emergency 207/596-8315); **Waldo County General Hospital** (118 Northport Ave., Belfast, 207/338-2500 or 800/649-2536).

Blue Hill and Deer Isle

Blue Hill Memorial Hospital (57 Water St., Blue Hill, 207/374-3400, emergency 207/374-2836).

Acadia

Maine Coast Memorial Hospital (50 Union St., Ellsworth, 207/664-5311 or 888/645-8829, emergency 207/664-5340); **Mount Desert Island Hospital** (10 Wayman Lane, Bar Harbor, 207/288-5081).

Down East

Down East Community Hospital (Upper Court St., Rte. 1A, Machias, 207/255-3356); **Calais Regional Hospital** (50 Franklin St., Calais, 207/454-7521).

AFFLICTIONS

Insect Bites and Tick-Borne Diseases

If you plan to spend any time outdoors in Maine April-November, take precautions, especially when hiking, to avoid annoying insect bites, and especially the diseases carried by tiny deer ticks (not the larger dog ticks; they don't carry it): **Lyme disease, anaplasmosis,** and **babesiosis. Powassan,** carried by the woodchuck tick, is so far extremely rare. As of late 2015, mosquito-borne **eastern equine encephalitis** has been diagnosed twice in Maine residents, once in 2014 and once in 2015.

Wear a long-sleeved shirt and long pants, and tuck pant legs into your socks. Light-colored clothing makes ticks easier to spot. Buy insect repellent with 20-40% DEET and use it liberally; pretreat clothing with permethrin. Not much daunts the blackflies of spring and early summer, but you can lower your appeal by not using perfume, aftershave lotion, or scented shampoo and by wearing light-colored clothing.

After any hike or prolonged time outdoors in the woods, thick grass, overgrown bushes, or piles of brush or leaves, check for ticks—especially behind the knees and in the armpits, navel, and groin. If you find one, there's a good chance the tick was infected with Lyme disease, a bacterial infection that causes fever, head and body aches, and fatigue and can lead to joint pain and neurological and heart problems. It usually takes 24-48 hours before an attached tick begins to transmit the disease. About 80 percent of Lyme patients get a bull's-eye rash that appears within a month of being bit. Anaplasmosis and babesiosis also exhibit flu-like symptoms. Anaplasmosis can, in rare circumstances, lead to encephalitis/meningitis; babesiosis can cause anemia and dark urine, and is especially problematic for those with weakened immune systems or who have had their spleen removed.

If bitten by a tick, wash the area thoroughly with soap and water and apply an antiseptic, mark the date on a calendar, then monitor your health. If you suspect any of these diseases, see a doctor to be diagnosed and treated immediately; don't put it off. For more information, consult the Maine Medical Center's Vector-Borne Disease Laboratory's **Ticks in Maine: What Do I Need to Know** (www.ticksinmaine.com) or contact the **Maine Center for Disease Control** (800/821-5821, www.mainepublichealth.gov).

Rabies

If you're bitten by any animal, especially one acting suspiciously, head for the nearest hospital emergency room. For statewide information about rabies, contact the Maine Center for Disease Control (800/821-5821, www.mainepublichealth.gov).

Allergies

If your medical history includes extreme allergies to shellfish or bee stings, you know the risks of eating a lobster or wandering around a wildflower meadow. However, if you come from a landlocked area and are new to crustaceans, you might not be aware of the potential hazard. Statistics indicate that less than 2 percent of adults have a severe shellfish allergy, but for those victims, the reaction can set in quickly. Immediate treatment is needed to keep the airways open. If you have a history of severe allergic reactions to *anything*, be prepared when you come to the Maine coast dreaming of lobster feasts. Ask your doctor for a prescription for EpiPen (epinephrine), a preloaded, single-use syringe containing 0.3 mg of the drug—enough to tide you over until you can get to a hospital.

Seasickness

If planning to do any boating in Maine—particularly sailing—you'll want to be prepared. (Being prepared may in fact keep you from succumbing, since fear of seasickness just about guarantees you'll get it.) Talk to a pharmacist or doctor about your options. Alternative precautions that may be effective include acupressure wrist bands and ginger.

Hypothermia and Frostbite

Wind and weather can shift dramatically in Maine, especially at higher elevations, creating prime conditions for contracting hypothermia and frostbite. At risk are hikers, swimmers, canoeists, kayakers, sailors, skiers, even cyclists.

To prevent hypothermia and frostbite, dress in layers and remove or add them as needed. Wool, waterproof fabrics (such as Gore-Tex), and synthetic fleece (such as Polartec) are the best fabrics for repelling dampness. Polyester fleece lining wicks excess moisture away from your body. Especially in winter, always cover your head, since body heat escapes quickly through the head; a ski mask will protect ears and nose. Wear wool- or fleece-lined gloves and wool socks.

Special Considerations During Hunting Season

During Maine's fall hunting season (October-Thanksgiving weekend)—and especially during the November deer season—walk or hike only in wooded areas marked No Hunting, No Trespassing, or Posted. And even if an area *is* closed to hunters, don't decide to explore the woods during deer or moose season without wearing a "hunter orange" (read: eye-poppingly fluorescent) jacket or vest. If you take your dog along, be sure it, too, wears an orange vest. Hunting is illegal on Sunday.

During hunting season, moose and deer are on the move and are made understandably skittish by the hunters invading their turf. Moose are primarily found inland, but deer are everywhere, and even the occasional moose strays into coastal areas of Maine. At night, particularly in wooded areas, these huge creatures often end up alongside or on the roads, so ratchet up your defensive-driving skills. Reduce your normal speed, use high beams when there's no oncoming traffic, and remain extra alert. In a moose-versus-car encounter, no one wins, and human fatalities are common. An encounter between a deer and a car may be less dangerous to the humans (although the deer usually dies), but some damage to the vehicle is inevitable.

Information and Services

MONEY

If you need to exchange foreign currency—other than Canadian dollars—do it at or near border crossings or in Portland. In small communities, such transactions are more complicated; you may end up spending more time and money than necessary.

Typical banking hours are 9am-3pm weekdays, occasionally with later hours on Friday. Drive-up windows at many banks tend to open as much as an hour earlier and stay open an hour or so after lobbies close. Some banks also maintain Saturday-morning hours. Automated teller machines (ATMs) are abundant along coastal Maine.

Credit Cards and Travelers Checks

Bank credit cards have become so preferred and so prevalent that it's nearly impossible to rent a car or check into a hotel without one. MasterCard and Visa are most widely accepted in Maine, and Discover and American Express are next most popular; Carte Blanche, Diners Club, and EnRoute (Canadian) lag far behind. Be aware, however, that small restaurants (including lobster pounds), shops, and bed-and-breakfasts off the beaten track might not accept credit cards or nonlocal personal checks; you may need to settle your account with cash or travelers check.

Taxes

Maine charges a 5.5 percent sales tax on general purchases and services; 8 percent on prepared foods, candy, and lodging/camping; and 10 percent on auto rentals.

Tipping

Tip 15-20 percent of the pre-tax bill in restaurants. Note that the tip is often added to the bill for groups of six or more.

Taxi drivers expect a 15 percent tip; airport porters expect at least $1 per bag, depending on the difficulty of the job.

The usual tip for housekeeping services in accommodations is $1-5 per person, per night, depending upon the level of service.

Some accommodations add a 10-15 percent service fee to rates.

TOURISM INFORMATION AND MAPS

The **Maine Office of Tourism** has an excellent website: www.visitmaine.com. You'll find chamber of commerce addresses, articles, photos, information on lodgings, and access to a variety of Maine tourism businesses. The state's toll-free information hotline is 888/MAINE-45 (888/624-6345). The state also operates **information centers** in Calais, Fryeburg (May-Oct.), Hampden, Houlton, Kittery, and Yarmouth. These are excellent places to visit to stock up on brochures, pick up a map, ask for advice, and use restrooms. All, except Hamden, offer free Wi-Fi.

The **Maine Tourism Association** (207/623-0363, www.mainetourism.com) also has information and publishes *Maine Invites You* and a free state map.

Peek in any Mainer's car, and you're likely to see a copy of **The Maine Atlas and Gazetteer,** published by DeLorme Mapping Company in Yarmouth. Despite an oversize format inconvenient for hiking and kayaking, this 96-page paperbound book just about guarantees that you won't get lost (and if you're good at map reading, it can get you out of a lot of traffic jams). Scaled at one-half inch to the mile, it's meticulously compiled from aerial photographs, satellite images, U.S. Geological Survey maps, GPS readings, and timber-company maps, and it is revised annually. It details back roads and dirt roads and shows elevation, boat ramps, public lands, campgrounds and picnic areas, and trailheads. DeLorme products are available nationwide in book and map stores, but you can also order direct (800/452-5931, www.delorme.com). The atlas is $19.95 and shipping is $4 (Maine residents need to add 5 percent sales tax).

PHONE AND INTERNET

Maine still has only one telephone area code, 207. For directory assistance, dial 411.

Cell phone towers are now sprinkled pretty much throughout Maine; only a few pockets—mostly down peninsulas and in remote valleys and hollows—are out of cell-phone range. Of course, reception also varies by carrier. Still, getting reception often requires doing the cell-phone hokeypokey—putting your left arm out, your right leg in, and so on to find the strongest signal.

Internet access is widely available at libraries and coffeehouses. Most accommodations offer Internet access.

Resources

Glossary

To help you translate some of the lingo used off the beaten track at places like country stores and county fairs, farmstands and flea markets, here's a sampling of local terms and expressions:

alewives: herring
ayuh: yes
barrens: as in "blueberry barrens"; fields where wild blueberries grow
beamy: wide (as in a boat or a person)
beans: shorthand for the traditional Saturday-night meal, which always includes baked beans
blowdown: a forest area leveled by wind
blowing a gale: very windy
camp: a vacation house (small or large), usually on freshwater and in the woods
chance: serendipity or luck, as in "open by appointment or by chance"
chicken dressing: chicken manure
chowder (pronounced "chowdah"): soup made with lobster, clams, or fish, or a combination thereof; lobster version sometimes called lobster stew
chowderhead: mischief or troublemakers, usually interchangeable with idiot
coneheads: tourists (because of their presumed penchant for ice cream)
cottage: a vacation house (anything from a bungalow to a mansion), usually on salt water
culch (also cultch): stuff; the contents of attics, basements, and some flea markets
cull: a discount lobster, usually minus a claw
cunnin': cute, usually describing a baby or small child
dinner (pronounced "dinnah"): the noon meal
dinner pail: lunch box
dite: a very small amount
dooryard: the yard near a house's main entrance
downcellar: in the basement
Down East: with the prevailing wind; the old coastal sailing route from Boston to Nova Scotia
dry-ki: driftwood, usually remnants from the logging industry
ell: a residential structural section that links a house and a barn; formerly a popular location for the "summer kitchen," to spare the house from woodstove heat
exercised: upset; angry
fiddleheads: unopened ostrich-fern fronds, a spring delicacy
finest kind: top quality; good news; an expression of general approval; also a term of appreciation
flatlander: a person not from Maine, often but not exclusively someone from the Midwest
floatplane: a small plane equipped with pontoons for landing on water; the same aircraft often becomes a ski-plane in winter
flowage: a body of water created by damming, usually beaver handiwork (also called "beaver flowage")
FR: Fire Road, used in mailing addresses
frappé: a thick drink containing milk, ice cream, and flavored syrup, as opposed to a milk shake, which does not include ice cream (but beware: a frappé offered in other parts of the United States is an ice cream sundae topped with whipped cream)

from away: not native to Maine

galamander: a wheeled contraption formerly used to transport quarry granite to building sites or to boats for onward shipment

gore: a sliver of land left over from inaccurate boundary surveys. Maine has several gores; Hibberts Gore, for instance, has a population of one.

got done: quit a job; was let go

harbormaster: local official who monitors water traffic and assigns moorings; often a very political job

hardshell: lobster that hasn't molted yet (scarcer, thus more pricey in summer)

HC: Home Carrier, used in mailing addresses

hod: wooden "basket" used for carrying clams

ice-out: the departure of winter ice from ponds, lakes, rivers, and streams; many communities have ice-out contests, awarding prizes for guessing the exact time of ice-out, in April or May

Italian: long soft bread roll sliced on top and filled with peppers, onions, tomatoes, sliced meat, black olives, and sprinkled with olive oil, salt, and pepper; veggie versions available

jimmies: chocolate sprinkles, like those on an ice cream cone

lobster car: a large floating crate for storing lobsters

Maine Guide: a member of the Maine Professional Guides Association, trained and tested for outdoor and survival skills; also called Registered Maine Guide

market price: restaurant menu term for "the going rate," usually referring to the price of lobster or clams

molt: what a lobster does when it sheds its shell for a larger one; the act of molting is called ecdysis (as a stripper is an ecdysiast)

money tree: a collection device for a monetary gift

mud season: mid-March-mid-April, when back roads and unpaved driveways become virtual tank traps

nasty neat: extremely meticulous

near: stingy

notional: stubborn, determined

off island: the mainland, to an islander

place: another word for a house (as in "Herb Pendleton's place")

ployes: Acadian buckwheat pancakes

pot: trap, as in "lobster pot"

public landing: see "town landing"

rake: hand tool used for harvesting blueberries

RFD: Rural Free Delivery, used in mailing addresses

roller-skiing: cross-country skiing on wheels; popular among cross-country skiers, triathletes, and others as a training technique

rusticator: a summer visitor, particularly in bygone days

scooch (or scootch): to squat; to move sideways

sea smoke: heavy mist rising off the water when the air temperature suddenly becomes much colder than the ocean temperature

select: a lobster with claws intact

Selectmen: the elected men and women who handle local affairs in small communities; the First Selectman chairs meetings. In some towns, "people from away" have tried to propose substituting a gender-neutral term, but in most cases the effort has failed.

shedder: a lobster with a new (soft) shell; generally occurs in July-August (more common then, thus less expensive than hardshells)

shire town: county seat

shore dinner: the works: chowder, clams, lobster, and sometimes corn on the cob too; usually the most expensive item on a menu

short: a small, illegal-size lobster

slumgullion: tasteless food; a mess

slut: a poor housekeeper

slut's wool: dust balls found under beds, couches, and so on

snapper: an undersize, illegal lobster

soda: cola, root beer, and so on (referred to as "pop" in some other parts of the country)

softshell: see "shedder"

some: very (as in "some hot")

spleeny: overly sensitive

steamers: clams, before or after they are steamed

sternman: a lobsterman's helper (male or female)

summer complaint: a tourist

supper (pronounced "suppah"): evening meal, eaten by Mainers around 5 or 6pm (as opposed to flatlanders and summer people, who eat dinner 7pm-9pm)

tad: slightly; a little bit

thick-o'-fog: zero-visibility fog

to home: at home

tomalley: a lobster's green insides; considered a delicacy by some

town landing: shore access; often a park or a parking lot, next to a wharf or boat-launch ramp

upattic: in the attic

Whoopie! Pie: the trademarked name for a high-fat, calorie-laden, cakelike snack that only kids and dentists could love

wicked cold: frigid

wicked good: excellent

williwaws: uncomfortable feeling

Suggested Reading

MAPS

The Maine Atlas and Gazetteer. Yarmouth, ME: DeLorme, updated annually. You'll be hard put to get lost if you're carrying this essential volume; 70 full-page, oversize-format topographical maps with GPS grids.

LITERATURE, ART, AND PHOTOGRAPHY

Curtis, J., W. Curtis, and F. Lieberman. *Monhegan: The Artists' Island.* Camden, ME: Down East Books, 1995. Fascinating island history interspersed with landscape and seascape paintings and drawings by more than 150 artists, including Bellows, Henri, Hopper, Kent, Porter, Tam, and Wyeth.

Maine Speaks: An Anthology of Maine Literature. Brunswick, ME: Maine Writers and Publishers Alliance, 1989.

McNair, W., ed. *The Maine Poets: An Anthology of Verse.* Camden, ME: Down East Books, 2003. McNair's selection of best works by Maine's finest poets.

Spectre, P. H. *Passage in Time.* New York: W. W. Norton, 1991. A noted marine writer cruises the coast aboard traditional windjammers; gorgeous photos complement the colorful text.

Van Riper, F. *Down East Maine: A World Apart.* Camden, ME: Down East Books, 1998. Maine's Washington County, captured with incredible insight and compassion by a master photographer and insightful wordsmith.

HISTORY

Isaacson, D., ed. *Maine: A Guide "Down East,"* 2nd ed. Maine League of Historical Societies and Museums, 1970. Revised version of the Depression-era Works Progress Administration guidebook, still interesting for background reading.

Judd, R. W., E. A. Churchill, and J. W. Eastman, eds. *Maine: The Pine Tree State from Prehistory to the Present.* Orono, ME: University of Maine Press, 1995. The best available Maine history, with excellent historical maps.

Paine, L. P. *Down East: A Maritime History of Maine.* Gardiner, ME: Tilbury House, 2000. A noted maritime historian provides an enlightening introduction to the state's seafaring tradition.

LOBSTERS AND LIGHTHOUSES

Bachelder, Peter Dow, and P. M. Mason. *Maine Lighthouse Map and Guide.* Glendale, CO: Bella Terra Publishing, 2009. An illustrated map and guide providing directions on how to find all Maine beacons as well as brief histories.

Caldwell, W. *Lighthouses of Maine.* Camden, ME: Down East Books, 2002 (reprint of 1986 book). A historical tour of Maine's lighthouses, with an emphasis on history, legends, and lore.

Corson, T. *The Secret Life of Lobsters.* New York: HarperCollins, 2004. Everything you wanted—or perhaps didn't want—to know about lobster.

Woodward, C. *The Lobster Coast: Rebels, Rusticators, and the Struggle for a Forgotten Frontier.* New York: Viking, 2004. A veteran journalist's take on the history of the Maine coast.

MEMOIRS

Dawson, L. B. *Saltwater Farm.* Westford, ME: Impatiens Press, 1993. Witty, charming stories of growing up on the Cushing peninsula.

Greenlaw, L. *The Lobster Chronicles: Life on a Very Small Island.* New York: Hyperion, 2002. Swordfishing boat captain Linda Greenlaw's account of returning to life on Isle au Haut after weathering *The Perfect Storm.*

Lunt, D. L. *Hauling by Hand: The Life and Times of a Maine Island,* 2nd ed. Frenchboro, ME: Islandport Press, 2007. A sensitive history of Frenchboro (a.k.a. Long Island), eight miles offshore, written by an eighth-generation islander and journalist.

Szelog, T. M. *Our Point of View: Fourteen Years at a Maine Lighthouse.* Camden, ME: Down East Books, 2007. A professional photographer documents in words and photos 14 years at Marsha Point Lighthouse.

NATURAL HISTORY

Bennett, D. *Maine's Natural Heritage: Rare Species and Unique Natural Features.* Camden, ME: Down East Books, 1988. A dated book that examines both the special ecology of the state and how it's threatened.

Conkling, P. W. *Islands in Time: A Natural and Cultural History of the Islands of the Gulf of Maine,* 2nd ed. Camden, ME: Down East Books, and Rockland, ME: Island Institute, 1999. A thoughtful overview by the president of Maine's Island Institute.

Dwelley, M. J. *Spring Wildflowers of New England,* 2nd ed. Camden, ME: Down East Books, 2000. Back in print after several years, this beautifully illustrated gem is an essential guide for exploring spring woodlands.

Dwelley, M. J. *Summer and Fall Wildflowers of New England,* 2nd ed. Camden, ME: Down East Books, 2004. Flowers are grouped by color; more than 700 lovely colored-pencil drawings simplify identification.

Kendall, D. L. *Glaciers and Granite: A Guide to Maine's Landscape and Geology.* Unity, ME: North Country Press, 1993. Explains why Maine looks the way it does.

Maine's Ice Age Trail Down East Map and Guide. Orono, ME: University of Maine Press, 2007. Information on 46 glacial sites, also available online (www.iceagetrail.umaine.edu).

RECREATION

Acadia National Park and Mount Desert Island

Monkman, J., and M. Monkman. *Discover Acadia National Park: A Guide to the Best Hiking, Biking, and Paddling,* 3rd ed. Boston: Appalachian Mountain Club Books, 2010. Well-planned and well-written guide, in the Appalachian Mountain Club tradition, including a foldout map.

Nangle, H. *Moon Acadia National Park,* 4th ed. Berkeley, CA: Avalon Travel, 2009. A Mainer since childhood and veteran travel writer is the ideal escort for exploring this region in depth.

Roberts, A. R. *Mr. Rockefeller's Roads,* 2nd ed. Camden, ME: Down East Books, 2012. The story behind Acadia's scenic carriage roads, written by the granddaughter of John D. Rockefeller, who created them.

St. Germain Jr., T. A. *A Walk in the Park: Acadia's Hiking Guide.* 3rd ed. Bar Harbor, ME: Parkman Publications, 2010. The book includes plenty of historical tidbits about the trails, the park, and the island. Part of the proceeds go to the Acadia Trails Forever campaign to maintain and rehabilitate the park's trails. The book is updated regularly; ask for the most recent edition.

Bicycling

Stone, H. *25 Bicycle Tours in Maine: Coastal and Inland Rides from Kittery to Caribou,* 3d ed. Woodstock, VT: Countryman Press/ Backcountry Guides, 1998.

Birding

Duchesne, B. *Maine Birding Trail: The Official Guide to more than 260 Accessible Sites.* Camden, ME: Down East Books, 2009. Authorized guide to the Maine Birding Trail.

Pierson, E. C., J. E. Pierson, and P. D. Vickery. *A Birder's Guide to Maine.* Camden, ME: Down East Books, 1996. An expanded version of *A Birder's Guide to the Coast of Maine.* No ornithologist, novice or expert, should explore Maine without this valuable guide.

Boating

Maine Coastal Public Access Guides. Augusta, ME: Maine Coastal Program, Maine Department of Agriculture, Conservation, and Forestry, 2013. Comprises three books: *Southern Region: South Berwick to Freeport, Midcoast Region, Brunswick to Hampden,* and *Downeast Region: Bangor to Calais.* Series covers more than 700 public access points along the coast.

The Maine Island Trail: Stewardship Handbook and Guidebook. Rockland, ME: Maine Island Trail Association, updated annually. Available only with MITA membership (annual dues $45), providing access to dozens of islands along the watery trail.

Taft, H., J. Taft, and C. Rindlaub. *A Cruising Guide to the Maine Coast,* 5th ed. Peaks Island, ME: Diamond Pass Publishing, 2008. Don't even consider cruising the coast without this volume.

Miller, D. S. *Kayaking the Maine Coast.* 2nd ed. Woodstock, VT: Countryman Press/ Backcountry Guides, 2006. Thoroughly researched guide by a veteran kayaker; good maps and particularly helpful information.

Hiking and Walking

AMC Maine Mountain Guide, 10th ed. Boston: Appalachian Mountain Club Books, 2012. The definitive statewide resource for going vertical, in a handy format.

Collins, J., and J. E. McCarthy. *Cobscook Trails: A Guide to Walking Opportunities around Cobscook Bay and the Bold Coast,* 2d ed. Whiting, ME: Quoddy Regional Land Trust, 2000. Essential handbook for exploring this part of the Down East Coast, with excellent maps.

Kish, C. M., AMC's Best Day Hikes along the Maine Coast: Four-season Guide to 50 of the Best Trails from the Maine Beaches to Downeast. Boston: Appalachian Mountain Club Books, 2015. Well-researched, detailed resource by a veteran hiker.

Roberts, P. *On the Trail in Lincoln County.* Newcastle and Damariscotta, ME: Lincoln County Publishing, 2003. A great guide to more than 60 walks in preserves from Wiscasset through Waldoboro, with detailed directions to trailheads.

Internet Resources

GENERAL INFORMATION

State of Maine
www.maine.gov

Everything you wanted to know about Maine and then some, with links to all government departments and Maine-related sites. Buy a fishing license online, reserve a state park campsite, or check the fall foliage conditions via the site's Leaf Cam. (You can also access foliage info at www.mainefoliage.com, where you can sign up for weekly email foliage reports in September and early October.) Also listed is information on accessible arts and recreation.

Maine Office of Tourism
www.visitmaine.com

The biggest and most useful of all Maine-related tourism sites, with sections for where to visit, where to stay, things to do, trip planning, packages, and search capabilities as well as lodging specials and a comprehensive calendar of events.

Maine Tourism Association
www.mainetourism.com

Find lodging, camping, restaurants, attractions, services, and more as well as links for weather, foliage, transportation planning, and chambers of commerce.

Maine Campground Owners Association
www.campmaine.com

Find private campgrounds statewide.

Maine Travel Maven
www.mainetravelmaven.com

Moon Coastal Maine author Hilary Nangle's site for keeping readers updated on what's happening throughout the state.

TRANSPORTATION

Explore Maine
www.exploremaine.org

An invaluable site for trip planning, with information on and links to airports, rail service, bus service, automobile travel, and ferries as well as links to other key travel-planning sites.

Maine Department of Transportation
www.511maine.gov

Provides real-time information about major delays, accidents, road construction, and weather conditions. You can get the same info and more by dialing 511 in-state.

PARKS AND RECREATION

Department of Conservation, Maine Bureau of Parks and Lands
www.parksandlands.com

Information on state parks, public reserved lands, and state historic sites as well as details on facilities such as campsites, picnic areas, and boat launches. Make state campground reservations online.

Acadia National Park
www.nps.gov/acad

Information on all sections of Acadia National Park. Make ANP campground reservations online.

Maine Audubon
www.maineaudubon.org

Information about Maine Audubon's eco-sensitive headquarters in Falmouth and all of the organization's environmental centers statewide. Activity and program schedules are included.

The Nature Conservancy
www.nature.org/wherewework/northamerica/states/maine
Information about Maine preserves, field trips, and events.

Maine Land Trust Network
www.mltn.org
Maine has dozens of land trusts statewide, managing lands that provide opportunities for hiking, walking, canoeing, kayaking, and other such activities.

Maine Department of Inland Fisheries and Wildlife
www.state.me.us/ifw
Info on wildlife, hunting, fishing, snowmobiling, and boating.

Maine Trail Finder
www.mainetrailfinder.com
Find trails by activity (hiking, snowshoeing, cross-country skiing, mountain biking, and paddling) and location, statewide.

Bicycle Coalition of Maine
www.bikemaine.org
Tons of information for bicyclists, including routes, shops, events, organized rides, and much more.

Maine Birding
www.mainebirding.net
A must-visit site for anyone interested in learning more about bird-watching in Maine, including news, checklists, events, forums, trips, and more.

Maine Windjammer Association
www.sailmainecoast.com
Windjammer schooners homeported in Rockland, Camden, and Rockport belong to this umbrella organization; there are links to the websites of all the vessels for online and phone information and reservations.

ISLAND RESOURCES

Island Institute
www.islandinstitute.org
The institute serves as a clearinghouse and advocate for Maine's islands; the website provides links to the major year-round islands.

Maine Island Trail Association
www.mita.org
Information about the association and its activities along with membership details.

ARTS, ANTIQUES, AND MUSEUMS

Maine Archives and Museums
www.mainemuseums.org
Information on and links to museums, archives, historical societies, and historic sites in Maine.

Maine Antiques Dealers Association
www.maineantiques.org
Statewide dealers are listed by location and specialty, along with information on upcoming antiques events.

Maine Art Museum Trail
www.maineartmuseums.org
Information on eight art museums with significant collections statewide.

FOOD AND DRINK

Maine Department of Agriculture
www.getrealmaine.com
Information on all things agricultural, including fairs, farmers markets, farm vacations, places to buy Maine foods, berry- and apple-picking sites, and more.

Portland Food Map
www.portlandfoodmap.com
A must for culinary travel in Maine's largest city. Information on anything and everything

food- and drink-related, including openings and closings and links to reviews.

Maine Lobster Promotion Council
www.lobsterfrommaine.com

All lobster, all the time, with links for lobster boat tours, lobster events, lobster bakes, and ordering Maine lobster, plus recipes for preparing lobster in more ways than you ever thought possible.

Wild Blueberry Association of North America
www.wildblueberries.com

Information on blueberries as well as numerous recipes.

Acknowledgments

This book is dedicated to all the underappreciated tourism workers in Maine, the volunteers and lowly staffers, the waiters, waitresses, toll collectors, gatekeepers, park rangers, traffic cops, ferry attendants, housekeepers, hostesses and front desk workers, tour guides, and everyone else who has contact with visitors. You make the state sing. We do appreciate you. You're the real face of Maine. Thank you.

I've lived on the Maine coast since childhood (yes, I will always be a "from away"), and have traveled extensively throughout the state for both work and pleasure, but every time I revisit a place, I find something new or changed, sometimes subtly, other times dramatically. Restaurants open and close. Outfitters change their offerings. Inns are sold. Motels open. New trails are cut. Museums expand. Hotels renovate. And on it goes. Which all goes to say, I couldn't have done this without the help of many people, who served as additional eyes and ears.

I'll start with the folks at Avalon Travel who shepherded me through the process: Bill Newlin, Grace Fujimoto, Kevin McLain, Sierra Machado, Elizabeth Hanson, and most especially to my team on this edition: editors Nikki Ioakimedes and Rachel Feldman, graphics/production coordinator Darren Alessi, and map editor Kat Bennett. Also thank you to marketing assistant Katie Mock, and to all the behind-the-scenes worker bees at Avalon Travel Publishing. I'm also eternally in debt to Kathleen Brandes, who wrote the original 2002 edition of this book. I valued her friendship and respected her work and dedication long before I began with the second edition.

More heartfelt thank-yous are due to those who sat down with me and shared insider info, sheltered me along the way, fed me, helped with arrangements, verified information, called me with updates, or simply encouraged me: Nancy Marshall, Charlene Williams, Abbe Levin, Raymond Brunyanszki, Lauralee Dobbins, Jennifer Forte Cuomo, Jean Ginn-Marvin, Chip Gray, Rauni Kew, Deb Lennon, Dale Northrup, Carla Tracy, Brandon Hussey, Marti Mayne, Anne and Peter Beerits, Sally Littlefield, Sarah Pebworth, Julie Van de Graaf and Jack Burke, Jim Ash, Aimee Beal Church, Pat and Chris Coston, Bill Haefele, Helene Harton and Roy Kasindorf, Susi Homer, Rosemary and Gary Levin, Richard Reith, Heather MacDonald-Bosse, Katherine Cassidy, Vern McKimmey, Greg Noyes, and Judy and Victor Trafford.

I owe more thanks to friends who joined me on day trips: Ellen Chandler, Claire Gosselin, Leah Hobson, and Sarah Wills-Viega.

I save my biggest thanks for my husband Tom and my frequent road-trip sidekick Martha Kalina. Between them, they drove me everywhere and didn't complain (too much) when I made them backtrack two or three times along the same stretch of road while seeking an elusive address; waited patiently while I visited practically every restaurant, inn, and bed-and-breakfast from Kittery to Calais; and supported me in every way possible throughout the entire process.

And you, dear reader, thank you for using this book to plan your visit to Maine's magical coast. Please, do me a favor, will you? Provide feedback to help make the next edition even better. Visit www.MaineTravelMaven.com to know what's new, changed, or happening in Maine and please, drop a line to share your thoughts and finds.

Index

A

B

C

D

E

F

G

H

M

N

O

P

QR

S

T

UV

WXYZ

List of Maps

Also Available